T5-AEA-809

THE OUTLINE OF KNOWLEDGE

EDITED BY

JAMES A. RICHARDS

THE ROMANCE OF THE ARTS

BY FREDERICK H. MARTENS

VOLUME III

J. A. RICHARDS, INC.
NEW YORK

Copyright 1924
J. A. RICHARDS, INC.
MANUFACTURED IN U. S. A.

Typesetting, Paper, Printing, Binding and Cloth
By THE KINGSPORT PRESS
Kingsport, Tenn.

CONTENTS

THE ANCIENT EAST

CHAPTER		PAGE
I	The Land of The Pyramids	11
II	"Towers of Babel" and Hanging Gardens	21
III	Persia's Towers of Silence and Royal Halls	24
IV	Architecture's Land of License	27
V	Where Nature is Architecture's Twin	34

GREEK ARCHITECTURE

VI	"The Glory That Was Greece"	39

ROMAN ARCHITECTURE

VII	"The Grandeur That Was Rome"	48

EARLY CHRISTIAN AND BYZANTINE ARCHITECTURE

VIII	From Catacomb to St. Sophia	58
IX	Gothic Architecture	66

MOHAMMEDAN ARCHITECTURE

X	Mohammed And The Mosque	74

RENAISSANCE ARCHITECTURE

XI	The "Rebirth" Architecture	85

THE BAROQUE

XII	The Last Great Style In Architecture	95

MODERN ARCHITECTURE

XIV	The Age Of The Discoverers And Explorers, Aztec Mexico	117

THE ROMANCE OF SCULPTURE

I	The Sculpture Of The East	140
II	The Great Sculptors And Statues Of Greece	145
III	From Praxiteles To The End Of The Hellenistic Age	149
IV	Sculpture From Ancient Rome To The Renaissance	154
V	The Sculpture Of The Renaissance	162
VI	Michel Angelo And Benevenuto Cellini	168
VII	Bernini And Canova	175
VIII	The Rococo, Empire And Italian "Classical Revival" in Sculpture	178
IX	Modern Sculpture In Europe	184
X	Modern Sculpture In France	191
XI	The Story Of American Sculpture	198

THE ROMANCE OF PAINTING

I	From The First Picture To The Gothic Age	206
II	Great Painters And Paintings Of The Gothic Age	212
III	The Great Painters Of The Renaissance	221
IV	The Great Painters Of The Italian High Renaissance	227
V	Titian And The Venetian School	238

CONTENTS

CHAPTER		PAGE
VI	The Italian Post-Renaissance Painters	245
VII	The "Flemish Revival"	248
VIII	Rembrandt And Dutch Painting In The Baroque Age	251
IX	Valesquez And The Spanish Painters Of The Baroque Age.	254
X	The French Painters Of The Baroque Age And The Eighteenth Century	259
XI	The Great English Painters Of The Eighteenth And Early Nineteenth Centuries	263
XII	Spain's Great Eighteenth Century Painter	267
XIII	Painters Of The Eighteenth And Earlier Nineteenth Centuries	269
XIV	Delacroix And The French "Romantic" Painters	274
XV	The French Barbizon School, Naturalism And Realism	276
XVI	British Painters	280
XVII	Other French Painters From Meissonier To Matisse	287
XVIII	German Painting From Cornelius To the Present Day	294
XIX	Modern Painting In Other European Lands	300
XX	The Romance Of Painting In America	307

THE ROMANCE OF MUSIC

I	Music In Ancient Egypt	320
II	The Laments Of Chaldea, The War-Pipes Of Assyria, And The Music Of Ancient Persia	324
III	Music In India, The Mongol Lands And Western Asia	328
IV	Music In Ancient Greek Legend And Life	334
V	Music In Republican And Imperial Rome	338
VI	From The Catacombs To Charlemagne	341
VII	Music And Mohammed	345
VIII	Cloister And Hearth In Music	348
IX	The Renaissance And The Baroque In Music	354
X	The Romance Of Song	358
XI	The Romance Of The Violin	362
XII	The Romance Of The Wind Instruments	368
XIII	The Romance Of The Piano	370
XIV	The Romance Of The Orchestra	375
XV	The Romance Of Music In America	379

THE ROMANCE OF OPERA

I	The Tales Of The Great Italian Operas	386
II	Tales Of The Great French Operas	409
III	Tales Of The Great German Operas	433
IV	Tales Of The Great Operas Of Other Lands	459

THE ROMANCE OF THE DANCE

II	Sacred And Profane Dances Of The Ancient East	478
III	The Light Fantastic Toe In Ancient Greece And Rome	482
IV	Dancers And Dancing In The Middle Ages	484
V	Court Dances Of The Renaissance And Baroque	486
VI	The Dances Of The Mohammedan East	489
VII	Aztec And Inca Dances	491
VIII	Rococo Dances And Ballets	493
IX	Some Great Dancers Of The Eighteenth And Nineteenth Centuries	495
X	Some Great Ballets Of Older Days	499
XI	Great Dance-Dramas Of The Russian Ballet Repertory	503

Note: This and the following page are exact reproductions of the letter-press page and paper used in THE OUTLINE OF KNOWLEDGE . . . . .

THE ROMANCE OF THE ARTS

BY

FREDERICK H. MARTENS

WHAT IS "ART" AND WHAT ARE "THE ARTS"

(Introduction)

VOLUME after volume has been written to explain the Arts. Enough, very likely, to build a "boardwalk" of books from the Atlantic to the Pacific coast. But, like most books dealing with "special subjects", they very often give us so much technical detail, that we don't understand them. We want a *clear idea* of what "Art" means, but though the scholars who write these books *know,* in many cases they *do not make their knowledge clear to us.**

Art and "the arts" are simply *Evolution* in other forms, a spreading out in other ways, getting other results. In "The Romance of Evolution" the great picture of the development of *life* was unrolled. For millions of years it was an Evolution, a moving up, from the lowest forms of life to higher ones. And, until man was marked off from the ape by a brain, it was just an *Evolution* of the *body, even though the dim, darkened half-brain of instinct moved along with the body in which it lived:*

But when man had a brain and began to *think,* to have "feelings", then there was no limit to his development. Since the men of the Bronze Age stepped over History's threshold, we have been pretty

---

* No average intelligent American wants knowledge "predigested" or "simplified" or put in "words of one syllable" for him. The average of intelligence, of "brains, in the United States probably is higher than in any other country. But the average American is a busy man. He leads a life full of many interests. He has no *time* for a college course in the Arts, based on four easy, pleasant "scholastic" years. But—he is entitled to what amounts to the same thing. With his own good brain to act the part of tutor and professor, he can "follow up" his own "college course" by the light of his own electric lamp, where the class-room does not make the education. And he has a right to clearness, interest, color. No subject is "dry" if rightly presented, and "Art" is one of the most fascinating and human of all subjects.

I

much the same in body. Eyes and noses, hands and feet, hair and skin, shades of color may vary, but when it comes to body, one race and one man is much the same as the other. When it comes to minds! . . . They differ because the brains and the feelings of individual men of different races vary in thousands of ways. The individual has just as many special "hall-marks" and "kinks" as the race has a hundred and one variations of "cross-breedings", "sports" and special developments. The arts, too, have bred among themselves and create new arts, just like the fishes and birds, the reptiles and mammals.

But what is Art and what are the arts?

If we drop rather "high-brow" phrases like "Aesthetic predilection", and "psychological associations", and "primal urges" and "subconscious phenomena" and get right down to plain facts—for *we* want to be able to talk about Art and the arts with *anyone,* intelligently and in a way that shows we know what we are talking about—it is easy to get a clear idea of what Art and the arts are. It boils down to this:

Everything that is or happens in the world belongs either to *Nature* or to *Art*. It is either Nature or Art. *And everything that is not Nature is Art—in some one way or another.* Nature is the expression of the *divine*—Sir Thomas Browne calls it "the Art of God"—but Art is the expression of the *human*. Nature has put *all* the matter there is in the world, into it. Man uses that matter—he combines it, but he cannot *add* anything to what Nature already has put here. The very root of the word "Art", the Latin AR, means "to put or fit things together". There you have the *difference* between Nature and Art in a nut-shell. Nature puts everything into the world, man *puts together* what Nature has put there.

When man's brain first began to work at "putting together" the material Nature supplied, *Art was born into the world:* But all of us—and early man was not a bit different there from the man of to-day—"put together" things for *one* of *two reasons:* for *practical* reasons or for reasons of *pleasure*. He "put together" things for *use,* or to *delight* himself or others. So one might say that the *Useful Arts* and the *Fine Arts,* the practical arts and the arts of beauty, were caveman *"twins"*. Now there is one thing that belongs to every human creature born and that never leaves it: it is his *shadow*. And each of these twins, *Useful Arts* and *Fine Arts* had a shadow, and the shadow's name was the same for each of these "Art" twins: *Science*.

For Science is "the knowing *how*" of any art, just as Art is the "doing!" Science is a mighty substantial shadow. It is a shadow mainly in the sense that it is the *companion thing* that never leaves Art: that stands *behind* all Art. In fact Science, the "theory", the "expert" knowledge of Art is its *backbone*. It is its skeleton, the dry bones that all the beautiful "flesh and blood" of art is built up on. Just as you can't have a blooming cheek in Nature, without a cheek-bone, or a golden head of hair without a skull, you can't have a glorious cathedral without its skeleton of pillars and arches to support the floating dome, or a wonderful painting without its "outlines", that the color fills in. Every Art has its shadow-soul of Science that is born with it and never leaves it, and is part of its own self. That is the relation between *Science* and *Art, or* between the sciences and the arts.

The useful arts, such as the art of agriculture, the art of navigation, the art of mining, the art of weaving, the arts of war and of government, and every other art that *produces things for use,* grew up out of man's ambition to *improve and perfect the practical ends and aims of life,* as life began to spread out before him in all its wonderful possibilities. And, in the bigger and broader sense of the word, *every man who cultivates a useful art is an artist,* if he practices his art *as an art,* if he *handles* it as an artist. He stands on a level, in his own special "art", with the sculptor, the painter or the poet. The locomotive engineer, the mechanic, the miner, the "man with the hoe", the men who have both *Science,* "the knowledge *how* to do" and *Art,* the actual "doing" of their work in the world at their finger tips, *are every bit as much artists* as the architect or the musician, the dancer or the opera singer. Old Plato, in fact, put such arts as *shoemaking, farming and medicine high above the Fine Arts!* For, said he, the Fine Arts only make "pictures" or "images" of things, while the Useful Arts *produce* things men actually can *use.*

But—the whole civilized world to-day agrees in the stand that the Fine Arts, the *pleasure* twin born of Man's desire to "put things together", has "an edge" on his serious, *useful* twin brother. Why? Because the arts that give delight to the soul seem to stand on a *higher level* than those which *serve the body!* The Fine Arts came out of man's *groping for beauty in all sorts of ways.* Sometimes they are useful, too, but beauty, the expression of what's in the soul, is the first aim in the Fine Arts. And it is the Fine Arts (with the exception of Poetry and the Drama, which are considered elsewhere) whose story is going to be told, and whose pictures are going to be seen.

The *first artists* were the *individual men,* here and there, in this tribe or that, who had a love for beauty in their souls *that had to come out.* That is another difference between the *useful artist* and the *inspired artist.* The men who follow the useful arts *can be made,* by training, though some of them have an *instinct* for their work or craft which *almost amounts to genius:* but the inspired artist is *born,* not *made.* Training will perfect him, training will make his shadow-soul, Science, strong; but *the art-instinct has to be born in him.**

The spirit that "creates", that "makes things" in Art is a germ, a spark, a breath of the Divine! It comes as God pleases, and not as man desires. No man can tell *where* the unknown sculptor who raised the Sphynx on the Egyptian sands found his vision. No man can tell *where* Beethoven found the music of those symphonies that move the spirit. No man can tell *where* or *how* Rembrandt found the pictures of gloom and affliction that wrung the heart, or Rafeal those paintings which carry the soul straight up to God! In the case of the great master-artists, between Science, "the knowing *how* to do" and Art, the "doing", a Divine spark, the Divine something which we "can't place", flashes forth in the "no man's land" of the soul. It trembled in the golden notes of Patti's throat. It sings in the golden notes of Fritz Kreisler's violin. It holds us spell-bound at first sight of the star-reaching, skyward striving Woolworth tower! It grips the heart in the sheer loveliness of the Taj-Mahal in India.

Which are the Fine Arts? They are the arts born of man's longing to express the beauty he sees in the things around him. The arts born of his need to "put together", in himself, and present "out of himself", the beauties of Nature, *his heart's emotions, his love for everything that is lovely,* the deepest dreams and longings of his soul.

The five greater arts are: Architecture, Sculpture and Painting—the arts which can be *seen* and *handled*—and *the arts of form;* and *Music* and *Poetry—the arts of time, movement and space.*

Sometimes we extend these five greater arts to seven, to include the art of the *Drama* and of the *Dance.* The arts of the *Drama* and *Poetry* (including Oratory and Literature) are considered elsewhere. We have to do with, in this volume, the *three great arts of Architecture, Sculpture and Painting—the arts of shape;* with *Music* (besides *Poetry* the greatest of the *arts of space*) and with two of Music's greatest *allied* arts: the Art of *Opera,* the child of Music and the Drama, and the Art of the *Dance,* the child of Movement and Musical Rhythm.

Among the great families of *reptiles* and *mammals* there were born of *new matings* of flesh and blood new forms or reptile and

---

* But—remember this: *you* may not be a musician. *You* may not be able to play the piano or cornet, or to sing, *but*—if you "get" Music's story, if you know the part it has played in *all life,* from man's beginning, you *can understand, enjoy and talk more intelligently* about Music than singer, pianist or cornetist. *You* will be on a higher level, as a *music-lover* than the "artist," the musician, who only knows his art "practically." This applies to all the arts.

mammal life, showing the traits of different ancestors. In the Fine Arts, the Evolution of soul and spirit, the "cross-breeding", or "putting together" of separate arts, has created all sorts of other, lesser art children, which take after father or mother or both, as the case may be. Yet, just as all mammals had certain things in common, so all the great arts have certain things in common. And so in unrolling the scroll of the past, which pictures the Evolution of Architecture, Sculpture, Painting, Music, Opera and the Dance—in a way that will make them all *clear* to you *and enable you to hold your own wherever they may be discussed*—we have tried to show two things:

First: that no one art is a separate thing, a thing by itself, which has grown up "all on its own", and has nothing to do with any other art. You will find as you follow the pictures of the great men, that the great artists and the great epochs of *Architecture, Sculpture, Painting, Music, Opera* and the *Dance,* that there is *a close, intimate connection between them all.*

Architecture has been called "frozen music", music, that is, which has taken *solid and permanent shape in stone and marble,* the loveliness of tone turned into cathedral and palace. The great difference between *Architecture,* the mother-art and *Sculpture,* the child, is that Architecture is an *original art*—it expresses *race feeling* and *individual emotion, race standards of beauty* and individual standards of beauty by "shaping up" masses of stone or other material in "ordered shapes". *Sculpture* is an "art of record". *It makes a record* of the beautiful that it sees around it—mainly the human or animal body. It imitates. Yet it clings to its mother, Architecture, as *Ornament,* to adorn and "fill in" its great spaces, to decorate its "lines". And *it takes movement and life* and holds them fast in beauty, in marble, ivory, clay or any other matter, for all time. *It catches up the rhythm of life as it passes,* the movement of its sister art, the Dance, for instance, and holds and keeps it for us for all time.

And *Painting?* To how many of us, when we hear the word does it only mean "putting color" on some sort of surface, in most cases the outside of a house or a window-sill? That's "painter work". *Painting is a Fine Art, is an "art of record", just like sculpture.* But it can "show more", and "go further" than sculpture. Painting is as free and unlimited—when it comes to expressing beauty or imitating things—as the skies. All we see, or think we see, can be put into painting. *Painting is a great magic "wonder frame", into which the artist can put anything and everything, and make it live and real:* man and all man's belongings, the animals on earth, the birds in the air, the fishes under the sea. In his painting the painter can reflect the masterpieces of *Architecture,* the glories of *Sculpture,* the movement of the *Dance*, field and landscape, skies, seas, mountains and wilderness.

And *Music?* Can you imagine a cathedral without the silver chime of bells? Can you think of a church without the voices of the choir, and the rounded notes of solo singers? *Music is an art of time.* It takes *sound*, and gives it meaning and beauty by "putting together" the notes our ears recognize *in combinations regulated by the same rhythm—the beat, the swing,* the time of movement—the same rhythm that is the spirit of the Dance. In some ways music is a more wonderful art than any other. It goes way beyond the senses, though we "take it in" with our ears. We "feel" Architecture, Sculpture, Painting, the Dance, the Opera (partly with our eyes.)

But though we "feel" melody and music in a "bodily" way, through our ear, *it has a magic power no other art possesses.* Something in "harmony", inside the arrangement of tones—as mysterious as the other something called "inspiration" which puts the soul into all Art—calls up pictures "in us", speaks to something mysterious in ourselves. It is not just that our ear enjoys the lovely sounds. The something behind the sounds calls up in us all sorts of dream-pictures and visions—colors, glorious crimsons and scarlets, or dull browns and greys; sun-gold yellows and autumn browns, purple twi-lights, towering ranges of whole mountain peaks, storms, spring countrysides, cities under the sea, strange faces! . . . That is the mystic side of Music. And again, Music gives its soul to the mute glories of the world's master-buildings—its temples, cathedrals and palaces. When Music sounds in the marble halls of architecture, then architecture is no longer "frozen music". It has a voice and it speaks. Music can be Architecture's voice. It can give Architecture the soul of tone!

Opera, like the Dance may be called a child of *Music,* for Opera is the child of Music and the Drama—*Opera is drama set to music!* And this child was born in the early days of the world, just like her sister, the *Dance,* which is rhythm usually "put together" in bodily movement with Music. *Opera, Architecture, Sculpture, Painting, like the Dance, all are blood-relations.* And all these arts—*Architecture, Sculpture, Painting, Music, Opera* and the *Dance*—express life!

That is one great, fundamental thing about Art—it expresses life! If you once realize that you will never feel ill at ease with Art. You always will feel "at home" when and where art is "talked." You will get the "feel" of the arts that can be "handled" with the eye or with the fingers—the "shaped-up" arts of form, *Architecture, Sculpture, Painting.* You will get to *"sense"* with eye and with soul *Music, Opera* and the *Dance,* arts of movements, time and space.

INTRODUCTION

The reasons why most of us "fight shy" of having anything to do with the arts, as a rule, is because we think they are hard to understand. We look on them as "dead things", things that have nothing to do with our own life, or with the life of our day. We "dodge" Art when anyone talks about it and are ill at ease. *And we are wrong!*

All of us can "understand" Art, and the arts—if we remember to use our *own natural intelligence and knowledge of life* to understand. Evolution is no mystery. If you dive down beneath the long and learned scientific names, titles and theories, if you "get from under" the thousand and one technical details, Evolution is a clear, easy proposition for every *intelligent* person to master. Besides it is the first and greatest story ever told. Art is one of the many sequels to Evolution's story—its monuments, its sculptures, its paintings, its music, its dances are each an Evolution, a separate Evolution, in one or another direction. And each of these separate Evolutions is as closely linked together as a string of sausages that all came from the same "dog".

We have a wrong "idea" of Art, most of us. That's why we avoid it. The fact that you are a mechanic (and being one means that you have *brains, good brains*), *does not mean that you can't talk Art,* if once you realize that the story of "Art", with all *its color,* all *its romance,* all *its human passion and tragedies,* is something you can understand.

The fact that you are a miner, farmer, or structural iron-worker, driller, fireman, brakeman, chauffeur, the fact that you are an artist in any field of *useful* art, does not mean to say that you cannot *understand, judge, and discuss the fine arts as well as the next man!*

Education, like everything else, is not a matter of *how or where* you got to know what you *do* know. If you get nothing out of a college course, then, so far as education goes, you have been cheated. If you get *the meaning, the essence, the gist, the real heart and soul of knowledge* out of enjoyable hours or half-hours spent with these stories of the great Arts—picture stories, every one of them—you have filled a dull evening with the gold of knowledge and the color of romance!

"Best Society", *in these big, broad days of democracy,* means "the most intelligent society". Are you less intelligent than any one else? White collars and flannel shirt-bands are not the dividing lines when it comes to knowledge of any kind, and that includes a knowledge of the *Arts. All the Arts are "live"!* Why? Because they express *human nature, race nature, the feelings of single men and of nations of men.* And the most fascinating thing in the world is to *go behind the picture in Art, and find the soul!* If you do that, you will know *why* the pyramids of Egypt are just as "live" as the

Woolworth Tower! You will know *why* there are no "dead masters", though the men who painted certain pictures long since may have moldered away! You will know *why* the lewd dances of Babylonian temples are as live as the modern Egyptian "Dance of the Bees", the hula-hulas of Polynesia, or the Jazz-trots whose rhythms we have borrowed from the gorilla-men of early African jungles!

A lot of *"art talk"* is just plain "putting on airs!" If you know the *actual facts, the human facts* and the *human things* about art, you need not fear to mingle with art-lovers in any circle. Dame Nature, "God's Artist", is not the producing director of the pictures screened in this "Art" series. The director is the Spirit of Art. But you will find that she makes Man "put his best foot forward", and that the *Divine as well as the human* in what he does, *the Divine as well as the human in Art,* "shines" through and "comes out" in every reel!

THE ROMANCE OF ARCHITECTURE

WHAT ARCHITECTURE MEANS

(Preface)

First of all, all the arts of *every separate people* of any age or time have something about them that makes them *related* to each other. That something is the *spirit* of the race, no matter *who* the individual artist may be. The *American race spirit* shows as clearly in the Woolworth Tower, the ideal of the "sky-scraper" as the Egyptian does in the *Great Pyramid*. And—no art ever fell "ready-made" from the skies! *Each worked itself out of the very souls of the artists and the races* by slow degrees. And *for the races,* in a big way, *the arts are what play is to the individual man.*

Why should the splendid pictures of *Architecture* be thrown on our screen before those of the other arts? *Because Architecture is the one big art that takes in all humanity. Architecture* is a double art: a useful art, an art of *service* and an art of *beauty*. Sculpture, Painting, the Opera, Music, the Dance—are more arts of beauty alone. But Architecture is bigger and broader. It is the art that gives us shelter and makes that shelter pleasing to the eye. It is the art that gives us human accommodation in space, in great public buildings and churches, while lending them the grandeur that the affairs of state or the worship of God demand. And it *brings together* the artist of the useful and the artist of the ideal, the *practical artist* and the *artist of* beauty under one roof.

The cave, hut or tent of the earliest days were more shelters than buildings. But hand in hand, as man progressed, the idea of beauty, of *something more than use,* and of *feeling,* went hand and hand with the idea of use. So we see the *menhirs,* the great stone "fingers" that betray man's first roping for God stretch up toward the sky. And the hut of boughs is made, heaped up into a fast uncovered temple, made by these groping fingers, *feeling for God, which had only God's blue sky for a roof.* They are rude, they are crude. Look at the great circle of clumsy stone blocks, thirty-two or more, all of them thirteen feet high, connected by oblong blocks laid across their tops. Inside the great outer circle are other stone blocks, some larger, some smaller. Some of them are the altars where the knife of the sacrificing Druid or priest ripped open the tender breasts of children, and the blood ran red over stones which still face the same sun, the sun-god to whom they were offered. That is English Stonehenge at Wiltshire.

In another great roofless temple in France, at Carnac (Brittany), a great avenue of the uncouth stone "finger" blocks leads up to the big temple circle. Up that avenue walked the long procession of priests with their white robes and serpent-masks, and the warriors and women whose little ones were to be slain, long, long ages ago! And everywhere, in the Old World and the New, man is beginning to give his dead "monuments". Instead of laying them away in the ground, he piles up great burial mounds over them, mounds so great, at times, that small forests of trees grow on their tops. And burial mounds and roofless temples, like the first gropings for religion, were pretty much the same the world over. We find them in Africa, in Asia, in Europe and the Americas, North and South.

Yet Architecture was not to stand still. At the end of the Bronze Age, when History begins, the single, huge block of stone that stretched up to heaven like a clumsy prayer, turned—in Egypt—to the finished *obelisk*. The avenues of shapeless blocks along which the blood-thirsty priests herded their little victims at Carnac, turned —*in Egyptian Karnac*—into a splendid avenue of crouching sphinxes, and the crude "uprights", the stones that made up the roofless temple circle, have changed into splendid towering columns ending with lotus capitals, that hold up a *roof*. The burial mounds covered with green vegetation have changed—*in Babylon*—to glorious hanging gardens, where queens love amid flowery bowers high above a monster city. In the earliest days Architecture is much the same everywhere. But when the races of men begin to break up into different tribes, each race *"works out" its own self, its own race-soul and individual soul in Architecture,* in the *way* it builds, just as it does in the way it *thinks* and *speaks,* the *way* it *worships* and everything else.

THE ANCIENT EAST

CHAPTER I

THE LAND OF THE PYRAMIDS

It was in the ancient East that man seems first to have found a separate great type of building to express himself, his soul, his longing for God, his dream of immortality. In Egypt he put his soul, his longing for the *Divine,* into his great temples. He put his hope of immorality, his longing for *eternal life* into his monster pyramids. His obelisks were stone prayer "fingers" that came before those other slender *towers of prayer, the thin minarets of the Mohammedan peoples,* many centuries later. The only difference between the two is that the Egyptian obelisks spoke silent prayer that went *up.* The minarets of Mohammed were *perches,* from which the priests *called* the people to prayer, five times a day, as their law is.

The first bricklayer was probably a yellow man, a Sumerian, but he may have been an Egyptian (one of the children of lost Atlantis?) In our own time and day the bricklayer is more important than the bricks he lays, but no bricklayer should take offence if we say that *in the story of Architecture, the first brick laid was more important than the man who laid it.* It was not much of a brick at that, probably. It was a clumsy, sun-dried thing, but—with bricks came temple walls and palaces, and houses in which people could live in comfort in the hot river-valleys of Egypt and Mesopotamia. The bricks the Hebrews had to make "without straw" were Nile river mud and chopped reeds mixed with water, dried in the sun, and no self-respecting bricklayer of to-day would handle such bricks.

The trouble with unburnt, "sun-dried" bricks was that—like some early forms of life—they had no backbone. Oh, yes, the sun would heat them up until they were like soft stone in the outside, but inside they were so soft they could not stand much pressure from the *top!* That's why these Egyptian, Chaldean and Babylonian city walls and temple-walls and tomb-walls were made much *thicker at the bottom than at the top.* The temples did not come first, of course. It was the plain every-day hut or house that gradually got itself "bricked up" from the ground. Then, one day, a man hit on the idea of taking the trunk of a palm-tree for a lintel over his door.

inscription "is shown in Egyptian characters, telling how much was spent *for radishes, onions and garlic for the workmen*. The interpreter", says Herodotus, "reading the inscription, told me it came to 1,600 talents of silver . . . How much more was probably expended for iron tools (we know now that the workmen sawed the hard stones of granite with bronze saws, set with jewels, diamonds, in the fine work) and clothes for the laborers?" And then—perhaps the interpreter had whispered it to him when they discussed the high cost of drafted labor in King Cheops' day—Herodotus adds a bit of ancient gossip: *"They say* that Cheops reached such a degree of infamy, being in want of money, he prostituted his own daughter in a brothel. She managed to get what money her father needed and then, by asking everyone who came in to her to give her a stone for the edifice she designed", she was able to build a pyramid for herself, a smaller one, it is true, "the pyramid which stands before the great pyramid" a shocking instance of what the desire for a splendid tomb could do! The private lives of kings have never been respected by gossip in any age, but perhaps the interpreter was "putting one over" on Herodotus when telling his tale. That *"they say"* looks like it.

THE MYSTERY OF THE PYRAMIDS

There no longer is a *mystery* of the pyramids. In Architecture, as in other arts, a perfect thing develops from a germ. In the earliest days a square room was sunk in the Egyptian ground, and the body of the king or pharaoh was put in it. It was roofed with brush and poles, and then covered with sand. Little by little, the pyramid grew up into the air, out of the underground chamber. The roofed wall that rose above the tomb grew into a higher mass of brickwork. Then came a pile of stone instead of bricks. The stones grew larger and higher and at last the true pyramid, the most impressive architectural monument any race has found for its dead, stood complete.

The real secret of the pyramids *is the manner in which it shows the Egyptian's belief in the immortality of the soul and of his earthly body as well.* The tomb was the place in which the Egyptian's soul "lived" (just as the temple was the place in which his gods "lived") until it entered the Egyptian paradise. This was called *Sokhet Earu,* "the field of reeds", and was just a greener and more fruitful Egypt of the skies, where the beloved green Nile of the homeland greeted the wandering soul. But every Egyptian believed that he had *two souls,* and the *Ka* was the soul *that might any day come back to its earthly home again.* And while the Pyramid was Egypt's supertomb, everywhere the necropholis, the city of the dead" spread out, vaster than the cities of the living, and even while the Egyptians endured as a nation, they grew larger and larger, filled with their mummied millions. No nation took as much pains to "keep" themselves "as good as alive", patiently waiting on the pleasure of Osiris, the King of Death, against the time when their souls would need their bodies again.

The Pyramids of Egypt all look out upon desert sands. The *Great Pyramid of Gizeh,* the pyramid of King Cheops, whose building Herodotus described, is the largest of all, and many other smaller pyramids have been built on the same idea.

THE TOMB OF TUTANKHAMEN

(Sealed 1375 B.C.—Opened 1923 A.D.)

The pyramid was the ideal tomb until about the 18th "family" of pharaohs came to the throne. After that the pharaohs built no more pyramids. *They built tombs cut in the rock.* Instead of "pyramiding" great blocks of stone, each king, as soon as he came to the throne, had great gangs of slaves toiling furiously, carving out his series of death-chambers in the mountain-side (Beni Hassan). Like the coral-insect, he spent his life building his tomb and—the minute he died all work stopped! The masons who were chiselling ornaments and "pictures" on the inside walls, the painters who were coloring them, dropped chisel and brush. Not a pick was lifted, not a blow struck, not a stone was moved. And Pharoah was laid away in his tomb—finished or unfinished. He had had his chance.

We live in a time when kings—living or dead—are treated in a very off-hand way. The discovery in 1923, of the tomb of one of the proudest and most splendid of the Egyptian Pharoahs by the late Lord Carnavon and Mr. Howard Carter, only drives home the fact. Over 3,000 years ago Tutankhamen was sealed up in his rock-tomb, in the Valley of the Tombs of the Kings, near Thebes. And there, overlooked by the unscientific grave-robbers of thirty centuries, he at last fell into the hands of the *archaeologists,* the scientific robbers of graves in the name of sicence.

The elaborate funeral ceremonies the priests of Ammon said and sang for him were powerless to protect him in the silence and blackness of his tomb, where he lay among all the riches sealed up with him in the stark, terrible *loneliness* which is so Egyptian, and which we cannot understand. For even in death *we* like the company of those *dear to us.* We like the idea of an open blue sky above our restingplace. We like the idea of green grass and flowers and a smiling sun.

There has been nothing new "out of Egypt" for some time, and the discovery of Tutankhamen's tomb came just at the right moment.

We are used to kings who have been "kicked out" of their countries and off their thrones. We are used to kings and princes who are living by selling or pawning crown jewels, or, perhaps, on the money they have married. We are used to "figure-head" kings of "constitutional" monarchies whose word carries equal weight when they are opening a church bazaar or a parliament. But Tutankhamen was not that kind of a king. He was a god and king both. When he passed his people flung themselves in the dust and trembled, and when they cried "Hail, Pharaoh!" their hearts beat fast, and a chill of awe and fear and worship, all mixed together, *one we do not know,* shook them. When Tutankhamen clapped his hands the highest in the land ran to serve him. If he frowned and waved his hand, heads fell. Like Sargon or Xerxes or Aztec Montezuma, the distance between Tutankhamen and the very princes of his blood was so great that nothing could bridge it. He was life and death in Egypt. He was Egypt!

But this we do not feel—*for we are not ancient Egyptians.* So as soon as the news of the discovery was made known "familiarity bred contempt". The wearer of the twin crowns of Upper and Lower Egypt was at once nicknamed "King Tut". He was dragged into popular dance-song numbers and "jazzed to death" there; he made his bow in the "funny sheet" as well as on the serious front page of the paper; toilet waters, dress models and all sorts of other things were named after him, and he turned into a kind of a "world joke", only to be forgotten once the excitement was over.

The most complete and gorgeous "funeral furniture" ever found in a royal Egyptian tomb was found in that of Tutankhamen: royal couches, splendid chariots of bronze, with wheels of gilded wood, a magnificent throne of gold, silver and precious stones, jewels, rich robes, all the luxuries that were a matter of course in the life of a great king, and that he would expect to find as a matter of course when his soul came back from its mysterious journey. Then his mummied body would throw back the wooden cover of his splendidly painted and gilded coffin-case. He would shake off the linen rags of his wrappings. The thousands of bats hanging on the walls would start up and circle around him. But he would walk into the outer room of the tomb. The life-sized images* of himself guarding the entrance to the inner tomb of wood, covered with black pitch, would start back. The staff and club would drop from their hands. From his linen box and garment-chest the king would take what he needed. He would rub himself with costly ointments in the great jars of ala-

---

*They stand in sandals of gold; and the royal Egyptian snake, the sign of immortality, is inlaid in bronze and gold in their foreheads. Their eyesockets and eyebrows are gold; their eyes aragonite, (a crystallised calcium) with obsidian pupils.

baster—one of these jars was opened, and this rich skin-cream *grew liquid in the sun's heat* and gave out the wonderful fragrance which *had been sealed up in it MCCC years ago!*—and would step toward his tomb-door. And through the power of the great god Ammon, the barriers of stone and earth would fall away. Out of the blackness of death, Tutankhamen would step into Egypt's golden sunshine. The courtiers, the lovely queen would be drawn up to greet him, and life would stretch out before him without end! . . .

But this was not to be. In another rock-tomb in the valley lies another king. But how? In a rock-chamber *lit with electric light,* his mummy in its coffin now is a "show" for tourists! Tip the guide and you can see Amenhotep II, a soldier pharaoh who boasted that none but himself could draw his great bow. On the bow are engraved his titles: "Smiter of the People who Live in Caves, the Over-thrower of Kush, the Great Wall of Egypt". Tip the guide and see him by *electric light!* And such will probably be the fate of King Tutankhamen. For we have no reverence for the dead of a dead past, and we make their tombs our pastime.

The pyramid, unlike the rock tomb, brings back again the idea of *flatness* in the Egyptian art and soul. No matter from which side you come up to a pyramid, it presents on each of its visible *three great flat surfaces a gigantic triangle*. And the inner arrangement expresses the Egyptian's idea *that all life is a path*—leading to "the valley of reeds". Usually an outside entrance on the north leads down, down, seemingly into the bowels of the earth, to the burial vault, with many stone drop-doors and doors that turn on pivots. And in the last and innermost room of all, lies the dead king. We *like* to be buried near and with those whom we loved in life. The Egyptian must have a tomb *by himself alone*. The Pharaohs slept *alone* in their cold, black chambers, in their gilded and painted mummy-cases, wrapped in precious spices and linens, in a night weighted down by countless tons of stone—the loneliest dead of earth, perhaps!

AMERICAN AND OTHER PYRAMIDS

But other races beside the Egyptians—perhaps related to them in some dim past—have piled up pyramids. In the valley of Mexico, at Cucuilco, preserved by the lava which destroyed the builders, some early Mexican Pharaoh was forcing his "conscript" labor to put up a mighty pyramid—1,000 years before King Cheops wrestled with the "production cost" of onions for a hundred thousand men. In Ixtlu (Guatemala), Chichen-Itza (Yucatan) rise the great "stairway" pyramids of the vanished Maya people. At Chichen-Itza four stairways of hundreds of steps lead to the temple shrine at the top. One stair was the feathered Rattlesnake God, Kukulcan. The head is at the bottom of the stairs, the body are the serpent "banisters", the tail-rattlers wind round a "newel-post" on the summit. Up the rattlesnake stair came the loveliest of the Maya girls in times of drought. Eighty-five feet below the pyramid lay a mysterious pool of black, unsounded water. One after another the bound and screaming girls were flung into the black pool below—where most of them never rose again. But if a girl survived the shock and did not drown, a rope was let down and she was hauled out. For now she was supposed to be able to tell the priests "when it would rain".

These temples—for all American pyramids are *temples,* not *tombs* like those of Egypt—rise in the buried jungle cities of the Mayas, and the tropical creepers force apart the great stone blocks at Tikal, Palenque and many other places. Everywhere, in the Toltec and Aztec (Mexican) pyramid temples, the *teocallis,* in Colombia and Honduras, there is the suggestion of human sacrifice and the knife of sacrifice. In Peru, too, we find the pyramid. In fact, as Humboldt has said: "One would think the same architect had built all these many monuments." Does the pyramid form, common to Egypt and Central America hint at a distant race "relationship"? It is hard to say. In Europe the dead and vanished Etruscan people destroyed by the Romans are supposed to have piled up great pyramids of red clay—but they have disappeared with their builders.

EGYPTIAN TEMPLES AND PALACES

Egyptian temples, the houses in which the "gods" lived, and palaces were much on the same order. But the old cities of Egypt are heaps of ruins, and though there are a few great temple ruins (Luxor, Karnak, Thebes) the "order of importance" in Architecture was: *pyramid and tomb, temple, palace or house.* The Egyptian temples, too, often lie on the edge of the desert. They turn their *backs* to the desert, and *front* on life. Always they make the *flat surface* the ideal of beauty.

A great pylon* rises on each side of a high gate, walls ornamented with figures of gods and kings "standing out flat" against the flat surface of the rock. It is a "front" without a "back" behind it. Entering the gate a new *front* faces on a great empty court, rows of columns on each side. They simply lead from the first gateway to the next. The next gateway is again set in a *flat wall-front.* Passing through it, we come at last to the image of the god himself, the inner heart of the shrine. *No wonder the Eyptian's ideal of life has been called "a path!"* It is so expressed in his temples. At

---

* Pylon: a gateway in pyramid form; in modern architecture a steelwork tower to hold a wire-end, like a telegraph pole.

Edfu the pilgrim, come to worship, lands from a riverboat. A *straight road* runs from the river to the temple, which towers before the pilgrim's eyes. Avenues of sphinxes and rams, their heads turned towards him, forbid him to leave the *straight path*. Thus he nears the temple, which grows larger and larger. He walks through one gateway after another, sees one great flat wall-front after another, and *at last stands before the god's image at the very end of the path!*

THE OBELISKS AND THE SPHINX

Egypt's obelisks were "passed on down" from the Neolithic past. Tall pillars, they were originally set up to honor the gods, and are even found in Abyssinia. Usually they stood in pairs in front of temples, though sometimes alone. Their tops often ended in a sharp point, sheathed in bright metals, copper, brass, or even gold, so that the sun-god whom they honored would reflect his face with dazzling light in these "sunrays in stone". Egypt could not "hold on" to her obelisks. The Roman emperors started admiring them—and carrying off the best to Rome. Augustus Cæsar moved two from Heliopolis, the old, dying city of the sun-god, and had them set up in Alexandria. From Alexandria *one* was taken to London (1877) and the *other*, "Cleopatra's Needle", to Central Park in New York City. There it still stands, its metal point *(pyramidion)* still reflecting the rays of the same sun it did in Egypt thousands of years ago. But the damp, moist air of New York eats into the stone and is gradually wearing it away. The largest known obelisk (set up 1500 B. C., in Heluipolis), stands in the court of the Church of St. John Lateran at Rome; it is 105 feet, 9 inches, high.

The Sphinxes of Egypt were granite statues of gods in a "laying-down" position, with beast-bodies that led to the temples, and the "head" usually was that of the particular Pharaoh who had "put them up", a royal portrait "bust". Little brothers of the true sphinxes were the *crisosphinxes*, which had lion bodies and ram's heads", and the falcon-headed sphinxes; and Herodotus tells us an Egyptian gentleman sphinx without wings is an *"androsphinx"*. The Sphinx among sphinxes is the Great Sphinx of Gizeh, 189 feet long, with a woman's head, looking out across the Nile valley. A famous French artist, Caran d'Arche, has immortalized her in a wonderful series of colored pictures, in which she is "on the spot" almost with the beginning of things, and—after the Napoleon's "forty centuries" pass in picture, the Assyrians, Greeks, Romans, Arabs, French, flooding Egypt in turn, she is left as they pass out of the picture, still looking across the Nile valley, frozen, hung with icicles, on a world of ice which is dead.

The Treasure-House of the Labyrinth

The famous "Labyrinth" was probably the most romantic thing in Egyptian Architecture. *Lope-ro-hounit*, "the temple at the entrance of the lake", was for Egypt what the United States Treasury would be like if the secret of where its gold were hidden were known only to a few clergyman who had a special guard of "religious marines" to treat any one "rough", *even the President of the United States,* who was "looking for information". The Labyrinth held the *national treasure of Egypt*—only to be used in the last extremity. And the priests—not Pharaoh—held the key to the secret of where it was hid. Near what is now the town of Medmet-el-Fayouin, lay a world-wonder of a lake, an artificial one, Lake Moeris. Hard by was the Labyrinth.

The lake was regarded as one of the wonders of the ancient world. Built by Pharaoh Amenemhat III (2,330 years B.C.), Herodotus says the Labyrinth was a building shaped like an immense horseshoe, surrounded by a single wall, with twelve courts and 3,000 chambers, 1500 above and 1500 below ground. The roofs were of stone. The "guide" priests, who took Herodotus through the *upper* rooms—he was not allowed to see the lower ones—said not a word about the treasure. Travellers were told that the *lower* rooms of the Labyrinth held mummies of pharaohs and sacred crocodiles, the crocodiles in long rows, with bracelets and ear-rings of crystal of gold. *But it also held the sacred treasure of Egypt, added to and never taken away from for centuries.* No one could reckon its value.

The Labyrinth was not closely guarded. It was not necessary. A small troop of soldier-priests, captained by the *Guardian Priest of the Labyrinth*, was its sole defence. What made the treasure safe was the fact that excepting two or three people in a generation, *no one knew where to look for it.* For the Labyrinth was a maze of rooms and passages. When a pharaoh became king, he paid a visit to the Labyrinth. There he *saw* the treasures of his empire with his own eyes. Yet even a pharaoh did not know the secret. The High-Priest of Ammon and the Guardian of the Labyrinth did, but they were sworn never to reveal it, except to the next man to hold their "jobs".

Flinders Petrie, the Egyptologist, discovered the *foundation* of the Labyrinth in the Fayum, in 1888, and somewhat beneath—or, perhaps, far beyond—this enclosure (1,000 feet long by 800 feet wide) there still may lie the gems, ingots and clay jars of gold-dust, whose sum total of value cannot even be guessed, waiting for the treasure-hunter who will bring them to light!

CHAPTER II

"TOWERS OF BABEL" AND HANGING GARDENS

(Chaldea, Babylon and Assyria)

The Assyrians were a "hustling" race. They were too busy with the "business" of *life* to give as much attention to the hereafter as the Egyptians. They were a Semite people (like the Jews) and the Semite is *practical*. Assyrian Architecture took over the Ziggurat, or *tower-temple in seven stories,* from the Chaldeans and built huge palaces. The ziggurates have something of the pyramid about them, but they are temples, never tombs.

The Ziggurat was made by taking one tower and putting another one on it, and so on up, each tower being a little smaller than the other until the seventh was reached. An outside spiral "way" connected all the tower platforms. The Egyptian built in stone; their pyramids stand. The burnt brick Ziggurats of Mesopotamia are gone. No doubt when one of these great Ziggurats was being built by the Chaldean priest-kings, the wild desert "cheap labor" they had hired and who could not understand each other's "talk", ran amuck and thus, as the Scriptures tell, the mighty edifice fell in ruins—and we have the legend of the "Tower of Babel". Under the bright stars, on the top-most tower of such structures a priest called down the hour of the night to the sleeping city below. Buried cities* in Chaldea and Assyria dating back to 5,000 B. C. have given us a good idea of the Architecture of Babylon and Assyria.

The Assyrian and Babylonian idea in Architecture was "Grandeur regardless of expense". Labor cost nothing. The bricklayers who put up the Assyrian and Babylonian buildings were slaves, prisoners of war. There were always plenty of them. King Cheops drafted his own peoples, but King Sargon or King Tiglath-Pilesar said: "Assyria first". The ideal was bigness, size, splendor, the true boastful Assyrian spirit of "the spectacular" shows in all their buildings.

* Sir A. H. Layard uncovered layer after layer of earth and in "mines" 90 feet deep, the ruins of ancient Ninevah were bared. Babylon and many other great Chaldean and Assyrian cities with palaces and temples have also been brought to the light of day.

Babylon was a "twenty million inhabitants'" town. Like the pyramids, the walls of Babylon were one of the seven wonders of the world, 300 feet high, 136½ feet wide. They enclosed 15 square miles—and outside them the "communities" lived in the suburbs. Ferryboats and drawbridges 30 feet wide carried people, as from "New York to Brooklyn" or "Oakland to San Francisco", over the Euphrates river, which ran through the city. Herodotus saw and marvelled at them. The little "dead towns" of that part of Asia still dig up the good glazed bricks of the old kings stamped with their names and "tally-numbers" to put up their own little "two by four" houses. But the "up-keep" of those walls was a terrible job. As long as Babylon was a city great gangs were busy repairing here, there and everywhere, for great rains and soft clay bricks (the inside bricks) do not agree. But there "was no money in it" for the bricklayers. It was before the good days of the Union and—they were slaves. It is enough to make a bricklayer of to-day weep when he thinks of the chances he lost. For the bricklayers also made up all the *books* of Babylon and Assyria "in the raw". They used bricks for books—engraved business records, school readers, (yes, they had them), hymns, prayers, "tales", royal proclamations, income-tax returns, everything—on burnt bricks. When an Assyrian bricklayer said: "I guess I'll burn a batch of books" it meant that he was preserving them. And our scholars read their wedge-letters (cuneiform) to-day. The Assyrians borrowed the sphinx from Egypt, gave it a beard—all Assyrians wore beards, while the Egyptians were beardless—and wings and "made a man of him". These, and the big buttresses they ran out from temple, palace and city walls to strengthen them are features of their building work.

Queen Semiramis, supposed to have built the wonderful Hanging Gardens of Babylon is a queen of legend, but the Gardens were a fact. Traces of the actual irrigation works that "screwed" the water up have been found. The great "roof-gardens" of our own cities are higher, for the Hanging Gardens rested on a tremendous series of arches 75 feet high. The earth of the wonderful gardens of trees and flowers, where Babylonian kings did more than "hold hands" with their harem beauties, was heaped on great lead plates, with a drainage system and aside from being another "world wonder" it raised royalty and its hidden pleasures high above the eyes of the crowd.

One little "human nature" story has come down the ages in connection with Babylon's Hanging Gardens to show that husbands were as good-natured thousands of years ago as now. King Nebuchadnezzar of Babyon had married (among others) a Median girl, a princess from the mountain wilds of Zagros. Chaldea was a low, flat hot country and the girl grew homesick for the pure mountain air and the cool shadows and the flowers of her home land. So her husband, to make her happy, had the great arches built and the wonderful garden planted high in the air, with a pleasure pavilion on the highest terrace. There is no reason to doubt the tale, nor that Architecture owes one of its most curious monuments to *human love!*

THE PALACES OF VAIN-GLORY

The Assyrian palace, crushing and overwhelming with its size, is at its best in the King Sargon's palace, "fifteen miles out" from Nineveh. Sargon was a very successful "war lord" king, and as he grew older instead of working away feverishly at a tomb, he decided to build him a new palace. He is really "human" about it. "Day and night I planned to build that palace and city", he says in one of his inscriptions. And he did, 712 B. C., throwing in a new city in front of it, on the Tigris River to protect it.

The river was led into a lake, and on a 650 foot terrace faced with stone rose a palace that "was a palace" even then. Thirty courts, 210 separate rooms, halls and galleries and with a special ziggurat of its own. The walls were wainscoted with great slabs of alabaster, the doors of palm and cypress were covered with polished bronze. Cedar, palm and ivory were used in the "interior work". His inscriptions tell us that there was any amount of calling down blessings and consecrating and dedicating when it was finished by the Assyrian priests; but "Man proposes and God disposes", and now its ruins only remain. But—he built in five years a palace no multi-millionaire of to-day could finish in *ten*, perhaps—but there were no labor unions in his day.

Sennacherib, a later King, had up-to-date modern ideas. He "made over" Nineveh in grand style, and one of his inscriptions reads: "Of Nineveh, my royal city, I greatly enlarged the dwellings. I renovated its old streets and widened those that were too narrow. I made it shine like the sun." The Emperor Napoleon III when he "did away with the narrow, dirty alleys of old Paris and gave it its beautiful Boulevards, did no more. Sennacherib also pats himself on the back in wedge-shaped letters by telling how he "cared for the health of the city by bringing streams of water into it", by 16 canals that piped in a little river.

Sennacherib built him a palace, too, that covered eight acres (700 B. C.) but Architecture which so boastfully shows Assyria's grandeur, shows her fall as well. After a great flood of wild Asian horseman had swept over the land we find that the palace of the king before the last is a small, mean, coarse building "evidently put up in great haste". And there, not long after (608 B.C.) the last king, Saracos, probably was burned alive when Nineveh fell into the hands of the Medes and Persians.

CHAPTER III

PERSIA'S TOWERS OF SILENCE AND ROYAL HALLS

The Medes and Persians were little mountain tribes, Aryan tribes, when they started to conquer the world. They brought with them from the high hills one characteristic thing on *Architecture*—their tower. For they were sun-god worshippers and the *Dakhma,* the "Tower of Silence", the tower of the dead, shows their race-soul in stone. These towers rose sixteen, twenty or more feet in the air. At the top was a circular platform, paved with large, flat, sloping stones, divided into three rows of "grooved box" receptacles. From the circle of stones, divided by ridges) liquid matter and rain-water drained into a deep stone-lined pit, in the centre of the tower platform. From the pit, underground, ran four drains, and at the mouth of each—*where anything coming from the tower might touch the earth*—were sand and charcoal, *to purify!* These four drains ran out to four wells sunk in the ground at equal distances from the towers.

THE TOWERS OF SILENCE

The "Dakhmas" these "towers of silence", *were the tombs of the Persian dead.* They still rise in Bombay, where the Parsees, descendants of the ancient Persians, hold to their old faith. How would you like to think that once the breath was out of your body, your nearest and dearest would tenderly take you to a "tower of silence", and lay you on a stone slab *for the vultures to feast upon?* We would *not* call this *burial.* The idea would be disgusting to us. Yet the ancient Persian *longed for it,* as the Parsee of Bombay does to-day. It is all the way you look at a thing. Why?

Because the great Persian god of light,* the sun-god, the fire-god, the god of all that was good, Ahura-Mazda said that *all the elements were holy.* Now death is impurity. *To bring the dead body into touch with any element was to corrupt it.* And that is how there came to be "towers of silence". The corpse could not be

---

* You may have wondered where the electric company which makes the *"Mazda"* lights got hold of the name. It is the name of the great Persian sun-light and fire-god, and a very appropriate one for an electric globe.

left "up in the *air*". It could not be buried in the *earth*. It could not be dropped "over the side", into *water*. At least of all could it be burned in the *fire*. That surely would have brought down Ahura-Mazda's curse on the whole land. So the ancient Persians had to leave the bodies of their dead ones, as their sacred books say "to the corpse-eating dogs and the corpse-eating birds". They weighed them down with brass, stone or lead, so that birds and dogs would not carry bits of flesh and bone to water or trees and defile them. If the ancient Persian mother could not afford a "tower" for her babe, the best she could do was to lay down her dead child on the ground, "clothed in the light of heaven" (naked) on its carpet pillow, and abandon it to the *carrion-feeding beasts!* And what seems *hideous* to us, the poor mother did *gladly*, knowing that her little one would enter into Ahura-Mazda's golden halls!

But after Cyrus the Great, the "towers of silence" seem to have lost their popularity. The great kings of his race had themselves laid away in burial chambers cut in the rock, "rock tombs", instead of leaving their bodies *for the birds to pick*. After all, a body laid away in coffin and sarcophagus* in a dry rock chamber could not pollute the air. Herodotus, who travelled in Persia in King Xerxes' time, said that the Persian dead were "covered with wax and buried in the ground." The *wax* the Magi priests no doubt insisted on, to "save the face" of their god and of themselves.

The Tower of Silence is a most characteristic thing in Persian Architecture. Persian rock-tombs are modelled after those of Syria, Asia Minor and Egypt. The huge palaces of the Persian kings are copied from the monster palaces of Assyria and Babylon, but the "tower of silence" is their own. Yet just as they outdid the Assyrians as a world-power, they outdid them in palace building. Of the many palaces of the Persian kings two, those of *Susa* and of *Persepolis,* have been discovered and unearthed, and in the last-named palace the *huge pillars of the Great Hall of Xerxes still stand,* the hall in which the "war-lord" of his time decided on the Greek expedition, which changed the course of History.

THE HALL OF THE "GREAT KING"

Persepolis means "the city of the Persians", but the city was just a "frame" for the big palace Darius II built, and in which Xerxes lived. A great, flat, rocky platform at the foot of a mountain, looking out on a plain is the building site. It was shaped up into three rising terraces, each twenty feet higher than the other, and back of the terraces was the towering mountain itself. The terraces were marble-fronted, and that human hands could get the

---

*Sarcophagus: a coffin made of stone.

huge stone columns and blocks out of which the palace was built up on the top terrace is as great a miracle as the building of the pyramids! The single stone-masonry blocks of the Persepolis palace are from thirty to fifty feet long (*your own house is probably no deeper*), eight feet high, and six feet thick. They were laid together by *cohesion* and by iron *clamps*: no *mortar*. The marble terrace stairs in double flights were so wide that ten men on horseback could ride up each stair without crowding. And with the fine "harmony" of great lines was combined the richest of colored figure ornamentation along the solid marble balustrades (parapets) that fenced in each stairway. The palace sits at the top: a central hall with two great "sets" of rooms on each side. Each "set" has an entrance door (portal), and four great windows that front on a porch with columns. But behind the palace, a thing apart, stands the great "Hall of a Hundred Columns".* *It "sizes up" in itself everything the proud Persian believed in: the undying glory of Persia, the "superiority" of the Persian race; the lordship over all the other nations of earth. It is in Architecture, the very spirit of pride, majestic, unshaken pride of race.* The great Assyrian palaces are just "bluffs in brick" compared to it.

It was one vast, tremendous hall—227 feet every way—with two great entrances and several windows in each great wall. One vast, flat roof of gold-plated cedar and cypress beams rose up on the hundred columns (72 feet still remain) that gave the hall its name—columns of *black marble, in ten rows of ten each.* Tall and slender, they seemed to grow out of flower "bases", and at their tops (unlike the bellshaped Egyptian columns) they ended in great bull and other animal heads, on whose necks the roof rested.

The Susa palace ruins show that the palace was much like Darius's; a great columned hall, with flat roof, with stone bulls guarding the entrance gates. If the columns of Susa could but talk! How often Haman, who was hanged high, passed between the huge bulls "on guard" before the palace gates, giving Mordecai a patronising look as he passed. And in that great hall Queen Esther, with her beauty and her cleverness, "sold herself" and her people's cause to the "monarch of all he surveyed". There, as the Bible tells us, "the heart of the king was merry with wine", and when Queen Esther was "raised up" the Jews slew their enemies by the thousands through all the provinces of Persia. It was a great day for the Jews!

---

* If you ever have seen a photograph of the Milan Cathedral—the modern building which most resembles it, you would have an idea of what the "Hall of a Hundred Columns" looked like in lines and size. At that the "floor space" of the Xerxes' Hall was greater, for the Milan Cathedral covers only 107,800 square feet.

CHAPTER IV

ARCHITECTURE'S LAND OF LICENSE

(India)

INDIAN *Architecture shows the race spirit* in an "exuberance ot fancy, lavishness of labor, and elaboration of detail found nowhere else." A strange land of architectural license, of monstrous gods and magnificent kings, its Architecture runs riot in stone. But not at first. At first, wood was all that Indian Architecture knew—until about 300 B.C. Stone or bricks were used at the most for foundations.

Then the Hindus began to build in stone the kinds of buildings they had built in wood. After Alexander's conquest of the world, from Indian travellers who had visited Persia, the Hindus learned to imitate the palaces and tombs of the Persian kings. But Asoka, the greatest of the Buddhist kings of India "rings a change" on the use of the *lats,* the great stone columns Babylonian, Assyrian and Persian kings set up for religious and royal proclamations, and added the Hindu *honeysuckle ornament* to the "bead" and "cable" ones of Persia.

He introduced the *Stupas* (*dagabas* in Ceylon) or *topes*—he is said to have put up 84,000 of them—the *Relic-Shrines for relics of Buddha.* They are simply low, circular brick drum-buildings, stone-coated, with a dome, and one at Bhopal is the largest and most elaborately carved one remaining. Then the Buddhists began to burrow underground, and dug them all sorts of Cave Temples and Cave Monasteries below the earth whose rock roofs were chiseled smooth, and supported by columns and pillars cut in the living rock. And, as often happens, when the followers of the god Brahma saw what the Buddhists were doing, they had to have Cave Temples too, and "went them one better" in cave-shrines like the celebrated cave temple of Elephanta Isle, a subterranean temple on a little island between Bombay and the Indian mainland.

THE LEWD GODS OF ELEPHANTA

The Elephanta Cavern-Temple is one of Architecture's most curious productions. Pillars cut in the rock flank its entrance, 60 feet wide

Mohammedan Architecture, the Mongol, and it seems preferable to consider it here.

Mohammedan Architecture in India runs from 1100, the date of the Moslem conquest, to the year 1700 A.D. and the castles, tombs and mosques that the great Mogul Emperors of India built, show the religious spirit of the Moslem in Architecture, in a special race form.

THE "WATER-SOUL" OF DELHI CASTLE

A glorious "left-over" of the oriental Middle Ages is the great castle of the Mogul emperors in Delhi. It is a palace-fortress. Fantastic walls and towers, dark winding gateways, guarded by stone elephants lead into what looks like a huge gloomy fort on the outside. But *within* are great, high, airy chambers; there is the magnificent hall where the emperors sat on the jewel-covered peacock-throne and held court. And while the terrible Indian sun burned down outside, inside the palace *the murmur of waters gave the building a soul of its own.* Everywhere, in the great Delhi palace, the crystal waters rill and run. Stone shells are carved in marble floors, and the fountain-jet leaps up and falls back with cooling splash into its basin. In a bed of marble, a silver brook *winds through whole suites of rooms,* disappearing under the pavement of the halls of ceremony to bring refreshing coolness to the intimate living rooms of the palace. *The brook is the life-vein of the great castle,* and connects all its many rooms and pavilions. The baths are more luxurious than anything we have today.

In shadowed vaulted rooms, deep, white marble basins ("tubs") are cut into the stone floors. There are rooms for hot and for cold baths, and quiet corners with couches of half-precious stones. Once the harem beauties lay there at ease, dreaming on pillows and costly stuffs, while slaves tenderly chafed the delicate limbs on which pearly drops of water lingered. *The Hindu artists knew how to use water as a living ornament in Architecture,* just as they spread the lovelier designs in colored marbles and half-precious stones over chamber walls, pillars and ceilings. And in this *Mohammedan Art* the beauty of the *whole as a whole* is never lost in the beauty of detail. In the Mogul emperor's splendid audience hall (its ceiling was once all of purest silver) every inch of wall-space is covered with the most bewildering ornament and yet—the high arched windows do not stop the eye from looking out on the spreading miles of plain below!

ANOTHER PICTURE! "THE HOME OF DREAMS"

Five miles from Agra lie the ruins of a great castle built by the Emperor Akbar the Great. Called Fatihpur-Sikri, it was a won-

THE ANCIENT EAST

derful combination of an emperor's palace hall and a poet's ideal of a private, "intimate" place in which to live. A narrow entrance leads through a mighty wall, too narrow for a horseman to pass. And then one stands in a great empty court, enclosed by shady "arcades." At the far end is a little raised hall through which the Emperor came from the *interior* of the palace, to seat himself on the marble throne beneath the middle arch of the far end of the court. His nobles and vassals could crowd the great courtyard—the grandest ever a king had—while Akbar sat only a few feet above them on his throne.

And, the audiences of ceremony over, he passed back through the little hall and—there he was among the fountains and gardens which surrounded the place of *his private life,* his "Home of Dreams," as he called it. It is a palace with cool, dim rooms, where crystal waters played, its walls covered with wall-paintings in the Persian style. At one side, is a delicate, filagreed little pavilion where his beloved "Turkish Queen" lived. And, a step away, through the burning, glaring garden is the cool, dim bath Akbar could enter, where "indirect" light filtered through unseen openings along the dome. In the middle of the inner courtyard of the "Home of Dreams" stands *one giant column* which supports a broad platform. Four bridges that seem floating in the air, connect the corners of the first story with the platform on the column. And there Akbar, *who loved the game of chess,* sat on the stone seat of his high perch with some favored courtier and—*the court was paved with great squares of black and white marble*—ordered about the slave-boys and slave-girls who were the living pawns of the chess-game he loved, as he made his "moves." No doubt the dark eyes of the harem women looked on at the game through the barred and gilded window peep-holes of their great bird-cage. And so that these harem women could pass down unseen to the gardens on the castle slope, a covered stone stairs led over pillars and arches, along the further side of the castle wall. But here, too, a rich gate of gilded iron work closes the entrance to the stairs. Any one trying to "get an eyeful" of forbidden beauty from a distance would see the lovely shape only *a second,* as it passed from the gate to disappear in the green bushes. Perhaps the finest single building of Fatihpur-Sikri is the *Dragon Mosque,* its pillars and arches reflected in the silvery marble of its floor as in a lake. And all around these principal buildings lie enormous palaces of courtiers, nobles, inns for merchants, great barracks for guards, elephants, camels, horses. And— a human touch—there is a cylinder-shaped tower from which elephant's tusks stick out on all sides. *It is the monument the emperor put up over the ground where his favorite elephants lie buried.*

CHAPTER V

WHERE NATURE IS ARCHITECTURE'S TWIN

(China and Other Lands of the Far East)

THE Architecture of China is a real product of the Chinese soul. There are few "ruins" in China—all buildings before 800 B.C. have disappeared. Egyptian Architecture shows that for the Egyptian life on earth was a pilgrimage with the tomb at its end. The Chinaman looks on life as a "stroll" through a world rich in beauties of nature.

So all that is *nature* around Chinese Architecture—mountains, rivers and lakes, trees, flowers, curiously shaped stones—is as important as gates, walls, houses and bridges. We use nature in Architecture as an "extra." The Chinese see it as a *part* of all they build. The arch is known to the Chinese but it is not used much: it is at its best in the graceful stone bridges near Peking. Especially Chinese are the *Pai-lou*—memorial archways or gateways put up to honor the great. The most famous are the *Pai-lou* of "The Sleeping Buddha's" temple and that at the avenue of tombs of the Ming emperors, both near Peking.

For the Chinese the roof of a house is more important than any other part: The one usual "house model" in China is called the *t'ing*. Many short columns are set up and the spaces between them "filled in" with stone or brick, but these walls are not "supporting walls." * But the columns, the walls, only are there for the sake of the roof. Chinese life centers in *the family,* and this may explain why the *roof,* which means protection, is greater than anything else about a house. The Chinese is an ancestor-worshipper, he prays to the spirit of the father who has gone before him. That is why he builds with wood and brick as a rule, instead of stone. He does not care about those who come after him: his spirit looks toward the past. But on the roof the Chinese architect gets in "his best licks." Roofs are raised in two and three "tiers": dragons crouch on the ridges and eaves; they are covered with carved and lacquered woodwork or with bright-colored glazed tiles. But most Chinese buildings are in "bungalow" style. They have only one story and there is only one "plan," and because they all look alike

* China and America meet here in a strange way, because this is the "construction" idea of our modern steel-frame building.

THE ANCIENT EAST 35

they weary our eyes, especially as all of them *must* face South. The greatest temple on this *t'ing* model is the Confucian Temple of Heaven (Peking), with a three-tier roof of deep blue tiles, and (outside) an open-air Altar of Heaven—three circle terraces with marble balustrades.

THE PAGODA

To us the pagoda* is the most interesting thing in Chinese Architecture. It is a tower with *eight* sides (usually on a brick foundation), thirteen "stories" high. Into the pagoda the religious fancies and dreams of the Chinese people, their religious "imagination," has created beauty in the Chinese way as fine as our Gothic cathedrals. In Chinese Architecture the pagoda shows us the Chinese instinct to express religious feeling in its noblest form.

THE PORCELAIN TOWER

The great Porcelain Tower of Nanking (it was destroyed in 1854, in a rebellion) covered with slabs of *faience*** coated with colored glazes was the wonder of all China. Longfellow, our own American poet, has described it:

Let us try and see it with the poet's eyes:
"The Tower of Nanking, strange and old,
Uplifting to the astonished skies
Its ninefold painted balconies . . ."

Just as the *Taj-Mahal* rose to express a lover's sorrow, the *Porcelain Tower expresses in stone a son's love for his mother.* For the Emperor Yung-Lo (1403-1428) raised it (260 feet in the air) as a memorial to his mother's virtues, and his tender memory of her,

"With balustrades of twining leaves
And roofs of tile, beneath whose eaves
Hang porcelain bells that all the time
Ring with a soft, melodious chime."

Its walls were bricks of the finest white porcelain, and the eaves of each of its nine stories were made of green glazed porcelain tiles.

---

* The Chinese word for pagoda is *taa*. Pagoda (fr. Pers., *but-kadah*, "the idols house") was a name the 16th century Portuguese in India gave any native temple. The name has stuck. But there was also an Indian gold coin, called the *pagod* or *pagoda*, worth about $1.68. And from that coin came the expression "shaking the pagoda-tree." When an Englishman had held a good "job" in the East India Company (18th and early 19th centuries) and came back to England with his pockets filled with gold, people said he had been "shaking the pagoda tree." The Chinese pagoda-tower is supposed to owe its strange shape to Indian Buddhist influence.

** Faience: a word for all *glazed* earthenware or porcelain.

Lanterns without number hung from the eaves, and the "porcelain bells," 152 of them, used to chime:

> "While the whole fabric was ablaze
> With varied tints, all fused in one
> Great mass of color, like a maze
> Of flowers illumined by the sun!"

It was topped by a gilt ball, and from five iron chains that ran from the roof hung five great pearls, "good luck" pearls, to guard the city of Nanking from danger. But alas, the pearls of "good luck" were powerless, and the Porcelain Tower, Architecture's fair white flower of motherlove and religious devotion, has vanished for all time!

THE GREAT WALL OF CHINA

The people of cities built walls with towers at an early date. One of the oldest towered walls was that of Nineveh (2,000 B.C.) but—the only nation which built a towered wall *around its whole country is the Chinese*. Twenty-one centuries ago the Emperor Khe-Hoangti set millions of workmen busy putting up this great architectural monument, 1,863 miles long (if it had been set up in Europe it would run from Scotland to the Dardanelles, or in the United States from New York to Omaha). Hundreds of thousands of laborers *died* building the wall, whose cubic feet of material would make 120 of the Great Pyramid of King Cheops. It runs uphill and down dale, over high mountains—up which the great stone blocks had to be carried—and through deep valleys, and any mason who left a crack in the stone-work large enough to admit a nail *was killed on the spot*. It is mainly brick, granite faced, and was meant to keep out all enemies—*and all the rest of the world was to China an enemy and a "barbarian."* And it did so until the middle of the seventeenth century. For fourteen centuries the Great Wall of China protected Chinese traditions, customs and life from foreign influence.

But now the Great Wall lies across the Chinese land like a big dragon that has died. Once its top was crowded with soldiery; military mandarins in fantastic armor raised their silken tents and gaudy dragon banners along its battlements. Its towers were filled with spearmen and archers. But now, where hundreds of thousands of soldiers once lined the granite wall-platforms on which twenty horsemen can ride abreast in many places, only a few wandering caravans pass. The practical usefulness of the Great Wall came to an end when the wild Tartar hordes of Timur Khan swept over it—there is an old legend that the cloud of Tartar arrows fell so thickly that a mandarin who stepped out of the tower at one place where the Tartars "rushed" the wall, *literally vanished in the air*—

shot into fragments by the tremendous number of arrows which struck him—and overran all China. Yet there is nothing in all Architecture more *moving* than this tremendous *dead* monument, this wall which "stood off" so many floods of enemy soldiers, and was put up at so great a cost of life and treasure to let the strange Mongolian soul and its civilization develop in its own way, protected by it.

THE HIDDEN VIOLET CITY

Yuang Ming Yuan, the "Hidden Violet City," is the "Summer Palace" where the Chinese emperors, the "sons of heaven," lived the life of earthly gods in a confusion of pavilions, pagodas, marble palaces and bridges, forests, lakes and gateways—*for here, too, Nature is part of Architecture*—where bronze temples and cinnabar-colored "summer-houses" smile down on the loveliest of green and flowering gardens. There the "Son of Heaven" dreamed away his idle hours in fairy pavilions with his lovely concubines, amid music, perfumes, rare birds and all that could delight eye and senses. There the riches of the ages were piled up for the soldiers of the foreign countries to plunder at the time of the "Boxer" troubles and some of the wonderful imperial "loot," silks and rare ivories, gems and miracles of jade and goldsmith's work, is still treasured in this land, undreamed of, in the womb of time when the Great Wall rose in its glory.

But the gods that grin from the eaves of temple and pavilion are dying in their gilding; the great marble junk which an emperor had built out into one of the lakes, will never again, perhaps, "take on a crew" of laughing young slave girls and squeaky-voiced eunuchs, to "sail" on its quiet "lake of dreams," in a golden Chinese afternoon. The "Hidden Violet City" lies deserted, one more marvel of Architecture which still expresses the life which has left it.

ARCHITECTURE IN OTHER LANDS OF THE FAR EAST

Architecture in *Japan is borrowed largely from China,* and its main peculiarity is the Chinese one of making Nature—the landscape, trees, lakes, hills, etc.,—part of the general "building" design. But what the Chinese do in this way on a grand scale, the Japanese carry out, very often, on a "reduced scale." So we see tiny gardens in which *dwarf* trees (sometimes hundreds of years old) and *dwarf* plants, and *dwarf* bushes, bridges, hillocks and lakes give us beauty as seen "through a microscope." Now the Japanese, a race of "imitators," build their great public buildings in our "Western" styles.

In the countries of Indo-China, Architecture shows often a double influence of the races. In Siam, the wonderful ruins of *Angkor*

Thom and *Angkor Wat*—*wat* means temple—great temples of an early race, the Khmers, buried in the jungle, are reckoned among the world's finest ruins. They are tremendous temple towers (*Angkor Wat* is 213 feet high), rising on enormous terraces reached by magnificent stairways. Inside and out, they are wonderfully carved with ornaments and figures of goddesses—*many of the images polished smooth by the pious lips of pilgrims of thousands of years ago*—and the many scenes of all sorts from Hindu mythology cut and carved in the stone seem to show that they were the shrines of an early race of Brahmin priest-kings, which afterward died and decayed, leaving its temples to fall in ruin. The *Wat Phra Keo* is considered the most beautiful modern *Siamese* temple—its woodwork all covered with gold-leaf, outside and in—but in *Siam, Cambogdia and Burmah,* architecture in its great pagoda-temples only follows more weakly and feebly, the grander style of the *Angkor* ruins. In *Java* many temples are Hindu (like *Chandi* Sewu, "the thousand shrines": really 240 small buildings around a middle temple) while others suggest China.

ORIENTAL ARCHITECTURE OF WESTERN ASIA

Syrians and Phœnicians, Lydians, Phrygians and Lycians built palaces like those in Assyria and Persia. Only *a few stones* of Solomon's temple in Jerusalem remain. It was built along the line of an Egyptian temple, and therefore (with all its gold and cedarwood fully described in the Bible) does not offer us anything new in Architecture. The rock-tombs of Asia Minor do not differ much from those of Persian kings or Egyptian Pharaohs. A *two-tier tomb-tower* (Amrith) seems to be about the only different and distinctive thing about these architectures, and it is Phœnician. Fancy would be going too far, perhaps, if it suggested that this tube-top fitting tightly into a round drum expresses the greed, the "all for the dollar" spirit of the Phœnician trading race!

GREEK ARCHITECTURE

CHAPTER VI

"THE GLORY THAT WAS GREECE"

If *beauty* is the most important thing in great architecture, then the Greek ideal is superior to that of the East, from the point of view to which our eyes have accustomed us. *Size* and the *majesty of size* impress us in the Egyptian pyramids, *order* and *beauty of arrangement* in the Greek temple. The Greeks probably sprang from the same race-stock as the Persians, in the dim ages before History, but their way of doing and thinking, in life as in art, changed completely in the course of ages. When King Xerxes invaded Greece each side called the other "barbarian!"

THE PALACES OF THE SEA-KINGS

Before passing to the Greece of History, we must consider the Architecture of the age before history, disclosed in the great palaces of the Cretan kings, of Knossus, Mycaenae and Tyrins, dug up on the island Crete. The Cretans were a sea-going people, with a big navy of merchant and war ships, and held their own from perhaps 3,000 B.C., until Knossus was destroyed by the forefathers of Homer's heroes before the year 1400 B.C. The Cretan kings were all called "Minos," and they and their people specialized in the *"art of living,"* which in their case meant the "art of having a good time," with every comfort and convenience, and they discovered and *used modern plumbing* in their castles long, long before any other nation dreamt that it was one of life's little decencies.

Flat and "gable" roofs, great "courtyards" with separate walls, "light shafts" (*like those in our big apartment-houses and hotels*), and "three-story" instead of "bungalow" floors gave the Cretan palaces quite a modern look. Fine cut stone and brick were the building materials used, and wooden beams supplied the "superstructure" in the palaces. But the architects had not discovered a "true" arch, and "got around" it by "building out" stones, each stone stretching out further than the one below it, until they met at the top. Great *wooden*—they have disappeared, of course—instead of stone columns supported the roofs, and animal figures, rosettes, palmetto leaf and other designs furnished rich ornamentation for the walls.

These Cretan palaces (there are great rock tombs as well), are not a "primitive" or "savage" art. They are a complete art *which expressed the Cretan's high civilization.* Of the great flight of steps, 45 feet wide, which led to the main entrance of the palace of Phæstos an authority has said: *"No architect ever made such a flight of steps outside of Greece!"* The vast walls of Tyrins are 57 feet thick in some parts, *and under one and the same palace roof a whole "small town" was "assembled,"* every department of the royal court, from the "private suites" of the king and queen to the cubby-holes where the stablemen slept. There were "chapels," stone underground dungeons (on the smooth surface of whose walls the clutching fingers of despairing prisoners could gain no hold), "offices" for the ministers of state, lodgings for hundreds of palace slaves, a great throne-room, its walls adorned with blue and green porcelain tiles, lapis-lazuli, and crystal panels. It was a high art, a great art, which *expressed the Cretan soul and civilization of its day!* And from this Cretan architecture the early Greek architects took the first of their three kinds of "columns" or "Orders"—Doric, Ionic and Corinthian—after which all the buildings they built are named.

WHAT GREEK ARCHITECTURE REALLY IS

The main Greek tribes appear in history around the year 1100 B.C., after the Cretans have dropped out of the ranks of living nations. The Doric (named after the tribes who occupied Central Greece) was that developed by the Athenians and other Greeks. The Ionians (on the Aegean Islands and coast of Asia Minor) "worked out" a style called the Ionian, which borrowed various things from the Asiatic nations, and the Corinthian style grew out of the other two.

The Doric* was a heavy fluted column, so heavy it did not need a special "pedestal" or support, but every portico or "porch" of Doric columns was always raised at least *one step* higher than its surroundings. After the Doric, and soon used with it came the Ionic column, very much more slender and graceful (both types had no fixed length, running anywhere from fifteen to fifty feet), and as time went by the joining of each part of the column, its decoration, its "end" (capital) and its base were improved until each became

* Earlier Doric temples and tombs are: the temple of Apollo; Syracuse, the temple of Corinth (650 B.C.), the temple of Neptune at Paestum. Early Ionic buildings are the old temple of Diana at Ephesus, the temple of Apollo in Naucratis, Egypt, and the tomb of Tantalais, near Smyrna.

GREEK ARCHITECTURE

more or less standardized, and with them certain styles of buildings. Latest of all came the Corinthian column and style.

In Egyptian and Assyrian buildings and temples there is, so to say, practically only "one general style." In Greek architecture there are three, named after the *kind* of column used, and the *way* in which they are formed. And now, as we go on to the "Romance" of Greek Architecture we will leave a footnote "by the way." It is for those who like solid fact as well as "Romance," and want to have a clear *mind picture* and a "good speaking knowledge" of what the three "styles" or "Orders" * (as they are called) of Greek architecture are.

* Nearly all buildings in ancient Greece came from a "germ-cell," the plan of the ordinary Greek *"house,"* consisting of a long narrow hall (not a "square," oriental one, with a court) supported by columns. Tile roofs on wooden beams rested on "inner walls" or columns. In marble temples stone ceilings and marble "beams" could be used for roof-work. Gable roofs (ridge-roofs ending in a gable—the end-wall roofing under the eaves) were common. The best walls were made of smooth-faced or "edge-dressed" blocks, and *each kind of column had its own molding.* The two *chief things* in a Greek building met in the door—the door-posts (columns) and the *lintel* (the horizontal beam lying across the top of the door-posts). As a rule Greek masonry is *"lintel construction,"* the opposite of *"arched construction,"* though the "true" arch was used in later days in bridges and gateways, and the old Assyrian "barrel vault" in tombs underground.

The *"entablature"*—everything between the beam-end of a column and the roof—and the *shaft* are the keys to each of the three "Orders" of Greek Architecture. The "entablature" is a "system," a group of parts. At the very top is the *"cornice of the roof,"* which juts out to protect the *"frieze"* or ornamental band running along *under* the cornice. Then comes the *architrave, the principal roof-beam,* which "sets" directly on the *capital, the ornamental top* in which the column-shaft ends. The column is made up of the *base* (or *pediment*), which is to the column what a foot is to the human leg; the *shaft* itself; and the *capital* or *"bearer"* (it has been compared by one authority to a hand stretched out open-palmed, to support the weight of the architrave).

The *Doric column* is fluted, with a "plain," undecorated architrave, and pedestals at the lower angles of the base hold small statuettes (little figures of animals or men).

The *Ionic column,* lighter and more slender, and with deeper "flutings" in the shaft, has an architrave in three separate "tiers," and the capital, instead of being plain like the Doric, has a *cushion-scroll with whorls (volutes) turning in.* Instead of the shaft running straight down to its floor, the Ionic column has an *independent base.* The Attic-Ionic is a richer combined column-form of this sort. The *volutes* look like a ram's horn.

The *Corinthian column,* with a separate base and even more slender than the Ionic column, blossoms out into a very rich and elaborate capital, shaped like a flower-cup, and decorated, as a rule, with stems, buds and *conventionalized* (shaped in a "set way") thistle (*acanthus*) leaves. In rare cases sculptured human figures of men (*Atlantes*) or women (*Caryatides*) were used as column-shafts to secure fine decorative results.

All the great architectural monuments of ancient Greece belong to one

THE TEMPLES OF THE "ORDERS"

(Parthenon and Erechteum)

The oldest (archaic) Dorian temple was one dedicated to Neptune, in Paestum, with the heaviest and clumsiest kind of Doric columns, and lighted through an opening in the roof. But the temple of Minerva (Athens) the goddess of wisdom, the temple of "Athene Parthenos," which still rises above the other ruins on the *Acropolis** ("citadel" or "fortress" of Athens) *is perhaps, the finest product of the finished Doric style.* The first important thing to notice about it is that *at last the architect—the artist who creates beauty in stone buildings—has come into his own!* Pericles, who ruled Athens at the time with the power of a king, was a bigger man than the oriental despots who denied the artist his rightful fame. He "ordered" the temple built (447–432 B.C.) and the architects *Ictinus* and *Callicrates* were the men to whom the glory of having planned and built it is due. Standing on a stone base, the Parthenon had seventeen columns on either side of its hall, and eight at each end. Steps led up to a great porch and in the central nave, in a space open to the blue sky of Greece, stood the famous gold and ivory statue of the goddess.**

The Erechteum was an architectural "oddity," a double temple on the Acropolis plateau of Athens, the home of both the goddess Athena and the god Poseidon (Neptune), who were supposed to be Athen's special friends. At the south end was a portico supported by column-maidens (the *caryatides* already mentioned) and in the one shrine was Athene's sacred olive-trees, and in the other Neptune's blessed salt well.

Most of us have seen plaster casts or statuettes of the "Winged Victory," the *Niké* of Samothrace. She had a little Ionic temple on the Acropolis, where her statue once stood, and, in fact, nearly every god or goddess of Greek mythology had a temple somewhere in Greece. We will consider a few of the more famous before pass-

or the other of the three great "Orders," Doric, Ionic or Corinthian: temples, theatres, civil buildings, tombs, market-places, etc., *and all are variations of the simple Greek house* which is the *"germ"* of all Greece's architectural deevlopment. And everywhere, in the separate states, "the Glory that was Greece" was shown in a wonderful architecture of marble and stone, whose ruins are still the inspiration of the world to-day.

* Nearly every Greek city has its *"acropolis,"* though that of Athens is best known. It was the "fort" which held the chief temples, public buildings, treasury, etc., of the town and usually stood on a hill.

**If you must have one long word for "gold and ivory," it is quite in order to say "chriselephantine," which is simply a contraction of two Greeks words meaning "gold and ivory" into an English one.

ing on to the other buildings. *Zeus (Jove)*, has a temple in Olympia much like the Parthenon, and a temple called the *Phillipeion* is curious because it is one of the few circular Greek temples and has Corinthian columns of great beauty. One of the most famous of all Greek temples stood in Asia Minor.

THE TEMPLE OF THE DIANA OF THE EPHESIANS

The first temple of *Artemis (Diana) at Ephesus,* in Western Asia Minor, was a little shrine, built toward the end of the eighth century B.C., which grew in size and riches until (650 B.C.) the wild Cimmerians, a savage tribe from Russian steppes, overran Asia Minor and sacked it. Then the Knossian architect *Chersiphron* and his son *Metagenes* rebuilt another temple that rose on the ruins—a glorious building covering 84,000 square feet, of purest white marble and surrounded by 129 beautifully ornamented Ionic columns, those at the entrance, 59 feet high, being arranged in three rows. Later it was enlarged, King Crœsus and all the cities of Asia giving gold for its erection, and after 120 years of construction work!—people took their time and produced masterpieces in those days—it was dedicated with a great deal of ceremony between 430 and 420 B.C.

And there it stood until an ordinary, everyday person named Herostratus made an end of it. Herostratus had a soul that thirsted for "publicity." He wanted to be in the "lime-light," wanted "to attract attention," to have "everybody talking about him." Since he did not have the *brains* to make a name for himself in some *legitimate* way, he decided *any way* would do. When his craving for "notice" got so great that he could stand it no longer, rather than keep on being ignored by the busy world about him, he decided *he would rather commit some horrible crime than go down to his grave unhonored and unsung*. So, one night, in October, 356 B.C., he took a torch and set fire to the glorious temple of Diana, and burned * it to the ground! The whole ancient world broke out into one cry of horror and despair—but Herostratus was satisfied. He knew that his name would go down in history as the greatest "firebug" that ever committed arson, and so it has.

Yet what can be burned can be rebuilt. While the ruins were still warm, Dinocrates—*the architect who planned and built Alexandria, the world-capital of Alexander the Great*—already was making blue-prints of the new temple to be erected. Dinocrates was an architectural genius whose mind worked only in a "big" way. It was he who constructed the tremendous funeral pyre, a huge building

* It is claimed that the fire would have amounted to nothing *had the goddess been on the spot.* Unfortunately, she was off in Macedonia, assisting at the birth of Alexander the Great!

of many stories, in which the body of Alexander's friend Hephæstian was buried. And he had a real American feeling for the *tremendous*—he offered to carve the whole of Mount Athos into a colossal statue of Alexander the Great with a left hand big enough to hold a city of 10,000 inhabitants, and a right hand holding a vase out of which a river would pour into the Black Sea. Unfortunately the king did not "take him up" on the proposition.

Dinocrates raised the old platform higher, he put in new columns, broader than the old, and over sixty feet high, and the new Ionic temple which was "building" when Alexander the Great came to Ephesus in 334 and offered to stand any further expense in connection with it, was looked upon as one of the world's wonders when it was finished.

With the temples should be mentioned the big enclosure gateways (*prophylæa*) with in- and outside porches, and the magnificent *altars of sacrifice,* special "buildings" in themselves, in front of the temples (open-air altars of this kind, 600 feet on a side, were to be found at Parion and Syracuse) and the little, separate "treasure" temples, to hold the god's coin and jewels, within the great temple enclosures, their white marble set off by groves of ilex and olive-trees among which gleamed beautiful statues. Often, as at Delphi, the "temple" was a mass of "temples," all cloistering around and about one larger than the others.

THE PROPHYLÆA OF THE ACROPOLIS

The Prophylæa of prophylæas is that of the Acropolis of Athens. It was a portico 58 feet wide, fronting the stairway that led to it with six Doric columns. Five entrances, two for persons walking, and a marble road with grooves on each side for chariot-wheels led to the entrances. Entering, one stood in a hall which six Ionic columns divided into three aisles. In the northern wing, called the *Pinothek** were paintings of Polygnotus on subjects from Homer's "Iliad" and "Odyssey."

THE GREEK THEATRE

From wooden benches along a hillside, sloping down to a ring in the valley the Greek theater turned into a building in which rows of seats sloped down to enclose a circular space or "stage"—much as in our own theatres of to-day, except that the Greek theatres were all "open-air" affairs. The Greek stage was known as the "orchestra," and there the actors acted. It was on a "ground level" and made of earth "tamped down," as in a tennis court, and the

* In the Bavarian city of Munich an "Old and a new *Pinothek*"—the name is borrowed from the Greek building—are filled with paintings, engravings and other art treasures.

only bit of permanent "stage property" was a small altar, that of Dionysius, god of the drama. Fronting the audience, back of the "orchestra," was the *skené* (at first a screen of wood and painted canvas, behind which the actors dressed) which later became a stone *screen* with a center door for entrances and exits of the chorus. Out of this *skené* modern theatrical scenery finally developed. The *leading man* or *men* (it was before the time of *"actresses"*) spoke and acted, mingled with the chorus, which moved around, or from the platform of the altar. Once the chorus was "on" the stage, it stayed "on" until the end of the play, but the principals came and went, according to the action. In the age of Pericles the theatre of Dionysius in Athens could seat an audience of 30,000 and that of Megalopolis—the largest theatre in Greece, though the Epidaurus theatre was considered the most perfect—seated 44,000. Sometimes special "seats of honor" were provided, as in the theatre of Dionysius in Athens, where 67 Pentelic marble seats of the "front-row orchestra" patrons, leading priests and officials of Athens, *each inscribed with the sitter's name* (like the china mugs in a barber shop), were discovered in 1864. The *Odeions*, on the general plan of the theatres, were the Athenian *"concert halls"*; the *Stadions* (two parallel tiers of seats enclosing a running course) were for the footraces, and accommodated from 12,000 to 50,000 people; while the *Gymnasiums* were pretty much what gymnasiums are to-day; and the *Palæstræ* were enclosed courts for boxing and wrestling matches, usually with an attached bathing tank.

THE AGORA

The *Agora* of a Greek city was its "market-place," or great public square. Often there was a fountain in the middle, and along the two sides ran *Stoas*, long "halls" or roofed passageways, with a wall on one side and columns on the other. There, on the raised steps of the *stoa* in the *agora*, as a rule, was the *boulenterion*, the house where the *council* met, with a speaker's platform, and seats facing it. In Miletus (the Greek city from which the Irish claim originally to have come) the council-hall was rectangular, but inside, the seats were arranged in a half-circle, as in a theatre, to face the platform. These buildings were all for the *living*.

THE MAUSOLEUM

One of the fine things about Greek architecture is its *big, democratic spirit*. In the oriental lands, excepting the temples, *everything played "second fiddle" in architecture to the king*. In the Greek cities, the *private individual* and *his house* stepped into the *background*. The pride of the Greek was in his *city*, his *country*.

And so he put all his *wealth,* all his *joy,* all his *effort* into making his public buildings, *the architecture which belonged to all in common,* great and wonderful and beautiful. Nor did death make a difference. Greek tombs were simply marked. A little slab, plainly carved with a honeysuckle, in the cemetery outside the city gates, answered every one's purpose. In the later days of Greece the oriental sarcophagus (stone coffin) appeared and little temples (such as we may see in our own cemeteries) were erected as memorials to heroes or soldiers. Yet—so *un-Greek* is the idea of a *private individual, no matter how wealthy,* "showing off" with a specially magnificent house or tomb, that we have to go to *Asia* to find the most famous of all Greek monuments.

How many of us know that our word *"mausoleum,"* would never have come down to us if the sorrowful widow of an ancient King of Cardia, in Asia Minor, had not made up her mind to give her "dear, departed" lord a monument which would make the world "sit up and take notice"?

King Mausolus's one claim to notice seems to be that he died and thus, 350 B.C., gave his wife (and sister) Artemisia a chance to win lasting fame as the builder of his tomb in Halicarnassus. *Satiros* and *Pythes* were the architects, assisted by five sculptors, and among them they put up a square basement supporting a temple-like vault surrounded by thirty-six columns, and crowned by a pyramid of twenty-four steps. At its top stood a group of four horses drawing a *quadriga* or chariot, containing colossal figures of Mausolus and Artemisia herself. The total height of the Mausoleum was 140 feet. When Newton did some digging there in 1857, he found the figures of the ancient royal pair, and took them back with him to the British Museum, where they now rest.

THE COLOSSUS OF RHODES

The Colossus of Rhodes* was the great bit of "freak" architecture (for it was "architecture" as much as "sculpture") of Greece. "Colossus" was what the Greeks called any statue of giant, or "colossal" size. It was a bronze statue of Helios, the sun-god, the work of the sculptor Chares, with walls inside the bronze, 96 feet high and put up in the year 290 B.C. Modern peoples, when they have won a war, sometimes "recast" the metal of captured cannon. So

* The Colossus of Rhodes was one of the seven wonders of the ancient world. These were: The Egyptian pyramids; the Hanging Gardens of Babylon; the Temple of Diana at Ephesus; the statue of Zeus (Jove) at Olympia, made by Phidias of gold and ivory and 54 feet high; the Mausoleum; the Colossus of Rhodes; and the Pharos—a great lighthouse of marble, 480 feet high, named after the island it stood on in the harbor of Alexandria. A great open fire burned at the top. Sosastros was the name of its architect.

GREEK ARCHITECTURE

the Rhodians took the metal of the big siege-instruments, the bronze armor and weapons left by a king who besieged them without success and "cast" it into this statue. In pictures you may have seen it "straddling" the harbor entrance, with ships sailing in between its legs. But that is a 16th century legend. It probably stood on a rock beside the harbor entrance. An earthquake knocked it down in 224 B.C. A thousand years went by, then the Arabs took the Rhodes; a Jew bought the huge pile of bronze "junk," lying in the water, from them, loaded it on 900 camels and disappeared. Collossus had been born of war weapons, and now it passed into war-weapons again, for that is what its "junk" was made into, probably with a good profit for the Jew who bought it. There is a moral—if you want to look for it—in the fate of this "victory" monument.

THE SPIRIT OF GREEK ARCHITECTURE

Greek Architecture is very different from Egyptian Architecture. In it man moves with freedom amid buildings divided into more important and less important parts, yet with these parts always *"in proportion."* They are not mere *flat* surface "fronts," like the temples of Egypt, but have depth. Beauty of outline and the ideal of the *curve*, not the *angle*, the *horizontal* and not the *vertical* line, *principle* and not *rule show the spirit of Greek* Architecture. Its buildings are each *a complete thing*, made up of parts that "belong together" in an ordered beauty we *feel* as well as *see*, and this gives it what oriental architecture lacks.

ROMAN ARCHITECTURE

CHAPTER VII

"THE GRANDEUR THAT WAS ROME"

ROMAN Architecture was not the first architecture that Italy knew. Before the Romans came to Italy, a race named the *Etruscans* (it is after them that Italy is sometimes called "Etruria") lived there. They were supposed to have come from Asia Minor, 1200 years before Christ, and they built great cities with temples, palaces, pyramids and tombs of brick and rubble masonwork which has gone the way of all clay, so that only a few ruins remain. They seem to have been a race kin to the earliest *Egyptians,* for their *race soul* expressed itself in the same way in their tombs.

THE TOMBS OF ETRURIA

The Etruscan tombs, sometimes in a pyramid mound of earth, at others carved in the rock, show that this people thought the dead man's soul "lived" there, that it was his "soul-house." And just as in Egyptian tombs, the "soul" of the dead was surrounded by carvings of all the little things it used and was fond of in life.

In Cervetri is an Etruscan tomb in which husband and wife probably were buried together. He was a soldier, a captain, perhaps, in the Etruscan army that put up such a hard fight against the Romans before it was defeated. On the walls are carved his favorite swords and helmets, and his wife's mirrors and jewelry, *and even her kitchen pots and pans*—and we know she was a good housekeeper and took a real interest in her husband's meals (there were no "delicatessen suppers" in those good old days) just as any real wife and mother does to-day—all those long centuries ago! But the gateways, town walls and tombs which have come down to us only show that this *Etruscan Architecture was a link between East and West*. Perhaps it might have moved in the direction Greek Architecture did, had the Etruscans "lived through" instead of being rubbed off the roll of nations. But the dying Etruscan race handed on the *arch*—the "curved structure closed above and open below"— and the arched ceiling, the *vault,* to the Romans.

BRICK AND MARBLE

ROMAN Architecture, as we know it, really dates from the day of Augustus, the nephew of Julius Cæsar, the conqueror of Antony and Cleopatra, who destroyed most of the old Roman city of his boyhood to rebuild it into a town fit to be the capital of the world. Augustus used to boast that he found Rome* "a city of brick and left it a city of marble." But there was a bit of "bluff" about this, for he used marble mostly as a *"facing,"* though there were a few small *solid* marble temples. Vitruvius, Rome's greatest architect of that time, wrote a book about his art, and this book gives us a good idea of the Roman ways of building. They were lucky in discovering an ideal "building material" in a *volcanic earth mixed with lime,* known as *pozzolana.* This formed a *natural concrete or cement* that turned as solid and hard as *rock,* and was used in brick or in liquid form for the walls, arches and buildings. This pozzolana was *not found* in most of the *Roman provinces,* where Roman mortar and other material was used instead, but Roman Architecture, the Roman *style* of building, spread throughout the Roman empire. Just as the Greek *style* was the same—with variations—*all through Greece in its days of glory,* so the Roman style was the same—with variations—*all through the Roman empire.*

WHAT THE ROMAN ARCHITECT WORKED WITH IN THE WAY OF FORM

Just like the Greeks, the Romans had their "Orders" of columns and "entablatures." The *Roman Doric "Order"* was the Greek Doric with a few "changes" of detail. It was too simple for the Roman taste and did not cut much of a figure in Roman building. The Roman Ionic "Order" ran the Greek Ionic into the ground of bad taste with *over-decoration,* and is seen at its worst, its most *"corrupt"* form (for to the architect and artist things not up to Beauty's standard are *"immoral,"* so he gives them harsh names) in the *temple* of *Saturn,* in the Roman Forum. The *Roman Corinthian* "Order" was a huge fluted or unfluted shaft with a very richly decorated entablature. It was so big that it made the ideal column for "monumental" works. The Roman *"Composite Order"* differed

---

* The few buildings of Augustus Cæsar's "ancient" Rome left, show how different early Roman temples, like the Etrurian temples, raised on a platform to which steps lead, were from the Greek. One such is the temple of *Fortuna Virilis,* the other a building called the *Tabularium,* in which the architect, Lutatius Catulus (78 B.C.) went back "on purpose" to the old style no one used any more, just to show what could be done with it. It is a simple, massive "house" on a high platform, with an arcade of arches of Doric columns.

from the Corinthian only in details of the capital decorations. The *"Arcade Order,"* which some architects call the "True" Roman "Order," was a combination of the *arch* (borrowed from the Etruscans) and the *column* (borrowed from the Greeks), the latter half-detached, but with a complete entablature, applied as a *"false front"* to walls, in one of two tiers (tiers of arcades). It was a *"decorative screen,"* put on the outside of Roman theatres and other public buildings.

The Roman architects had more *"forms,"* more *"shapes"* and *"designs"* to work with than the Greeks. They had the Greek columns and entablatures to "develop" in their own way, and they had the Etruscan *arch* and *vault*. *But there is something in the race soul of the world—conquering nations which makes them feel they must "show" their greatness!* So Roman Architecture is often more splendid, larger, bigger, more magnificent, *grander* than Greek, but it has not the same *"unity of design,"* which means *it does not form as perfect a "whole,"* one in which every part *dove-tailed* into another part so that we know and feel they belong together. It has not the same *"beauty of symmetry,"* which means that every part is in exactly the right proportion, neither too long nor too short, too wide or too narrow, when compared to any other part, but that all *"fit"* in every way.

The Greek architects combined the *practical and the beautiful*. The Roman architects combined the *practical and the magnificent, the grand*. The lines and proportions of the great Greek buildings are perfect, like the perfect fit of clothes to the human shape. The good lines of great Roman buildings often are *hidden* by all sorts of rich and splendid *decorations,* like clothing made of the very richest materials, cloth of gold or silver, covered with embroidery and jewels, but *not "fitting"* the wearer.

And now we shall see what the Roman architects produced with all they had to work with in the shape of "Orders" and ideas.

THE PANTHEON

ROMAN temples were always raised on a platform, and—as the Romans did not, as a rule, take their "religion" as seriously as the Greeks—were looked on more as "public monuments" and put up in prominent places: facing the *Forum**—or some big city "avenue."

---

* The *Forum* in any Roman city was like the *Agora* of a Greek city. It was a public square or "market-place" where popular gatherings were held, and speeches made. The most famous of all was the *Forum Romanum,* "the Roman Forum," which was the heart and soul of the life of ancient Rome, between the Palatine and the Capitoline Mounts (two of the "seven hills" of Rome). Besides *the* Forum, there were seventeen other forums or market-places, open squares with collonaded porticos of columns, in ancient Rome.

ROMAN ARCHITECTURE

Roman temples were first *square*, then built in the oblong form of the Greek temple and *some* were *round*. The most famous of all Roman temples, perhaps, was the *round* Pantheon,* now the Church of St. Maria Rotunda. M. Agrippa was the architect who put up the first building which burned down and which the Emperor Hadrian had rebuilt, 25 B.C. It is just one immense *rotunda—a circular hall with a dome*—142 feet in diameter, and with a dome 140 feet high. The walls were 20 feet thick, with alternate semi-circular and rectangular "niches" in them. In the middle of the dome a round opening 30 feet every way showed the blue sky and gave the building its light, for there was *not a window in it*. There are two "stories," with pillars and on the second "story," which runs around the great dome-hall, are doors leading into rooms in the wall. The roof of the dome was once covered with bronze plates, and an eight-column porch stood before the entrance. The immense dome, with its thirty foot eye of light in the top, towers so high, that no matter how great the storm that may rage outside, *one hardly feels a breath of air when standing inside,* and as a great French architect says: ". . . the rain falls down slowly, through the immense emptiness of air in a cylinder of drops, but only marks the pavement with *a circle of moisture!"*

A few among many other great Roman temples were: the *Temple of Vesta* on the Forum (circular), the *Temple of the Sun* at Palmyra (on a 16-foot platform, 735 by 72 feet), the *Temple of Jupiter* at Baalbek (rectangular and Corinthian) raised on a 25-foot platform, 400 feet wide and 900 feet deep; and the square Roman temple known as the *"Maison carrée"* ("Square House") in Nimes, France. Most of the great temples (outside of crowded Rome, where space was too precious) had magnificent enclosing walls and porticos.

---

*Just as the great *Mausoleum* supplied all nations with a word for a large funeral monument, so *Pantheon* is the name we give any building (the Roman one contained statues of heroes and gods) in which the famous men of a nation are buried, or which holds statues of them. Westminster Abbey is called "the British Pantheon." The great rotunda of the Eicoreal palace where the Spanish kings are buried is called the Pantheon. A German Pantheon (Valhalla) stands near Regensburg. The famous Paris Pantheon has had a good many "ups and downs." It started out as St. Genevieve's Church (1764) but when the French Revolution came it was made a public building, called *Le Pantheon,* and dedicated to the great men of the nation—it is since that time the people have used the word in the sense mentioned—but in 1828 the church got hold of it again. In 1830 in the game of prisoner's base that the Church and State played with the building, it was once more made "civic." But in 1851 the Church had her innings and resprinkled it with holy water. In 1870, the State again got hold of it and (1885) made a law which will keep it national property. The Pantheon of the United States, existing only since the World War, is a grateful country's memorial to its "unknown soldier," in Arlington Cemetery, near Washington.

From the justice (or injustice) of the gods to the justice (or injustice) of man is but a step. The Roman *Basilica* was the court of justice, a rectangular hall with columned aisles and a raised platform at one end called the *tribune*. The principal Roman basilicas were the *Basilica Julia,* a central hall surrounded by a double aisle of arches on piers; the *Basilica Ulpia,* built by the Emperor Trajan; and a third great basilica commenced by the Emperor Maxentius and finished by the Emperor Constantine. The early Christians turned these "court houses" into churches, and that is why their churches are still called *basilicas.*

THE ROMAN COLOSSEUM

The Roman *Colosseum,* the Flavian Amphitheatre, is probably as famous as any single building in the world. No *one* building expresses the "grandeur that was Rome" better. The Colisseum itself, the huge four-storied (tiers of arches, held up by Doric, Tuscan, Ionic and Corinthian columns) ovular building which framed the arena—600 feet long and 500 feet wide—of "blood and sand," was the biggest, *the most stupendous thing the architects of the empire ever built.* And the very heart of Rome pulsed within those tremendous walls when the emperor sat in his "box" of marble and "the whole town" crowded the rows on rows of stone seats, while the blood of the gladiators ran red on the *gold dust* the emperors often scattered.

Let us work up from the cellars. These held the underground stairways, wild beast cells and keepers' rooms, and vaulted rooms and passages from which the gladiators and wild beasts were raised up on "elevators" (movable platforms) passing through trap-doors to the level of the arena. And under the ground, too, were the great pipes which let the water of the Tiber in to *flood* the arena when a naval battle was the "sport" furnished the crowd. The arena itself was enclosed in a wall faced with *polished* marble (to give no "hold" for wild beasts to climb up) topped with a metal railing. The lowest tiers of seats, nearest the arena, were the "best" seats. There was the emperor's box, the *podium,* and around it clustered the "boxes" and seats of all who were great, wealthy and powerful in Rome. Then came the gallery of the Roman "knights," and after that up to the "peanut gallery" under the big awning, the *velarium,* spread out as a protection against the sun and rain, the seats of the rest of the people. After 45,000 spectators had crowded in, there still was *"standing room" for* five thousand more.

Amphitheatre is another "architectural" word we use to-day for any building in which the seats of the "lookers-on" surround the stage or arena. But the huge size of the *Amphitheatrum Flavium* did it out of its rightful name, and it always has been known as the "Colosseum," which means "colossal."

There are other famous Roman amphitheatres. There is the *Castrense Amphitheatre* in Rome itself; the *Amphitheatre of Pompeii* (with thirty-five rows of seats in three tiers, and a seating capacity of 20,000), and others at Verona, Capua, Arles and Nimes in France, Italica (near Seville) in Spain, Pola in Istria and El Jem in North Africa but there is only one Colosseum.

THE BATHS OF CARACALLA AND DIOCLETIAN

Whether or not the Romans of the empire believed that "cleanliness was *next to godliness*" they *did* appreciate the bath. The *Thermæ*, the immense public baths the emperors built to "make themselves solid" with the people of Rome, were the finest the world knows. There were *Balnæ* (ordinary bath buildings) in Roman cities all over the world, but the *Thermæ* were on a much larger scale.

Except the Colosseum no buildings saw more of Roman "life" than the *Baths of Caracalla* and the *Baths of Diocletian* in their day. *The ancient Roman bath was more than a bath: it was a club, a place where you could shop, lunch, have your hair "marcelled" and your nails manicured, talk "art" with the "artistic crowd" or "philosophy" with the "high-brows"!*

The hardy early Romans, after they had exercised, simply took a plunge in the cold Tiber river and came up smiling after their dip. But the Romans of the empire had to have swimming tanks, warm baths, hot air baths, vapor baths! There were dressing rooms, there were rooms where the *aliptæ*, the "rubbers," rubbed you in with oils and pomades (they had them in the Baths, but you could bring along your *own* if you preferred, as many did.) There were *frigidariums*, rooms with cold baths, and *Tepidariums* or warm rooms where you "rested," after bathing. There was the room for the hot bath, and the "sprinkling room," where the bather sprinkled himself with water to help rub off perspiration. One old Roman writer said that a *Thermæ was a whole "province" in itself!* He was not far from the truth. *A single room* of the Baths of Diocletian still exists, *turned into a large modern church,* and the faithful now pray where the pagans once washed. The Baths of Caracalla had 1600, and those of Diocletion 3200 marble seats for bathers. And included in the "Baths" were: a *Stadium* for athletic games, inside of open colonnades with raised seats for those looking on, *long colonnades and seats* where "writers" and "thinkers" could read their "latest" to each other, or talk over the news of Rome. There were *gardens;* there was a regular *"ball-ground";* there were *"tanks"*

200 feet long, made of the most beautiful marbles, while the great *halls* were crowded with statues. In the Baths of Diocletion there was a *big library*. But with all the grandeur of their baths the Romans were "behind the times" in one respect: *they had no soap!* Oils and pomades, yes, but no "true" soap and those who were not rich had to use "flour of lentils." Sad to say, it seems historically correct that in Rome itself, and in some of the "provincial" cities, *women were in the habit of intoxicating themselves in the public baths!* It is no wonder that the *early Fathers of the Church* wrote that people should bathe for the sake of *health* or *cleanliness, but not for pleasure!*

NERO'S "GOLDEN HOUSE"

The "Golden House" of Nero, the *Domus aurea*, as the Romans called it, built at Nero's command, by the architects Severus and Celer, was perhaps the most magnificent of imperial Roman palaces. Its stones were cemented with the tears and blood of the Roman people. Nero's cruel "commissioners" gathered in the special tax to build it with such harshness that the Roman provinces were practically "looted" to pay the price. The "Golden House" stretched from the Palatine Hill across the low ground (afterward occupied by the Colosseum) to the Esquiline Hill. The tremendous gardens in which the palace buildings stood included meadows and lakes, great hills and shady forests in their distant views. Three great pillared colonnades, each a mile long, ran through the huge park, swarming with tame and wild animals of every kind, and with the "Golden House" in its heart. Gold, gems and the finest marble statues of Greece—robbed from all the Greek cities, by the commissioners—adorned the inside of the palace, and a bronze "colossus" statue of Nero—120 feet high—by Zenodorus, the best sculptor of the day—stood in one of the porticos. There were dining-rooms with ivory roofs which, as they turned, scattered roses down on the drinkers below or sprinkled them with perfumes. One ceiling revolved all the time to the movement of the stars in the heavens. Into the great palace baths was piped sea-water from the distant sea, fresh water from the Tiber, and sulphur-water from the Tiber springs. Floors and furniture were of gold or mother-of-pearl shell. And the "Golden House" was the actual *"prison" of the poor painter Amulius,* for Nero never gave him a *"furlough,"* but kept him at work till the brush dropped from his hand! It was the greatest and grandest thing in Rome before the Colosseum was built, was the "Golden House."

But the people of Rome hated it. It blocked up many important streets and roads, and took up land much needed *for the houses of the poor*. Anything else Nero did made the Romans—from whose city this huge stretch of land was literally stolen—despise him more. So Vespasian knew what he was about when he destroyed the "Golden House" and put up the Colosseum and the Baths of Titus, *buildings in which the people had a share,* on the same ground where it had stood. Vespasian, who was a very *saving* man, also turned the great statue of Nero to good account. He had the face and head "altered" a bit and—there was a fine statue of the god Apollo, all ready for use! Twenty-four elephants had to work hard to move it from its old place to the new spot where it was to stand.

TRIUMPHAL ARCHES AND TOMBS

The Romans built many more different *kinds* of buildings than the Greeks. Some of the finest *bridges* in the world were built by them, and solid masonry and a graceful arch mark the bridges of Augustus at Rimini and Alcantara in Spain, which have "lasted through" to our day. Roman *aqueducts* are so fine that they have a right to be classed as "monuments." A combination of "big-scale" construction and usefulness and nobility shows in those of the Pont-du-Garde (Nimes) and Segovia, Tarragon and Merida, Spain. Roman theatres are like those of Greece: the theatre of Marcellus in Rome and at Orange, in the South of France, are among the best. Other useful architectural works are city *entrance gates, drains, harbor works, fortifications, archive* ("record") *buildings* (the *Tablarium* or "Hall of Records" in Rome is the finest example); the *Curias* or "House of the Senate," on the order of temples; *Circuses,* special long, narrow "course" *stadiums* for chariot-races—the oldest "sport" the Romans had—with a "barrier" down the middle to separate the courses; *sewers*—the *Cloaca Maxima,* the "great sewer" of imperial Rome, was a wonderful engineering feat; and *roads,* spread all over the empire.

Military glory was more of a "moving power" to the Roman than to the Greek, and out of this feeling in him came the "Arch of Triumph," which was *a Roman way of expressing the pride of victory in stone and marble; in a different fashion than the simple Greek column or trophy shaft.* The arch was bigger, richer, more decorative. To leave *memorials* of their victories, the emperors and generals of Rome put up the triumphal arch throughout the empire in the principal cities or on battle-fields. It was a great arch supported by columns, with every foot of its walls and columns carved with "pictures" in low relief of the events of a victorious campaign or battle. The great triumphal arches are: the *arches of Titus, Septimus Severus, Marcus Aurelius,* and *Constantine* at Rome, *Trajan's* famous arch of triumph at Ancona, and the *Arch of Caracalla* in Tebessa, Syria. Trajan and Marcus Aurelius, too, each set up *triumphal columns* in Rome famous for their beautiful reliefs. These arches were symbolic of the "yoke" under which conquered armies had to pass.

EVERYDAY AND IMPERIAL DUST

Roman tombs are of all kinds. When they are underground, like the tombs called *Columbaria*, they are on the funeral "hotel" idea, the vault consisting of a number of little *pigeon-holes* or *niches* for the vases which held the *ashes of the dead*. We have somewhat the same system in some of our large *Crematoriums*. But "the thing" as a rule, was to be buried along the *via sacra*, the "holy street" of your town (every Roman town had one), in Rome itself the "Appian Way." There the "first families" were laid away in big, fine family mausoleums, the bigger and finer the better. No simple headstone with a honeysuckle engraved on it for the magnificent Roman! In some respects the world has not changed much since the days of the Roman empire, and one still has "to have the price" for a big tomb, now as then. If you had only two rooms in one of the great Suburra *tenements*, you had to be satisfied with a pigeon-hole in some *Columbaria*. If you were an emperor or noble you could have a splendid mausoleum along the Appian Way, with circular seats of marble and beautiful sculptures. In the long run, of course, it came to pretty much the same thing: it was *"ashes to ashes and dust to dust" for Roman workman and noble alike!*

In Palmyra the Romans built their tombs in the shape of great towers as high as seventy feet in the air and in Central Syria and Roman Judea they cut them in the rock. But in general they lined the "sacred street" of Roman towns everywhere throughout the empire.

THE CASTLE OF SANT' ANGELO

(Hadrian's Tomb)

Augustus had built himself a great mausoleum in Rome (28 B.C.), between the Tiber and a street called Flaminia. There the emperors were buried until Hadrian. But Hadrian wanted a handsomer monument. So he put up *the greatest of Roman tombs, the Hadrian Mole,** a large circular building with enormous, thick walls, faced with marble and surrounded by a colonnade crowned with statues. The statues in the time of the Emperor Justinian broke many a head (and disappeared themselves) when the Romans, defending their city, threw them down on the hard skulls of the Goths

---

* As a general thing a "mole" means a jetty or breakwater or the well-known animal that ruins our gardens. But the massive old Roman tombs, like Hadrian's, are also called "moles," and it is quite correct to call them so when you are "talking architecture."

below. In the seventh century the *pagan emperor's tomb* was turned into a combination of *Christian fortress and church* which shows the Pope's idea that earthly and heavenly power ought to go together. At the top of Hadrian's tomb, the *Church of St. Angelus* rose into the clouds, but the fortress part was below, fitted up with *every weapon of defense and offense* a good castle in the Middle Ages needed. It is in this form—as the Castle of Sant' Angelo—that Hadrian's tomb still exists, shorn of all its former magnificent decorations, without having lost its massive grandeur.

THE SPIRIT OF ROMAN ARCHITECTURE

Greek Architecture was the architecture of one race and land. Roman Architecture was that of a world. For, speaking broadly, there was a time when Rome *was* the world, from Britain to the Nile, from Spain to India. And this makes Roman Architecture a thing of the universe, *universal*. It varied in the provinces in East and West but the main ideas of plan and construction were the same. The Romans were the first people to "lay out" whole cities in a big, modern engineering way. And in its bigness, its grandeur it touches our own modern life—our architecture has something in common with it. Like the Romans we put mass, practical needs, before detail and delicacy. And its ideals influenced succeeding generations. It was continued after Rome fell in the Byzantine Architecture of the Emperors of Constantinople and in the building of the barbarian tribes who divided the spoils of Rome's empire.

EARLY CHRISTIAN AND BYZANTINE ARCHITECTURE

CHAPTER VIII

FROM CATACOMB TO ST. SOPHIA

The word "catacombs" did not at first mean what it does to-day—"underground burial vaults." It came from the Latin *catacumbæ* which is "a hollow." It was just a low-lying section of Rome, near the Appian Way. Nor did the Christian "dig" the catacombs as a place of refuge. The Romans burned, the Christians buried their dead. That meant big burial vaults under their first churches. At the same time they probably did use old Roman burial vaults, too, or any hidden place for meeting and services in the days when the Roman emperors made life miserable for them.

THE CATACOMBS

St. Jerome, when he was a schoolboy in Rome (354 A.D.) was the first man to describe the "catacombs": "When I was a lad I used to go with other boys at school on Sunday . . . many a time . . . down into the catacombs, deep in the earth . . . the bodies of the dead *buried in the wall*. It is all so dark there that the words of the prophet: 'Let them go down quick into hell' seem to have come true."

They are a vast maze (labyrinth) of narrow galleries, four to five feet wide, broken by small rooms, all cut out on different levels in the volcanic rock. Vertical shafts give light and air. In Pope Damasus's day when St. Jerome lived, Christians made pilgrimages to them to see the tombs of apostles and martyrs. But in the *cubiculum,* the small room a family often had to itself, the *early* Christians too often acted like *late* Romans. The "funeral feast" was a pagan custom the Christian Church had taken over. And St. Augustine in some of his writings has spoken his mind about the "gluttony and insobriety" of people who "made themselves drunk in the chapel of the martyrs" in these feasts. Perhaps the early Christians were no better than we are. Under all the early churches ran these vaults and winding passages and corridors, these suites of rooms, chapels and halls, and in the days when the wild beasts were wait-

BYZANTINE ARCHITECTURE

ing for them in the Colosseum, the Christians met, prayed, celebrated the sacraments, were baptized, married and buried in their underground maze. All catacombs had several entrances and exits for escape. But the early Christians never lived in them for months at a time, working like moles to "pray down" the Roman empire. It is a romantic idea, but not a true one.

THE EARLY CHRISTIAN CHURCHES

In the catacomb days the Christian churches were small, hidden and "run on the quiet" so to speak, for the lions might get you in those times if you didn't "watch out"! When the Christian religion was established, they took the big basilicas and temples in Rome and Greece and "made them over" into churches: that is why the Parthenon in Athens and some of the big buildings in Rome have come down to us. But they would build churches, or basilicas as they called them, too, and the first Christian Church built in Rome was the Lateran. Next came "old St. Peter's," taken down in 1506, to make way for the present St. Peter's Church. Church after church was built—often the splendid marble columns of the old temples were used for them—the St. Paul Basilica, Santa Pudenziana (Saint Modesty), Saint Sabina, Saint Agnes. In Ravenna rose the church of San Vitale. And much attention was paid to beautiful decoration and mosaic floors and the like. In some Italian cities the "style" of the East, of Constantinople (Byzantine) showed if the architect came from that city. And in Syria, too, the churches with domes, for that is the church-mark of the Eastern church, was the rule. In Syria and in Egypt great monasteries were built, but the churches of the Copts (the Egyptian Christians) were on the basilica plan (See Chapter VII, Roman Architecture) like those of Rome. The Copts, especially after the Mohammedans, who persecuted them, came to Egypt, hid themselves behind big enclosure walls. The "White Monastery" (Deir-el-Abiad) and the "Red Monastery" (Deir-el-Akhmar), 240 by 130 feet, are the most remarkable of the Christian churches in Egypt, with nave and aisles separated by big columns taken from old buildings.

THE CHURCH WITH THE DOME

(Byzantine Architecture)

The Byzantine church is the church with the dome. After Constantine made Constantinople the capital of the Greco-Roman empire (324 A.D.) it developed there. There were (and are) many famous Byzantine churches in Rome. The prostitute-empress Theodora, one of the worst women in the world, built a Church of the

Holy Apostles. But all that is left of it is a description and the knowledge that it was the model for the Church of St. Mark in Venice. Everywhere in Greece and the Greek East, the emperors of Constantinople built these Byzantine churches. Those attached to the Mount Athos monasteries are famous. So is the Catholicon (Cathedral) in Athens, and the Armenians developed a variation of it that shows at its best in the Cathedral of Ani (1010 A.D.). But the three great world monuments of Byzantine Architecture are the Church of St. Sophia in Constantinople; St. Mark's Cathedral in Venice (technically known as "Byzantine Romanesque"), and the Cathedral of the Assumption in Moscow (technically known as Lombardo Byzantine); and some of its companion buildings.

THE CHURCH OF SAINT SOPHIA

St. Sophia is the greatest thing in Byzantine Architecture.* It is *the high-water mark of the Byzantine style,* the model for all Greek churches, and even the Mohammedan mosques (after 1600) built in Constantinople. Anthemius of Tralles and Isidorus of Miletus were the architects, and they solved the problem of carrying a *dome 107 feet in diameter on four arches.* When the Emperor Justinian, who gave it its final shape in 561 A.D., visited it for the first time after it was finished, he cried "Solomon, I have beaten you!"

The Mohammedans believe in "beauty unadorned." After the bloody massacre that followed the taking of Constantinople by the Turks in 1453, when the blood of men, women and children who had taken refuge in the great Christian church ran over the crimson and purples of the marble floors, they whitewashed the gold mosaics of walls and ceilings, and the inlaid floor-tiling, though the columns of colored marble that came from great Roman temples still stand. St. Sophia's is one of the most romantic churches in the world. Coronations of emperors in stiff robes of cloth of gold, waves of the people's rage (as when the party of the "picture breakers" in the Greek Church got the upper hand, and would sweep

---

* The main architectural facts and ideas in Byzantine architecture are the following: 1. It is a grand art, an imperial art, combined out of Oriental and Roman and Greek ideals. 2. It gave the *individual* architects every chance to express themselves. 3. Brick, mortar, concrete and cut stone were its building materials. 4. The *dome,* over the center of the church, around which the other parts of the building are grouped, *is the "lead" feature.* 5. *Pendentives*—vaulting to connect the angles of the square enclosed by the four arches—form the support of the dome, and *capitals* are the support of the *pendentives* or *vaulting.* 6. The square, the "Greek cross," or the "Greek cross" *inside* the square, is the ground-plan of most Byzantine churches. 7. A great central court, with a *narthex* (porch or vestibule) entrance section, a great nave, and an *apse* (altar-end), surrounded by tiers of arcades, is the "building" idea.

BYZANTINE ARCHITECTURE

through the great building destroying the costly jewelled and golden *icons,* images of the saints, that cover the walls), bloodshed, murder, intrigue and assignation, all have played their part under that great dome. And then St. Sophia "changed her religion," and began a brand new life as a Mohammedan instead of a Christian building. To show that the "Saint" had been *converted,* the Turks "stuck up" four ungraceful minarets outside, at the corners. No doubt now that the great "Christian" powers have had to let them do as they want inside their own country, the Turks look at these minarets with a good deal of satisfaction. No other Byzantine building equals St. Sophia's, or ever equalled it, not even the palace of the *Blachernæ,* the vast "Golden House" of the Greek emperors, whose great walls with their towers, barracks, courts and other buildings ran down to beautiful green gardens that fronted a sea-wall on the Bosphorus, where the palaces of Turkish sultans now stand.

Two other Byzantine buildings should be mentioned, before moving on to Venice and St. Mark's Cathedral. There are the famous *Reservoirs*—a tremendous underground system of pillared aqueducts (some are still in use) and chambers, so vast and complicated that they often served as a refuge for whole bands of Byzantine "gangsters" and criminals. Old legends record grisly tales of prisoners held for ransom, and *tortured to death where the* living waters flowed. And there is the equally famous *Hippodrome.**

THE HIPPODROME

The Hippodrome (Constantine the Great completed it) was known as "the *hub* of the Byzantine world," just as we call Boston "the Hub" to-day. Politics, religion, everything in Greek Constantinople turned on what happened in the Hippodrome, the long race-course arena enclosed with its arched tiers of seats. The members of the "Blues" and the "Greens," the two big "racing parties," hooted, cursed and assaulted each other there. For you could tell what a man's religious and political opinions were by the racing "colors" he sported. Practically everyone in Constantinople, even the emperor, was a "Blue" or a "Green," but when it came to destroying each other they both were "Reds"! So in the Hippodrome the emperors were cheered or hissed, and sometimes murdered. There

*The *Hippodrome* was the Greek equivalent of the Roman *Circus*—a racing course. But the Greeks of Constantinople went the Romans six better in their great Hippodrome: where the Romans raced *four* chariots at a time, *they* raced *six.* We still use the word for "circus," but when we say someone is "hippodroming" we mean that he is trying to put over a race, prize-fight or sporting event which is "not on the square," but has been "fixed" beforehand.

criminals *writhed on,* and martyrs were *burned at,* the stake. The Colosseum sands at their worst ran no redder with blood than those of this "circus"—the last word in the world we now connect with horror or suffering!

ST. MARKS IN VENICE

St. Mark's (it was put up by Byzantine architects) *has five of the great Byzantine "domes"* and though it is one of the "mixed styles" called Romanesque ("near-Roman") which sprang from the Byzantine main idea, it reproduces *so many* of the features of the Byzantine Church of the Holy Apostles in Constantinople (which the most wicked woman in the world built), that it seems right to rank it with the great *Byzantine* buildings. There are many other old Italian churches—Torcello, Murano, Ravenna, etc.—which show the Byzantine "influence," and a number of palaces in Venice and elsewhere, but St. Mark's is the greatest of them all. Inside, the thing that stands out about it is *its wealth of color;* color in mosaics, transparent alabaster, polished marbles, in veneer, sculpture and glass, everywhere set off by gold and gems. So rich is it in color and decoration that great authority on Art, Ruskin, calls it *"encrusted architecture,"* architecture where the beautiful ornament is *so rich* that it actually forms a *"crust" of splendor* over lines and curves. No other building in the world is as rich in its material and decoration. Why? Because in the golden days of the Republic of Venice a *law* was passed. Every merchant, every trader who sailed to the East, *had to bring* back some costly gift for the great cathedral. For hundreds of years every Venetian ship which came into port brought with it a gem, a jewel, a costly bit of goldsmith's work, rich stuffs, brocades of cloth-of-gold or cloth-of-silver, pearls, corals, carved woods. All went into the cathedral for the greater glory of God and Venice.

Compelled by law to "do the right thing" by their saint, his church —were it not for the great beauty of all that it contains—would seem like one vast "pirate treasure hoard," so varied is the pious plunder the old Venetian sea dogs dragged back with them from the Orient. *How* they got what they gave the saint, did not matter to them! They had to get it—*there was the law to reckon with*—and they *did!* The high altar, the *Pala 'doro,* is probably the most magnificent specimen of goldsmith and jeweller work existing. The *robes* of its figures of Christ, the prophets and saints—who really walked about the earth bare-footed or in sandals, with *a single robe of coarse linen*—include 1300 great pearls, 400 garnets, 90 amethysts, 300 sapphires, 300 emeralds, 80 rubies, 4 topazes and 2 cameos. But with all this splendor goes a feeling of the worldly. St. Mark's (at least in later days) was a place where fond lovers kept "dates."

One went there to hear good music, read an old inscription on a tomb; and to "flirt in church" had the thrill so often given people when it is *"sinful."* Nor did the Council of Ten and the Doges hesitate to *use their most sacred shrine as part of a stage setting* to entertain some foreign monarch. When the Emperor Joseph II of Austria visited Venice, the whole Square of St. Mark was turned into a fairy lake and garden, with little islands, and groves of myrtle and laurel bushes and—everywhere nymphs, lovely Venetian girls in classic undress, sported about among the grottos and bushes! Can we imagine such a scene along the steps and in the squares surrounding any of our great cathedrals to-day?

THE MOSCOW CATHEDRAL OF THE ASSUMPTION

(Russian Byzantine Architecture)

Byzantine Architecture "took out citizenship papers" in Russia, between 1473 and 1479, when the Italian architect Aristotle Fioraventi put up the *Cathedral of the Assumption* ("The Virgin's Rest") in the Kremlin, the imperial enclosed pile of palaces, churches and other buildings which is Moscow's *Acropolis*. For the kremlin of the old Russian city was its "fort" or "fortress," just as the acropolis was the fortress of the Greek city.

Some speak of Russian Architecture as a *"degraded version"* of the Byzantine. It is certain that the nobler Byzantine *"dome"* looks like a *"bulb"* on the Russian cathedrals, and this may be called its *"Tartar form."* All these Russian cathedrals have three parts, a narthex, a "body," and a "shrine," separated from the body by a screen. The *Church of St. Basil* in Moscow; the Kremlin *Cathedral of the Archangel Michael,* and the *Cathedral of the Assumption*—where fresco pictures on the wall of the passage leading into the church show *Homer* and *Plato* as *forerunners of Christianity*—and the Kremlin Palace itself *all have the golden "bulb" domes.*

The Cathedral of the Assumption is the church in which all the czars of Russia (while Russia had czars) were crowned, and Alexander III had the whole inside *"regilded"* for his coronation, though it was almost as rich in gold and colors as St. Mark's. One cannot help wondering whether the fact that St. Jonah lies buried in a tomb in one corner of the cathedral, may not have had something to do with the *"bad luck"* of Russian czars in general. Perhaps if Nicholas II, the last Romanoff, had let himself be crowned anywhere else but in the Russian Rheims"* he might have done better.

---

* So-called because all the old French kings used to be crowned in the Cathedral of Rheims which the Germans "shot up" during the World War.

The Cathedral of the Assumption is full of gold and gems, mosaics, tombs, holy *ikons* (images of the saints), legend, tradition and history. It is a marvel of art and a gold-mine, though the architect who built it and who, besides cathedral-building, understood bell-casting, cannon-founding and coining, only received $35.00 per month for his work. Among its relics is *the seamless coat our Saviour wore on the Cross*. The seamless coat our Saviour wore also exists in the Cathedral of Treves but it is easy for the devout Christian to tell *which is the true coat:* if he is a *Greek Catholic* it is the one in *Moscow;* if a *Roman Catholic,* it is the one in *Treves!* In the *Cathedral of the Archangel Michael* the Czar Alexis, father of Peter the Great, used to pray for five or six hours at a time, getting down on his knees from 1,000 to 1,500 times; and in the great *Tower of Ivan Velike, a tower in pure Byzantine style,* with the finest belfry in Russia (269 feet high), the peal is struck which sets all the thousands of Moscow bells ringing on the midnight of Easter Eve. The gorgeous group of the Kremlin palace buildings—against one of them the bloody *Red Stairway* where the murdered bodies of many a Russian prince was flung down to be cut to pieces in the courtyard below—are architecturally less important than the cathedrals. In one palace building room, *two great names known to us* are brought to mind: there is a magnificent chariot sent by *Queen Elizabeth* of England to Boris Godounoff, Czar of Russia in her day; and *Napoleon's* vamp-bed, captured when he fled back through the Russian snows to France in 1812. The *earliest* Russian cathedrals in the Tartar-Byzantine style are those of Kiev and Novgorod.

THE MELTING OF STYLES INTO ONE ANOTHER

(Romanesque Architecture)

Romanesque Architecture is one in which different styles are melting into each other here, there and everywhere in picturesque confusion. It is the "groping," during the Middle Ages, toward the *Gothic Style* which follows. There is *Lombard* and *Byzantine Romanesque* in Italy, *Sicilian Romanesque*—which has a touch of the Mohammedan Orient in it—in Sicily, *Rhenish Romanesque* in Germany, *Norman Romanesque* in England, and *Romance Romanesque* in France. We will mention a few of its great buildings, and pass to the greater Gothic style which follows:

ROMANESQUE CHURCHES

Europe is full of Romanesque churches. Three-naved basilicas, vaulted stone roofs, massive "cellar" (crypt) pillars and piers, doors sunk in walls, "rose-windows" (round windows above doors) and towers to top the church are main features of the Romanesque styles.

The Cathedral of Pisa,* in the shape of a Latin cross, with an "egg-shaped" dome, the Florence Church of San Miniato, San Ambrogio in Milan, and St. Michele in Lucca are all fine examples of *Italian Romanesque*. The finest example of *Sicilian Romanesque* is supposed to be the Cathedral of Monreale (1176) five miles from Palermo, with *Norman* towers and *Saracen* (Moslem) decoration. The most famous Romanesque monument in Italy, is the well-known "Leaning Tower" of Pisa.

The *Pisa Campanile* (Bell Tower) is considered the noblest one Southern Italian Romanesque produced. It is 179 feet high, with an inside stairway winding with the walls, and was 16½ feet *"out of plumb"* in 1910. The architects Bonanno and William of Innsbruck did not mean to make it "lean," but it began to do so while they were building it, and the habit has grown on it ever since. Perhaps the fact that the foundations are only ten feet deep, and their circumference only that of the tower itself has something to do with it.

One of the greatest monuments of *Rhenish Romanesque* is the Cathedral of Spires. Begun in 1030, it was "building" 100 years, was ruined by the French in 1689 and restored in 1772. The earlier Saxon churches of *England* had a long, narrow nave with a square-chancel end. The Romanesque churches of Norman builders are, perhaps, best represented by Durham Cathedral (St. Cuthbert's) with its towers *all the same size from bottom to top*, thick walls, windows "splayed"—widened by "slanting" the sides and stone vaulting. In *France* the abbey church of Vezeley, in Burgundy; St. Trophime in Arles, and St. Martin at Tours, are fine examples of the "mixed style," while in *Spain* the Church of St. James of Composttella might be mentioned.

---

* The pious Pisan can be buried in *actual "holy ground,"* without taking the trouble to go to Palestine. The *Campo Santo* (churchyard), north of the cathedral was made especially sacred in or about the year 1200, when Archbishop Ubaldo had 53 shiploads of earth brought from Mount Calvary and "filled in" there.

CHAPTER IX

GOTHIC ARCHITECTURE

(The Great "Pointed" Style of the Middle Ages)

GOTHIC Architecture has nothing to do with the *"Goths,"* a savage people of the early Middle Ages. But the word suggests *rude, original strength* and *grandeur,* in the meaning of Emerson's line: "The Gothic church plainly originated in a rude *adaptation of the forest trees with all their boughs, to a solemn and festive arcade."*
When "rib-vaulting," the *ogive,* which is the "pointed arch" and the "pointed window" was put into Romanesque buildings, the Gothic style was produced. The Italians built no great Gothic cathedrals. The Gothic Milan Cathedral, so big that it looks awkward and clumsy, is not the noblest Gothic. The best Gothic buildings in Italy are the Gothic palaces in Venice, Florence, Bologna, Genoa and other cities, and the town halls in Perugia, Placenza and Siena.
Gothic Architecture is a Northern art: it is in France, Germany, England and Spain that it found its finest expression.

THE CATHEDRAL OF NOTRE DAME

(French Gothic)

Victor Hugo, one of France's master-writers, has painted the greatest picture ever written in a chapter of his famous novel, "Nôtre-Dame de Paris," * a chapter devoted to this greatest of Gothic cathedrals. Since it could not be improved upon, we will quote from it in our description:

"Its front showed in succession and together: three *ogive* (pointed) carved-in great doors; the embroidered and lace-worked ribbon-band of its twenty-eight niches for the statues of kings of Israel and Judah; an immense rose-window flanked by two side-windows, as a priest is by his deacon and subdeacon; the high, frail gallery of trefoil arcades carrying a

* Any reader who has seen the carefully and accurately "staged" moving picture, the "Hunchback of Notre-Dame," will have an excellent idea of *how the great cathedral actually looked, outside and in.*

GOTHIC ARCHITECTURE

heavy platform on its slender colonnades; and finally, the two black, massive towers with their sloping roof-sheds. *All these were the harmonious parts of a magnificent whole, piled up one above the other in five gigantic stories,* broadening out before the eye without confusing it with all their countless details of statuary, sculpture and carving, all powerfully 'drawn in' to help along the quiet grandeur of the whole building. It was *a vast symphony in stone,* so to say, the colossal work of one man and one people, *a complete, composite whole like the 'Iliad' whose sister it is.* The prodigious product of a union of all the forces of an age, on whose every stone we see stand out in a hundred ways *the fancy of the workman disciplined by the genius of the artist.* In a word, it is a human creation as strong and as fruitful as the divine creation from which it seems to have borrowed its double nature: variety and eternity. And what has been said of the whole church, of the Cathedral of Nôtre-Dame, applies to all these Christian churches of the Middle Ages. All is contained in this art developed out of itself, logical and well-proportioned. *If you measure the giant's big toe, you have measured the giant!"*

Founded in 1163, the cathedral (it was a "Temple of Reason" for a time, during the French Revolution) is 139 yards long and 52 broad, with a central spire 148 feet high, and consists of a main body flanked by square chapels. Of its decorative roof-work the *Gargoyles,* odd and hideous figures *carved at the ends of the waterspouts,* attract the most attention. Sometimes these figures with grinning goat's or devil's faces or loose-lipped monk's heads are *obscene* and *blasphemous.* It is supposed that, since the great Gothic cathedral was built by wandering bands of workmen, who were not very *churchly* in their thought, in these carvings they "spoke their mind" about the monkish tyranny of their time. Inside the building, however, all is reverence. The beautiful colors of stained glass, in which the Gothic artists "painted," took the place of gold backgrounds of the pictures of Byzantine and Romanesque saints. The altar in the Gothic cathedral is a shrine—under it are kept the precious bones of holy saints, enclosed in caskets of gold and silver. And the altar is large and imposing.

Many French cities, among them Laon, Senlis, Rouen, St. Omer, Chartres, Troyes, Beauvais, Amiens, Cahors, Nantes, Langres (many of them familiar to members of the A.E.F.) send their immense pointed spires towering to the skies. But, somehow, the Cathedral of Nôtre-Dame of Paris is the Gothic church of all France, though the pathetic fate of Rheims called special attention to it during the war.

CANTERBURY CATHEDRAL

(English Gothic)

The cathedrals of Lincoln, Wells and York, Glouchester and Ely, and the wonderful Salisbury Cathedral all are noble examples of the *English Gothic*. Salisbury is, perhaps, the one most "all in one piece," and the best proportioned among them. But Canterbury,* really begun in 1174 by a French architect, William of Sens, is the one which appeals most to our imagination, for it is the most romantic of them all.

Its most striking feature is its Perpendicular Tower, 235 feet high, the "Angel Steeple," as it used to be called, from the golden figure of an angel that stood on the top. Inside, dark marble and light stone give contrast and the Trinity Chapel behind the altar is the shrine of St. Thomas of Canterbury, the murdered archbishop Thomas à Becket. It was to this shrine that Chaucer's *"Canterbury Pilgrims"* (like thousands of others, from kings and emperors to pious souls without a farthing to offer) made pilgrimages, telling their stories as they went, for there was no rushing along the beautiful English country roads in autos then. In this shrine, King Henry VIII, who has his axe so handy for his wives' necks, got his "biggest haul" in the way of gold and gems in all England, when he *combined business with pleasure* by making himself the head of the English Church and *"looting"* the rich cathedrals and abbeys of the faith he had cast off.

Westminster Abbey (the Abbey of St. Peter's) in London, England's Pantheon, where most of the famous men are buried or have monuments, and where all the English kings have been crowned since William the Conquerer (except Edward V), is a splendid example of the "pointed" style. It is shaped like a cross with a central nave and six chapels opening off it. The Abbey is 531 feet long and has two western towers and a low central one. Poor, weak-minded Edward the Confessor built it in 1050. The coronations—the magnificent one of King George V, the last celebrated there—do not seem nearly as important as the great army of soldiers, statesmen, poets, authors, scientists and others who are honored in Westminster Abbey by tomb or tablet.

---

* The word "canter," by the way, which means going at an easy gait on hoseback, came from the phrase "Canterbury gallop," used to make fun of the comfortable way the pilgrims "rambled along" on horseback when they were making the Canterbury pilgrimage.

GOTHIC ARCHITECTURE

THE CATHEDRAL OF COLOGNE

(German Gothic)

Cologne was known in Germany during the Middle Ages as "the holy city" and the "German Rome." It was and is a city of churches and relics. In St. Ursula's Church, for instance, are preserved the bones of 11,000 English virgins* who were massacred near Cologne on a pilgrimage to Rome. But if the Cologne Cathedral can boast no "virgins," it has a greater treasure: the shrine containing the bones of the "three kings of Cologne," *the three Magi kings* of our Christmas carols. They were carried off from Milan, in March, 1192, by the Emperor Frederick Barbarossa, who presented them to his chancellor, the archbishop of Cologne, while the defeated Milanese wrung their hands in despair.

That must have been one of the great moments in the history of the huge cross-shaped cathedral, one of the purest monuments of Gothic architecture in Europe, when with all the pomp and ceremony of the Middle Ages, with priests in rich robes, and knights in armor, and the sun streaming in through the stained glass windows, the bones of the three Magi kings—*stolen* from the people to whom they belonged—were solemnly laid in their magnificent shrines to sound of bell and chant as the white clouds of incense rose.

Gerhardt von Rile (d. 1295) was the architect of the original of the present cathedral, which after stops of a century or more at a time, and with many additions—it is 480 feet long, 282 feet wide, with two towers each 511 feet high—was opened in the presence of the German Emperor William I and all the then reigning German princes. That was another high moment of the cathedral's story. The heaviest of its seven bells, the "Emperor's Bell," weighing 543 cwt. and cast of the metal of the French guns taken in the war of 1870, pealed out loudly and triumphantly, but the times have changed since then. The Hohenzollerns have disappeared—there is no German emperor, and French bells do the triumphant ringing now.

But there is another spirit in the Cologne Cathedral as well—a more human one, neither fanatically religious nor proudly triumphant. It breathes out something of the human feeling the

---

*It seems that these English girls, in the time of the Roman Emperor Maxentius, either came swarming to Cologne "chasing up" the Theban Legionary soldiers ("the military do, no doubt, exercise an irresistible attraction upon girls," says the Rev. S. Baring-Gould in his 'Lives of the Saints,' dealing with the legend) or were passing on their way to Jerusalem or returning from the Holy Land, when the soldiers slew them.

townspeople, who built the great Gothic domes, had for these great churches. In cathedrals like that of Cologne it was not thought wrong to exchange a loving glance, the saints often were the confidants of lovers, and it was proper, when trying to make a fair maid's acquaintance, to offer her the holy water.

The cathedrals of Mainz, Worms, Treves ("the first pure Gothic church in Germany"), Erfurt, Regensburg, Spires and Ulm, as well as the Cathedral in Munich and the Church of St. Lawrence in Nurnberg, all deserve mention, and in Vienna the Cathedral of St. Stephen has the Gothic dome, with a 450 foot tower.

THE CATHEDRAL OF SEVILLE

(Spanish Gothic)

Third largest of *any* cathedral in Europe and the largest Gothic cathedral, larger than Cologne and Milan, is the Cathedral of Seville. Juan Gil de Hontanon was the architect who rebuilt it in 1511, five years after the dome of the first unknown builders had given way. Though a Christian church it has a Moorish tower, the Giralda. A great French poet, Théophile Gautier, has given us a pen-picture of it:

"The most extravagant and most monstrously prodigious Hindoo temples are not to be mentioned in the same century as the Cathedral of Seville. It is a mountain scooped out, a valley turned upside-down. Nôtre-Dame of Paris could walk erect in the middle aisle, which is of *frightful* height! Pillars as large round as towers, and which appear so slender that they make you shudder, rise out of the ground or descend from the vaulted roof, like stalactites in a giant's cave."

The people of Seville determined that their cathedral should outdo every other in Spain, and to this day, while the Toledo Cathedral is called "the rich," and Salamanca Cathedral "the strong" and the Cathedral of Leon "the beautiful," Seville Cathedral is known as *"the great."* Like Nôtre-Dame, it has three entrances (*puertas*), the middle one the largest. Its great dome rises above a roof studded with pinnacles, flying buttresses and towers: "Like a high-pooped and beflagged ship rising over the sea with harmonious grouping of sails, pennons and flags," says a Spanish writer.

Within, rich and poor alike *stand or sit on the marble floor,* there are no "class distinctions" before the majesty of God in the Seville Cathedral. In its eighteen chapels are vast treasures of art, the most wonderful paintings, the most glorious examples of the goldsmith's and jeweller's work, carvings, statues, stained-glass windows—all the great artist names of Spain are represented. There

GOTHIC ARCHITECTURE

are tombs in a kind of Pantheon: among them that of Don Pedro the Cruel, King of Spain, with the mistress he betrayed and the brother he murdered on either side.

"The hour to enter the cathedral is at the *Ave Maria,* when the sun is low, its rays trembling on the burnished wall in irises of gold, when the great painted windows stand out in a pale light, alive with the venerable forms of law-givers, prophets and kings." That is the time to see this Saint Fernando—he was so pious that he used to set fire to the faggots to burn heretics *with his own royal hands*—where he lies in a shell-shaped vault, under a gold-encrusted dome, in a coffin of crystal. The body is wonderfully well preserved, with the "pointed" crown and the mantle Fernando wore in life, his sword on one side and his sceptre on the other.

THE GOTHIC IN OTHER LANDS

Burgos, Barcelona and Valencia, Leon, Gerona, and other cities have Gothic cathedrals—usually darker and more gloomy inside than those of France and Germany—and Alcobaza is the great Gothic cathedral of Portugal. Toward the end in all countries the Gothic style ran to more decoration, more flowing lines and tracery and the buildings that show this very rich decoration are said to be built in *Flamboyant Gothic.*

THE GOTHIC CASTLE

Everywhere, during the Middle Ages, men went about arms in hand. Their cities and towns were surrounded with great walls and bristling with towers, and cascassonne in Southern France, is one of the best examples of the old fortified town still to be found. In Carcassonne there are fifty round towers and a great central tower or "keep," the citadel or "fort" itself, towers above them. The great nobles lived in castles and these in France, Germany, Spain and England were square or round, with big ditches filled with water around them, with a drawbridge that could be let down and pulled up, and walls (as in the Castle Couci) as much as 34 feet thick. Later on, in the Age of the Renaissance, these castles were turned into *chateaux,* great country houses. The two most famous Gothic castles in the world are probably the *Tower of London* in England, and the former *Paris Bastile* in France.

THE TOWER OF LONDON

The old fort known by this name is thought to have stood on the East side of London, on the North bank of the Thames, ever since Julius Cæsar conquered the island. It is a record in stone of English history, and in it are kept the crown jewels of England.

Gundulph, Bishop of Rochester, put it up in 1078 for William the Conquerer, though, much later, it was *restored,* as to its *outside,* as it now looks, by Sir Christopher Wren. To Gundulph's first great "White Tower"—the finest example of Norman Gothic tower architecture in England—succeeding kings added walls and other towers until now there are twelve in all.

The White Tower, the big inside keep or fortress, was Sir Walter Raleigh's prison. In the Wakefield Tower the crown jewels are kept. The Middle Tower and Byward Tower are the main fortress entrance, over a bridge that crosses the moat (a deep ditch filled with water that surrounded Gothic castles), and the Lion Gate is so called because from Norman times to 1834 a menagerie of wild beasts was kept in the Middle Tower. On the South, giving entrance through the St. Thomas Tower and Bloody Tower, is the "Traitor's Gate." Here prisoners of high rank were let in, and the Beauchamp Tower was for a long time the prison tower. The Tower of London was used as a prison—like the Paris Bastile—from Norman days to the end of the eighteenth century.

THE PARIS BASTILE

The gloomy *Paris Bastile** was first given the shape it had when destroyed by King Charles V, whose architect, Hughes Aubriot, 1369, added six big heavy towers to the original one, and connected them all with thick walls, with a 25 foot outside moat, and Aubriot was *the first man to be jailed in the prison he had built.* As the centuries went by it was sometimes used as a fort, and King Henry IV kept his treasures there, but more and more, like the Tower of London, it was used as a prison.

With Louis XIV the terrible and monstrous abuse of the *lettre de câchet* the "jail order" started. From the fourteenth Louis on these "jail orders" were easy for anyone with influence at court to obtain. They superseded the *law*—for they expressed "the king's will," which was above the law in those days. Any great noble who had a grudge against some lesser man could get a "jail order." Then the poor victim—it might be a father or lover who had defended the honor of daughter or sweetheart, it might be a creditor who asked for payment of the money due him, it might be anyone who had offended the great lord—was seized and the gates of the Bastile closed behind him with iron clang. Often he was entirely forgotten—and men lived and suffered a life-time in the Bastile, *without even knowing why they had been sent there!* Besides these poor sufferers the writers who wrote against the tyranny of the government also were sent there. It is no wonder that when the Revolution came, the

* In Gothic days a *bastile* was any fortified building or fort.

first thing the Parisians did was to capture the hated fortress, the dark prison of tyranny, and raze it to the ground on July 14, 1789. Now a splendid column of bronze dedicated to the patriots of 1789 rises where it stood, crowned by a gilded figure of Liberty.

THE SPIRIT OF GOTHIC ARCHITECTURE

Gothic art is a *socialistic* art. Not in the *present-day political* meaning of the word. It is a *socialistic* art because it expresses the soul of *all the human society of its age*. It is an art of the *people*.

There was only *one* Christian Church in Europe when the great Gothic cathedrals were built: but they did not spring up at the command of the Roman pope. They were the expression of the *people's own deep religious feeling* and belief, the belief of the ordinary human being as well as of the monks and clergy, the kings and emperors who put them up.

But under the sculptured and embroidered "envelope" of a Gothic cathedral, we always, as in all Evolution, find its germ, the Roman basilica. And in shape and arrangement the Gothic Cathedral is a *confession of faith*. Nave and aisles are a *sign* of the Trinity (or the sacred number seven); like the *three* entrance doors and the *three* towers; the rose-window meant unity; the building itself was *cross-shaped*. The altar-shrine stood for the *Presence of God*. The black vaults (crypt) below were the darkness of "the valley of the shadow of death," where in its coffin the body of king and commoner awaited the Resurrection. And in the great bells of the cathedrals the soul of the cities sang. They not only rang out the churchly hours of prayer and devotion: they chimed the joys and sorrows of the "whole town": they pealed for baptism, wedding and death, for festivals as well as penances. The Christian Architecture of the Middle Ages is a younger sister of the great masonry works of the older Orient. Out of its Romanesque "zone" grew the Gothic, that "adaptation of the forest trees, with all their boughs, to a festal or solemn arcade."

MOHAMMEDAN ARCHITECTURE

CHAPTER X

MOHAMMED AND THE MOSQUE

The Greeks took their "everyday" house and "built it out" into a *beautiful temple*. The Romans took the Greek temple and "built it out", in their way, putting *grandeur* before perfect proportion in using it. The early Christians took the Roman court of Justice, the *basilica*, and made it Christian. So the Romanesque, Byzantine and Gothic styles all go back to the *old pagan basilica*, "baptized" and made Christian.

The *Mohammedan* mosque, its plan and its "features" were *born* out of Islam, the faith of Mohammed, not baptized into it. During the first 100 years Mohammedanism did not work out a fixed building "style" of its own. But in the year 643 A.D. the mosque of Amr at Cairo, *once and for all* seems to have set the general style *all* mosques were to take in the future.

The "church rules" a Mohammedan has to observe *outwardly*, are few in number. Four times a day he has to pray. He flings himself down, his head turned in the direction in which Mecca, the "sacred city" of the Prophet lies, and says his prayer. And before he prays he has to "purify" himself by washing. A Mohammedan *does not even need a mosque* to "do his religious duty," day by day, as he should. In the desert, the Bedouin simply throws his little praying carpet on the sands, under the burning sky, and if he is "pointing" in the right direction, *toward Mecca*, all is as it should be. So no matter how *different* one mosque may be from another in *detail* of decoration, or any other detail, they are all planned for *just one thing—prayer*, in the way the Prophet's law demands. All Mohammedan mosques are the same. They turn *inward*—they have nothing to do with the world!

The whole Mohammedan mosque grows out of *one wall!* This wall is not just a wall: it is an *idea*, the *soul of Mohammedanism*. It is the wall built at right angles to *a line drawn toward Mecca*. For Mecca, the "holy city", where the prophet is buried—though it may lie thousands of desert miles away, though the eye of the flesh cannot see it, only the eye of the spirit—is for the Mohammedan *the great truth for which the mosque is only the sign-post*. And the little, empty niche sunk in the wall, the *mihrab*—found in every mosque—is as much the *altar of the mosque,* as the *shrine* is the *altar* of the Gothic cathedral.

The other walls help the *mihrab-wall* form the covered prayer chamber to protect worshippers from the weather. And the large, square open court in front of the prayer chamber *really* exists to hold the *fountain* or *well* for washing, because the Mohammedan must make himself clean in body before he can draw near to Allah. The approach to each side of the court and the entrance are roofed. In the "sanctuary" itself is the *mimbar* or pulpit, from which the priest addresses the faithful, and the *kiblah,* the place where the holy Koran (the Moslem Bible) is kept. But they are secondary. The *mihrab, the Mecca-niche,* is the *shrine*. When they have washed, the faithful enter in rows, to turn toward Mecca to pray, and therefore the floor or pavement of the mosque is covered with rugs or matting. The columns are like a pattern which is repeated again and again. They are like the date-groves in the desert oases, and *express the spirit of a church in whose eyes men are equal, caliph and commoner, sultan and slave*. Sometimes the roof columns support *square dies,* carrying ranges of arches and *even these arches all run in the direction of Mecca*. The minarets, the slender towers from which the priest calls all the faithful to prayer four times a day, *also turn toward Mecca*. And if we get this—*that the whole mosque is simply a turning of the soul of Islam*—in stone or marble—*toward its shrine, toward Mecca,* we have the whole idea of the mosque.*

THE MOSQUE OF THE KA'BA IN MECCA

(Arabia)

In telling the romance of the great mosques, we would naturally begin with *the mosque* toward which *all* other Mohammedan mosques, the wide world over, in Europe, Asia and Africa, and the millions who pray in them, turn. That mosque is the Great Mosque of the Ka'ba in Mecca.

For ages in the dim past there had stood in the city of Mecca

---

* The main architectural ideas of Mohammedanism are: 1. There are two styles of mosque: one with a big square court closed in by corridors (here, too, the corridors are deepest in the direction of Mecca); the other with a central Byzantine dome. 2. Pointed arches are the rule, though "horse-shoe" and wedge-form arches also are used. 3. The Mohammedan dome has a sharper point than the Byzantine. 4. The word "Saracen" (Arab) is sometimes used for Mohammedan.

an old stone building, without windows. No one knows who raised it or prayed in it, for it was some *old heathen temple.* And the shrine mosque of this religion, toward which all other mosques turn, was originally an *old, forgotten temple of idol-worshippers!* And the small black stone of volcanic rock, fixed in the southeast corner of the building, is the *holiest thing in the Mohammedan faith.* Once it was just a fetish stone—for before Mohammed came the Arabs worshipped fetish stones. Mohammed was a clever man. He turned the old temple into a mosque, by charming that *Abraham had built it* at Allah's (God's) command. And while he broke up the other idols that stood in it, he kept the old black stone and fixed up a story for it. It seems that the Angel Gabriel made a gift of it to Abraham and, coming direct from the Mohammedan heaven, so to say, it was holier than holy. It is fixed in the wall in a silver setting, so that any one can kiss it. *And it has been kissed by millions and millions of lips*—the lips of white, black, brown and yellow men. The lips of caliphs and camel-drivers, of sultans and scavengers, have been pressed to that cold bit of lava stone with a passion they never gave the lips of women: millions and millions and millions, for the pilgrims have crowded to Mecca by the hundred thousands ever since Mohammedanism began. These kisses stand for a treasure of heart's devotion (a horribly unsanitary one from our point of view) seldom equalled in any faith!

And these hundreds of millions of *passionate kisses,* the religious kisses of uncounted, devout lips, have worn the rough stone so smooth that it is *softer than silk!* The old building in the mosque of the Ka'ba is the shrine of Islam (Mohammedanism). Around it the magnificent mosque has been built, with a great colonnaded court, and more than 500 costly pillars from Egypt and Syria. There are various "holy spots" in the Ka'ba besides the black stone itself. And the Zamzam well—a deep well-shaft enclosed in a heavy vaulted building—is an especially holy well: the Mohammedans say that from it *Hagar* drew up water for her son *Samuel.* To the Mohammedan the water from this well is as sacred as the water from the river Jordan is to many Christians, and its healing and wonder-working quality (?) makes the idea of the individual paper drinking cup ridiculous to an Arab. Rich marbles, costly silken hangings and brocades, silver and gold adorn the shrine and mosque inside, and the pilgrim who has made the *twaf* (walked around the shrine seven times) and other "stunts" he has to go through, and has returned to his native land, has acquired *the only class distinction recognized in Islam.* He is a *hadj,* a pilgrim, and a person to be respected forever after. Other mosques may be more splendid, but there is none which so holds the fancy as this one with its millions of pilgrims who for nearly thirteen centuries—white, black, brown and

MOHAMMEDAN ARCHITECTURE

yellow—have been pressing *burning* lips of religious worship against the *cold* black lava of the Ka'ba, until their devout caresses have worn the hard stone to the texture of satin.

THE MOSQUE OF EL-AZHAR IN CAIRO
(Egypt)

Of the two hundred mosques of Damascus, that old city of the "The Thousand and One Nights," we will mention only the Mosque of the Ommeyad rulers. It was an old Byzantine church, so it still has Byzantine arches and—strange to say!—there, where the Moslem prays to his Prophet, the old inscription the masons of the Emperor Arcadius carved over the great entrance door can still be read. It says: "Thy Kingdom, O Christ, is an everlasting kingdom, and thy dominion endureth throughout all generations!" And in Syrian Mosul the Great Mosque has a "Leaning Tower," like that of Pisa. But in Pisa the architects just naturally "figured wrong." In Mosul the great minaret tried to *bow* to Mohammed, once, when he was passing, and never got back "to plumb" again, so they say!

Cairo is another wonder city of "The Thousand and One Nights," and much of its charm remains. It is a city of many mosques, but the Mosque of El-Azhar, "The Splendid," built toward the end of the tenth century, is not only a grouping of great, open courts, prayer chambers and minarets, but also *the great college of Islam,* where to-day all that remains of the learning of Arab civilization is taught the thousands of Mohammedan students who flock to it. Mohammedan boys also have their "college days"—though they are not like ours. But it is a *dead* learning—to us at any rate—"cut on the bias" of religion, and *looking backward,* in a dream toward the past.

The *finest* mosque in Cairo is the mosque of the Sultan Hasan, with four immense halls; the oldest *brick* mosque, the Mosque of Tulun (879 A.D.); the *biggest,* perhaps, the Mosque of *Amr,* and the most *graceful,* the Tomb-Mosque of Kair-Bey, with a roofed central court. And if Brooklyn has a good claim to its title of "the city of churches," then Cairo has an even better one to that of "the city of mosques," for there are 3,000 mosques in Cairo. In general, all Mohammedan architecture in Egypt is more *heavy,* more *massive* than in other Mohammedan lands. The spirit of the ancient temples of the Pharaohs seems to cling to the buildings there.

THE MYSTERIOUS MOSQUE OF KAIRAWAN

More mysterious, more jealously kept from prying Christian eyes than any mosque in Cairo, is the great Moslem sanctuary of Northern Africa, the Mosque of Kairawan (675 A.D.), almost as holy as the *Ka'ba* itself. There "holy wars" against Christianity still are preached, to the 20,000 worshippers it holds, by fanatic *marabouts,* as the Moroccan and Tunisian priests are called. Its roofs resound night and day to the confused murmur of chant and prayer, and *for centuries riches of every kind, gold, silver and gems* have piled up there. Through the great *ogive* entrance portal may be seen at a distance—for this mosque is too holy to be defiled by a Christian foot—the stretching forest of columns and arcades, covered with the exquisite geometry *"pattern"* figure-decoration of Arab Art, known as *Arabesques.* In it—since the Mohammedans are forbidden to use the figure of bird, beast or man in Art—the beautiful curves of Arab writing are woven into lace-work, tracery patterns of lines, in all sorts of rich, glowing colors, blue, green, crimson, gold, etc. From the roofs hang thousands of silver and copper lamps and the murmur of prayer, rising with a sound like that of the waves of the sea, never stops. The mosque covers 38,000 square feet, and to the Mohammedan the most wonderful thing about it is the fact that it is set *absolutely true to the Ka'ba in Mecca.*

THE MOSQUES OF PERSIA, CONSTANTINOPLE AND JERUSALEM

The mosques of Persia were probably *the most beautiful in the world* in their prime. Like those of Egypt, they are falling into ruins. *Color,* every kind of color, in the enamel tile-work which covers their walls, is the beauty of the Persian mosques. Outside the city of Tabriz lie the ruins of the *"Blue Mosque"* (1437), named after the blue tiles which cover it. In the town of Koum, is a mosque covered with *golden* enamel, with *rose-colored* minarets, where holy Fatima, the Prophet's grand-daughter, lies buried. In Ispahan, where the muezzin's chant tells the hour from the minarets just as our bells chime them from our bell-towers, there are two great mosques: the *Imperial Mosque,* built by Shah Abbas the Great in 1612, is one. It has a huge entrance portal which seems to lead into *a blue gulf of color,* with outside walls of the bluest of sky-blue enamel tiles and *blue* lapislazuli stone, topped with *blue* domes and minarets—all the minarets of Ispahan are blue. The other is the *"Friday Mosque,"* dressed in golden yellow tiles, with a touch of *green and black.* In the south of Persia the domes of the mosques all are *green* and *gold,* instead of *turquoise blue,* and the minarets *rose-colored.* In Shiraz, there is an immense mosque with a great entrance gate entirely made of *old-rose tiles.* Everywhere in Persia these beautiful mosques, like the Persian palaces, all color, are falling into ruin, and like them all are set in the *green* of trees and the *silver* water of fountains that rise in their courts, while the crimson red of Persian roses grows around them. Three things mark out the Persian mosque: the wonderful *rainbow color* in their tilework, the use of the *"ogee"* arch (an arch formed of *two long S-curves, joined*) and the "bulb" dome, borrowed from India.

The greatest mosque of Constantinople always will be its Christian mosque—*Saint Sophia*. The Turkish emperors built them mosques of their own, influenced by the *Byzantine* style though they turn away in spirit to the Arabian desert where Mecca stands. The greatest Turkish mosque probably is that of the Sultan Mahommed the Conquerer (1459, rebuilt in 1768). Still, all the Constantinople mosques are copies of the great Byzantine church, and while more of "a picture" than Mohammedan mosques in some other countries, are, perhaps, not as truly Mohammedan in looks.

The mosques of Sultan Selim, Rustem Pasha, Sultan Bayazed II, Sultan Ahmed I, call for mention. The Mosque of *El-Aksa,* in Jerusalem, was put up out of the ruins of a Christian church, but *its Mecca-end is true to plumb!* The so-called "Mosque of Omar," *is really no mosque at all,* but just a shrine put up over the Dome of the Rock.

THE GREAT MOSQUE OF CORDOVA

(Spain)

When the Christians took away their cities from the Moors, they turned their mosques into churches. The mosques still look toward Mecca, but the people who worship in them do *not*. In all the former cities of the Moors, Seville, Cadiz, Granada, Cordova, the mosques showed forth the piety of the great Spanish Moslem kings and sultans. Of all, the *Great Mosque of Cordova*—the Caliph Abderrahman built it in 780 A.D., *after the model of the great African Mosque of Kairawan*—was the glory of its day. When the Caliph Hakim II had finished "enlarging" it and gave it the name of *Zeca,* "The House of Purification," the prayer-chamber alone (135 feet wide by 220 deep) covered 148,000 square feet. It was the next largest mosque in Islam, after the *Ka'ba,* and a little less long and broad than St. Peter's in Rome.

In the golden days the big *mesquita* (the name the Spanish Moors gave their mosques) was one of the most wonderful temples in the world. A courtyard 500 feet long, shady with palm, orange and cypress trees, watered by five marble fountains, led into the hall of 1600 marble columns of all colors. Four thousand seven hundred lamps of gold and colored glass, fed with perfumed oil, blazed down upon its twenty-nine great aisles. Great alabaster bowls threw out the fragrance of musk and attar of roses on the air. In the heart of the mesquita was the holy niche, the *Mecca-niche,* the *Mihrab,* with a great marble conch-shell for a roof. Its sides were bright with polished gold, and the feet of centuries of pilgrims had worn a rut—one can still see it—in the white marble pavement in front of it.

The great mosques, like the great cathedrals, all have had their high *moments of romance*. Let us close our eyes and open them inside the Great Mosque of Cordova, in the year 939 A.D.

The Caliph Abdurrahman III has proclaimed a "holy war" against the Christian "dogs." In the morning he rides with his captains and *emirs* (lords) to join the army which already has left the city for the field. The Great Mosque is crowded with the people of Cordova, for this is the last time the Caliph will pray there until the campaign is over. Where the standards ending in golden crescents stand, the priest mounts the *alminbar* or pulpit, about to speak the first words of the opening prayer. There is a stir at one side. Two huge gates of gilded bronze open out in the wall. And *up and out*—for they are the gates of the underground tunnel which connects the mosque with the Caliph's great palace, the Alcazar—comes Abdurrahman. A tall, haughty, brown-faced man, he walks along the rich Persian carpets sewed with jewels, spread from the gates to the *macsurah*, the golden throne set in a stone frame of wonderful lace-work carving, opposite the marble conch-shell shrine that looks towards Mecca. Abdurrahman's fierce black African guards, with their bared, curved swords, close around him. Beyond them stand the great men of his court: Moorish knights in armor, African chiefs with golden head-bands; *emirs* in splendid green, red and golden brocades; wandering *dervishes*, in dirty linen gowns, but of pure and holy life! And from the open gallery which runs around the *Giralda*, the high minaret-tower outside, floats down *the creed that is summed up in ten words:* "There is no God but God, and Mohammed is his prophet!" And—caliph and all, *for are not all men equal in the sight of* God?—every man in the magnificent mosque flings himself down on the floor *and beats against it with his forehead,* and answers "God is Great!" And when Abdurrahman rises and sits down on his throne again, he *knows* he will give the Christians a beating! But—he is wrong, for if he could look into the future, he would see himself, with a small band of his *emirs,* and a face as black as night, galloping off as fast as he can from a lost battlefield. Behind his fleeing back, the soldiers of Castile are putting his men to the sword until their arms are too tired to kill. And the pleasure-loving Caliph, soiled with the dirt and sweat of the fight, thinks of the green, shady gardens of Zahra, with their blue and yellow china gates, where twelve statues of pure gold, set with precious stones, spout their perfumed water in a court of crystal columns. He thinks of the soft white arms of his women—and when he does so he thinks an *armful*—for Abdurrahman has 6,000 wives and concubines! Yet there is nothing in the Koran

MOHAMMEDAN ARCHITECTURE

to prevent his doing so, and still being a member "in good standing" of the congregation in the Great Mosque.

THE ALHAMBRA

(Moorish Spain)

Many are the great palaces of Mohammedan sultans and kings. There is the Alcazar of Cordova, fortress palace of the Cordovan caliphs, and there are the ruins of Zahra, Abdurrahman's garden palace-town three miles north of the city, named after *one of the* 6,000 of whom he was especially fond. On it 10,000 workmen toiled for 25 years and there, in spite of his women, and every other luxury, Abdurrahman said he had known *but 20 days of happines in 50 years of life!*

There is the Alcazar of Seville, now one of the palaces of the King of Spain, once the royal palace of a Moorish sultan. There Don Pedro the Cruel, once a King of Spain, lured his younger brother and, safe behind a barred door, had him shot down by the bowmen of his guard. There that gloomy religious fanatic, King Philip II* of Spain, while the orange-blossoms in the gardens below sent up their fragrant perfume to his window, with his own hands made out lists of heretics to be burned at the stake for the greater glory of God!

There are the ancient Mohammedan palaces of Egypt, the ruins of the palaces of Haroun-Al Raschid, the caliph of "The Thousand and One Nights" in Bagdad. There are the rainbow tile palaces of the Persian shahs, the silver-white marble palaces of sultans of Oman and of Zanzibar. There are the marvel palaces of India (See Chapter 4) and the vast ruined palaces of older Moroccan sultans, finer than those of the present one. But all these palaces, in spite of their size, splendor and luxury are just the *Mohammedan houses* on a larger scale (courts surrounded by shady porticos and gardens, and provided with fountains and marble water-basins, and the halls and rooms opening on these courts). But the key-note of the palace as well as the ordinary Mohammedan home is *strict seclusion of the women in the harem,* the women's apartments. The men's quarters are jealously shut off from all communication with those of the women, and *only the master* (and his eunuchs) can "get in." Of all the Mohammedan palaces, there is one which is beyond compare. It is the *Alhambra* of Granada.

---

*Any one who has seen the moving picture dramatization of Marion Crawford's novel, "In the Palace of the King," will have an excellent idea of how King Philip looked and acted, though in this picture he is shown in his palace in Madrid.

"A PEARL SET IN EMERALDS"
(Moorish Saying)

The Alhambra is a fortress-palace on the top of a high hill overlooking the city of Granada. It is made up of fortified walls and many Moorish towers of all sizes, covering a great platform. The palace itself hardly seems to be *a solid building*. It is the loveliest palace ever built by an artist and its architect's name was Aben Cencid. It dates from the end of the thirteenth century. As in the Delhi palace of the Mogul emperors of India (See Chapter 4) water *is used as a "building material."* The palace of the Alhambra itself seems to sit among the clouds, the sky above and the sky below it. To see and be in the entrance Court of the Myrtles, and the great Hall of the Ambassadors, which is full of majestic calm, brings peace to the soul. But each hall has a soul of its own.

The Hall of the Ambassadors was the great throne-room of the palace and the sultan's throne was set up opposite the entrance door. It has known its dramatic moments. At the very moment Columbus was trying to move the King of Portugal to give him a ship to discover America another scene was taking place there. Under a dome where silver stars gleam on a ground of crystal and tortoise-shell, sits the fierce old Sultan Hassan, on a golden throne. Around it hang jewelled curtains fringed with pearls. Around him are Moorish knights and courtiers and African guards. And before him stands Don Juan de Vega, come to demand tribute from Muley Hassan for Ferdinand and Isabella. And a deep sigh of satisfaction comes from every Moslem breast as the old fighter on the splendid throne cries out: "Tell your masters that the kings of Granada who paid tribute are *dead*. My mint coins only sword-blades and lances!"

The Court of the Lions was the great hall of the *harem,* where the beauties of the king's court enjoyed their happy dances and games. It has hidden corners and spraying fountains, while rooms filled with the fragrance of their orange-gardens open on it from all sides. In the middle of the Court of the Lions is the round alabaster basin which gives the place its name, for under it—*contrary to strict Mohammedan law which forbids figures in sculpture*—stand twelve marble lions. The Court is surrounded by a low gallery raised on 124 pure white marble columns and two lovely Arabesque pavilions stretch out into it, one from each end. There the women and children of the Kings of Granada led their happy, carefree lives, in a spot which combined sunny freedom with cool, twilight shadow. Rose-red terra-cotta bricks and turquoise-blue tiles form the pavement, while the stucco walls are rose-white in color.

The alabaster basin in the Court of the Lions stands in the lowest part of the palace, and to each new suite of chambers a step leads

MOHAMMEDAN ARCHITECTURE

upward. And as one goes on, *the running water which is the building's living soul* rises from the pavement of the floors in basin fountains and runs in open channels cut in the stone back to the basin, whose well receives it in four pools, and the lions once more cast it out again from their twelve mouths.

The most famous chamber opening from the Court of the Lions is the Hall of the Abencerrages, a perfect square. This was the name of a great noble family or *clan* of the last days of Granada. King Boabdil had thought one of his sultanas had been untrue to him with a knight of his tribe, and so at a festival he brought the whole clan together. Then, in that pleasant court, he had them massacred by the black Africans of his Guard. The Abencerrages were clad in gay silks for the dance. They carried no weapons. The Africans wore heavy breast-plates of silver and had massive clubs studded with brass nails. . . . The visitor is shown certain *dark stains* on the pavement *which water will not wash out:* it is the blood so unjustly spilled there centuries ago. Other famous rooms of the Alhambra are: The Hall of Justice, the Council Chamber Court, and Court of the Vestibule, and the Queen's Dressing Room. And further up and on are the baths and bedrooms of the harem beauties, a labyrinth, *a whispering gallery*, and funeral vaults.

An outlying building which belongs to the Alhambra is the *Palace of the Generalife*, with hedges, grottoes, fountains and cypress avenues, and on another hill is the *"Martyrs' Villa,"* where the poor Christian slaves who spent their wretched lives toiling to put up the fairy palace of the Alhambra were herded together in underground cells at the end of the day. The "Vermilion Towers" were once strong forts, with underground stables and cisterns. The Alhambra decorations—among the richest of their kind—are *Arabic inscriptions,* and curved and straight lines and figures worked out into the most beautiful *Arabesque* patterns, in filagree-work of white, blue, red, brown and gold. The roof of the dome in the Hall of the Abencerrages is like *the honeycomb of the bees*—it is "cut in" with more than 5,000 little cells of different shapes, *the famous "stalactite vaulting"* of Oriental Architecture. Sun and light flood the wonderful airy rooms everywhere, and the view from balconied windows is magnificent. A great art-lover once said: "The Alcazar of Seville with its 'bluff' and unimportance, is more nearly related to any Moorish café in a World's Fair Exposition than to that fairy palace, the Alhambra!"

THE BAZAAR[*] AND THE MYSTERY OF THE ORIENTAL STREET

The Bazaar is the Oriental idea of the *ideal business street*. It

[*] We use the word now for charitable and benefit "fairs" or "sales."

simply means a street of stores, shops or stalls under one roof. The "arcades" in business buildings in so many Western cities, where an arcade runs through a building from end to end, lined with stores facing the arcade passage, have borrowed this idea from the East. You pass through the gates of an Oriental town, take its "main street" and soon find it branches off into these *bazaar* streets, covered streets, where stone vaulting keeps away the heat of the sun. The bazaar and the mosque are the two places of a Mohammedan's public life. And each *bazaar* has its own kind of stores. In our cities we have variety: in the Mohammedan cities the booths of the swordsmiths, the silk merchants, the shoemakers, the jewellers, the tailors, each have their bazaar. It is a labyrinth of streets each with its own colors, noises and smells. The ring of the hammer tells you you are in the swordsmith's bazaar; clouds of fragrance let you know you have reached the bazaar of the perfume-seller who deals in attar of roses and Indian essences. And the bazaars are lighted from above by narrow openings in the vaulting.

But only the "main" streets are real public streets, leading to the bazaars. The streets that lead off from them, the streets that are lined with houses where people live are just *passages,* that keep branching off into alleys. And the larger alleys all end in smaller blind alleys and these alleys each end in some lonely, closed and silent door. These streets are not streets like ours. They are just *passages* to houses. Mohammedan houses (in spite of their entrance door) really *turn their backs on the streets.* The streets are the passages on which the same unchanged backs of houses front. That gives them the mystery and romance we feel in an Oriental town: the secrets which lie behind the rows and rows of white houses with doors that seem never to open. They all turn the same blank doors and heavily barred windows on the streets of passage. But inside! Passing through a vestibule one steps into an open court full of flowers and trees, where marble columns gleam and fountains play. All the rooms open on this court. It is the place where in the cooling shade, to the murmur of waters the Mohammedan lives his *private* life, with his wives and children. All that is beautiful in his art is here, hidden from the eyes of others. Our *habits* of life are more public. The Oriental values *privacy* like a jewel. And because of it we feel the charm of *mystery* behind the rows and rows of high-walled houses with their doors that seem never to open.

THE RENAISSANCE

CHAPTER XI

(The "Rebirth" Architecture)

In the great buildings of the Renaissance—the word simply means "a being born again"—the old classic architecture of Greece and Rome are born again. But they are "shaped up" differently because the artists of this "rebirth" art were *not* the artists of Greece and Rome. They had different minds and souls, and different ideas. So they gave the great *building forms* of Greece and Rome a "shaping" that came out of their own genius. The Gothic Architecture (especially in Northern lands) *stands for the soul of the Middle Ages*. It is a soul sincere and devout, but ignorant. The world of the Middle Ages was a world in which the Pope at Rome (and under him his bishops and priests) *held the keys of heaven and hell!* The pope was lord and master of all things of the *spirit,* but he claimed the earth as well! The *German* emperor of the "Holy *Roman* Empire"—it has that name because it was supposed to continue the *old* "Roman Empire"—was the first among all the kings of the earth. When the *lord high spiritual ruler* and the *lord high earthly ruler* "got together," they seldom could agree. Battle, murder and sudden death marked the course of their little arguments, and gradually came a general *loss of faith* on the part of the people *in both—the idea of the papacy and the empire* began to "count for less." People everywhere were beginning to do a little thinking for themselves, instead of letting priests do it for them; they were beginning to think the whole "feudal system" a bit silly. People were getting to think more and do more "out of their own heads."

The Renaissance was the age, too, in which people began to think and speak more of themselves as *"nations,"* and less as *subjects* of some king. It was an age of change and restlessness and advance.

And in the Renaisance the artist, the great architect, *gets full credit* again for what he does. In the Gothic Age the architect usually was forgotten in the work. The idea of the Renaissance was born in the great city of Florence, Italy. Later it spread to France,

THE CATHEDRAL OF FLORENCE
(Early Renaissance Architecture)

Filippo Brunelleschi (1379-1446), is the one big name in the first of "Early" Renaissance Architecture (1420-1500). His father was a lawyer, but Filippo—like so many of the great Renaissance artists—was "a jack of all trades and *a master of all.*" He became a first class goldsmith and a wonderful sculptor before he handed in the blue-print plan for the Florence cathedral "dome," that won the prize, and gave him the glory of putting up the first dome of the Renaissance. To this day the Florence Cathedral is simply called the "diomo" (The Dome), and the "dome" became the leading feature in Renaissance Architecture.

Filippo, while he was "studying up" for his life work, did so much digging among the old Roman ruins in and about Florence, that most people thought he was looking for buried treasure. In a way he was, but they did not know it until his cathedral was built. Brunelleschi was one of the very first architects to use *perspective* right in his work.

Another architect and sculptor, Ghiberti, had finished the cathedral, *all but the famous dome,* and as Brunelleschi felt that too many architects spoil the building, just as too many cooks spoil the broth, he managed to get rid of Ghiberti (with whom he had to work) in a "foxy" way. When his great dome was done, he never had the satisfaction of knowing what people said—that it was a more

---

* The following are important points about Renaissance Architecture. 1. Symmetry—Right measure and *proportion* combined with classic beauty of shape are the guiding spirit in Renaissance buildings. The *Gothic* architect looked only at his cathedral. *The cathedral was the only important thing in the town or city.* The other buildings and houses "herded up" around it any which way, and the cathedral over-shadowed and looked down on them all. But the *Renaissance* architect looked *out* from his church, cathedral or palace, to see "how it would fit in" *with the rest of the street or square.* He not only wanted every bit of the building itself to be in the right proportion: doors with windows, height of roof, length of building "balancing." He also wanted his building to "balance" with the street, the square, the city itself, as a part of a complete whole. 2. The classic columns and "Orders" (Greek and Roman) are used to decorate the "fronts" of buildings. 3. Windows and doors are "grouped together," to make the best "picture" effect. Wood was a favorite building material, and much plaster cornice and molding-work was done, and "facings" to make the best "picture" effect. Wood was a favorite building first: beauty of any special part second. 5. Painting influenced architecture because the painters were no longer painting everything *flat.* They were painting "room" and "space" into their pictures. So the architects had to shape the inside of their buildings with this in mind.

striking looking dome than St. Peter's in Rome—for he died just sixty years before St. Peter's corner-stone was laid.

Brunelleschi's other best works were the small "true Greek style" Pazzi Chapel in the St. Croce churchyard of Florence—with a real "pantheon" dome; and some splendid palaces in Florence. Best is the *Pitti Palace,* a long building in three great stories, with an even row of windows along its front It was built of big square blocks of rough-cut stone. The *Strozzi Palace* was designed by the architect Cronaca (1498), and has a top story with a massive cornice—to prevent its escaping up into the sky like the Gothic buildings do—and doors and windows with half-circle arches. The architect Michelozzo built the Palace Riccardi, also with an "antique" or "old Roman" cornice. Leon Battista Alberti (1404-1472), another "Early Renaissance" architect, made the front of his *San Francesco Church* in Rimini a regular Roman "Triumphal Arch," and imitated the Roman amphitheatre columns in front of his *Rucellai Palace* in Florence. Though they were not in Rome, these Early Renaissance architects were all "doing as the Romans did."

ST. PETER'S CATHEDRAL IN ROME

St. Peter's Cathedral in Rome is the high-water mark of "High Renaissance Architecture," which came after the "Early" and was a *richer* development of it. The greatest church of Roman Catholic Christianity owes its "being there" to the ambition of Pope Julius II to put up a cathedral which would throw everything Europe had thus far seen completely in the shade.

Bramante (1444-1514), painter as well as architect, who had done some building in Rome for Julius II, called on him to build St. Peter's. Before death overtook him, Bramante had finished four big piers and their arches. But Michel Angelo, who finally succeeded Bramante—poet, sculptor, painter and master of a dozen arts beside—*was the greatest genius of the whole Renaissance!* So far as one man could, he expressed the *Renaissance soul,* and its ideals. As a sculptor he will be elsewhere considered.

Michel Angelo superintended the building of St. Peter's for eighteen years, until he died—but even then the great cathedral church had not been completed.

For a time after Bramante's death, *Rafael* had charge of building St. Peter's. He kept the Greek Cross which was Bramante's choice for the *shape* of the church. *Baldassarre Peruzzi,* the architect who followed Rafael, chose the *Greek Cross.* San Gallo, who was in charge a short time, chose the *Latin Cross.* But Michel Angelo went back to the *Greek Cross* of Bramante, and it was according to Michel Angelo's plans that the work on St. Peter's continued up into the seventeenth century. In 1620 the architect *Maderna,* under Pope Paul V, lengthened the nave and managed to shape the building as a *Latin* instead of a *Greek* cross. And 120 *years after the foundation stone had been laid,* Urban VIII consecrated the new cathedral (Nov. 18, 1626), on which twenty succeeding popes, and the greatest architects of the age had worked together. Great architects have said that if Michel Angelo's original plans had been carried out "all the way," the dome would be far more impressive. The walls of St. Peter's are faced with colored marbles, and it has four monster "bays" in the middle nave, a bay for each transept and one for the choir. The great court which the Neapolitan Bernini—a great architect of the *Baroque*—(See next chapter) added in 1661, as an "approach" to the front entrance, made his reputation. It also added greatly to the "looks" of the whole building. Pope Urban VIII, aside from the dedication of St. Peter's—his family name was Barberini—is remembered for *two* other things. He took the beautiful Greek bronze works of art of the Pantheon and *cast them into cannon for his papal castle of St. Angelo,* something which made the Romans say: "What the *barbarians* did not *do, Barberini did!"* He is also the pope who had the Inquisition make poor Galileo *"take back"* his statement that *the world was round and that the world "do move."*

Among other great buildings of the "High Renaissance" in Italy is Bramante's Vatican Palace, and the courtyard of the papal Palace of the Cancellaria. The Vatican Palace, the palace of the popes (the Quirinal, the palace of the present Italian kings does not amount to much as architecture) was partly Italian Gothic, but Bramante and Bernini added to and changed it. There the pope lives and *not* in the old Lateran Palace, which was used for an orphan asylum in the 18th century and is now a museum. Rafael's Vidoni Palace, and the Farnese Palace of Sangallo, perhaps the finest in Rome, were only two of many magnificent palaces the princes and nobles of Italy had built for them. During most of the 15th century the Venetian palaces that looked down on the waters of the Grand Canal, where the lovers of a light-hearted city passed swiftly and silently in the black gondolas, were Gothic. But later on they changed to Renaissance, and the great architect San Sovina built the wonderful Library of St. Mark's. In the Palace de' Diamante, "of the diamonds," at Ferrara, the square faces of the outside stones are "bevelled in" toward the middle as though the masons had been set to work diamond cutting. In Bologna is Peruzzi's Albergate Palace. The "marble palaces of Genoa" are of white marble with magnificent vestibules, among them the Cataldi, Pallavicini Dora, and Durazzo palaces, many by the architect Galeazzo Alessi, who also built the noble *Marino* (Municipal Palace) of Milan. The *big-*

RENAISSANCE ARCHITECTURE

gest in Italy, the Caserta of Naples (1752) by Vamvitelli competes with the Spanish Escurial for the honor of having the *most* tiresome, "the same thing over and over again," design of any palace in the world.

FONTAINEBLEAU AND THE LOUVRE

(Renaissance Architecture in France)

The French kings Charles VIII, Louis XII and Francis I, during the fifteenth century had been making military "raids" into Italy. When our boys came back from France in 1918 and 1919 they brought with them all sorts of things they had "picked up" in a land new and strange to them: wives (some of them), new notions, a well-known perfume. The French did the same in Italy in the fifteenth century. And among the things, good and bad, they brought back with them was the Renaissance idea in building. The French kings saw the magnificent Renaissance buildings in Rome, in Naples, in other cities, and so did the French nobles. When they got home they were no longer satisfied—they wanted castles in which *beauty* and not *strength* came first. And so the Renaissance Architecture began in France. But the French gave it a touch of their own and the *chateaux**—"castles"—of the French kings and nobles are French Renaissance, not Italian Renaissance, in style. The main difference was that while they often kept the entrance gates, towers, walls, etc., of the *Gothic fortified castle;* they covered and changed their looks with rich Renaissance ornament and decorations.

King Francis I, who loved art almost as well as women and wine, was fond of the great hunting forest of Fontainebleau and began to build him a great palace there in 1526, and it expresses the spirit of the French Renaissance in spite of the changes and additions all the French rulers who succeeded him, made. In one of the series

---

* A group of these French royal castles, with Fontainebleau the most magnificent, show Gothic and Renaissance styles "fermenting" together and producing French Renaissance. There is the great *Chateau of Blois,* on the Loire, with a famous spiral staircase tower and a room in the northeast wing where the degenerate King Henry III had the Duke of Guise daggered before his eyes; there is a room where the Queen Catherine de Medici, who set the blood-rivers of St. Bartholomew flowing, died, old and lonely, amid the ruins of her schemes. There is the *Chateau of Chenonceaux,* which King Henry II gave his beautiful *mistress* Diane de Poitiers, only to have his wife take it away from her as soon as he died. Like the Chateau of *Acy-le-Rideau,* its beautiful entrance gate, towers and walls are Gothic in form, but Renaissance in detail. The *Chateau of Chambard,* a great block of buildings, with so many towers, turrets, spires and dormer windows to its roofs that they are its most striking "feature." There is, finally, the *Chateau of Amboise,* where the great Italian artist Leonardo da Vinci is said to be buried. All these *chateaux* are 14th century castles *outside* and 16th century palaces *inside*.

of courts surrounded by buildings, the "Court of the White Horse," Napoleon wept when he said farewell to his Old Guard in 1814. Gilles the Breton, the architect of Francis I, erected many of the palace group of buildings, and the Salle des Fêtes is considered the finest room known. Other famous rooms are the *Galerie de Diane* (Diana's Hall) and the library the *Galerie des Cerfs* or "Deer Gallery."

Gardens and "ornamental waters" (lakes and fountains) surround the great *chateau,* and nearby are the beautiful woods of Fontainebleau, where the kings of France hunted in pomp and ceremony, according to the laws of court etiquette. It is a building of memories, grave, and gay, joyous and tragic.

The Palace of the Louvre—those parts built by the architect Pierre Lescot under Francis I and his successors, the south and west courtyard wings—rank among the finest specimens of French Renaissance Architecture, though other additions were made by later kings. The *Palace of the Tuileries,* (*tuileries means tile-kilns,* and before Catherine de Medici had the great engineer-architect Philebert de l'Orme build the palace, a tile-kiln stood on the ground) is the one from which poor Louis XVI was dragged to prison, and in which Napoleon III, *the last French emperor,* held his gay and dissolute court. It was burned by the French Communists in 1871. But the south end wing (*Pavillon de Flore*) escaped; and the *Pavillon de Marsac,* the north end wing, has been rebuilt since. The cities and countryside of France are rich in other fine Renaissance buildings: big *chateaux* (country houses and palaces) and *hotels* or city palaces of former great noble families. The noble families have largely disappeared, their palaces belong to private persons (some to Americans) and many of the great *hotels** are now public buildings. The Paris Church of St. Eustache (1533), a Gothic church, wears a robe of Renaissance carving and decoration. At first much of the fine art-work of the French Renaissance was done by Italian artists. The French kings coaxed them to come with them from Italy for big pay—and since "big pay" is a strong "moving" power, they came.

HEIDELBERG CASTLE

(Renaissance Architecture in Germany)

Ask any German what the finest monument of German Renaissance Architecture is and he will not stop to think. He will say, "Heidelberg Castle"—though much of it lies in ruins.

The Castle of Heidelberg, 330 feet above the Neckar river, was

---

* The word "hotel" now means a building for the entertainment of "paying guests." The French *hotel* of the 17th and 18th century was a private residence where "guests" *never* paid.

the residence of the German princes known as the "Electors Palatine" (*Electors* because they belonged to a little group of princes who chose or *"elected"* the German emperors, and *Palatine* because they ruled the *"Palatinate,"* one of the German countries). It was the grandest and largest of all old German castles before the French under Marshal Turenne, who ravaged the entire Palatinate with merciless cruelty, burning, destroying and looting, reduced the two wonderful wings (of which one, the "Otto-Henry Building" was Renaissance) to ruins. One of these wings was "restored," at huge cost and labor between 1897 and 1903. In a cellar entered from the courtyard of the restored building is what those who "look upon the wine when it is red" would consider the most important thing about the castle. It is the *Great Tun of Heidelberg,* built in 1751, and holding 49,000 gallons, but which had been "filled" only *twice* since it was built.

The other wing, the "Friederich Building," is in the *Baroque* style (See next chapter). It was a gay, wasteful life in Heidelberg Castle before the unjust ambitions of Louis XIV brought war and destruction to all its beauty. There was dancing in the great castle halls, and the gaming tables were piled high with gold wagered by noble players—*gold which the tax-ridden farmers of the country had to furnish*. There was love-making in the splendid gardens by moonlight, there was joy and laughter. There were parades and reviews of splendidly mounted and uniformed guards of the Prince Palatine in the great courtyard.

The long line of gilded carriages drove up to the castle entrance. Out got ladies and gentlemen. Bright-colored satin slippers tapped the marble pavement, heavy silk dresses rustled. The court ladies and court gentlemen moved along in a costly confusion of furred collars, ermine and marten, high-built, shaking French *coiffures* (head-dresses of hair and ribbons), great pompous wigs, hats with long feathers, and glittering uniforms, while the air was filled with French perfumes. It was a wonderful "mix-up" of bright color that moved from the empty carriages into the high, candle-lit halls, where the sound of violins and cembalos (the earliest kind of piano) greeted their ears. Thousands of candles, as dusk was falling, drove away the shades of night. They stood in silver candlestick holders along the tapestried walls, and while some danced the minuet, others bent over the card-tables and watched the gold pieces flow toward or away from them. And then—in a few months' time—the French general Montglas's troops had taken the splendid castle. It was set afire, its flames reflected in the waves of the Neckar below, lit up the whole countryside for miles around!

THE ESCORIAL

(Renaissance Architecture in Spain)

In Spain the Renaissance ideas, when the Renaissance influence began to be felt there, were mingled with the *architecture already in existence*. This itself was a mixture of *Gothic* and *Moorish* (this *Arabesque Gothic* style was known as the *Mudejar* style). Then came the Renaissance, and out of the three styles the Spanish Renaissance developed, first a so-called *"Platcresque"* (from *Plate-makers*—that is, *silversmiths*—because its ornamental work in stone and stucco was as delicate and rich *as the work of the finest silversmiths in silver*). The *Town Hall* of Seville, and the great gateway of the *University of Salamanca,* are among the best examples of the *Plateresque*. In a Spanish way it is the same thing as "Early" Italian Renaissance.

The Spanish "High" Renaissance was another thing, still very rich in decoration, but more cold and stately, and more along the ideas of two Italian architects named Palladio and Vignola, who were all for *"big forms,"* and imitated the *"colossal"* things the ancient Romans built too slavishly. The Plateresque Spanish style has "plain" outside walls and towers, and "goes in" for bright colored stucco and rich gilding in the inside of its splendid halls and courts. As we know (See Chapter 10) this idea of having the beauty on the *inside, and showing a plain face to the outside world,* is a Moorish or Oriental one. Chilly, solemn magnificence is the soul of the Spanish "High Renaissance" and its great building is the *Escorial*.* (The palace in the style of the Emperor Charles V built in Granada is completely overshadowed by the wonderful Alhambra.) Never did *one* building reflect more exactly a cold, formal, stiff and austere human being than this Escorial does its builder, King Philipp II of Spain.

It is a combination of royal palace, church, monastery and tomb. In the battle of St. Quentin, August 10th, 1537, King Philipp's army had given the French a bad beating. Phillip thought the victory was due to the fact that Saint Laurence, whose "name-day" it was, had "helped him out." So he swore to build a convent-palace and give it the Saint's name. Saint Laurence was martyred to death by being *fried alive on a gridiron,* and so Philipp insisted the palace take the shape of a gridiron, which it did.

Juan Baptista de Toledo, a Spanish architect trained in Italy, drew the plans and the first stone was laid in 1563, under the eye

---

* The correct Spanish title of the Escorial is: *El real monasterio de San Lorenzo del Escorial* ("The Royal Monastery of Saint Lorenzo of Escorial"—*Escorial* being the name of the village near which it was put up).

RENAISSANCE ARCHITECTURE

of the royal fanatic. Toledo's favorite pupil completed the building after that master's death in 1593, but many Spanish kings have added to it since. The whole Escorial covers 396,782 square feet, and has 7 towers, 15 gateways, and 12.000 windows and doors. The Escorial Church is the finest building, and *one of the greatest Renaissance churches in Europe,* with a dome 60 feet in diameter. Under the high altar is the royal mausoleum, where some 20 *black marble urns in niches* are reserved for the *dust of kings or their mothers.* Many Spanish kings are in these urns, but some still are empty. A separate vault for other members of the royal family has a rather horrible name, *El Pudridero* (The Rotting Place), and is known as such to every Spaniard. But the royal palace is but one smaller group among the other larger groups of buildings of the Escorial. The church has ten chapels, one of them dedicated to the 11,000 Virgins; then there is a tremendous group of buildings which make up the *Seminary,* and there is the huge *Convent,* with its Clock Tower. In the palace, the room which best *expresses Philipp* is his cell—he had to have a cell even there—from which he could "attend" at high mass, even while sick in bed. Of course, with the *lack* of church buildings near at hand, there is a special *Royal Oratory* or *Chapel* in the palace, too! The great *Library* (in the Convent) contains wonderful treasures in manuscripts.

The *Palacio Real* in Madrid, originally improved by Charles V, and which his son King Philip II enlarged in the Spanish Renaissance style (it is the one in which Crawford has staged his famous novel "In the Palace of the King," which has been very popular as a moving picture), has something *more human* and *less monkish* about it than the Escorial. The present palace (King Philip's burned down in 1734), was built by the Italian architect Sachetti of Turin, in the Tuscan style of the "High Renaissance," and is a building of white granite, 470 feet square and 100 feet high.

The *Town Hall* of Seville, the Palace of the Counts of Monterey in Salamanca, and the Palace of the Bishop of Alcala de Henares are other fine examples of Spanish Renaissance.

ST. PAUL'S CATHEDRAL IN LONDON

(Renaissance Architecture in England)

The *Tudor Style* in England (called *Tudor* after the family name of the English kings from Edward IV to Queen Elizabeth) was really the last rich kind of Gothic Architecture developed in England. But in the time of Henry VIII artists and architects from Flanders (Holland), Italy and France were coming into the country and bringing new ideas along with them. And so English Renaissance buildings began to go up and the great nobles of England began to prefer Renaissance country houses to their heavier castle-like Tudor mansions, just like the French.*

The English Renaissance in building may be said to have begun with the Tomb of Henry VIII, put up in Westminster Abbey (1516) by the Italian Torrigiano. Its greatest and most finished work, perhaps, "the most successful great church built in Europe during the Renaissance" is St. Paul's Cathedral in London.

Like any old Roman architect Sir Christopher Wren (1632-1723) who planned and built St. Paul's Cathedral after the Great Fire of London (1666) built around the idea of a great central dome, like that of the Roman Pantheon. Its ground plan is Gothic, its style Italian Renaissance, the later Italian Renaissance of the Vignano kind, that "went in" for Roman *grandeur*. The 216-foot dome (above the inside stone dome is an outside wooden dome), had a stone *lantern* (a roof tower, open below and letting in light from the sides) 360 feet from the pavement below. Some architects consider it finer, with its great central dome, its two huge square front bell-towers, with "pyramid steeples," its portico with columns and the two flights of steps leading to it, than St. Peter's in Rome. It is Sir Christopher Wren's greatest work.*

* Among many of these might be mentioned: Holland House, Kensington; Montacute House, Somersetshire; Castle Ashby, Northampton. In Kirby Hall, John Thorpe, the architect, like some of the French architects, kept the plan of the old fortified castle, with rich outside decoration. The English Renaissance style, which came in after the Tudor is often called *Jacobean* (Jacobus is the Latin for James, and as it came in with James I, the first Stuart King of England, it was given his name).

* He built besides many other churches of which the "Bow" Church, was the first London church put up on arches. Any Londoner born in hearing distance of the "Bow" bells is known as a "Cockney." Eight colleges, 35 "halls" for city companies, theaters, Hampton Court Palace (East front) and Greenwich Hospital were erected by him and his architect followers built hundreds of noble English mansions and churches: Vanburgh built Blenheim Palace, where the American wives of the Duke of Marlborough have lived. Sir William Chambers built Somerset House (1776), among others. The famous St. Paul's Church in New York City (1764) is a church in the Wren style.

THE BAROQUE

CHAPTER XII

THE LAST GREAT STYLE IN ARCHITECTURE

The *Baroque* is the style of the Seventeenth Century. To know what the style means, we must know what the *word* means. Renaissance buildings, inside or outside, whatever the "picture" was that meets the eye, give a feeling of *depth*. You get the contrast of *lights* and *shadows*. With old Greek and Roman building *shapes* in mind, the Renaissance architects tried to make everything look *"natural,"* rightly balanced. *The Baroque style tries to outdo Nature.* The word "Baroque" comes from the Spanish. The Spanish word *barrueco* means *a large, irregularly shaped pearl.* And while some authorities on Art think Baroque a style so fantastic and *"overloaded"* that it offends the rules of *simplicity* and *good taste,* others consider it *"a pearl"* of a style, even if it is an "irregularly shaped" one. Those who can appreciate the great, even in the wild fancy and extravagance in Baroque Architecture, will admire it. Those who do not will not like it.

The Baroque style tries to outdo Nature. It makes forms and lines *bigger than big.* It extends itself in *every* direction, *up* toward the sky, *out* into gardens and parks. Like the Chinese, the architects of the Baroque make great gardens *a part of their buildings.* The Baroque is really the last, biggest development of the Renaissance ideas. It is a style full of life, of color, of actual movement— *in pictures, in statues, in decorations,* which cover every inch of the inside and outside of buildings. In Baroque the architect does not care so much whether his column *is a real stone column or a painted column on a wall*—so long as it *rises up* and *holds the eye!* Everywhere there are moving figures, stucco groups hanging from ceilings or bending over balustrades. The ceilings in Baroque buildings look right into *the vast painted skies of heaven* (in the churches) or into the cloudland of Mount Ida, where the Greek gods lived.

Some have called the Baroque style a "theatrical art"—which means a "showy," unreal one. But if it is theatrical, it is theatrical in the *grandest way.* What the last, richest kind of Gothic, the so-called *Flamboyant Gothic* (which we have described in a preceding chapter) was to *earlier Gothic,* the *Baroque was to the earlier Renaissance* Architecture. It takes what is *grand* and *big* in the Renaissance building, and makes it *grander* and *bigger*—to the eye, at any rate. Mountains are just pedestals for Baroque architects, lakes are only there to reflect buildings. They take in the sky, the sun and the stars into their painted ceilings. They make garden and countryside part of their architectural plan. Terraces, alleys, hedges and bushes are "trimmed" into designs, into vases and figures to "fit into" their building schemes. They even use *cages full of wild beasts as building material.*

The Baroque may be called *the first style that was used everywhere.* Its buildings rose from Seville to Petrograd, they stood in Mexico, Constantinople and Peking. The Baroque has been called a "style of great lords," and it was universal, used everywhere during the later seventeenth and earlier eighteenth centuries, because the great lords of the age all wanted to be kings, and Baroque palaces made them feel that they were kings.

VERSAILLES

(The Baroque Style in France)

The Baroque is a wild, mad, extravagant style. But—the stiff, formal, ceremonious Louis XIV of France managed to build the hugest Baroque palace *inside* in the world and combine it with a grand and simple *actual* outside building of two enormous wings flanking a central portion, and then show the *real Baroque* feeling again in the *tremendous gardens,* still the wonder of France, which take in the surrounding countryside and make it part of the palace. Jules-Hardouin Mansard, was the *architect of the Palace of Versailles.* Charles Le Notre was the architect of the *Versailles Gardens,* and Louis XIV himself—the greatest Baroque king that ever lived—supplied the *idea* of the largest palace in Europe.

The men who may be said to have "started" the Baroque style, were the Italian architects Palladio and Vignano (already mentioned), with their striving for the *tremendous size and grandeur* of old Roman buildings like the *Colosseum* and the *Pantheon.* Bernini, who added the colonnaded square to St. Peter's, carried their ideas of size and grandeur ever further, and was one of the greatest of the real Baroque architects.

Inside, the palace of Versailles—where the lords and ladies of King Louis' court once revolved about the "grand monarch," like lesser stars around the sun—is crowned with a collection of art works commemorating the *great persons* and *great events in French*

THE BAROQUE

history, a collection whose value *cannot be expressed in dollars and cents.* In these rooms the famous "decorator" Lebrun, who might be called *the architect of the Baroque* inside of the palace of Versailles, "let himself go" in the most magnificent wall and ceiling decorations, as in the famous "Hall of Mirrors" or "Glass Gallery" —with its 34 arches, 17 of them great windows looking out into the gardens, and 17 huge mirrors. The "Apollo Room" was the throne room, but Louis XIV sometimes used the "Glass Gallery" instead. Often, in novels, whose scene is laid at the French court in Versailles, you see the words *"Oeil de Bœf"* ("The Bull's Eye"). This was an anteroom with a big *oval* window, like "a bull's eye," in which the courtiers waited for the king, who was dressing, to come from his bed-room. In the "Battle Gallery" hangs a *picture record* of great French victories. It would be impossible to describe all the great halls and rooms of this historic building. One can imagine the shades of great kings, generals, admirals, priests and lovely women filling them when night has fallen, and the huge palace is shrouded in silence and darkness!

Le Notre, the architect of the Versailles gardens, *included the rivers and forests about Versailles in his plan.* Everywhere in the gardens, silver water (carried by innumerable pipes and conduits under the ground) played in fountains, sparkled in lakes and pools, and ran in streams. When the king gave a garden party by night, the waters of Versailles threw back the light of Bengal fires and thousands of lanterns. Inside the vast Versailles park also lies the *Grand Trianon* (another big palace in the style which had the Baroque soul under an old Roman *outside dress of stone*), and Louis XV had a *Petit Trianon* (Little Trianon) put up. The *machinery* is still shown there which, without a sound, sent up a suppertable covered with rich wines and delicious dishes to a private room above, where King Louis XV, *the most depraved and dissolute monarch of his age,* is said to have eaten with his mistress in a state of nature. The *Chateau of Marly,* five miles from Versailles, was another of Louis XIV's magnificent *"concealed Baroque"* palaces. It was burned down in the French Revolution, when the sight of the splendid building raised by their blood and their tears drove the French peasants mad with rage.

Marley is said by those who lived at the time to have been the most wonderful "water palace" in the world. It was one vast room or suite of rooms *in the open air.* The architect Mansard extended the *actual* rooms of the palace right out into the woods. "Panels" and "niches" in which marble statues of white marble stood were cut into the great masses of green forest leaves. The thee-tops were made to look like *domes* and *cupolas.* One walked along walls and through colonnades of green leaves. And all these great open-air chambers had names. The "Ladies' Cabinet," the "Green Hall," the "Prince's Cabinet," etc. Everywhere the fountains played: there were basins, jets and cascades. The cascade called "The Green Carpet" flung up a great column of crystal water *at the highest point of the forest view,* from a huge vase held by bronze figures of water-gods. And the mass of water flowed in a foaming white torrent down long marble steps, set off by the thick background of green so dark as to be almost black. There, in an open-air *water-theatre,* where the chandeliers and hanging lamps were high jets of crystal water, and the "footlights" a diamond fringe of water pouring into a bed of grass, Louis XIV gave great garden-parties with magic illuminations which turned the whole out-of-doors into a dream of fairyland. Yet for Louis XIV this gorgeous creation of the Baroque style, that turned all Nature into a palace was—just a "little country place." He went there for what to him was *"simple"* amusement, to get out *"into the country."*

The famous *Hotel des Invalides* in Paris (where Napoleon lies buried), the *National Library* (once a palace of Cardinal Mazarin), the *Institute of France,* the *Hotel de Toulouse* (now Bank of France), and the great square called the *Place Vendome* as well as other buildings in Paris, and buildings in the big cities of the French provinces, were put up in the age of the Baroque, the seventeenth century, most of them, like the *Luxembourg Palace,* with their Baroque on the *inside* rather than the *outside.*

THE JESUIT CHURCHES IN VIENNA AND THE DRESDEN "KEEP"

(Baroque Style in Germany)

The grand Baroque style in French Architecture has a "back-fire" action in Italy, Germany and Spain, for France, during the time of Louis XIV, was the "boss" country of Europe. Every king and every prince imitated the "grand style" of Louis XIV in his buildings. Even under his successor Louis XV, when the French reputation in war and politics reached a "bottom level," the *"Rococo"* style of that king (a kind of "dialect" Baroque—just as an "up-Maine" way or a "down-Georgia" way of speaking to-day is still English, but a "dialect" English) ruled the taste of the princes of other lands. And—besides this Baroque of palaces, there was a Baroque of the *Church.*

In church architecture of the seventeenth century we find the Baroque is largely the architecture of the great churches built by the *Order of the Jesuits.* It was a style that "fitted in" well with their ambitious plans of ruling the whole world and even the pope, who was supposed to be above them. (The Vicar-General of the

THE BAROQUE

Jesuits was so powerful for a time that he was known, from the black gown he wore, as "the Black Pope".) In their churches you can fairly see the ambition, the wish to rule and dominate in the buildings, their plan and decoration.

The University Church of the Jesuit Order in Vienna, St. Ignatius, Church of St. Peter and other churches built by the architect Fischer von Erlach, are the greatest examples, perhaps, of this vast and *worldly* style of building turned to *sacred* uses. In these churches, and in that of St. Charles Borromeo, *the ceilings open* up and show the interior of the heavens. The whole architecture, the columns, arches and supports seem to be there only to *hold up another world*, a painted world vaster and bigger than any of earth. This *Religious Baroque* is given up to the *appearance of things,* how they look, and everywhere the richest decoration is arranged to give constant "new views," from new angles, to make the whole magnificent interior seem *endlessly large,* endlessly extended out into the distance. The Religious Baroque has a deep meaning. After the Thirty Years' War, the Catholic Church made new efforts to dominate and control. The great Baroque churches, especially those of the Jesuits, express the very spirit of Roman Catholic *propaganda*. They advertise the splendor, the magnificence, the power and the glory of their faith! Often this "picture" architecture is boastful and pompous, with its "doubling" columns and "double-doubling" arches, and pillars wherever they can be crowded in. Flights of steps are "foreshortened" to make them *seem larger* (like the steps in the *Vatican*). Up on the roofs, or in niches of the wall, stand *excited saints,* who are preaching their propaganda out into the world or at the man who passes them inside. When one enters the House of God, the huge and heavy ceiling is loaded with gold and painting. As already has been said, "the heavens open," and there are whole regiments of angels, drawn up in rank and file, and saints in ecstacy are walking on great banks of clouds. It seems as though religious feeling had run mad. And yet there is a *wonderful amount of fancy and imagination,* there is a grand swing in these Baroque churches.

Besides the Vienna Jesuit churches, there are fine Baroque churches elsewhere: the Holy Trinity Church and Catholic Court Church in Munich, and others in Prague, Passau, Bamberg. It is odd to notice that many a *weak-kneed* Protestant was affected by the saintly magnificence, the "picture" advertising and art propaganda of the Catholic Baroque churches. The effects of the hysterical decorations "took him" back into the arms of the Mother Church.

So the Protestant architects decided they would offer something "just as good." That is why we find the Dresden *Frauenkirche* (Women's Church) and the *Michaelskirche* (St. Michael's Church), in Hamburg, "going in" for Baroque just as hard and just as heavy as the Catholics. Art, like everything else, always has been used by people to "put over" the ideas they want to see win!

When it comes to Baroque palaces, Germany is full of them. Some were the palaces of great princes of the Catholic Church—for a prince was a prince in those days, whether he was the ruler of a kingdom or an archbishop—and these palaces of the religious "princes" are no different from those of any other. One of the most famous and magnificent of these is the Palace of *Mirabel*, where the Austrian archbishops of Salzburg (Mozart was the orchestra leader of one of them, for they had their private orchestras and theatres in Salzburg) lived in the summer, and had another splendid palace in the town itself. In Berlin, the architect Schluter built the *Berlin Palace* for the first King of Prussia, and in the Petrograd of Peter the Great the same architect built one for that monarch in the city he founded. Petrograd has many a huge Baroque palace—the *Winter Palace,* by Rastrelli (1784), with fine proportions, the *Anchikov,* and others. In Vienna, the finest Baroque palace is probably the *Belvedere*—the palace of Prince Eugene who, when Louis XIV refused him a commission in the army, went into the Austrian service, and later "beat up" some of Louis's best generals with special feelings of satisfaction. He never forgave the proud French king for the haughty way he had spoken of him (his parents had meant to make a priest of Eugene) as "the little Savoyard *abbé*" (abbot). But if the *Belvedere Palace* (now a museum), is the finest example of the "Princes' Baroque" style (as they used to call it) in Vienna,* there is a Baroque palace in Dresden which outdoes it. This palace is the "Keep" in the Saxon city.

THE DRESDEN "KEEP"

When the Swedish king, Charles XII had been badly defeated at the battle of Pultowa, the Elector Augustus of Saxony and King of Poland (he had *inherited* one crown and been *elected* to the other), felt so happy that he decided to celebrate by building *a second Versailles*. He called his architect Poppelmann, and commenced with a tremendous court, the so-called *"Keep"* which, besides colonnaded walks, great rooms and halls, had a museum, a library, great gardens and "keeps," where wild beasts were kept in pits and cages. This court was to be only the *"start"* of the whole thing—it was to be a German Versailles which would make the French king turn green with envy.

* The celebrated Vienna *Hofburg,* the imperial palace of the former Hapsburg emperors of Austria, is a huge collection of buildings of so many ages and epochs, that it does not seem to belong to any "fixed" style.

THE BAROQUE

But—*Augustus's money gave out!* And so the vaster Versailles of Saxony never really came to be.

Yet this "keep" which remains is a tremendous and glorious triumph of Baroque building all in itself. For it already is a tremendous palace though it was meant to be only the *vestibule* to one. There is a newer *Royal Palace,* the *Georgenschloss,* in German High Renaissance style, and a beautiful *Bruhl Palace* in Baroque, but the "Keep" is the real monument of the style in Dresden. Its statues and decorative figures are "chockfull" of Baroque energy and movement. On the top of the main pavilion a huge statue of Atlas is carrying the world on its shoulders. Satyrs (Greek woodland gods with goats' feet and horns) seem to be straining their muscles to support easy balustrades; and the columns and Baroque "half-columns" are without number. Gods, goddesses and heroes, all in some attitude of movement, fill niches and hollows in the walls. And everywhere the stone and marble is turned into flatteries for the great Augustus— he was called Augustus the Strong, and he could take a silver dollar between his thumb and forefinger and bend it in two—for his electoral sword of state, and his royal crown of Poland, and the royal and princely orders and decorations he wore are all "cut in" the stone as ornaments. The Dresden "Keep" has been called *"a champagne supper in stone,"* and it does seem like a stone fairytale of the time of Louis XIV. Perhaps, if the magnificent Augustus had ground out his *poor, suffering people* he might have out-Versailled Versailles. But he had so many other ways of spending it: many, many expensive "lady friends," idiotic wars, other mad building plans, and the "upkeep" of his personal pomp and magnificence.

Ludwigsburg, the Baroque castle of Karl of Wurtemburg, was another Versailles on a smaller scale. The vast palace was tremendous, its buildings grouped around three large courts, with great gardens and a tremendous park in which (as Versailles had its *Grand Trianon* and *Petit Trianon*) there was a "Little Favorite Castle." The Opera House of this Baroque palace was so large that *whole regiments of cavalry* could cross the stage at a time without rubbing the walls and columns, all covered with mirrors. There, too, as at Versailles, was an "Orangery"—tremendous hot-house gardens under glass, where a dream of the Southland grew in German winters, with green magic walks and spraying fountains, lit by a starry artificial sky of hundreds of thousands of glass lamps! And so it was in the capitals of the German states while the Baroque magnificence of Louis XIV ruled the world of kings and princes.

THE WHITEHALL OF THE "MERRY MONARCH"

(The Baroque of England)

Inigo Jones, who built Covent Garden (still London's leading Opera House, a solid, massive building), the *York Stairs Watergate,* and *Ashburnham House,* is England's great Baroque architect. He had studied in Rome, was enthusiastic for the "grand" Roman style of Vignano and Berini, and did achieve the great Baroque palace structure England owns—the fine banqueting Hall of Whitehall Palace, the Whitehall of Charles II,* the "Merry Monarch."

Whitehall Palace, destroyed in the great fire of London (1666) had originally been Cardinal Wolsey's palace, but King Henry VIII, who usually managed to lay hands on anything well worth having, took it after Wolsey's disgrace, and lived there. It always has been associated with the "high jinks" and revels of the court of Charles II. After Inigo Jones's second visit to Rome, he submitted to the king a plan for *an immense palace,* 1150 feet by 900 feet, but the only part built was the splendid Baroque *Banqueting Hall* (1622), which has survived fires which destroyed the rest of the building. Inigo Jones, like the other great Baroque architects thought only in a "large way." After London's great fire he submitted a plan for rebuilding London, but it was so tremendous that it was rejected.

Sir William Chamber's *Somerset House* (1776), in London, is also magnificent enough—it is second only to Inigo Jones's Whitehall Palace Banqueting Hall—to be admired as a great Baroque creation. It still faces on the Thames river, and has many historic memories.

THE CATHEDRAL OF MEXICO

(Spanish Baroque)

The tremendous Seville Cathedral makes all other buildings in the city look "small," but there are some fine Baroque palaces and churches in Seville. One is the handsome *Sagrario,* an addition to the north of the Cathedral, built by Miguel de Zumarraga and Fernandez de Iglesias, as a separate parish church. And the *Palace of the Archbishops of Seville* (1697) is a splendid example of *Spanish Baroque,* especially its doorway and staircase. There are fine Baroque buildings in other large Spanish cities, such as Madrid and Cordova, as well. In Salamanca there is José Churriguera's *Town Hall,* and in Madrid the *Royal Palace* and the *Church of San Marco el Grande* (1761).

---

* *Buckingham Palace,* where the English royal family now lives, is a modern one, having been built in 1835, by John Nash.

THE BAROQUE

The architect José Churriguera (1650-1723) has given his name to Spanish Baroque, for the buildings in that style are mostly called *"Churrigueresque,"* and the word seems to imply that they are *most wild and extravagant in decoration and ornament.* The "religious" Baroque of Churriguera, with its "display ornament," and picture "advertisement" of heaven and the saints, is seen at its best in the high altar of the *Church of San Salvador* in Seville. The *"Churrigueresque"* Baroque even stretched out its influence to the New World, where its greatest monument, perhaps, is the *Cathedral of Mexico,* which stands on the ground where the temple of the Aztec war-god once stood.

Its foundations—it is in the shape of a Greek cross—were laid in 1573, its towers completed in 1791, and it was completely finished in 1811—a year before the outbreak of our second war with England. It has two great naves, 20 side chapels and a magnificent Baroque high altar, supported by marble columns, and surrounded by a *tumbago* balustrade with 62 *tumbago* statues of saints holding candelabra made of a rich alloy of gold, silver and copper. But what is a *tumbago* saint? A *tumbago* saint is a saint whose statue is made of *an alloy of copper and zinc,* a composition of metal sometimes known as *"Mannheim's gold."* The choir is enclosed in *tumbago* railings made in Macao, weighing 26 tons—and they were brought all the way from the town where they were cast, at the entrance to the *Canton river in China,* to their distant place of destination. The vaulted roof of the cathedral is held up by 20 great Doric columns, and the whole interior is richly painted and decorated and carved in the highest and most luxurious Baroque style, and its walls covered with rare paintings.

ROCOCO AND EMPIRE

(The Styles of Louis XV and Napoleon)

In the Rococo style (the word comes from *rocaille*—"shell-work" in stucco or stone carving) the wild, fantastic, magnificent *Baroque* turns into delicate, graceful but *meaningless ornaments,* pretty shells, ribbons and scrolls, all mingled together.

The *Empire* style is a return, along lines already laid down in the Renaissance, to the old Roman temple. Of these two styles—they are *"dialects,"* in a way, of the last great original style, the Baroque—the *Rococo* is more "trifling, the *Empire* more "noble."

THE "HERMITAGES" OF LOUIS XV, AND THE CHATEAU OF LUCIENNES

(French Rococo)

The Rococo style—in architecture, in furniture, in goldsmiths' work, in ornamental art of every sort—centers around the mistresses of the French King Louis XV, as in Germany, in most cases, it does about the mistresses of the various German "princelings" who imitated Louis XV, as their fathers had imitated Louis XIV, as hard and as "fast" as they could.

There are no dark shadows in the light, elegant parlors of the Rococo palaces, their salons and "boudoirs." Walls and furniture are in white and gold, delicate, baby-blue or sky-blue or dainty pink. And Rococo—as might be expected, seeing that it is more a *"dialect"* than a real original style—has not so much to show in the way of architecture, in buildings. *It expresses itself mainly on the inside of buildings, in the decorations.*

Versailles and Marly were too "heavy," too "solemn" for the taste of Louis XV. He was a king who devoted a long, useless, idle and disgustingly vicious life to having "a good time." And he wanted everything smooth and pleasant around him. The grand oppressed him. Perhaps it suggested *work* or *effort* to a man whose most strenuous work in government consisted in reading secret police reports to see who had been visiting the disreputable houses of Paris the day before! A man who was led around by the nose by his mistresses, as long as he did not tire of them, would naturally feel oppressed in the great halls which Louis XIV had filled with the canvas and marble record of the military glories of France. Louis XV had very little in the way of "military glory" to brag about during his long reign.

That is how the "Hermitage" came to be built. Louis XV was too lazy to build even these "retreats," where the heavy grandeur of Versailles would not annoy him. But Madame de Pompadour, his mistress, did so for him with the gold he supplied. There was the *Chateau of Celle,* the "little chateau," as it was called, not far from Versailles; where Madame de Pompadour entertained her royal lover with gondola parties on the canal; there was the *Chateau of Crecy*. "In June, 1751," says the Duke of Luynes, a member of Louis's court, "the King made a trip to Crecy, with part of the court. The journey took six days. We played for high stakes, and a good deal of gold was lost at cards. The Duke of Chartres alone lost 600 gold pieces."

The "Hermitages" were much smaller, simpler buildings. The one near Versailles was *quite a small house,* and the Fontainebleau "Hermitage" (a pretty hermit Louis XV made!) had on its ground floor only a dining-room, and a parlor which would hold ten card-tables, and in its second story only two bed-rooms. Smallest of all was the "Hermitage" of Compiegne. All three, of course, were decorated with the "fanciest" of Rococo ornament, though the Fontainebleau "Hermitage" had a big—chicken yard! There are other Pompadour *chateaux—Bellevue, Choisy*—but the "Hermitages" are the most Rococo of all. Nor should *one* little building (romancers and even historians are fond of making out that it was *a whole set of harem buildings, but it was not*) which has gone down in history as *one of the most infamous in the world,* be forgotten. This is the notorious *Parc aux Cerfs* ("The Deer Park"). It was a small house with an attached garden, near Versailles. There Louis's infamous valet Lebel installed the young girls who had attracted his master's eye, and there they were seduced and ruined to gratify Louis's base passions. Madame de Pompadour herself, his mistress, encouraged these diversions, and tried to "control" the choice of the girls who entered the *Parc aux Cerfs*. Her ambition was to rule the kingdom through the king, no matter who ruled his senses for the moment.

LUCIENNES

Luciennes was, perhaps, the most beautiful of all Rococo "love-nests" (though it housed a debased and sordid love). It was a square pavilion, a palace-"boudoir," put up by the architect Ledoux in three months. It was a Rococo *temple of pleasure,* filled with priceless art-works in the most luxurious Rococo style, in gold, silver and precious woods. White marble walls were broken by columns of bronze, and on the ceiling of the great room—for the portico opened directly on a great dining-room—jolly little Cupids, little figures of the god of love, played among white and rosy clouds. Between the columns the coats-of-arms of the Du Barry and King Louis were *entwined!*

Under Louis XVI there is a return to simplicity, the Rococo is beginning to fade, and will soon vanish altogether in the blood and flame of the Revolution. Yet even in England the Rococo influence was felt in *furniture*—the well-known *"Chippendale"* furniture is Rococo—and in Germany the German princes imitated French Louis XV, even after he had passed away on his revolting death-bed, one of the worst libertines of his libertine age.

In Germany we have in the *Castle of Wilhelmsthal* near Cassel, the *Palace of Amalienburg* in Munich, great rooms decorated in the most extravagant Rococo ornament. Near Stuttgart, in Wurtemburg, besides the great *Palace of Ludwigsburg,* the Dukes of Wurtemburg built their "Hermitages"—tiny Rococo palaces—and gave them *sentimental names,* such as *"Monrepos"* ("My Repose") and *Solitude*—for the eighteenth century was "long" on *sentimentality* which is *affected sentiment*, even if it "went short" on the real thing, *true sentiment!* There was one German prince, however, who could not bear the wasteful Rococo style, with all its expensive gilding and colors. This was Frederick William I of Prussia, the father of Frederick the Great. Frederick William was a very saving king, and he preferred to "put his money" into the foolish regiment of "giant" guards that was his "hobby," instead of into gold-leaf. So he built buildings when he *had* to, for *useful* purposes, that were the stiffest and least Baroque-like kind of Baroque, all straight lines, *to take in as much room at as little cost as possible*. And because he liked to have his buildings all look alike and stand up stiffly in rank and file, as he did his soldiers, with their pigtails standing out straight behind, he is known as the inventor of an architectural style all his own—the *"Pigtail Style"* (*Zopf*), as it is called in Germany.

Frederick the Great *liked the Rococo*. His *Castle of Rheinberg* on the Rhine was a Rococo castle, and his architect Knobelsdorff was the builder of the famous *Potsdam Palace* and the old king's favorite *Palace of Sansouci*. But Sansouci was no white and gold setting for base pleasures like Luciennes. *In the latter* the old French king's ignoble young mistress taught him to drink the fiery *cognacs* which he had not touched—being a wine-drinker—before he met her. In *Sansouci*, the aged Frederick the Great, though it was a Rococo palace, studied, worked at state papers, played his flute, rode in the great park and played with his greyhounds when he was not entertaining learned men and guests of high rank. Some architects consider the Palace of Sansouci as one of the finest of Rococo palaces, with its famous marble hall, its Study in cedar-wood, and its Library. But it was a "bachelor's hall," for Frederick the Great lived separated from his wife, being a peculiar and erratic man in various ways.

But the Rococo was to give way to a *new style*—a style born of the admiration the greatest soldier in the world felt for the *Roman grandeur*. And, though the *"Empire"* style of Napoleon was only a *"dialect"* of the Baroque, it gave rise to at least *one* great building to commemorate and keep its memory green in France.

THE EMPIRE

(The Napoleonic Style)

The Rococo had "gone under" in the blood and flame of the Revolution. Gilded stucco, lacquer-ware, dainty porcelains, shell and ribbon and scroll ornaments in light colors had "had their day," and it was over. In Germany people had stopped reading Voltaire,

THE BAROQUE

the great "radical" of his time, and were reading Homer's "Iliad" again. And with Homer came a new love for *Greek* ideals in Architecture and in Art. The Baroque was too *pompous*, too theatrical, the Rococo was too *"trifling."* A shoe-maker's son, *Wickelmann*, went to Rome, where the Italian sculptor *Antonio Canova* was making statues in the spirit of the old Greeks, and came back to rouse enthusiasm for Greek art in Germany. A master of drawing, Carstens (1754), drew Homer's heroes, gods and goddesses in charcoal. The Dane Thorwalden (1798), the "Northern Praviteles," began to reshape the world of gods and heroes in marble, and the architect *Schinkel* built the *Berlin Museum* and the *Royal Theatre* in Berlin along the simple, classic *Greek* lines. But this was a Greek not a Roman revival, with Greek beauty, not Roman grandeur as its aim. In France the arts, during and after the French Revolution, also went back to Greece. For Greece had been the ideal land of freedom. The Rococo style "tied up" with royalty and a privileged class of nobles that had been swept away. It seemed even more "old fashioned" than Baroque. But when Napoleon made France an Empire, the arts turned to Rome, because in Napoleon, the French emperor, the spirit of grandeur and military glory we think of in connection with the *old Roman empire seemed to be expressed in one man*. One man created the "Empire" style in France, and that man was Napoleon. The Greek ideas, before he came to power, were mainly shown in *women's fashions*, in the "Greek style" dresses the ladies wore, and these dresses really were quite as much Roman as Greek. The main idea in the Empire style is a combination of classic dignity and splendor, and the Empire style may be said to have been *inaugurated* by Napoleon's coronation at Nôtre-Dame. As he stood there in the cathedral, the laurel wreath the jeweller Biennais had made on his head, dressed in a tunic of white atlas satin, wearing an amaranth-colored velvet mantle, embroidered in an old Roman pattern in gold thread, and lined with white ermine, with the long sceptre ending in a gold eagle, he seemed the Cæsar of a Rome new-born. The Empress Josephine, too, looked the "Empire" part. Her white satin dress was what we still call an "Empire" gown and all the diamonds that covered her did not "kill" its effect, for she was a tall, slender woman. After the coronation this "Greek style" dress as it had been called before, was given *a new name,* and has been an "Empire" dress ever since.

With the "Empire" style, to the great joy of all the Paris men's and ladies' tailors, and others, came splendid uniforms for several dozen marshals, generals and crown dignitaries, court costumes for a brilliant crowd of chamberlains, officials, ladies of honor and other court ladies, lackeys, liveries for the grooms of the great imperial stables, magnificent coaches, special guards, and what not.

And the imperial splendor shown at Napoleon's coronation in Nôtre-Dame made itself felt in the *buildings* put up during his reign. After his victorious campaigns the *Palais Bourbon* in Paris was rebuilt in the shape of a *Greek temple,* with a portico of twelve Corinthian columns. The *Paris Bourse* (Stock Exchange), was provided with a peristyle of 66 Corinthian columns, in imitation of the *Emperor Vespasian's temple* in Rome. And, just as the Roman emperors put up great triumphal arches and victory columns, so did Napoleon. The *Triumphal Arch* in the Place du Carrousel in Paris was built on the model of the *Triumphal Arch of Septimus Severus,* another great "Roman" Triumphal Arch was erected in the Place de l'Etoile, the *Vendome Column* was an imitation of *Trajan's Column,* and Roman, too, were the *Fountain of Victory* and the *Column of Palms* in the Chatelet Square. It almost seemed as though the Rome of the emperors had been transplanted to Paris!

In interior decoration the Empire style dropped the ribbons, scrolls and gilt shell-work of the Rococo in favor of other figures, ornamental figures that were *symbolical*—that meant "Napoleon" and "Empire." The imperial initial *N* was often used decoratively. The *obelisks* and *sphinxes* introduced in monuments or public buildings were meant to recall the Emperor's victories in the land of the *pyramids.* The *laurel leaves* and *wreaths* meant the battles gained in all the lands of Europe. And *branches of palm, ears of corn, cornucopias full of fruits,* and the *golden Napoleonic bees* were all signs of the *blessings* the "Empire" had showered on France. Napoleon's bed-room in the *Grand Trianon* and his throne room in *Fontainebleau* are "Empire," though the *Elysées Palace,* where he lived in Paris, is not; but the great "Empire" building in Paris is the *Church of the Madeleine.*

THE CHURCH OF THE MADELEINE

The Church of the Madeleine is *the* church of the Empire style. It was built by Napoleon's order in the grand Roman manner of which the emperor was so fond, on the foundation of an old eighteenth century church, and was not completely finished until long after Napoleon's death. The emperor meant it to be a "temple of glory," and so it is built on the lines of a *Roman temple,* with a noble colonnade of columns surrounding it.

MODERN ARCHITECTURE

CHAPTER XIII

INTRODUCTION

THE great styles of architecture have passed in review before us, from the *earliest times* to the end of the *Napoleonic age,* with all their romantic, historic and human interest. The end of Napoleon's time is the beginning of the nineteenth century, and the beginning of Modern Architecture.

But—there are *no new original styles* in Modern Architecture. Modern Architecture *uses* and *develops the styles that have gone before.* It has not originated a new one. The styles and the beauties of Greek and Roman, of Romanesque and Byzantine, of Gothic and Renaissance, of Baroque and its "dialects," Rococo and Empire, are used as the individual case seems to call for them. There have been in the principal countries of the world, all sorts of "revivals" in architecture, just as "fashions" are "revived" in woman's dress. There have been "Greek" revivals, there have been "Roman" revivals, there have been "Gothic" and "Renaissance" revivals— which means that the architects have used the one or the other style in shaping up their buildings.

But these forms and shapes in nineteenth century architecture express a different spirit. When the magnificent Gothic cathedrals rose towering to the skies, a *one and only Christian church* in all Christian lands was the religious centre of *all men's thoughts, hopes and aspirations* for heaven and a life beyond the grave. The church and religion were a thing so strong, so real, so wonderful in the human soul, that we find it hard to realize the depth of religious feeling in the Middle Ages to-day. *Now* Christianity is divided *into many sects,* into many branches. We build fine new temples in one or the other style (the *Roman Catholic* Cathedral in London is in *Greek Byzantine* style and the remarkable Church of the Holy Heart in Paris (*Sacre Cœur*), on the heights of Montmartre is *Byzantine Romanesque,* with Byzantine domes, while the great *Protestant* Cathedral of St. John (still building in New York), the white marble *Roman Catholic* Cathedral St. Patrick's, in the same city, and Trinity Church, the most venerable of the Episcopal churches, are *Gothic*). But the style does not mean that those who pray in these churches do so in a Byzantine or Gothic *spirit*.

And, in Europe as well as in America, *the spirit of our age* is not Gothic or Renaissance or Baroque or Byzantine, though we use all these styles. The *Romance of Architecture* rests in *the old castles and palaces* of kings, in the *old fortresses and towers* of the great nobles of the time gone by, in the *temples, cathedrals, mosques,* the hundred and one great buildings which express *the spirit of ages and times that have passed forever*. Modern Architecture expresses the *realties* of life. For romance is something we seldom think of in connection with our *own* day and our *own* lives. Our own time always seems humdrum to us, "the same old thing, day in day out."

And yet, both in Europe and America, *there is romance in the new modern* trend which architecture has taken during the nineteenth and twentieth centuries. Certain ideals have, more or less, passed away. *Royalty* in the living world to-day even in countries where there are kings, is *a dead issue*. A European king now is merely a bit of human furniture, decoration, a "costume figure," which "represents" *the nation* in a splendid display of gold and silver, gorgeous uniforms and court dresses. *Democracy* has come into her own. The *People* rule. And this is reflected in architecture. All over Europe great royal palaces have been turned into *national museums,* they serve as *art galleries*. They have become *public property,* the property of the *People*. And the same holds good of celebrated *castles* and *palaces* of great nobles, and of the greatest *churches* and *cathedrals:* even those in which worship still goes on. Once, in the *Cathedral of Seville*, in the *Cathedral of Cologne,* in *St. Peter's* at *Rome,* in *Canterbury,* every soul that entered the holy place was a devout worshipper: the church was a *shrine* to him. Now, in the great cathedrals of ancient faiths, thousands of visitors, every year—*though their attitude may be one of deep respect*—*do not come to worship* (for often it is not their church). They come to *see* and *admire* the wonderful paintings, the statuary, the carvings, the decoration: they visit the Gothic and Renaissance and Baroque shrines, as *sight-seers,* as *tourists*. The great churches have, in a way, become the *artistic property of all mankind,* and in the Vatican itself, the *Palace of the Popes,* visitors are admitted to the Library as they would be to any other great art museum. And our *modern churches* and *modern palaces* are built with *twentieth century comfort and convenience,* as well as artistic beauty in view. The spirit of a democratic age is always more *practical* than that of an autocratic one. We must have *sanitary plumbing* in our *churches* and *palaces* to-day, as well as shrines blazing with gold, and panels by great masters on the walls.

MODERN ARCHITECTURE

So the great architecture of modern times uses the great styles of the ages gone by. It combines and varies them. It works out a hundred and one new "patterns," but all these patterns are based on "old forms," even though the architects borrow from the ancient East, from Egypt, China or India, when they tire of Western styles. And with the use of *new building materials*—especially *iron and steel structural work* for the "skeletons" of buildings—all sorts of new ways and means of building have developed. The Romance of Architecture in the United States, our own country, will be considered in a final, closing chapter, but before going on to it, we will select a few of the great *modern* buildings, a few of the great *public* buildings, the building of the *newer democratic age* in the European countries, in order to show what Modern Architecture* has produced.

FRANCE

I

Out of the many hundreds of great modern examples of architecture a few which cover the *forms* of building that express *modern life* shall be mentioned. In general, the architects of all civilized nations are more or less in touch with what is being done in each country in their "line", and so far as style goes, modern buildings, especially public buildings, houses of parliament, courts of justice, and the like, lean as a general thing, to the classic (Greek or Roman) or the *Renaissance* styles, though the *Baroque* was the first world-wide style. The *Gothic* and *Byzantine* are still favorite styles for modern cathedrals and churches, though the *Romanesque* is also used, and we often find new *Town Halls* in older cities in *Gothic* style. These styles are used in a broad, "free" way, however, and are subject to many changes which the individual ideas or tastes of the architect suggest.

In Paris modern architecture runs in "periods". After Napoleon

---

* The main things that make Modern Architecture "different" from what went before are: 1. Kinds of buildings, big factories, stores, office buildings, banks, hotels, schools, hospitals, asylums and prisons. 2. Great bridges, vast *terminal* railroad stations, and Expositions, "temporary cities" of plaster, stucco. 3. The use of steel and iron in construction giving bigger "spans" and more "interior space" to buildings. 4. The vast "covered court" building of steel construction, roofed with glass (Crystal Palace, Syndenham, 1825; Palace of Industry, Paris Exposition, 1855) for museums, shops, libraries, etc. 5. Combined steel and concrete work and the use of "fireproof" building materials. 6. New theater *inside* constructions, with huge "revolving stages," and special *kinds* of buildings for special art purposes (the Wagner Festival Play House in Baireuth). 7. The development of landscape architecture in connection with *modern* building demands.

had been sent to St. Helena, the old Bourbon king Louis XVIII—a brother of Louis XVI, who had his head chopped off—came back, and tried to "carry on" *as though there had been no French Revolution* in between. He favored the *Rococo* a bit, but it was not much used. In 1830 came the "Greek" craze, which left some fine results in the west front of the *Palais de Justice* (by Duc), the Library of the *"School of Fine Arts"* (by Duban), and the *St. Genevieve Library* (by Labrouste). A little later Paris architects "went in" for the *French Renaissance* style. As a result we have the splendid *Grand Opera House* in Paris and the famous (or *infamous,* according to how one looks at it) "Casino" at Monte Carlo, where more American gold has been lost than won over the gaming tables. Both were put up by the architect Charles Garnier. Paul Abadie's *Church of the Sacred Heart,* Byzantine, also dates from 1873. Next came some "functionalist" * buildings: Labrouste's *National Library (Bibliothèque Nationale),* the Buildings of the Paris Exposition of 1878 and 1899 (Victor Baltard), and the famous *Eiffel Tower* (1899), by the architect Alexandre Eiffel; and also the *stations* of the *Paris Subway* ("Metro") by Hector Guimard, and the *Champs Elysées Theatre,* by Auguste and Gustave Perret. Of these "functionalist" buildings the Eiffel Tower is the most celebrated.

THE EIFFEL TOWER

The *Eiffel Tower,* in the Champ de Mars, whose elevator many an American soldier or sailor boy has taken to the top during the years of the War, is *the highest architectural structure in the world.* It is 984 feet high, built of uprights rising on huge piers of masonry and concrete, at first curving at an angle of 54 degrees, then growing straighter until they run into a perfectly straight shaft about halfway up. On the first enormous platform (5860 square yards) is a variety theatre, a restaurant and a café. A stairway of 1,798 steps leads to the tower—but *most* people use the elevators. The third platform, at the top of this great tower, composed principally of iron lattice-work is a great glass-framed and covered "observation-hall", under its lantern, in which 800 people at a time can look out and get a bird's eye view of Paris and the surrounding country. In the "Observation Room", you can buy your souvenir postal cards, minia-

---

*It is well to know what this word means. Then you will not be at a loss if someone "airs" it in conversation. *Functionalism* is not a *style* in architecture: it is *an idea* behind the actual way the architect "shapes up" his building. It means keeping in mind, before anything else, that the building to be built, *must suit its purpose.* The style comes second to the idea of giving the building the shape best suited for *the special purpose for which it is to be used.*

ture "Eiffel Towers" and other mementos in the little booths which line the walls. Above this room is a big scientific laboratory for weather observations and astronomical research and study, with all the necessary instruments. The constant pressure of the wind against the surface of the Eiffel Tower is tremendous; yet *the* vibrations at the top of the tower never exceed six inches.

ENGLAND

II

In England Modern Architecture went through a Roman period first, which among others, produced the *Bank of England* in London (1788-1835) by Sir John Soane, the *University Buildings* in Edinburgh (1778), by Robert Adam and *Saint George's Hall*, in Liverpool, by Harvey Lonsdale Elmes (1814-1854). The greatest building of the Greek period which followed was the *British Museum* in London, built by Sir Robert Smirke (1825-1847), probably the most famous museum in the whole world. The "Romantic" time which followed, among many churches, court houses and the like, saw Sir Charles Barry's *House of Parliament* (1840-1860) put up. Then came a time of "mixed styles", during which Sir Charles Barry built the *Travellers' Club* in London (1829-1831) in a combination of Italian and Greek designs; and the "Queen Anne"* period, with Eden Nesfield's *"Lodges"* in Regent's Park (1864) and Kew (1866).

The English architects of the "Functional" kind (1850 to the present date), are represented by the *Bishopsgate Institute,* London (1893-1894), by Harrison Townsend, the *Horniman Museum,* by the same architect, and by the *London Crystal Palace* (1851) of Sir Joseph Paxton.

THE CRYSTAL PALACE

The *Crystal Palace,* in Sundenham, London, is a building chiefly made up of iron and glass, and a wonderful view of London can be obtained from its two high towers. It is 1608 feet long by 384 feet wide across the transepts, and was opened where it was put up for the great London Exposition of 1851, when the late Queen Victoria opened the great hall in person.

* "Queen Anne" style is another phrase we often hear used—*and very often the people who use it could not tell you what it means.* The "Queen Anne" style, is the style in which private houses were built in England in the early part of the eighteenth century, during Queen Anne's reign. It was very popular in the United States during the nineteenth century, and the main points about "Queen Anne" houses are their *many gables, angles, irregular* windows; and other *"quaint"* features.

GERMANY

III

In Germany, the "Greek" period in building is principally represented by the use of Greek ideals as to form and ornament in buildings dedicated to the greater glory of the *House of Hohenzollern*. There was the *Brandenburg Gate* in Berlin (1788-1791), Friederich Gilly's proposed *Memorial to Frederick the Great* (1797); Leo von Klenze's Greek *Walhalla*—a German Pantheon—in Regensburg, and his *Glypothek* in Munich. A "Gothic" revival produced the *Gothic Cathedral of Berlin,* by Schinkel (1819), and Friederich von Schmidt's *Vienna Rathaus* (Court House).

Probably no great modern city covers all the architectural styles in old and new buildings as completely and fully as the Bavarian city of Munich. A famous architect, Maurice Carriere has said that "a walk through Munich gives a picture of the art and architecture of two thousand years." There is an *Egyptian* obelisk to commemorate the 30,000 Bavarian soldiers who perished during Napoleon's Moscow campaign (Bavaria was the ally of France at the time). One of the city gates, the *Prophylaea,* is a reproduction of the gates of the *Acropolis of Athens.* The *Glypothek* is the Ionic and the *Art Exhibition Building* (1845) in the *Corinthian,* while the *Rummeshalle* (Hall of Fame), a Bavarian *Pantheon,* is a splendid Doric colonnade. *Roman* is the "Victory Gate", a modern imitation of Constantine's Arch of Triumph in Rome. *St. Boniface Church* is a copy of an *Early Christian Basilica,* the *Ludwigskirche* is a reproduction of the *Italian Romanesque style,* the *Allerheiligen Hofkirche* (All Saints' Court Church), a *Byzantine* church building. The *Town Hall* is modern *Gothic,* the Parish Church of Au (Early Gothic), and Gothic is the *Church of St. John* in Haidhausen and many others. The *Royal Wittelsbach Palace* (1843-1850), is also *Gothic* (*Early English Pointed*) in style. The *Renaissance,* too, is a favorite Munich style, and there is a whole magnificent street built up in the *"composite"* style introduced by King Maximilian II, *who tried to create a pure Munich style for his city.* The old Royal Palace consists of the "Old Residence" (*Rococo*), the *Festsaalbau* (or Festival Hall Building) is *Italian Renaissance* and the *Konigsbau* a copy of the Pitti palace in Florence. And the *Church of the Theatines* is a magnificent *Baroque-Rococo* structure which contains the royal burial vaults. These, with other buildings too numerous to mention, crammed with art treasures, made Munich one of the most important cities, architecturally speaking, in Europe. To cap all, Munich has its own *Crystal Palace* (*Glaspalast*), built in 1854, and used for art and other exhibitions. Before leaving Bavaria, the wonders of beauty wrought in stone and marble by *a mad king*—one of the real romances of architecture—should be mentioned.

A MADMAN'S VISIONS OF BEAUTY IN STONE

King Louis II of Bavaria was a royal madman who, *because of the turn his madness took,* left some of the most beautiful buildings in the world as a legacy to posterity. He was an insane *Baroque* king 300 years behind the times in which he lived. Mentally he dwelt in the *Gothic* days of the knights of the Middle Ages, or in the *Baroque* ones of the "Sun King", Louis XIV. Architecture was his hobby, architecture and *solitude*—and when he began to withdraw more and more from the society of other human beings, his craze for putting up magnificent buildings, whose cost of construction was almost beyond the power of Bavaria to pay, brought about his ruin. It was this wild extravagance, together with *fits of destructive rage,* and a tendency to the most cruel forms of abnormal vice, which led to his being placed under restraint in 1886. But Louis's *love for beauty*—though it plunged him into financial ruin—also brought material profit to Bavaria in the end. And this madman also had some lovable traits. He was *kindly,* and had a real understanding of art and architecture. The visions of his brain took their most wonderful shape in five castles in particular.

The *Castle of Berg,* gay and white, raised its towers among dark pines and light green meadows on the banks of the crystal lake of Starnberg—in which Louis was to drown himself one day—facing the snowy Tyrolean Alps. This charming little *stucco* castle did not burden the crown with debts. But it soon seemed too trifling for his dreams. So *Hohenschwangau* (The High Place of the Swan) was projected in the exact style of the *great Gothic castle of the Middle Ages.* King Louis had been to the Paris Exposition (1867), invited by Napoleon III, and there had seen the great French architect Viollet-le-Duc's restoration of the Gothic Cathedral of Nôtre-Dame and the French Gothic *Castle of Pierrefonds.* The architect Jank was chosen to build *Hohenschwangau* and on a steep granite rock amid the Tyrolean Alps—where to please the caprice of an insane king—rose one of the most towered, turreted, walled, moated and battlemented Gothic castles, fantastic and mysterious, that ever was conceived. It was also a compliment to the composer Wagner (See "The Romance of Music": Wagner) but—it cost a fortune! Once it was completed, the mad king went right on building.

Linderhof was a kind of *Grand Trianon* lost amid the snows of the Tyrolean Alps. *Linderhof* had various "Hermitages", yet it is no more than a very rich French eighteenth century palace, in *Rococo.* But *Nenschwanstein* ("New Swanstone") was greater, vaster, more luxurious even than *Hohenschwangau*. It was ruinously expensive *Wagnerian Gothic* castle, another mad musical dream in stone, with vast halls, and a great domed basilica and its cost was so immense that it never was completely finished. The vast throne of ivory and gold which was to have stood under the domed cupola was never made, as the king's extravagances had drained the royal treasury. And then, still not content, Louis hit on the idea of his *Bavarian Versailles*. The mad Bavarian had a fanatic admiration for the great French King, and made a secret and hasty pilgrimage to the great palace of Versailles before returning to his own land, to get *his* Versailles started. He gave it the name of *Herrnchiemsee* (Lord of Chiemsee Castle), and building began in a vast, deserted countryside, on a barren island in the Chiemsee Lake, where his palace long was in danger of sinking beneath the waves, because of the difficulty the architects had in building a firm foundation. The huge building was begun in 1878, when Louis was already unable to finish *Neuschwanstein* because of his financial straits. But, somehow, the money was raised to go on with the palace. It was a bottomless pit. *It swallowed gold as fast as it could be put into building material.* It ate up all King Louis's own revenues and began to devour the revenues of the State. The *French* Versailles had an *object:* it was *alive*. It was the *actual residence* of a king and his court, and the government of France was conducted from it when the king Louis XIV was there.

The *Baroque German revival* also developed works of greater *practical* importance than the unfinished dream of *Herrnchiemsee*. Gottfried Semper made it notable with his *Vienna Burgtheater* (Court Theatre) 1871 to 1879; while Paul Wallot put up the Reichstag (Parliament Building) in Berlin, (1882-1894); and Ludwig Hoffmann the *Imperial Supreme Courts Building* in Leipsic (1884-1895). Nor should the magnificent *Vienna Hofopernhaus* (Court Opera House), built by Van der Null and A. Von Siccardsburg (1861-1869), be forgotten. It may be regarded as the most beautifully and artistically finished opera house, inside as well as out, in the world.

In Germany, "functionalism", has found expression in some great buildings. They include the Postal Savings Bank of Vienna (1905), by Otto Wagner, the *Werthelm Store* (1896-1907), by Alfred Messel, and the great *Turbine Factory* in the same city (1909) by Peter Behrens, as well as Joseph Olbrich's *"Succession Art Gallery"* in Vienna (1897), and the *Fictz Store* in Dusseldorf (1906-1908).

AMERICAN ARCHITECTURE

CHAPTER XIV

THE AGE OF THE DISCOVERERS AND EXPLORERS
AZTEC MEXICO

I

THE earlier "Romance of Architecture" in America must not be looked for among the Indians of the Eastern forests or the Western plains. It lies in the great palace and temple ruins of the Maya civilization in Yucatan and Guatemala (See: Chapter I, The Pyramids), in the remains of *Aztec* splendor in Mexico, and the monuments of *Inca* grandeur in Peru. And, too, there are the mysterious cities of the *Pueblo* Indians, in New Mexico. Before architecture was thought of in "our own United States" (for they did not exist at the time) *unknown architects* raised great buildings that rival and exceed the Egyptian pyramids and the Assyrian palaces in size and magnificence, where now the jungle creepers cover the faces of stone gods whose very name has passed from the memory of man. Among all these relics of a distant past some stand out because *men who saw them in their prime* handed on the tale to us who have come after. First among these are the buildings of Aztec Mexico.

THE GRAND PALACE OF MONTEZUMA

When the Spaniards came to Mexico they found the Aztec land filled with rich and beautiful cities of stone houses, the walls whitened and polished so carefully that at first they thought they were of *silver*. The houses or castles of the nobility were large, had many rooms, were built on solid masonry foundations, and surrounded by extensive gardens. Often they had strong towers and their walls were crowned with battlements. Walls, ramparts, stockades, parapets, ditches and trenches were used to fortify cities: the town of Cuanhquichollan had 20 foot walls of stone and mortar, 12 feet broad. In Mexico itself were four great arsenals, and the great causeway that led into the city had stone parapets and was broken by drawbridges over the canals. One remarkable thing about the houses, *the palaces* in which lived the sub-kings who obeyed Montezuma, the Aztec emperor, and *the homes of the poor,* is that none of them had *doors.* Neither of the two entrances (one usually giving on a street, the other on one of the great canals or water-fronts of the lake amid which the city of Mexico stood) had a door. Why? Because the *laws against theft* among the ancient Aztecs were so *severe* that every one felt safe. No one *dared steal!* So all that hung in the doorways of the houses were light curtains, to hide the inside of the house from the curious eye of those passing.

The columns which supported the Aztec buildings were square or cylinder shaped. They had neither bases nor capitals, always were cut from a single block, and were ornamented with carvings and sculptures. The roof-timbers were usually cedar, the columns of the ordinary houses stone, and those of the palaces marble. And so rich and beautiful was this fantastic *Aztec Baroque* which, just like *European Baroque,* drew lakes and ponds and water-ways, hills and gardens and forests into its architectural plans, that Cortez, in a letter to the Emperor Charles V said: "The King, Montezuma, owns in Mexico such vast and wonderful mansions that I cannot give a better idea of them than by saying that their equals are not to be found in Spain!"

Besides their great temples and palaces, their noble *arched* public baths—for the Aztecs knew the use of the *arch*—and other public buildings, this strange and romantic people raised splendid *aqueducts,* worthy of the Romans. The double aqueduct which carried the waters of Chapultepec from two miles away into the city of Mexico, had stone conduits five feet high and two feet across.

MONTEZUMA'S HUEI-TECPAN

The Aztec word for palace was *tecpan* and the palace of Montezuma, the emperor, was called *Huei-Tecpan,* which simply means "Grand Palace". We will draw on a German novelist for a vivid and romantic yet historically accurate picture of Montezuma's *Huei-Tecpan:*

"The *Huei-Tecpan* was a castle amid the waters, on a great foundation reached by steps. It was a city within the city, a tremendous labyrinth of richly tapestried and painted rooms, with roofs of cedar beams, with reception halls, armories, shady courts with playing fountains—fed by distant springs which rose in the mountains and were led to the palace by the great aqueduct—broad throne rooms, whose walls shone with jasper and silver, dance courts and a wild animal park. There were gardens washed by the great lake, under whose ancient trees pleasure pavilions were hidden. There was a bath-house where baths could be heated, a house for the ball play, and a 'House of Sorrow'. The palace had thirty gates and there was room for several thousand people in its largest court. The most wild and fantastic arabesques and figures of gods in all sorts of distorted positions, grinned and stared at the passer-by from the polished stone of the outer wall.

"Every one who went in had to leave his sandals with the doorkeepers and then was given a stone seat in one of the three great waiting-rooms. A secretary wrote down his request in a book, and if he was fortunate enough to be allowed to pass into the presence of Montezuma, he had to put on a coarse, grey mantle of cheap and common agave-fibre. For in the eyes of Montezuma all other men—even the greatest, even other kings—were only slaves and beggars! . . ."

THE TEOCALLIS

The *teocallis*, "Houses of God", the Aztec temples, rose by the hundred in every Aztec city. They were great mounds of earth, cased in brick or stone in the pyramid form of Egypt. The bases of some were more than a hundred feet square, and they towered even higher into the air. Steps led to the top, at an angle of the pyramid on the outside. At the top was a broad platform from which rose one or two towers, forty or fifty feet high, *shrines* in which stood the images of the gods. In front of the towers stood the terrible stone altars of sacrifice. On those *dreadful altars* the living heart was torn from the victims by the priests, and held up dripping to the sun-god. On the altar of the *Great Teocalli* or temple of *Huitzilipochtli*, the wargod, as many as 70,000 captives were said to have been slaughtered at one of the religious festivals, which lasted for several days.

INCA PERU

II

Peru, like Mexico, had a civilization and an architecture when the Spaniards came there. In old Peru the progress of architecture is shown in no less than *five* different styles. *First* come forts, consisting of walls of unhewn stone and mud, on platforms or rocky terraces. *Secondly* come ruins of huge temples and palaces built of *giant blocks*, enormous stones, not cut, except so that they "fit" together exactly. There are giant statues, too, but very rudely cut, and great flights of stairs hewn in the rock. A later development of this style is the great imperial fortress of the Incas on a high hill called Sacsahuaman, above the city of Cuzco. Three lines of strong and massive walls each support a terrace with angles (cut in and pushed out) for the length of 600 yards. The walls are 28, 18 and 14 feet high, with platforms between, and their total height is 60 feet. They are built of huge blocks of blue limestone, some as large as 27 by 14 feet, cut with the greatest exactness and very carefully joined. The *Sacsahuaman Fort* is as strong as any of the great Gothic castles of the Middle Ages, and when the Spaniards came was complete with all its walls and towers. The *third Peruvian* style showed that the Inca kings saw the waste of labor caused by dragging and raising stones weighing so many tons. They kept the "patterns"—used stones with rough outside surfaces—but made the single blocks smaller, so that they could be lifted and carried with ease. There are various palaces, with stone lintels to their doors, slanting inward, at Cuzco and Yucay. In the *fourth* style we have upper and lower stone blocks "dove-tailing" into each other, and real *cornices*. Then, the *fifth* and last style, used when the Spaniards came, shows buildings with perfectly *horizontal courses,* with stones beautifully "fitted", and right-angle doorways, windows and wall recesses, with serpents often carved on the walls in relief. Temples and palaces, fortresses with circular towers and loopholes, *chupas,* or "burial towers", some 24 feet high, faced with limestone blocks with an inside room ten or eleven by thirteen feet—for the Peruvian *chupas* were no Persian "Towers of Silence", nor were the dead *laid out for the vulture's beak*—all show how well advanced the Peruvians were in the art of architecture. There is one exception— the most splendid Peruvian palace, the most magnificent Peruvian temple, *had a roof of straw or thatch.* Yet their irrigating works and aqueducts are admirable. "The Inca masonry is unequalled throughout the world, some of the monuments of the Peruvians are as durable as the pyramids of Egypt; their designs were tasteful and elegant, and their engineering works, especially those for irrigation, show skill and ingenuity and an advanced stage of civilization."

CUZCO'S TEMPLE OF THE SUN

When Pizarro, the Spanish conquerer, entered Cuzco, the Inca capital, he was surprised at the large number of handsome stone houses. The walls of the palaces "were painted or stained with gaudy tints" and according to one of the Spanish soldiers, "the doors were of red, white and other colored marbles". Some of the adventurers, when they laid aside their arms and settled down in Spain in their old age, took pleasure in writing an account of the most wonderful adventure their hot youth had known. Says one: "In the fineness of their stone work the natives excel the Spanish stone-cutters, though the roofs of their dwellings instead of tiles, are only of *thatch,* yet put together with the greatest art." From the Great

Square of Cuzco four principal streets ran out and passed beyond the city walls into four great high roads of the empire. The Great Square itself and many parts of the city were paved with a fine pebble. Through the city's heart ran a river of clear water, its banks on each side faced with stone, crossed by bridges with broad flags.

There was one building in Cuzco in the Inca days which surpassed all others. That was the great *Temple of the Sun*. It was covered with plates of pure gold—not a bit of alloy—and to this day you will find many private families in Cuzco in which one of these gold plates, *beaten as thin as paper,* and highly polished, has been handed down as an heirloom for generations. This gold-covered temple was surrounded by the convents of the virgins of the sun, the priest's dormitories, and magnificent gardens. Twenty-four hours after the Spaniards had entered all that was left of the gold in and on the great temple was a gold frieze or band, set in the stone of the temple wall, which the spoilers had not yet been able to pry out. Nothing was spared. The decent repose of the mummies of the dead queens and princesses of the royal Inca race, resting in this Temple of Coricancha, were not spared. The jewelled and golden ornaments were stripped from their shrivelled fingers and shrunken necks. When all the precious metal, gold and silver, had been collected, it was put in a great heap and (after the King of Spain's share, one fifth, had been set aside) it was divided among the soldiers.

THE SECRET OF SACSAHUAMAN

In the great granite fortress of Sacsahuaman, which always was commanded by an Inca prince of the blood royal, there was a winding labyrinth of underground passages and tunnels which led, far beneath the ground, to hidden stone cellars in the Inca's great palace in Cuzco. Only those of the royal blood had the secret key to these winding passages, and especially the one which led to the secret underground hall,* where an immense treasure in gold was concealed.

Now in the years after the Spanish conquest of Peru, the daughters of Spanish nobles married princes of the Inca blood, and Inca princesses gave their hands in marriage to Spanish knights and noblemen. Among the Spanish girls who married native princes was Dona Maria de Esquivel, who had married Don Carlos de Esquivel, known as "the last of the Incas". But Dona Maria was not satisfied, for her husband did not live in the style and splendor which a man who had come down from the Peruvian emperor should. So she often would reproach him, saying she had been tricked into marrying a gentleman

* The author (his name is unknown) of an old Mss. *Antiguidades y Monumentos del Peru* (Antiquities and Monuments of Peru), is the authority for this tale.

with the proud title of *Prince* and *Inca,* only to find out that he was nothing but a *poor Indian*. As ladies sometimes will, she harped on this one string so long and so often, that one night her husband, Don Carlos, lost patience and said: "Well, Dona Maria, you must know whether I am rich or poor, it seems, so I will show you!" With that he covered her eyes with a handkerchief, led her down into the cellars of his house, made her turn around three or four times, and then, taking her by the hand, led her along in a certain direction for a time, and then down a short flight of steps. Suddenly he tore the handkerchief from her eyes and, to her amazement, she saw she was in a great square hall of stone. It was so large that the four sides and ceiling were lost in the darkness, but by the light of her husband's torch she could see, ranged on stone benches along one side of the wall, the statues of all the Inca kings who ever had worn the *lorla,* the Inca crown, in Peru. Each statue was the size of a twelve-year old boy, and was of the *purest, most solid gold*. Heaped up around the golden statues were all sorts of basins, cups, bowls and other vessels of gold and silver. Dona Maria looked at her husband and cried: "It is the most magnificent treasure in the whole world!" And Don Carlos smiled. "It is the treasure of the Incas", he answered, "a sacred treasure. If I had not given up my claim to my birthright it would be mine. But now it waits some other Inca prince of the blood (and there are others) who will rule the land as it was ruled before your people came to it. The treasure cannot go to our children, for they are half Spanish. I myself would rather starve to death than *sell a single cup* of the hoard to buy me bread. And now", he added, as he firmly tied the handkerchief over Dona Maria's face again, and prepared to lead her back the way they had come, "let me hear no more talk of 'poor Indians!' For I am richer than all the Spaniards in Peru, including His Excellency the Viceroy himself, put together!"

THE ARCHITECTURE OF THE CLIFF-DWELLERS

Before the Spaniards came to America, from Jalisco and Chihauhau in old Mexico to Colorado, were to be found the *cliff-dwelling Indians,* whose towns, granaries, outlook towers, shrines for sun- and snake-gods and dwelling houses were carved out high, high up in the face of great cliffs, at a height which often ranges between the height of the Washington Monument and that of the Paris Eiffel Tower. The people who lived in them were farmer people, who raised grain, and it is thought that war-like tribes who had no fixed places where they lived, drove them desperate, so that they took refuge from them by building these *nests of stone, high up above the clouds*. There, on the edges of plateaus so steep that they were

AMERICAN ARCHITECTURE

almost impossible to climb, under the vast overhang of a mountain hundreds and hundreds of feet high up a canyon wall, they made themselves a safe place in which to live.

The tribes who built these "cliff-dwellings" are called by the general name of the Pueblos, and the Hopi, Zuni and Pueblo Indians of to-day are probably their distant descendants. It is not known whether the hunted and harassed red-skinned farmers of the plains were driven up into their eagle-nests 500 or 5,000 B. C. To-day the Pueblo—pueblo is a Spanish word meaning "village"—Indians are to be found mainly in New Mexico and Arizona. They are still farmers and herdsmen and build houses of adobe brick, shaped either as hollow squares or pyramids, and many of their towns are still built on steep mountain plateaus which can be reached only by break-neck trails.

The ruins of the ancient Cliff-Dwellers are among the most interesting and romantic that architecture can show. Made of sandstone or lava-stone, the cliff towns usually were groups of separate houses of many small rooms, built in tiers or terraces, so that your neighbor's roof, on the house below you, was *your* "front yard", so to say. To make sure that they had a "fighting chance" even if an enemy did climb their cliff, the houses which formed the *lowest* outside tier, *showed never a door in their walls.* One could get into them only by using a ladder or a hatchway in the roof. The houses of the tiers above were entered by ladders or by stone steps built against the outer walls and resting against the roofs of the houses below. The floors were paved with smooth stone slabs or with smooth mortar which made up the walls and roofs. The *kiva*, the temple chamber and building, is supposed to have been the germ around which the whole town grew. But if these towns cut into the rock rise as much as a thousand feet into the air, how did the people who lived in them "make the grade"? As a rule, where the trail is very steep, yet possible to follow with some trouble, nothing further was done. But where it could no longer be followed, *foot-hold stairs were chipped into the rock,* and ladders of notched logs were used. An enemy—with the arrows of the hidden Cliff-Dwellers whistling about his ears—had really no chance of ever reaching the top, except by surprise, and watchmen guarded against that.

The ancient cliff-dwelling Pueblos have vanished. Their towns are empty. Yet we know how they lived—their water-jars, the dried corn in their store-houses, their pottery, their tombs, where they were laid *midway between heaven and earth,* to sleep the eternal sleep, their fire-places in the middle of the main front room, around which the family life centered, and the children played, all still are as they were, and make these wonderful ruins the most interesting, perhaps, we have in the United States.

There are many cliff towns. There are the *Casa Blanca* (White

House) ruins in the Canyon de Chell, Arizona, and in Colorado there are the *Mesa Verde* (Green House) canyon ruins, those of *Hovenweep, McElmo* and *Montezuma* canyons, others in *Utah* and along the San Juan river in Mexico. The *Montezuma Castle* on Beaver Creek, Arizona, the *Cliff Palace* in Walnut Canyon, the *Spruce Tree House* in Navaho, Colorado, are among the finest of the Cliff towns.

In one spot, in the famous *Mesa Verde* ruins, the Pueblo people, instead of *climbing up* into the clouds, went *down, down, down into the very depths of the bottom of the canyon,* to make them a place of refuge. There, protected from above by the overhang of the canyon side, the people of the Chaco lived, loved and died through the centuries. Only a few years ago an underground entrance was found that led into the "town". This Pueblo "built in a cave" in the *Mesa Verde,* shows one extreme, the ruins of the high cliff towns in the Canyon del Muerto, a branch of the Chelly Canyon, and the *Pueblo Bonito,* Chaco Canyon, represent the other extreme.

THE COLONIAL AGE

In Florida, Louisiana and California the influence of the Spaniards is shown in the old buildings they put up there in the days when these states were Spanish "crown-lands", loyal provinces across the sea of the Spanish kings who reigned in Madrid. In Florida, in St. Augustine, the *Fort of San Marco* (1757), renamed *Fort Marion* in honor of the Revolutionary general, is a fine specimen of old seventeenth century Spanish military architecture. To contrast with it, and with the old Roman Catholic Cathedral, are the great modern *Ponce de Leon Hotel* (Spanish Renaissance), and the Hispanic-Mooresque (Mudejar) *Alcazar Hotel.* The buildings bring home the *contrast* between the ages which produced them: the king's fort and the state church for loyal and devout *Spaniards* on the one hand and—the great hotel which is open to all who can pay their way, without regard to *nationality* or *creed*.

In New Mexico, in the City of Santa Fe, the *Cathedral of Saint Francis* (1713-1714) is a larger kind of early Spanish mission church in adobe brick, without much ornament on its doorway and twin towers, though its rich altar recalls the Baroque cathedrals of Spain and of the city of Mexico.

In old Spanish-French New Orleans, the French influence is most noticeable in the street names—Toulouse, Orleans, Maine, Conti, Bourbon, Dauphine, Chartres—while the Spanish shows in the architecture, in stucco walls with iron lattices, arches and gratings, in old Spanish houses with balconies, inner courts surrounded by flowerbeds and trees, with fountains and basins of water, and statues half-hidden by roses and flowering vines. The old *Cabildo* (City Hall) is

AMERICAN ARCHITECTURE

in classic style, two stories of open arcades, and Lafayette stayed as the city's guest when he visited New Orleans in 1825. The *Cabildo,* where in 1803 the French governor handed over the keys of the city to the United States commissioners, is one side of the *Cathedral of St. Louis* (1792-1794) and on the other side is the old *Calaboza* (1810), the jail, while near the Cathedral stands a brick building, the Convent of the Holy Family, for *negro sisters,* founded in 1835, and formerly the scene of New Orlean's famous "Quadroon Balls". The Palace of the *Archbishop of New Orleans* (1730), is supposed to be the *oldest* building in the Mississippi Valley.

THE CALIFORNIA MISSIONS

Robert Louis Stevenson when he was in California wrote: "The Carmel river, a clear and shallow river loved by wading kine, runs by many pleasant farms and at last, as it is falling . . . toward the great Pacific, passes a ruined mission on a hill. . . . The roof has fallen . . . the holy bell of St. Charles is long dismounted! . . . "

Carmel Mission, near Monterey, is the oldest but one of the romantic old California missions built by the Franciscan fathers for the greater glory of God and the conversion of brutish Indian souls in the California of the Spanish kings and Mexican viceroys. It is the most poetic of the mission ruins, with its bell-tower from which the bell has fallen, and its great star-shaped frontal window through which the candles of midnight masses once shone brightly out into the night. In its chancel lies buried Father Junipero Serra, who has been called "the American St. Francis", and who created the chain of beautiful old religious buildings which are the most notable architectural relics of Colonial California. The foundation-stone of the Carmel Mission was laid in 1770, a few months after the Boston Massacre, but *San Diego Mission,* built in 1769, where the Franciscan fathers landed, was the *first* of the old mission chapels, and there in a rude chapel-hut of reeds and boughs the *first mass said on California soil was celebrated.* As a historian of the Franciscan Order has said: "instead of the music of the organ we discharged our firearms, and for incense we had the smoke of our muskets!" Carmel lies near the sea on the "Old Spanish Trail", and " if you are in luck" the mellow tone of a bell may come drifting from its neighbor, *San Bonaventure,* spacing the roar of the surf, to delight your ear.

Much has been written about the Franciscan fathers and the Indians. The fathers have been accused of treating their converts harshly and using the whip too freely. Yet—the Californian Indian was anything but an angel. And to wean him, idle and dissolute as he was, from his naughty heathen ways, the whip was probably the best persuader, for it seems clear that the whip was more effective in controlling these great crowds of "mission Indians" who fetched and carried, ploughed, sheep-herded, and worked at useful crafts and industries and *knew no law but the fathers' pious will,* than gentle words and prayers. It is true that the Indians made the great missions more prosperous while they were gaining their own soul's salvation, but the object of the Franciscan fathers was a lofty and noble one. The spread of the Christian faith was their first and great aim and any gain that may have come to the Church was secondary. And it is probable that whipping* was not used as a cruel and barbarous punishment, but was really needed to hold down the brute multitudes who toiled for the fathers. At the San Diego Mission the great church front is the only portion of the building which has survived. Near it is shown a cistern connecting with the cloister by means of a tunnel, through which two of the first band of fathers escaped when the San Diego Indians attacked and burned down the mission in 1775, putting to death, with horrible tortures, the *first Californian martyr, Father Jayme.*

The *Mission of San Juan Capistrano,* with a splendid stone church of seven domes was looked on as the finest building of its kind in America before an earthquake tumbled it down in 1812. The echo of the Pacific surf is carried to its poetic ruins, where under the arches of the bell-tower there still hangs the four bells first hung there in 1776, with the gleaming white cloister buildings for a background. But the San Juan Mission is less well known, perhaps, than the famous San Gabriel.

San Gabriel Mission was built in 1771, and with the exception of Carmel and Santa Barbara, is probably the best-known of the old California missions. There "The Bells of San Gabriel", sung by the good American poet Charles Warren Stoddard, still take the visitor back to the early pastoral days, when after mass had been said, on a Sunday afternoon the mission courtyard was filled " . . . with friars, with converts in their blankets, with dignitaries of state and smart army officers, and the brilliant robes and mantillas of Mexican ladies—all applauding the bull-fighters or the *caballeros* who tilted at

---

*Father Junipero himself, it is true, had been an official of the Spanish Inquisition. In an anonymous book, "Life in California, by an American," published in 1846, the unknown author, telling of a visit to the *Mission of San Luis Rey,* says: "Mass is offered daily, and the greater portion of the Indians attend . . . It is not unusual to see numbers of them *driven along* by the alcades (police officials), and *under the whip's lash forced to the very door of the sanctuary!* . . . Many attempt to escape the severity of the religious discipline at the mission. When taken they are flogged, and an iron clog is fastened to their legs." But anonymous authors are not always to be believed. The bulk of evi-

rings, or the contestants in the national sport called *carrera del gallo* ("coursing the cock"). In this the body of a live cock with head and neck well greased, was buried in the ground. The object was to lean from the saddle and pull it out while tearing by at full gallop." Beautiful twin towers, with pierced belfry walls, are a feature of San Gabriel as of the San Juan Capristrano Mission.

Santa Barbara Mission, also provided with twin bell-towers, is enshrined amid trees and flowers. Lemon, gum, palmetto, and bougainville bloom around its ancient walls, and eucalyptus trees tower behind it against the mountains. There at Santa Barbara, as at San Bonaventure Mission, its neighbors, the sweet voiced mission bells still ring out at matins and vespers, the brethren still work in the mission gardens, or walk the cloister paths telling the beads of their rosaries. It is the same at the *Palmdale Mission,* with its great garden grounds laid out with palms, at *San Fernando,* at *Pala,* at all of the twenty-one old missions which the Franciscan fathers planted along the "Old Spanish Trail", as the American pioneers called it, the *Camino Real,* "The King's Highway" of the Californians of the royal Spanish land-grants. There are no longer any "heathen" to convert in California(?), but the good fathers still, in the "restored" older mission buildings or in more modern churches and chapels adjoining them, carry on the life monastic of the "Little Brothers of St. Francis", in an age which has long since cast away the monastic ideal. The *Mission of San Gabriel,* not so far removed from *Hollywood,* near Los Angeles, in actual mileage, is as far away from it in spirit as monasticism is from "free-thinking", or *Pope Gregory the Great* from Charles Chaplin. But the poetry, the romance and the glamor of the old missions remains. The good fathers whom some of the tourists visiting the cloisters may regard as mere "costume figures", in reality add the *human atmosphere and interest* which makes their former great work of civilization *real* to us. When we see and talk with these gentle, kindly old men we get a clearer idea of what those who went before them did in bringing a higher ideal of life to the Indian tribes sunk in brute superstition and ignorance.

In Quebec, Canada, we find old French and English buildings. It seems sufficient to mention that the oldest and most interesting is the *Church of Nôtre Dame des Victoires* (1688), named in honor of Phipps defeat 1690. The Dutch influence hardly makes itself felt in America outside of New York. The brick Stad-Huis of New Amsterdam (1642-1653) with a simple open cupola in which hung the town bell, has vanished. And just as the English colonists and the

dence seems to favor the idea that, as a general thing, the good fathers treated the Indians kindly, or as kindly as they thought Indians should be treated.

English colonies were the ruling ones in the Colonial world of America, so English Architecture was, naturally, the ruling type of building

THE COLONIAL STYLE

American Colonial Architecture may be explained in a few words —it is a *variation of English Renaissance,* changing according to locality and colony, adapting itself to weather and other conditions of climate, soil and building material. Jones and Wren influenced its development in the American colonies from old England across the Atlantic.

But with the eighteenth century, the Colonial roofs grow less steep, sash windows take the place of leaded casement windows, cornices and doors grow richer in ornament. Especially in the South did the newer Colonial style flourish, and there are fine old houses of this type preserved in Virginia, Maryland, North and South Carolina and other towns. There is much *Baroque* ornament, and Palladio's designs for villas are used for the great country houses of American gentlemen, as in Thomas Jefferson's famous villa at *Monticello.* The churches and public buildings are modelled after the London ones of the day *St. Michael's,* in Charleston; *St. Paul's,* New York; *Christ Church* (Philadelphia), and in Independence Hall, Philadelphia (1732-1752), *where the Declaration of Independence was signed;* but *Faneuil Hall,* in Boston (1742), stands for a move in the classic direction. And everywhere brick and wood, not stone, are the chief building materials. We associate the "Colonial" idea in architecture with *the free-standing porch or portico of tall white pillars in front of a Colonial mansion.* This style of portico did not exist in the beginning. It did not "come in" until 1760, and people did not use it much until after the Revolution. Thomas Jefferson's villa at Monticello, and many another Virginia Colonial house may be a more exact, or a larger or a more richly ornamented example of the colonial style at its best, but *before any other Colonial house we think of Mount Vernon,* Washington's home on the Potomac, a national shrine.

MOUNT VERNON

In the Mount Vernon which Washington enlarged to its present size and appearance in 1784-1785, we recognize the Colonial mansion of the stately type which is so impressive in its proper setting. "The mansion built by Lawrence Washington and called a 'villa' by the General, was of the old gable-roofed style, with only four rooms on each floor. The mansion when completed by General Washington (as it now appears) was of the most substantial frame-work, two stories in height, ninety-six feet in length, thirty feet in depth, with a piazza fifteen feet in width, extending along the entire eastern or river front, supported by sixteen square columns, twenty-five feet in height. Over this piazza is a balustrade of a light and pleasing design, and in the centre of the roof an observatory with a small spire.

In making his improvements Washington was his own architect and drew every plan and specification for the workmen with his own hand.

It was fitting that American women should take the lead in making Mount Vernon, Washington's home, a national shrine. And Mount Vernon as it now stands, a place of national pilgrimage, the one home and house Americans reverence above all others, owes its restoration "in the condition in which it was in Washington's lifetime", to the devotion of the Women's Mount Vernon Association of the Union, and the efforts of Edward Everett, statesman and scholar, on its behalf.

DEMOCRACY AND AUTOCRACY MEET IN THE PLAN OF THE NATIONAL CAPITOL

With the new age of Liberty, the "National Age" that began after the winning of the War of Independence, a noble thought filled the mind of Thomas Jefferson. He wanted to show that the United States did not have to borrow the *idea* of her public buildings—national and state, government, prison and asylum, from the style of *any European monarchy.* So, as the French of Napoleon's Age turned to ancient imperial Rome, with the idea of its grandeur and military glory in mind, Thomas Jefferson turned to ancient Greece and the Roman *Republic.* Their great buildings, their style of architecture were the proper ones for a free and independent people to take as a model.

And in the severe, clear, simple beauty of the *Capitol of Virginia* at Richmond (1785), he created *the first of our great modern government buildings.* After that American architects worked along the lines of the old "classic" styles, the Colonial was long forgotten, and State houses and other public buildings in various states reflected Jefferson's idea in noble and imposing buildings. The *University of Virginia,* with its fine, classic colonnades leading up to a central library modelled on the Pantheon, is regarded as the finest example of this movement in the classic direction. In a general way it may be said that with few exceptions, the *classic Greek or Roman style* has held its own for *public* buildings in the United States ever since.

THE CAPITOL AND THE WHITE HOUSE

With its glorious Dome, with its great sculptured portico of tall white Corinthian columns, the Capitol, the stately home of the Congress of the United States is worthy of the American nation. The Capitol faces east, and another sculptured Corinthian portico leads to the Senate Chamber, the north wing; while a plain Corinthian portico leads to the Hall of Representatives, the south wing.

As we walk up the broad flight of white marble steps that lead to the central portico of the Capitol and reach the top, a huge statue group in marble stands at either side. One shows the sculptor's Persico's statue of "Columbus and the Indian Girl", the other an American Pioneer struggling with an Indian savage. And on the great bronze entrance doors the hand of Randolph Rogers has carved the tale of Christopher Columbus's deed. In figures which seem to live we can trace the story of the man who gave the world he knew a new world unknown to it, from his start into the mysterious ocean distances in 1492, to the death royal ingratitude prepared for him in the old Spanish town of Vallodalid in 1506.

The great bronze entrance doors let us into the big round hall of the Capitol, the Rotunda. The Rotunda is 96 feet in diameter and 180 feet high, and an American's heart beats higher when he admires the eighteen great historical paintings it contains. For they are all paintings of high moments in our history. They fill our eyes with the actual figures and movement of the men whom we have learned to reverence in school. We admire them the more, these fine, big one hundred per cent Americans of the past—when we think of our own day and time. There is John Vanderlyn's "Landing of Columbus" (1492), William Henry Powell's "De Soto Discovering the Mississippi" (1541), and "The Baptism of Pocahontas" (1613), by John Gadsby Chapman. There is the "Embarcation of the Pilgrims from Delft-Haven" (1620) by Robert Walter Weir, John Trumbull's "The Signing of the Declaration of Independence" (1776), his "Surrender of Burgoyne at Saratoga" (1777), his "Surrender of Cornwallis at Yorktown" (1781), and his "Washington Resigning His Commission at Annapolis" (1783). They are pictures whose sight makes us feel —what we sometimes are inclined to forget—that "American" is a word with a great meaning, that it stands for something high, and proud and fine!

GEORGE WASHINGTON'S UNUSED TOMB

There is a tomb beneath our feet as we stand on the Rotunda floor. It could be the tomb of only *one* man, George Washington! But the tomb, standing in the middle of a room of Doric column is *empty*. Congress had planned to make this tomb the Nation's shrine, to place there the remains of the greatest American. But Washington himself had asked in his will to be buried at Mount Vernon, on the grounds of that "home" on the banks of the green Potomac. It seems right for Napoleon to rest in military state with a guard of old

AMERICAN ARCHITECTURE

soldiers, under a dome in the heart of Paris. But Washington was more than a soldier. His shrine should lie apart yet near the great capitol he founded, for the liberty of every American home and every one who lived in an American home, was his ideal, a higher and nobler one than imperial grandeur. And so he sleeps at Mount Vernon, on the little green hill that overlooks the river.

THE CEILING OF THE ROTUNDA

Above the great historic pictures the ceilings, the canopy of the Dome, is aglow with color. Raising our eyes we see Burnside's great fresco painting—Washington surrounded by all the Arts, Sciences and Industries. And we think of Washington, and the great Americans of his time, and feel that we need not despair of our dear native land in times when men are small instead of great, when cheap personal or political ambitions and greed of gain seem to come first, and good of country last. The little men of the moment will pass and be forgotten, but the country will go on, growing in greatness and prosperity, in spite of pettiness, in spite of politics, in spite of everything. For the example of a Washington is something we all feel in our *hearts,* and *what the great body of the nation feels, sooner or later, finds expression!* Washington admired the *Arts,* he practised the *Sciences,* but he never stooped to draw political or any other kind of capital from the *Industries.* "Washington Surrounded by the Arts Sciences and Industries" is a great, commanding figure full of dignity.

OTHER BUILDINGS

And as we stand in the "Whispering Gallery" to which we have climbed, just below the canopy of the Rotunda, it almost seems that "Washington" is the word which should sound back to any we utter, so full is the place of his personality.

In the columned *National* Statuary Hall—where each State of the Union has a right to put up the statues of "two of her chosen sons"—the decorations of the 57-foot domed ceiling are copied from the Roman Pantheon. Many of the men whose statues stand here were great and good men, but some of of the *statues* themselves are very bad art. The one which stands out, because it is the only one of its kind, is that of Frances Elizabeth Willard—the American reformer who devoted her life to the cause of *Prohibition*—the only woman who stands in this hall. Above the door to Statuary Hall is the sculptor Franzoni's clock, a winged chariot resting on a globe. The chariot is the chariot of "Time", and it holds the female figure of "History".

We will spare only a glance for the Supreme Court Room, and the Senate Chamber and Hall of Representatives. These are places where the *business* of the nation is attended to. We will find no *romance* there. But on the West Stairway—on our way to the President's room—we stop to admire a picture, for it goes straight to the heart of any of us who may have seen the great moving picture founded on Emerson Hough's novel, "The Covered Wagon". This picture is called "Westward Ho!" It is a scene in a wild, desolate pass of the Rockies, a stony village where an emigrant train has stopped to rest on its toilsome "hike" into unknown country. Yet where the valley opens there is a glimpse of the green and rolling land of promise beyond, the new land which will reward them for all their hardship and suffering!

The President's Room is quiet and dignified in decoration. The Senators' Reception Room, the "Marble Room", a room all marble, its walls colored marble from Tennessee, its ceiling marble from Vermont, its columns of marble from Italy, is richer. And most colorful of all, with its arched ceiling covered with fresco paintings of Peace, War, Liberty, Power and Plenty, Prudence, Temperance and Justice, is the Public Reception Room. And there are other buildings into which we will only glance to-day, on our way to *the most famous private home* in America, the *White House*. First, there is the magnificent white marble, Italian Renaissance *Library of Congress*, filled with glorious paintings on walls and ceilings—we stop for a moment to look at the series of paintings in the Reading Room Lobby, paintings which show the results of good and bad administration. There we can make a mental comparison between great George Washington's day and our own. Aside from the books, the pictures in the Library of Congress are wonderful. We will only describe two, on the Northwest Gallery (third floor) walls. The first picture is one of "Peace". The followers of the goddess are bringing her an offering, and carry her statue in their midst, a lad leading an ox winding up the procession. The other picture is "War". The king is riding back from the battle. First come his grooms with great hounds tugging at the leash, then the footmen with their long spears and shields, next the king himself, his white horse trampling the bodies of the slain under its hoofs as it moves along, and last, the sad "tail" of the procession, the wounded carried along in litters by their comrades. Opposite the White House stands the huge granite building that houses the Army, Navy and State Departments, and not far from it is the Corcoran Art Gallery, built of white Georgia marble. We will stop at none of them, but move on to the Executive Mansion.

THE WHITE HOUSE

George Washington laid the cornerstone of the White House (1792) and lived to see the two-story building of white Virginia freestone finished by James Hoban. The White House* is simple in its

AMERICAN ARCHITECTURE

style. The architect followed the plans of the fine country palace of an Irish peer, that of the Duke of Leinster, near Dublin (and as has been the case with L'Enfant's plan for Washington itself when new executive offices and a Cabinet Room were built in 1902-1903, and connected with the main building, by an esplanade). Hoban's original plan was followed. There is no finer lesson in patriotism than the *faith* of these early architects of ours, and that of Washington who inspired and approved their plans, in the magnificent *future* of our country. They felt, deep in their hearts, that the structures of the last years of the 18th century would not answer the needs of the 20th, and so they planned *ahead* to meet those needs. It is worth remembering when we look at the portico of Ionic columns with its balustrade, the only outside ornaments of the "Executive Mansion".

A PALACE OF WIVES

Washington never lived to "move" into the White House, but it owes its name to Martha Custis Washington, his wife. For it was named "The White House" after the old colonial mansion home, where Washington claimed his bride.

Martha Washington never ruled in the White House. The first lady of the White House was Mrs. Abigail Adams, who held the first New Year's reception there in her lace cap in 1801. And ever since the White House has been a palace for *wives*. The old palaces of European royalty, Versailles, Fontainebleau, and the great French *Crateaux*, Whitehall, Spanish Aranjuez, the Rococo palaces of German and Italian princes have only too often been palaces of *mistresses*. The White House always has been a palace of *wives*, the home of an American wife.

A HOME WITHIN A HOME

There are two "homes" in the White House. In a way it is *the* home of the United States, and in a way it "belongs" to every American. So we have the great "Public Rooms" which every American has a right to enter. We enter the long East end colonnade and see the pictures of the many "first ladies of the land", and some of the historic china they used in the Basement Corridor, and climbing the central stairs to the central hall of the building come to a beautiful large room. It is the great East Room, where big formal presidential receptions are given, and where many an American bride has been married. The State Dining Room is another great formal room where the President entertains at State dinners and over 100 guests can be seated around the great mahogany table. Three rooms are filled with intimate relics of our national history. There is the Blue

* 170 feet long and 70 feet deep.

Room, hung in blue silk. It holds the magnificent clock Napoleon once presented to Lafayette. The Green Room, hung in green velvet, contains pictures of many of our presidents and splendid gifts sent by foreign rulers. These gifts are made to the "President", not to the man who holds the office, and he leaves them when he leaves the White House, for they are "presidential", not private property. In the Red Room is *one picture* that has been the model for millions of copies. It is the wonderful Stuart oil-painting of George Washington, the picture which Mrs. Madison saved from the British burning. That is the one home in the White House.

The other is made up of the rooms of the President and his family. In them he enjoys the privacy which every American citizen can claim for the home, and no visitor expects this "home" to be "shown" by a guide.

Washington the city in which the heart of the country beats, has its two great buildings, the Capitol and the White House, which in a national and patriotic sense are the two greatest buildings in the United States. It has a hundred and one wonderful "functional" buildings in addition: government buildings, art galleries, scientific and charitable institutions, temples, memorial halls, statues, museums, the great Union Station, baths. And Nature, as at Versailles, has been made a part of the city's building plan, with gardens, parks and fountains. And, aside from these, Washington has its monuments.

Washington's Monument, put up in 1884, a tall, plain, noble obelisk shaft, as simple, solid and unpretentious as the man whose memory it honors.* It is lined outside with marble from the various states, and is itself a shaft of the purest white Maryland marble, 55 feet square at its base and 555 feet high. Elevators take us to the top where a bird's eye view of the city is obtained. And from the platform where the elevator stops, 105 feet up, we see the City of Washington's other great monument, the Lincoln Memorial Building and the green slopes of the nation's "Field of the Dead", the National Cemetery.

The Washington Monument and the Lincoln Memorial link together the memory of the two greatest men America has had in a way that Architecture alone could do. Both Washington and Lincoln "belong to the ages", the ages of America, past and to come. For ten years the Lincoln Memorial was building, a great massive columned hall with simple Doric columns of marble outside, on all its sides, and simple Ionic columns inside, in keeping with the pure and simple beauty of Lincoln's character. The great memorial hall is

*It was of this monument that Winthrop said, when he laid the cornerstone, "Build it to the skies, you cannot outreach the loftiness of his principles. Found it on the massive and eternal rock, you cannot make it more enduring than his fame!"

AMERICAN ARCHITECTURE

156 feet long and 84 feet wide and all its marble was quarried from the Colorado Yule quarry, whose stone is of the finest texture and of a glowing white purity. The great allegorical paintings on the inside walls of Lincoln's shrine are by Jules Guerin, the colossal statue of Lincoln himself, of Georgia marble, by Daniel Chester French, both American artists. These two monuments, Washington's and Lincoln's, are the greatest in Washington and in our whole United States.

MODERN ARCHITECTURE IN AMERICA

The private town palaces of our multimillionaires, and their vast country villas are French or Italian Renaissance, Baroque or Gothic as individual taste prefers. Gothic too—and not without reason, for the Gothic is a *more military style than any other*—is the *United States Military Academy* at West Point. A long list of names of celebrated American architects could be given,* and a still longer one of great buildings they have put up. But the "Romance of Architecture" is neither a text-book nor a dictionary. It aims to give the big things and the big ideas which count for the average reader— the *meaning* and *spirit* of architecture, the romance of the great buildings of the world, *ability* to tell one style from another, a good idea of what each is and means, and enable its reader to *talk intelligently* about a great subject. It is enough to say that after the middle of the nineteenth century the use of different styles became as *free* and unhampered in the United States as anything else. American architects went to Paris and to London to study their art, and came back with the broader and more decorative ideas of the French Renaissance or Baroque, or with English Pointed and Gothic Norman preferences, as the case might be. Henry Hobson Richardson developed a Spanish Romanesque style (*Trinity Church,* Boston, 1872), and—quite aside from *public* buildings our *suburban* and "*small town*" houses have indulged themselves ever since the "late seventies" in a variety of every kind of smaller house and design and style. American taste in larger public buildings is a *universal* one, it is a world-style, a composite and an adaptation of *every* style, plus *special American "functional ideas"* which have found their most original and *most truly American development* in the *"sky-scraper"* type of building. When it comes to the smaller dwelling "the private house", especially in suburban communities or towns, the *average American pleases himself*. He has a Colonial, a Queen Anne, an Italian, a Swiss or a Gothic style house, as he may choose. This

---

* There might be mentioned, however: James Hoban, the *White House,* Washington (1792-1829); Charles Bullfinch, the *Massachusetts State House,* Boston (1795-1798); Benjamin Henry Latrobe, the *Baltimore Cathedral* (1805-21); Joseph Mangin and John McComb, the *New York City Hall* (1803-1812); Robert Mills, *Washington Monument,* Washing-

is called *eclectism*. In the houses of the rich, where the surrounding country, the landscape "fits in", Chinese and Japanese, Moorish and other Oriental styles have been used with effect.

WORLD WONDERS OF AMERICAN "FUNCTIONAL" ARCHITECTURE

Though they lack the romance of old history, legends of weak and lovely women and splendid and wicked princes, our great "functional" buildings have a romance all their own It is the romance of high achievement. The structural iron-worker, carelessly swinging his legs from a steel girder on the top story of the Woolworth Building as he explored the contents of his dinner-pail makes the patient work of the stone-carver under the eaves of Fontainebleau look tame. The men who tossed the red-hot rivets on the tops of the iron skeletons of the Singer Building, the "Flatiron" Building, the tower of the Equitable Building in New York and on sister buildings in Chicago, Denver, Cincinnati, Cleveland, Seattle—a hundred and one other great cities in the United States—are the most romantic of adventurers—risking life to put a nail in position—compared to the old chisellers and masons who toiled on Gothic and Renaissance cathedral towers. The building of our "sky-scrapers", the idea of them alone, is a romance, a romance of the conquest of the dizzy heights of the air. These are structures which for sheer height, exceed any buildings the world has yet known.

The Hudson Terminal Building in New York, a city of 10,000 inhabitants above and under the ground, with its own shops and banks, its post-office and police—4 stories under and 22 stories over the surface—is only one sample of our functional railroad building. In Galveston we have an example *of a whole city raised to a higher level*. There were 11,000 cubit metres of sand pumped up by airsuction from *the bottom of the sea* and when the water it contained evaporated a firm foundation was left. No flood as in 1900 can again destroy the city. What is more romantic than the thought that Galveston to-day, standing on the *bottom of the Gulf of Mexico*, is

---

ton (1836-77); William Strickland, *Tennessee Capitol*, Nashville (1850); Thomas W. Walter, *Wings and Dome of Capitol*, Washington (1851-1865); Richard Upjohn, *Trinity Church*, New York (1839-1846); James Renwick, *Grace Church* (1843-1846), and *St. Patrick's Cathedral*, New York (1850-1879); Richard Morris Hunt, *Biltmore*, N.C.; Charles B. Attwood, *Fine Arts Building*, Chicago Exposition, (1893); Charles F. McKun, William R. Mead, Stanford White: *Newport Casino* (1881); *Villard Residence*, N. Y. (1885); *Boston Public Library* (1888-1895); *Madison Square Garden* (1891); *Pennsylvania Station*, N. Y. (finished 1910); John M. Carrere, Thomas Hastings: *New York Public Library* (1897-1910); Cass Gilbert, the *Woolworth Building*, New York, (1911-1913); Ralph Adams Cram, *West Point Military Academy* (1903) and *Saint Thomas Church*, N. Y. (1906).

AMERICAN ARCHITECTURE   137

notwithstanding raised high above the ocean tides? Brooklyn Bridge is still the longest suspension bridge in the world and the stone pillars of Washington Bridge, crossing the Hudson, are still the highest the world has seen, higher than the tip-top point of the great cathedral dome of Ulm. And, most romantic of all is the American railroad that runs over the ocean, on the Florida Keys.

In Asia and Africa, "time" as a unit of value hardly exists. In Europe there always is "time enough" for everything. Time moves along easily, slips by comfortably, is measured out for everything in big, liberal doses. In the United States time is almost the most valuable thing we have. No American, rich or poor, looks on "time" as something that "comes in unlimited quantities. He wants to get the benefit of *every moment of his time,* at work or at play. And out of this driving, time-saving, time-wanting American spirit, the spirit that is at the bottom of our American energy, our "push" and our "hustling", was born the Florida East Coast Railway. Louis XIV could give up a lifetime building Versailles, he could spend *ten days,* "easing himself along" in a great gilded state coach from Versailles to the Chateau of Compiegne. But the American millionaires who wanted to bathe at Key West found the trip by yacht from Miami too slow, it cost too much "time". They were not French kings of the Baroque, they were American kings of the "minute". And so, using the coral islands under the sea—also built by creatures who could give a lifetime to one "job"—as foundations, the magic road across the water was built. In one stretch about 28 miles long the foundations go clear down to deep-water rock-bottom. And what can be more romantic than gliding along in the middle of the ocean in a railroad coach—for no land can be seen anywhere in the middle of the openwater stretch—and seeing nothing but blue sky and blue waves through the window! And these are only a few outstanding examples of what American engineering and other "functional" architecture has done.

THE SPIRIT OF AMERICAN ARCHITECTURE

The admirable thing about *modern* American Architecture is that it has been able to build according to *its own needs,* and that American architects *using their own originality and skill,* their own invention and imagination, have been able to set new lights of beauty burning in the old lamps of form. They have followed the spirit of the race and of the times in creating buildings which, while they use the shapes of the decorations, the lines or the domes which the rest of the world had developed in its long history, are yet different, *truly American,* and as fine as anything modern architecture in general has produced abroad. Styles and revivals of styles may come and go. But there always will be the genius of the individual artist in America as elsewhere to create beauty in stone and in steel out of his own heart and mind, and to express his own and the *American spirit* so that it cannot be mistaken for any other. For the great modern buildings of the United States express *us,* the American people, the *race,* just as much as the pyramids and temples of ancient Egypt did the Egyptians, or the temples of Athens the ancient Greeks. If we look for this *human* interest in architecture all architecture is romantic. Its great monuments are no longer masses of building material, but hopes, dreams, visions and ideals realized in enduring marble. They are life and beauty expressed in stone.

THE ROMANCE OF SCULPTURE

THE EARLIEST SCULPTURE

(Introduction)

In the caves where early man lived in Europe, the first step toward sculpture was *engraving,* the tracing out of cutting in on a stone wall, or a flat bit of stone of the *outline* of a figure, the figure of some beast the "engraver" knew well by sight, or the figure of some other "human" like himself.*

After a time men found that by digging in *deeper* with their eolith tools, they could make the figures of bear or tiger or man *stand out* more, stand out "in relief".

In this way a beginning was made toward coaxing the *statue out of the stone,* instead of leaving the figure a flat tracing *in the stone.* And, in the course of time, instead of chipping out his figures of men and beasts in the wall, or in a bit of stone or ivory, the early sculptor took his stone or his big ivory tiger-tooth, and by chipping and cutting turned the tooth or the stone *itself* into a figure. The first figure of bird or beast or man thus shaped out of a mammoth tusk or a stone of some kind was *the first statue,* and the man who carved it was *the first sculptor.* After that it was only a question of time and evolution—the *idea* of sculpture was there. In the Stone Age of Neolithic man, and in the Bronze Age of civilization's dawn, sculpture already had moved from ivory, bone and stone statuettes, "little statues", to big statues of stone, and the earliest and oldest of the huge stone statues of Egyptian gods and kings are probably the work of unknown artists of the dawning days of history.

*See: "The Romance of Evolution," Chapter XXVII, "How Art Came Into the World."

THE SCULPTURE OF THE EAST

CHAPTER I

THE CHISELLERS OF EGYPT

THE old Egyptian chisellers are nameless: we do not know who they were. But their carvings tell us how their brains and hands "worked". They chiselled as their architects built: with the *flat ideal* in mind. Most of their work was "cut in" the wall to be decorated: figures did not "stand out" beyond the surface of the wall. They made everything flat, as we show countries on a map. The head of a lady looks and walks toward or away from you *in profile*. But her eyes and her body *front face*. Why? Because the *first idea* in Egyptian sculpture was *not* to be *true to life,* but to make a good *record,* to show as *much* as possible of what there was to show. Besides "cut in" work, there also were *reliefs,* in which the figures and ornaments "stood out" from the stone. But as a rule they do not "stand out" very far, for the *flat ideal* prevents it. On the *figures and scenes* from Egyptian life, family, war, religious, battle, processional, etc., pyramids, temples, obelisks, and other ruins, "cut in" or "standing out" from the stone, much of our knowledge of Egyptian history is based.

Of actual "statues", the *Sphinx* may be the oldest work of sculpture in existence.

But Egyptian sculpture, like Assyrian and Indian, is *anonymous*. No one knows who chiselled the Sphinx or the carved "pictures" on temple walls and obelisk. The Great Sphinx (described in "Architecture"), is *thought* to be a portrait of the Pharaoh Chephren, who built the second pyramid about 3,700 years B.C. But poets, though the Sphinx has a *man's body* and a *lion's head,* like to think of it as "her". And the fact that she has lost her "beard" in the course of centuries, makes this easier. But who the sculptor was that conceived the great statue and executed it is one of Sculpture's mysteries.

In the Museum of the Vatican stands perhaps the most touchingly "unknown" bit of "Egyptian" sculpture known. It evidently is the work of a Greek artist, and he must have known and loved his Egypt. It is called *Father Nile*. A fine, big figure of a man, with wavy hair and beard, he is stretched out in his "river-bed", leaning against the Sphinx. To give Egypt a fruitful harvest Father Nile had to rise sixteen feet. So sixteen tiny "kids", without a stitch on them, are playing about in the mud at Father Nile's feet with the crocodiles, looking for "something to eat". And as the water creeps up Father Nile's body, they begin to find different vegetables and to show what happens when it gets to the "high-water mark", one little fellow has climbed into the big cornucopia behind the sphinx, and found it filled with delicious fruit. It is a fine, *human* idea, and one beautifully carried out—but *no one will ever know* the name of the artist who chiselled it! An unkind fate has deprived him of the recognition of the ages!

STATUE-MAKERS OF CHALDEA, BABYLON AND ASSYRIA

Chaldean and Assyrian chisellers were *recorders* of Nature, like those of Egypt. They even give their big stone bulls and lions five legs and feet—no matter from which angle you look at them they always show *four* legs and feet, anyhow. Their carved stone work and statuary is "grander" in spirit than the Egyptian, and they have done spirited work in "hunting scenes", with kings riding horses as full of life and spirit as anything stabled to-day, dashing ahead, while their masters, standing in two-wheeled bronze chariots, send their arrows into the lions.

Have you ever seen a real "tapestry", whole "pictures" woven into heavy drapery stuff? The old Assyrian chisellers used big *alabaster slabs,* "squares of stone ten or twelve feet square", joined together, in their royal palaces for "tapestry" wall coverings. Instead of *weaving in* their pictures of battles, processions, feasts and festivals, they *carved them out.* Such carvings show some very "live" figures.

Relief Carving of King Sennacherib (dug up at Koyunjik), wearing a royal turban and a very richly embroidered robe of state (the chiseller has not left out a thread), sitting on an armless chair, its feet resting on a footstool. The heavy beard does not quite hide the pleased expression on the king's face—for while one hand rests in his lap the other holds out a cup, from which he seems about to drink. One cannot help connecting the *pleased expression* with *what the cup may contain!*

Wounded Assyrian Lioness (British Museum), a stone panel carving, comes from the Nineveh palace of King Assurbanipal. With two arrows piercing her spine and another in her shoulder, the great beast drags along her paralyzed hind legs, her jaws curled in a snarl of rage and helplessness. But this is no "game" killed in the hunt. It is one of the trained "battle lionesses" of the king, carried with the army and "let loose" on the enemy when the fight started. It is quite likely that the Prophet Jonah who got to know the whale so well, saw this lioness carried on the outside wall of the king's palace in Nineveh, when he "did" the great city (it took him three whole days), for the carving was there at the time, and no one who making a tour of Nineveh would have "passed up" the royal palace.

The curse of *being unknown* rests on all these artists who faithfully and beautifully "recorded" in stone, the life of their time. In those days a *king* got credit for everything. The *worms*—artistic or other—beneath his feet were supposed to be *glad that they were alive!*

MONGOLIAN ARTISTS OF THE CHISEL

(China and Japan)

Before Buddhism came to China, the Chinese seemed to have done relief work in bronze and stone. All true Chinese sculpture dates from the *fourteenth* century. The carving and inlay work on Chinese bronze vases, mirrors, incense-burners, is the most beautiful *of a special race type* the world knows, and *solid figures* of animals: elephants, frogs, oxen, tortoises, and of men, appear on the vases of the emperors of the Han family.

There are some fine *Buddha statues* in Chinese temples, and the giant stone human figures guarding the tombs of the Ming emperors near Peking (15th century), have often been pictured. But in general, the Chinese artist of the chisel preferred to carve and cut in ivory, jade, rock-crystal, wood and horn. Some of this carved *ivorywork* is wonderfully well done, other, later pieces are ruined by being "over-ornamented". What is supposed to be one of the finest Chinese sculptures is an ivory group known as *Kwanyin and Child* (South Kensington Museum, London), which *in its small way*, is as lovely and sincere as any great bronze statue might be.

The Japanese, like the Chinese, have huge *Buddha* statutes (the *Lochana Buddha* at Nara weighs 550 tons), and great sculptors of vases, incense-burners and the like, Seimin, Masatune, Kesai, Takusai, Gido and others made a name for themselves during the 18th century. Somewhere in the middle of the nineteenth century "swords went out" in Japan and "guns came in". Then many skilled sword-chisellers took up bronze-work. (Among them Sanseisha, Eisuke, Joun and Sessai—who has cast huge "panels" in high sculpture relief—might be mentioned). Japanese bronzes are considered one of the great art products of the country. Marble statues do not "go" with wooden houses. But graduates in the Imperial of art in Tokio have made "models" in our style, and native bronze-casters have cast memorial statues in Japanese parks and squares quite as *hideous* as *some we have in our own public parks!* Of course there is nothing really Japanese about them except the bronze.

THE PERSIAN STONE-CUTTERS

The Persian stone-cutters borrowed ideas and ways of working from Egyptians and Assyrians, peoples whom they conquered. Practically all that exists of their work is in great palace ruins.* The most famous bit of Persian sculpture known, perhaps, exists in Persia, near a little village at Murghab, near which stood Parsagardae, the oldest royal city of Persia. It is a stone portrait of Cyrus the Great, founder of the Persian empire, cut in relief on a heavy stone pillar.

We know it is Cyrus, because the inscription engraved in three languages on the stone reads: "I am Cyrus, the King, the Akhaemenian!" (*Akhaemenia* was Cyrus's "family" name: just as, since the war, the royal English family name is *Windsor;* the imperial Russian *Romanoff;* the German *Hohenzollern;* and the Austrian *Hapsburg.*) The head-dress rising from his helmet is Egyptian, and the *four great wings—the sign of power*—which grow out at the back of his body, as well as his fringed robe, are Assyrian. But the face of Cyrus is not an Assyrian or Egyptian one. It is an Aryan face. In fact, one may say so, he looks something like a brainy American "king" of industry or captain of finance.

Sculptures of the Sassanian Age are represented by a few rock-carvings. In one of them (Nakshi-Rustem) a Sassanian king, (Sapir I) on horseback, wearing *trousers* which look very much like a cow-boy's fringed *chaps,* is receiving the humble submission of the Roman Emperor Valerian (260 A.C.D.) But nowhere do we meet with a letter or *sign* to show that *some one man* carved a certain piece of work. All individual glory is lost in that of the king's majesty!

HINDU CARVERS OF MAD GODS

(India)

"The further we go the more fantastic we get! The more we sculp, the madder our sculpture! The more horrible our god the higher our art!" These seem to have been the *mottoes* of the Hindu stone-carvers who have peopled temples and caverns with *beast-gods* of every kind.

What is best known to us in Hindu statuary are figures of the "great god Budd". We may see them in any "oriental goods" shop window. The white-robed, seated Buddha, with a more *Mongolian* cast of features if he comes from China or Japan, and a more *Hindu* face if from India, seated lost in thought, calm,

* See "The Romance of Architecture," Chapter III.

quiet, meditative is, perhaps, the *one great achievement* of Buddhism in sculpture.

The worship of the *Brahmin gods* to this day seems to be coupled with the grossest immorality and obscenity. The figures of Black *Kali,* the "patron saint" of the stranglers or "thugs": the immoral *Krishna,* and the loathsome *Vishnu,* have debased the Hindu art of sculpture for centuries in the celebration of "the union of male and female energies". An eminent English authority, Dr. Hunter, says: "The most deplorable corruption of Vishnu-worship to-day is that which has *covered the temple walls* with indecent sculptures . ." Yet, from a purely *artistic* standpoint, and apart from their mad license and extravagence, many of these sculptures are *full of life, vigor* and *technical skill.** The viewpoint, which looks at Art *as* Art, does not admit of a moral issue in connection with it. But it has not prevented pious and pure-souled earlier *Christian* and *Mohammedan* missionaries from defacing many sculptures in the Elephanta Isle caverns. The *antiquarian,* the *artist* and often even the *student of religion,* however, see in them most interesting examples of the effect wild religious license has on the art-work of the sculptor!

A few great Japanese sculptors *in wood* have managed to handle the chisel "our" way without losing their own *race* feeling or their own "personal" genius.

The greatest sculptor, *in wood,* Japan ever knew was Matsumoto Kisaburo (1830-1869). He was a natural born genius, never had a chance to "study" art, and yet his carvings of *human* figures, *every muscle showing beneath the skin,* are so perfect that any professor of anatomy could use them for models. And they are just figures of "everyday" men and women, covered—strange to say—with thin lacquered *muslin,* which makes them look something like dolls. They are "realistic"—an "art lingo" word for "true to life". Japanese do not seem to care for them, but hundreds have been sold in the United States and Europe. The best *netsuke*— tiny wood and ivory figures in all sorts of funny and pathetic poses (as any "art fan" who collects them will tell you) are all old. The proper thing to do when the *netsuke* are mentioned is to sigh and remark: "Yes, you can't get good *netsuke* any more since they are making them by the thousand for the inexperienced American buyer!" This will at once show that you are at home in the subject of *netsuke*. With many individual differences Chinese and Hindu art ideals have influenced and controlled sculpture and carving in the Indo-Chinese countries.

---

*See Romance of Architecture," Chapter IV.

THE GREAT SCULPTORS AND STATUES OF GREECE

CHAPTER II

FROM THE BEGINNING TO THE END OF THE GOLDEN AGE

THE Eastern sculptors were "nameless". No one knows who they were. They worked in darkness for some "great king", and were *cheated* out of the credit they deserved. But the Greek sculptor was a sculptor in a *democracy,* where the *individual artist* who could create beauty out of his own brain and heart, and with his own skillful hands, was *honored* as he deserved to be.

The only difference between the statues of gods and the statues of men and women the Greek sculptor chiselled was that he tried to make his gods "finer", and "nobler" than his human beings. Otherwise they were much alike. In fact, the Greek sculptor turned around the words of the Bible: instead of making *man* in the *image of God,* he made *gods* in the *image of man!*

THE THREE GREAT SCULPTORS OF THE GOLDEN AGE

Myron

The Golden Age of Greek sculpture is the age of three men, Myron, Pheideas and Polycleitus, when the artists of Greece began to portray *the human form* in all sorts of attitudes, with all its youth and beauty, in the shape of manlike gods and of godlike men.

Myron was a "nature-sculptor". He sculped men and animals oftener than gods and heroes. His most famous work, *The Cow,* stood on a hill in Athens, but not a trace of it is left today. "The Cow" was so life-like that horseflies would settle on her bronze skin, and every farmer boy who passed tried to lead her away. A statue of *Ladas,* a runner, falling dead at the moment of victory in the great Marathon athletic games at Olympia is another *lost* Myron. Most of Myron's statues were statues of athletes. He was the great Greek *sporting* sculptor—but only one statue has come down to us.

The Discus-Thrower, (Vatican, Rome; British Museum, London), is a naked youth with the *discus**, much the same as our "quoit", swung back with the full arm, about to be thrown. But—though every muscle is strained in the act of throwing, and the left foot is ready to swing relax in rest the minute the discus leaves the hand holding it—the throwers head has been "put on" wrong. It is not *looking back* at the discus. Life and motion in figures of athletes or animals were Myron's masterpiece. But he did not portray *feeling* in his statues, only *action*. He was a sculptor of muscle, not of *mind*.

With Myron might be mentioned *Pythagoras*. He, too, was a sculptor of athletes; his specialty being pugilists. When it came to muscles, veins, hide and hair of pugilists he could not be outdone. He sculped all the Dempseys of his day. Pythagoras' statue called *The Limping Man* has kept green in bronze the memory of Philocetes. He, poor fellow, would have been at the sack of Troy, with the rest of Homer's heroes, had it not been for a wound in his foot. This statue stood in Syracuse, and the old Roman naturalist Pliny, who saw it said it "made you feel the pain of the wound". One supposed work of Pythagoras has come down to us.

Apollo (Chosieul-Gouffier, in British Museum) is a noble looking bronze "bruiser" who masquerades under that name. But he is no Apollo. He is a real "pug", and is quietly waiting in his corner of the "ring" for the other man so show up. We even know the name of this ancient John Sullivan: it is Euthymos!

Calamis the Athenian kept away from the "ring". His *Sosandra* (the name means "Saviour of Men"), which no eye has seen since the downfall of Rome, was a figure of the goddess of love, and on its face *a Mona Lisa smile* was carved in stone *for the first time!* Calamis was a great "horse" sculptor, so much so that even one of the greatest who came after him, Praxiteles, acknowledged him as a master.

Myron's name seems to stand out above those of his two fellow artists. His "Cow" has been called by ancient writers "a real cow with a skin of bronze" and "a bronze cow with a living soul". But —the soul in sculpture, the emotions, were to be expressed by a greater sculptor than Myron, the sculptor Pheidias.

PHEIDIAS

Pheidias is considered the greatest of all Greek sculptors, though he seldom touched chisel to marble. His material was gold and

---

* Discus-throwing was revived in the Olympic "Marathon" Games at Athens, in 1896, and ever since there have been discus-throwing contests at athletic "meets" in the United States, and in certain European countries. There is a set of "American rules" for the game.

ivory, or bronze. He "rode the crest of a splendid wave of art", that of the Age of Pericles, the Golden Age of Greece. Born in Athens, about 500 B.C., his works were his life. We do know that he was a bit of a politician—for Art's sake. Pericles, who was an art lover besides being a politician, was his friend, and Pericles, for Art's sake, would do *anything*. Pheidias' gold and ivory was expensive stuff to work with—but Pericles did not hesitate. He took the money Athens's allies had furnished *for the common cause,* the fight against Perais, and let Pheidias use it to *make his home town beautiful*. At the worst, it was better than the unscrupulous politician's idea today: taking civic money to put into his own pocket. The greatest of Greek sculptors has left *not a single statue*. The three on which his fame rests are:

Zeus (Jove) a colossal figure in ivory and gold at Olympus. The god sat on a throne, every bit of it beautifully carved. His body was ivory and his robe gold. This we know because the figure was reproduced on small Greek coins. The other colossal statue was that of *Athena Parthenos,* in the Parthenon of Athens. Besides these, there was a statue in gold and ivory of *Aphrodite (Venus)*—oh, the lost beauty of that Venus! Pheidias' giant bronze image of *Athena* with spear, helmet and shield, stood by itself on the Acropolis. It stood three miles inland, but could be seen far out at sea, so huge was it. And there were groups and other statues cast in Persian bronze gathered on the victory field of Marathon, where the Greeks defeated the Persians, and a statue of *Athena,* that went by the name of the "Lemnian", in which he made the goddess of wisdom *so beautiful* that she was *fairer than Venus herself!*

THE VENUS OF MILO

There are many "Venus" statues, originals and copies of works by famous Greek sculptors. There is only *one* Venus of Milo. It is supposed to be a copy of a wonderful statue of Venus by Pheidias. It was found in a grotto in Italy, by a bare-foot Italian goat-boy, in the early nineteenth century. The Venus of Milo should really be called the *Aphrodite* of Milo, for she is the Greek and not the Roman goddess of love. In spite of her missing arms, the Venus of Milo, with her noble, serene face, and her drapery chastely gathered about her lower limbs, is regarded among all other Venuses as the one who stands for the *purest, finest, highest* and most *ideal* marble figure of the great goddess of human love in its *diviner* sense.

The Frieze of the Parthenon. The frieze—the ornamental strip below the cornice—of the Parthenon is a great work Pheidias supervised which has survived the ages. It shows the great religious procession that carried a sacred veil to Athena's temple once every four years, a scene from the "home" life of the city, which runs around the whole building. On the *West* side, the procession is starting. Men are mounting their horses, or reining them in looking for friends who are late: On the *North* side come the victors in the great athletic games, in chariots and on horseback; and members of the "foreign" population of Athens, with chairs, parasols, pitchers and the like, to show that they were not *native-born*. On the *South* side come the chief magistrates of the city, in chariots and on horseback, with deputies from the "colonies", leading cattle to be sacrificed. From North and South these two bands are moving toward the front. In the *East* panel the "marshals" direct the two "columns" of marchers, and virgins are carrying gifts to the middle of the panel, where the chief priest takes the sacred veil from a boy's hands, while the twelve gods look on. Worn by the passing centuries, (British Museum: Elgin Marbles) the sculptured groups are beautiful, but they do not look as they did when the chisels of Pheidias and his sculptors had touched them for the last time. Then the horses' reins, the staves and weapons in the hands of the horsemen, were made of bronze, and the hair and gowns of the figures were colored and gilded. To this day Pheidias is associated with the Parthenon frieze, and it is considered one of the finest group sculptures of ancient Greece.

POLYCLEITUS

Myron was the sculptor of action, muscular action. In Pheidias' statues the *soul*—spiritual beauty, majesty, sublimity—shone through the ivory of his gods and goddesses. Polycleitus was the sculptor of *perfect proportion*. Polycleitus's:

Dorypohrus (Naples Museum) a youth with a spear over his shoulder, and

Diadumenos (British Museum), are athletes in quiet movement or at rest. And he was a sculptor of Amazons, the warlike women who "did without" men and loved battle, according to ancient legend.

The Amazon (Vatican Gallery) is, perhaps, the finest of three we have. She is fair of face, and about to leap on her horse to ride into battle. In the greater art he almost rose to Pheidias' level in his colossal lost statue, gold and ivory, of *Hera* (Juno). The goddess sat on a throne, richly draped, on her head a splendidly carved crown. It owed its existence to a careless woman's blunder. Chrysis, the priestess of the temple of Hera in Argos, fell asleep while on duty, and the temple caught fire and was burned down. A new statue had to be made for the temple and so Polycleitus' masterpiece was created.

CHAPTER III

FROM PRAXITELES TO THE END OF THE HELLENISTIC AGE

PRAXITELES

PRAXITELES, of Athens, the greatest Greek sculptor of the fourth century B.C., that age which succeeded the "Golden," is said to have left more than fifty statues and statue groups—only *one* and copies of three others have come down to us. We know but little of his life. He worked altogether in marble, and not in gold and ivory. His great works are:

Hermes Carrying the Child Dionysius. About two thousand years ago, Pausanius, a Roman traveller, made a "tour" of the old Greek cities, among others visiting the town of Olympus. We have his book of travels, and in it he says that in the temple of Juno was "a marble Hermes, carrying the infant Dionysius, by Praxiteles." Centuries passed and Olympus became a "deserted village," fell into ruin, and was forgotten. Then, in 1875, while digging there for art treasures, this very statue the old traveller had written about two thousand years before was found. The boy is not a great success—perhaps Praxiteles was not fond of children—but *Hermes* (Mercury) is a noble figure, full of "dreamy grace," as art critics say, and every muscle under his skin shows in the marble as it did in life.

Apollo "the Lizard-Slayer" (Vatican), is a Praxiteles copy. A young, slender Apollo is leaning against a section of tree-trunk up which a little lizard is climbing. Apollo's hand, resting against the trunk, holds an arrow, and he is about to drop it on the poor little reptile crawling up the bark. Aside from the art value of the statue, we would probably consider Apollo "too handsome" for a man, and busy doing nothing in rather a cruel way.

The Faun (Capitol, Rome) another Praxiteles copy, is of special interest to *Americans*. It is a statue of one of the Greek woodland gods, the *Fauns* or *Satyrs,* a "wild" lot who, according to Greek mythology, spent most of their time playing the pan-pipe (the great god *Pan* was their leader), and chasing charming Greek nymphs through green forest glades. But this *Faun* inspired a great American writer, Nathaniel Hawthorne, to write his famous "The Marble Faun." Praxiteles' Faun is not one of the "low-brow," brutish, half-animal fauns of earlier Greek sculpture. He stands leaning in a dreamy, gentle way against a tree-trunk, and is human—like any other handsome youth—except for his little *pointed, furry* Faun's *ears!* These mark the difference between Faun and man, and show that he is "all but" human.

Aphrodite (Vatican). This copy of Praxiteles' most famous statue was the wonder of his time. It stood in the city of Cnidus, in a grove of trees, and people from all over Greece and Asia Minor made long journeys just to have a look at it. The goddess was represented nude, laying aside her drapery to take a bath. The Roman writer Lucian who saw the statue speaks of her eyes, and their "melting" gaze, full of brightness and charm. Kings tried in vain to buy the statue from the citizens of Cnidus, and a King of Bythnia fell so deeply in love with the marble lady that he offered to pay the national debt of the people of Cnidus if they would hand her over to him. The *Capitoline Venus* (Capitol, Rome), and the *Venus dei Medici* (Florence), are by *later* sculptors, who copied Praxiteles's ideas, but did not carry them out as well. Art critics say that they have given too much attention to the hair-dressing of these statues.

SCOPAS

Scopas was a sculptor of Praxiteles' time, and his *Aphrodite* is said to have equalled his rivals.

Warrior's Head with Helmet (Athens Museum), from a pediment group, "very powerful, with a massive *bony* framework," is regarded as his *own* work. But he made a bronze Aphrodite riding a goat for the people of Elis, and we have what is thought to be a copy of his:

Maenad or *Bacchante* (Athens Museum), a "wild woman" celebrating the religious festival of Dionysius, the god of wine, her draperies fluttering, her hair streaming, intoxicated with religious frenzy, and the juice of the grape. In her hand she holds the little kid (of the goat variety) she has torn apart, "not knowing what she was doing", as an offering to the god, Greek writers claimed the statue was so life-like "the frenzy mingled with the marble."

Laocoon (Uffizzi Gallery, Florence) is by or may be by Scopas. It is considered one of the most famous examples of "pathos in marble." Laocoon was a priest of Apollo. When he uttered the gods' names in vain, the latter sent two serpents to punish him. The statue shows these snakes winding around the limbs of Laocoon and his two unfortunate sons, the father in the middle, his face convulsed with terrible agony. Belonging to this period (The Hellenistic), and though by sculptors unknown, supposed to be copies of works by sculptors of the cities of *Rhodes* and *Pergamos* are the:

Gigantomachia Reliefs (battles between giants and gods), in the Pergamos Museum, the:
Dying Gladiator (Rome), the
Farnese Bull (Naples Museum), the:
Friezes from the Mausoleum at Halicarnassus (British Museum), which show Greeks fighting Amazons (women warriors), and the:
The Victory of Samothrace (Louvre).
Leochares did a fine statue of *Alexander the Great* (Munich), and:
Ganymede and the Eagle (Vatican). Ganymede was a Greek shepherd lad. Once, when out with his sheep, an eagle, at Zeus' command picked him up in its claws and carried him up to Mount Ida. The Greek god had noticed his pleasing looks, and decided he would do to keep the cups of ambrosia, the liquor of the Greek gods, circling around their table. Leochares' work was so well done that one can see how carefully the eagle is carrying the boy, in order not to tear his garment.

Bryaxis ran to colossal bronze statues of gods, *Silanion* carved a statue of a *Dying Jocasta*, making the paleness of death shine through the bronze by mixing in silver. *Apollodorus* is *the first Greek sculptor* on record who had what we now call the "artistic temperament." When he had finished a bit of work and it did not suit him, he would fly into a fit of rage and smash it. Perhaps that is one reason why *none* of his statues have come down to us. *Demetrius* was a "realistic" sculptor. That is, he sculped persons just as they looked to him. His statue of the Corinthian general, C. Pellichus, showed the famous military man as he was: bald, ugly, fat, half-clothed, and with bloated veins. We do not treat great generals in this "realistic" style now, preferring to make them appear as they *should* look, at times, rather than as they *do*.

LYSIPPUS

(The Hellenistic Age)

Lysippus of Sicyon worked in bronze. Whenever he finished a statue he put a gold coin in a Greek vase. When his heirs opened the vase they found 1,500 gold coins in it. Of the 1,500 statues a *copy* of *one* has come down to us. From a humble bronze-caster, who worked for his daily wage, Lysippus became the favorite sculptor of Alexander the Great. This was not strange, however. Alexander had a slight cast in one eye, and his neck was oddly set in his shoulders. Lysippus, by making him look *up,* turned these two drawbacks into advantages. No wonder Alexander used to complain that other sculptors never "did him justice," the way Lysippus did.

Apoxyomenos (Vatican), a Lysippus copy, is a standing athlete. He is busy scraping off the oil and sand (the Greek athletes rubbed themselves in with them, and scraped them off just before going into action) with a metal scraper. From Greece it was carried to Rome, and set up in one of the great baths. There the Emperor Tiberius saw it and carried it off to his palace, but had to return it because the people mobbed him in the theatre, insisting that he put it back. Lysippus' colossal statue of *Zeus* in bronze, set up in Tarentum, was sixty feet high: a bronze statuette he made of Alexander the Great was less than twelve inches long. The figure of the king "a mighty god shut up in a little image of bronze", showed Alexander as Hercules, sitting with his club in one hand and a cup in the other. It stood on Alexander's table during his great drinking-bouts, and long after his death became the property of Hannibal. *Chares* of Lindos, one of Lysippus's made the *Colossus of Rhodes* (See "The Romance of Architecture", Chapter VI).

The "Hellenistic Age" runs from Alexander the Great to about 100 B.C. During it, Greek Art spread into Egypt Asia Minor, and Alexandria, the Greek-Egyptian city Alexander founded, became its center. But the great art of the Golden Age was gone. Gold and ivory gods, bronze giants and huge reliefs went into the discard. The sculptors sculped "little things," and "little scenes," and their marbles and bronzes now show all sorts of folk doing "every-day things." But if Greek Art during the "Hellenistic Age" was less divine, it was all the more *human* because of it.

BOETHUS

Men of the chisel now carved old fishermen with their nets, old peasant women carrying lamps, boys "shooting alleys" in old Alexandria, drunken old women hugging wine-jars, and coy young girls protecting harmless little snakes—the kind of thing supplied the Alexandrian palaces and private houses of the rich. Boethus' name stands out among them. He was a Carthaginian by birth, a favorite "child sculptor," and copies of two works of his have come down to us:

The Boy With a Thorn in His Foot. There is as much "human nature" in this marble copy of the original bronze (Capitol Museum, Rome) made in the second century B.C., as in any figure carved to-day. It shows a shock-haired country boy, sitting on a bank. He was just ready to "jump in" some regular "old swimming hole" out in the countryside near Alexandria when—he got a thorn in his foot! And there he sits, the foot with the thorn across his knee, digging it out, while his face says "Ouch!" plain enough for any one to hear. No doubt the rest of his "gang were yelling for him to "come on in, the water's fine," a few feet away, somewhere.

The Boy with the Goose. This boy is a little chap, not more than ten or twelve, with a big goose—the goose was a kind of a children's pet around the Greek home of the period, as our cats are today. He has her neck caught in a strangle hold. It is another marble copy of a Boethus' bronze original.

There are some statues, by unknown sculptors, which may belong to this Hellenistic period. One is the:

Venus of Melos (Louvre). She is simple and dignified, and her lower limbs are draped. It is evident that she takes clothes more seriously than some of her predecessors. There is the:

Apollo Belvidere (Vatican). *The Apollo Belvidere* was once supposed to be the very *ideal* of manly beauty in marble. But the ideals of Art change, and now the Parthenon statues and reliefs are supposed to be superior. This former model of manly beauty is now considered "too graceful and too smooth," and his unknown sculptor is reproached for having "fussed" too much over Apollo's hair.

The Artemis, or *Diana of Versailles* (Louvre), hurrying along holding a deer by the horn, is also thought to be Hellenistic.

Greek Sculpture may be said to end with this age, for Greek Art leaves Greece for Rome. When the Roman general Paulus Aemilius, the conqueror of Macedonia (168 B.C.) rode in his chariot in a Roman triumph before *250 wagons* filled with the great paintings and statues he had "gathered up" in Greece, the Age of Roman Sculpture may be said to have begun.

CHAPTER IV

SCULPTURE FROM ANCIENT ROME TO THE RENAISSANCE

"ROMAN SCULPTURE" made an easy beginning by *not* lifting the chisel on its own account, but "lifting" the statues of Greece and carrying them to Rome instead. Following Aemelius, a thousand bronze and marble statues were brought to Rome in the year 189 B.C., by another Roman general. In 146, the general Mummius bared Corinth of her treasures of sculpture, and under the earlier emperors the Greek cities—Athens, Delphi, Olympus and a hundred others—were stripped of anything in the way of art works worth having. Then, when a good many statues "passed out" in the Nero's great fire in Rome, Greece once more had to make good the loss. One of the Roman emperors even had a *number* of magnificent Greek bronze statues *melted down* to supply metal to cast *one* ugly, inartistic statue of himself. But, first Greek sculptors and then native-born Roman ones created new works, at first, especially, copies of the great statues of earlier times. And these Greek-Roman copies of the famous Greek originals are the statues which fill our museums today.

PASITELES

We know that Pasiteles was a Greek artist who settled in Rome and took out his citizenship parchments in 87 B.C. He did a number of things: wrote a "History of Greek Sculpture," founded a school for artists, sculped figures in marble, clay, gold, silver and ivory. But none of his works remain:

The *Statue of a Youth* (Villa Albani, Rome), signed Stephanus and of a *Mother and Son* (Rome) signed Menelaus, are supposed to be by pupils or artists of his "school", as well as a group, *Electra and Orestes* (Naples Gallery).

ARCESILUS

Arcesilus, who lived at the time of Pasiteles, is associated with Julius Caesar. Caesar ordered him to make a great statue of *Venus Genetrix*, for the Temple of Venus in the Forum Julium.

Venus Genetrix (Louvre). Of the many copies of this statue, the beautiful figure in the French capital, is the most famous, draped in a delicate and transparent robe which hides only to reveal the perfect proportion of her limbs. Arcesilus had quite a vein of fancy in his work. One group is said to have represented a marble lioness, imprisoned by a number of Cupids, who, in the part of little winged "cutups", are trying to make the poor beast drink out of the horn and putting slippers on her feet.

ANTINOUS

The story of Antinous (there is a bust and a statue in the *Vatican:* a statue in the *Capitol,* Rome: a bust in the *Louvre,* France; and a head in the *British Museum)* is the great romance of Roman sculpture.

Antinous was a beautiful Bithynian boy whom the travel-mad Emperor Hadrian found in Asia Minor, and made his inseparable companion. There is a choice of versions as to how Antinous came to his sad death. One tale is that when Hadrian visited Egypt (130 A.D.), the Egyptian priests told him that unless a substitute volunteered to die for him, he must die himself. So Antinous nobly cast himself into the Nile and, unable to swim, was drowned. The other story says that the country lad, soon after his arrival in Rome, became so saddened at the corruption and wickedness of the Imperial court, that he committed suicide. The shift from his pure and simple life on the Bithynian farm to the vicious revels of the great city had been too much for him.

In either case, the Emperor Hadrian's grief at Antinous's death knew no bounds. He put up temples to the boy in Egypt and Greece, and had sculptors, Greek and Roman, working overtime to make the busts and statues of his lost favorite with which he surrounded himself. But, strange to say, the busts and statues which have come down to us do not show him with the glad smile of sacrifice, the smile of one, happy to lay down his life for a friend! All show a brooding face, a face full of gloomy and distracted thought, a face that seems to mourn an innocence cherished and lost!

In a way (the face of the beautiful, unhappily brooding Antinous shows it) the Romans did, perhaps, excel the Greeks as *portrait* sculptors. They were "realists", they made a man look as he looked in life. And that is why the busts and statues of Roman emperors (they are to be found in many European museums and galleries) are so interesting. The cruel *Nero,* the bestial *Caracalla* reveal themselves in the bronze in which they were cast. From the busts of three Roman empresses—*Plotina, Julia,* and *Faustina* (Rome) a woman's keen eye (given a slight knowledge of Roman history) could read serious defects in *character.*

Augustus Caesar (Bracchio Nuevo, Rome). One of the best

Roman works is the famous statue of the Emperor Augustus, with one hand raised, about to make a speech to the legions, while the other holds the staff of command. His armor is richly carved and chased, and the statue shows traces of the original colors in which it was painted: yellow, brown, blue, red and pink. The figures on the great Roman Triumphal Arches are often not so good. They do not compare with the Greek *Parthenon Friezes*. Among the many, many statues by unknown Roman or Greek-Roman artists to be found in museums, one should be mentioned. *Orpheus and Eurydice* (Villa Albani, Rome, Naples Museum, Louvre) is a relief which shows the famous musician saying farewell to his wife, who is about to go to Hades (See "The Romance of Music,) a marvel of lovely simplicity and true feeling. It is a fitting art-work with which to bid farewell to Roman Sculpture.

SCULPTURE FROM EARLY CHRISTIAN DAYS TO THE GOTHIC AGE

From Early Christian days to the Gothic Age the art of sculpture is practically an art of the *Church*. That means, that instead of lovely women or heroic men, such as the sculptors of Greece and Rome had carved, we have figures of the Christ and his Apostles, of saints, popes and martyrs. Stone on marble coffins of the Early Christians (sarcophagi) are mostly imitations of the richly carved pagan ones. Instead of scenes from *Homer,* there are scenes from the *Bible*: the *Sacrifice of Isaac, Daniel in the Lion's Den, Jonah and the Whale,* or *The Sermon on the Mount* and the *Entry of Christ into Jerusalem.* The finest, perhaps, is one taken from the vault of old St. Peter's in Rome. It contained the body of an aged Christian named Junius Basseus, and dates from the year 359. There was also, besides tomb sculpture, carving in ivory (ivory thrones for popes and bishops), and church doors, carving with pious scenes in *wood*. In the sixth century the Byzantine artists did their best work in colored *mosaics*, stone pictures made up of the joining thousands of little bits of stone, and in metal and ornamental screen-work. In the eighth century the big wall relief sculptures in hard *stucco*, like those in the *Church of Cividale* (Trieste) stand out. Here long rows of very handsomely dressed saints, female with jewelled crosses, crowns and wreaths, move along in procession. Two big reliefs in *Chichester Cathedral*, England, show a very stiff and clumsy Byzantine version of the *Raising of Lazarus,* in which the figures have bits of colored glass for eyes.

NICCOLO PISANO

(1206-1278)

Niccolo Pisano is the *first* among all these religious sculptors whose name stands out. Not much is known of his life. His great works are:

The Marble Pulpit for the Baptistry (Pisa). Supported by nine marble columns, three of them resting on marble lions, the pulpit has five panels, the finest, perhaps *The Adoration of the Magi*. It shows he had studied the old Greek statues. The Virgin Mother recalls the goddess Juno; and the standing and kneeling Magi kings look like an Apollo and a Jove. This pulpit is the most *beautiful* of Pisano's works.

The Great Pulpit (Siena Cathedral). An octagonal pulpit with columns and arches, overloaded with sculpture and crowded with figures, it is the most *magnificent* of Pisano's works.

Fountain in Perugia. Opposite the west end of the cathedral, it is a series of basins, rising one above the other, each with sculptured bas-reliefs. Pisano was a great architect (Pistoia Cathedral), and a skilled engineer as well as a sculptor.

Stone and marble pulpit work, bronze door, panel and choir screen work, and *hard stucco saints* in gold and colors on choir screens *(Choir Screen,* Mildesheim Cathedral), and gates *(Golden Gate,* Freiberg Cathedral), with free-standing statues of saints on nave pillars, in Germany and in France, lead up to the great sculpture of the Gothic Age. In France rows of large statues on cathedral fronts *(Poitiers Cathedral),* sometimes covered with painting and gold *(Châstres Cathedral),* beautiful sculptured doors (Bourges Cathedral), and the clumsy marble statues (Knights Templars in *Temple Church,* London), and Robert, Duke of Normandy, *(Gloucester Cathedral,* 1134 A.D.), show Romanesque Art moving over into Gothic.

CLAUS SLUTER

(Gothic Sculpture in France)

The Gothic Age is an age of *unknown* artists. Only a few names of men who carved lovely angel figures *(Sainte Chapelle,* Paris), noble statues of Christ and the Apostles *(Amiens Cathedral),* the majestic row of kings along the front of *Notre-Dame in Paris,* the nude St. Sebastian and the gracious Christ *(Rheims Cathedral)* in the Gothic Age, are known to us.

Claude Sluter was a Netherlander born, but Philip the Bold, King of France, coaxed him to his city of Dijon with shining gold and there Sluter's two great works are to be found:

The Moses Fountain. A fountain in the Carthusian Monastery of Dijon (1399), carved with six life-sized figures of prophets, the stone painted and gilded in the style of the Middle Ages.

Alter Tomb of Philip the Bold. A white marble tomb whose arcades contain forty small alabaster figures. It is a question whether Philip was greatly mourned in France when he died, but there figures show mourners of all classes and conditions and Sluter, being a "realistic sculptor, has managed to make them very life-like in their grief. Above them, on the top of his tomb, lies Philip, majestic and silent, his mantle gathered about him. On some of these French Gothic religious sculptures the artist's sense of humor gets the better of him. On the Rheims entrance portal good St. Remigius is "shooing" away some devils, and one little devil is so paralyzed with fright that he has grabbed a bigger devil's foot and is holding on for dear life.

THE SCULPTOR WHO NEVER WAS

(Gothic Sculpture in Germany)

In Germany there are fine Gothic sculptures, but who are the sculptors? The Germans have invented a certain *Sebald Schönnofer*, a "sculptor who never was," but the stories told of him probably are all "made up". Fine statues—there are getting to be more and more *human* as well as *religious* statues, even in the Gothic Age—include: a statue of the German Emperor Conrad III on horseback *(Bamberg Marketplace),* Henry the Lion and Queen Mathilda *(Brunswick),* a relief group of the "Death of the Virgin," with "sorrowing apostles", *(Strassburg (Cathedral),* and a rich crop of statues *(Church of St. Sebald, Frauenkirche,* Nuremberg).

The Beautiful Fountain of Nuremburg. This is a striking example of German Gothic sculpture. The "Fountain" has eight pillars on which, under canopies are sixteen statues: Clovis, Charlemagne, and Godfrey of Bouillon are Christian heroes; Joshua, Judas Maccabacus are Jewish heroes; Hector, Alexander and Caesar are Pagan heroes. "Higher up" stand Moses and the seven greater prophets, and in addition there is a rich variety of gargoyle heads of bestial men and manlike beasts.

There are statues of Christ, the Virgin, the Apostles and altar reliefs with figures in white against a background of black marble. *(Cologne Cathedral)* A colossal figure of the Virgin *(Marienburg Castle Church),* of a hard stucco, a bronze St. George and the Dragon *(Prague),* and a fine portrait-statue of a great prince of the church, the Archbishop Conrad of Cologne *(Cologne,* 1261), and a Gunther of Schwarzburg *(Frankfort Cathedral,* 1349), are statues by *unknown* sculptors, the more's the pity! The Gothic Age was a coarse age, not like our own *refined* one, and the humor in this sculpture is a little vulgar at times. In one cathedral panel, St. Peter with the huge key of the heavenly gates in his hand, is receiving the blessed dead. But those blessed souls already in heaven are shown crowding their windows, just eaten up with curiosity, to see who the new arrivals may be.

ENGLISH GOLDSMITH SCULPTORS

(Gothic Sculpture in England)

England had plenty of unknown Gothic sculptors. In *Wells Cathedral* alone, are over 600 figures separate or in relief groups, kings, queens, bishops, knights, saints of the less and the more deadly of the species, but we do not know who carved them. There are 60 reliefs from *Bible* history in *Salisbury Chapter House* and the massive reliefs of angels, both in *Lincoln Cathedral* and *Westminster Abbey*, are famous. The age is rich in *portrait statues* of great historical folk. There is *King Edward III* (d.1377), who originated the famous saying "Evil to him who evil thinks" *(Honi soit qui mal y pense)*, when he picked upon a lady's garter at a ball, and made the remark to his grinning courtiers. He lies in *Westminster*, in gilt bronze. And at *Canterbury*, on his own tomb, is a fine bronze statue of Edward's son, the *Black Prince*, the knightly hero of his day. In *Westminster*, near King Edward, are King Richard II, the son of the Black Prince, together with Anne of Bohemia, the good wife of a bad, weak and dissolute husband. They too, are in bronze gilt, and in their case we know the sculptors' names: *Nicholas Broker* and *Godfred Prest*, "goldsmith citizens" of London. The alabaster tomb where *Ralph Nevill, Earl of Westmoreland*, and two wives are represented in marble *(Staindrop Church, County Durham)*, and the tomb figure of *William of Wyckham* (d. 1404), in *Winchester Cathedral*, are good, but finest of all fifteenth century bronze portrait statues is that of *Richard Beauchamp* (d. 1439), in his family chapel in *Warwick Castle*. Another "goldsmith sculptor", *William Austen* of London, modelled and cast the figure, and the gilding and engraving was done by assistants.

SILVERSMITH SCULPTORS OF SPAIN

(Gothic Sculpture in Spain)

Three Spanish sculptors lived and worked in early Gothic Spain. One was *Aparicio* (11th Century), who executed a *Shrine of St. Milian* for the *Monastery of Yuso*. Another is *Mateo* (12th Century), whose noble statue of *St. James* in the *Cathedral of Santiago de Compostella*, together with other statues of saints and beautiful religious relief carvings on the three church portals, have made him famous. Mateo in our own day is reverenced as a *saint*. He sculped a statue of himself kneeling, at the back of the central church pier. Time goes on and people are forgotten. The Spanish peasants, who know no better, think Mateo is a very holy saint of olden times, and his head has been kissed so often, by so many thousands of pious believers through the centuries, that it is nearly worn away. The third earlier Spanish sculptor is *Bartolomé*, with nine stone statues in the *Cathedral of Tarragona* to his credit.

The *fourteenth century* was the century of the Spanish "silversmith sculptors", chief among them the Valencian *Bernec*, who made the great silver retable—an altar panel—in *Gerona Cathedral*. It is all silver, part cast, part hammered, three tiers of statuettes and reliefs of saints and holy personages, each in a canopied silver niche. The *fifteenth century* in Spain produced the sculptured *Main Door of Salamanca Cathedral,* and the fronts of *San Juan* (Valladolid), and of *San Juan de los Reyes* (Toledo), regarded as the most gorgeous examples of church sculpture in the world. Among the sculptors who worked on them were: two *Diaz* brothers, *de Sahagun, Rodriguez* and *Gonzales*. The sculptors *Juan* and *De La Mota* carved the marble altar-piece of *Tarragona Cathedral* (1426), and *Gil de Siloe* did the poor statues (considered as *human* figures), but very rich and beautiful alabaster carvings of the altar-tomb of King John II and his queen *(Certosa Monastery,* Miraflores). Beginning with the sixteenth century the Spanish sculptors took to *wood* and we have fine carvings of big historical scenes, such as *The Taking of Granada,* by the Master Rodrigo.

SACRED AND PROFANE

(Italian Gothic)

The marble *Shrine of St. Augustine* (Pavia Cathedral), and the marble *Shrine of Peter the Martyr* (San Eustorgio, Milan, 1339)— by Balduccio of Piśa; Bartolomeo Bon's huge statue of the Madonna (Victoria and Albert Museum); with a number of kneeling worshipers crowded together under her great mantle; and Andrea Nicola's *Bronze South Gate of the Baptistry* (Florence), are all monuments of Italian Gothic chisel work.

ANDREA DI CIONE (ORCAGNA)

(1308(?)—1368)

Painter, sculptor and architect, Andrea di Cione, usually called Orcagna, is the *last great master of the Gothic period.* As a sculptor his one great work is in a chapel in Florence.

The Tabernacle (San Michele Chapel, Florence). A man by name of Taddeo Gaddi, in an age that knew nothing of the connection between sanitary engineering and the plague, had built the chapel as a thank-offering when it had run its course in Florence. In this chapel Orcagna built the big marble Tabernacle considered the finest monument of the Italian Gothic style. It is an altar shrine, and with a vaulted canopy. The canopy ends in a spire, topped by the figures of St. Michael, and below him, on the roof are statuettes of the Apostles. As a sort of "signature", Orcagna carved his own portrait as one of the Apostles. The relief panels of the altar show scenes from the life of Christ and in the shrine is a miracle-working picture of the Madonna. Many other beautifully carved figures of angels, prophets and virtues adorn the Tabernacle and the sculptor by "inlaying" glowing colored bits of glass mosaic in his marble makes it look as though it were finished in jewels. *No sculptured shrine in Italy* is more magnificent or beautiful, and it cost 96,000 *gold florins*, a tremendous sum in its day.

CHAPTER V

THE SCULPTURE OF THE RENAISSANCE

LORENZO GHIBERTI

(1378-1455)

GHIBERTI has been called the first great sculptor of the Renaissance. He was everything a sculptor should be: scorned money, tried to reflect "Christian truths" in his work, and never tired of studying the great works of the Greek masters.

Gates of the Baptistry (Florence). Though Ghiberti chiselled a St. John the Baptist, a St. Matthew and a St. Stephen for the tomb in the San Michel's Chapel, his one *great* work is the bronze gates of the Florence Baptistry. One gate had been carved by Andrea Pisano 100 years before, and Ghiberti's design for the second gave him the work, though other sculptors* competed. His first gate shows the "Sacrifice of Isaac". When the first gate was finished (it took the artist twenty years to finish it), the Florentines were so proud of the work he was asked to do a second. A century later, when they were still shining in the brightness of their original gilt, Michel Angelo said: "They are worthy of being the gates of Paradise!"

LUCCA DELLA ROBBIA

(The Sculptor in Terra-Cotta)

The Della Robbias were a whole Florentine family which chose baked clay instead of marble as material for their work, though Lucca della Robbia (1400-1482), did fine work in marble and bronze in his early years:

Singing Gallery, Florence: This is a gallery of ten wonderful panels in the Florence Cathedral, of singing angels and dancing boys (real, *human,* natural looking boys), and he also did other reliefs and a bronze door with figures for one of the cathedral sacristies. An old bishop of Tiesole, Benozzo Federighi, is kept green in the memory of art-lovers by a marble tomb in Saint

---

* One of them was *Jacopo della Quercia* (1374-1438) a goldsmith's son, whose finest works are a monument of *Ilaria del Coretto,* a now forgotten lady of Lucca, and the *Fonte Gai* fountain in Siena (1409).

Francesco di Paolo Church outside Florence. He lies in marble on a marble sarcophagus and angels are holding the wreath he is to wear above. But then, in later life, Lucca della Robbia turned from marble to terra-cotta. He covered his reliefs with a wonderful enamel of many colors. His most famous enamel reliefs include:

Medallion of René of Anjou (Victoria and Albert Museum). This was a "special order" from the city of Florence. It was a big medallion (a medal-shaped relief put up on the Pozzi Palace (1442) in honor of a royal visitor, just as a *modern hotel* floats the flag of his country when it has a royal guest. René was a spendthrift, merry, music-mad monarch. He was king of Sicily and Jerusalem in name only; another man had the first kingdom "in hand," and the Turks held the second. But he was Count of Provence in France and there he lived as a rule. No doubt, for he loved splendor and bright colors, his medallion pleased him. It showed his coat-of-arms, surrounded by a wreath of fruit and flowers, with apples, lemons, oranges and pine cones all glistening in enamel in brilliant colors.

Madonna Between Two Angels (Via del 'Aguolo, Florence). A tympanum-relief of exquisite beauty, showing the Madonna standing between two angels.

Medallions of the Virtues (Chapel of St. Miniato, Florence). These four colored medallions are not inappropriate since the young cardinal-prince of Portugal whose tomb they adorn, died young.

ANDREA DELLA ROBBIA

(1435-1525)

This sculptor Lucca's heir, nephew and pupil, kept on working in terra-cotta, and his reliefs were on a bigger scale than his uncle's work. His most remarkable work, one often seen reproduced is:

Series of Bambino Medallions (Foundling Hospital, Florence). Almost everyone has seen reproductions—they are easy to get—of these lovely medallions, of little children in white against a blue enamel background. The lovely child-figures are modelled with wonderful skill and *no two are alike!* Among his many other reliefs in colored enamel (terra-cotta), the Virgin and Child is a favorite subject and his faces always are sweet and full of expression. He seems to have been a man who loved children.

GIOVANNI DELLA ROBBIA

(1469-1529?)

Of Andrea's seven sons two, Giovanni and Girolamo, stand out. The best thing Giovanni did is:

The Last Judgment (St. Girolamo's Church, Volterra). The modelling of the figures, especially of the Archangel Michael and a nude youth who has just risen from his tomb, is very fine. There also is a frieze "The Seven Works of Mercy" (Del Ceppo Hospital, Pistoja).

GIROLAMO DELLA ROBBIA

(1488-1566)

Girolamo, besides enamel, worked in marble and bronze and was an architect. In 1528 he went to France. There he built for Francis I the Bois de Boulogne known as the Chateau de Madrid. It was a four-story Italian Renaissance monument to a broken promise. Francis, while the prisoner of Charles V, in Madrid, gave his word he would not leave that city. When he broke it, he built the chateau he called Madrid as a cheap bluff to pretend he had kept it. But every one knew better. There are fine collections of Della Robbia ware in European Museums and in the United States, (Boston and New York). Most of it, however, is still in the Italian churches.

DONATELLO

(1386-1466)

Donatello is probably the greatest of the early sculptors and artists of the Italian Renaissance. His name, Donato di Niccolo di Betto Bordi, was shortened by all who knew him (Can one blame them?) to Donatello, "little Donato", and by that name he is known to this day. He started as a boy and worked in a goldsmith's shop as an apprentice. Then he went to Rome and studied the old statues there. On his return to Florence he chose sculpture, as his friend Brunelleschi chose architecture, and produced his great works.

Donatello was not one of the "artistic nighthawks" of the Renaissance. He was no roysterer, no wine-bibber. There were no "wild women" in his life. Kindly, simple, unmarried, he lived at home with his mother, widowed sister and her son. He cared nothing for money. How many of us would do what he did? In a basket hung by a cord from the roof, he kept his money, and from this *all his assistants* as well as his *friends* took what they needed without being expected to say anything about it. Friends with such baskets are rare in our day, in artistic or any other circles!

The statue Donatello liked best, among his works, seems to have been the figure incorrectly called "King David", which he made for the great Florence Bell-Tower, the *Campanile*, built by Giotto. Donatello was a "realist"; he made his saints and sinners look like *human beings*. His model for this figure happened to be a homely-looking, old, bald man, and that was the way the prophet (for he was a prophet) turned out. He called in Florence *Il Zuccone*, which is the same as "Baldy", and Donatello made him so life-like, that while he was putting the finishing touches to this statue he often would say: "Curse it, why don't you talk!"

Donatello lived a fine life, full of great works of art and good works of Christian charity. He died in his little house, not far from the great Cathedral of Florence, (December, 1466), as cheerfully as he had lived. Donatello was buried in the Church of San Lorenzo, near the tomb of Cosimo dei Medici, as he had asked to be.

St. George (Nat. Museum, Florence). A marble statue so lifelike that when Michel Angelo saw it for the first time he cried: "Move on!"

The Annunciation (Santa Croce Church, Florence). A bas-relief in soft grey stone, the background picked out in gold. The Madonna, rising from her seat, turns to listen to the angel bending a knee before her.

Playing and Singing Angels (Church of St. Antonio, Padua). Twelve beautiful bronze panels of playing and singing angel children, each child busy with its own song or instrument, "like a poem in twelve stanzas in honor and praise of childhood."

The Child Jesus (Church of Saint Francesco de' Vanchetoni, Florence). A little marble bust of a lovely baby face with nothing to show *why* it should be called *Bambino Gesù* (The Baby Jesus), and thought it to be the bust of the child of a friend—Donatello loved children—given to its parents.

David (Nat. Museum, Florence). With a body worthy of Praxiteles, and a helmet fit for a Roman hero, this bronze David—*the first nude bronze statue of the Renaissance*—shows a youth whose legs, graceful in act and outline, contrast with bony shoulder-blades and thin, awkward arms, seemingly copied from some young Florentine boy model.

Singing Gallery (Cathedral of Florence). This "Singing Gallery" (*Cantoria*), is opposite the one by Lucca della Robbia, already described. Lucca's children have been called "pictures of life", and Donatello's dancing young ones "life itself". The children are tumbling, whirling, jumping and reeling about in liveliest movement, to the music of their horns.

St. John the Evangelist (Cathedral of Florence). A heroic marble statue of "Gothic character."

Gattamelata (Square in front of Church of Saint Antonio of Padua, Padua). A professional soldier instead of a saint, Erasmo da Nardi, known as Gattamelata, was a Venetian soldier adventurer. The statue (1446), is *the first bronze statue of a man on horseback since old Rome* produced the statue of the Emperor Marcus Aurelius. It is a portrait of a hard military man who lived by the sword.

Lesser artists influenced by Donatello were *Mino da Fiesole,* the two *Rossellini, da Maiano, da Settignano, Civitali, di Duccio, di Giovanni, Laurana,* and *die Pollaiulo,* who sculped papal tombs, but *Andrea del Verrocchio* stands out among them.

VERROCCHIO

(1435-1488)

Verrocchio did sculptured tombs and altars, and a "realistic" *David* (Bargeloo, Florence), in bronze, but his master work is the great horseback statue of the Venetian general Bartolommeo Colleoni.

Equestrian Statue of Bartolommeo Colleoni (Piazza of Saints Giovanni and Paolo, Venice). Colleoni was a soldier of fortune who had feathered his nest so nicely by "professional services" rendered various towns and princes, (Venice alone gave him great estates), that when he died he left a large sum to that Republic, to be used in fighting the Turks. There was a "string" attached to the money, however. He wanted his statue *set up in the Saint Mark's Square.* The Republic of Venice hated to lose the good money. They decided to take it, have the statue made and—since it was against every rule to put up a statue in *St. Mark's Square,* they humored the dead soldier by putting it up in the *Square of St. Mark's Hospital.* The statue came near never being put up, at that. First the Venetians gave the job to Verrocchio, then they changed their minds, and told a sculptor named *Alexander Leopardi* to take the hero in hand. But Verrocchio was not the kind of man to stand for such treatment. He had finished his horse, a magnificent animal. When he heard the news, he sawed off the horse's head, shook the dust of Venice from his feet and taking the head with him, left the city. The Venetians wrote threatening letters: he *must* restore the missing head (Leopardi could not make one), or they would cut his *own* head off. But Verrocchio wrote them: "With my head on my shoulders I can put on the horse's head again, but with it off you will never get it!" So the Venetian authorities gave in and after they had agreed to pay a much larger price for the work, Verrocchio returned and made the statue of a soldier on horseback which is considered *superior to Donatello's in some ways.* So if you see *Alexander Leopardus Fecit Opus* ("Alexander Leopardi made this work") engraved in the horse's belly-band, you need not believe it—it is not true!

LEONARDO DA VINCI

(1452-1519)

The Statue That Never Was Cast

Architect, musician, engineer and natural philosopher, painter of "The Last Supper", was Leonardo da Vinci. The model of the great statue on horseback of the Duke of Milan, *Ludovico Sforza*, greatest of all Renaissance equestrian statues, was ready for casting in bronze. Leonardo could stop his work on "The Great Horse" to build a bathing pavilion for his master's young duchess, so lovely and so ingenious that her own beauty seemed *doubled* in it. He could turn from his original model of the Duke on horseback, 26 feet high, to play for him on the marvellous silver lute with a horse's head he had made and brought with him to Milan. Leonardo could do the Duke a problem in geometry, draw him a plan for a new sewer system for his city, or write a little play for his Court to perform. For Leonardo did everything, and did it as a master. When the great model of the Duke's statue was finished and set up in the castle courtyard, the world flocked to see it. No one could look at it without a gasp of admiration. Another day and it would be cast in bronze, to go down through the ages, to be *our* delight! But the morrow of the casting never came. Instead the French, under La Trémouille sacked Milan, and Gascon archers used the clay body which was to have been reborn in enduring bronze as a butt for their arrows! Two years later a Duke of Ferrara begged the French general to let him have the poor mutilated masterpiece for his own city, to be its greatest art treasure. He was refused. The noble model fell apart, and the heavy boots of soldier feet kicked the fragments of the world's wonder about the castle courtyard. Leonardo da Vinci's statue of Duke Ludovico of Milan—the statue that never was cast—is one of Art's tragedies!

CHAPTER VI

MICHEL ANGELO AND BENEVENUTO CELLINI

AMONG other sculptors of the time, *Giovanni Francesco Rustici* (1476-1550) "the Raphael of Sculpture", has given the world a model of what a Pharisee looked like in the group of *St. John Addressing a Pharisee and a Levite* (Baptistry, Florence). His *Baptism of Christ* (Baptistry, Florence), is famous as well. But Michel Angelo's fame outshines that of all the men of his day.

Michel Angelo was a Florentine (1475-1564), and he himself said —he had been put to nurse with a marble-cutter's wife—that he "sucked in his love for art with his foster-mother's milk." He worked and fought his way (a fellow art-student hit him with a wooden mallet and ruined his nose for the rest of his life), until in 1496 he made a marble *Cupid* so good that he passed it off for a large sum as a genuine "antique" Greek statue. When the fraud was discovered the Roman cardinal who had bought *Cupid* insisted that the young artist come to Rome. There art-loving princes of the church kept him busy until 1501, when he did his famous *David*, for the city of Siena. *The David is the great statue of his youth.*

Including difficulties with Pope Julian—artists and priests quarrelled royally, but always got reconciled—Michel Angelo from 1505 to 1513 was busier with his great *fresco-paintings* and *architectural* works than with sculpture. A colossal bronze statue of *Pope Julius II*, the keys of St. Peter ready to smite with if the hand he raised in blessing did not secure results, was cast (1508), and put up over a church porch in Bologna. But the people tore it down and broke it up three years later in a revolution. In this period three of the figures for pope's tomb were finished, among them the *Moses,* one of the most famous of all existing works of sculpture.

The greatest sculptures done by Michel Angelo from 1516 to 1534 are the statues of the *Tomb of the Medici* princes in Florence, and during most of that time he was in his native city.

When he returned to Rome in 1534 seven years were claimed by his great painting of "The Last Judgment". His unfinished "sketch in marble" called *Mercy* (Pietà), showing a mourning mother and her dead son (Palazzo Rondini), is more appealing than the group statue of the same name, Christ collapsing in the arms of those trying to hold him (Florence Cathedral). They are the statue fruits of this final period of his life.

A heroic old man, mighty as a sculptor, painter and poet—Michel Angelo's *Sonnets* are well worth reading, for his poems sing the *Christian religion,* the *joys of Platonic love,* and the *power and mystery of Art.* He had a noble heart, though solitary, masterful, and stern, and ended a long and not very happy life as the chief architect of St. Peter's in Rome, *whose dome is still his monument.* Michel Angelo's greatest works are:

David (Florence Academy) known as *il Gigante* ("The Giant"). Out of a huge "cast-off" block of marble another sculptor had unsuccessfully tried to do something with forty years before, Michel Angelo hewed his *David.* He was not like other David statues before him, not historical or "Jewish". He was just a huge, frowning, well-balanced and watchful figure of a young lad, who knew that he was going to win his fight. If you wish to say the right thing about it: "Science of execution", and "Victorious energy of expression", are good phrases, because they express the *truth.*

Moses (Saint Pietro in Vincoli, Rome). First Michel Angelo had his troubles with Pope Julius, who was eternally changing his mind and his plans about the great tomb he had ordered Michel Angelo to do for him. Then he had to dicker with the pope's heirs, who when he had died, wanted the monument carried "out on the cheap". It finally was "done in a hurry", (1545) part of the work being handled by the master's pupils. But though statues of *Leah* and *Rachel* sit on either side, Art knows no "ladies first". *Moses* stands out, not only on the tomb, but in general. The figure is a compliment to the dead pope. Like the Hebrew prophet he was a lawgiver, priest and soldier. It is a seated figure. A long, flowing beard descends to the waist, it has *horns* on its head (the *Latin Bible* of the Roman Church calls the "rays" of the *English Protestant Bible* "horns"), and deep-sunk eyes, "blazing with the light of the Burning Bush". Two figures of *Slaves* (Louvre) originally meant for this monument, whose faces show deep suffering, got into the possession of King Francis I of France. It was at the foot of his *Moses* that Michel Angelo used sometimes *to meet the lady of his heart* the *motive power* behind his *later picture* and *poetry.* But this was *no affection of the flesh.* It was a *Platonic feeling* of the deepest and purest kind. When *Victoria Colonna,* that was the lady's name, died, (1547) Michel Angelo's hopes and ambition left him!

Tomb of the Medicis (San Angelo, Florence). A Madonna and child presides over two separate tombs. Above each sarcophagus in a niche, is a seated figure. Resting on each side of *each* sarcophagus is an emblematic figure—*two* figures, for each tomb. Duke Lorenzo in armor is the image of the crafty brooder and plotter. Duke Guliano is the image of the practical "man of action". At Lorenzo's (he is called *Il Penseroso*, "The Thoughtful") are his two figures, a female *Night* and a male *Day*. At Guliano's feet are his two figures, a male *Evening* and a female *Morning*.

Many, many other marble and bronze statues have come from Michel Angelo's chisel, but these *three* are the ones the common consent of artistic mankind has declared his greatest.

BENEVENUTO CELLINI

(1500-1572)

Benevenuto Cellini was a master goldsmith, he was a great sculptor, but his greatest work of art was his famous "Autobiography", the story of his life by himself. That book *is* a work of art. It is the greatest art romance written. Benevenuto was all that an artist should and should not be. At fifteen he already had figured in what might be called the Florence "police court" of the time for disorderly conduct, and was told to get out of town, for six months at least. He went to Siena, worked as a goldsmith for a while, then moved on to Bologna. In Bologna he became an accomplished flute-player and a better goldsmith. After visiting Pisa and Florence again, he took a trip to Rome. Here a silver casket and a silver vase established him in the good graces of the Bishop of Salamanca. He was introduced to Pope Clement VII, and appointed one of the papal court flutists. Shortly after, Rome was taken by the army of the Emperor Charles V, whose soldiers stabled their horses in St. Peter's, and used the altars for drinking bouts and worse. Cellini (he tells us so himself in his "Autobiography", was one of the leading defenders of Rome. With his own artistic hand he fired the cannon shot that killed the enemy general, the Constable de Bourbon, and then killed the second in command, Prince Philibert of Orange. It seems strange when we read his pages, that the enemy managed to enter Rome at all. History is silent about these "large" claims, but Benevenuto, who believed in blowing his own trumpet, saw to it that the rumor of his great deeds spread. Florence invited its police court graduate to return. He did, and being a really great artist as well as a great braggart, he did some wonderful gold medals there (*Hercules and the Lion,* and *Atlas Supporting the World*). From Florence to Mantua, and back to Florence, and then to Rome he went, doing jewel and medal work, and making wonderful coin dies for the papal mint. But always, sooner or later, he was in trouble. In Rome (1529), some one killed his brother, and Benevenuto promptly, and with great joy slew the slayer as a matter of course. This was not a serious offense: but when he wounded a lawyer, Ser Benedetto, he had to flee to Naples. Yet several cardinals got together—lawyers were plentiful, but there was only one Cellini—and he was pardoned. The accidental murder of a goldsmith—Cellini did not have it in mind to kill the man—was too trifling a matter to be taken seriously. Pope Paul III overlooked it. More serious (on his return from a visit to the Court of King Francis I of France), was the charge that he had helped himself to some of the choicest rubies and diamonds in the papal tiara. The charge was probably false, but Cellini was jailed in the Castle of Saint Angelo, escaped, was recaptured, and expected to be put to death from day to day. At last the Cardinal d' Este of Ferrara— Cellini had made him a present of a magnificent chased cup—got him pardoned. The great goldsmith now left the unhealthful air of Rome, and went to France. But his years at King Francis' Court were years of constant quarrels with the king's favorites. They were too highly placed for him to use the sword on them, though his hand often itched to do so, and after five terrible years of having to quarrel without being able to kill, he retired to Florence in disgust in 1545. His stay in France, among other works, produced the famous *Silver Saltcellar of Francis I* (Vienna); a gold Medal of *Francis I*, and large silver statues of *Jupiter, Vulcan* and *Mars*. Back in Florence, Cellini promptly started fighting with his fellow-artist, the touchy sculptor Bandinelli. The latter accused Cellini of "gross immorality" before Duke Cosimo. But immorality, like murder, was not taken much to heart by any one in the golden days of the Renaissance. It is useless to call the kettle black when all the pots are the same color. There is little doubt that Cellini had numerous mistresses, but therein he only followed an established Renaissance custom. Be that as it may, Cellini had a healthy confidence in his own goodness. He tells us that a marvellous halo of heavenly light surrounded his head at dawn and twilight after he had gotten out of Saint Angelo, and while he was jailed there he had visions, and angels seem to have come down to visit the great artist. In the end, Cellini died in Florence (1571) unmarried, leaving no children, and was buried with great pomp and ceremony in the Annunciation Church. Be it said for him, for he had his good points, that he always had supported his widowed sister and her six daughters. As a sculptor, he cast several big bronzes: one is a masterpiece:

Perseus Holding the Head of Medusa (Loggia dei Lansi, Florence). Perseus was a son of Zeus (Jove) and Danaë. When Perseus grew to manhood King Polydectes began to cast sheep's eyes at Perseus' mother, Danaë; and to rid himself of Danaë's son, who was always in the way. The king sent him off to bring him Medusa's head. Medusa was one of the three Gorgon sisters. They lived on the rim of the Western ocean, and anyone who looked at their terrible heads was turned to stone. Cellini's statue shows Perseus holding up the gory head, as he stands on the body of the slain monster, his sword in his hand, while the blood spouts from the severed neck. It has "the fire of genius and the grandeur of a terrible beauty." It is one of the great monuments of Renaissance sculpture.

Another notable sculptor of the Cellini's time was Giovanni da Bologna, or John of Douai (1524-1608). His great works are:

Flying Mercury (Bargello, Florence). A bronze statue of the god, flying upward; his finest work.

Rape of a Sabine Woman (Loggia dei Lanzi, Florence).

Great Fountain (Bologna). Two tiers of boys and mermaids, topped by a colossal statue of Neptune.

Equestrian Statue of Cosimo de' Medici (Florence). A fine bronze.

We already have mentioned many "portrait" statues, by various sculptors. Vincenzio Danti's:

Pope Julius III (Perugia). A colossal seated statue (1555), is considered one of the best of his time.

JEAN GOUJON

(Renaissance Sculpture in France)

The Italian Renaissance sculptors at the court of King Francis I and his successors "killed" the Gothic style, and native French sculptors also began to chisel along Renaissance lines. Germain Pilon did a marble group of *Three Graces* holding up the marble urn containing the heart of King Henry II. Queen Catherine de Medicis had the work done—though Henry's heart never was hers and she knew it. Barthélemy Prieur carved a fine "lying down" tomb statue of the Duke of Montmorency (Louvre) in armor, a 1570 marble "portrait." Francois Dusquenoy, Il Fiammingo, of Brussels (1594-1644), failed at big statues, but carved lovely boys and Cupids in ivory. Jacques Sarrazin did *Caryatides* (Louvre pavilion), and the Netherlander Jan de *Bekker,* a *Bronze Tomb of Mary of Bergundy* (Bruges).

JEAN GOUJON

(d. 1572)

Jean Goujon is the *French Cellini.* But a tragic fate was his in life, and pursued his works after death. His graceful nude:

Diana Reclining by a Stag (Louvre), makes a similar *Nymph* by Cellini look "second-hand." But with the exception of a lovely *Bust of Diane de Poitiers* (Versailles), and some bas-reliefs for altars, buildings and fountains, the work of the finest French Renaissance sculptor has vanished! He was driven from the bigoted Catholic court because he was a Huguenot, and seems to have died obscurely in Italy. Then, when the French Revolution came, the fine statues he had cast, and they were many, were destroyed.

THE VISCHER FAMILY OF NUREMBERG

(Renaissance Sculpture in Germany)

Wooden figures of saints without number, carved and gilded, and all sorts of carved wood-work are features of German Renaissance sculpture. Jörg Syrlin sculped gorgeous choir-stalls with statuettes, (*Ulm Cathedral*), and Veit Stoss of Cracow, a man of the vilest character, carved divine reliefs of the *Heavenly Host,* and scenes from the Bible (*Cracow Cathedral*), The Great Albrecht Dürer, with a carved relief of *Christ* (Landau Monastery), and Adam Krafft, "picture-like" figure carvings (*St. Sebalds, Nuremberg*), are among these sculptors in wood.

It was the *Vischer Family* of Nuremberg, however, which for three generations did the best bronze figure work in Germany, during the fifteenth and sixteenth centuries.

Hermann Vischer came to Nuremberg in 1453, did a baptismal font in Wittenberg (1457), with figures of the Apostles, and retired from history. But his son Peter, "the elder" (1455-1529), soon got to be *the only man* in Germany the princes of the land would have sculpture their figures on their tombs. He was the fashion, his work was the rage. An archduke, cardinal, or elector who did not have Vischer "do" him in bronze after he had "passed on," was looked down upon by the rest of the crowned heads of good society. With the aid of his five sturdy sons Peter Vischer, among others, provided *Bishop Johannes IV* (Breslau Cathedral), *Archbishop Ernest* (Madgeburg Cathedral), *Cardinal Albrecht of Brandenburg* (Aschaffenburg Church), the *Electoral Prince Frederick the Wise* (Wittenberg Castle Church), and many more with realistic "portrait" figures for their tombs.

TORRIGIANO

(Renaissance Sculpture in England)

The best English Renaissance sculptors seem to have been Italians. As in Italy, France and Germany, so much attention was paid by everyone of princely rank to having a *well-decorated tomb,* that we sometimes feel that nothing else mattered much to those who were to sleep in them. The Florentine Torrigiano (1472-1522) came from Italy to build King Henry VII's magnificent black marble tomb in

Westminster, and make splendid "portrait" figures of himself and his queen, to lie on it. Henry VII was the first "Tudor" to rule England, and with the exception of Queen Elizabeth, the stingiest. His great idea in life was never to let a shilling "get away" from him, and when he died he was the richest prince in Christendom. Of course, on his tomb he spared no expense, but he was known to higgle and haggle with his workmen, and no doubt "beat them down" well, on his monument. Torrigiano's bronze "tomb statue" of Margaret of Richmond in the same chapel is very "true to death," for it shows that it was done from a plaster cast of her dead face and hands. Da Maiano was another Italian sculptor of the English Renaissance. Poor Cardinal Wolsey! The marble sarcophagus da Maiano made for him, in St. Paul's Cathedral, now holds the body of Lord Nelson!

JUAN MONTANES

(Renaissance Sculpture in Spain)

In Spain we also see Torrigiano's fine Italian hand. His *St. Jerome* (Buenavista Convent, Seville) so Goya, the great Spanish painter said, was a better statue than Michel Angelo's, but that's as it may be. But there were plenty of Spanish sculptors, and so in Spanish churches and royal places we find many fine statues, especially of saints, by Berruguete, Becerra, *Our Lady of the Solitude* (Madrid), Jordon, Hermandez, J. Morlanes, who did wooden statues in Dürer's style, Cespedes, Alonzo Cano, and Montañes (d. 1614), probably the ablest Spanish sculptor of his time.

Montañes, a "realistic" sculptor, carved magnificent altars (Santa Ponce, Seville; San Miguel, Jerez; Seville Cathedral) and tombs. He executed most of his statues in *wood,* then covered them with a surface of *polished gold,* and colored them. He also made the model of a great *Equestrian Statue* of King Philip IV of Spain (Madrid), cast in bronze by Tacca, in Florence.

CHAPTER VII

BERNINI AND CANOVA

(Baroque Sculpture)

JUST as Baroque Architecture (See "Romance of Architecture"), in many cases was all *violent* movement, *too much* movement, "flutter" and "putting on side," so was Baroque Sculpture. Giovanni Lorenzo Bernini (1598-1680), who had as many "assistants" to help him make his statues as Alexander Dumas did to help him write his novels, *might* have been a Michel Angelo if he had had more "balance" and repose. His imagination ran away with him and—he had a *coarse* mind. Great art is often *nude,* but its nakedness is never *vulgar.*

The gifted Neapolitan began with refinement. His:

Apollo and Daphne (Villa Borghese), his earliest figure group, is his finest. He never improved on it. As he grew older his art became more *coarse,* in which respect it was more in keeping with the times in which he lived. But his age thought him the *one* and *only* sculptor, and that it did more than "think" so is shown by the fact that, in spite of his extravagance, he left a fortune of more than $500,000. To-day, if we look at his clumsy, colossal saints and angels in the churches of Rome, the Colonnade of St. Peters (his work, for he was a famous *architect* as well as sculptor), and the Bridge of Saint Angelo, they *shock* us.

Pluto Carrying off Proserpine (Borghese Gallery) saddens us. It is a fine group, so far as the artistic workmanship of violence goes. But it is the opposite to the lovely *Apollo and Diana,* and shows how his work has *coarsened.*

Saint Cecilia (Saint Cecilia's Church, Rome), by Maderna, is one of the most *"life*-like" statues of *death* known. Its *pose* (the way the figure lies) and realistic drapery are wonderful. Alessandro Algardi, Brunelli, Guidi, and Mazza are other better-known sculptors of the Italian Baroque.

THE "VEIL" TRICK

A "trick" idea to give a little more spice to the clumsy, agitated statues in the Baroque style was hit on by three Neapolitans,

Queirolo, Corradin and Sammartino. They produced (St. Maria de' Sangri Chapel, Naples) a lot of marble statues covered with thin *nets* of *veils,* to make them more "interesting"; a cheap trick and a most inartistic one, though the "veils" were very skillfully carved. In the 19th century, Monti, an Italian sculptor, exhibited some "veiled" statues (London Exposition, 1851), and every one crowded around them with "Ahs!" and "Ohs!" of admiration. But— for your benefit be it said—"veiled" statues are not considered "fine art."

PUGET AND GIRADON

(French Baroque Sculpture)

The monumental Baroque style was also developed in France by *native* French aritsts. The two Coustons, and Coysevox (1640-1720), did fine statues. It is a question, though, whether most Americans who were in Paris between 1917 and 1919, studied what critics call "the exaggerated elegance in their treatment of the female figure" from the examples they have left of their work.

Pierre Puget (1622-1694) of Marseilles in his statues showed that the Baroque style could be grand and strong as well as "fluttery" and exaggerated. Engineer and architect as well as sculptor, he not only carved many huge figure-heads for the men-of-war of Louis XIV, but also painted many pictures (Aix, Toulon and other cities), before he gave up painting for sculpture. His most famous statues are:

Hercules; Milo; Perseus and Andromeda; Alexander and Diogenes (Louvre), his bas-relief, *The Plague of Milan* (Council Chamber, Marseilles); and his *St. Sebastian* (Genoa). Puget was a "realist" sculptor. He took his models off the street or farm, and dressed them in saintly gowns or classic nothing. *St. Sebastian* and his *Virgins* are just every-day "farmer types." His *Hercules* (speaking from a human, not an *artistic* standpoint, of course) is just *scum;* a "branded galley slave," a criminal, the sort of model easy to get in Marseilles, where in his day the harbor was filled with galleys, floating prisons whose inmates were "used up" at the oar, and then thrown overboard weighed with a stone.

François Giradon, of Troyes (1628-1715), sculpted things which have all the "pomp and ceremony" of the Baroque style in spirit and expression. Naturally, he sculpted the princely tombs of France, and was the *Peter Visher* of his day. He did a great deal in Versailles, and worked in the sunshine of royal, princely and aristocratic favor. His most famous works are:

Tomb of Cardinal Richelieu (Church of the Sorbonne, Paris).

THE ROMANCE OF SCULPTURE

Tomb of the Marquis de Louvois (Church of St. Eustace, Paris).

Tomb of Bignon, Louis XIV's librarian (St. Nicolas de Chandonneret, Paris).

Rape of Proserpine (Versailles); and *Bull of Apollo:* two fine bronze groups.

Marble *Busts of Louis XIV* and his queen, *Maria Theresa* (Troyes). His great bronze statue of Louis XIV on horseback, which once stood in Paris, was melted down to make bullets to shoot at royalists during the French Revolution, but a small model of it exists (Louvre).

Jan de Juin (d. 1614), Pedro de Mena and Zurcillo did big *wooden statues* during the Baroque period in Spain; while in other European countries Baroque statuary was often provided by lesser Italian and French sculptors.

BAROQUE SCULPTURE

In England, Germany and Austria

In England Nicholas Stone was the chief sculptor of the Baroque Age. Handsome alabaster and colored marble tombs for the English nobility, with rich carving but poor statuary, were his "specialty." The French sculptor Hubert Le Soeur (d. 1670) did a fine bronze horseback statue of *Charles I* (Charing Cross, London); but a "standing" statue of *King James II* (formerly Whitehall Banqueting Hall) by Grinling Gibbons (1648), is poor. Gibbons did better carving, life-like pears, apples and flowers, in white wood.

In Germany the Baroque produced a few good "portrait" statues. Andreas Schuter did a colossal Baroque horseback *Statue of the Great Elector* (Berlin Bridge); and Rafael Donner in the *Donner Fountain* (Vienna), lead figures of Providence and the four greatest Austrian rivers, created a fine example of Baroque grandeur. Friedrich Drake put over into the 18th century a bronze colossal horseback statue of *King William of Prussia* (Cologne).

In Austria, too, the Baroque feeling for the colossal, the immense (as well as the Empire classic "military" spirit) makes itself felt in the eighteenth and early nineteenth centuries. Franz Zauner (1746-1822), *Tomb of Leopold II* (Augustinerkirche); *Tomb of Marshal Landon* (Hadersdorf; and "Empire" busts; and Joseph Klieber (1773-1850) stand out. Joseph Klieber had such a "big name" for colossal statues, triumphal arches and tombs that he "got the order" for the huge Louis XVIII catafalque (Paris), when that fat old king died. Johann Martin Fischer (1740-1820), was strong in anatomy. His statue called *The Muscle-Man* (Vienna Academy) still is used as a model for students.

CHAPTER VIII

THE ROCOCO, EMPIRE AND ITALIAN "CLASSICAL REVIVAL" IN SCULPTURE

THE French sculptor Falconet (1716-1791), was still Baroque in his work, which includes a statue of *Milo of Crotona* in the grand Baroque manner, and a colossal *Equestrian Statue of Peter the Great* in bronze (Petrograd, 1766), "ordered" by the Empress Catherine. But Clodion or Claude *Michel* (1745-1814)—we should not confuse him with another *Michel,* Clémence, a French female anarchist (1830-1905), known as the "Red Virgin of Montmartre," whose only idea about sculpture was "carving up" members of regularly organized governments—leaned more to the sensuous *eighteenth century Rococo* taste. He worked largely in terra-cotta, and has done much charming decorative work, besides statues of *Montesquieu, Dying Cleopatra* (South Kensington Museum), and an affecting group showing poor old *Blind Homer Driven Away by Fishermen* (Paris, 1810).

PIGALLE AND HOUDON

The two most important sculptors of the Rococo eighteenth century are Jean-Baptiste Pigalle (1714-1785), and Jean-Antoine Houdon, the latter being a "forerunner" of the finer modern school of French sculpture.

Pigalle, the seventh son of a carpenter, was probably the most popular sculptor of his day in France. He showed that he could sculp "the sort of thing the people liked" in his bronzes *Mercury Fastening His Sandals* (Berlin), and his "touching" *Bird in a Cage* (Sèvres); but rose to serious dignity in his *nude* statue of *Voltaire* (Institute of France) a skinny but imposing old gentleman who would bring a blush to no cheek. His tomb statues, the *Count d'Harcourt* (Notre-Dame), and *Marshal Saxe* (Lutheran Church, Strassburg), are considered good examples of eighteenth century French sculpture.

Houdon was the "real" sculptor of the French Rococo and a good one. In fact, he was so good that after he managed to get through the French Revolution without losing his life—the artistic associate of kings and princes was naturally an object of suspicion—he worked for Napoleon, and changed his style to "Empire."

He studied sculpture from the bronze and marble statues Louis

XIV had put up in the gardens of Versailles, instead of from teachers. And he did everything well. Pope Clement XIV, when he saw his statue of Saint Bruno, said: "He would speak if the rules of his order did not prevent him!" The list of Houdon's marble busts reads like a list of all the famous folk of his century. There were: *Catherine II of Russia, Diderot* the philosopher, and *Prince Galitzin* (Salon, 1773); *Gluck,* with the small-pox marks on his marble face, and the famous actress *Sophie Arnould* (Wallace Collection, London); *Prince Henry of Prussia, Buffon* the naturalist (Louvre); *Rousseau* the philosopher, and *Count Maribeau, Molière* (Theatre Français, Paris); and in the same theatre, a *draped* statue of *Voltaire.* He also did a bust of Benjamin Franklin, and in 1785 went to *Mount Vernon,* where the *Father of his Country* sat for him, a sitting which later produced the fine marble statue of *George Washington* which stands in the State Capitol, Richmond, Virginia.

Other famous statues of Houdon's are: *Diana* (Louvre), a proud, chaste and noble statue, which the Paris Salon refused to exhibit. The judges said that since Diana *wore no clothes,* she was merely a "follower of Venus," and so could not be entered!

La Frilleuse ("The Shiverer"), a nude female figure embodying "shivering cold," was done for the King of Prussia; and Houdon saved his neck from the guillotine when the French Revolution came by turning his statue of *Saint Scholastica* into a *Goddess of Reason.*

ENGLISH ROMANS IN WIGS

The English sculptors of the Rococo were mostly Flemings: Roubiliac, Peter Sneemackers, J. M. Rysbrack, and Nollekens (1737-1823), are the best known. The good English sculptor John Bacon (1740-1799), also deserves mention. What made many of the statues of Rococo times in England look silly was the custom of sculping English dukes, noblemen, generals and others in *Roman* gowns and *Roman* armor, and then putting large, clumsy *English* wigs on their heads. They looked as though they had been begun in 70 B.C. and finished in 1770 A.D. In Germany, the able sculptor Gottfried Schadow of Berlin (1764-1850), at least saw to it that the clothing his statues wore was up-to-date and did not combine *Roman* gowns and *German* wigs. If the German sculptor Christian Rauch (1777-1857) was sentimental in the true Rococo way, in his reclining statue of *Queen Louise of Prussia* (Charlottenburg), and *General Bülow* and *General Scharnhorst* (Berlin), his splendid monument of *Frederick the Great* (Berlin), modern in feeling, shows not a trace of Rococo weakness.

JACQUES PRADIER AND FRANCOIS RUDE

The Empire Style

The imitation of old classic art, Greek and Roman, "came in" with the Revolution and Empire, but most of the work done by the sculptor imitators was shallow and poor. Under Napoleon, of course, "imitation Roman" was the thing. Houdon, who from royalist had turned republican, now turned imperialist, and made some colossal reliefs for a proposed *Grand Army Column* at Boulogne; and then produced a statue of *Cicero,* and busts of *Marshal Ney,* the *Empress Josephine* and *Napoleon* himself, which brought him the legion of honor. He also sculped a *nude statue* of the *Man of Destiny* (Dijon).

Josef Bosio (1769-1845) seems to have been Napoleon's "own choice" among the sculptors of his time. He did the bronze spiral reliefs on the famous *Place Vendôme Column* (Paris), and the *Napoleon* statue on its top. Jacques Pradier represents the softer, more sentimental side of Empire Art. His *Chained Prometheus,* and his *Niobe* (Louvre), are *sensuously beautiful,* while Joseph Duvet, with a *Dancing Fisherlad* (Luxembourg), may also be mentioned in this connection.

François Rude (1784-1855) did his Roman work with more freedom. Celebrated are:

Bronze Mercury (Louvre); *The Song of Departure* (a high relief on the *Arc de Triomphe,* Paris). But his statue of *Marshal Ney* (Luxembourg Gardens), and of *General Cavaignace* (Montmartre Cemetery), make art-lovers shake their heads.

JEAN BAPTISTE CARPEAUX

(The Empire of Napoleon III)

Carpeaux (1827-1875), a mason's son, was the most popular sculptor of the Third Empire. His statues are considered clever but "unsculpturesque"—which means that his work is sometimes too violent and extravagant in gesture. His Bust of *Princess Mathilde,* his *Valenciennes Repelling Invasion* bas-relief, and his *Statue of the Prince Imperial* (which got him the Legion of Honor), are his *Bonapartist* works. Classic are: *Hector Bearing in his Arms his Son Astyanax;* while his "life-scenes" include: *Neapolitan Fisherman* and *Girl with a Shell* (1864). His last important work was a fountain, the *Four Quarters of the World* (Avenue de l'Observatoire, Paris), four female figures, Asia, Europe, Africa and America, holding up the globe. His group of *Nude Dancers* sculptured in relief on the outside of the Grand Opera House in Paris (1869), though a "sound" work and full of motion, was received with loud cries of indignant protest, because the Dancers were *nude!* In this connection the subject of the nude in Sculpture might well be considered.

THE NUDE IN SCULPTURE

The nude in Art, in sculpture as in painting, stands for the *idea* that the *unclothed human figure, in its perfection, is an ideal of beauty*. This ideal originated with the sculptors and artists of ancient Greece and Rome. The human form "in native worth and honor clad," was a commonplace in their lives, and no moral question of presenting its details ever entered their minds. Beauty justified everything!

Christianity, which brought in new ideas of what was *right* and what *wrong* in life, and art, looked on nudity in Art as something *immoral* and *impure*. To this day it has given us, where nude sculptures are concerned, an angle which seems to make the museum fig-leaf a necessity. To the real artist, that which tradition has taught us to regard as an objectionable detail, is just a detail of a complete figure, nothing more. He sees no *moral question* involved, and asks us not to create one where none exists. But if we allow there is no immorality in his unclothed figures, there still remains the question of *propriety*, of what is *proper!* Here conscience must be the art-lover's guide. If, like most of us, you feel that certain details of statuary should be shrouded with a decent reserve, lest they bring the blush of shame to the modest cheek of youth, you reflect the great body of *sane*, well-balanced opinion which thinks that the truth need neither be "shown" nor "spoken" at all times. If you are a bolder, more free spirit, and *can* look at any nude with the clear, pure eye of *absolute artistic*, not *sensual* enjoyment, your conscience may also say you are right.

CANOVA

(The Classic Revival)

The revival of antique Greek and Roman ideas and ideals in sculpture in Italy in the eighteenth century, the classic revival which succeeded the Rococo in Italy, as well as in other European countries, is largely represented by one great, tremendously popular sculptor, the Venetian Antonio Canova (1757-1822).

A stone-cutter's orphan son, placed in the household of a Venetian nobleman, the lion he molded in butter saved the day at a great banquet for which a splendid "fancy dish" for a middle of the table ornament had failed to arrive. His master then saw that he had lessons (with Toretto, a good sculptor), and when he was twenty-three his first work, *Dædalus and Icarus,* made his reputation and sent him to Rome. There one great work followed after another:

Theseus Vanquishing the Minotaur (Vienna Museum). Heroic size figures. Theseus is shown exhausted, sitting on the monster he has slain. The keynote of the work is grandeur and truth.

Monument of Pope Clement XIII and *Monument of Pope Clement XIV.* These tombs, with their figure-work, made people hail Canova as the *first* artist of his age.

Psyche. A butterfly on her right hand is held by the wings with her left. The figure, which represents man's *soul,* is considered Canova's most faultless work. Two other groups show *Cupid* and *Psyche* (his bride): in one they are standing, in the other lying down.

The Parting of Venus and Adonis (Naples); a very famous group.

Perseus with the Head of Medusa (Vatican). Fine, but not considered equal to Cellini's *Perseus.* The attitude is the same, the hero holds up the Medusa's head in one hand, and grasps his sword in the other.

Hercules and Lichas. This is a struggle group, and the most terrible conception of angry passion Canova's mind originated, far exceeding his *Hector and Ajax.*

When the shock of the French Revolution made itself felt in Italy, Canova retired to his native Venetian village of Passagno, and there, for a while, turned to painting. Travels in Germany improved his health, which had been shaken, and on his return to Rome he worked hard and produced more masterpieces.

The "portrait" statues and busts produced throughout his career include many great men:

George Washington, King Ferdinand of Naples, on horseback (Naples), the *Princess Esterhazy* and *Alise Bonaparte* (as "Polyhymnia), *Pope Pius VI,* a colossal figure, the *Empress Marie Louise* and *Napoleon's Mother,* and—at Napoleon's *personal request* (1802) Canova, to whom he gave "sittings" in Paris, did a colossal statue. His tombs include a nine-figure *Archduchess Maria Christina Monument* (Vienna), and a small model for a tomb for Lord Nelson. There are also some "fancy" busts: *Helen of Troy, Sappho, Laura,* etc.

His lovely female figures include *Hebe*—four times! There are four separate statues of the goddess of youth, and each is beautiful in delicacy and finish. His *Dancing Girls,* the *Three Graces* and *Hebe,* copied in plaster, to use the words of a stern art critic, "disfigure the stairs of countless hotels and other buildings on the Continent," and show "Canova at his worst!" But most of us would find them charming.

The fate of what might have been Canova's greatest statue, *Religion*, is curious. He had made the model for his colossal work, a model which all Italy admired. But—the priests of Religion fell out as to where the great statue was to be put, and—it never was cast! Canova reached the highest point of artistic development, and many honors were heaped on his head. The pope made him a "Marquis of Ischia," he was "registered" among the nobility of several states, and decorated with all sorts of orders of knighthood. But he kept on producing statues till he died (Venice, 1822) from a disease caused by the continual depression of the ribs owing to the use of chisel and carving-tools. His last period works were: *Mars and Venus*, *Pietà* (Mercy), *St. John*, and a *Recumbent* (lying) *Magdalen*. Some of his statues and busts are considered "artificial." He did, to some extent, give in to the taste of the "high society" of his day. But most of what he did is great art. Personally, he was one of the kindest and most generous of men. The major part of the vast fortune he accumulated was spent in helping the needy, the aged and unfortunate, and founding prizes or pensions for poor artists.

The greatest sculptor influenced by Canova was Bertel Thorwalden (1770-1844), an Icelander, buried under a bed of roses in the court of the Thorwalden Museum in Copenhagen, which contains many of his statues and models. His biggest work is the colossal group of *Christ and the Twelve Apostles* (Fruenkirche, Copenhagen), his most popular the bas-reliefs *Night* and *Morning*. His *Tomb of Pope Pius VII* is in St. Peter's, Rome; but his statue of *Lord Byron* was refused a place in Westminster. His pagan heroes and gods are considered very fine.*

In England, John Flaxman (1755-1826) is the classic reviver. His "cameo" reliefs on Wedgewood chinaware, showing old Greek subjects, are beautiful; his big marble statues less so. Baily (1788-1867) was Flaxman's best pupil. He carved a nude marble figure of *Eve*, the mother of mankind. John Gibson (1790-1866) was Flaxman's most successful follower. He made an attempt to gain public favor for the "painted" statues the old Greeks liked. But the public verdict "turned down" his *Venus Victrix* (London), the "tinted Venus" as she was called, and the white marble won out. Probably the finest work of the time was Alfred Stevens' *Wellington Monument* (St. Paul's Cathedral).

---

*Marchesi, Carradori, Pacetti, Rinaldi and Fabris were Italian sculptors of Canova's school as well as Thorwalden. Pietro Ternarini (1789-1869) a "naturalist," has a fine *Descent from the Cross*, in St. John Lateran, Rome.

CHAPTER IX

MODERN SCULPTURE IN EUROPE*

In a general way, old masterpieces of Greek art supplied the ages which followed with ideals and models for expression. Byzantine art, however, "worked out" special Christian ideals, and Mohammedan art, also "religiously" developed, turned in sculpture entirely toward "decorative patterns"; because figures—men and animal—sculpture's chief *subjects*, were forbidden it. Yet underlying the sculpture of other periods was the Greek ideal.

Modern sculpture, however, has developed other *besides Greek* ideals. The world of thought, of emotion, in Art has grown bigger with every passing century. Even the greatest of the Greeks presented their gods as superior *men*. Beauty of form, the human form, was their ideal. Now we have a thousand ideals where they had one. And the modern sculptors put in marble the *deepest emotions* of the *mind*. *Labor,* the working man, the farmer, in a democratic age, has supplied new art ideas and ideals; Actual human life, history, Nature, new ways of "feeling" and "expressing" classic Greek art, *modern* ways of developing the art and race spirit of other peoples beside the Greeks—the Egyptians, the Assyrians, even African negro art—are "live" influences for sculpture to-day.

BARTOLINI

(Modern Sculpture in Italy)

The greatest sculpture of modern times, the later nineteenth and twentieth centuries, probably has been produced in France, and will be considered in a separate chapter. Yet in other European countries great things have been done and modern Italy can point to some important men.

Lorenzo Bartolini (1777-1850), took Italian sculpture along a new road. He broke away from Greece and Rome and went "back to Nature," whom his statues copy exactly. He also did his *Napoleon,* a colossal bust; but the figures in his *Faith in God* and his *Charity groups* are taken from actual life, as are many busts, including those

---

*French Sculpture is considered separately in the chapter succeeding this one.

of the musicians *Méhul* and *Cherubini.* Even his classic *Hercules and Lichas,* and *Cleobis and Biton* are figures of modern Italians, and not ancient Greeks. Other "naturalists" are: Belliazzi, a Neapolitan, *The Sleeping Boy* (Gallery of Modern Art, Rome); Gemito, *The Gamester* (Capodimonte), and Barbella, who did peasant subjects: *Three Peasant Girls* (Royal Villa, Monza), the *Conscript's Departure* and *The Conscript's Return* (Nat. Gallery, Rome). Perhaps a little *too natural* is the Neapolitan d'Orsi's *The Parasites* (Naples). It is a horrible example of two gluttons as drunk as drunk can be. The more dignified Jerace, among other works, has a *Beethoven* (Venice, 1895), and a *Donizetti* (Bergamo, 1897).

Force of gesture and facial expression mark Civiletti's (b. Palermo, 1846) statues: *The Young Dante, The Young Cæsar, The Dead Christ.* Ettore Ximenes (Palermo), chose subjects which ranged from his grand statue called *Revolution* to one of *The Scullion.* Monteverde, besides a charming group of his own children (Piazzo Blanco, Genoa) has a *King Victor Emmanuel* statue (Bologna). The Roman Ettore Ferrari's work is a model of "finish." His *Roman Slave* stands in the Campo di Fiori, Rome; his *Abraham Lincoln* in the New York Museum. Emilio Gallori did the *Garibaldi Monument* (Rome). Antonio da Zotto (b. 1841), is ranked as the best Venetian sculptor of the nineteenth century. He has done statues of *Galileo, Titan, Goldoni* and *Petrarch* (Venice), and a monument to the violinist *Tartini* (Pirano). Oroardo Tebachi (b. Turin, 1831), toiled with Antonio Tantardini on the *Cavour Monument* (Milan), in more serious moments, and sculped *The Bather* (Milan, 1894), in his lighter ones.

MODERN SCULPTURE IN GERMANY AND AUSTRIA

Reinhold Begas and Max Klinger

Royal and princely patronage and the new German feelings of "nationality" which followed the Franco-Prussian War of 1870, called forth much "monumental" and portrait work in Germany. Without dwelling on many lesser talents Reinhold Begas (b. 1831), who produced some fine, but much hasty and pretentious work stands out with: *Emperor Wilhelm I Monument, Schiller Monument,* and a colossal *Bismark* all in Berlin. Joseph Uphues (b. 1850) *Moltke Monument, Monument of Frederick the Great* (duplicate in Washington—he was friendly to us during the War of Independence, but his statue was promptly hustled out of sight in 1917) was a Begas pupil. Fritz Klimsch: *The Triumph of Woman, The Kiss;* Seffner, Christ, Kurz, Hahn, Kaufmann are newer men. August Gall (animal statuettes), Louis Tonaillon (horses) are specialists. Adolf Hildebrand (b. 1874) did a *Wittlesbach Foun-*

tain (Wittlesbach is the name of the royal family of Bavaria), as Begas did his great Hohenzollern, *William I, Monument.* Franz Stuck's massive *Beethoven,* however, yields to that of Max Klinger (b. 1857). His *Beethoven Monument* (Leipsic) shows the great composer sitting, the eagle of Jove at his feet, in colored marble. Busts of *Liszt* (Leipsic Museum), and *Nietzsche,* the philosopher (Weimar), and a group of three wonderful life-size nudes, *The Drama* (Albertinum, Dresden) are among his great works.

Modern Austria is rich in sculptors. In Vienna there is much "monumental" sculpture and many "portrait" figures of historical persons. Anton Fernkorn, statues on horseback: *Archduke Charles, Prince Eugene; Johann Meixner, Albrecht Fountain;* Zumbusch, *Beethoven, Empress Maria Theresa;* Edmund Hellmer (b. 1850) *Turkish Monument* (St. Stephens); Arthur Strasser, oriental figures, Japanese, Egyptian, Hindoo; Anton Wagner, *The Goose Girl;* Friedl, *The Horse Tamers;* Pendl, colossal statue of *Justice;* Bitterlich, *Gutenberg Monument;* are a few among many.

RUSSIA, SCANDINAVIA, SPAIN AND BELGIUM

Tremendous and moving statues of great figures of history—*Ivan the Terrible, Louis XI of France, Peter the Great*—soul portraits, represent Marc Antokolsky (1845-1902) probably the greatest of Russian sculptors. He considered his *Spinoza,* the philosopher, and his *Mephistopheles,* probably the greatest Satan ever sculpted, his greatest statues. His *Christian Martyr* shows the beautiful soul of a woman, ugly of features and deformed in body, and is one of the greatest and most affecting figures a sculptor ever carved. Liberich, Bach, Mikechine, Tourgenieff yield in interest to the original genius Naoum Aronson (b. 1872), with a *Beethoven* (Bonn), and many other works to his credit. The Swedish sculptor Fogelberg, unlike Sergell and Byström, has gone to the Valhalla of the old Norse gods for inspiration instead of Greek Olympus, and Bissen, *King Frederick VII,* on horseback, and Jerichan, *Man Assailed by Panther,* are Danes.

Of Spain's many modern sculptors a few might be singled out: There is the Catalan Novas, *The Dead Torero;* Querol, *Tradition,* and a great Baroque *Monument of King Alfonso XII;* Blay, *Miners' Monument* (Bilbao), and many beautiful marble busts; and Joseph Llimona, perhaps the greatest of Spanish modernists, who has done large monument work as well as a small marble *Pain* which is so expressive that those who see it can almost feel the emotion it expresses. Embil, Alen, the Osle brothers, Gragera, Alcoverio, Fuxa y Leal and Pages y Serratora are other modern names of note among Spanish sculptors.

In Belgium, Simonis, with his *Godefroid de Bouillon* precedes Paul de Vigne (1843-1901), whose best work is the figure of *Immortality* (Brussels Museum) among many. Charles van der Stappen (b. 1843), *A Group of Tired Workmen;* Thomas Vincotte, *Music, The Horsebreakers* (Brussels); Julien Dielens, *The Lansquenets* (Brussels); Jules Legae, *The Kiss;* Jean Marie Gaspar, *The Abductor* and *The Brave,* a Western Indian on his mustang; and the Fleming Jan Lambeaux (1852-1908), who carried his sculpture from colossal reliefs of great strength like *The Passions of Humanity,* down to unpleasant statues like *Intoxication,* are important names. Perhaps the greatest of Belgian sculptors was "the workingman's sculptor," Constantin Meunier (1831-1908)). In wonderful groups and statues—*Fire-Damp* (Brussels Museum), *The Mower* (Botanical Gardens, Brussels), *Puddlers at the Furnace* (Luxembourg Museum), and others—he expressed the strength and *dignity of labor* in a masterly way. Jacques de Lalaing, a sculptor of merit, should be mentioned as the creator of the statue of *La Salle* (Chicago).

MODERN SCULPTURE IN ENGLAND

The examples of Carpeaux, Jules Dalou, another Frenchman, Alfred Stevens and Lord Leighton, first led modern English sculptors to put more "flesh and blood" into their marbles. J. H. Foley (1818-1874), got away from the stiff and formal altogether in a spirited *General James Outram* (India), on horseback, and a *Sir Joshua Reynolds* (Tate Gallery, London). Henry Hugh Armstead (1828-1905), together with many "big" statues, did a fine *David and the Lion* tomb bas-relief (Guards' Chapel), in the flat style the old Nineveh chisellers used; and a lovely marble statuette of *Remorse* (Chantrey Collection). One of the best modern Scotch sculptors, George A. Lawson, has a classic *Daphnis,* and *In the Arena* and a *Weary Danaid;* and a modern *Old Marjorie* and *Robert Burns* (Ayr), to his credit; while Sir Edwin Landseer, the painter, did the four colossal *Lions* (7 tons apiece of stone), at the corners of the *Nelson Monument* (Trafalgar Square). *Dionysius Astride His Leopard* is George Simonds' (b. 1844) finest work. His *The Falconer* stands in Central Park, New York, and his undraped females such as *Anemone,* always are *refined*.

Thomas Brock

Thomas Brock (b. 1847), is one of the great modern English sculptors. One of his best groups, *The Moment of Peril* is American in subject. It shows a Red Indian attacking a serpent which had thrown his horse. Brock has done numerous fine "portrait" statues: *Robert Raikes* (Thames Embankment), *Henry Philpott,*

Bishop of Worcester, Sir Richard Temple (Bombay Town Hall), *Sir Richard Owen* (Nat. Hist. Museum, South Kensington), *Thomas Gainsborough* (Tate Gallery) and *Sir Henry Irving*, the great English actor. His loveliest and most delicate *single* figure, perhaps, is *The Genius of Poetry*, his most colossal work, the *Queen Victoria Memorial*,* a big sculptural monument, 70 feet high, with many large figures. A noble sleeping image of *Lord Leighton* (St. Paul's Cathedral), should not be forgotten.

Sculptors who have specialized in *animals* and in *primitive man* include: Sir Joseph M. Swan (1847-1910), whose chief works are: *Leopard Playing with a Tortoise, Leopard Running, Puma and Macaw,* and the human figure *with* animals, *Orpheus* and *Boy and Bear Cubs*. Harry Dixon, *Wild Boar* (Tate Gallery), *A Bear Running,* and *Otters and Salmon,* chisels animal life in vivid statuary; *The Slain Enemy* shows a prehistoric man with the wolf he has killed. Robert Stark's *Indian Rhinoceros* (Chantrey Collection), Captain Adrian Jones's, *Duncan's Horses,* and horseback statue of *The Duke of Cambridge* (Whitehall, London), and W. R. Colton's bronze *Tiger,* are works of great strength and truth. Herbert Ward's bronzes of South African savages, among them *The Idol-Maker,* might be mentioned in this connection.

Sir Charles B. Lawes-Wittewronge (b. 1843) has done a large group, *The United States of America* (1890). His colossal group, *The Death of Dirce* both in bronze and in colored marble, very strong and robust, was exhibited at the Franco-British Exhibition (1908). W. Hamo Thorneycroft's *Gladstone Memorial* (Strand, London), and Edwin Roscos Mullins' *Cain,* are regarded as their best works.

F. Onslow Ford

Onslow Ford (1852-1901) is one of the greatest of British "portrait" sculptors. In his portrait statues he showed "flesh, bone, hair, clothing" just as they are, and did his more "ideal" work in smaller forms. His great portrait statues are: *Henry Irving as Hamlet; Gordon*—he is riding a camel—(Chatham, copy in Khartoum); *Shelley* and *Huxley*. In his last figures, *Glory to the Dead,* he has

---

*There are so many Queen Victoria statues, that it might be well to list the most important. Nearly all are "collossal" in size: *Queen Victoria* (bust) considered one of the noblest of its kind, and the statue *Queen Victoria* (Manchester), by E. Onslow Ford; *Queen Victoria* (Winchester), by Alfred Gilbert; *Queen Victoria* (Calcutta), *Queen Victoria* (Leeds), by Sir George Frampton; *Queen Victoria* (India), *Queen Victoria* (Australia), *Queen Victoria* (Blackburn), by Bertram Mackennal; *Queen Victoria Memorial* (Liverpool) by Charles J. Allen (1906); *Queen Victoria* (Aden) by John Tweed; *Queen Victoria* (Dublin) by the *Irish* sculptor, John Hughues.

been reproached for bringing *nudity* into *funeral* art, something the Greeks did not do.

Other "portrait" statues by British sculptors are: H. R. Hope Pinker, *Dr. Martineau* and *Henry Fawcett;* Harvard Thomas, *Edward Burke;* Harry Bates, *Homer;* Sir George Frampton, *Socrates Teaching* (1884), a *King Edward VI*, in bronze and marble, *Charles Keene, R. Stuart Poole, Leigh Hunt, Passmore Edwards;* A. G. Walker, *Adam and Eve* (1910); Frederick W. Pomeroy, colossal statues of *Admiral Blake, Dean Hook* (Leeds), *Oliver Cromwell* (St. Ives, Huntingdonshire), *Robert Burns* (Paisley), *Gladstone* (Lobby of Parliament House); Albert Toft, *Gladstone;* W. Birnie Rhind, *Lord Salisbury, King James V of Scotland;* W. Goscombe John (b. 1860), *Duke of Devonshire* (Eastbourne), the horseback *Viscount Tredgar* (Cardiff), the *Sir Arthur Sullivan Monument* (London); Henry C. Fehr, *James Watts* (Leeds); J. Pittendrigh Macgillvray: *Robert Burns Memorial* (Glasgow), and *John Knox Memorial* (St. Giles Cathedral, Edinburgh); John Tweed, *Cecil Rhodes;* G. F. Watts—considered one of the finest sculptors of the nineteenth century—*Lord Tennyson, Bishop Lonsdale* (Litchfield Cathedral), and *Hugh Lupus* (Eaton Hall) for the Duke of Westminster.

Frederick, Lord Leighton

This great English painter (1830-1896) was able to give Greek beauty expression in marble as well as on canvas. His important statues are three in number: His *Athlete Struggling with a Python* (Chantrey Collection), created great excitement when it was first unveiled. *The Sluggard* (1886). The model who had been "posing" for him as the *Athlete,* in his first group, was tired one day and took a good "stretch." Leighton was so charmed with the new pose that he made him "hold it," and thus the statue came to be. His third piece of sculpture is a very attractive nude* statuette of

---

* British nudes, as a rule, have a quality missing in many French ones: they are *decent* and *refined* in expression, and make us feel that the artist thought no evil when chiseling them. There are many fine British nudes: J. Harvard Thomas' *The Slave Girl* has been called "full of grace and well-felt realism." Andrea C. Lucchesi (*Destiny, Flight of Fancy, The Myrtle's Altar, Carthage, 149 B.C., Verity and Illusion*) by his *refined* treatment of the female form beautiful "succeeded in interesting a public—the English public—usually indifferent to this branch of sculpture." Albert Toft, *Antigone;* Harvard Thomas' *Lycidas;* F. Derwent Wood, *Psyche;* F. W. Pomeroy, *The Potter* and *Feroniae* (1909); Edouard Lanteri, a very dignified nude *Pax;* Bertram Mackennal, *Diana;* David McGill, *The Bather;* F. M. Taubmann, *The Sandal,* a small nude kneeling figure; Charles F. Hartwell, *The Rising Tide, The Bathers, Sirens* (1910); Harold Parker, *Ariadne* (Tate Gallery), are a few among many refined nudes by British sculptors.

III

a young girl looking over her shoulder at a frog, and is called *Needless Alarms*.

Gilbert, Frampton, Pomeroy and Watts

Alfred Gilbert (b. 1854) reintroduced the "lost" process of casting bronze statues (he had learned it in Italy) in England. His work is noble and displays the *spirit* as well as the *flesh* in beauty. Of many colossal statues and monuments the *Tomb of the Duke of Clarence* (St. George's Chapel), is considered the finest thing of its kind in England. Of many smaller works, his most touching display of feeling is the bronze group called *Mors Janua Vitæ* ("Death is the Gate of Life"), in the Royal College of Surgeons' hall (London).

Sir George Frampton (b. 1860) produced masterly statues in every field and of every kind of subject. His works range from practical subjects, his bronze *The Steamship* (Lloyds' Registry, London), to "mystery" figures, full of "symbolic meaning," like *The Mysteriarch*. His "ideal" figures, like *Music* and *Dancing* and *The Angel of Death*, are as well chiselled as his *Maternity* (1905) group and *The Sailing Ship*. Elegance, simplicity and breadth mark Frampton's work.

Frederick W. Pomeroy shows mastery in colossal monument and ideal statuette. Among his "ideal" works are: *Love the Conquerer* (Walker Art Gallery, Liverpool), *Boy Piping* (Tate Gallery) and *Nymph Finding the Head of Orpheus*. His *Perseus* is an echo of Cellini, but *The Spearman* is original. Alfred Drury (b. 1857), has done exquisite children's busts (*The Age of Innocence*) as well as colossal figures and monument carvings. Richard Garbe's work might be called brutally strong. His "powerful" statues include: *The Egoist, Man and the Ideal,* and *The Idealist*.

G. F. Watts is another sculptor of force. His great horseback group, *Physical Energy* (Kensington Gardens, London), cast 1902, after twenty years of labor, was sent to South Africa in duplicate as a memorial to Cecil Rhodes. His bust of *Clytie*, in the classic Greek style, has been called the finest work in the Greek *spirit*, for grandeur, simplicity and beauty, that England has produced.

CHAPTER X

MODERN SCULPTURE IN FRANCE

FRANCE, before all others, is the land of modern sculpture, and the French influence in developing the art and its ideals is the one which has been most strongly felt in our own United States. Modern French sculpture may be said to begin after the Franco-Prussian War of 1870, in a great revival of national feeling in art. This earlier school of sculptors,* in general, clung to the old established way of doing things, the "classic" traditions of their art; and achieved many beautiful works in so doing.

But others ** were not content with Greek, religious, or "fantasy" subjects treated in the "classic" way.

Emmanuel Frémiet

Emmanuel Frémiet (b. 1824), is one of the great names among the artists who "pulled away" from the older traditional style of using the chisel, and the old traditional choice of subject and presentation. He may be said to represent *all* the sculptors who put the "inside" portrayal of the "soul's" emotions, of *human* feeling, be-

* Among them are: Paul Dubois (1829-1905), *Tomb of General Lamoricière;* Chapu—with a wonderful figure of *Youth,* on the *Henri Regnault Tomb;* Falguiere (1831-1900), statues ranging from a pathetic *St. Vincent de Paul* to a spirited *Hunting Nymphs;* Delaplanche (1836-1890), *The Virgin with the Lily;* Barrias (1841-1905), the patriotic group, *Defence of Paris;* Mercie, the *Victory Monument;* Idrac (1840-1884), *Mercury Inventing the Caduceus, Salâmmbo;* Verlet, *Monument to Maupassant;* Lanson, *The Iron Age;* Peinte, *Orpheus Charming Cerebus to Sleep;* Longpied, *Immortality;* Sicard, *Hagar and Ishmael,* Muchel, *In a Dream.*

** Other members of this group of artists who tried to express "the spirit within" rather than the outer appearance of things were: Christophe (1827-1892), *Fortune, The Human Comedy, The Supreme Kiss,* chiselled in "symbolic" style; Injalbert, *Christ on the Cross;* Desbois, *Leda;* Becquet (1829-1907) *Ishmael;* Dampt, *A Grandmother's Kiss.* A special French interpretation of the spirit of freedom is the colossal bronze *Goddess of Liberty,* by the sculptor Bartholdi, a gift of the French government, which stands on Bedloe's Island, in New York Harbor, and is dear to the New Yorker's heart.

fore an attractive "outside" showing in statuary; and who tried to express *themselves* in everything they did, whether their subjects were from mythology, religion, poetry or history, or just showed people and events happening around them all the time. Frémieux was great both in *animal* forms and in the *human* form—he had learned anatomy in a ghastly place, the Paris morgue, as "painter to the Morgue"—and his chief works (no matter what their subject) always represent his ideals:

Wounded Bear; Wounded Dog (Luxembourg Museum).

Gorilla and Woman (Salon medal, 1887).

A striking "primeval man" group, *She-Bear and Man of the Stone Age*.

Orang-Outangs and Bornean Savage (Paris Museum of Natural History) are among the most spirited, "true to life" statues ever devoted to savage man, and the savage beasts of his time. Military statuettes for Napoleon III occupied him from 1855 to 1859; but his great equestrian statues are:

Napoleon I, St. Louis of France, Louis of Orleans (Pierrefonds), *Joan of Arc* (Place des Pyramides, Paris), and the equestrian *Velaquez* (Louvre).

Antoine-Louis Bayre

Bayre (1796-1875), earlier in point of time than Frémiet, felt the same need to express his personality *away* from the classic models. He turned to animal sculpture and became the greatest *animal* sculptor, perhaps, that France has produced. Bayre gave animals *souls*. Before his time they had been looked on as "decorative" forms and figures, to be introduced in ornament. He made them *live*, and first expressed Nature in animal life as she is. While working for a fashionable goldsmith, Bayre cultivated his hobby. He made the old head-keeper at the Paris Menagerie his friend, and spent all his spare time there, studying the wild beasts "from life." When a visitor once called to see him his wife said: "There is no use trying to see him for three weeks—a new tiger has just come from Bengal!" But when he sent his *Tiger Devouring a Crocodile* (1830), to the Salon, and in 1833 his *Lion Crushing a Serpent* was put up in the Tuileries Gardens, many sculptors who were *not* made Knights of the Legion of Honor as he was, were indignant. "Why turn our public gardens into menageries?" was their war-cry. At the same time Bayre was making exquisite small statues and groups in bronze. But so great was the professional jealousy he excited that the jury refused to accept them at the 1834 Salon: they were "goldsmith's work, not statuary," they declared. When King Louis Philippe's son asked him to interfere, the king said: "I can appoint a jury, but I can't force them to recognize works of genius!"

Though Bayre's stone *Tiger* (1835), and his *Seated Lion* (Louvre)*
were grudgingly admitted, some of his finest single figures, more of
his small bronzes were refused, and Bayre, deeply wounded, did not
exhibit again until 1850, when he was so famous that a refusal
was out of the question.

Bayre's works include one *poor* one: a bronze equestrian statue of
Napoleon I (Corsica), and many *wonderful* single statua and groups,
large and small:

Elephant of Senegal Running (Bulk and heaviness coupled with
agility and grace; bronze, 5½ inches high; *Panther Seizing a Stag*
(Vivid in force and movement; bronze, 15 inches high; *Theseus
Slaying the Minotaur* (Brute force, a half-man, half bull creature,
struggling against human intelligence, finely and proudly shaped;
bronze, 18 inches high). *The Standing Bear* (9½ inches), and *The
Walking Lion* (13 inches), are only a few among a great number
of smaller bronze animals, including horses, camels, alligators,
eagles, jaguars, gazelles, buffalo, pythons strangling crocodiles, etc.

Among the larger bronzes not already mentioned are: *Tiger Devouring Virginia Stag* (Marseilles Museum); *Lion Devouring an
Antelope (Paris)*. Bayre has been called "the Michel Angelo of
animal sculpture." A bronze cast of his *Lion Crushing a Serpent*
has been presented by the French Government to the Metropolitan
Museum, New York; and in Washington (Corcoran Gallery), are
120 bronzes, duplicates of his best works, cast by Bayre himself,
owing to the efforts of Mr. Walters of Baltimore. When the old
sculptor received the commission his eyes filled with tears and he
said: "My own country never has done anything like this for me!"

THREE SCULPTORS OF DEMOCRACY

Dalou and Meunier and Bartholomé

Three men of the newer group stood for the more individual
freedom which Frémiet represented, developed their individuality
each in a very distinct manner.

Jules Dalou (1838-1902), who during his stay in England (1871-1879), exerted a great influence on English sculpture, may be said
to have had two styles *different* and *distinct*. One is a *democratic*
style in sculpture which expresses the *people* in a simple, natural
way: *Woman of Boulogne Telling Her Beads, The Reader, French
Peasant Woman* (this last a terra-cotta). In the other, he tries to
revive the splendid dreams of the Age of Louis XIV: the relief

---

* The *Seated Lion* and four noble human figures (Louvre) of *War,
Peace, Order* and *Force*, have been put up in duplicate in Mount Vernon
Square, Baltimore, U. S. A.

Mirabeau Replying to M. de Dreux-Breze (Palais Bourbon); *Procession of Silenus,* and the vast monument, *Triumph of the Republic* (Place de la Nation), the work of twenty years. There also are monuments, *Alphand, Delacroix, Victor Hugo, Floquet,* in which portrait expresses the inner spirit of the men it represents. In all his work Dalou is a master of taste, "carrying out" an idea.

Constant Meunier has been considered in the preceding chapter, among Belgian sculptors. But the sweeping democratic feeling of his art had an influence in France. *Labor,* probably the most important thing in our life to-day, and the "laboring man," his toil, his power—portrayed as the heroes of the thousandfold effort on which all modern society rests—seemed to Meunier the *highest subject* for artistic treatment. And the sincerity, truth and feeling shown in his glass-blowers, miners, puddlers and smiths and other "industrials," as people who write about "the people" call them, makes his statues and statuettes, art in the highest sense!

Albert Bartholomé, originally a painter, answered the *democratic appeal* in monumental works of the highest and noblest kind. His idea was to create large and lofty monuments which would lead the popular heart *upward,* fill it with noble *images,* teach it to find the sublime in *human life itself.* His greatest work in this field is the magnificent *Monument to the Dead*—the dead,[*] all human dead, not any particular dead person (Père Lachaise Cemetery, Paris). In carrying it out his mind did not turn to the ancient Greeks. He allowed his "shaping up" to be influenced by the one people which among all others has paid Death the greatest respect—the Egyptians!

August Rodin

It is not too much to say, perhaps, that what Shakespeare and Dante represent in Literature, Auguste Rodin represents in Sculpture. Born in 1840, he attended the sculpture classes which Bayre taught, but animal sculpture did not attract him. The portrayal of individual man and of humanity always was his dream and ambition. In him French sculpture produced its *greatest figure,* just as

---

[*] The funeral monument and statue in which French sculptors have excelled, is represented by hundreds of works in all the towns and cities of France. Among the greater might be mentioned: Saint-Marceaux, *Genius Guarding the Secret of the Tomb;* E. Barrias, *The First Funeral;* Chapu *Daniel Stern;* Mercie, *Tombs of Baudry, Cabanel, King Louis Philippe* and *Queen Amelie;* François Sicard, *Monument of the War of 1870, Monument to Bertagna;* Bartholomé's *Monument to Jean-Jacques Rousseau* (Pantheon), is one of the finest examples of this art. Fine French "portrait" studies include: L. Gérome, *Bonaparte at Cairo;* Emile Bourdelle, *Beethoven;* Jean Boucher, *Renan.* Alfred Lenoir's specialty has been to present great men, *Berlioz, Marshal Canrobert, César Franck,* in sculptured "clothes that fit!"

Saint-Gaudens may still be said to represent the highest that American sculpture has achieved.

The great thing in Rodin's art, which makes it different from all other sculpture, is that in his figures and statues the marble or bronze *turns to human flesh,* and in this quivering flesh *the very soul shines forth!* He "throws away" all that is conventional, clothes, traditions, "period costume," anything and everything which may interfere with his showing humanity as it *lives* and *breathes,* humanity as it is. Every mystery of the human soul is revealed in his inspired works. From 1863 to 1885 Rodin's chief works are: *The Man with the Broken Nose* (1864), which first showed his strong *individual* bent; some *Caryatids* for the interior of the Paris *Bourse* (Stock Exchange); *The Bronze Age* (Luxembourg Museum); and busts of *Victor Hugo, Jean-Paul Laurens, Dalou* and *Antonin Proust.* Then, for twenty years, he devoted himself to the tremendous decorative piece of sculptuary (entrance of the *Musée des Arts Decoratifs*), in which Dante's poem seems to live in stone. All the suffering and terror, the anguish and despair expressed in the line "Abandon hope all ye who enter here!" has been put into this great work. Dante himself is seated at the top, and below him writhe the crowd of the damned, torn by frenzies of suffering, contorted by the anguish of lost hopes. The lower portion of the work consists of two special bas-reliefs, where show two tortured faces, around which runs a frieze of women and centaurs, while three men cling to each other in despair above the door.

It was while carrying out this tremendous relief that Rodin also found time to do a statue of *Bastien Lepage* (Damvilliers) and a *Monument to Claude Lorrain* (Nancy). In the *Burgesses of Calais,* which he did for that city, instinct forbade his "grouping" the citizens huddled together, according to tradition—so he made them walk in *Indian file!* The bust of his friend *Puvis de Chavannes* (1892), his *Contemplation,* and *Caryatid* lead up to the *Victor Hugo Monument.*

Victor Hugo had already been immortalized in a *bust* by Rodin and—he was a wonderful *etcher* as well as *sculptor*—his etched portrait of *Victor Hugo* is considered the best etching he ever did. The *Monument of Victor Hugo* (Luxembourg Gardens), however, is the most famous of the three. Rodin's *Victor Hugo* is another striking protest against the ordinary, everyday in art when it comes to representing great men. The immortal author of "Les Miserables," is stripped of the protective covering of practical but hideous clothing we wear (French trousers in life are usually "baggy," which would have made it worse), and stands forth as a majestic *nude,* an old man full of power and dignity, his right hand stretched out in a commanding gesture, while the Muses stand respectfully behind him.

Rodin's *Victor Hugo*, like his *Whistler* and his *Balzac*—*Balzac* was made to look "in character" by a flowing dressing-gown—excited much criticism. The "Society of Men of Letters" which had "ordered" the *Balzac* took offense at the dressing-gown, and refused to regard it as a statue. But opposition never had any effect on Rodin. He felt he must create as his instinct and conscience told him.

The passionate and voluptuous in human life were not forgotten or neglected by Rodin. His marble group *Paolo Malatesta* and *Francesca da Rimini*, is as fine in one way as his bronze *St. John* is in another. His greatest nude is *The Kiss*, no frivolous, "jazzy" expression in marble of the idea of lips meeting; but two unclothed human figures clasped in an intensity of emotion, in tenderest affection. There is, also, an *Eve*, and a nude *Danaïd** (Luxembourg), in marble.

Three great "ideal" works of Rodin's imagination are: *The Hand of God* (1905); *The Thinker*, in front of the Panthéon, and *Les Ombres* ("The Shades").

Before he died Rodin, the greatness of his art generally acknowledged, had the satisfaction of seeing the City of Paris put up a special building and present it to him, to house all his models and works, finished and unfinished, which were not elsewhere placed. And the French Government bought some twenty-five of his great works and put them in the Luxembourg Gallery. Rodin, more than any sculptor before him, used the methods and produced the results of the great art of Michel Angelo, and in the wonderful expression he has given the *divine* as well as the *human*, he probably never has been excelled.

Some Special Developments in French Sculpture

Following in the footsteps of Bayre and Frémiet, a number of French sculptors have devoted themselves to the *animal* instead of the *human* figure. Among them Gardet: *Fighting Panthers* (Luxembourg), *Lions, Dogs*, etc., is perhaps the most important figure. Medallion work, little statues and busts in the pathetic vein were a specialty of Theodore Rivière. *The Vow, Charles VI and Odette, Salâmbo and Maltho*. Rivière combined precious stones and other

---

* The nude female figures of French sculptors often are voluptuous and seductive to a degree which makes it hard to say whether there is an objectionable *intention* in making them so, or whether the sculptor's fervid fancy has *innocently* run away with him. Famous French nudes include: G. Michel's *Dreaming*; Bartholomé's pure and virginal *Young Girl Dressing Her Hair*; D. Puech's *The Siren*; L. Marquette's *Galatea*; H. Gerber's *Narvissus*; Maillot's *Stooping Girl*. Louis Convers, Segoffin, Aimé-Octobre and Landowski have also displayed a fine feeling for the graceful curve in this field.

metals with his ordinary material, and in this has had followers: Agathon Leondard, *The Dancers* (in Sèvres China); the painter Gérome (a little *Tamerlane*), and others who inlay marble or bronze with wood, ivory, gold and gems.

Other sculptors who have devoted themselves to showing the beauty and dignity of *Labor*, or the incidents of everyday life are: H. Greber, *Le Grisou* (The Fire-Damp); Alexandre Charpentier, *Woman Suckling Her Infant,* the stone bas-reliefs, *Bakers;* Hippolyte Lefebure, *Summer,* a young girl with a parasol, and *Winter,* an old lady in furs; Henri Bouchard, *The Quarry,* and *Turning the Sod;* Emile Bourdelle, *Wrestlers of Tarn and Garonne;* and Roger Bloche's *The Accident,* a city street "happening," with a man stretched out surrounded by a crowd of some twenty others, such as may be seen in any metropolis almost any day in the week.

"CUBIST" SCULPTURE

Anarchistic developments in modern painting, the names of whose greater masters, Cézanne and Picasso (*Cubism*), Matisse (*Fauvism-Savagery*) "distil the fundamental *geometric* shape (whence 'cubes' and 'cubism') out of their subjects and by seemingly making it more important than anything else, produce what is recognizable as to a cubist *as* a picture." There is also some "cubist" sculpture. A few names might be mentioned: Laurent, *Guitare* (1918), *Woman's Head* (1921), "works in the block," keeping its original form, and "establishes" his "sculptures" on two or three axes. Lipchitz does the same (*Sculpture, Nudes*) (1919, 1920). Czaky "idealizes" little Egyptian statuettes so that they seem to be caricatures. The uncultured person who looks at a Laurent nude, would never blush, for the idea of the human figure is so cleverly concealed in the "geometric plan" that one can recognize it neither as human, nor as a figure.

Like all art that is sincere, cubist sculpture has a claim to respect, but many people who have seen it do not like it, though "pity is akin to love." Useful phrases, if you find it necessary to speak of "Cubist" sculpture as though you liked it, are: "Laurens style is grace itself;" or "Laurens makes a crowd of details arrange themselves according to very free inner rules of rhythm;" or "What I like about Laurens is that his angles all turn so smoothly on their hinges." Of Lipschitz, you say, with a smile: "I think he is so fond of playing with abstract light and shade that he forgets the *human element,*" and of Czaky: "His geometrizations seem very forceful."

CHAPTER XI

THE STORY OF AMERICAN SCULPTURE

For a nation so young, we have a record in sculpture in which we can take pride. In the early Colonial days the average American father in New York and in the South had a healthy dislike to seeing his child "take up" anything as "unpractical" as Art in any form, except, perhaps, for amusement. In New England, Puritan prejudice threw a damper on artistic ambitions. The descendants of the Pilgrim Fathers uttered loud cries of horror when the first nude Greek casts were brought to this country. Merely to look at them was a sin, to say nothing about trying to sculp such abominations! Besides, there were no sculptors in the country with whom one could study, marble had hardly been quarried, and the art of casting in bronze was unknown.

FROM SHIP'S FIGUREHEAD TO THE FATHER OF HIS COUNTRY

It is probable that when the famous Houdon came to Mount Vernon to "sculpt" Washington, and the news that his statue brought him $4,620 plus expenses leaked out, that practical American fathers looked with greater favor on an art which paid such returns. Even the stern Puritan conscience may have been softened. At any rate, sculpture begins to come into American life—by way of the sea! For William Rush (1765-1833), a founder of the Pennsylvania Academy of Fine Arts, did good work in wood-carving, and the ships of our Navy at that time were victorious with *figure-heads* of his providing: the *Genius of the United States* (Frigate "United States"), *Nature* (Constellation), *The Indian Trader* (*William Penn*), and others.

A nation, however, cannot produce sculptors out of hand. Horatio Greenough (1805-1852), even if we would not call him a great sculptor to-day, and his statue of George Washington (Capitol, Washington) gives him an "ancient Greek" look he probably never had, did much to bring the *spirit* and feeling for fine sculpture to his native land. The marble statue in his father's garden which start him out on his career led him to Rome, where he worked and studied with Thorwaldsen, Canova's pupil, drank in the artistic "atmosphere" of the Roman capital, and prepared himself to make sculpture *respected,* at least, when he went home again. He, as well as Joel T. Hart, S. V. Clevenger, and Clark Mills, all men of his own generation, did their bit in a modest way, and prepared the way for better native artists.

PUTTING OVER BEAUTY UNADORNED

Hiram Powers (1805-1873), from modelling wax figures for a dime museum, worked his way up to portrait busts, and made enough to go to Florence to study. His portrait busts (*Webster, Franklin, Clay*) are excellent likenesses. But though he had skill, and handled a cleverer chisel than Greenough, his art is what some call *gentle* and others *tame*. His graceful and pleasing *Greek Slave* (Rome, 1843), Thomas Crawford's (1814-1857) pleasing and graceful *Dancing Girl,* and William H. Rinehardt's (1825-1874) *Latona* helped to moderate the feeling against the antique, and to induce the national sense of propriety to let out a notch in its belt. Especially did Powers, *Eve Before the Fall,* show Americans that the nude could be devout and pure. The old feeling against the beauties of the undraped human figure began to yield (aided by the fact that copies and photographs of the great masterpieces of European sculpture, old and new, found their way into American homes).

THE FIRST AMERICAN EQUESTRIAN STATUE

Our first sculptured "man on horseback" was the work of Clark Mills (1815-1883), a New York country boy who, after a hard youth as lumberman, farm hand, millwright, and what not, reached a point where the city of Charlestown bought his bust of *John C. Calhoun*. The most famous among his many works (not all of them "inspired", by any means) is the *first equestrian statue in America,* a bronze General Jackson (Washington), fittingly cast of old British cannon the hero had captured in the battle of New Orleans. It brought the sculptor $12,000.

THE SCULPTORS OF THE NATIONAL PERIOD

The sculptors who follow these pioneers might be called the men of the "national period". Their work is able to stand on its own pedestals, and does credit to any country. It shows that in the Art of Sculpture a genuine *American* spirit, a real *race* feeling, an American manner and method of expression had developed. The sculptors of the United States knew and were proud of the fact that they were Americans.

One of the finest equestrian statues of Washington, the heroic mounted figure in Union Square, New York City, was the work of Henry Kirke Brown (1814-1886); while Thomas Ball (b. 1889), a Boston house-painter's son, did some vigorous "portrait" statues and groups: *Washington* (Public Gardens, Boston); *Daniel Webster* (Central Park, New York); *Emancipation Group* (Washington). Erastus Palmer (1817-1904) showed grace in his girl-figure, *The White Captive,* and an "ideal" relief, *Peace in Bondage,* while among his good portrait busts are: *Alexander Hamilton, Commodore Perry* and *Washington Irving.* J. Q. A. Ward (1830-1910), whose first model was an old negro on his father's Urbana, Ohio, farm, is best known by his *Indian Hunter* (Central Park), and his *Washington* (Wall Street, near Sub-Treasury), and Olin L. Warner (1844-1896), was the sculptor of a portrait statue of *William Lloyd Garrison,* some fine medallions, and the classic figures of the *Portland Fountain* (Oregon). Workers along classic lines are: Randolph Rogers (1825-1892), with *Blind Nydia;* William Wetmore Story (1819-1896), *Cleopatra, Lybian Sybil* and *Semiramis;* and *the first* American *woman sculptor,** Harriet Hosmer (1830-1908), with a very popular *Puck* and a reclining *Betrice de Cenci* to her credit. J. S. Hartley, George Bissell, Howard Roberts, Lant Thompson, John Rogers, and Martin Milmore are other American sculptors of note.

AUGUSTUS SAINT-GAUDENS

Augustus Saint-Gaudens (1848-1907), though there are great American sculptors who have "come up" since he died, is a name that still stands out in this country. Saint-Gaudens' father was a French shoemaker and the great American sculptor was born of an Irish mother in Dublin (on the first, not the seventeenth of March), and he was still a baby when his parents came to this country. After studying in New York he started to earn his living when only thirteen as a cameo cutter's apprentice, attending the night classes in drawing and modelling in Cooper Union and the Academy of Design. He went to Paris in 1867 where he was one of the sculptors of the great "express truth in Art as you see it; never mind tradition" group of men described in the preceding chapter. After two years' hard work at the Paris "School of Fine Arts," he spent three years

---

* American women have done notable work in sculpture. Besides Mrs. Potter Vonnoh and Mrs. Clio Hinten Bracken, who have done beautiful work in miniature figures and statuettes, are Miss Yandell; Mrs. Hermon A. McNeil; Miss Helen Mears; Miss Evelyn Longman; Mrs. Kitson and Mrs. Elsie Ward. In particular, there might be mentioned, Evelyn Beatrice Longman, bronze figure *Electricity* (Western Union Building, New York City); Anna Vaughn Hyatt, *Joan of Arc* (New York).

in Italy with his friend the French sculptor Mercié, studying and working, and it was in Rome that he executed his statues *Hiawatha* and *Silence*.

Saint-Gaudens had no trouble in "finding work" when he came back in 1874. In New York, where he settled, and in his studio in Cornish among the New Hampshire hills, he began to produce one great piece of sculpture after another, marrying in 1877. The first thing that called general attention to his work was the big relief he did for St. Thomas' Church, New York. Saint-Gaudens was equally great in "portrait" and in "ideal" work. In the first field he did a bust of *William M. Evarts,* the statesman and orator, and medallion portraits of *Robert Louis Stevenson,* the authors of "Treasure Island", (St. Giles, Edinburgh); the French painter *Bastien-Lepage, Garfield* (Garfield Memorial); *General Logan,* (Chicago); *Peter Cooper* (Peter Cooper Memorial, New York), who had founded the night-school in which Saint-Gaudens "learned his trade" and— *Charles Stewart Parnell* in Dublin.

His great portrait statues are five in number. There is the famous statue of *Admiral Farragut,* standing (Madison Square, New York) just as he did on the quarterdeck of his ship, on a fine pedestal by the architect Sanford White. There is his equestrian statue of *General Sherman* (1903), at Fifth Avenue and 59th Street, with a Victory striding on ahead of him. His *Lincoln* (Lincoln Park, Chicago) unveiled in 1903, is one of the finest Lincoln statues in the country. And in Springfield, Mass., stands his Deacon Chapin, known as *The Puritan*. Besides these there is his *Philip Brooks Memorial* (Boston) and the *Shaw Memorial* (1897).

No one who visits Boston fails to see this great bronze relief. It is eleven by fifteen feet, and shows Robert G. Shaw, the young colonel of a negro regiment in the Civil War on horseback, leading on his men, while a female figure points upward to the clouds.

In the "ideal" field Saint-Gaudens' greatest work was one single, beautiful figure, for the *Mrs. Henry Adams Memorial* (Rock Creek Cemetery, Washington, D.C.). People call it *Death,* and *Grief,* and the *Peace of God*. But it is the combination of the two last titles which really expresses its beauty best. It is *Grief*—a woman grieving, and her grief is so simple, natural and touching that it moves the heart and yet, at the same time, we see that *The Peace of God* is there to console. And, as a contrast to this spiritual carving, we have the joyous, happy Diana,* known to every New Yorker, on the tower of Madison Square Garden.

All that Saint-Gaudens did, revealed beauty in one shape or an-

* Her namesake, Olin Warner's statue, and his *Venus and Cupid* relief, are ranked among the purest and loveliest nudes American sculpture has produced.

other, of heart, mind or soul, and his right to be considered our greatest sculptor is generally admitted.

FRENCH AND MACMONNIES

Daniel Chester French (b. 1850), and Frederick MacMonnies (b. 1863), the latter a Saint-Gaudens' pupil, are two other great names which stand out in American sculpture.

French, from carving turnips as a boy, reached his best-known statue in *The Minute Man* (Concord, Mass.), unveiled on the centenary of the battle of Concord (April 19, 1875). Among many other fine works *The Minute Man*, with the plough he has just left to seize his gun; the beautiful *Death Staying the Hand of the Sculptor* (a memorial for the young sculptor, Milmore's, tomb, in Forest Hills, Boston); and the colossal *Statue of the Republic* (Columbian Exposition), are the most famous.*

MacMonnies from a clerk in a Brooklyn jewelry store, also rose to a great patriotic inspiration in statuary, his *Nathan Hale* (City Hall Park, New York). MacMonnies has told the idea in the back of his head in carving this great figure of the martyr for Liberty's cause, his hands bound, about to be led off to be shot. "I wanted to do something that would make the newsboys and bootblacks around the Park *think* . . . something that would make them want to do something fine in life!" Among his other works** none, perhaps, has attracted more attention than the wonderful *Bacchante* (Metropolitan Museum of Art, New York). It is a mad, glowing nude figure, full of the "joy of life", combining realism and imagination to a wonderful degree. In Boston the "joy of life" always has been regarded with a certain amount of suspicion, and the Boston Public Library for which it has been done, was *shocked* by the *Bacchante* and rejected her. But New York's more liberal Metropolitan Art Museum welcomed the splendid art work with open arms.

ANIMALS, THE WILD WEST AND AMERICAN INDIANS IN SCULPTURE

Quite a group of American sculptors have devoted themselves to

---

* His portrait statues include: *Dr. Gallaudet and his First Deaf-Mute Pupil* (Washington), *General Grant* (Fairmount Park, Phila.), *General Joseph Hooker* (Boston), the *Washington* he modelled together with Edward C. Potter, presented to France by the Daughters of the American Revolution, and many more.

** A noble *Diana*, which shows the influence of his splendid French training, Columbian Fountain (Chicago World's Fair), the three great bronze groups of American soldiers and sailors that decorate the *Soldiers and Sailors Memorial Arch* (Prospect Park, Brooklyn) and—many fine *paintings* are among MacMonnies works.

"animals". Paul Wayland Bartlett (b.1865), who studied animal modelling under Frémiet in Paris, did many beautiful *patinas* (green coated bronzes) of reptiles, fish and insects, and two wonderful statues: *The Bear Tamer* (Met. Museum, New York), and the *Dying Lion* (Penna. Academy, Phila.). MacMonnies, too, has a fine *The Horse Tamers* (Prospect Park, Brooklyn), T. Massey Rhind, a *Bohemian,* (Metropolitan Museum, New York), showing a man trailing a bear; and among other animalarians are: the fine Southern sculptor Edward Kemys, who has also done Indians, Phimister Proctor, Frederick Roth and Edward C. Potter.

The "Wild West" of the Indians and the cowboys has given "a square deal" in bronze and marble by: Frederick Remington (1861-1909), who was "with the army" on the Western Plains, and made a specialty of statuettes of the U. S. Regular and Western Indian, the Cowboy and Trapper as they lived and were. These statuettes are brimful of life and character, though Remington is better known by his Western life paintings.

Solon Borglum (b. 1868, in Utah) is another, who as a "wild cowboy" on his father's ranch learned to know Western life from A to Z. He has caught and held the romance of the "vanishing frontier" in vivid original works, whose thrill even the old Westerner feels. His great groups and statues are: *Lassoing Wild Horses, Stampeding Wild Horses, The Last Round-Up, The Lame Horse, On the Border of White Man's Land* and *Burial on the Plains.* His best military statue perhaps, is *Captain Buckley O'Neill* (Prescott, Arizona). The soldier is reining in his spirited horse and leaning forward in his saddle. It is a thoroughly natural statue (or in "art lingo" *naturalistic*).

The American Indian has been given special attention in a number of statues. There is P. W. Bartlett's *The Ghost Dancer,* (Penna. Academy, Phila.) Hermon Macneil Atkins' *The Moqui Runner, A Primitive Chant,* and the *Sun Vow.* Cyrus Edwin Dallin, though he has done other fine things *(Pioneer Monument),* is also best known as a sculptor of the North American Indian, and his superb horseback statue *The Appeal to the Great Spirit, The Signal of Peace* (Lincoln Park, Chicago), and *The Medicine Man* (Fairmount Park) are famous.

THE MAN WHO TURNED A MOUNTAIN INTO A MONUMENT

Gutzon Borglum, (a brother of the "Wild West" sculptor), is probably the leading representative of the heroic, the colossal, and the superbly grand in American sculpture to-day. But he combines with heroic size the most intimate picturing of the *soul*. His colossal *Head of Lincoln* (Capitol, Washington), makes any one who sees it realize all the sadness with which the strife of brothers weighed down the noblest of his kind. His *Twelve Apostles* (Cathedral of St. John the Divine, New York) are the true expression of *simple grandeur of spirit*. Among his many works the most stupendous is the great *Memorial to the Horses of the Southern Confederacy*. Begun in 1916, it is a conception worthy of a Rodin or a Michel Angelo, for the sculptor had taken a *mountain*, Stone Mountain, Georgia, and on its face carved in relief the great Southern heroes, chief among them General Robert E. Lee, on a vast scale of feet and yards instead of inches, though they seem only life-size to the eye, seen from below. No Egyptian colossus, no Persian rock-sculptures compare with this magnificent monument American genius has raised to Southern heroism!

THE SCULPTURE OF AMERICAN PATRIOTISM

In no field has there been finer or greater work done than in this. Great men identified with our glorious past are without number, and fully represented: Paul Wayland Bartlett: *Equestrian Statue of General Lafayette* (Place du Carrousel, Paris), presented to France by American school-children; *Columbus* (Congressional Library); Charles Henry Niehaus: *President Garfield* (Cincinnati); *James A. Garfield* (Capitol); *Hooker, Davenport* (State House, Hartford, Conn.); *General Forrest* (Memphis, Tenn.) *Lincoln, Farragut* (Muskegon, Mich.); *McKinley* (Canton, Ohio); George Gray Barnard: *Lincoln* (Cincinnati); Daniel Chester French: *Lafayette* (Brooklyn); John Paulding, *General J. B. McPherson* (McPherson, Kansas); J. Massey Rhind, *President McKinley* (Niles, Ohio); William Orday Partridge, *Thomas Jefferson* (Columbia University, N. Y.); John J. Boyle, *Commodore John Barry* (Washington); Karl Bitter, *Signing of the Louisiana Purchase Treaty, Jefferson Memorial* (St. Louis, Mo.); Francis Herman Packer, *General Nathaniel Green* (Greensboro, N. C.); J. Massey Rhind, *General Webb* (Gettysburg). In Richmond, Va., is a whole galaxy of Southerners: the English sculptor Foley's bronze *Stonewall Jackson;* the Frenchman Mercié's *General Robert E. Lee;* Frederick Monyhan's *General J. E. B. Stuart;* E. V. Valentine's *Jefferson Davis;* Joel T. Hart's marble *Henry Clay*, and Thomas Crawford's equestrian statue of *Washington*, surmounting the great *Washington Monument* in Capitol Square. These statues are only a few among many others.

Patriotism in its more "ideal" and less "personal" form also has been largely represented by works like MacMonnies' *The Pioneer*, (Denver, Col.); Edward C. Potter's *Mounted Bugler* (Soldiers' Monument, Brookline, Mass.); the "temporary" *Victory Arch* (Madison Square, N. Y.) that welcomed the 27th Division back to its home town at the end of the Great War; Andrew O'Connor's *Boy Scouts of America* (Glen View, Chicago), a Theodore Roosevelt Memorial, and the same sculptor's fine *Patriotism* (Duluth, Mich.); and Raymond Averill Porter, *The Green Mountain Boy* (Rutland, Vt.)

SCULPTURE THAT HONORS LABOR AND DEMOCRACY

It is not strange that the United States, like France, should have produced some fine sculpture that honors the workingman and democratic ideals. Much of it has taken shape as carved relief work on great buildings, yet there stand out works like: Douglas Tilden's *Mechanics Fountain* (San Francisco); C. H. Niehaus, *The Driller* (Titusville, Pa.) in honor of Col. E. L. Drake, who sunk the first oil-well in Pennsylvania in 1850; Gutzon Borglum's *Governor John P. Altgeld* (Chicago, Ill.), and Myra Reynolds Richards, *James Whitcomb Riley* (Greenfield, Ind.), the statue of the "Hoosier" poet who sang the simple life of the American countryside, the life of the farmer, in immortal verse.

THE "IDEAL" SUBJECT IN AMERICAN SCULPTURE

The American sculptor has created great works of art in this field. A few might be mentioned: Daniel Chester French's *Memory*, a seated female figure, one of the most beautiful of American nudes (Met. Museum, New York), and his *Mourning Victory, Melvin Memorial* (Sleepy Hollow Cemetery, Concord); MacMonnies' *Indian Corn;* George Gray Barnards's marble group, *The Two Natures of Man* (Met. Museum, New York), which shows our higher nature rising triumphantly and spurning with its foot our *lower* nature, lying defeated on the ground. It is a noble presentation of how our higher self *ought* to overcome our lower one. *Brotherly Love* and *The Hewers* are two other great "ideal" statues by this sculptor. Among these statues might also be placed J. Massey Rhind's *reproduction* in bronze of Verrochio's famous *Colleoni* (Newark, N. J.); Bela Lyon Pratt (d. 1917), symbolic figures of *Science* and *Art* (Boston Public Library); Edmond A Stewartson, *The Bather;* and some of the great sculptured fountains: Roland H. Perry, *Fountain of Neptune*, Charles Grafly, *Fountain of Life,* and Lorado Taft, *Fountain of Time* (New York).

THE ROMANCE OF PAINTING

CHAPTER I

(Introduction)

FROM THE FIRST PICTURE TO THE GOTHIC AGE

The very first "picture" in the world was one that *could* be seen—and at the same time *could not* be seen. Some savage, primitive man, in order to give a companion an idea, a *picture* of what was in his mind, drew an outline with his finger in the air—the first painting! Next, the outline was drawn in the ground with a pointed stick. Then it moved to the stone wall of the caveman's cave, traced in with a flint-stone. And then—came color. What was the first color used? Probably *red*—the bright, exciting *blood-color* (we know that primitive man often stripped flesh from the skeletons of his dead, and rubbed the bones with red ochre or red clay to decorate them, just as he smeared his own living body). He began to fill in his "outlines" on the cave wall with colors—red, green, brown and others. In the Altamira Caverns, near Santander in Spain, are wall-paintings 50,000 years old, painted in *three colors,* and we can still look at a great bison bull of that day, with his winter coat of hair showing *black,* and *red* patches where, with spring coming on, he had *rubbed away* some of his *black* winter coat. So true to nature were those painters of 50,000 years ago!

Next (after pottery had been invented) man "painted" picture-patterns and figures on his clay jars and then, with the first empires of civilization, we find colors used to decorate the stone bas-reliefs, stucco-coated, or the thin coats of plaster in Egyptian palace and temple walls. But this really was *coloring* stone carvings. "Paintings", however, were also put together of "mosaics", individual colored baked tiles, yellow, black, blue, and green in Assyrian, Babylonian and Persian palaces. But all this early oriental art is still not "painting" as we understand it.

The Hindoos, too, used painting to decorate walls with processions, battle and hunting scenes, like Egyptians and Assyrians, and when Buddha became a god his picture was painted on walls in all sorts of gay colors: red, blue, white and brown. The Chinese have done beautiful paintings on silk instead of canvas, and like the Japanese who also paint in water-colors on silk or paper, they do not put up their paintings on the wall to hang there year in year out. A fine painting to a Chinaman or a Japanese is a rare and costly, almost a sacred thing. It usually is rolled up on a rod, and is brought out on special occasion to be hung on the wall or from a screen, and each and every one of its beauties is studied and enjoyed at leisure. For the Oriental does not believe in enjoying beauty in a hurry as we do. He takes his time. Hokusai has the reputation of being the greatest of later Japanese painters and his paintings on silk are famous for showing Japanese life as it is.

There never was any painting among the Jews of the Bible (except such personal painting as Queen Jezebel did—we still hear the expression "a painted Jezebel") because their religion forbade them to practice *painting* and *sculpture*.

THE PAINTERS OF ANCIENT GREECE

The Greeks painted their vases and—something that sculptors, with a few exceptions have given up—they painted the draperies of their *statues,* and gilded their hair. Besides this they also painted the walls of their temples and private houses with frescoes. The first great Greek painter lived at the time of the famous sculptor Pheidias, in the middle of the 5th century B.C., and his name was Polygnotus.

An Athenian, Polygnotus was famous in his day as a painter. But what he really did was to "color" reliefs on walls, using only a few simple colors. For he lived before *perspective*—showing people and things in painting as they really look to the eye—and before light and shade had been discovered, though he did draw beautiful figures. His most famous works were great frescos, wall paintings, in a building at Delphi. People came from all over to see them. They showed Odysseus' adventures in the lower world, and the taking of Troy Town.

ZEUXIS

Zeuxis (420-390 B.C.) of Heraclea, we know more about. Not one of his paintings has come down to us, but we have some stories of what he could do. He painted a boy holding a bunch of grapes, and the birds flew to peck at them. But, the Roman author Pliny, who tells the story, can't help adding that if the boy had been painted as well as the grapes, the birds would not have come near them! Yet they must have been great painters in those days, for Parrhasius painted a curtain that looked so real that even Zeuxis tried to raise it by mistake. Zeuxis is famous for having painted a wonderful picture—the first of which we know—of lovely *Helen of Troy*, "making up" his Helen out of five beautiful young girls of Croton, who were his models. What ever was best about each of the five he put into his Helen. This picture was exhibited, and admission charged and from this source of revenue and the high prices his paintings generally brought, Zeuxis grew so rich he could afford to make presents of his pictures to kings and other great folk, instead of selling them. And when he turned up at Olympus to enjoy the Games, his robes were embroidered all over with his name in golden letters.

Of Parrhasius, already mentioned, the story is told that the grapes at which the birds pecked was Zeuxis' picture in a competition between the two, while the curtain that Zeuxis tried to raise (he thought it hung before Parrhasius' picture), was the latter's picture itself. So Zeuxis has to admit himself beaten. Of Parrhasius' many pictures none have come down, and this may be a good thing, for history says he spent his spare time painting obscene subjects, something unworthy of a great painter's art.

APELLES

Of all the painters of antiquity, Apelles was probably the greatest. Both he and his friend the Rhodian painter Protogenes lived in the days of Alexander the Great, whose court painter Apelles was. Apelles is thought not to have used many colors but to have excelled in the *line* and *curve* beauty of his figures and their charm of expression. Of all the many wonderful paintings he is supposed to have done, and do not survive, two may be regretted especially: one the picture of *Alexander* in which the *hand* fairly *stood out* from the canvas; the other his *Aphrodite Rising from the Sea*. Both Apelles and Protogenes laid great value on beauty of outline. Protogenes took his time painting, some of his pictures costing him seven years of labor to finish. During the whole time that King Demetrius of Syria was beseiging Rhodes (305-304 B. C.) he was busy painting a "Satyr", though the enemy had camped all around the garden outside the walls in which he painted. But King Demetrius saw to it that he was not disturbed. When Protogenes had finished his "Satyr" the Satyr was leaning idly against a column, and on the column was a partridge—the partridge was so *natural*, that no one even thought of the rest of the picture. "If you go a step nearer he'll fly away! Did you ever see a partridge look more like life itself! I don't believe it is painted!" was all the crowds said that surrounded the picture. And gradually, little by little, Protogenes grew very angry. He had put his very best brush work into the "Satyr" and—no one even gave him a glance; Protogenes began to dislike his partridge more

THE ROMANCE OF PAINTING

and more. At last, one fine day, he grew so disgusted with the bird, that while the usual crowd was gaping around it and talking about its "naturalness", he came along with a brush, swept the painting with one stroke—and the partridge was gone, "Yes, he was so natural, he just spread his wings and flew away!" he told the astonished crowd as he left. Apelles admired Protogenes greatly, and one of the finest things he did, which shows his noble nature, was to raise the market value of Protogenes' paintings by spreading the report that he meant to buy them from him and sell them as his own. A curious survival of Apelles' *time* are real *portraits* painted on mummy-cases, found near Kerki (Fayoum) in Egypt. They are by Greek artists of the period, and it is strange to think that we now know just how these dead and gone Grecian Egyptians of Alexander's day looked, for the mummy cases have survived the mummies.

ROMAN PAINTING

The Etruscans, who lived in Italy before the Romans, decorated the walls of their tombs with colored outline sketches, and the Romans themselves covered the walls of their houses with frescoes. We have historical, landscape, mythological and decorative figure-work preserved in all its freshness beneath the ashes of Pompeii and Herculaneum, the Roman cities Vesuvius buried. Three are famous: *The Aldobrandini Marriage,* discovered 1606 (named after its first owner, a Roman cardinal). It is a Pompeiian wedding scene. The veiled bride sits on a nuptial couch, the bridegroom at her right. On one side women are preparing a sacrifice, on the other a bath. The *Odyssey Landscapes* are frescoes (discovered 1848) showing Odysseus in the nether world; and the "Battle of Issus" pictures Alexander's victory over the Persian king Darius. This last picture is a mosaic. The next Roman paintings we find are on the walls and ceilings of the Catacombs. Christ is represented in these pictures by "sign" figures, such as a lamb or a fish, or as Orpheus. And the tale of Jonah and the Whale is painted as a "symbol" of the Resurrection. Byzantine painting is mostly mosaic, with figures of Madonnas, saints, prophets and angels against a background of fine, pure blue or bright gold, a magnificent kind of painting in colored marble, stone and glass. But all this *painting* was *less human* than that of the *Greek* or *Romans.* It was only religious—much of it beautiful and dignified, but allowing no chance for gayety or humor. Yet strange to say, a quarrel within the Byzantine Church itself led (for a time) to the substitution of the most gay, human, and non-religious scenes on church walls. Certain Greek emperors (they are called iconoclasts—"image-breakers") took the part of one group of the Byzantine clergy which said that all these sacred figures led to *image worship* and was wrong. Like all questions of religion in the old days, this immediately led to all kinds of bloodshed. There were floggings, blindings, beheadings and murderings; there were great riots in Constantinople among those who thought it better for any amount of fellow-Christian blood to flow, rather than have Christ and the Saints shown "on painted walls", and those who felt that the best thing for the people who objected to holy images and *ikons* (small metal placques on which the Madonna, Christ or the saints were painted) should be killed outright. Leo the Isaurian (726) ordered the "holy and venerable images" in the churches to be overthrown. And—the *women* in one city, Chalce, objected so that they killed an official who had destroyed an image of Christ in the imperial palace there. This led to a riot in which a number of persons were killed and wounded. These were the pleasant things which happened in the old days, when there was no religious toleration, and when men were ready to cut each other's throats for a matter of religious opinion. So, in Constantinople, when the Greek *iconoclast* emperors were in power, instead of images of saints, the walls were covered with gay pictures of hunting scenes, and of men picking fruit in pleasant gardens with birds singing in the branches of the trees. Then an emperor who *believed in images* would seat himself on the throne (usually murdering his predecessor to do so), and out would go all the merry hunting scenes, and in would come the saints again! The only other Byzantine painting which we know is the *painting in books.* There is a great *Natural History* by Greek Dioscorides (Vatican), who lived about 500 A.D., which contains a beautifully drawn series of plants, delicacy colored in pink and blue.

MOHAMMEDAN PAINTING

We usually take for granted that, like the Jews, the Mohammedans were forbidden to practice the arts of painting and sculpture. But the Arab priests did not forbid showing the human figure, birds and animals in painting and sculpture until the ninth century. Before that time they covered the walls of their mosques with mosaic paintings, showing scenes from the life of Mohammed and the prophets. And the Moors in Spain (with their lion fountain in the Alhambra), did not take the law against animals in sculpture or painting too seriously. One thing the Mohammedan artists did was to add to their arabesques—their geometric figures, and scrolled and curved lines—fantastic beasts of fancy, which never existed save in their imagination, to supply the place of real ones. And the Persian Mohammedans, in older times, paid hardly any attention to the law *against the human figure in painting at all.* In museums we find the most beautiful Persian miniatures, painted in various colors.

THE ROMANCE OF PAINTING

These miniature paintings were the delight of Persian Mohammedan shahs and princes, and they lavished gold on the great painters who created these pictures. One charming miniature (British Museum) has a special interest because it gives us the Persian version of the story of *Joseph and Madame Potiphar*.

According to the Persian Mohammedan tradition, when Joseph dropped his mantle he did not do so to run away from Madame Potiphar. But the Egyptian lady's aristocratic friends all shook their heads, and blamed her for falling in love with a mere Hebrew slave. In fact, they said so much that Potiphar's wife made up her mind she would prove she was excusable. She invited all her friends to a little afternoon affair and, when they were all seated on cushions, and each one with a citron in her hand, about to peel the fruit, a certain curtain was drawn. There stood Joseph! And Joseph was so exceedingly handsome that every one of the ladies present, *without a single exception,* and at the selfsame moment, cut her finger instead of the citron with the fruit-knife! And after that Madame Potiphar was no longer blamed for having lost her heart to the Hebrew slave. And—in the Persian miniature in question, which shows the scene—*there is a tiny drop of blood on each little white finger* to prove the story true!

Painting in Mohammedan Art is mainly expressed in one direction, architecturally: in connection with mosque and palace, and in one way, color. The great charm of Mohammedan architecture, in fact, lies in the glory of the many colors which are poured out over it with the most lavish extravagance, so that all its surfaces glimmer, shine and radiate with a wealth of gold, crimson, blue, green, rose and purple, like the richest of oriental rugs. But this glory of color painting in Mohammedan architecture reached its climax in the Persian mosques and palaces, the Indian Mohammedan palaces, and the glorious Moorish Alhambra (See "The Romance of Architecture", Chapter X), and then rapidly decayed.

CHAPTER II

GREAT PAINTERS AND PAINTINGS OF THE GOTHIC AGE

IN the Gothic Age we pass from the "mosaic" paintings of the Romanesque and Byzantine churches to the more human religious wall-paintings of the Gothic cathedrals. They are for the most part, only outlines, "filled in" with flat tints, and there is no attempt at perspective nor "modelling"—rounding out of figures—either in the saints and prophets on the church walls, or the figures in the worldly scenes painted on the walls of Gothic castle halls. But the colors were bright and pure, and the pictures often pleasing to the eye. Besides wall paintings, wooden panel painting, and (especially in Germany) painting wooden figures of the saints with colors was cultivated. In Italy painted and gilded wooden panels and great carven chests, painted with all sorts of scenes from mythology or actual life were common. Yet in the great Gothic cathedrals there was but little wall-space, so instead of doing their painting on the walls, the church artists let their light shine before men in the beautiful "pictures" they made in *stained glass* where the sun, shining through the glowing panes, gave them that glory, beauty and softness which still moves the heart in our churches to-day.

CIMABUE AND GIOTTO DI BONDONE: THE FIRST GREAT PAINTERS

Florence and Siena were the two great painting centres in Italy during the Gothic Age. The Italian painters painted great "panel pictures", "in tempera"* on the white plaster walls of churches, in books ("illustrated missals", etc.) Most of these paintings have disappeared. Niccola Pisano (better known as a sculptor), and the Roman Cavallini (1923), painted a fine *Last Judgment*, recently uncovered in the Church of St. Cecilia in Rome, and Florence and Siena respectively produced the two great Italian painters of the Gothic Age.

* "In tempera" simply means that against a gold background they painted their pictures in water-colors mixed with white of egg and other substances to "bind" them, and prevent the colors from flaking off when they dried. When they painted on *dry plaster* their painting was called *in secco* (dry) painting; when they painted on *damp plaster,* it was known as *fresco* (damp or fresh) painting.

THE ROMANCE OF PAINTING

CIMABUE AND GIOTTO DI BONDONE

Giovanni Cimabue (1276-1337), the head of this early "Florentine School", is often called *the first great painter*. Cimabue's saints—especially the great St. Francis, who founded the order of begging monks known as the Franciscans, and whom the painter knew personally and loved—*are human,* and not stiff and lifeless like those of Byzantine mosaics. Cimabue painted St. Francis just as he was, going about Italy doing his "miracles" in a kindly, human way, and we may still see his paintings *The Infant Christ Appearnig to St. Francis on Christmas Eve and St. Francis Defending the Rules of His Order* (Florence Museum). Among the people of his time Cimabue had a great reputation. His greatest painting, done *in tempera* is the colossal *Madonna and Child* (Rucellai Chapel, St. Maria Novella, Florence). Charles of Anjou, the bloody King of Sicily, one of the most cruel monarchs of his time, came to see the great work in the painter's studio, before it was removed to the church, and tears of emotion came into his eyes when he looked at it. The Virgin, in red tunic and blue mantle, sits in a chair hung with drapery flowered with gold and blue. The Infant Saviour, in a white tunic and purple, gold-shot mantle, is in her lap. Her face is tender and melancholy. With the king came all the great folk of Florence to see the picture, and it was then carried to the church in a great procession of the people with trumpets blowing and drums beating.

Cimabue's fame, however, is overshadowed by that of his pupil Giotto di Bondone. Giotto di Bondone (1267-1337), was an even greater "humanizer" in painting than his teacher. A little goat-herd, he was grazing his goats one day on the grassy slopes of the Apennines when Cimabue, riding over the hills found him—like a cave-boy of primitive days—drawing the outline of a goat on a rock with a sharp stone and took him home with him. There he soon called attention to himself: Cimabue tried to brush off the fly he painted on a picture! For the pope's envoy (who had been sent to inquire about his marvelous skill), he dipped a pencil in red ink and with a single "free-hand" movement drew so perfect an *O,* that the Roman could not get over his astonishment. He painted great frescoes in Florence, Padua, Rome (where he enjoyed the favor of Pope Boniface), and Naples. Busy his life long, he still found time to marry and raise a brood of children as small and homely as himself, for his homeliness was a joke among his friends. He had a merry wit and once, when a drove of pigs came rushing along the road and upset him, he said as he got up and brushed off his clothes: "I can't blame them when I think how many thousands of their bristles I have used without even giving them a pail of slops!" His wit could take a sarcastic turn, too. Like other artists of his time he could use the pen as well as the brush. His poem "Voluntary Poverty" not only denounced the vice and hypocrisy often found beneath the monk's cowl, but honestly admitted that he *could not see that poverty was a virtue*—something many artists who pretend to despise money are hypocrites about, to this day! Coming from the chosen painter of the monastic order of St. Francis, it shows what an independent sort of man Giotto was.

Giotto's last great work was the design for the *Campanile*, the great tower of Florence. Giotto's greatest merit lay in his close imitation of nature, and in his pure, well-tempered colors. He always painted human faces *as* human faces, so some of his saints and angels look a bit vulgar. On the other hand, this makes them appear only the more real. Other fresco works are the *Death of St. Francis* (Bardi Chapel, Santa Croce Church, Florence), which shows the soul of St. Francis borne to heaven on angel wings, while his monks weep around his body; the *Nativity, Entombment and Resurrection* (Arena Chapel, Padua), *Herod's Feast* (Santa Croce Church, Florence), Salome stopping her dance while a soldier offers King Herod, John the Baptist's head; and *The Birth of St. John the Baptist* (Santa Croce Church, Florence).

There are four great allegorical frescoes—frescoes that tell something in an indirect way, using figures or signs to explain their meaning (St. Francis' Church, Assissi).

Allegory of Poverty. St. Francis is marrying Poverty, a bride with patched and torn clothes. Children throw stones and dogs bark at her, but the roses and lilies of paradise bloom round her, and St. Francis looks on her with divine love. Above the wedded pair, two angels are handing to the Almighty a bag of gold, a garment and a miniature palace—worldly goods the bridegroom is giving up.

The other frescoes are: *St. Francis Enthroned in Glory,* an *Allegory of Charity* and an *Allegory of Obedience.*

FRA ANGELICO

Among the painters of the "Sienese School", Simone Martini (he has been called the "Sienese Giotto"), whose most famous picture is a great fresco of the *Madonna Enthroned* (Public Palace, Siena), with his followers Taddeo di Bartoli and Ambrogio Lorenzetti (middle of 14th century) are the most noted. Ambrogio Lorenzetti is thought to be the painter of several great allegorical frescoes on the walls of the cloister court of Campo Santo, the old public burial ground of Siena. They include a *History of Job, The Triumph of the Hermits in the Thebiad* and *The Last Judgment.* But the greatest is:

The Triumph of Death: It shows a procession of high-born

knights who have suddenly run across a corpse in the road. One knight holds his nose in disgust, another is turning his horse, and the third is evidently making some low and ribald jest at the corpse's expense. In the picture's middle ground some wretched beggars are imploring Death—a winged female figure. (It seems strange that this old painter should have anticipated Kipling and made "the female of the species more deadly than the male" at so early a date!) She is mowing down with her scythe a happy pair of lovers sitting with friends beneath a tree. In the air above, angels and devils fight for the souls of the dead, while some old monks stand about busy with one thing and another.

The "Holy Brother Giovanni Angelico of Fiesole" (1387-1455), is a Renaissance painter in *point of time* only. In his *style* of painting, his *choice of subject,* and in every other way he is a painter of the Gothic Age which went before the Renaissance. "Friar John", was a Dominican monk with a marvelous gift for the brush. He seems to have come as near to sainthood on earth as a man could and still continue to live. "He shunned the worldly in all things, and during his pure and simple life was such a friend to the poor that I think his soul must now be in heaven", wrote a great historian of painting of him. Fra Angelico's one idea was in his paintings to lead the thoughts of the brethren—all too apt to stray—to heavenly things. He never was idle, no one ever saw him angered. He painted only *sacred* subjects. He always muttered a prayer when he took up his brush, and the tears never failed to stream from his eyes when he painted a Crucifixion. The faces of most of his saints are pure and lovely, though sometimes *so* pure that they are quite sexless and dehumanized, and seem sleek, prim and smirking. The angels in his *Last Judgment* have been called "celestial dolls, thin as paper and stuck fast to their gold background". And—Fra Angelico was only at home with saints, angels, prophets, evangelists, the Saviour and Madonna. Knowing what wickedness was only by *heresay,* he found it hard to paint it. No painter since Fra Angelico has reached the spiritual plane, either in his life or in his work, that he did. When Pope Nicholas V invited him to breakfast (a meat breakfast) he excused himself, though the pope was ready to grant him a dispensation on the spot, because the prior of his monastery had not given him permission.

Fra Angelico lived in a world of his own, outside the world of flesh and blood around him. He could not paint simple, vigorous peasant girls full of animal life, such as Raphael's celestial virgins are. He was a monk *for whom the nude body did not exist* (monks were forbidden to study it), and so he "sprinkled holy water in the face of the antique" as one critic has said. In the innocent, dreamy atmosphere of his convent enclosure, while prayer sang in his soul, he painted "mystic gardens" not of this world, where ransomed souls embraced. He painted angels dancing "on the lawns outside the city of the Lamb", lawns "never trodden by the foot of man in any paradise on earth". His most famous paintings are:

The Coronation of the Virgin (Louvre, Paris). Christ on a throne of colored marbles holds a rich crown above the kneeling Virgin's head. Around them angels play musical instruments in a glory of heavenly light, while on both sides of the throne are apostles, bishops and founders of monastic orders, with a group of female saints—visible souls rather than bodies—in chaste draperies of rose, white and blue.

Dance of the Angels in the Last Judgment (Florence Academy). While devils push the damned into the hell below, Christ thrones surrounded by saints and seraphim and watches the angels dance on a flowery meadow in robes glistening with golden stars, and with forms that have no earthly taint.

Madonna dei Linajuoli (Uffizi Gallery, Florence). The most popular best-known of Fra Angelico's works. The art-lover and critic who knows, looks with scorn on the twelve "doll" angels along the border of the central panel of the altar-piece. And yet—the majority of people who see these graceful angels playing musical instruments like them. The greatest of his frescoes, *The Crucifixion* (San Marco Convent, Florence) the smaller *Annunciation* (San Marco Convent, Florence), as well as the wonderful *Scenes from the Life of St. Laurence* (Nicholas V Chapel, Vatican, Rome) are considered his finest work—though he painted them at the age of sixty. But they yield in *human* interest to a little panel fifteen inches square:

The Flight into Egypt (Florence Academy) is in Giotto's style. The Virgin, wrapped in a long blue mantle, rides an ass, clasping the Child tenderly in her arms, while St. Joseph, in a yellow tunic, trudges on behind. The faces are simple and sweet, and the feet of the holy personages tread a ground grown with wild flowers.

ALBRECHT DURER AND THE HOLBEINS

Gothic in spirit, though in point of time falling within the Renaissance are the great German artists, Albrecht Dürer (1471-1528), and the Holbeins, Hans, the elder (1460-1524) and Hans the younger (1497-1543).

Albrecht Dürer was one of a family of eighteen. He learned to be a goldsmith, spent three years as a "wandering journeyman", saw Venice and returned to marry a pretty girl of Nuremburg, Agnes Frey,* and begin to turn out his great woodcuts and other works.

* How careful we must be about accepting the opinion of a man's

Dürer's greatest works were his famous *woodcuts.* Among them is his fantastic *Four Horsemen of the Apocalypse* (1498) which has inspired a modern novel by the Spanish author Ibanez, and been turned into a spectacular motion picture. The simple grandeur of its design has never been surpassed. *The Knight, Death and the Devil* (1513), *The Virgin, Child and Monkey,* the last-named symbolizing the devil (1500), and *The Repose in Egypt* (1511), a pretty detail of which is the crowd of little angels picking up and carrying off the chips that fly as Child Jesus plays at being a carpenter with an axe and a bit of wood. Nor should the celebrated *Melancholia* (1515) a sombre woman with a great wolf-hound at her feet, the *Passion on Wood* (1511), and the *Passion on Copper* (1512) be forgotten. But Dürer painted as well. His best known paintings are:

The Feast of Rose Garlands or "Adoration of the Virgin", (Strahow Monastery, Prague). Dürer painted it in Venice to show that he could *paint* as well as *engrave,* but—the Venetians still claimed, and were right, that he was a greater engraver than painter. In Germany they thought more of the picture, for in later years the Austrian Emperor Rudolph bought it and had it carried all the way to Vienna on men's shoulders for safety's sake. It shows—a Gothic idea—pope and emperor kneeling to left and right of the Virgin and Child enthroned.

The Virgin with the Goldfinch (Berlin), *Christ Disputing with the Doctors* (Barberini Gallery, Rome,) yield in value to the *Adam and Eve* (Madrid), the life-size *Virgin with the Iris* (Richmond), and a great, crowded canvas *The Massacre of the Ten Thousand Virgins of Nicomedia* (Vienna). The *Madonna with the Pink* (Augsburg), and two noble pairs of saints, *St. John with Saint Peter* and *Saint Paul with Saint Mark*—on altar panels—these last regarded as among the finest examples of early German painting—complete the tale of his more important works.

The older Hans Holbein did a few good "portrait" paintings, and some excellent saints, but ends his life under circumstances that seem to throw a cloud over him. He does not pay his taxes in Augsburg, and his brothers and others sue him for debt, which looks very much as though he had formed the bad habit of never paying his bills!

friends regarding his wife is shown in Dürer's case. For centuries poor Agnes had been put down by art historians as being the worst kind of a nagger, and suspected of worrying Albrecht into his grave. All because Albrecht's friend, Willibald Pirkheimer wrote in a letter which had come down through the ages, that "he himself would have preferred to Agnes . . . A *light* woman who behaved in a friendly way, instead of a nagging, suspicious, scolding, *pious* woman." Recently these charges have all been proved false. But for centuries poor Agnes has been despised because Willibald Pirkheimer did not like her. We do know, however, that Agnes was thrifty, and had a peep-hole in the floor over her husband's studio and would start rapping whenever he stopped work.

When he slinks off out of life, and his son claims his paints and brushes from the monks of Issenheim (for whom he was to do an altar piece) they said they themselves had not been paid for them and refused to give them up.

Hans the Younger was a far greater artist than his father. Though born in Augsburg he made Masel, Switzerland, his headquarters, married a widow there, and painted the walls of the Basel Town Hall with historical frescoes. He painted many great pictures but only his drawings, woodcuts—including the famous *Dance of Death*—as well as designs for stained glass windows, have come down to us. Many of the great paintings he painted have not come down to us. In 1537 Holbein went to England, settled in London, and from that time on was in touch with all the great of the land. Bluff King Hal had him paint a family picture of himself, his father and his son, and gave it a place of honor in Whitehall. He painted Jane Seymour, King Henry's third wife, and painting royalty paid in those days! When Hans revisited Basel in 1538, he turned up in silks and satins.

His principle paintings are: *Lais,* and *Venus and Cupid* (Basel Museum), in Italian style; *Virgin and Child* (Solothurn); *The Ambassadors* (Nat. Gallery, London); *The Madonna with the Meyer Family* (Darmstadt, Ducal Palace), perhaps his greatest painting and, *The Dead Christ* (Basel Town Hall fresco), a realistic dead corpse on a dissecting-table.

HUBERT VAN EYCK

Of the two brothers who are the founders and greatest masters of the "Early Flemish School" of Painting, Hubert (1366-1426) belongs to the *Gothic Age,* while his brother Jan represents the aims and trends of the *Renaissance.*

Hubert, though not quite so angelic as Fra Angelico, always worked on a lofty plane, and his religious paintings have the true, devotional Gothic spirit, the spirit of the Middle Ages. Known as "the Father of Flemish Painting", he spent nearly all his time working in Ghent, in Flanders. Court painter to the Duke of Burgundy, and with a number of rich citizen patrons, Hubert knew no material wants. His greatest picture, which he and his brother painted together is:

The Ghent Altarpiece (St. Bavon's Cathedral, Ghent). Originally there was a central piece, divided into four middle panels and eight "side" panels. The four middle panels remain: When closed, the upper of the two outside panels shows the Virgin and the Archangel Gabriel kneeling in prayer, one on each side, facing each other. In the lower panel Jodocus Vydt and his wife (who had the altarpiece done for their private family chapel), kneel to St. John the Baptist and St. John the Evangelist. In the upper inside panel sits God the Father, in red, with the Virgin in dark blue on one side, and St. John the Baptist in green, on the other. In the lower panel the Lamb is shedding His blood in the presence of angels, apostles, prophets, martyrs, knights and hermits. The eight "side" panels are scattered. One showing Adam and Eve in the days before the fig-leaf (now in the Brussels Museum) was thought unfit for a church in a day that pretended to be more refined but was not, and was hidden away in the cathedral cellar. Others were sold abroad. When the great altar-piece was first shown (1432) crowds flocked to see it. "On festival days", writes an old chronicler, "it was hard to get near the picture. Painters old and young and all lovers of art flocked around it like flies around a basket of grapes!"

Jan van Eyck (1386-1440), his brother's pupil, was a more worldly person. Jan's saints and virgins all had a thoroughly human anatomy. He studied the nude from nature, and painted bodies as they were, even sacred ones. That is why his Madonnas are fine likenesses of the homely Flemish women who were his models, but have little of the purity and spirituality we associate with the Mother of God. Jan was court painter to Philip, Duke of Burgundy and well paid, and his master placed such confidence in him that he married the Princess Isabella of Portugal on the strength of the picture Jan painted of her in Lisbon and sent on to him. Jan seems to have dealt more fairly by Philip than Holbein did by Henry. His best paintings are: *Madonna* (Louvre), the *Man with the Pinks* (Berlin Museum), a *Madonna with Saints* (Dresden), and his portrait of his wife:

Jan van Eyck's Portrait of his Wife. The great painter's wife is shown in a scarlet dress trimmed with grey fur, with a green girdle and a white fringed kerchief on her head. She has a kind, intelligent face, and the whole picture is finished with loving care. Three words beneath her husband's signature may still be read on the canvas. They show how deeply Jan loved her. *"Als ixh xan...."* they read. It is the first part of an old Flemish proverb: "As well as I can, not as well as I would like to!" was what the loving husband wrote on his picture when he finished it in 1439.

The greatest service the two Van Eycks did art was to discover the *secret of real oil painting*. This lay in a subtle mixing of oil and varnish when moistening colors and pigments, and did not come into the possession of the Italians until the close of the fifteenth century.

THE DUTCH RENAISSANCE PAINTERS

Jan Van Eyck, the first Flemish painter of the Renaissance was followed by many others. Van der Weyden, Diereck Bouts, Quentin Mathys, Lucius van Leyden (1494-1533), a friend of Dürer, who made a wonderful engraving when fourteen years old of St. Sergius being killed by Mohamet while carelessly sleeping where the Arabian prophet hung about. There is also Hans Memling (1425-1494) whose two famous paintings are the panels of the The Shrines of St. Ursula (St. John's Hospital, Bruges). But these and others—Mabuse, van Scorel, Vermeer, Floris, the Breughels and many more—are merely preparers of the glory of Flemish painting which begins with the Rubens.

CHAPTER III

THE GREAT PAINTERS OF THE RENAISSANCE

The great painters and paintings of the Renaissance fall naturally into two groups. One, the first group, includes the painters who are *striving to perfect* the new ideas and ideals the Renaissance brought with it. They are the painters of the Preparatory Period, the Early Renaissance. The second group have *realized* the ideals the first was trying to attain: they are the painters of the Period of Perfection, the High Renaissance.

THE FLORENTINE SCHOOL OF EARLY RENAISSANCE PAINTERS
MASACCIO

There are many notable names among these early Renaissance painters of Florence. Masaccio, in his *Peter Baptizing,* shows that the drawing of the male human figure had at last been mastered. Masolino, his contemporary (1403-1440), painted an *Adam and Eve Before the Fall,* and his figure of Eve has been called "the first really beautiful nude figure of modern art", just as Masaccio himself has been termed "the Father of Modern Painting". Domenico Ghirlandajo (1449-1494) who excelled in draperies, Lorenzo di Credi (1459-1537), Paolo Uccello (1337-1495), Cosimo Roselli, Benozzo Gozzoli, Signorelli (an Umbrian who painted in the Florentine style), however, are less famous than Sandro Botticelli and Fra Lippi Lippi.

SANDRO BOTTICELLI*

Botticelli, after good training in his artistic home town, painted portraits for the magnificent Medici rulers of Florence and for the churches, and made a great name for himself. The most famous picture Botticelli ever painted (1478) in his *Primavera,* "Spring", (Florence Academy). Venus, very fancifully draped, stands in an orange and myrtle grove welcoming the approach of Spring, who enters

---

* Properly Allesandro di Mariano dei Filipepi, a struggling tanner's fat child, he was nicknamed *Botticello* or "Little Barrel", by the rest of the street urchins of Florence, and the name stuck to him through life.

ushered in by Mercury, while Flora and Zephyr urge her to step forward to meet him. Above Venus a Cupid hovers in the air.

Botticelli did this picture for young Lorenzo di Medici's villa at Castello and (true or otherwise), the story is that the Venus in it was a very lovely Florentine lady, known as *La Bella Simonetta* (Beautiful Simonetta), the wife of a gentleman called Marco Vespucci, and that Flora and the Zephyrs knew what they were doing when they were urging her to meet Spring, in the likeness of young Duke Giuliano di Medici himself. The assassination of his patron Duke Giuliano di Medici, strange to say, was a stroke of good fortune for Botticelli. He got an order—after the murderers had been hung!—to paint them in effigy on the wall of the Town Hall, the *Palazzo del Podesta*. But his painted criminals hung there only 16 years. Then they were destroyed in a political upheavel. Yet Botticelli got a good price for them and was paid as soon as he had painted the ropes around their necks. In Rome Botticelli worked on the paintings of the Sistine Chapel, and the list of his many works is a long one. Chief among them are:

Birth of Venus and *Virgin with the Pomegranate* (Uffizzi Gallery, Florence), *The Nativity* (Nat. Gallery, London), the *Madonna Enthroned* (Berlin Gallery), and the great *Altarpiece of San Marco* (Florence).

THE LIPPIS

Fra (Brother) Philippo Lippi usually known as Lippo Lippi (1406-1469), was a butcher's son, and though a Carmelite friar, he was a different kind of monk than Fra Angelico. In letters he calls himself the poorest friar in Florence, and speaks of the six girl nieces whom he has to support; but the truth is that he made plenty of money—only it seemed to get away from him as soon as he got it! Fra Lippi's fancies did not stray to celestial meadows and bodiless angels. He led an adventurous and romantic life. Flitting about in Ancona and Naples, he was captured on the high seas by Barbary pirates, and supposed to have owed his release to his skill in drawing portraits of the bearded Algerian *bashaws* and *beys*. While painting in a convent chapel near Florence (1458), he saw a lovely novice whom the pious nuns had in charge. Fra Lippo did not look at her with the spiritual eye of a Fra Angelico. He at once coaxed the nuns to let her be his model for the Madonna he was painting, and then improved the opportunity to make such passionate love to her, that she completely forgot her vows. He abducted her in spite of the nuns' cries and—took her home as his lady-love, though, owing to his clerical estate, he could not marry her. The only excuse for Fra Lippo Lippi's straying from virtue was their son, Filippino Lippi, who inherited all his father's talent as a painter. So, while outraging morality, Fra Lippo at least did Art a service. He was buried in Spoleto and a monument was put up to him by Duke Lorenzo the Magnificent of Florence, for the Medici had been his patrons. But the poet Robert Browning raised a greater monument to him in his poem called "Fra Lippo Lippi", which is worth any one's reading who wants to get an insight into a Renaissance painter's life and feelings. The tale of his life leads us to believe that what the critics say of his work may be true: "His pictures show a strong, rich nature full of lively observation. He approaches religious art from the *human* side". A *Virgin* (Uffizzi, Florence), a *Vision of St. Bernard* (Nat. Gallery, London) and a *Coronation of the Virgin* (Florence Academy) are among his more famous paintings.

Filippino or Lippino Lippi (1460-1505), the natural son of the Fra Lippo and the lovely novice Lucrezia Buti, inherited all his father's talent and painted virgins, saints and prophets in Florence and Rome, among them a *St. John in the Cauldron of Boiling Oil* (St. Maria Novello, Florence), which prove his gifts.

A third Lippi, Lorenzo (1606-1664), lived in the Baroque Age. He excelled in portraits, but his most famous painting is a "word painting", a burlesque romance, full of Florentine slang called *Malmantile Racquistato,* which Italians consider a good "language test".

THE EARLY RENAISSANCE SCHOOLS OF PADUA AND UMBRIA

ANDRIA MANTEGNA AND THE PADUAN SCHOOL

Cosimo Tura (1430-1496), a court painter for Duke Borso d'Este at Ferrara; Francesco Francis (1450-1518) of Bologna, who painted like a goldsmith; and Francesco Squarcione (1394-1474), originally a tailor, who was better at collecting antique statues than painting pictures, are all of the Umbrian school. The one great artist of the school, however, was Andrea Mantegna (1431-1506), whose best work is the *Scenes from the Life of St. James* (Eremitani Chapel, Padua), a fine series of frescoes, though he painted many secular pictures, notably his *Roman Triumphs* (Hampton Court). He was a pupil of Squarcione, but probably learned more from himself than from his teacher. As many as 147 students passed through his own school and spread has fame. The influence of Mantegna and the Paduan School was felt in Genoa, Verona, Modena, Brescia, Parma and Bergamo.

PERUGINO AND PINTORICCHIO AND THE UMBRIAN SCHOOL

Perugino (1446-1524) is one of those painters whose character forms a strange contrast to his pictures. In his *Pavia Altarpiece* (Nat. Gallery, London), the Virgin looks with ecstatic devotion at her Holy Child. In his *Transfiguration* (Perugia Chapel), and *Assumption* (Florence Gallery), the faces of the holy personages are full of sweetest religious devotion and dreamy spiritual ardor. And yet—Perugino himself *had no religion in his soul!* He did not, in fact, believe there was such a thing as an immortal soul, died without confession, and was buried in unconsecrated ground. As soon as he had made a name for himself, he turned to "factory production". He was satisfied to put all his poetic feeling into his heavenly-faced Madonnas, but when it came to driving a bargain there was not a bit of poetry about him. Then his Madonnas only meant money, his saints shekels, and his cherubs cash to him. In 1493 he married a handsome young wife, Chiara Fancelli, whom he loved to hang with jewels and dress in pretty clothes. But though he drove such hard bargains for his pictures and owned houses and real estate in Florence and Perugia, he always was "hard up", and always was engaged in brawls and quarrels. He outlived his famous pupil Raphael by three years, dying of the plague.

Bernardino di Benedetto di Biago, called Pintoricchio ("the little painter") for short, knew something of the intimate life of the Vatican at one of its most romantic periods, the pontificate of the Borgia Pope Alexander VI, for Pintoricchio was his court painter. He painted many fine works in Perugia, Florence, Rome and Siena, and won fame and money, but his life does not seem to have been happy. When over forty he married a lady named Grania, and then it became even less happy than it was before. It is to be feared that Grania was not a perfect wife. Pintoricchio's friend, Signismondo Tizio, a Sienese historian and writer, tells us a sad tale of his end. As is somtimes the case with young wives of elderly celebrities, Grania's fancies strayed to another. Pintoricchio fell ill (1513), and could not rise from his sick bed, so Grania improved a welcome opportunity. Her lover was a young soldier in the Sienese Guard, and selfish as lovers are, the two carefully locked up poor Pintoricchio in his empty house to die of hunger and neglect. Some women of the neighborhood heard his cries, and went to help him, but he died shortly after his rescue.

His paintings include: *Portrait of a Boy* (Royal Gallery, Dresden), *Holy Family* (Siena Academy), The *San Severino Madonna* (San Severino Cathedral) *Scenes from the Life of Cardinal Piccolomini* (Library, Siena Cathedral), great historical frescoes brilliant with color, of proud moments in the life of Pope Pius III; *Journey of Moses* and *Return of Ulysses* (Petrucci Palace, Siena). But the most romantic painting of all is the one he did for the private rooms, the "'Borgia Apartments", a suite of six chambers, of Pope Alexander VI in the Vatican:

The Dispute of St. Catherine (Vatican, Rome). Pope Alexander

VI was a gorgeous and splendor-loving half-barbarian. He wanted the glitter of gold and the costly richness of ultramarine blue around him. And Pintoricchio, who was a master-decorator, could give it to him. Pintoricchio lived in an age when it was wise to keep one's mouth shut about what one chanced to see or hear in the private apartments of the great. But we wish he had kept a diary of the three years he spent painting frescoes in those Borgia rooms. The subjects, though the dweller in those rooms was one of the most *unsaintly* of men—were scenes from the lives of the *saints*. In the finest of the frescoes, *The Dispute of St. Catherine,* a great crowd of people are gathered in a sunny landscape. There are Eastern kings, Turks, philosophers, courtiers and great lords, pages, soldiers and splendidly harnessed horses. To the left of a triumphal arch in the middle of the picture sits the Emperor Maximinus on a throne. Before him that pure and innocent virgin, St. Catherine of Alexandria, in red, gold-embroidered robe, is very earnestly explaining the true inwardness of the Christian religion.

And who was the *model* for this slim, innocent girlish figure of the spotless Christian girl *saint?* None other than Pope Alexander's lovely and infamous daughter, Lucrezia Borgia, the lady who passed out the poison-cup to so many victims with a sweet and candid smile! The Emperor Maximinus, a Christian persecutor, has not much reputation to lose. So it does not seem wrong for the terrible Caesar Borgia to have served as his model. *But Lucrezia as a Christian saint and virgin?* A turbaned figure on horseback near the Emperor is Prince Djem, son of the Turkish Sultan Mohammed II, whom Pope Alexander—seeing that he was paid a good sum in gold every year for so doing—held as an informal prisoner at his court to oblige his Mohammedan friend.

THE EARLY RENAISSANCE SCHOOL OF VENICE

Among early Venetian painters we find Antonelli da Messina, a Van Eyck pupil, who introduced the Van Eyck secret of laying on oil colors in his native town; John and Antonia da Maurano, Luigi Vivarini, Carlo Crivelli Conegliano (b. 1460) and Carpaccio (b. 1450), but the two greatest are the two Bellinis, Gentile and Giovanni. Carpaccio was a religious painter, and his most famous work was a series of nine pictures illustrating *The Legend of St. Ursula* (Venice Academy), while he also did a fine, blond-haired, black-armored *St. George* (Church of St. George the Slavonian, Venice), riding full tilt at the dragon.

THE BELLINIS

The fame of Jacopo Bellini (1400-1470) is overshadowed by that of his sons. Gentile Bellini's finest paintings are a *Miracle of the Holy Cross* (Venice Academy), which shows his home city when it was rich and famous, and a portrait of the Venetian girl who married a king, and became Queen of Cyprus, Catherine Cornaro. Besides this is a souvenir of an interesting trip to Constantinople in the days when the Turk was in his glory under Sultan Mohammed II. It seems that "the Grand Turk" had asked the Venetians to send him a good painter to work at his court (1479). Gentile Bellini went, stayed a year, gave full satisfaction, and came back with a knighthood, lots of rich clothes, a gold chain and a pension. One of the best fruits—for posterity—of his trip was a striking likeness of *Sultan Mohammed II* (Louvre), and also a great painting, *Reception of an Ambassador in Constantinople* (Louvre). Giovanni Bellini has been called "the Giotto of Venetian painting". He was equally at home in the sacred and secular, and could paint a *Deluge with Noah's Ark* (1570), or the *Bacchanale* he was working on at the time of his death, with equal ease. His great historical paintings have not come down to us, only a few portraits, among them the masterly portrait of the Venetian *Doge Lorendano* (Nat. Gallery, London), but many of his Madonnas have, the finest among them perhaps the *Madonna* in the San Zaccaria Church, Venice.

CHAPTER IV

THE GREAT PAINTERS OF THE ITALIAN HIGH RENAISSANCE

The Florentines

Leonardo da Vinci

THAT artistic wonder of the Renaissance, Leonardo da Vinci, was a man who knew the *theory* of all art and science so well that the *execution* of works of any kind seemed easy to him. He could build bathing pavilions, plan monster sewer systems, write dainty court plays, chisel golden dagger hilts, or play a silver flute in tones that moved the heart, or design artillery which no stone towers could resist. As a painter Leonardo has left two great finished works and one unfinished one.

Leonardo da Vinci is still a mystery. He was the natural son of a Florentine lawyer and a village girl, but acknowledged by his father, and brought up in his house. He grew to be a winning, handsome youth, with a restless craving for knowledge. As painter, sculptor and goldsmith Verocchi was his teacher; but he also studied music, engineering, natural philosophy, and excelled in all. Even-tempered, amiable, honorable, his curiosity about the *why* and *wherefore* of everything gave him no rest. It was his life. Gathering knowledge and *knowing* seemed more important to him perhaps, than putting knowledge into practice. It was hard to find time for both. He could bring tears to eyes that never shed them with his music. He excelled all the youths of Florence in feats of strength and horsemanship. He was a natural-born story-teller, and would hold the crowd in the market-place spell-bound while he stood golden-haired in a rich rose mantle, and told them the wonder-tales his ready fancy called up. His mind was full of all sorts of images of beauty. He was kind to animals. He was a generous, loyal and devoted friend. He cared nothing for money, fame, power. Like Michel Angelo, he had no *love-life,* unless it be that pure soul affection for the famous *Mona Lisa,* whose portrait was his one cherished possession. Vile insinuations have coupled his name with that of handsome pupils, but they seem baseless. All that we know of Leonardo reflects a spirit high, pure and noble. He was tried once, in his youth, for immoral practices—and in the Italy of that day this was a real accusation—but fully and honorably acquitted.

The tale of his great paintings is the tale of his life, in a way. At the court of the art-loving Duke Francesco Sforza of Milan (1483) Leonardo was busy as political cartoonist, designer of bathing-pavilions, writer of court plays, masques and pageants and as civil engineer; and there he designed his famous equestrian statue of the Duke. Yet there also, in 1494, he did the one painting of its subject which never has been excelled:

The Last Supper or *Il Cenacolo** (Church of St. Maria delle Grazie, Milan). Fra Angelico, among others, has painted a *Last Supper*. But these apostles of Leonardo's are human. They are no bodiless souls. At the long table Christ sits in the middle, at either side of him six apostles. And he has just uttered the words: "One among ye shall betray me!" The apostles have dropped their medieval halos—the little rings of heavenly flame around their heads—and they are only struggling, questioning, doubting, human beings. Their excited gestures and questions directed to the Master contrast with the wonderful repose of Christ's divine face and figure. This picture shows Leonardo, not as the magician and sorcerer some legends made him out to be, but as the serene Christian who received the sacraments before he died.

The Virgin of the Rocks (National Gallery, London) is a picture of the Milanese period, but *The Virgin of the Rocks* (Louvre) was the one first painted. In a rocky countryside, all basalt caves and arches, grown with exquisite clumps of flowers and shrubs, the Virgin stands in a strange mysterious light. It is one of the most romantic settings ever given the Mother of God.

Between the time he left Milan—when his patron, Duke Ludovico, was carried a prisoner to France—and 1502, Leonardo drew many sketches for pictures, and did much other work. In 1502, he entered the service of the notorious Caesar Borgio, Duke of Valentinois and the Romagna, as military engineer and artillery founder. After spending months studying the countryside of the heart of Italy, which Caesar planned to conquer, Leonardo showed him the six large-scale maps he had drawn with his own hand. And there, before the great soldier's astonished eyes, lay the land just as a bird might see it from the clouds. The sea was painted blue, the mountains brown,

---

* Leonardo painted it *in tempera*—in water colors—not in oils, and with the years it began to flake and scale off. In the 18th and 19th centuries attempts were vainly made to restore it, and D'Annunzio, the Italian poet, wrote a despairing ode about it called The Death of a Masterpiece. It became a *ghost* of a picture—though a ghost more impressive in its faded beauty than many a painting of richest color. At last (1904-1908) Cavenaghi managed to restore it, and now with beautiful, freshened colors it seems likely to endure.

THE ROMANCE OF PAINTING

the rivers pale blue, the cities light red, the fields green, and everywhere towns, towers, villages set down in the most exact detail. Caesar was so delighted with these wonderful maps, which seemed to place within his hand the countries he intended to conquer, that he treated his engineer with the most splendid liberality. But in 1503 came Caesar's downfall, as a result of his father's death, and Leonardo was once more cast on his own resources.

The Struggle for the Standard (Palazzo Vecchio, Florence) is the unfinished fresco which (1503) together with Michel Angelo's *Bathing Soldiers*, also unfinished, adorns the wall of the Palazzo Vecchio, Florence. The painters were competing with each other. But Leonardo—though his mad, dramatic, terrible mingling of raging men and steeds is glorious even in its uncompleted state, did not care for his first color-cheme. Abruptly flinging down his brush, he walked off, just as Michel Angelo was summoned suddenly to go to Rome by Julius II. So neither fresco was completed.

Mona Lisa, Leonardo's wonderful portrait of Madonna Lisa, the young Neapolitan wife of the Florentine merchant Francesco del Giocondo (the portrait is also known as *La Gioconda* or *La Joconde*, Louvre) remains one of the great mysteries of the painter's art. It took the artist three years to fix that haunting, secret, provoking smile —a smile whose meaning none can read, which has a charm that compels the heart, a lure that rouses the imagination!

Leonardo did trivial things for one and another, Louis XII of France, Pope Leo X (a pontiff who did not know enough to value his services) and poor, and unappreciated in his own land, at last accepted a flattering offer from the French King Francis I (1515), and went to his court as court painter. There he painted his last picture, a young, half-length picture of *St. John the Baptist*, with the haunting Mona Lisa smile (Louvre), his finger beckoning skyward. But he was stricken with paralysis of one hand and arm before he completed it. Among his great store of notes, his scrapbooks, etc., Leonardo had brought with him the one thing he valued above everything else in the world, his *Mona Lisa*, the picture of the mysterious smile. One day King Francis, to pass an idle hour, visited the aged artist in the little castle he had given him near Amboise. Leonardo was painting on his *Saint John*. But Francis went straight to the picture of *La Gioconda*—and could not drink his fill of it! He looked at it with the eyes of a sensualist, but even he was haunted with the secret smile which seems to ask a question he longed to answer. He felt he must have it. In a splendid burst of generosity he told Leonardo he would give him 4,000 gold pieces for it, and to send it to the Chateau. Leonardo said nothing, but for hours after the King had gone sat in silent despair. At last, sick and weak as he was, he made his way with a pupil's help, to the royal castle in the darkness of night. Francis was supping gaily with his court, among the ladies being his sister the Princess Marguerite. Leonardo begged the king piteously to let him keep the picture until he died. It would not be long, and he would formally leave it to him in his will. The King frowned. But Princess Marguerite, who had a kind heart, whispered to him: "Be generous! Grant the old man's prayer. He deserves it." And when her brother raised his eyebrows she said: "He still loves her!" "But she is dead!" was Francis' answer. "Suppose she is. Do we not love the dead? And you yourself said she was alive in the picture. Be kind, brother, let the old man keep his one memory!" So Francis had one of his generous moments. "Keep your picture, Leonardo, and come for your gold to-morrow. Only remember that when you need it no more it is mine." Then a happiness so innocent and childlike glowed in Leonardo's eyes that the King was touched, patted him on the shoulder, and told him: "Do not fear, dear master. I give you my word no one shall touch your Mona Lisa!"

So Leonardo died content on Easter Eve, not long after, in 1510. It is said that King Francis wept when the news of his death came. But he got the *Mona Lisa,* as Leonardo had promised. Though the artist had cared little for pomp and ceremony, he had arranged his funeral in a way befitting the great servant of a great king. Masses were to be said for his soul, and candles offered in three churches of Amboise. Sixty poor men were to serve as torchbearers at his funeral. And when they lowered him into the vault at St. Florentin's, Leonardo already had solved the mystery of that smile which had haunted him even while he painted it, whose secret no living man since has ever guessed.

Bernardino Luini (1475-1533) was Leonardo's chief pupil. He is called "The Rafael of Lombardy" and classed with the "Lombard School", but he painted in Leonardo's style. He was one of the best of Renaissance painters. But—he worked for almost nothing. It is said he fled from Milan, for having murdered a man. Going to the town of Saronno nearby, the monks of the convent there got him to paint them a wonderful *Nativity*—for thirty cents a day, plus bed and board. And the modest artist was content. When he left the brethren said: "It is almost a pity Bernardino did not commit a few more murders, so that he could have done more paintings for us!" His pictures like a note of music, draw a chord from the heart. Among the best are: *The Madonna of the Rose Hedge* (Certosa, Pavia); the vast fresco *Crucifixion* (Santa Maria Church, Lugano), and four blonde Salomes, *The Daughter of Herodias* (in Florence, Milan, Paris and Vienna), each different and not one with the Mona Lisa smile Luini had learned to paint from his master.

MICHEL ANGELO BUONARROTI

Michel Angelo's life story as a sculptor, architect, and human being already has been told (See "Romance of Sculpture", Chap. 5), but the great paintings he has painted, among the world's wonders, cannot be overlooked. Into two great fresco works Michel Angelo crowded what other painters have spread over hundreds of canvases. First come the frescoes he painted on the high, tunnel-shaped ceiling of the Sistine Chapel of the Vatican at Rome. No more wonderful story ever has been told by the painter's brush than this:

Frescoes in the Sistine Chapel (Vatican, Rome). What Michel Angelo did in this work was to tell the tale of *Genesis* in glowing, romantic color, tell it in a way that in painting is as inspired as the words of Holy Writ. Older artists of the Early Renaissance, Ghirlandajo, Pinturicchio, Perugino, already had painted the upper half of the walls with scenes from the Bible, the life of Moses and the life of Christ. Now Michel Angelo was to show the world the Creation.

First, with his brush, he changed the great stone vault of the roof into the blue, open, spreading sky, framed with his own *painted* stone edging. And there, as we look up, in the heavens above, we see the glorious scroll of the Bible tale unrolled! There are five great Creation pictures:

God Almighty floats over all in majestic loneliness. As though longing for creatures to love, he stretches out His arms. With a single glance of love he looks into nothingness—and there is light! *Michel Angelo shows us that God is Love.*

On the wings of the storm-wind God now sweeps through space, angels peeping out from beneath his mantle. He is everywhere. Worlds take shape about Him. We sense His Presence in the whirling globes of fire. Tremendous, overpowering, He lifts His finger, His forehead heavy with thought, His eyes aflame—and at His command *matter takes shape*.

Again God floats in the heavens, but no longer on the wings of the storm. Now His hands are raised in *blessing*. He is preparing Man's earthly home. Mercy and kindness shine in His glorious features. He has taken pity on earth, even before it is formed.

Man, the first man, has been created. But he is unfinished—he does not move his limbs. Again God draws near, resting on a cloud. And with infinite compassion he stretches out a divine finger, touching the timid finger-tip of the creature He has created. With that touch we see life and strength rush through the creature as though from an electric spark. A moment, and Adam, the first man, will rise, raised to life by the magnetic touch of the finger of God!

Woman has been created, while Adam slumbered. Now for the

first time God sets foot on earth. He advances with fatherly kindness toward Eve, who bows timidly before Him and, still hardly aware that she is living, folds her hands in prayer. The Creation has been accomplished and God sees that it is good.

The five smaller of the nine oblong ceiling pictures are: *Noah's Drunkenness, The Deluge, Noah's Sacrifice, The Fall* and the *Expulsion from Paradise*. And then, over the windows and between the windows are other pictures. The darkness of a hopeless night falls on a sunny earth. Yet rays of hope gleam on the horizon, among the people of Israel and those of the pagan world. On a tremendous stone battlement, a high stone wall, as though raised on the edge of the world, prophets and sybils are watching. Beneath their feet all is twilight. We see the tribe of Jesse, men and women, with their first-born. They seem asleep, but a smile of divine joy lights their faces. And round about them the race of Israel seems waiting, waiting for the great Messiah who is to come. All faces are turned with hope and expectation toward the light. And everywhere, in every corner, in every bit of space left, are countless other figures looking, longing, expecting! They turn the whole series of great frescoes into one mighty Advent poem, into one great voiceless melody of human longing for the divine.

When after twenty months of tireless labor the great frescoes were completed (1520) all Rome rejoiced. But if the ceiling frescoes of the Sistine Chapel are Michel Angelo's *song of Christian hope,* we have in the wonderful *Last Judgment,* the altar-picture of the Sistine Chapel, Michel Angelo's *song* of despair. Michel Angelo, in spite of his gloomy nature, was a lover of his fellowmen. His thoughts were lofty and noble. The break in the Church had grieved his soul. And the attempts to bring about a reconciliation between Rome and Luther failed. The gloomy and fanatic Cardinal Caraffa set alight the first fires for the burning of heretics. Dark shadows rose over Italy. Michel Angelo's noble-hearted friend, the Lady Vittoria Colonna, died of a broken heart. And Michel Angelo despaired of humanity. The *Last Judgment* is the picture of his despair. It is a picture that grips the heart.

The Last Judgment (Sistine Chapel, Vatican, Rome) is a terrifying vision of the day when the dead will rise from their graves. No later painter has ever painted its equal, though many have tried. It is a picture of stern and terrible judgment. The martyrs draw near as accusers, and all heaven seems to tremble with their chorus of accusation. Angels drag up instruments of torture. Those who have been flayed alive, broken on the wheel, impaled on stakes, hold out the things which have done them to death. Yet from below the damned rush up, daring and defiant, to the bar of heaven! We see all hanging on the words that come from the lips of the Supreme

Judge. Even the blessed saints seem to freeze in attitudes of awe as He speaks. And the Virgin Mary turns away from her Son in fear: never has she seen Him thus. Like some warrior god he has leaped forward. He does not give the company of the saved a single glance. Only three words, words that sink into the very marrow of the evil-doers, come from His lips: "Hence with ye!" Struck as though by lightning, the damned plunge into the abyss! They sink faster and ever faster, torn and pulled down by legions of devils! The heart stands still when we see this terror of the guilty conscience, this glow of the soul, this burning passion. Far below, Charon, the ferryman of the dead, carries the lost across the river of hell. At the right side of the great picture, it is true, there are beautiful, heavenly scenes of Paradise. The joyous resurrection of the dead, the happy recognition of those who have loved each other on earth, the rising to the eternal glories of Paradise. But—the general effect of the great picture is one of superhuman terror and majesty. In these two great paintings Michel Angelo—his knowledge of anatomy is such that the flesh and blood of his bodies seem more real than our own—created enough to make the reputations of hundreds of lesser men. *The Last Judgment* was his last great picture.

Among the Florentine painters of the High Renaissance several others stand out. There was Fra Bartolommeo (1475-1571). A poor mule-driver's son, he was a follower of the great Florentine reformer, Savonarola. When the latter (1497) bade the Florentines burn up all worldly things—musical instruments, dice, playing cards, toilet articles, etc.—Fra Bartolommeo threw into the flames all his beautiful mythological nudes. Savonarola's reforms were soon forgotten (in fact he himself was burned in Florence, in 1498), but the loss of Fra Bartolommeo's beautiful paintings to Art could not be made good. His finest religious painting is the *Descent from the Cross* (Pitti Palace, Florence). Mariotto Albertinelli (1474-1515), and Andrea del Sarto (1486-1531), the latter in particular, also deserve mention. Del Sarto was called "the faultless painter", but though his color-work was fine his figures have been accused of lacking spirit.

RAPHAEL SANZIO

Raphael (1483-1520) has a name that stands out in painting as Alexander's does in war, Demosthenes in eloquence, or Phidias in sculpture. A painter's son, his works fall into three periods. The first is the "Perugian Period". As Perugino's pupil (1499-1503), as a boy of seventeen or eighteen he helped paint Perugino's fresco of the *Resurrection* (Vatican), and the *Diatolevi Madonna*, sold to the Emperor of Russia by the Perugian Count of Connestable in 1871, for something like $45,000.

During his so-called "Florentine Period" Raphael dropped Perugino's style for that of Leonardo and Fra Bartolommeo, with whom he studied in Florence, improving his figure work by drawing from nude models and dissecting corpses. As a result Raphael's Madonnas became beautifully earthly women and mothers, and the finest of them, painted during this period has quite a worldly name, *La Belle Jardiniere*, "The Lovely Gardener" (Louvre), showing the Virgin seated in a green and flowery countryside, Child Jesus beside her knee, and little St. John kneeling at her side. This and other Madonnas, Raphael painted in the so-called "pyramid style"—that is the figures are so grouped that they shape up, vaguely, into a pyramid of forms. The *Madonna del Baldachino*, "The Madonna of the Canopy", and a number of "portraits" also belong to this time.

In his third, or "Roman Period", Raphael produced what are considered his greatest works. In 1508 Pope Julius II called him to Rome and there, in the Vatican, he painted his great frescoes. These paintings were allegorical and historical. On the walls and the ceiling of the room in which the papal "bulls" (the infallible orders and commands the popes sent out over Christendom) were signed, he painted *Adam and Eve, Astronomy, The Judgment of Solomon,* Apollo and Marsyas, as well as Theology, Poetry, Philosophy and *Justice*. On the right wall went the *Disputa* not really a "discussion", as the Italian word seems to imply, but a "glorification of the Christian faith"). It has been called the highest expression of *Christian* painting. It reveals the idea of the *Trinity*. God the Father in glory on golden clouds, surrounded by prophets, patriarchs and archangels, is above Christ enthroned between the Virgin and John the Baptist, while the Dove bears to earth the Gospels. There saints, confessors, learned doctors, fathers of the church, painters, poets, old men and young, are grouped around an altar on which are the mystic tokens of Christ's presence. And Raphael—noble hearted and an admirer of the free and the great of soul, has placed among his popes and cardinals the figure of the pure and selfless monk Savonarola (for a great painter dared to take liberties in those days no one else could have taken) burned to death as a heretic in Florence by the Church only eleven years before. Dante, Fra Angelico and Bramante, his friend, the architect of St. Peters, are also among the figures about the altar. Opposite the *Disputa* is *The School of Athens,* and on the other walls, *Parnassus* (Apollo with the Muses and other creatures of Greek mythology on his mountain), and *Jurisprudence*.

The *Church History Frescoes* in another Vatican apartment also are wonderful. *The Retreat of Attila,* shows the fierce King of the Huns stopped near Rome by the imposing figure of Pope St. Leo. *The Deliverance of St. Peter* pictures the escape of Pope Leo X after the battle of Ravenna. Greatest of them is: *The Miracle of*

Bolsena. It has a story. When Urban IV was pope, a German priest doubted the doctrine of *transsubstantiation*—the actual turning of the body and blood of Christ into the wine and waters of the sacrament. Raphael shows him kneeling before an altar, looking with astonishment at the holy blood flowing from the Host—the "Miracle". Behind him a crowd of eager faces gaze with awe. On the other side of the altar kneels Raphael's friend, Pope Julius II, with cardinals and princes of the church in the background, and Papal Guards with their shining weapons in the foreground.

The Sybils (Santa Maria della Pace Church, Rome), *The Triumph of Galatea* (Farnesina Villa, Rome), a "Greek" picture, with the lovely nymph sailing over the sea in a dolphin-drawn shell, and *Scenes from the Life of Cupid and Psyche,* in the same Villa, are among Raphael's other famous frescoes. His most famous "easel-picture" is the celebrated *Sistine Madonna* (Dresden Gallery), though he painted other lovely Madonnas, sweet-faced and smiling, which fill the soul with joy: the *Madonna of Foligno* (Vatican), the *Diademed Virgin* (Louvre), the *Garvagh Madonna* (Nat. Gallery), and the *Madonna de la Pace* (Madrid). The lovely *Madonna of the Pearls* (Madrid) once belonged to King Charles I of England, but when his head fell in the basket, Cromwell, a man who had but little use for Madonnas, no matter how beautiful, sold it to a Spanish bishop, and it hangs in Spain (Royal Gallery, Madrid), with the *Madonna of the Roses,* the most perfect in *color* of all Raphael's Madonnas. Ten tapestry cartoons, many other paintings, portraits of popes, princes and private persons, designs for silver articles, drawings and pottery came from the hand of this genius, as well as the 52 small frescoes called *Raphael's Bible,* scenes from the Old and New Testament, in the Vatican Loggia.

THE GREATEST PAINTER EARTH HAS KNOWN

Raphael's name still remains the greatest in the Art of Painting. He could paint anything and everything, and paint it to perfection. Even in his own day, his fame outshone that of Leonardo da Vinci and Michel Angelo, yet he was celebrated for the sweetness, nobility and generosity of his nature. Gold poured in on him, popes, kings and princes sent ambassadors to him begging for pictures. He lived in a great Roman palace like some royal personage, with a court of fifty chosen pupils, whom he treated like a father. And—his genius understood and could express the gay, joyous freedom of the old Greek spirit as well as the lofty sweetness and grandeur of Christianity. His nudes are beautiful, natural, palpitating human flesh and blood. His female saints and his Virgins are lovely, divine women, whose divinity still does not deny their earthly origin. His versatility—his perfect skill in passing from one subject to another absolutely different—is best shown, perhaps, in two pictures. One is his great "fire picture".

Incendio Del' Borgo (Vatican, Rome). In the quarter of Rome called the Borgo, a quarter of old wooden houses, a tremendous fire once broke out in the days of Pope Leo X. On the steps of St. Peter's stands the pope and about him crowd the terrified fugitives, fleeing from great, red, devastating flames, the heat of whose fierce burning seems to strike out from the canvas and singe the onlooker.

And, as a contrast, we have the *Transfiguration* (Vatican Gallery). This was Raphael's swan-song on canvas. He painted it in all its beauty, while he was dying. And there is something touching in the thought that the transfigured Christ, who with tender, loving face floats in the air above the Mount of Transfiguration, almost seems to be waiting to carry with Him to His Paradise the pure and noble soul of the painter who had done so much for the glory of His faith, both by his life and his works. All Rome flocked to see the "divine painting" when Raphael died, April 6, 1520, of a fever, gotten so it is said, by dancing attendance in the vast, cold halls of the Vatican Palace. He died on his birthday, Good Friday, and the whole world mourned his loss.

Giulio Romano (1492-1546), was Raphael's best-known pupil. He preferred classic Greek subjects to religious ones.

THE SIENESE SCHOOL

Il Sodoma

Giovanni Antonio Bazzi (Il Sodoma, 1477-1549), continued the style of Pintoricchio and Spanzotto, Giovenone, and other painters of the Sienese school in an original way. His most famous pictures are *St. Catherine in Ecstasy* (St. Catherine's Church, Siena), fainting with joy as an angel hands her the Eucharist, and a *Christ Scourged* St. Domenico, Siena). As his name indicates Bazzi had a bad moral reputation. Vasari says that he also was known as Il Mattaccio, "The Madman", dressed like a mountebank, had a regular Noah's Ark of all sorts of queer animals in his house, was fond of singing unseemly poems whose words he had written, and was extremely lazy.

THE SCHOOL OF PARMA

Correggio

One of the most original, daring, restless and vivid painters of the Renaissance, Antonio Alleggri (Correggio, 1494-1534), used only the richest and costliest color for paintings he did on fine canvas or on sheets of copper. His works in many cases combined the qualities of Leonardo and Raphael. Vast religious frescoes in the cupolas of Parma's churches so moved the Venetian painter Titian that seeing the authorities did not think as highly as they might of Correggio's talent he told them: "Turn your church domes upside down and fill them with gold—you still will not have given him his money's worth for his pictures!" Correggio loved rich, glowing colors and he was a master of the human form. He painted lovable souls in lovely bodies, as in his nudes *Diana Returning from the Chase* (Nat. Gallery, London), his *Venus, Leda, Danae, Vice and Virtue,* five paintings done in 1526—*The Leda* with charming figures of girls bathing—as well as religious subjects. And his life bears out the soul-qualities of his paintings, for the young sixteen year old girl he married in 1520—she sat as the model for his famous *Zingarella* or *Madonna del Coniglio,* "The Gipsy" or the "Madonna *with the Rabbit*" (Naples Museum)—and he were very happy together, and she gave him four children. Sometimes Correggio got good prices for his works—as when King Augustus III of Poland paid him 6,000 gold pieces for his *Magdalen Lying at the Entrance to her Cavern* (Dresden Gallery); sometimes he was poorly paid. Legend says that he came to his death because a customer, meaning to hurt and wound him, paid him the big purchase price of a picture in copper coin. Weighed down with all the copper, Correggio walked on a hot, dusty day the long road from the neighboring town to Parma, and when he got home his fatigue led to a mortal illness.

Among his imitators and belonging to his "school" were his son Pomponio, Francesco Capelli, Giovanni Giarola, the Parmigiani and Bernardo Gatti, the last considered the best painter in his style.

CHAPTER V

TITIAN AND THE VENETIAN SCHOOL

IN 1540 Venice was at the height of her power. She was a rich, splendid city, and the Venetians seemed to be born painters. The shadows that flitted and trembled over the blue waters of her lagoons, the playing lights, the warm, tender veils woven in the air out of the mist and golden sun-motes, coaxed them to paint. And there was the oriental splendor of St. Mark's, the marble palaces adorned with glowing mosaics, all the wealth and color that filled the Venetian marketplace. There was all the glory of the festival life—and life was one great festival—with its display of splendid stuffs, laces, and jewels, all the colorful splendor of existence to teach them to paint, and to paint with colors that were glorious and brilliant.

Giorgione (1478-1510) or Giorgio Barbarelli, a fellow-student of Titian, was one of the first to paint pictures that did not "tell a story", that just expressed the mood he was in, or the poetry of beauty in itself. Just as "absolute" music puts moods and feelings into sounds, so Giorgione pictured romantic feeling and poetry in color. He was a figure of romance, a great lover, great musician. He painted religious paintings, yes—a *Christ Bearing the Cross* (Church of San Rocco, Venice), with a Jew dragging at the rope around his neck; and a beautiful altarpiece with the *Virgin* (Castlefranco), but his was a worldly soul. His idea was to live and love, and enjoy living and loving to the full. And so—out of many pictures he painted—his greatest pictures are pictures in which profane and not sacred beauty is the ideal.

Giorgione's greatest pictures are: *The Sleeping Venus* (Dresden Gallery). The goddess of love and pleasure lies dreaming on a sweep of white drapery, but so sweet and chaste is the rhythm of her sleeping body that only a debased mind could see anything wrong in its pure nudity. This Venus is one of Giorgione's earlier, more pure and slender nudes. Later, influenced by Titian, who preferred voluptuously rounded figures, Giorgione's nudes swelled to ampler and more rounded physical proportions.

The Pastoral Symphony (Louvre). Here we have a picture of a concert in the open, and like the equally famous *The Concert* (Pitti Gallery, Florence), it proves that a song dwelt ever in the painter's soul. In the last-named picture only one figure has survived the cruel hand of time—it shows a monk, playing a clavichord, with head thrown back, and his face is the very incarnation of musical rapture. We can see that his soul is away in heavenly regions, borne on the wings of tone.

The Mystery (Giovanelli Palace, Venice). This picture *is* a mystery. Many have tried to guess its meaning, and many theories have been advanced about it. It seems to be an allegory. Anonimo Morelliano, who saw it in 1530, described it as "the small landscape with the storm, a Gipsy woman and the soldier". But who and what the Gipsy woman and the soldier were, what tale of passion, tragedy or sacrifice they carry with them through the storm, is a mystery still, like *Mona Lisa's* smile.

Sebastiano del Piombo (1485-1547), who began life as a musician, was the pupil of Giorgione and Michel Angelo, and his greatest painting is a *Raising of Lazurus* (Nat. Gallery, London). Plama Vecchio (1480-1528), painted in Giorgione's manner personal portraits of lovely Venetian women as saints, *Santa Barbara* (St. Maria Formosa, Venice); and Pordenone (1498-1539), another Giorgione pupil—all yield to the great Titian in fame and celebrity.

TITIAN

Titian, "The Divine" (1477-1576), Tiziano Vecellio of Cadore, in the Ventian territory, near the Tyrol, was one of the world's very greatest painters. Bellini's pupil, his first work to excite attention in the world was the *Assumption of the Madonna* (Venetian Academy), painted in 1518. It created a sensation all over Italy, for it was the *largest* altarpiece, and the most vividly and brilliantly colored one that ever had been painted. It at once established his fame. After he had done his *St. Sebastian* (Brescia), in 1521, he was flooded with orders. Up to 1524-25 he hbdaeen a most irregular liver, not a difficult task in the Venice of his day. But in that year he "settled down" with the lady with whom he had entertained common law relations—her name was Cecilia*—though, the following year, he made an anything but edifying acquaintance, with the depraved Pietro Aretino. After his wife's death in 1530, his sister Orsa kept house, or rather "kept palace" for Titian and his children, for he lived in a beautiful palace at one end of Venice, with gardens that ran down to the sea. There—during a long life, for he lived to be nearly a hundred—he painted many of his famous pictures, and these we will consider before resuming the colorful tale of his romantic existence.

Sacred and Profane Love (Villa Borghese, Rome) is probably the best-known of many of Titian's paintings. It has also been called

*Considered in "Romance of Life Through the Ages" (The Renaissance)

Artless and Sated Love. In the warm glowing light of a summer evening, a light the painter loved to introduce in his works, lies a smiling landscape with a fountain in the center, in which a little Cupid is dabbling fat, baby hands. Over the edge of the fountain leans a woman, scantily draped. In her hands she holds a vase of crystal, and turns a face of innocent, artless happiness to another woman, seated at the other side of the fountain. The happy, innocent smiler is *Artless Love.* *Sated Love* is a proud lady. Richly dressed, but with a discontented face, and gloved hands, she does not even spare the baby Cupid a glance. Her lute lies unnoticed at her elbow, by her side is a fading rose. The picture is painted somewhat in the style of Palma Vecchio, and the rumor goes that one of the two loves pictured Palma's daughter, one of the many fair women whom Titian loved. Another interpretation of the picture is that which makes *Artless Love* a Venus who is tempting a stiffly coy maiden to take the step which will initiate her in love's mysteries, and has suggested the title *Love and Longing.* Titian painted equally well the rich flowing draperies of saints and Biblical characters, and the beautiful, rounded nude figures which have made his fame as the portrayer of feminine beauty. But—we notice that he has painted more Venuses than Madonnas. We have:

The *Assumption of the Madonna* (Venetian Academy), the *Madonna of the Rabbit* (Louvre), and the *Presentation of the Virgin in the Temple* (Venetian Academy). On the other hand there are: *The Worship of Venus* (Madrid Museum), *Venus* (Darmstadt), the lovely *Venus Anadyomene* (Bridgewater Gallery), the *Urbino Venus* (Uffici Gallery), of all the most famous, and the *Venus and Cupid of Florence,* a *Venus and Adonis,* and the *Venus del Pardo* (Madrid). It almost seems, if we are to judge both by his life and by his works, that the great painter preferred *Profane* to *Sacred Love.* Quite a few of the Venuses and other lightly clad ladies of antiquity (one is a *Danae,* clad only in the rain of gold the Greek god Jove showered on her) Titian painted for that pious fanatic King Philip of Spain, who seems to have been as diligent a student of the nude in painting as he was of religion.

Many other fine paintings, religious scenes, mythological scenes, great battle-pictures (among the last he did was one of the *Battle of Lepanto* (Madrid), in which the Christian fleet defeated the Turks at sea) and portraits of popes (Paul III), kings, dukes and great personages—for he was the foremost "portrait-painter" of his day—were among his works.

In his palace on the Adriatic Titian lived, loved and painted. When he went to Bologna to paint Emperor Charles V, (1532) the latter made him a Count Palatine and a Knight of the Golden Spur, and gave his children hereditary nobility—something unheard of for

THE ROMANCE OF PAINTING

a painter in those days. His splendid mode of life cost money, and Titian always was keen to get a good price for his works. But the lord of the Indies, Emperor of Germany, King of Spain, Sicily and Jerusalem, who was so free with titles of nobility (which cost him nothing) was very poor pay, and his son Philip was worse. The very year of his death poor Titian was sending dunning letters to the royal Spanish "dead beat" to beg for payment of pictures supplied for the last twenty years. But we must not think of Titian as a person small or mean. He was more royal in his generosity than many a prince. When the Valois King Henry III passed through Venice from Poland, to take his place on the throne of France, Titian entertained him in his splendid villa. Henry looked at a number of the fine pictures on the walls, and priced them. And Titian with a splendid gesture, made the Valois a gift of all the pictures he had priced. And in spite of his many love affairs, Titian was happy in his family life. He loved his children and they him, with the exception of his oldest son Pomponio, who was worthless, a "tonsured profligate" as he has been called, and who, after his father's death squandered his fortune. Titian lived to be ninety-nine and then died suddenly (1576) of the plague raging in Venice at the time. No sooner had Titian and his son Orazio died, than the beautiful palace on the Adriatic was plundered by the thieves who prowled about the city uncontrolled. Great art critics seem to waver between calling the *Presentation of the Virgin in the Temple* (Venice Academy), or the stupendous *Entombment of Christ* (Louvre), his greatest picture, and many consider him the greatest of all painters.

Paris Bordone (1500-1571), and Bonifazio were Titian's best pupils. Jacopo Bassano da Ponte (1510-1571) was the great Venetian "landscape" artist and "animal painter" of Titian's name.

VERONESE

Paolo Veronese (Paolo Cagliari, 1528-1588), though born in Verona, belongs to the Venetian School. In Venice (except for a short stay in Rome), he lived and painted, died and was buried. He was the best all-around draughtsman and decorative painter among the Venetians, and his Christs, Marys, saints and martyrs all are "serious, well-fed" and well-dressed people. No plain linen garments and sandles for Veronese. His men are coarsely powerful, and his women are voluptuous in rich garments instead of in the nude. "All things that burn and glitter in the sun" he likes to get into his pictures.

The *Marriage at Cana* (Louvre) is probably his most famous picture, one of various sacred marriages-feasts (for a feast always gave him a chance at glory of color, pomp, gold and glitter) he painted.

Christ and the Disciples only seem to happen to be there, and do not cut much of a figure. The splendid architecture, the gorgeous costumes, the crowd of musicians, gold and silver plate, silken canopies and banners are borrowed from the life of the wealthy Venetians of Veronese's own day. There is not much difference between the Marriage at Cana, and a marriage in some great Venetian noble's house. And on the back of one of Veronese's drawings a note in his own handwriting has been found that says: "If I ever have time, I want to show a sumptuous banquet in a superb hall. The Virgin, the Saviour and St. Joseph will be present. They will be served by the most brilliant retinue of angels you can imagine. They will be offered the daintiest viands and abundance of splendid fruit in gold and silver dishes. Other angels will hand them precious wines in transparent glasses, and gilded goblets, to show with what zeal blessed spirits will serve the Lord". As Veronese says: "The Virgin, the Saviour and St. Joseph" *will be there,* but the "service" is the main thing.

The Vision of St. Helena (Nat. Gallery), a charming picture, shows us the mother of the Emperor Constantine, but—as a nice young Venetian girl asleep at her window.

The Family of Darius Before Alexander (Nat. Gallery, London). A glowing, gloriously colored picture—its colors the best preserved of any by Veronese. The wife and daughters of Darius kneel before Alexander, in armor and crimson dress, surrounded by his generals. In its noble male figures, beautiful women, fine dog, and even Alexander's monkey, in the gem-like gold and silver tones of its costumes and architecture, it shows Veronese at his best.

Christ at Emmaus (Louvre). There is no deep religious feeling, no moral suffering in this beautiful picture. It is a Christ in Venice, sixteenth century Venice. In a rose-colored robe, with a halo around His head, He is blessing wine and bread, which the numerous waiters are passing to the well-dressed disciples. In the foreground two little girls in brocaded silk dresses are playing with a big dog.

The Holy Family with Saints (Church of San Zaccria, Venice). Here too, we find a Holy Family which has spent a good deal of time with some of the very best sixteenth-century Venetian tailors. They seem to be attractive lay figures meant to display the beautiful colors, crimson, yellow, green, blue, gold, red and pale rose, of the rich garments they wear.

The Rape of Europa (Ducal Palace, Venice) is not a very passionate affair, but it is a most beautiful picture, full of youth, beauty, lovely ladies in silks and pearls. One great writer had said that "it fills the heart with joy". We see blonde Europa, the classic nymph, dressed as a young Venetian girl of the highest society, in a rich silk robe, being helped to the divine bull's back by her attendants, that gentle animal lovingly licking her foot. About her are a crowd of companions who have come to "see her off", while Cupids drop flowers from the air.

The Triumph of Venice (Ducal Palace, Venice), a ceiling fresco, shares with the *Marriage of Cana* the reputation of being Veronese's masterpiece. Venice, golden-haired and radiant, a female figure, is throned between marble columns. Angels crown her, while the virtues, arts and sciences gather round her and all the people of Venice pay homage to their queen.

Honored and beloved, lavish in expenditure, affectionate and amiable in disposition, Veronese led a happy married life, and never was at a loss for work, counting great kings and nobles among his customers. One of his sacred feast pictures got him into trouble with the Inquisition. They said it would have been more fitting to have painted in a Magdalen where he had put a dog. Poor Veronese answered that he had the greatest respect for the Magdalen, but a dog "fitted" better into the corner in question. Then he was called to account for the figure of a drunken German, trying to stop his nose from bleeding. "Why, I had meant no irreverence", said Veronese, "it was to show that the master of the house had so many servants they had time to quarrel among themselves." But—the Holy Inquisition ordered him to paint out his dog and his German, and paint in his Magdalen instead. And Veronese did so, for people who disobeyed the Inquisition were apt to get in trouble.

TINTORETTO

Jacopo Tintoretto (1518-1594), "The Thunderbolt of Painting", is the most passionate, profound, and rich in thought among the great Venetians. His art was not the lordly decorative art of Veronese. He was a greater-souled man. He refused the title King Henry of France offered him. He was indifferent to emperors, and princes, wrapped up in his work. His skill lay in his knowledge of anatomy, his genius in handling the lights and shadows of night. And he was impracticable, for all he cared about was getting his great thoughts down on canvas, whether it paid him or not. This could not have met with his wife's approval, and she may have improved him in this respect, for he left his children a decent fortune when he died. He had much of Michel Angelo's savage originality and energy, but when his wife, Faustina, every day, tied up his little allowance of money in a handkerchief, and bade him account for it when he returned home, he obeyed meekly enough. His studio was hidden away in the furthest corner of the house. He did not want to be bothered when he worked, and could only be reached by going up a dark staircase, and through long, dark passages. His greatest paintings are:

The Marriage at Cana (Church of St. Maria della Salute, Venice). A purer, nobler picture than Veronese's with the same name. It was painted for a monastery dining-room so that the monks might feel the Saviour always was eating in their company. Christ sits at one end of the table, and the intense, clear light which comes through the windows is so arranged that it falls the full length of the table, on a line of young Venetian women, making the whole centre of the picture "one broad sunbeam made up of fair faces and golden hair".

The Crucifixion (San Rococo Scuola, Venice). Ruskin says this picture is beyond all analysis and all praise.

Marriage of Bacchus and Ariadne (Ducal Palace, Venice). Painted in what artists call Tintoretto's "silver manner"—the Venetians said he had three pencils, "iron, silver and gold"—it is a poem of exquisite feeling, in which Ariadne on her island is offered a wedding-ring by the god Bacchus. Symonds, an authority, has called it "the most beautiful oil-painting in existence."

The Miracle of St. Mark (Venice Academy). St. Mark comes from heaven to aid a Christian slave who would not stop worshipping at his shrine, and is about to be tortured. The middle of the canvas —it is glorious in colors—glows "as if a topaz had burst there!"

Paradise, the last picture Tintoretto painted, is probably the largest oil-painting in the world (35 feet high by 74 feet long), with 500 figures. Time has much darkened and confused it, and it has lost much of its original beauty.

CHAPTER VI

THE ITALIAN POST-RENAISSANCE PAINTERS

(The Painters of the Baroque)

PAINTING in Italy after the Renaissance represented a decline. It is known as the Post- (or After) Renaissance Age, that of the so-called "Catholic Revival", the Baroque Age, the age of the Counter-Reformation. The ideas of the Baroque in Art already have been explained (See "The Romance of Architecture, Chap. XII), and the Baroque painters of the later sixteenth century painted in the same extravagant style the architects used in building, and the sculptors did the same in their statues and decorative works. The more important Baroque painters are known as the "Mannerists" (because their painting represented a more or less artificial "manner"). Chief among the "mannerists" was Agnolo Bronzino (1502-1572). Certain among the Baroque painters of Bologna stand for a nobler type of work (they are also called the Bologna School) and led by Lodovico Caracci (1555-1619), are called "Eclectics" because they tried to combine in their style the fine points of all the great artists who had gone before them.

They may be "Eclectics", like Ludovico and his brother Annibale of Bologna, Domenico of Domenichino Zampieri (1581-1641), whose most famous work is a *Communion of St. Jerome* (Vatican), Barbieri, called Guercino (1590-1666) or Salvi. They may be "Eclectics" like Guido Reni (1572-1642) and Carlo Dolci (1616-1686). Or, they may be "Naturalists" like Caravaggio, Ribera or Carlo Rosa, men who tried to show everything "naturally", just as it was, and sometimes overdid the terrible and horrible in showing it. But they all used their gift as a weapon in the great counter-reaction of the Church against the Protestantism of the Reformation.

GUIDO RENI AND CARLO ROSA DOLCI

Sweetness and tender sentiment is the keynote of the religious paintings of these two great artists, Guido Reni's *St. Sebastian Pierced with Arrows,* dying in agony (Capitoline Gallery, Rome), his plaintive, weeping, sorrowing Madonnas, *Ecce Homos* (Christs), Magdalens and saints were all appealing to the hearts of the people, pleading for their abandoned altars, with their beauty and gentle, suffering grace, winning back hearts to the Roman Church. Carlo Dolci—a man who worked very slowly and turned melancholy mad when he found that another painter, Luca Giordano (1682), could get more painting done in four or five hours that *he* could in four or five months—was another artist whose pictures fairly brought tears to the eyes. He, too, did a *St. Sebastian* (Florence), a *St. Cecilia* (Dresden), his most famous composition being *St. Andrew Praying Before the Crucifixion* (Pitti Gallery, Florence). It is said that during Passion week, every year, he painted a half-length figure of the Saviour. Guido Reni's most famous "worldly" pictures are an *Aurora* (Rospiglo Palace, Rome) and—an odd, merry little picture surprising in a painter who loved to dwell on saints in agony—a *Youthful Bacchus* (Pitti Palace, Florence). The *Aurora* is regarded as his masterpiece, and she is sailing happily along on golden clouds instead of turning a sorrowful, heart-torn face to the skies.

Beatrice Cenci (Barberini Palace, Rome). It is a sad, lovely face that looks out from the canvas, and the heroine—said to have been painted by Guido on the eve of her beheading—was the central figure of a terrible tragedy which shook Rome at her time. Young and motherless, Beatrice was the daughter of a Roman noble, Francesco Cenci, whose vice and wickedness of every sort startled even the Rome of his day, which was not easily shocked. Francesco kept his poor daughter shut up in a lonely castle in the Apennines. There he treated her so barbarously and, so it is said, with even incestuous violence, that the poor, tortured girl felt her only salvation lay in killing this monstrous father. When seventeen years old, she managed to have her father murdered by some bravos she hired, and in spite of the horrible nature of the crime, one cannot help feeling that it was a "good riddance" of exceedingly "bad rubbish". Her beauty did not save Beatrice from torture nor the axe, but it is clear that she was driven to do as she did. And her haunting beauty, her dark eyes, saddened by the crimes committed by and against her, still look out from the canvas as Guido fixed them there in his day.

CARAVAGGIO AND RIBERA

If Guido Reni and Carlo Dolci aimed at the hearts of the people, and tried to bring them to the Roman fold with pictures of Madonnas and Saints that wrung the soul with tenderness and melting sentiment, two other painters, "naturalists", did religious pictures whose wild, passionate, exciting nature was an even more powerful means of appealing to the religious sentiment of the beholder. The Church was glad to place these strong, emotion-arousing works over its altars, there to fill sinning souls with a useful terror, by making their hearts miss a beat when they looked at them.

Michel Angelo Amerighi Caravaggio (1569-1609), a Lombard, flung into his canvases the same wild, fierce fury which led him to kill a man in his youth in a gambling quarrel in Rome. His *St. Sebastian* and his *Entombment of Christ* (Vatican), are filled with dark and suspicious secondary figures. For he chose as his models the scum of the underworld, an underworld he knew from actual experience, and not from "say-so". These figures he presented with dramatic force and a magic handling of sinister shadows which his followers so exaggerated that their school has been called that of "The Darklings".

Giuseppe Ribera, often called Il Spagnoletto, or "The Little Spaniard" (1588-1656), a leading painter of this "Neapolitan School", was a pupil of Caravaggio, the famous "shadow-painter", and painted in his style, dramatic and exciting. When his first picture, a *Martyrdom of St. Bartholomew* was exhibited from his father-in-law's balcony, the people gathered in the streets in such crowds, to gloat over its terrible details, that the Spanish Viceroy of Naples, the Count of Monterey, thought a revolution had broken out. After that Ribera had orders and to spare. Incidentally he had some excitement in his own life, for Don Juan de Austria, son of the Spanish King Philip IV, came to Naples, saw and conquered Ribera's lovely daughter Maria, and abducted her. Maria, however, was socially reinstated in the graces of good society by being married to a Spanish nobleman, and Ribera died wealthy. Ribera's *Descent from the Cross* (Certosa, Naples), is considered his masterpiece, and his most "shuddery" painting probably is his *St. Januarius Emerging from the Furnace*. His best pupils were Salvator Rosa and Luca Giordano.

Salvator Rosa (1615-1673) a Neapolitan, was one of the most romantic of painters, and created the style of the "romantic landscape". He did not run to saintly horrors, like his teacher, and though he did some religious paintings, his wild desolate beaches, cavernous and romantic countrysides, peopled with all sorts of wild and savage folk—sailors, fishermen and soldiers, doing all sorts of wild things—and great historical and battle-pictures were his favorites. Still, his trend of mind was toward the savage and terrible. *Democritus Among the Tombs, Regulus in the Spiked Cask* (England), *Saul and the Witch of Endor* (Louvre), his great *Battlepiece* (Louvre), show his trend. He was a musician and a writer as well as painter, and in one of his "Satires", dealing with painting, he talks about the indecency of painting "sprawling, half-naked saints of both sexes."

CHAPTER VII

THE "FLEMISH REVIVAL"

Peter Paul Rubens

PETER PAUL RUBENS (1577-1640), and the artists of his "school", are the masters of the so-called "Flemish Revival". In Flanders, during the Baroque Age, in the Netherland provinces which remained true to Spain and Catholicism (present-day Belgium), the name of Rubens leads all the rest. "Does this painter mix blood with his colors?" Guido Reni asked, when he saw his pictures, so dramatic and so forceful are they.

Rubens was another "king of painters," like Titian, a monarch of art. His father had been a humble Antwerp druggist, and had flitted from his native land when he was in danger of losing his head for having become a Protestant. But Rubens was brought up in a noble household as a page, and once his genius became known moved from honor to honor, was knighted by King Charles I of England, and was the familiar of princes and potentates.

Rubens was a true Dutchman, strong and healthy, full of life and action. He had none of Reni or Dolci's sentimentality. All his figures are alive, and full of dramatic movement and vigor. Rubens painted well in every field. Among his thirteen-hundred-odd paintings, his greatest religious pictures are:

The Descent from the Cross (Antwerp Cathedral), and the *Assumption of the Virgin* (Antwerp Cathedral), every outline bathed in light in the latter picture, so that the Virgin seems raised in a dazzling glory no other master has shown; his dramatic *Massacre of the Innocents* (Munich Gallery), would move any mother, for it shows devoted mothers defending their little ones tooth and nail; his splendid *Martyrdom of St. Peter* (Cologne), and his *Martyrdom of St. Thomas*. Rubens' religious pictures were no "propaganda" paintings. They are hardly *religious* in many cases, so intent is the painter on handling some *dramatic* action or moment in the most effective way. His *Adoration of the Magi* (Madrid Gallery) is an instance. It is a magnificent processional picture, with 28 life-size figures—Rubens liked to paint on the largest scale, always—with the kings and their nobles in gorgeous dresses, soldiers in armor, slaves, camels, etc.

Animals, incidentally, Rubens painted like one who loved them. He has painted animated lion, tiger, hippopotamus and crocodile hunts, and his Flanders horses and dogs are "the best of their breed". And he was a favorite portrait painter of kings. For Louis XIII of France he painted 24 great historical pictures, showing the life of Marie de Medici, his mother. When he was in France in 1625, busy with other works, he saw the marriage of Princess Henrietta Maria at Nôtre Dame in Paris, and when the scaffolding on which he stood gave way, was just able to catch an adjoining pillar and save himself. His purely "fancy subjects" include two beautiful paintings *The Garden of Love* (Madrid) and *The Village Feast* (Louvre), and one of his happiest smaller fancies is the *Children with Garland* (Munich), eight laughing little naked tots, dragging and pushing along a huge garland of flowers, many times too large for them.

Some of Rubens' pictures from Greek mythology are glorious. He has one called *Quos Ego* (Dresden), in which old Neptune is driving along in a huge conch-shell, drawn by fantastic sea-horses, while moist damp mermaids play around him. The uproar of Nature is so well painted that one almost hears the storm-wind whistle and the slapping waves clash in foaming billows. In his *Neptune and Thetis* (Berlin), the same old god, after the storm, is sitting with his water-bride in the shade of a wreck's sail, and the sea is rolling all its treasures to her feet.

His nudes have been criticized, and have been called "blowsy" by some. Yet Flemish women generally were of a large build and lacked the grace of the Italian sisters, and Rubens painted nature as he saw it. His *Feast of Venus* or *Helen Fourment Ready to Enter the Bath* (Vienna), are beautiful in their coloring and breadth of touch.

"The Fleming" as he was called, was twice happily married, and both Isabella Brant (1609), and Helen Fourment, the sixteen-year old girl he married when fifty-three, were beautiful women and acted as his models. He was the friend of kings, of Philip IV of Spain, with whom he once spent nine months, Charles I of England, and Louis XIII of France, and all the great of his time. Besides being a painter, he was a courtier and diplomat, and to the end of his time moved and lived in an atmosphere of splendor, courtly favor and consideration. In his time there was no painter to equal him, and for a century after his death the Flemish school was merely an echo of what he had done. He died in the fulness of his glory in 1640.

Jacob Jordans and Franz Snyders (1579-1657), who painted animals and "still life", and the two Teniers, David the Elder and David the Younger, who painted "low life" subjects in a refined style, the latter more celebrated, may also be mentioned. Two great Flemish portrait painters stand out.

SIR ANTHONY VAN DYCK AND SIR PETER LELY

Van Dyck (1599-1641), born in Antwerp, though he painted tender, religious pictures, a *Holy Family* (London), *Crucifixion* (Florence) *St. Martin Dividing his Cloak* (Windsor Castle), and others, is more famed as one of the greatest of portrait painters. His religious pictures, some of them, were done for the greater spread of the Roman faith, like the *Mystic Marriage of the Blessed Herman Joseph* (Vienna), and the *St. Augustine in Ecstasy* (Antwerp), both painted for the Antwerp Jesuits. In Brussels he soon shared the title of court painter to the Regent of the Netherlands with Rubens, but he spent much time in London and English earls, dukes and lords, as well as Flemish and Dutch and French nobles, have been immortalized by his brush, and his refined and dignified portrait of *King Charles I* (Nat. Gallery & Louvre) is famous.

Van Dyck painted a tremendous number of portraits, for he loved pleasure over-well and always needed money. His mode of life was dissolute, though to it we owe the beautiful picture of an English professional beauty, Margaret Lemon, as *Herminia Putting on Clarinda's Armor* (Hampton Court). Margaret was the most beautiful and famous, though far from only mistress of Van Dyck. The great artist, in fact, loved beauty in every form, and found the seduction of female charms irresistible. Margaret lived with him in his house at Blackfriars (near London). In 1636, largely because his friends thought Margaret and others of her kind were not doing him any good, Van Dyck married the Lady Ruthven, grand-daughter of the Scots Earl of Gowrie. (He has painted her in white satin, playing the 'cello.) Then Margaret resented the end of their Blackfriar days so deeply that she bit and tried to maim Van Dyck's right hand! In 1641, his health began to fail, and in the same year he died. Stone and Dobson, Reynolds, Gainsborough, Lawrence and Raeburn owed much of their superiority to the study of his works.

Lely (1617-1680), was the court painter of King Charles II, as Van Dyck had been to King Charles I. He was a favorite with "Old Rowley", and his most famous work is the group collection of portraits of the gay and giddy court ladies of Old Whitehall, ladies drowsy with languid sentiment, known as *The Beauties* (Hampton Court Palace). As might be expected of a court painter of the "Merry Monarch", the subject he felt drawn to in the historical field was *Sushannah and the Elders* (Burleigh House).

CHAPTER VIII

REMBRANDT AND DUTCH PAINTING IN THE BAROQUE AGE

The painters of the Dutch School do not show the magnificence and splendor of court life in their pictures, as do the painters of the Flemish School. Holland was a land of the Reformation. The painters were naturalistic. They painted tender, intimate pictures of every-day life, of nature, and portraits, and their art shows that they had cut themselves off from ceremony in worship, and splendor in court life. Rembrandt is the great name that stands out above all others, in Holland, just as that of Rubens does in Flanders.

REMBRANDT

Rembrandt Harmens Z. van Rijn (1606-1669), a miller's son, goes under the name of "The Shakespeare of Holland" in Art, so great is he both as realist and poet, and so deep an understanding has he of humanity. He painted the living history of his day, the life that went on around him. The subjects of his religious paintings he drew from the Bible, not from the legends of the Roman Church. In 1631 he already was regarded as the first portrait painter in Amsterdam. His great groups of individual portraits include the famous *The Lesson in Anatomy* (1632), his landscapes the poetic *Castle on the Hill* (Cassel), his "realistic" ones, the *The Woman Taken In Adultery* (Nat. Gallery, London), and the religious paintings the lofty and dignified *Christ Healing the Sick*. His most famous "realistic" picture is:

The Night Watch (1642) which should really be called "The Day Watch", for it only seems like night because the background has been so darkened by time. It shows a crowd of city night watchmen, arquebusiers (men armed with muskets) pouring out of their "community club house", in red uniforms, with a lieutenant in citron yellow, a captain in black velvet, and a girl and drummer in green, to go about their duties.

In his earlier years he often turned to the subject of Susannah. But though *The Bather* (Nat. Gallery, London), and other nudes of his are coarse and lumpy in figure, his "modelling is soft and round". His *Danae* (Petrograd) is considered the answer to all who claim he could not paint the nude human figure and give it beauty, for one can see the blood pulse beneath the warm skin. Many are the pictures of serious beauty, of striking dramatic force, of lofty nobility and "true to life" character he painted, more than 700 in all. Some of his pictures have a great human interest. There always was a loving woman in Rembrandt's life. First his mother, whom he often painted in earlier years. Then came his wife. Her name was Saskia van Uylenborch, a beautiful, blonde Frisian girl, whom he married in 1634. They were very happy together, and Rembrandt loved to introduce her on his canvases. He painted her sitting on his knee, or doing her hair, he painted her covered with the gold and Indian pearls he would have liked to have hung around her neck. And, he painted a sad, very touching picture of her in 1641, the year before her death, in which his brush sorrowfully records her failing health, and makes us feel his own grief.

The Marriage of Samson (Dresden Gallery). Here Rembrandt has made the historical scene a mere excuse to paint Saskia and himself as happy lovers. Saskia (as Samson's bride), sits calmly on a raised platform, with the light shining on her golden hair and jewels, while the bustle of the wedding festival flows around her. Rembrandt, as Samson, leans over a chair and puts his riddle to the Philistine lords.

But Saskia died in 1652. In 1654, two years later, unfortunately, we find the painter involved in a scandal. His maid-servant, a peasant girl named Hendrickje Stoffels had a child, which he recognized as his own. But he did not marry the girl, because if he had, Saskia's fortune would have passed from him. There seems little doubt that otherwise they would have wed. The picture known as *Rembrandt's Mistress* (Edinburgh Nat. Gallery), showing a sweet-faced girl in bed, raising herself to draw the curtain as a loved footstep draws near, is supposed to be that of Hendrickje.

In 1653, Rembrandt, though declared bankrupt and stripped of all he had, produced some great religious pictures, among them *John the Baptist Preaching in the Wilderness* (Berlin), and, painting to the last, died in 1669, having outlived his popularity. His work today is, however, valued very highly for the unique mellow, golden "tone" which marks his paintings.

FRANZ HALS

Franz Hals of Haarlem (1584-1666), with his vivid *Corporation Pictures* (Haarlem Town Hall), group portraits of the members of various military guilds or associations, his merry scenes taken from popular life, men drinking, boys making music, scolding market-wives and fish-women was, perhaps, the greatest of Dutch artists after Rembrandt. His daylight always has a silvery sheen, just as Rembrandt's great point is a golden glow based on artificial contrast of low light against darkest gloom. Hals' *Laughing Cavalier* (Wallace Collection, London), his *Bohémienne* or *Gipsy Girl* (Louvre), and many others have subtle smiles—but not the wonderful smile of *Mona Lisa!* These smiles are subtle smiles of a *lower* order, and one feels that one can interpret them in the terms, perhaps, of Hals' own life. For he was more or less of a high liver and low thinker. He so ill-treated his first wife that she died prematurely, and he just saved the reputation of his second by marrying her in 1617. But though drink was one of his main interests in life, he managed to raise ten children until 1652, when he became poverty stricken, and even the three mattresses the family owned were taken to satisfy his creditors. He put all his spirit into his fine paintings: his wife had to beg her bread, and died in a hospital. People are apt to judge an artist during his lifetime by his own personality. For two centuries after he died Franz Hals' pictures were so little thought of that you could buy one at auction for a couple of shillings. In 1908 the London National Gallery paid nearly $100,000 for a single group picture!

Other more important "light and shade" Dutch seventeenth century artists and painters of *genre* pictures—genre pictures are pictures of *real, ordinary, everyday life*—are Gerard Dou (1613-1675), Rembrandt's pupil, *The Young Mother* (Hague); Nicolaas Maes, Pieter de Hooch (he excelled in pictures showing one room opening into another), Gabriel Metsu, Jan Steen (1626-1679), crowded "life" scenes, *The Parrot Cage,* (Rijks Museum), Van Goyen (1596-1656), one of the first Dutch landscape artists, Hobbema, *Road to Middleharnis* (Nat. Gallery), and Jacob Ruisdael, another great landscape painter, *Mill near Wyck.* Paul Potter (1625-1654), though he lived before the days of Durham, painted in *The Young Bull* (Hague Museum), one of the finest of its kind, Philip Wouverman (1619-1668), did hunting and horseback scenes, Gerard Terborch, and Jan Vermeer of Delft (1632-1675), in his famous *Young Woman at a Window* (Met. Museum of Art, New York), showed a skill in handling color values in the *genre* style—the last named in particular —which few other painters can equal. During the eighteenth century Dutch painting did not produce anything very remarkable.

III

CHAPTER IX

VALESQUEZ AND THE SPANISH PAINTERS OF THE BAROQUE AGE

In Spain, during the seventeenth century, each of the main schools of Spanish painting, those of Valencia, Seville and Madrid (or Castile), produced one great painter. The great painter of the Valencian School, José de Ribera, made Naples his home, and already has been considered with the Italian painters. His influence, however, had its effect in Spain, and there the Valencian School brought forth Francisco de Zurvaran (1598-1662), a painter of noble, beautiful and human religious paintings, whose masterpiece is the *Apotheosis of St. Thomas Aquinas* (Prov. Museum, Seville) and Murillo. Before Murillo an "independent", El Greco, should be mentioned.

EL GRECO

Dominico Theotocopuli, known as El Greco (1548-1625), a Cretan, and a pupil of Titian's who had settled in Toledo, considered a madman in his own day, occupies a unique place among Spanish painters. He was a reverent Catholic, and his pictures are mainly religious ones. He was eccentric and loved to paint livid, gaunt and extraordinarily spectral figures. But though his pictures are extravagant and fantastic, they are always haunting and thrilling, and are now highly regarded. So great an American artist as J. S. Sargent claimed that he learned more from El Greco than from any other painter. More famous than his *Disrobing of Christ* (Toledo Cathedral), is a splendid picture, one of the finest in all Spain, which has been turned into a little dance-drama by the Swedish Ballet, to music by the French composer Inghelbrecht, a picture come to life: *Burial of the Count Orgaz* (San Tome Church, Toledo). It is a wild, weird and fantastic work. The pious Count of Argas is about to be buried, amid the raging of a terrible storm, and the saints Augustine and Stephen, in a frankly naturalistic way, are putting his body into the grave, while a crowd of mourners assist. Dark and lowering, mysterious and gloomy is the scene on earth below, while above the clouds are parted and the naked soul of the sainted Count kneels at the Saviour's feet, the Virgin begging for him, while the angels of heaven and the holy dead crowd around. The great picture makes a weirdly terrifying effect.

BARTOLOME ESTEBAN MURILLO

A wonderful painter (1617-1682), one of the most popular painters of all time, Murillo's paintings fall naturally into two classes: *genre* pictures and scenes from "low" life, and religious paintings. His father was a Sevillian working-man, and poor art students had had a hard time of it in Seville when Murillo was young. For models, the boys had to strip in turn and give other members of the class a chance to draw "from life", because none could afford to hire models. He grew up as one of the "street painters" who did *pinturas de la feria* (pictures for the fairs), generally daubs whose "clumsy saints and unripe Madonnas" were a regular Seville industry, and shipped by the cartload to convents and missions in Mexico, Peru and Cuba. But Murillo was not destined to stay a "street painter". In 1642 he bought a lot of canvas cheap, cut it up in strips of different sizes and, as fast as he could, painted pictures for the "American trade", until he could afford a trip to Italy. When he came back he took his first step on the road to greatness by painting eleven large pictures of saints (afterwards stolen by the French Marshal Soult, when he was in Seville, and sent back to his Paris home in baggage-wains) for the Convent of St. Francesco. They reflect the influence of Ribera and Caravaggio, and are painted in what is known as Murillo's *frio* or "cold" style. They "made him" among the rich and noble in Seville.

In 1648 Murillo married a wealthy lady, and for the next twenty years turned out one noble picture after another. His first picture in the calido or "warm" style was *Our Lady of the Conception* (1652), soon followed by *San Leandro and San Isidro*, his very famous *Nativity of the Virgin*, and the vast canvas known as *San Antonio de Padua*, all in the Seville Cathedral. In the picture of *Our Lady of the Snows* (St. Maria la Blanca Church, Seville), he painted one of the first pictures in his *vaporoso* or "misty" style, in which outlines are lost in a misty blending of light and shade. His *frio* and *calido* styles, however, alone or in combination he used during the best period of his life.

Murillo's Masterpieces. Murillo's masterpieces owe their existence to the fact that a vicious profligate had a change of heart. In 1661, Don Manuel Miguel Marana Vincentelo de Leca, one of the greatest nobles of Seville, and a debauchee of the wildest and most fantastic immorality, turned suddenly from sinner to saint. One of the first things he did was to commission his friend Murillo to paint eleven pictures for the Seville Charity Hospital. Of these eleven eight—*Moses Striking the Rock, The Return of the Prodigal, Abraham Receiving Three Angels, The Charity of San Juan de Dios, The Miracle of the Loaves and Fishes, Our Lord Healing the Paralytic,*

St. Peter Released from Prison, and *St. Elizabeth of Hungary*—are regarded as Murillo's master works. He was four years painting them, and was paid about $4,000 for them (a sum which looks better in Spanish *reals*—78,115). Among them *The Prodigal* and *St. Elizabeth* are considered the most perfect. *The Charity of St. Thomas de Villanueva* (Capuchin Convent, Seville), Murillo used to call "my own picture", and for the same church he painted (it has disappeared) a *Virgin of the Napkin,* so-called because it was painted on a napkin, and presented to the cook of the convent—he probably was a good cook—as a gift from the artist. His most *human* sacred painting is probably *The Angels' Kitchen* (Louvre). Old St. Felix, the saintly cook is holding the Holy Child in his arms in an ecstasy, while the angels are busy about the kitchen, and his *Madonna on the Half-Moon* and *Madonna with the Mirror,* are the most tenderly human as well as chaste of young girls. Murillo painted few portraits, but the few are beautiful and the dog lying at the feet of his friend, the *Canon Justino,* is known to have drawn a snarl from a living spaniel! A fine character, brave, pious, hard-working, Murillo fell from a scaffold in Cadiz in 1681, while he was painting a big picture for the Capucins of that town, received an injury from which he did not recover, and went back to Seville to die there the next year.

He was one of the greatest painters who fought the cause of Catholicism with brush and colors. The ecstasies of his Madonnas touch the heart, and though sometimes the self-mortifying details of his saints are repulsive, his pictures are not "artificial". They are real, honest and broadly human, and express the Catholic idea of life in a broadly human way. That is why they were a power, and held the hearts and minds of high and low, rich and poor. His Virgins are young Spanish girls of Seville, young working girls, but idealized, and while human, always removed from all suspicion of the sordid or worldly. His ragged street Arabs of Seville (*Beggar Boys,* Munich) and other "low-life" bits from the streets, in most cases belong to his earlier days. There are 45 of his wonderful canvases in the Prado Museum, Madrid.

VELASQUEZ

Diego Rodriguez de Silva y Velasquez (1599-1660) is the greatest master of the Madrid and Castilian School, the lordly painter and aristocratic star of painting in Spain, as Titian was in Venice and Rubens in Flanders. He was for 36 years the great court painter of one of the most splendid and extravagant of Spanish kings, King Philip IV, and developed "unity" and the giving of "essentials" in painting—the idea of *not painting in more* than the eye can grasp at first sight—as no painter before him. The people who lived at his time called him the "King of Naturalistic Painters", and he did manage to lend the second-rate human beings and the horrible costumes of the seventeenth century Spanish court a dignity and interest that is not theirs by right. Velasquez is a realist. In his *Crucifixion* and his *Christ at the Column* for all their pathos, the Saviour is intensely human rather than divine, and one can hear Velasquez' dogs bark, and feel his horses move. Velasquez was no brat of the streets, but a lawyer's son. While studying at the best school of Seville (1618), however, he married his teacher Pacheco's daughter, Juana. He deliberately painted *bodegones*—"tavern pictures"—because he said he would rather be the *first painter of common things* than the *second* of things nobler. And to be able to give every shade of meaning to the human face, he hired a simple farmer boy as a model and servant, and took down every change of expression brought out by the emotions and feelings city life awoke in the boy from the farm, as in his *Breakfast* (Petrograd, Hermitage), which shows the boy laughing and the youngest of the *Musicians* (Berlin Museum). In *St. John in the Desert* (Madrid), the same farmer lad is turned into a saint. In 1624, the weak, worthless, but art-loving King of Spain called Velasquez to court, and when he painted him on horseback (1623), he became a member of the royal household. In 1628 he was Rubens' guide to the art treasures of Spain, by the king's command—but the Spanish painter did not change his style.

His *Expulsion of the Moors from Spain* (destroyed by fire in 1734), made him a gentleman usher, and got him a daily allowance of 12 *reals*—the same amount paid the dwarfs, jesters and players in the palace. The picture showed King Philip III pointing with a bâton to a crowd of unfortunate Moriscos, men, women and children, driven off by soldiers, while Spain, as a majestic female looks calmly on. On a visit to Italy (1629) Velasquez copied Tintoretto's *Crucifixion* and *Last Supper,* and paintings by Michel Angelo and Raphael for the Spanish king, and sent them to him and also did some beautiful, silvery landscapes, returning to Madrid in 1631.

The Court Portrait. The picture of a princely boy, Don Baltasar Carlos, (Grosvenor House, London), heir to the Spanish throne, exists in many portraits. The best known is the one that shows the boy, proud and haughty even in childhood, dressed as a little field-marshal, on a galloping horse, in the palace riding-school, while his father and mother look down on their son from a balcony. The poor little prince died when only seventeen. The *Count of Olivares* (Madrid Gallery) with his proud, haughty face—a kind friend to Velasquez and who first had called him to court—is splendid in a great horseback portrait.

Las Meninas (Madrid Gallery). Velasquez is standing in his studio. He is painting the portraits of the king and queen, whose figures are reflected in a mirror at the end of the room, when in comes the little princess, the Infanta Margarita Maria, daughter of the new queen, Mariana of Austria, with her maids of honor, and her big mastiff. The child has just asked for a glass of water, and one of the maids has handed it to her. After this picture Velasquez was made a noble, and a knight of Santiago (after his ancestors had been carefully looked up to see that there was no taint of Jewish or Moorish blood in his veins), and stood at the height of his fame.

The jealous Spaniard has always shrunk from having the portraits of his lovely women painted. "Painters? Well . . . it is better to take no chances", seems to have been their motto. So we find few portraits of lovely women among Velasquez's personal pictures. There is one painting of a surpassingly beautiful woman, however, *The Brunette Lady* (Wallace Collection), which shows a superb brunette, whose bosom seems to rise and fall, and whose blood seems to pulse through her veins, and whose flesh has a beautiful glow.

Velasquez' greatest historical painting is without question *The Surrender of Breda* (Madrid), while his portrait of *Pope Innocent X,* is considered one of the greatest portraits, when it comes to the insight a bit of painted linen gives us in a man's soul, that ever has been painted. *Las Lanzas,* "The Lances", as the *Surrender of Breda* sometimes is called because of the lances that tower against the sky, shows Justin of Nassau, in front of the Dutch soldiers, surrendering the keys of the city to the Marquis de Spinola, the Spanish general, the lances of whose men rise like a forest, while behind them stretches the vast Lowland countryside, dotted with fortifications. The light and the air of the famous picture are a silvery blue.

Christ on the Cross (Madrid Gallery) is usually considered Velasquez's greatest religious painting. The Saviour's head hangs down on his breast. Yet though he did various others, notably a *Coronation of the Virgin* (Madrid), Velasquez was not the *church* painter. Murillo was the brush-child of Holy Church, while Velasquez was the *court* painter.

Venus and Cupid (Nat. Gallery) is a fine example of his treatment of the nude. In his nudes and half-nudes (*Forge of Vulcan*), he painted the "very essence of living flesh". His last great "realistic work" was *Las Hilanderas,* "The Spinners" (Madrid), and shows the interior of the royal tapestry factory in a wonderful scene full of light and life, in a harmony of red, blue-green, grey and black.

Velasquez died rather suddenly of a fever, at the splendid marriage festivities of the Spanish king's daughter and the French king's son, on the swampy Island of Pheasants (Bidassoa), and in contrast to Murillo, the painter of the Church who died with hardly anything, Velasquez left a large fortune to his wife. His slave Pareja, was his best imitator, and did good work in his style.

CHAPTER X

THE FRENCH PAINTERS OF THE BAROQUE AGE AND THE EIGHTEENTH CENTURY

French Painters of the Baroque Age

GREATER names in French painting do not appear much before the seventeenth century. Fouquet (1415-1490), one of whose *Virgin* (Antwerp Museum) was modelled after Agnes Sorel, the mistress of King Charles VII of France, and has a strangely haunting expression; and Clouet (b. 1500), with a *Portrait* of *King Francis I* (Louvre), showing a sly and sensual face, seem to be the outstanding Renaissance artists. But with the seventeenth century we have a group of French artists. Lesueur (1617-1655), called by those of his own time "The French Raphael", however, is not given that name now, though he did paint religious pictures. Lebrun (1619-1699) was more a decorator than a painter, as his work in Versailles shows. Philippe de Champaigne did historical canvases, and Pierre Mignard (1610-1695) and Nicolas Lagrilliere (1656-1746), were the French Lelys of the age, painting the vapid French court beauties in their velvets, satins and laces, their pearls and jewels, powder and patches. Hyacinthe (1659-1743), is chiefly known by his pompous and stately picture of the greatest king the Baroque Age knew, Louis XIV, (Louvre), with a tremendous wig, in a white satin suit, with a splendid blue velvet mantle falling around him, embroidered with the silver lilies of France. It is a magnificent example of the great court painting. The genre painter of the day is Le Nain (1588-1677) who did simple life scenes of haymakers on the farm or village blacksmiths. Two great artists stand out in France during the seventeenth century. Both lived mainly in Italy, but their art was individual and French.

POUSSIN AND CLAUDE LORRAINE

Claude Gelee (1600-1682), a poor Lorraine orphan boy and pastrycook's apprentice, rambling to Italy, became the greatest French landscape painter of his time. Amiable, gentle, patient, his work came into great demand, and he is considered the inventor of the so-called "classical" landscape. He gave his great landscape picture historical names, but that was merely a little trick to allow him to introduce small groups of human figures. In his *Landing of Cleo-*

patra at Tarsus (Louvre) the river Tarsus and its surroundings are more important than Egypt's queen. He himself considered his *Villa Madamma* landscape and a *Feast of Esther and Ahasuerus*—which he refused to sell though Pope Clement IX offered to cover the whole surface of the big canvas with gold pieces—as his finest works. There are some ninety-two paintings scattered in European art galleries. He died of the gout, in Rome, at the age eighty-two, leaving a considerable fortune to a nephew and niece.

Nicholas Poussin (1594-1665) was also a French Roman. His works represent the grand style of the Baroque at its best, great religious and mythological paintings in the large, bold manner of the splendid Renaissance artists, and he produced a great number of works. But he coupled the Italian grand style with a great love for Nature and also did some very fine landscapes. His historical paintings include: *The Death of Germanicus* (Barberini Palace), his religious paintings the *Vision of St. Paul* (Louvre), a *Last Supper* (Versailles), a *Seven Sacraments* (Bridgewater Gallery), and a *Holy Family* (Louvre) while among his mythological scenes are: *The Triumph of Flora, Labors of Hercules* and *Bacchanal* (Louvre).

WATTEAU AND THE PAINTERS OF THE ROCOCO AGE

The one great figure among the French painters of the Rococo eighteenth century, is Watteau. But there are not many other *peintres de l'amour* or "painters of love" as the French call them—for love was the one great interest in French life, a love not always of the higher kind—and we have Jean-Honore Fragonard and a whole group of painters whose names are familiar for their light and graceful, if often sensual works.

Jean-Honore Fragonard (1732-1806), was a follower of Rubens, but his charming pictures all have the true Louis XV spirit. He delights in all sorts of graceful nudes in more or less compromising positions: *La Chemise Enlevée*, "The Shift Withdrawn", *The Sleeping Bacchante,* or still more provocative groups of flounced and furbelowed lovers as in *The Dangers of the Swing, Feeble Resistance, The Shepherd's Hour, The Tumble* (Louvre). These scenes of love and voluptuousness, in demand at the licentious court of Louis XV (he also decorated the private apartments of Madame du Barry and la Guimard, the dancer), brought Fragonard far greater fame and more money than his earlier *Christ Washing the Feet of the Apostles* (Grasse Cathedral). In Fragonard's time a chemise properly placed was more important on canvas than the noblest historical or religious scene, and so the painter gave up the religious for the raw. Nicolas Lancret (1690-1743), Pater, Van Loo, and François Boucher (1703-1770) all ran to unclad nymphs and mythological figures. Boucher was especially famed for his voluptuous and smiling nymphs, and was given the name of "The Anacreon of Painting". Jean Baptiste Chardin (1699-1779) was a man of a different type, a true painter, who excelled in fine *genre* works which, however, in his own day did not bring him the golden rewards and the favor shown the lighter and more frivolous brethren of the brush, whose naughty nudes and still naughtier dishevelled beauties were the rage.

WATTEAU

(1684-1721)

Watteau, the greatest French painter of the eighteenth century, followed Rubens in a way of his own. A Chopin of painting, consumptive, a poetic, melancholy nature, hard to get along with, yet of a fine, noble disposition, he hurried through his short life, painting, painting, painting with frantic energy, as though he knew Death's hand was stretching out to stop him. He has painted, with hardly an exception, pictures free from licentiousness, and his chief creation is a type known as the *fête champêtre*—the "country festival". In these lovely pictures gallant gentlemen and beautiful ladies of the time (even though they may be disguised as shepherds), wander through the greenest and serenest of park landscapes, with song and laughter, with lute-music and graceful flirtation. These *fêtes champêtres* of Watteau have inspired great poets like Paul Verlaine to set them in verse, and great musicians like Claude Debussy to retell them in tone. Watteau has other pictures, military scenes, genre bits, religious paintings. When he was in the last stages of his disease, and about to die, he was completing his *Crucifixion* but it is by his *fêtes champêtres* that he is remembered. The ex-emperor William of Germany was supposed to have the finest collection of Watteau paintings, but there are many beautiful ones at the Louvre in Paris. In his own lifetime they did not bring high prices; now a genuine Watteau may run into the thousands of dollars.

L'Embarkement du Cythère. "The Embarkment for Venus' Isle" (Berlin, Imperial Palace). This is the loveliest of those dreams of gallant innocence in which eighteenth century moral degradation is clothed in the beauty of poetry. The gay gentlemen and ladies who are setting out for the Island of Love are the children of some Rococo Venus, with red-heeled shoes, three-cornered hats, silken costumes, shepherd staves and powdered hair. The clear, shining water calls them. In the tender blue skies above hover fluttering cupids. We look at the picture, and are in what Hunecker has called "a land out of time, a No-Man's land of blue skies, beautiful women, gallant men and lovely landscapes". It is a poem of the joy of youth in love.

GREUZE

The Painter of Artificial Innocence

(1725-1805)

Louis XVI, who followed Louis XV on the throne of France, was a dull, stolid, highly respectable family man, who looked with horror on immorality and loose conduct. Since the king set the style, the tone of the French court at once changed to one of outward innocence. Virtue and modesty, though those who pretended to cultivate them may not have been sincere, became the fashion. In fact, virtue was exaggerated to the most vicious sentimentality and when Marie-Antoinette played at village innocence and pretended to be a milk-maid at the Trianon in Versailles, the painter of artificial innocence, Jean-Baptiste Greuze, came into his own. To do Greuze justice, he did not want to be the painter of "innocence". He wanted to be a great historical painter, but—people did not want Roman emperors just then. They insisted instead on having enticingly soft, healthy, tender and innocent young girls (not of *The Shift Withdrawn* kind), preferable mourning over some dear, little departed bird or animal friend. So Greuze painted *Innocence,* (Wallace Gallery, London) a charming young girl holding a little white lamb in a somewhat affected way, *Young Girl Weeping Over her Dead Bird, Young Girl With a Broken Pitcher, Young Girl with a Black Dog,* and others. His first picture in the popular virtuous style *Father Reading His Bible to His Children* (Louvre), roused good society to frantic admiration. The writer Diderot said of *The Good Mother* that "it preached raising children". How seriously Greuze took his pictures is proved by one incident. Madame Geoffrin once called a picture of his, showing a young mother surrounded by many little ones, a "fricassee of children". Greuze was furious. "I shall paint her as a school-teacher, whip in hand", he cried, "and children *for all time* will fear her!" But these, as well as *The Village Bride* (Louvre), *The Father's Curse,* (the degenerate boy is receiving it, while the rest of the family stand by in horror-stricken attitudes), and the *Wicked Son Punished* (returned from war, the "cursed" son sheds tardy tears over his father's dead form,) (Louvre), though they brought him plenty of money did not make him happy. He was extravagant and his money always melted away. But soon young French girls had more than broken pitchers to shed tears about, and fathers were too busy stuffing their hungry mouths with grass to read the Bible. When reality broke through society sentiment with the French Revolution, Greuze was forgotten for a long time.

CHAPTER XI

THE GREAT ENGLISH PAINTERS OF THE EIGHTEENTH AND EARLY NINETEENTH CENTURIES

The Portrait Painters

IN England Sir Peter Lely, and Sir Godfrey Kneller (1648-1723), who held the position of court painter from Charles II to George I, and is known chiefly by his *Ten Beauties of the Court of William III* (Hampton Court), which has led to the well-established opinion that Charles II was a better selecter of court beauties than Dutch William of Orange, were succeeded by other masters of portrait painting as time went on.

William Hogarth (1697-1764), though a fine painter, is best known by his wonderful series of engravings which show the life and manners of his time and provide each painting with a moral. The originals of three of these sets of engravings: *A Harlot's Progress, A Rake's Progress*, and *Marriage à la Mode* (Nat. Gallery), are oil paintings, and the vices and depravity of his age are lashed in them in a dramatic and gripping way.

Sir Joshua Reynolds (1723-1792), a man of polished and amiable manners, was by 1760 the most fashionable portrait painter in all London. He was hand in glove with all the great men of English society, the admirals and captains, the generals and bishops, the playwrights and poets. As a painter he stands with Gainsborough *just behind* those of the *very first* rank. Besides his society belles, the *Duchess of Devonshire and her Baby, Three Ladies Wadegrave* (Nat. Gallery), *Nelly O'Brien* (Wallace Collection), his *Mrs. Siddons* and other stage beauties, his *Gibbon, Burke, Sterne, Fox, Johnson, Garrick* and other portraits have been called "historical monuments" so fine are they, so natural and speaking.

Thomas Gainsborough (1727-1788), was both painter and musician —he played several string instruments—a lover of home life and a man of many friends, who shared Reynolds vogue as a society painter. For him, too, the great of the time sat, and his two most famous portraits are, probably, *Georgiana, Duchess of Devonshire* (Morgan Collection), a beautiful, sparkling picture of one of the greatest society beauties of her day, and *The Blue Boy* (Master Nuttal) in the same collection, a beautiful, dreamy picture of a boy in his 'teens, whose wonderful "blue light" is said to have been the result of a remark of Reynolds' that *blue* as a color was not suitable for the main light of a work. Many of Gainsborough's landscapes are as fine as his portraits, and among his scenes of English country life, the *Waggon and Horses Passing a Brook* (Nat. Gallery) was the painter's own favorite.

George Romney (1734-1802) was the third of the great English painters of the eighteenth century. His ladies of fashion are more alluring, more soft and feminine, than those of either of his predecessors. Romney was married, but the love of his life was the famous (or infamous) Emma Lyon, better known as Lady Hamilton. He met her in London, in 1782, after she already had acquired notoriety as the mistress of various English gentlemen. And after that the beautiful portraits of his brush idealized his "divine friend" as he called her (though Emma, if anything, was decidedly earthly). He painted her as *Magdalen,* and *Joan of Arc,* as *Cassandra, Circe* and a *Bacchante.* Later, while the wife of Sir William Hamilton, she became Lord Nelson's love, and finally died, broken by gambling and dissipation, a coarse, bloated caricature of her once lovely youthful beauty, in Calais, in 1815. Romney's wife had an amiable nature. When he returned to her in Kendal, after thirty-seven years of London life, broken in mind and body, she cared for him tenderly until his death. His finest portraits are, perhaps, his *Parson's Daughter* (Nat. Gallery), and his *Duchess of Gordon and her Son* (Nat. Gallery). Sir William Beechy, John Opie, and John Hoppner yield in importance to the sentimental society portraits of Sir Thomas Lawrence (1769-1830), and those of Sir Henry Raeburn, a Scotchman, whose *Lord Judge Newton,* is considered one of his finest works.

William Blake (1757-1827), was a great visionary poet and painter, who applied his painting to illustrating his poetry. His strange, weird poems he accompanied by water-color drawings and engravings of fine quality and great original power of invention. Some of his finest designs are contained in his own book of poems "Songs of Innocence" and his brother poet Blair's "The Grave". The *Illustrations* to his *Book of Job,* done when he was twenty, are usually considered his greatest work.

ENGLISH LANDSCAPE PAINTERS

Constable and Turner

Old Crome (1768-1821), Stark, Cottman, Vincent, Richard Wilson (1714-1782), are among earlier English landscape painters who did worthy and beautiful work, but two great names, Constable and Turner, stand out in special glory in this field.

John Constable (1776-1837), was one of the oil-poets of Nature and of the English countryside. In England art critics first made a great deal of fun of the greens, browns and yellows of the landscapes he painted *as he saw them,* and spoke of his "eggs and spinach"; but his pictures won immediate appreciation in France when they were shown there, and influenced the growth of the French school of nature painters known as the Barbizon Fontainebleau School. Constable made money painting portraits to enable him to marry the girl of his choice, but his greatest paintings are his landscapes and horse pictures. *The Leaping Horse* (1826) is generally considered his masterpiece, but there are in addition *The Haywain* and *The White Horse* (1824-1825), *Salisbury Cathedral* (1823), *The Lock* (1824), *The Cornfield* (1827), *The Valley Farm* (1835), and *Arundel Castle and Mill* (1837), his last painting, completed the year he died. Most of Constable's pictures are the property of the British nation, and preserved in its great national art galleries.

Joseph Mallord William Turner (1775-1851) is probably the world's supreme water-colorist, and in oil has been called one of "the world's seven supreme colorists", while as a landscape artist many hold him to be superior to all others. A London barber's son, his earlier works (until 1820), while many are very fine, do not show him the great colorist he afterward became. He was often rough and rude in manner, but had a singularly kind heart. He never married, though his enemies accused him of being "excessively addicted to sensual indulgence"; and his life, in general, was a lonely, secretive and solitary one. One of the most pathetic remarks he made in his old age, when sight and hand were failing him, and his pictures were severely criticized was: "A man may be weak in his age, but you should not tell him so!" But this was long after he had produced the works which had made his name immortal.

He loved the sea, and many of his finest landscapes are sea-scapes. Beautiful is his *Garden of the Hesperides* (Nat. Gallery), from Greek mythology, his *Frosty Morning,* his *Crossing the Brook* (1815), of which he was especially fond, the *Childe Harold's Pilgrimage* and *The Golden Bough,* one with an ever increasing richness of color. Some of the great sea pictures show him in the full glory of his genius:

Ulysses Deriding Polyphemus (Nat. Gallery). In the centre of the picture is Ulysses' gallery, oars thrust through the oar-locks, sailors swarming up the mast to furl the sails. The giant Polyphemus, whom Ulysses has just escaped, rises dark and huge on the cliff above the sea, while Ulysses waves a blazing olive-branch at him in defiance.

The Venetian Pictures: Venice, to use Turner's own words, seemed to him "a city of rose and white, rising out of an emerald sea against a sky of sapphire blue". And so he has painted her in: *The*

Bridge of Sighs, Ducal Palace and Customs House, The Sun of Venice Going to Sea, the Approach to Venice, and *Venice, Evening, Going to the Ball,* poetic dreams and glorious miracles of color.

The Slave Ship (1840), and the *Burial at Sea* (1842), as well as *The Fighting Téméraire Lugged to her Last Berth to Be Broken Up* (1839), are among his great sea pictures. In this last painting we see an old three-decker of the kind that Captain Marryat has described so well in his novels of eighteenth century English navy life. Like the ghost of a ship in the wan evening light, it is slowly towed along by a fiery, puffing little steam tug—the new kind of ship that killed the grand old wooden ships as surely as though they sunk them with a round of shot and shell. And behind the wreck of the old order, the battle-ship of a day gone by, the sun is setting red in a bank of mist.

When Turner reached his sixty-seventh year his health and his powers failed. He was sensitive. His lonely and secretive habits grew on him, and the day after a friend had discovered his final hiding-place in a Chelsea lodging house, where he lay sick, he died. Ruskin has said of him: "During all the ten years I knew him, when he was suffering most from the evil speaking of the world, I never heard him say one depreciating word of any living man or his work." And surely that is a fine epitaph for a great man, failing in obscurity, loneliness and sorrow.

CHAPTER XII

SPAIN'S GREAT EIGHTEENTH CENTURY PAINTER

Goya

(1746-1828)

FRANCISCO GOYA LUCIENTES of Madrid, born at Fuendetodos, near Saragossa, is the one great name in Spanish painting during the eighteenth century, or rather, from the days of Murillo and Velasquez to those of Fortuny. Rafael Mengs (1728-1779), the German artist who was court painter to King Charles III of Spain, and whose twenty children did him more credit than the many more paintings he painted (for his style was strained and artificial) secured the royal favor for Goya, and he painted four Spanish kings—Charles III, Charles IV, Ferdinand VII, and "King Joseph". But the painting of royal nincompoops was merely a trifling detail in his production. His great works, though his skill in portrait is remarkable, show him wonderfully gifted in every direction. From a peasant boy to an accomplished courtier, his life was a romantic one. When a young student in Saragossa, he took pleasure in playing his part, cudgel in hand, in the unseemly street rows which disgraced the religious processions of rival saints. When he went to Madrid at nineteen (after friends had picked him up one fine night in the Saragossa street stabbed in the back), he carried on wildly. He may have painted during the day. At night he was swarming about, guitar in hand, serenading the beauties caged behind their iron window-bars. But though he enjoyed the favor of the ladies the police did not approve of him. He found it well to go to Rome where his quarrelsome, passionate nature, his wild sensuality and equally savage blood-thirstiness gave rise to all sorts of legends. In 1771 he returned to Saragossa and, the last man in the world to make a woman happy, married a golden-haired Spanish girl, Josefa Bayeu, whom he deceived, ill-treated and neglected systematically though she bore him twenty children. When called to Madrid, he painted canvases for the king's tapestry factory, frescoes for a church, court and society portraits, and many wonderful genre pictures. He painted portraits of princes and nobles, of the great ladies and great (?) men of the most immoral and corrupt court of Europe, and quite naturally when he was appointed court painter in 1789, was drawn into that life. A romantic tale, whose truth has not been proved, shows him spending an idyllic year of love with one great court lady, the *Duchess of Alba*, in the castle of San Lucar, till a royal order called him back to Madrid. Her picture in the Duke of Alba's palace in Madrid, shows her to have been a very lovely woman, and there is no question that there were many women besides his faithful wife Josefa, aristocrats of the bluest blood and *majas* and *manolas*, girls of the streets and of the people, in Goya's life.

Goya's great genre pictures include: The *Al Fresco Breakfast* in Watteau's style, the *San Isidrio Fair* (Prado Museum), the *Carneval* (San Fernando Academy, Madrid), the realistic massacre scene in the Madrid streets, *El Dos de Mayo* (Prado, Madrid), the striking *Curate Feeding the Devil's Lamp*, the charming *Watercarrier* (Budapest), and many others. In a class by themselves are his wonderful bull-ring sketches and drawings (Tauromachia), and his terrible satirical etchings, which show the horrors of the Spanish mad-house, and the terrors of the Spanish Inquisition. They are known as *Los Caprichos* (The Caprices), and some of them make one shiver, so powerful and repulsive are they. His great group picture of the *Spanish Royal Family* (Prado Museum, Madrid), shows them "as they are" with cruel and absolute truth: Queen Louise as a vulgar, vile woman; King Charles IV as a silly, fat-witted, old incompetent, and the faces of others all reflecting their various degrees of degeneracy or stupidity. It is hard to imagine that the royal "sitters" were not indignant. But we seldom "see ourselves as others see us". They were highly pleased with their family picture, which they often had copied and presented as gifts. Nor did Goya paint them as terrible as they look to us today, intentionally. But he was a realist. He painted what he saw and, in this case did not dream of analyzing the dreadful faces he saw about him every day. Goya died in 1848, in Bordeaux, but in 1900 his body was brought to Spain, and one May morning taken in solemn procession through the Madrid streets to the Church of San Isidro, where it was again laid to rest. The procession was costumed in eighteenth century style. The hearse was drawn by eight splendid black horses with waving white ostrich plumes, and accompanied by eight lackeys in eighteenth century gold-embroidered liveries and white wigs. All Madrid stood along the streets to see the greatest Spanish painter since Velasquez, and one of the greatest painters of all time, taken to his last resting place in the style befitting him, and one which his haughty and color-living soul would have enjoyed.

CHAPTER XIII

PAINTERS OF THE EIGHTEENTH AND EARLIER NINETEENTH CENTURIES

THE FRENCH "CLASSIC" PAINTERS

AFTER the Revolution had shattered more human "pitchers" than sentimental Greuze ever painted on his "innocent" canvases, and the Empire came in with Napoleon, there was in painting, as in sculpture and architecture, a return to the *classic* "Roman" style. David is the great Napoleonic painter of this classic revival.

JACQUES-LOUIS DAVID

(1748-1824)

His father killed in a duel when he was nine years old, little David was put in Boucher's studio to learn the painter's art. But Boucher soon realized this was no boy for the nymphs. Though he won the Roman Prize with a painting (1775), entitled *The Loves of Antiochus and Stratonice,* feminine charms were severely rather than loosely displayed. His early pictures, *Brutus, The Death of Socrates, The Oath of the Hoartii,* all show his historical bent, and even in his *Loves of Paris and Helen,* we have no passionate lovers. As a red republican he painted *The Oath of the Tennis-Court.* And he voted for the death of Louis XVI as a member of the new government, the Convention. David could only think "Roman", even in his religious paintings. Once he painted a *Christ,* induced to do so by a charming lady. When it was finished she cried: "Why, He looks like a Cato!" David shrugged his shoulders, and said with a superior smile: "My dear woman, there is no inspiration in Christianity now!" While he deplored the death of one of the Revolution's most blood-thirsty monsters, who perished by a young girl's dagger in his bath-tub in his *Assassination of Marat,* he became Napoleon's most enthusiastic admirer when the latter rose to power. He commemorated his *Passage of the Alps* (Berlin), in a picture showing the conqueror on horseback, pointing out the Italian plains, and (when appointed court painter to the emperor) produced his *Josephine's Coronation* and *The Distribution of the Eagles.* When the Bourbons returned to power, David promptly turned to classical subjects of a non-Napoleonic kind again, and painted *Mars Disarmed by Venus,* and *Cupid Quitting Psyche.* A great artist, who expressed the spirit of his time when that spirit was pulsing with life, many of his splendid compositions now seem cold and dead because we no longer can feel as the men of the Empire did. David was not too modest. When a head he had drawn of *Leonidas* was shown him as he lay dying, he looked at it, whispered "None but I could have conceived the head of a Leonidas!" and died happy with that consoling thought.

Paul Prud'hon, David's contemporary, took Correggio and Raphael as his models, and painted "classical" subjects from Greek mythology in a refined, misty and poetic way. One of his best is *The Abduction of Psyche* (Louvre). Antoine Jean Gros, (1771-1835), whom Napoleon made a baron of his empire, was David's pupil, but grouped the people in his pictures in a more natural way, and did not have them strike as many attitudes as did his teacher. He got the material for his battle-pictures at first hand—the *Bonaparte at the Bride at Arcola,* the *Bonaparte Visiting the Victims of the Plague at the Jaffa Hospital,* and the effective romantically natural *Napoleon at Eylau* (all in the Louvre). Another "Napoleonic" painter was Antoine Charles Horace Vernet (1758-1835), usually known as "Carle". His vast picture of *The Battle of Marengo* made him famous in his day and his *Morning of Austerlitz,* brought him the Legion of Honor from Napoleon. Jean-Hippolyte Flandrin confined himself to religious subjects, and Charles Gabriel Gleyre clung to mythology, while Alexandre Cabanel (1823-1889), because an "academic naturalist", was one of the most popular portrait painters of his day, and painted a *Birth of Venus* (Luxembourg) which made him famous. Jean Jacques Henner (1829-1905) was a popular and sentimental painter of the nude, with a fine feeling for color. Some of his pictures are hung in the New York Metropolitan Museum of Arts: *The Bather Asleep, Chaste Susannah, the Magdalen, Byblis Turned into a Stream, A Dream* (1900), *Christ Entombed* are among his best-known works.

BOUGUEREAU

(1825-1905)

Adolphe William Bouguereau is one of the French painters of the nineteenth century whose pictures are most popular with the general public, and have been spread about in thousands of reproductions. Boubuereau was a sort of combination of Boucher and Greuze. While his nymphs or nudes are not intentionally provocative as Boucher's they are quite as clotheless, but his figures always are graceful.

Girl Bathing, Nymphs and Satyrs, Triumph of Venus (1865) *Bacchante, Youth of Bacchus, A Girl Defending Herself Against Love, Biblis Love Disarmed, Love in a Shower, Love Victorious, Bacchante Teasing a Goat,* and *The Return of Spring*—this last picture sprang into fame because an American collector bought it and a poor, misguided fanatic who objected to its nudity afterward slashed the beautiful painting to pieces in his mentally unbalanced condition— are examples of the "Boucher" Bouguereau. In his Greuze moments we find him producing charming sentimental pictures of children and young girls with almost factory-like regularity. *Charity, Prayer, Fraternal Love, The First Discord, An Indigent Family, Remorse, Little Beggar Girls, First Jewels,* and others are among them. Bouguereau has also painted a number of religious pictures: *The Martyr's Triumph* (Luxemboug), which shows St. Cecilia's body being carried to the Catacombs, a *Holy Family, the Holy Women at the Sepulchre, Jesus and John the Baptist,* and others.

GÉROME

(1824-1904)

Jean-Leon Gérome, a painter of great technical mastery, has painted a number of fine historical *genre,* and oriental pictures. He was one of the artists who made the Orient (West Africa and Egypt) fashionable in painting, but his pictures have a coldness which has led them to be accused of looking like colored photographs. Among his *genre* pictures *Pifferaro, A Russian Concert, Egyptian Recruits crossing the Desert, Turkish Butcher,* and *Camels Drinking* might be mentioned. His *Virgin with Christ and St. John* contrasts with his mythological *Bacchus and Venus, Drunk.* Historical paintings deal with Egypt in *Memnon and Sesostris,* with Greece in *Phryne Before the Areopagus,* and *Socrates Discovering Alcibiades in the House of Aspasia.* He remembers Rome in his *Caesar, The Age of Augustus and the Birth of Christ,* the Baroque Age in Louis XIV and *Moliere,* and *the Reception of the Siamese Ambassadors at Fontainebleau,* and the Empire in his *Death of Marshal Ney.* His most famous oriental picture is, perhaps; *The Slave Market.* Gérome too may be classed with the painters who mingled classic and natural ideas of treatment in their work.

Ingres

Jean-Auguste-Dominique Ingres (1780-1867), was the greatest of David's pupils, and far greater than his teacher, a master of the enchanting line in the nude, and the greatest *classical* painter of modern France. His ideal was a "living line", and exquisite charm of form, and he has illustrated it in paintings which call forth admiration in the beholder.

Ingres was one of the painters whose romance lay in their works. A long richly active and honorable life, in which he knew first poverty then fame, he was a tender and affectionate son, the devoted husband of two wives who were devoted to him, and a noble character who lived only for his art and the intimate love his home life gave him. In his early "Empire" days, as might have been expected, he produced Napoleonic pictures: in 1802 *The Ambassadors of Agamemnon in the Tent of Achilles* (Ecole des Beux Arts, Paris): in 1804 his *Portrait of the First Consul* (Liège Museum): and in 1806 his *Portrait of the Emperor* (Invalides). His study years in Italy brought forth the wonderful *Oedipus and the Sphynx* (Louvre), which showed him to be a genius. But in 1815, when the Spanish ducal family of Alva commissioned him to do a portrait of the cruel *Duke of Alva* who had so bloodily carried on in the Netherlands as the governor of King Philip II of Spain, such a loathing and disgust for "that terrible man" grew on the painter, that at last—in spite of the large money return it meant to him—he gave up the work, and wrote in his diary: "Necessity drove me to undertake such a dreadful picture. Thank God it has remained a mere sketch!"

His many fine historical and religious canvases, however, all yield in beauty and merit to his wonderful paintings of the nude feminine beauty, and aside from his *Grande Odalisque* (Turkish harem favorite), a delicate "feminine animal" as one art critic has called her, full of languorous health and drowsy vitality; and his *Odalisque with a Slave* (Coll. of Sir Philip Sassoon, London), in which a slave sweeps the strings of a long guitar which the lovely half-draped figure of the *Odalisque* her eyes lost in a dream amid the fragrance of sunny gardens and sparkling fountains seen in the background, calls up visions of the Arabian Nights as she lies stretched out on her cushions, there are *three* great paintings:

La Source, "The Spring" (Louvre), is one of the loveliest half-child, half-woman figures of all nude art. It is a girl holding a jar from which the water escapes over her shoulders, and we *see* the shiver in the delicate flesh of the modest, timid girlish figure. In some ways *La Source* (painted in 1862, and so admired that the Emperor Napoleon III made Ingres a senator of the Empire after seeing it) is a little sister of the even lovelier *Venus* to which Ingres' genius inspired him:

Venus Anadyomene (Chantilly Museum). This pure, exquisitely virginal Venus, standing on the ocean foam, while Cupids cling to her knees, is the perfection of Ingres' ideal of lovely womanhood. All her delicate "paganism" is expressed in a trembling, innocent smile of the flesh. A caressing tenderness seems to come from the horizon. It touches the waves on which she stands, enwraps her, and gathering in her lovely white form, radiates a touching grace. It is almost as though one could sense the goddess through the tissue of her warm, pulsing skin. In this painting Ingres has expressed the feminine dream of his days of loving happiness. His first wife, whom he worshipped, was his model for the painting. She was a washerwoman when he married her: he made her the *Venus Anadyomene!*

Le Bain Turc, "The Bath in the Turkish Harem" (Louvre). Curiously enough, in point of time of production (1859), this "Bath" picture comes between two *Virgins, the Virgin of the Adoption,* and the *Virgin with the Host,* which last shares with his *Venus* the honor of being considered Ingres' greatest painting. The *Bain Turc* is the lovely swan-song of his secular painting. We smile when we learn that it so alarmed the modesty of Prince Napoleon (the former loose-lived King of Westphalia) and brother of the great Napoleon, that he exchanged it, though it had been painted for him, for a portrait of Ingres, by himself. For it is not an immodest or objectionable canvas, though the most voluptuous that Ingres ever painted. It shows the crowd of harem beauties in the intimacy of the bath. Most of them are resting, one is still seated on the edge of the pool, another dancing. The scene breathes the languor of the seraglio, the enervating warmth of tepid waters, in a heaping-up of lovely nude white figures whose beauty glows in an indolent realm of the senses, of languid, passionate dreams. A soft light caresses these creatures of a paradise which lies outside all the boundaries of a stricter moral law. It is a hymn to beauty, to feminine loveliness, into which Ingres seems to have put his whole soul. It is the one great painting of the harem interior. And it is a canvas as sane and healthy as the vision of a youth, though painted by an old man of eighty-six. "Its splendor of design and innocence of evil intention places it above all malignant criticism" a great art critic has said, and some have called it "Ingres' testament!"

CHAPTER XIV

DELACROIX AND THE FRENCH "ROMANTIC" PAINTERS

ROMANCE—the sense of the glory and beauty of *emotion* in life—was a contradiction of the classic spirit. And romance in France made itself felt, first in literature and then in art, toward the end of the eighteenth and the early part of the nineteenth century. Goethe, the great German romantic writer, had an effect on Sir Walter Scott and on Lord Byron in England, and Scott and Byron, translated into French, woke the spirit of romance in great French writers, in Victor Hugo, Theophile Gautier, Alexandre Dumas. And from the writers and dramatists, from the poets and novelists, the spirit of romance, which insisted on a more *personal* expression of what the artist felt, which objected to restraint and classical "traditions", which looked for new ways of expressing beauty, passed to the sculptors and *painters*. Different men, "romantic" painters, expressed this new spirit of revolt and independence in different ways.

Gros (as already has been mentioned), is considered the link between the "classic" and the "romantic" schools of military painting. Thédore Géricant improved on Gros in spirit and color in *The Raft of the Méduse* (Louvre), a picture of romantic horror and tragedy, showing the survivors of the wreck of the battle-ship tossing on the waves in the last stages of suffering and exhaustion. It is like a trumpet-call of the romantic cause. Géricaut did some fine military *genre* pictures: *Wounded Cuirassier,* and *Officer of the Chasseur Guard* (Louvre), and was a marvellous painter of horses. One of his greatest pictures is the famous *Race of Released Horses* (Louvre).

Emile-Jean-Horace Vernet (1789-1863), usually known as "Horace" Vernet, is considered one of France's most individual military painters. He was a brilliant "free-hand" sketch artist rather than a great painter, but his work is spirited and exact. The most famous of his many pictures of military life during the Empire, and of the French campaigns in Algeria, are largely represented by three years' work on the walls of the Constantine Room in Versailles. Perhaps his best-known work is the *Defense of the Barrier at Clichy* (Louvre), which made him immensely popular.

THE ROMANCE OF PAINTING

DELACROIX

(1799-1863)

Ferdinand Victor Eugène Delacroix may be called the real leader of this whole romantic movement. Byron and Shakespeare were his literary heroes, and Byron inspired some of his finest paintings. Once he survived his childhood, he painted in a fury of production, and as a colorist and romanticist ranks among the greatest of French painters. "Survived his childhood" may truly be said. When a baby he was nearly burned to death. A nurse fell asleep reading a novel, and let a candle fall on his quilt. He carried the scars of his burns on his face through life. Next he nearly died of poison, then was nearly choked to death and, finally, with no idea of suicide tried to hang himself. He had seen an engraving of a man hanging, and wondered what it was like! Delacroix's first great tragic picture was *The Massacre of Scios* (Luxembourg), and with his *Greece Lamenting on the Ruins of Missolonghi*, reflected his own and Byron's enthusiasm for the Greek struggle of independence against the Turks. His tremendous *Marino Faliero Beheaded on the Giants' Stairway of the Ducal Palace in Venice* is considered one of his greatest works, as is *The Crusaders Taking Constantinople* (Louvre); and *Drawing Lots in a Boat at Sea*, after Byron's "Don Juan" should not be forgotten. He could also produce glowing gem-like pictures of women, however, when he felt inclined. His *Algerian Woman* (Louvre), is an example. One who knew Delacroix declares there were no women in his life: "It is hard to imagine a poet, and especially a painter-poet, without an absorbing passion for *some* woman—not necessarily the *same* woman. To my knowledge Delacroix had no such passion, for his housekeeper, Jenny Leguillou, could scarcely have inspired such a feeling." A splendid, overwhelming romantic vision of tragic voluptuousness, with its many nude figures, is his greatest painting, *Sardanapalus*:

Sardanapalus (1827), is the very expression of Byron's drama which suggested it. It pictures the self-destruction of the last Assyrian king, with the beauties of his harem and his treasures, on a vast funeral pyre. It was much criticized when first exhibited, and the artist said: "I became the abomination of painting, and was refused bread and salt," and then added with a smile, "But I was tickled to death with myself!" Though he produced an immense number of paintings in oils and water-colors, Delacroix had no immediate successors. But he was a great influence in the encouragement of *individual* ways of expression in painting, and the choice of the romantic subject.

CHAPTER XV

THE FRENCH BARBIZON SCHOOL, NATURALISM AND REALISM

TURNING from human romance to Nature certain French artists went out into the fields and forests, and there founded what is known as the Barbizon-Fontainebleau School—which idealizes landscape painting. It is not surprising that the pictures of Theodore Rousseau (1812-1867), a tailor's son who had married a woodland girl who went mad, are sombre and melancholy. This leader of the Barbizon School * created his greatest painting in *The Edge of the Forest* (Louvre). Cows drink at eve in tree-grown meadows in the red glory of the setting sun. It has the charm of Nature in an intimate hour, and has called forth a French phrase which the art-lover may find useful in conversation, *paysage intime* (*pay-ee-sahje* en-teem) meaning "an intimate landscape". Charles François Virgille Diaz de la Pena (1807-1876) who married Boucher nymphs in scanty draperies to his verdant landscapes, as in *The Bathers* (Louvre), did pictures which have a Correggio-like quality of color. He also likes to wander from the countryside to the harem interiors, and let up peep at the secluded beauties they hide. Other famous pictures of his are: *The Pearl Fairy* (Louvre), *The Forest of Fantainebleau* (Leeds), *Storm and Sunset in the Forest*. Joseph Dupré (1812-1889), a painter of storm-clouds and leaves tossed by the wind, is best known by his *Morning and Evening* (Louvre) and *The Big Oak*.

Corot

Jean-Baptiste-Camille Corot (1796-1875), is more of a "classic" naturalist, and like Diaz, loves to paint the human figure as well as trees. He is classed with the Barbizon painters, however, and is usually regarded as the greatest representative of their school, greater even than Millet. Up to the age of fifty, Corot was a "tight" painter—not in the vulgar sense so often associated with the word in the United States, but in the sense of being very *exact, clear* and

---

* A retired and lonely man, Georges Michel (1763-1842), had already given up his lifetime to putting on canvas the flat and spreading Montmartre plains, beneath cloud-filled skies. But Rousseau and the later Barbizon painters knew nothing of his fine work, which has been recognized only in comparatively recent times.

definite in his outlines. After fifty he became mystic and poetic in his paintings. He painted several hundred landscapes, and his works are scattered over France, the United States, the Netherlands and Great Britain. Among them are: the landscapes: *Morning* (Louvre), *The Lake, The Shattered Tree, Pastoral: An Italian Souvenir* (Glasgow Gallery, and among his figures *Macbeth* (Wallace Collection, London), and *Biblis*.

MILLET

Jean-Francois Millet (1814-1875) was the man who put the soul of the French peasant into the landscape of the French Barbizon School. Himself a peasant boy, he grew up working in the fields beside his father. A hard youth spent in study led to his first small success in 1844, when his *Milkwoman* attracted attention in Paris. Then came years of poverty, during which he was cheered and encouraged by a noble wife, Catherine Lemaire, and learned to paint with a brush which he had dipped in the bitterest hardship and suffering of the very poor. To this period belong his *Bird Nesters, Young Girl and Lamb, Bathers* (Louvre), his *Mother Asking Alms, The Blue Monday* and *The Winnower*. With the money the last picture brought, Millet was able to go to Barbizon and establish himself there in a three-room cottage on the forest's edge. And there he shaped, in canvases that will live, the hard story of the peasant's life. He painted the French peasant as he is, a poor, toilworn, miserable creature, whose life is hardship and struggle from beginning to end. In a letter written at the time Millet's own peasant soul speaks from the heart: he is through with "mythological subjects, and undraped nude females", he says. And so we have his *Man Spreading Manure* (1853), *The Reapers* (1854), *Peasant Grafting a Tree* (1857), *The Woodcutter and Death* (1860), *Sheep Shearing* (1861), *Woman Feeding a Child* (1862), *Potato Planters, Winter and the Crows* (1863), *Shepherds and Flock, Peasants Bringing Home Calves in the Fields* (1869), *The Knitting Lesson* (1870) and *Buttermaking* (1871). But Millet has studied the nude so thoroughly and so well, that the clothes he puts on his figures are no more than draperies, through which the forms and movements of the bodies show clearly, though always with serious and noble intention and breadth. It has been said that even his *Washerwoman at her Tub* shows the grand action of a *Medea*. When Millet died on January 20, 1875, he was buried beside his friend Rousseau in the churchyard of Chailly. The two pictures of his which are best known, aside from three, toil-stooped figures of *The Gleaners* (1859), and *The Sower* (Met. Museum of Arts, New York) are:

The Man with the Hoe (Louvre). Here Labor, in the form of a peasant toiler, has been presented with pathetic seriousness. The stooped, heavy figure of the farmer boy who has just plunged his hoe into the soil makes a narrow angle compared to the immense landscape breadth of the picture's background. It is just this *narrow angle* which makes *The Man with the Hoe* breathe forth such a deep feeling of pathos and poignant hardship. The picture is one that has inspired an American poem which is among the finest written, and equals in verse Millet's "cry of the soil" on canvas, Edwin Markham's "The Man with the Hoe".

The Angelus (Met. Museum of Art, New York). This is Millet's most popular picture and—his one great picture of deep, heart-felt sentiment.

Harassed by debt and illness, Millet was sometimes haunted by the idea of suicide. On one such occasion he said to his wife: "Suicide is the act of a bad man. Come let us go and see the sunset. It will make me feel better." And out in the fields at the twilight hour, out of the consolation of his mother earth and the echo of the vesper bells, we make take it that the idea of *The Angelus* was born.

More recent "impressionistic" Barbizonites include: Jean Charles Cazin (1840-1891), the serious André Dauchez, Emile René Menard, who peoples his landscapes with lovely nudes, Henri le Sidamer, with "moonlight effects".

Famous animal painters usually considered in connection with the Barbizon School include: Constant Troyon (1810-1865), who made cattle, heavy, placid cows, great bulls and oxen the living inhabitants of his pasture landscapes; Emile van March, Marie Dieterle, and Charles Jacque (1813-1894), who chose sheep and poultry by preference, and put them in barnyard and stable as well as in the meadows.

ROSA BONHEUR

Rosa Bonheur (1822-1899). *Deer in the Forest: Winter,* a study of deer in the Fontainebleau Forest, is only one of her links with the Barbizon School. Troyon and Bayre were greater animal painters than she was; both had more original charm, more inspiration, more "style". But what has been called "dignified realism", the photographic character of Rosa Bonheur's painting has always endeared her to the multitude. She was conscientious and always truthful in her work. She already had made a reputation for herself when in 1849 the French Government bought her *Ploughing in the Novernais* Luxembourg) and after a visit (1855) to England and Scotland (where her *Horse Fair* already had made her famous) she bought an estate on the border of Fontainebleau Forest, and there with a great menagerie of animals tame and wild, settled down at the Chateau de By for the rest of her life as an animal painter, in a retired spot, free from worldly interruptions, and surrounded by creatures she loved. So great was her fame in her own day that during the Franco-Prussian War of 1870-1871, the Prince Royal of Prussia have strict orders that the Chateau of By and the property of the studio of Rosa Bonheur remain undisturbed. So thorough a student was she of animals she painted that she figuratively (not literally) "skinned them alive" in order to reproduce the exact "feel" and color of the texture of their skins on the canvas. Where others have painted dramas of human life, she has painted dramas in the lives of the lower animals, and her aim always was to express all that she saw with truth and exactness.

Sheep in a Meadow, A Family of Lions (one of her finest pictures, painted from a caged African lion who always purred a welcome when she drew near him) *Highland Sheep* (1855), *Cattle and Sheep in the Pyrences* (Orleans Museum), *Andalusian Bulls* (Walters Gallery, Baltimore), *Cattle at Rest* (Chicago Art Institute), *Deer Drinking* (Lennox Library, New York), *Deer in the Forest, Twilight, Weaning the Calves* (Met. Museum of Art, New York), are among her more important pictures.

The Horse Fair (Met. Museum of Art, New York). First exhibited in the Paris Salon in 1853, this famous picture did not at once find a buyer, though much admired. It was almost from the first in American hands, though the painter wished to sell it in France, and though numerous replicas and copies have been made of it, the only true, *original* large-size *Horse Fair* is the one which passed from the William P. Wright to the Stewart Collection, and when the latter was sold at auction in 1887, was bought for $55,000 by Mr. Cornelius Vanderbilt, and by him presented to the Metropolitan Museum of Art. There is no fair crowd, there are no flags or banners, but only a few onlookers in the background, while in the middle of the picture half a dozen horses—brown, gray and sorrel—with three or four grooms in blue blouses are in movement. They are not thoroughbreds, but big Normandy dray horses, thick-necked, round-backed, heavy-hocked. One horse-boy is running alongside a nervous beast which is pulling a man off his feet. Another is having his troubles holding down two great gray Percherons. The horses have no bridles, only halters and bits of rope to lead them, and are jerking along with the restlessness all horses show when they are being taken to quarters strange to them. The great popularity of the picture, no doubt, is largely due to its truth, its honest realism.

CHAPTER XVI

BRITISH PAINTERS

(Earlier Nineteenth Century to Present)

The Genre Painters

MOST important among the British painters of the first half of the nineteenth century were the men who developed an English school of *genre* painting. Some men tried to graft the grand style of the Italian Baroque on the English historical subject as a result of travel and study in Italy. But they did not produce works of the quality of the *genre* painters. Among the "historical" painters we have:

Daniel Maclise (1806-1870) of Cork, who beside much illustrating: Shakespeare's "Scenes", Lord Lytton's "Pilgrims of the Rhine", Moore's "Irish Melodies", produced two large stiff paintings: *Meeting of Wellington and Blucher after Waterloo*, and *Death of Nelson* (Houses of Parliament, London). The American Tory, John Singleton Copely (1735-1815), a Bostonian, though the leading portrait painter of Colonial days, wisely expatriated himself and settled in London in view of his political opinions. He had two "deaths" in the grand historical manner, *Death of the Earl of Chatham* and *Death of Major Pierson*. William Etty (1787-1849), preferred the allegoric to the historical, and his sentimental *Youth at the Prow and Pleasure at the Helm* (Tate Gallery, London) is his best-known work. Eastlake, Dyce, Haydon, and Hilton are other followers of the men who painted pictures in the grand historical style.

Among the *genre* painters we have George Morland (1763-1804), indoor and outdoor scenes of English country life; the Scotchman David Wilkie (1785-1841) whose *John Knox Preaching* is not a very happy try at the grand manner, and far less honest and natural than his *Blind Fiddler, Village Festival, Rabbit on the Wall*, and other simple village scenes. The Irishman William Mulready (1785-1863), gave expression to humble life as he saw it with a fluent brush in *The Barber's Shop* (1811), *Idle Boys* (1815), *The Interrupted Fight, Interior of an English Cottage, Choosing the Wedding Gown, The Last In*, and *The Toy Seller*. Thomas Webster (1800-1886) in his *Dame's School* and *The Truants*, and William Collins (1788-1874) in *Boys with a Bird's Nests*, and *Boys at Breakfast* chose children rather than grownups. Charles Robert Leslie (1794-1859) and William Powell Frith (1819-1909), drew largely on literature for the subjects of their paintings. Well known paintings by Leslie are his *Uncle Toby and Widow Wadman*, from Lawrence Sterne's "Tristram Shandy" and *Sancho Panza in the Duchess' Apartment*, after Cervantes' novel. Frith painted a famous *Scene* (1843) from Goldsmith's "Vicar of Wakefield"; then his realistic *Derby Day* (1847) and *Railway Station* (1851).

SIR EDWIN HENRY LANDSEER

Edwin Landseer's (1802-1873) animal pictures have been more popular and are, probably, better known than the pictures of all the rest of the *genre* artists just mentioned. At times stiffly drawn and often hard in color, the painter succeeded in making his animals so dramatic and true to life, and lent them so much "character", pathetic, joyous and humorous, that (especially in the form of engravings) they keep their hold on popular affection.

His *Fighting Dogs Getting Wind* (1818), made Landseer the fashion in London. After that his life was a long productive series of paintings, with increasing appreciation and honors, including knighthood, until after producing his *Swannery Invaded by Eagles* (1869), he died after four last years of ill health, which affected his mental and artistic powers, and was buried in St. Paul's Cathedral (1873). His first *humorous* animal picture *The Cat's Paw* (1824), made a tremendous sensation. It was followed by *The Larder Invaded* and *The Monkeys Who Had Seen the World* (1827), which fixed the artist as one who could do fullest justice to the humorous animal subject. By the time *High Life, Low Life* and *The Highland Whiskey Still* had appeared (1829), Landseer's dogs and "even his birds and lions" were often more human than animal, and often rose to high expressions of nobility. A picture of this kind is his *Suspense* (South Kensington Museum), which shows a dog watching by his sick master's closed door. This picture, and another of deep sentiment, *The Old Shepherd's Chief Mourner* (1837), may be chosen as Landseer's finest works. *Boton Abbey in Olden Time* (1843), and the grewsome *Man Proposes, God Disposes* (1864), a dreadful subject in which polar bears prowl and clamber clumsily about among the bodies of the dead of Sir John Franklin's Polar Expedition; *Dignity and Impudence* (1839), *Laying Down the Law* (1840), two "humor" pictures; the lovely *Eos*, a "portrait of Prince Albert's greyhound", *Shoeing the Bay Mare* (1844); *The Stag at Bay* (1846), and *Random Shot* (1848), a pathetic picture of a dead kid lying in the snow; as well as *A Piper and a Pair of Nutcrackers* (1864), are among his most famous paintings. His romantic and pathetic deer subjects are numerous. They include the celebrated *Monarch of the Glen* (1851), *Night, Morning, The Sanctuary* (1842), *Deer Pass,* (1852), *Children of the Mist* (1853) *Bramaer* (1856) and others.

THE ENGLISH PRE-RAPHAELITES

The Pre-Raphaelite Brothers (so they called themselves) were three English painters, Dan Gabriel Rossetti, William Holman Hunt, and John Everett Millais, who decided the simple truthful "nature" painting of the Early Renaissance artists ought to be the real inspiration in *all* painting. They claimed even Raphael strayed from the true path in painting when he left Florence and the Florentine manner for Rome and his Roman style. But together with Nature, unlike the French naturalist painters like Millet and Courbet, they felt they must express *mystic* rather than *physical* beauty. Rossetti and Burne-Jones (who followed him), were *sensuous mystics* in their paintings. Millais was a *sentimental naturalist,* Ford Maddox Brown an *emotional realist* and Holman Hunt was an *ecstatic realist*.

ROSSETTI AND BURNE-JONES

Dante Gabriel Rossetti (1828-1882), though his technique and anatomy were often faulty, had what is called *vision*—the power of *physically* seeing dramatic objects and events, and *of making others see them*—and this is what lends greatness to his art. His greatest painting, probably, is his *Dante's Dream* (Liverpool Gallery). Many of his loveliest canvases idealized his wife, a sensuous, Titian-like beauty, with the very shade of red hair the Venetian painter had made famous. Elizabeth Eleanor (Siddal) looks down from the canvas as *The Beloved, Lady Lilith, Bocca Baciata* (The Kissed Mouth), *Venus Verticordia* and *Dante's Beatrix*. Great as a poet as well as a painter, he wrote sonnets (The House of Life), and romantic ballads "Sister Helen", "Troy Town", "Rose Mary", etc. When his wife died he turned to what he has called "the painting of the soul".

To this period belongs his *Blessed Damosel,* illustrating his poem. It shows his lost love leaning out from the casements of Paradise and prophesying their meeting. The French composer Debussy has set the poem to exquisite choral music as a cantata. Many are the beautiful pictures Rossetti painted, aside from those mentioned, but in the end—perhaps the never-dying yearning for the love he had lost drove him to it—he took narcotics, shattered his health, and died from a complication of disorders in 1882.

Edward Burne-Jones (1835-1898), was a mystic with a Gothic strain, though he did not confine himself to Gothic subjects, but loved all romantic subjects that held a thrill of sad, tender and delicate beauty. He once said: "I mean by a *picture* a beautiful, romantic *dream* of something that never will be! . . ." *King Copethua and the Beggar-Maid* (Nat. Gallery), tells in gorgeous color a romantic tale we all know, of the King in Babylon who raised the Christian slave to his throne because he loved her. In *The Depths of the Sea,* a mermaid is carrying down to the deeps the body of the youth whom her impetuous love has killed. In his religious *Annunciation* and the gloomy *Wheel of Fortune,* the *Mirror of Venus,* the *Beguiling of Merlin*—in all his lovely paintings breathes the soul of romance.

William Morris (1834-1896), who wrote wonderful prose romances of the early Middle Ages, was a Gothic Pre-Raphaelite. His influence was exerted largely toward creating beauty in decoration— furniture, hangings, wall-paper, stained glass and tapestry, and his finest designs were drawn at Merton Abbey, the workshop of the firm to which he belonged. Walter Crane (b. 1845) carried out the ideas of the Pre-Raphaelites in many lovely book illustrations, tapestry and stained glass design, painted easel pictures such as *The Bridge of Life, Neptune's Horses* and *The Rainbow and the Wave.* George Frederick Watts, shared with the Pre-Raphaelites only their love for the visionary, the ideal and the spiritual. He painted many great allegorical pictures, among them *Love and Death,* which shows Love, a beautiful boy, trying in vain to bar the door against the mighty figure of Death and being thrust back with crushed wings (Met. Museum, New York); and more than forty wonderful portraits of the great men of his time.

JOHN EVERETT MILLAIS

Millais (1829-1896) was the manly, human painter of sentiment among the Pre-Raphaelites. His idea of the movement was "to present on canvas what he saw in Nature". His many charming pictures are story pictures. *The North-West Passage* has been called his masterpiece. It shows an old sailor listening to a tale of Arctic voyage in a room overlooking the sea, strewn with charts. His *Eve of St. Agnes* is one of the loveliest of "moonlight" pictures known. *The Carpenter's Shop* is a simply realistic picture of the Christ (and was much abused when first exhibited). *The Rescue* was a sensation because of the brilliant glow of the fire, and the frantic glare in the eyes of the mother whose child is saved from the flames. *The Yoeman of the Guard* (a simple love-story) is considered his finest bit of color, and *Chill October* his loveliest landscape; while among his many pictures of children are *Cherry Ripe* and *Sweetest Eyes Ever Seen.* Mallais also painted many notable portraits of great public men, and drew Charles Dickens after his death.

Ford Maddox Brown (1821-1893) was a realist of Pre-Raphaelite painting and a friend of the workingman. His great historical canvases, like the *Execution of Mary Queen of Scots* show one side of his creative genius. His *Work*—navies digging a drain in Hampstead Road, with idlers watching them, and a lady and gentleman riding by on horseback—and *The Last of England,* an emigration scene, show another. His paintings in nearly every case have the drama of truth.

Holman Hunt (1827-1910) is a religious mystic who mingles realism with mysticism in his work. He painted many fine sacred and secular pictures but one stands out:

The Light of the World (1854). It shows Christ knocking at the door of the human soul, and is said to have produced the greatest effect of any religious picture of the 19th century. It was the talk of England when first exhibited and has been shown all over the world. Christ, lantern in hand, is seen against the full moon, knocking against a door overgrown with brambles and creepers. Hardly less impressive, in a human way, is Hunt's famous *The Awakening Conscience* (1854). It shows a tragic moment in the life of a girl who has gone wrong, and who, suddenly conscience-stricken by the memories of her innocent childhood, is rising from her lover's knee. These are but two among the many powerful realistic pictures born of Hunt's devout inspiration.

MODERN BRITISH PAINTERS

The names of men notable in modern British painting are numerous. A few of the best-known stand out by reason of works which have won very general appreciation.

SIR LAURENCE ALMA-TADEMA

(1836-1912)

Laurence Alma-Tadema (1836-1912) though born in Belgium, was a naturalized British subject and lived in London. With his picture of the three young children of King Clovis hurling the axe beneath their mother's eye—she is training them to *avenge* their father's murder, *The Education of the Children of Clovis* (1861) Alma-Tadema sprang into fame, and in many pictures of great beauty has recreated the life of ancient Egypt, Greece and Rome: *The Mummy, The Pyrrhic Dance, The Wine Shop*. Among his many famous canvases are *The Roses of Heliogabalus, Hadrian in Britain, Sappho, An Earthly Paradise, The Way to the Temple, A Reading from Homer* (Met. Museum of Art, New York), in particular, a lovely classic scene, whose figures are warm and human, shows his skill in painting marble with such a tone that one can almost *feel* it.

The chief beauty of his pictures of *ancient* life is that he fills them with *modern* feeling and sentiment.

There are many modern British painters. Stanhope Forbes (b. 1857) is one of the best-known of the "Newlyn School" of realists along French lines: *Fish Sale on a Cornish Beach* and *Soldiers and Sailors*. Orchardson (1835-1910), an "illustrative" painter, has a *Napoleon on Board the Bellerophon*. Hugh Cameron did a famous picture of *A Lonely Life*, an old dame opening her cottage door in the fading twilight. Sir Luke Fildes, *The Doctor*, belongs to the "Glasgow School". Ernest Crofts, *Napoleon at Ligny, Napoleon Leaving Moscow;* Lady Butler, *The Dawn of Waterloo;* A. C. Gow, *Cromwell at Dunbar,* Frank Bramley, *A Hopeless Dawn;* Furse, *Diana of the Uplands;* Caton Woodville, John Gilbert, Frank Dicksie, Frank Brangwyn, Leslie Thompson, are only a few among other well-known modern British painters. Brandwyn, in particular, is famed both as etcher and painter, for his great mastery of design.

THE FRENCH NATURALIST PAINTERS

The French painters of the Barbizon School were naturalist painters—but they tried only to express *actual* Nature in a poetic and romantic way. They expressed Nature without any "program" or "propaganda". As they painted her, Nature was just Nature. But the French naturalist painters led by Gustave Courbet started a movement *away* from anything but *the most radical expression* of Nature as they saw her—not "poetized", not made poetic or romantic, but absolutely, for better or for worse, *as she was*. In a way this feeling that developed was an inheritance of the American and French revolutions which first set up the principle that the everyday, individual man, no matter how lowly his station in life, has equal rights with any other class of persons who, for one reason or another, may claim superiority. This feeling was actively expressed in the art of the French *naturalist* painters.

Gustave Courbet (1819-1877) objected to the *aristocratic* art of Raphael. He objected, in fact, to any art which "improved on Nature", which was not uncompromisingly *realistic*. But his somewhat brutal realistic pictures. *The Stone Breakers, Peasants of Flazey, Burial at Ornans, Wrestlers, Bathers,* and his activities as a Communist, which led to the destruction of the Vendome Column* are not what artists remember him by, but his noble *Stag-Fight, The*

---

* A council of war condemned him to restore the Column at his own expense and rather than work for the rest of his life raising the money Courbet went to Switzerland and died there in 1877 of liver trouble due to excessive drinking. The German painter Leibl (1844-1900) was so impressed by Courbet's work that he became a peasant and is known because of his nature paintings as the "German Millet".

III

Wave, Haunt of the Does, landscape and sea paintings. The lack of feminine grace that Courbet's nudes show is proved by an amusing story. When the Empress Eugénie stopped in front of his picture of heavy, ungracious women called *The Bathers,* in the Paris Salon (1835) she asked, alluding to the heavily built Norman draft horses: "Are they Percherons, too?"

Bastien-Lepage (1848-1884) is a "peasant" painter, with a lovely country girl, *Joan of Arc* (Met. Museum of Art, New York). Certain of these "realists" invaded the Paris *salons* and instead of peasants, painted society ladies. Carolus-Duran (b. 1837) became one of the best known of French society portrait painters, one of his best pictures being *The Lady with a Fan* (Luxembourg) a portrait of his wife. Alfred Stevens (1828-1906) was also a drawing-room poet of the brush, and James Joseph Jacques Tissot (1836-1902) who began with pictures of the feminine "half-world" of the Paris cafés and Boulevards, ended with very honest and realistic, though not very "moving", scenes from the Bible, based on actual studies in the Holy Land. He realized an enormous sum for these 700 watercolors for the Scriptures, far more than from his earlier Parisian naughtinesses. Léon Bonnat painted honest and unflattering portraits of the great men of his time, and Jules Adler may be said to have made himself (in *On the Bench*) the Millet of the Paris workingman. In the realist *genre* picture François Bonvin, Theodore Ribat and Joseph Bail as well as Honoré Daumier (1808-1879) whose "Third Class Railroad Coach" is owned in the United States. Eugène Carrière, a very fine modern *genre* painter, might also be mentioned here.

Léon Auguste Lhermitte (b. 1884) and Lucien Simon (b. 1861), are other *realist* painters of peasant life. Jules Breton—*Women Gleaning, Blessing the Fields, Potato Gatherers, The Shepherd's Star, The Return of the Gleaners* (Luxembourg, painted the Artois peasants more as they ought to be, perhaps, than they were, with a "poetry" that French peasant life (if we are to believe Zola's novels) is apt to lack.

CHAPTER XVII

OTHER FRENCH PAINTERS FROM MEISSONIER TO MATISSE
JEAN LOUIS ERNEST MEISSONIER

(1815-1891)

MEISSONIER is the painter who created the special *genre* of the oil miniature, the "microscopic" painting in oils. (One critic said of him: "He could paint a battle-scene on a gold piece!") He painted hundreds of lovely smaller genre pictures of a historical and costume interest, but is best known as a great military artist whose paintings glorify the First Empire in the year of whose downfall he was born, and the Third Empire, whose fall he survived. As a military painter he was attached to the staff of Napoleon III during the Italian campaign, and at the beginning of the Franco-Prussian War, and during the siege of Paris in 1871 he was colonel of a marching regiment.

His great military and battle-pictures are: *Desaix and the Army of the Rhine* (1867), *Moreau and his Staff before Hohenlinden* (1878), the *Cuirassiers,* (1805), *Barricade, The Outpost of the Grand Guard* (1814), *The Emperor at Solferino. Friedland,* (1807) (Met. Museum of Art New York) is his most famous picture. In order to make the grain trampled down by the hoofs of the cavalry horses in the foreground of the picture "true to life" Meissonier is said to have bought a wheat-field and tipped a troop of cuirassiers to charge over it. He himself rode beside them noting the attitude of horses and men. It is a great historical moment. Napoleon sits motionless on his white horse, his marshals—Bessieres, Duroe, Berthier—about him, just behind him General Nausonty, waiting to command the "defile" for his division. Further back is the "Old Guard' in black bearskin bonnets and white breeches, and beyond them squadrons of cavalry spread as far as eye can reach. And before the Conquerer defile the triumphant cavalry of the Imperial Guard. "I did not mean to paint a battle," said Meissonier. "I wanted to paint Napoleon at the height of his glory, the love of the soldiers for the great Captain for whom they were ready to die!" And in *Friedland* Meissonier has done so.

Alphonse-Marie de Neuville (1836-1885), was one of the most

celebrated military painters of the army life of the Third Empire. He had lived the army life himself, and painted in a realistic and convincing manner. *The Battle of San Lorenzo, Attack in Magenta Streets by Zouaves and Light Horse, Light Horse Guards in the Trenches of the Mamelon Vert* (before Sebastapol), *The Cemetery of Saint-Privat, Bivouac before Le Bourget, The Last Cartdirge, Fight on a Railroad, Attack on a House at Villersexel, Surprise at Daybreak, The Intercepted Dispatch-Bearer, Attack on a Barricaded House* (Luxembourg), among his best, are painting scenes from the Italian, Crimean and Franco-Prussian Wars.

Jean-Baptiste-Edouard Detaille (b. 1848), was another truthful and spirited interpreter of French military glory. The First French Empire he has remembered in his fine *Bonaparte in Egypt* (1878), and *The Skirmish with Cossacks* (Met. Museum of Art, New York) and the *Engagement Between Cossacks and the Imperial Guard, 1814* (1870). The Third Empire lives in *The Defence of Champigny by Faron's Division, Charge of the 9th Regiment of Cuirassiers in the Village of Morsbronn, 1870, The Marching Regiment,* Paris, December, 1874 (1875), and the great panoramic study *Evening at Rezonville.*

Charles Bargue, Ferdinand Roybet, Paul Baudry (1828-1886) and Paul Albert Besnard may be classed as "decorative" painters. Besnard is not an "impressionist"—not agreeing with the *realism* of the impressionist group. But he has used impressionist ways of applying *light* and *color* in big decorative frescoes (Paris Sorbonne School of Pharmacy, etc.) and one of his finest "light" studies is *Woman Warming Herself* (Luxembourg).

PUVIS DE CHAVANNES

(1824-1898)

PIERRE-CECILE-PUVIS DE CHAVANNES, with his first greater panel paintings *Peace and War* (1861), showed that decorative mural painting was the field he had chosen. After that his life was given up principally to the many commissions he received to decorate the walls of important municipal buildings in France and abroad. In the Paris *Sorbonne, Hotel de Ville* and *Panthéon* (City Hall) are some of his finest decorative frescoes. Of particular interest to Americans, however, are the great mural paintings he did for the Boston Public Library.

The Boston Library Panels. The great stairway panels Puvis de Chavannes painted for the Boston Public Library (1895-1897), comprise one large composition and eight smaller panels. The large composition is entitled: *The Muses of the Inspiration Hail the Spirit, The Harbinger of Light.* The eight smaller panels include: *Dra-*

THE ROMANCE OF PAINTING

matic Poetry, Epic Poetry, Pastoral Poetry, Astronomy, Philosophy, Chemistry, Physics and *History*. In some ways *History* is, perhaps, the finest one among these panels. Crowned with a wreath of golden laurel leaves, *History* is calling up the vision of the past from the buried entrance to an ancient temple ruin. An attendant spirit holds torch and book beside her. The foreground hills are toned in russet and brown which turn to grayish green where vegetation covers the upper slopes, while huge trees raise their limbs on the horizon against a sky as blue as turquoise.*

The romance of Chavannes' life was his love for the Princess Marie Catacuzene, whom he met in his thirtieth year, "loved" as one of his biographers has said, "as Michel Angelo might have loved Vittoria Colonna," and whom he made his wife. She settled his doubts when he asked her about the arrangement of a group in one of his pictures. She sat for him, for pictures professional models were unable to pose. She watched over him in health and illness and when she died (1898), it was clear that Chavannes did not care to survive her. He followed her to the grave in two short months. His lover's tribute of art is the sweet-faced, gravely beautiful *Saint,* in the Pantheon picture of *Saint Genevieve Watching Over Paris.*

THE FRENCH "IMPRESSIONIST" AND OTHER MODERN PAINTERS

"Impressionism" in painting is "naturalism" in painting developed in what has been called "a more natural way." But—impressionist paintings are often difficult to appreciate or to understand because they represent *one man's* "impression" of a certain thing or scene at a certain given moment. He paints his pictures the way the landscape or person he is looking at "impresses" him. The permanent things in a landscape, for instance, trees, stone walls, bushes, etc., *shift* and *change* in appearance and color with changing lights and shadows. They look different from one moment to another, at times. It is these "changing", less permanent glimpses, and minute to minute shiftings of the face of nature that the "impressionist" painter catches and puts on canvas. So it often happens that while he has recorded a vivid momentary glimpse of a particular scene at a particular time under particular circumstances, we may never have seen the like, and hence his picture does not have sense or meaning to us. Yet this does not apply to all impressionist pictures by any means.

* A kind of German Chavannes was Hans von Marées (1837-1887), who combined nudes and the landscape in grand decorative panels.

EDOUARD MANET

(1833-1883)

Edouard Manet was the head of the "Batignolles School", so-called because the artists, all "impressionists" who composed it, gathered at the Café Guerbois in the Batignolles Quarter of Paris. Manet had a simpler, "naturalistic" way of painting, in Velasquez's style (of which his *Boy with the Sword*, Met. Museum of Art, New York, is a fine example). But he saw Japanese art prints, in which the light and shade of the pictures were "spotted in" with the brush* instead of being "built up" along a carefully planned scheme of proportion. This "spotting in" process meant putting in "values" of light and shade in *flattish patches,* and with emphasis on a *leading* color *note* and *patch,* to mark each figure in a scene. It allowed the "impressionists" to catch the swift, passing moment of life as it passed, and to set down the changing face of nature as it changed. And by painting in the open air, (plein air) open-air painting, which impressionism first introduced in modern art, many new color schemes and color arrangements were discovered in Nature!*

Manet's first paintings in the new style, *Déjeuner sur l'herbe* (1863), "Breakfast on the Grass," a "country festival" from the life of his own time, and his realistic *Musique aux Tuileries,* did not please the public. And his famous *Olympia* (1865) aroused a perfect storm of hooting and laughter. It showed a nude woman lying on a couch, behind which rose the head of a negress holding a bunch of flowers, while a black cat at the woman's feet made the white sheet on which she lay seem twice as white. But gradually Manet's honesty and earnestness and the high artistic value of his works brought people around. Now his jolly *Bon Bock* (1873), a real Parisian "type" sitting over his glass of beer, which created a great sensation when it was first exhibited, his *Fifer of the Guard, A Bullfighter, Young Girl*, the portrait of *Lola, The Music Lesson, Railroad, Nana,* and *In the Conservatory* have long since been properly appreciated. His great historical pictures include *The Execution of the Emperor Maximilian,* whose public exhibition (since Maximilian died in Mexico because Napoleon III had lured him there) was forbidden by the government. He also has painted a fine *Battle of the Kearsarge and the Alabama.*

Claude Monet (b. 1840) carried Manet's theories further. He improved the "broken" character of the impressionist "touch" in painting. And he sacrificed delicate form and continuousness to brilliant light and color. Monet was a "pointillist." Pointillism** is using the

---
*The Japanese call this "spotting in" of light and shade *notan*.

**The use of *pontillism*, that is, dotting on oil pigment, though the painter Pissarro tried it (and then dropped it) and Signac, Vincent van

six primary rainbow colors and "dotting" them on canvas with a brush, unmixed. Then to the eye they look like *light* not *colors*. But the dotting is course and has many drawbacks. Monet was a landscape impressionist, and aside from his painted views of *Vetheuil* (1875), *Pourville and Cliffs of Entretat* (1861), *Bordighere* (1886), *La Creuse* (1889), *Le Meules* (1891), his chief work is a series known by the name of *Cathedrals*, showing the Cathedral of Rouen under all sorts of different lights. The only interest of the picture is in its *lights*, and how they shimmer, glow and color the stone of the cathedral front. The architectural details are treated as unimportant.

Firmin Auguste Renoir (b. 1841), is an impressionist whose pictures are especially rich in beautiful and sumptuous color. He is the most unequal of the impressionist painters, though his best works have been called masterpieces. He painted in every style—landscape, modern life, the nude—and his nude *Bathers*, and others have the lovely pink and ivory flesh tints of Boucher's nymphs. His "modern life" scenes include *Ball at the Moulin Galette, Rowers' Luncheon, The Box;* his portraits *Jeanne Samary* and *The Ingenue*.

Hilaire-Germaen Dégas (b. 1834) a "courtesy" impressionist, though his was one of the first to use the Japanese patch "dotting" is *the* Parisian painter of the ballet-girl, the dancer of the Grand Opera, and the theatre, as well as of Parisian "behind the scenes" and night life. Facial beauty, grace of figure is not what he aims at, but he does try for and catch *the fluid motion of life in the instant of living*. His *Singers at the Café-Concert* and his *Ballet Girls*, his *Rehearsal* and *Races*, are as realistic and truthful as his *Criminals* (set of portraits), his nudes, workingmen, and jockeys, and he has even made a distinctly American contribution to impressionism in his *Interior of a Cotton-Broker's Office in New Orleans* (Pau Museum), exhibited at the Centenary Exhibition in 1900.

Paul Gaugin is, perhaps the most romantic of the Neo-Impressionists.* Disgusted with Paris he went to Tahiti, where after making love to an "absinthe-drinking native princess," he took refuge in the interior of the island, married a brown Tahitian girl and free, and happy—he had left a wife and children behind in France— roamed the island "in the native girdle", unashamed and rejoicing.

Gogh and van Rysselberghe have used it, is tending to disappear in impressionist painting.

*A group of impressionists had made a special "scientific application of the principles of impressionism for the development of pointillist technique by using *divided* colors and a *divided* touch of the brush in painting. It includes Seurat, Cross, Dubois-Pillet, Signac, Rysselberghe, Van der Velde, Luce, Paul Albert Besnard (b. 1849) already considered. They are known as Chromo-Luminarists or *Neo-Impressionists*.

For he found that he could paint again. One of his pictures turns Manet's Olympia black-side foremost, so to say. It is a picture of the *Black Goddess of Evil,* who lies on a couch with a white background. In his "Noa Noa" (which he wrote after his return to civilization, together with the pictures he had painted in his South Sea Isle), he told many startling details of primitive life there. His South Sea paintings are full of the brilliant, glaring sunlight and hard shadows of a crystal-clear air, and show the female and floral forms about him in bold strokes of a luminous brush.

CÉZANNE, MATISSE AND THE "WILD MEN",

PICASSO AND THE "CUBISTS"

Paul Cézanne (1839-195) was a genre painter who led a movement away from "impressionism". He painted ordinary, every-day people and landscapes in a way that aimed to represent their inner soul and meaning, rather than give a mere outward "impression". His landscapes have been called "leaden", and his nudes, for example his *Bathers,* "merely women in their natural pelt, uglier than the females of Degas and twice as truthful". On the other hand, on an apple or a cabbage he would "lavish his palette of smothered jewels". As Huneker has said "an onion for him is as beautiful as a naked woman". His Orans and other Provencale landscapes *impress* or *depress* according as one reacts to them.* The saying that the heaven of art holds many mansions, and that Paul Cézanne may be remembered "as a painter who respected his material, and a painter pure and complex," may be called a fair summary. He has had a very great influence on many landscape painters of to-day.

Henri Matisse (b. 1862), the leader of the so-called "Wild Men", who follow his ideas, took the stand that a painting should suggest the *idea* of what it stood for, that a picture is first of all *decoration,* a combination of pattern, color and form pleasant to the eye. So in the decorative panels *Music* and *The Dance,* we have nude crimson flesh dancing on a green hill against a background of blue sky. Glow of bright color and rhythm of line are Matisse's ideals.** Among his better-known paintings are *Girl Seated* (a nude) which

---

* A principle of Cézanne's painting is that every shape and color has a definite relation to every other shape and color in the picture, and to the collective grouping of all the shapes and colors.

** Others who share his ideals or have special original use of them include André-Derain, the Basque painter Tobeen (*Circusrider*), Albert Marque, Marie Laurencin, Viaminck, Othon Friesz, Raoul Dufy, Charles Camoin and Henri Mangui. The principles of this art has been expressed as "the giving of rhythmic life to surfaces by skeleton forms, within which pure, hot colors burn."

has been called his finest work, *Road to Villacoublay, Woman at the Window, The Sea.*

Pablo Picasso and "Cubism" appear about 1910 (though after 1914, Picasso returned to a more academic style as well). Cubism makes geometric picture architecture, "cubes", the principal medium of expression in painting. It has been called "a system without an aim". For those whose mental eye is able to grasp the inner meaning of form, pictures expressed in all sorts of squares, oblongs, elipses and other geometric forms, cubist painting offers its own beauties. Numerous *Still Lives,* by Picasso, Braque's *Chopin,* Leger's *Card Player, Three Women at their Toilette,* Gleize's *A Man in Town,* and paintings by Gris, Metzinger, Herbin and others must be seen to be appreciated or understood. Even seeing does not bring understanding in many cases.

Futurism, a very modern theory in painting, attempts to show beings or objects *in actual motion* on the painted canvas. In one and the same picture we may see an arm or a leg in six or seven successive positions. It does not seem to be a movement, however, which will live. In pictures, at any rate, most of us prefer to know where the eye can find an arm or leg and not see it dispersed in space. Futurism has many branches. One futurist gem at an exposition was entitled "Noise No. 5." Noises, perhaps, are better heard than seen.

CHAPTER XVIII

GERMAN PAINTING FROM CORNELIUS TO THE PRESENT DAY

RAPHAEL MENGS, the court painter to the Kings of Spain, and a few other lesser German artists (including the artificial Angelica Kauffmann), where about the best names German painting had to show during the eighteenth century. But with the revival of a national spirit and the German War of Liberation (1813-1815), various German schools developed mainly along the line of nationalism and the patriotic subject in art. Peter Cornelius (1783-1867) of Düsseldorf was the leader of the first of these groups which included Friedrich Overbeck, Philipp Veit and Wilhelm Schadow, and appointed director of the Düsseldorf Academy, made that town for a time the art centre of Germany. In his great wood-cuts illustrating the "Song of the Nibelungs", the German national epic, and Goethe's "Faust", he stressed national German ideals in art. Later he passed to Munich, and made that city the centre of his school of great historical pictures on a large scale. Cornelius' most important pupils were Alfred Rethel (1816-1859) and Wilhelm von Kaulbach (1805-1874).

Alfred Rethel, mentally deranged and hovering on the borderland between madness and sanity, produced some of the weirdest, most terrible and striking paintings known. His tendency toward the horripilant was first shown in great historical canvases, a series showing *Hannibal Crossing the Alps* (1842), and he drew on Dürer's technique of terror in carrying out his work. His painting *Nemesis Pursuing a Murderer,* shows a flat, dreary stretch of country with a slaughtered body, away from which an assassin is hurrying off into darkness, while above him hovers the angel of vengeance. The legend goes that this picture was won at a lottery in the city of Frankfort by a nobleman of high rank, who had been guilty of a secret murder, and that the sight of the terrible prize which had fallen to him drove him insane. Another of Rethel's pictures, *Death the Avenger,* showed a grisly skeleton appearing at a masked ball, daintily scraping away at two human bones as a fiddler might on a fiddle. The mere sight of this gruesome fancy so haunted the minds of his friends that it disturbed their dreams until, for Rethel himself was of a gentle disposition, to make up for it, he produced another, pathetic and tender scene, *Death the Friend*. His striking *Dance of Death,* in Dürer's best manner, was suggested by the Belgian Revolution of 1848.

WILHELM VON KAULBACH

(1805-1874)

Wilhelm von Kaulbach—who also could depict the terrible and horrible with exciting realism, as in his *Narrenhaus* (Madhouse), the series of pictures recording the memory of what his eyes had seen in a certain insane asylum near Düsseldorf—is famous chiefly for his tremendous historical frescoes. In splendid and at times showy style, and with remarkable power and imagination, he presented in great wall-paintings more than thirty feet long some of the greatest historic dramas of the world's story. He painted these pictures of a rich and imposingly theatrical art along the grand stairway of the *New Museum* in Berlin. The wall had a granulated surface, specially prepared with an infusion of silicia securing permanence, a technical treatment known as the "water-glass" or "liquid flint" treatment. It was afterward borrowed by English painters, though a German invention, to prepare the wall for the wall-pictures in the Westminster Houses of Parliament. It took the artist ten years to complete the great series of pictures which show—just as a dramatic poet, a Shakespeare or a Dante tells his story—the *Tower of Babel, The Age of Homer, The Destruction of Jerusalem,* the *Battle of the Huns, The Crusades* and *The Reformation,* each picture containing more than one hundred life-size figures, and surrounded by small pictures, twenty in all. About these great dramatic pictures the painter grouped allegorical figures of the Arts and Sciences, and of the lawgivers of the nations, from Moses on. It is *the world's story told in painting,* and makes a tremendous effect on the observer, so dramatic and stupendous is it, like a great moving narrative. A melodramatic series of pictures illustrating *Goethe,* and a magnificent seascape, *The Sea Fight at Salamis,* painted for the Maximilianeum in Munich—a thirty-foot canvas— are among Kaulbach's other great works. His great painting, *The Battle of the Huns,* where the dead lie heaped up on the ground while their souls continue the struggle in mid-air, inspired the famous composer Franz Liszt to write the symphonic poem for orchestra by the same name, expressing the picture in music!

The Düsseldorf "visionaries", under the leadership of Shadow (the fellow-student of Cornelius) devoted themselves to a more delicate type of "easel picture". The artists of this school included Lessing Bendemann, Hildebrandt, Sohn and Hübner (1806-1882), who devoted especial attention to historical subjects; while among the *genre* painters were Henry Ritter, Rudolf, Jordan, Kral Hübner, Jacob Becker and Adolf Tidemand. A kind of German Millet was the Hamburg painter Hermann Kauffmann (1808-1889); landscape was cultivated by Heinrich Burkel; while sentimentalists of German popular life were: Spirtweg (1808-1885), Hess (1792-1871), Eduard Meyerheim (1808-1879) of Berlin, and Johann Georg Meyer (1813-1886) of Bremen.

PILOTY

Rich color, splendor of design and power of imagination showed in the work of a group of famous German painters who specialized in historical subjects. The Munich painter Karl von Piloty (1826-1886) did great canvases, including: *Seni the Astrologer at the Dead Body of Wallenstein* (1855). *Nero Dancing on the Ruins of Rome* (1861), and a notably fine *Discovery of America* (1874). Franz von Lenbach is another historical painter and Mikaily de Munkacsy (1844-1900), a Hungarian trained in Düsseldorf, in his *Christ Before Pilate* (1881), and his *Golgotha* (1883), both owned in the United States, as well as his *Death of Mozart* (1884), reached the high-water mark of his dramatic power. Adolph Menzel (1815-1905) was a coldly correct glorifier of Prussian and especially Hohenzollern history, notably in his painting *The Coronation of King Wilhelm I at Königsberg*, and in his scenes from the life of Frederick the Great (400 drawings), and scenes from contemporary life including *The Tuileries, The Ball Supper*, etc. Perhaps the most imposing figure among the historical painters is that of Hans Makart.

HANS MAKART

(1840-1884)

An Austrian, Hans Makart, was one of the great princely figures in painting. Like Titian, Rubens and Velasquez, they appear from time to time. He was the leader of the artistic life of Vienna, and reigned in that city like an uncrowned king beside the Austrian emperor who was his patron. In the days of his glory the appearance of one of his great historical canvases was a more important event than any mere political happening. *Catherina Cornaro, Death of Cleopatra, Entry of the Emperor Charles V into Antwerp* (1879) are, perhaps, his best-known canvases. At the great festivities in Vienna in honor of the old Emperor Franz Josef's silver wedding, Makart designed the medieval costumes worn by the thousands in the great street processions. Mounted on a white horse, glittering with gold, he led the procession of the artists past the imperial box, costumed as Rubens, with the great Fleming's white-feathered hat. In the nineteenth century Makart once more made the *prince of* *painting the equal of the kings of earth.* He flung away a fortune—his studio was always filled with silks, ivories, carvings, gems, and precious Eastern stuffs to recall "one hour of the world of Rubens, so bright in color, so princely in splendor!" He dominated Austrian literature, art and the stage. The great actresses would only appear in the costumes he had designed. The great writers wrote in "the Makart style". All Vienna wore Makart hats, bouquets, dresses. And with him passed the last great "royal" painter, a medieval survival in a modern age.*

OTHER MODERN GERMAN PAINTERS

Among the many painters of modern Germany,** four perhaps, are better known than others, irrespective of qualities of merit, interest or style. They are Klinger, Stuck and Udhe and Böcklin.

KLINGER, STUCK AND UDHE

Max Klinger (b. 1873) is a poet, musician and philosopher who, aside from his genre pictures has expressed a great thought—the writer Strindberg's conception of the real *unity* of *Greek beauty* and the *Christian ideal* in a famous picture:

Christ in Olympus, in which he combines Greek simplicity and beauty of form with a wealth of Christian truth and sentiment. Franz Stuck (b. 1863) is closely related to Klinger in spirit. In

---

* Other Austrian moderns include: Leopold Karl Müller (1834-1892), who draws his subjects from the Egyptian Orient; Heinrich von Angeli (b. 1840) who has painted all the crowned heads of the nineteenth century of Europe; Gustav Klint: *Philosophy* (Ceiling of Vienna University), a fiery head with serious eyes looking down from heavens where nude human forms cluster among green clouds and golden stars; Moll, Zettel, Hänisch, Friedrich, Ticky (landscape), F. König, enchanted princes in romantic groves; the Bohemian, Gabriel Max (b. 1840) is a painter of morbidly beautiful girl martyrs: *Female Martyr on the Cross* (1867) and the suffering insane; Hans Schwaiger (Bohemian legend) and Orlik (genre scenes from Old Prague) are other Czechs. The strange Austrian painter Kokoshka, in Vienna, paints portraits and other pictures hard to grasp, in which he tries to express the *inner heart* and *mind* of sitters and scenes in a *psycho-anayltical* way.

** Hans Thomas (b. 1839) was a modern Dürer, romantic medieval fairytale and legends of chivalry and mythology his favorite subjects. Genre painters are Liebermann (b. 1849)—*Net Menders; The Shoemaker's Workshop;* Skrabina, Lesitikow, Keller, Herterich, Zugel, Erbe, Putz, and Hengeler (a great animal painter). Theodor Hagen and Gleichen-Russwurm (b. 1866), are landscape artists and Albert von Keller (b. 1841) has been called the *only modern* German painter who has caught the *charm of modern woman's movement and expression,* Exter (b. 1863) his best known work a *Paradise Lost*—two nudes grovelling on the ground in the sunlight, Habermann (b. 1849) is pensively morbid—*Child of Sorrow* (Berlin Gallery).

religious pictures *Pietà, The Guardian of Paradise* (1889), a slim, beautiful angel figure; in classic and modern subjects primitive, even brutal strength and Greek simplicity are combined. His most famous picture is an allegorical one: *The Conqueror*. A telling pictorial argument against War, it shows a cruel nude figure, spear on shoulder, astride a beast half-horse, half-swine, trampling the naked bodies of the dead who have fallen in battle.

Fritz von Udhe (1848-1911), is a naturalist of religion, staging his realistic pictures from the life of Christ among the hills and hamlets of Bavaria. Famous among them are *The Sermon on the Mount* and the tender *Suffer Little Children to Come Unto Me*. Böcklin, though a Swiss, was of German descent, and is usually considered a German painter.

ARNOLD BÖCKLIN

(1827-1901)

Böcklin is a painter who stands alone as *one of the very greatest of modern times*. He is, perhaps, the most wonderful painter of dramatic and romantic landscape modern times have known. But landscape does not alone answer his creative needs. He makes his landscapes live with the life of all the fanciful creatures and folk of mythology and romance. The gods and half-gods of the ancient Greeks *Prometheus, Ulysses and Calypso,* the *Battle of the Centaurs* (Basel Gallery, one of his most famous paintings), *Tritons* chasing the daughters of Neptune in the billowy waves, are not the only ones to appear. There is *The Sea-Serpent, Death Playing a Violin,* Saracens storming flaming castles, Knights of the Middle Ages on adventurous journeys, *Moorish Horsemen* (Lucerne Gallery), an *Anchorite in the Wilderness* (Basel Gallery) romantic subjects that caught his fancy, all painted in a glorious glow of color. In fact to all the romantic creatures the imagination of the ages has called forth, that dwell in Nature's trees or lonely rocks, that live on slimy sea-bottoms, he gives a body and a soul. He runs the whole scale of the human emotions, from merry laughter to deepest tragedy and —he has painted the *most moving, heart-stirring, ardent religious pictures of the nineteenth century* in *The Magdalen and the Christ.* (1868), the *Pietà* (1885), and his *Saint Catherine*. He excelled in the "radiance of far stars, the vivid grotto-blue of the sea, the copper-brown of a faun's skin". Weingartner wrote a symphonic poem for orchestra inspired by his picture *The Elysian Fields*. But the one great painting of Böcklin which the whole world knows is:

The Island of the Dead (Paris). In this famous painting the rest of the dead in a place forgotten by the world is expressed with sombre beauty. A great rock towers in the sea, but the sea is still, there is no cry of bird, no fluttering of wing, no sound of voice. A boat, with a single white and quiet passenger, is being rowed silently to the island. There blue-green cypresses shadow the mysterious recesses of the rock amid the brooding waters, and the dead may sleep on undisturbed with the lapping of sighing waves to lend music to their eternal dream. It is this picture which has inspired the noble symphonic tone-poem of the same name by the Russian composer and pianist Rachmaninoff.

Wilhelm von Kobell (active after 1870) has painted magnificently spirited battle-scenes on a colossal scale, *The Battle of Wagram, The Siege of Cosel* (New Pinatholek, Munich). Ferdinand von Rayski (d. 1890), landscapes, portraits, animals; Willy Jaeckel, who is a realist of El Greco's type in religious pictures—*St. Sebastian, Rest of the Flight,* and others, *Toledo in a Storm;* Leo von König, a Berlin impressionist; Ludwig von Hagn, historical paintings *Philip of Orleans in Versailles* (Munich), Walter Klemm, *genre;* Edvard von Munch, one of the greatest of German impressionists, represent only a few among the many other important names in modern German painting.

CHAPTER XIX

MODERN PAINTING IN OTHER EUROPEAN LANDS

In other European countries painting reflects, more or less, the more important "trends" or "movements" in the countries already considered, plus various developments of a special individual and national kind.

SPAIN

The first great Spanish painter to follow Goya* was Mariano Jose Maria Bernardo Fortuny (1838-1847). A poor boy who toiled hard at his chosen life-work, a Moroccan campaign gave him his lasting fondness for the brilliant glitter of the African sun, and in his clever use of glowing color he is at times extravagant. Among his famous pictures are *Choosing a Model, Vicaria* ("Spanish Marriage"), *The Snake Charmer* and *Moors Playing with a Vulture*.

Ignacio Zulaoga (b. 1870), has been called a "modern Goya". Girls and old women, bull-fighters and *manolas*, the lower type of Spanish city girl he paints with mastery. He is Spain's greatest national artist and has the Goya ability to call up the weird and horrible as well as the piquantly feminine. One of his best-known pictures is the portrait of Lucienne Breval (an opera singer). She is shown in "Carmen", bowing behind the footlights which glow on her blue shawl. The painter Columbano, who illustrates scenes of Portuguese actual life, has been termed a "Portuguese Goya."

BELGIUM

Belgium always has been influenced by French art and has always been a country rich in painters. Among the many, many artists of

* Other Spanish artists include: Eduardo Zamacois (1842-1871); Casanova (b. 1847); de Madrazo (b. 1841); José Villegas (b. 1848), painters of Spanish and French Rococo scenes; Pradilla, *The Mad Queen Juana;* Carbonero, *Conversation of the Duke of Gandia;* Casado, *The Bell of Huesca;* Vera, *Last Day of Numantia;* Cabello, *Inez de Castro;* Checa, *Barbarian Onslaught*. Benliure y Gil, *Vision of the Coliseum,* cultivated the big historical canvas. Rico applied Fortuny's glowing color to Venetian scenes. Realist painters of the *genre* are: Agrasot, with truthful pictures of Spanish low life, and Sorolla y Bastida. Sorolla did fine sea-pictures, especially a large *Fishing* (Luxembourg) full of truth and realism. A Portuguese peasant scene painter is Carlos Reis.

name and reputation associated with painting in Belgium during the nineteenth century several stand out.

Constantin Meunier, the Millet of the Flemish workingman, with *The Peasants' War* (Brussels Gallery); Xavier Mellery, an "inner life" painter, *The Drawing;* Charles Verlat, *Godfrey de Boulogne at the Siege of Jerusalem* (Brussels Gallery). Among more modern painters, Hoeterickx, who paints "the crowd in the park"; Marcette, marines; J. de Greet, realistic landscapes, *The Pool at Rouge-Cloitre* (Brussels Gallery); Van Rysselberghe, already mentioned with the French "impressionists"; Laemaens, who has been called "a Daumier with anchylose ('stiff') joints," and numerous others.

HOLLAND

Joseph Israels (b. 1827), a Jew, who for thirty years (after he gave up the historical subject) painted the joys and sorrows of the poor, especially those of the Dutch seafaring man, is the greatest painter of nineteenth century Holland. All his pictures tell a tale of every-day life, of toil, of the bowed and broken backs excessive labor brings, of the melancholy lives of the down-trodden. In his eloquent paintings the past of his own lowly and oppressed race is revealed to the eye of the beholder. One of his most touching and intimate pictures is *The Bashful Lover* (Met. Museum of Art, New York), a solemn-faced country boy walking beside a pensive country girl, without finding courage to utter the words his lips are burning to speak. Among others, Christophe Birschop has painted *genre* pictures of colorful costumed Friesland life; de Hoogh, the dreamy stillness of Dutch interiors; Gerk Henkes, the life of the foggy Dutch canals; Cortz, the gray-green and yellow-flowered Dutch countryside.* Jan Toorop, a "revolutionary" Dutchman in painting, is regarded as a master of the drawn line. In his picture of the *Sphynx* he reveals "all phases of unbridled desire," and in his *Three Brides,* we have contrasted the convent demureness of the nun, the chaste devotion of the honest affection, and the unbridled voluptuousness of the harlot at heart.

ITALY

Among the artists of modern Italy were and are many talents. Michetti, Capri and Dalbono have painted the sun and froth and colorful gayety of Neapolitan popular life in convincing colors. Favretto and Barberino have recreated the splendid glow of Venice in the days of the eighteenth century; and Tommassi and Dall'oca

* The names of Jongkind, Tholen, Jan Veth, Havermanns, Jacob and William Maris (landscapes), Matthew Maris (mystic figures), Neuhuys (women and children) and the wonderful "colorist" Anton Mauve, also should be mentioned.

Branca have illumined the lagoons and streets of Venice of to-day with the light of their art. Signorini has painted the Piedmontese landscape. The Neapolitan de Nittis (who died in Paris in 1884), painted *French* street life in its more sensuous moments. Pasini painted the East; Muzzolini, Roman antiquity; Monticelli equals Fortuny in the glow of his colors. Portrait painters include Stefani, Giusti, Tallone and Boldoni: *The Whistler* (Brooklyn Museum). Distinguished landscape painters are: Costa, Morelli, Nono, Gioli, de Maria Cairati, Pelliza Fraggiacomo and Ciardi. But Italy's one great modern painter who towers head and shoulders above the rest, is Biovanni Segantini.

GIOVANNI SEGANTINI

Segantini (1866-1899) is one of the greatest examples of the truth of the saying that "The artist is born and not made." He was one of Nature's artists, like Millet, and living in the Italian Alps, in the village of Val d'Albona, he created his greatest oil-paintings amid the solemn loneliness of the towering mountain. How earnestly and seriously he regarded his art is proven by his own words about how he came to paint some of his finest pictures.

> "To comfort the sorrow of the parents of a child that had died, I painted my *Consolation of Faith*. To bless the union of two young lovers I painted my *Love at the Source of Life*. In order to express the whole fulness of mother love I painted the fruit of love in *The Angel of Life,* and to show the bad mothers, the selfishly barren and unfruitful ones, who live only for *pleasure,* I painted them whipped by hellish furies. Then, to show the source of all evil I painted my *Vanity*. I felt that men should love the brave breasts that give them milk, flesh and skins, and I painted *The Two Mothers* (it shows a human mother drowsing over her babe by the light of a stable lamp which reveals a mother-cow with her little calf), and the patient horse at the plough that works for man in *Ploughing in the Engadine*. I have painted work and rest after work, and especially the good beasts with their kind gentle eyes."

Segantini painted with the moral outlook of a St. Francis of Assissi, and when he died the history of art "lost one of its rarest geniuses!"

RUSSIA

The late nineteenth century showed that Russia had some painters of striking originality. Elias Repin (b. 1844), has given the dramatic soul of Shakespeare to great historical paintings: *Ivan the Terrible, the brutal Cossacks' Reply to the Turkish Sultan,* the beast-featured men *Towing a Ship along the Volga,* and in his *genre* picture, *Sowing on the Volga.* Victor Vaznezov besides gold-glowing Byzantine religious paintings, also has cultivated the historical scene. *The Scythians* show wild horsemen fighting on the steppe with lance and battle-axe. Schischkin, Vassiliev, Savrasso, are landscapists, as are Kuindski (birch woods), Sudkovski (marines), Albert Benois (Finnish water-color scenes) Apollinaris Vasnezov (primeval Siberian plain and forest). A brutal, realistic painter of Russian *moujik* (peasant) life was Philip Maliavine. His *Laughter* is a horrible picture of witch-women in flaming red, and his hulking peasants are creatures of brute and beast-like force. The Russian painters best known in the United States, perhaps, include Vassili, Vereschagin, and the "decorative" painters of the Russian Ballet, Léon Bakst and Roerich.

VERESCHAGIN

Vereschagin (1824-1904) was the soldier painter of a Russia vanished probably for all time into the past, the Russia of the Czars. A painter of the old military school, the school of the Frenchman Gérome, a stern realist and naturalist, in his showing of fact, a noble ideal filled his work. He was the soldiers' friend, and his ideal was the *end* and *abolition of war,* whose horrors he had witnessed at first hand in the Russian military expedition against Smarkand, and in the war against Turkey. Vereschagin is, perhaps, the only military painter who in his pictures has deliberately *preached against fighting* by representing with startling fidelity the *horrors* of war. His pictures have been exhibited in the United States, and he was a guest with the American troops in the Philippines during the Spanish-American War, and perished when the Russian flagship "Petropavlovsk" was sunk by the Japanese in the Russian-Japanese War, on April 13, 1904. His most impressive pictures are:

The Pyramid of Skulls or *Apotheosis of War* (1874), a realistic pyramid of skulls, dedicated to "all conquerors, present, past and to come"

Left Behind. A picture of a dying Russian soldier abandoned by his comrades during a retreat in the Turkestan campaign.

Sepoys Blown From English Guns in India. A horrid picture of the cruel method of execution used by the English authorities in the suppression of the Indian Sepoy Mutiny.

Execution of Nihilists. A drastic "real-life" rendering of the scene. He also did paintings inspired by the New Testament (not forgetting, of course, a *Crucifixion,* which was a subject especially attractive) and other pictures revealing the horrors of Napoleon's 1812 campaign in Russia.

SOME MODERN RUSSIAN PAINTERS

Léon Bakst, Nicolas A. Roerich, A. Golovine and Alexander Benoist are best known by their brilliant water-color (aquarelle) costume designs, rich in the most glowing and barbaric color, for the Diaghileff and other Russian Ballets, and their fantastic stage-settings for these dancers. But they have done "easel pictures" as well, and Nicolas A. Roerich, whose paintings have been exhibited here is, perhaps, one of the most important figures among these modern Russian artists.

His great paintings are fantastically Russian. He paints the ancient Russia of legend and fairytale in throbbing, glowing colors. *Welcome to the Sun, The Idols* (white horse-skulls glistening on the poles of a stockade within which rise barbarously painted totem-poles) call up the days of primitive Slavic man. *The Enchanted City*, with its golden walls and towers aglow in the red light of a surrounding sea of flames, and *The Treasure* are visions of fairyland. *St. Procopius Blessing the Unknown Traveller* (a solitary figure seated on a hill overlooking a great river, with hand raised in blessing on the boat about to turn around a bend in the stream far beneath its feet), is one of his finest religious-legendary thoughts.

K. A. Korovine, *Spring, Summer in the Country, In the Garden;* A. Golovine, *Spanish Girls;* Bogdanoff-Belsky, *Peasant Girl;* F. Maljawin, *Peasant Women;* Ivan Bunin, the series of pictures called *The Russian Village;* Somov, *Lady in the Blue Dress; Alexander Block* (portrait); Alexander Benois, *The Hunt;* Streletzky, *The Boyars,* are works by modern Russian artists; some of them—like the ultra-modern Soudeikine—are equally or even more famed as painters of stage settings.

POLAND

The French artist Jean-Pierre Norblin de la Gourdaine, who established himself in Poland during the eighteenth century, may be regarded as "the spiritual founder of Poland's national art". He was followed by native painters, Orlowski, Michalowski, Kossak, Malczewski, Chelmonski and later, by Kucharski and others. But the first really important painters of Poland are Arthur Grottger and his contemporary Jan Matejko. Grottger, who has been called "the Chopin of Polish paintings," created great historical "cycle" pictures: *Varsovia* (1861), *Polonia, Lithuania,* and a *Valley of Tears* (Paris Exposition, 1867), which painted with glowing realism all the horrors and miseries Poland suffered in her wars of independence in a series of eleven paintings. Matejko is a painter of great historical canvases: *Albert, Duke of Prussia Swearing the Oath of Vassalage to King Sigismund of Poland* (Cracow Museum), *Etienne Bathory, King of Poland, The Battle of Grunwald* and *King Jan*

Sobieski's Triumphal Entry into Vienna (Vatican, Rome). He was a realist in his models, going to the Warsaw streets to find them. Partly owing to this fact, perhaps, his historical pictures are vivid and full of life. Brandt has specialized in the life of the Zaporogian Cossacks; and Joseph Chelmonski, in his *In the Steppe* and *Winter Journey* give magnificent pictures of spirited horses in tremendous gallop. Antoine Kamienski with a wonderful imaginative gift, shows the worn and discouraged artist glancing from his straw bed toward *The Uncompleted Work*, while Death's grisly hand stretches out to seize him. Jean Styka, a pupil of Matejko, like Elviro Andriolli, has also produced great historical canvases: *Polonia, Bem at Siedmiogrod, The Rome of Nero*—inspired by the Polish novelist Sienkeiwicz's "Quo Vadis".

Other names eminent in Polish painting include: Weiss (portraits); Wehssenhoff; Ruszczyc (landscapes); Falat (hunting scenes); Tetmayer (peasant life); Malczewski (symbolic pictures), and Gerson (historic paintings). A critic has said: "We see in Polish pictures a great deal of fighting, a great deal of weeping, but what there is peculiar to the Poles in the expression or technique of their works it is hard to discover."

THE SCANDINAVIAN COUNTRIES

DENMARK

Karl Bloch (1834-1890) and Christian Zahrtmann (b. 1874), are the greater Danish historical painters. The second, especially, has painted simple and moving pictures of the tragic life of the Danish Princess Eleonora Christina, that make his historical scenes far more human than they are historical. Viggio Johansen (b. 1851) paints *genre* pictures of Danish home-life, simple and tranquil (*An Evening at Home, Grandmother's Birthday*) and silvery landscape scenes. Peter Kroyer shows the life of the Danish sea-coast sailor, in ocean sunshine or lamp-lit tavern. Copenhagen "actual life" has been painted by Ring, Haslund, Syberg, and Irminger. Thorolf Pedersen, Locher and Micheal Ancher are sea-painters. Symbolism is represented by Slott-Moller (b. 1864), and Willumsen (b. 1863) who paint ancient folk-legends with a mystic modern touch. The ideal of religion on a grand scale is cultivated by Joakim Skovgaard (b. 1856), in great canvases like *Christ Among the Dead*, and *The Pool of Bethseda*.

SWEDEN

Swedish art is more elegant and Parisian than the homelier Danish. And the Swedish landscape artists, Kreuger, Nordstrom, Ekstrom, Prince Eugen of Sweden, Wallander and Wahlberg treat their more southern countryside with a more coquettish brush. Bruno Liljefors (b. 1860) is famous as an animal painter, but in general Swedish artists, Pauli, Bergh, Josephson, Bjorek, do not confine themselves to one type or *genre,* though Anders Zorn (b. 1860) has made a speciality of the study of sunlight effects on naked bodies and dancing waves in oil and water color: *Dance Before the Window,* and *Ripple of the Waves.* Younger experimenters in glowing, mosaic-like brilliancy of color, are Gustav Fjalstad (b. 1868) and Hermann Normann.

NORWAY

Norwegian painters might be divided into two classes: the *rougher* and more direct realists,* and the more *elegant* and *polished* ones. They first paint the open-air scenes of their land, often in rough-hewn style. Pine forest and fjord, sparkling snowfields, mountain twilights, realistic peasants and fisher men.

The more "elegant" realists** include painters who paint light rivers and pools, night skies, dark green meadows contrasting with the colorful dresses of female figures, and simple Nature lying in deathlike repose.

* Adolf Tildemand (1814-1876), first introduced such pictures in Europe. Other names include: Normann, Jorgensen, Wentzel, Kolstoe, Krohg, Nilsen, Eilif, Pertesen, Skredsvig, Tjaulow.
** Thaulow, Borgen, Hennig, Hjerlow, Stenerson, Strom, Werenskjold and Gerhardt Munthe (as well as some of the "rougher" painters who softened their brushes) belong in the second category.

CHAPTER XX

THE ROMANCE OF PAINTING IN AMERICA

AMONG eighteenth century American painters must be mentioned John Symbert (1684-1751) who painted many a crabbed-face Colonial preacher and bishop, and the Tory John Copely (considered with the English painters), as well as the Anglicized Benpamin West who, though born in Pennsylvania, deserted his homeland to paint pompous pictures in the grand historic manner in London. But the first really *American* painters are the Peales and John Trumbull.

THE PEALES AND JOHN TRUMBULL

There were really no less than five Peales, and *three* are especially associated with the *patriotic* subject in American painting. Charles Wilson Peale (1741-1826), a pupil of Gustavus Hesselius, a Swedish portrait-painter living near Annapolis (Peale himself was born in Queen Anne County, Maryland), painted at Mount Vernon, in 1772, *the earliest known portrait of George Washington,* in the uniform of a colonel of Virginia militia (Lee Memorial Chapel, Washington and Lee University, Virginia) and, besides two miniatures of Martha Washington, did in all fourteen paintings of the Father of his Country, and portraits of other celebrated Americans of the time. Charles Peale was a painter who fought as well as painted for his country, and his most famous picture of Washington (he was captain of a company of Continentals in the battles of Trenton and Germantown) he painted during the winter of Valley Forge (1777-8) with stiffened fingers in bitter days of cold and suffering. At eighty-one this hale and hearty pioneer of American painting did his *Christ Healing the Sick at Bethseda,* and at eighty-three a portrait of himself (Academy of Fine Arts, Philadelphia). His brother, James Peale (1749-1831), also painted two portraits of Washington, one of which is in Independence Hall, Philadelphia.

Rembrandt Peale (1778-1860) the son of Charles, and his father's pupil (he also studied in Paris and with West, in London) was a better draughtsman but a poorer colorist than his father, and one of the first American lithographers. His Washington portraits include one in the Capitol at Washington, and an equestrian picture (Independence Hall, Philadelphia). Among his other portraits are:

President Jefferson, the charming *Dolly Madison, Commodores Perry* and *Decatur, Houdon,* the French sculptor, and *General Armstrong;* and his *Court of Death* hangs in the Detroit Art Gallery. His one brother Raphaelle (1774-1825) painted still-life subjects, one of the first Americans to do so, and his other brother Titian Ramsey (1800-1885), did animals in water-color.

John Trumbull (1710-1785), an aide-de-camp to George Washington and to General Gates during the War of Independence, painted pictures even more popular than those of Charles Peale. Trumbull, like the modern Russian painter Vereschagin, was less interested in painting as an *art* than as a *means of influencing* men. But where Vereschagin's "purpose" in painting was to abolish war's horrors, Trumbull set himself the task of stimulating and glorifying American patriotism by making a glowing record on canvas of great moments in our national struggle for freedom. The very titles of his great historical paintings are a record of American military and civic glory:

The Battle of Bunker Hill, The Death of General Montgomery (both in Yale School of Fine Arts), *The Surrender of Burgoyne, The Signing of the Declaration of Independence, The Surrender of Cornwallis, The Resignation of Washington* (Capitol, Washnigton), and a collection of fifty other historical paintings (Yale College), also tell the story of American history at its high-water mark.*

His fine portraits include numerous pictures of Washington: *George Washington* in the New York City Hall; in Charleston, S. C., Yale (in full military costume), and the National Museum, Washington. Besides he painted portraits of *Governor George Clinton, Hamilton, Jay, Adams* (City Hall, New York), *John Quincy Adams* (Yale), a second *Alexander Hamilton* (Met. Museum of Art, New York), and numerous others.

Gilbert Stuart (1755-1828), however, was not only the greatest of the portrait painters of the Age of Independence, but also has painted the *one generally best-beloved portrait of George Washington.* It hangs in the Boston Museum ("the Athanaeum Portrait") and the story goes that when he had finished his noble head, he felt it was the best thing he ever had done, and would not touch it again with the brush to finish the bust for fear of spoiling it. He would

---

*With these should be mentioned the most famous pictorial record of a great scene in American history, *Washington Crossing the Delaware,* by the German artist Emanuel Leutze. Leutze (1816-1868) born in Germany came to Philadelphia when a child. Eastman Johnson (1824-1906) who studied in Düsseldorf and Holland has painted fine pictures of Civil War days, and *genre* pictures of Negro farm and fisher life, among them his *Old Kentucky Home* (1867), *Husking Bee* (1876), *Nantucket Cranberry Festival,* while among his portraits are: *Daniel Webster, Emerson, Longfellow, Hawthorne, and Presidents Hayes, Arthur, Cleveland and Harrison.*

not part with it during life. "I copy the works of God and leave clothes to the tailor," he once said when some one asked him why he seldom painted more than the head and bust of a sitter. It is claimed that Stuart, who had painted King George III and his son in London, and Louis XVI in Paris, as well as an uncrowned American queen, Madame Patterson-Bonaparte, the disowned wife of King Jerome of Westphalia, and most of the great of their day in the Old World and New, found in George Washington the *only sitter* who ever made him feel "embarrassed" and unimportant, and that for this reason his first attempt to paint him was a failure. John, and John Quincy Adams, Thomas Jefferson, James Madison, James Munroe, John Jay, Generals Gates and Knox, are some of the other great Americans whose faces Stuart's brush has immortalized.

SOME POST-REVOLUTIONARY PAINTERS

John Vanderlyn (1776-1852), one of Stuart's pupils, set the fashion for American painters, like American sculptors, to study in Rome. His best-known canvases are a nude *Ariadne*, a portrait of his companion *Washington Allston*, and *The Dead Man Restored to Life*. But the trend of these artists, like that of Thomas Cole (1801-1848), in his pompous allegorical *Course of Empire* and *Voyage of Life;* of Daniel Huntington (1816-1906), *Mercy's Dream*, and Henry Peters Gray (1819-1877) *Wages of War and Cleopatra's Dissolving the Pearl*, were rather in the direction of big, pretentious pictures in the inflated Italian historical manner.

THE HUDSON RIVER SCHOOL

Meanwhile a group of American painters who lived and worked along the Hudson River in the earlier nineteenth century, preferred Nature to the grand historical style, and were the first Americans to take *landscape painting* seriously. Asher Brown Durand, Thomas Doughty, Thomas Cole (before he abandoned landscape for allegoric and historic subjects), John Frederick Kansett (especially identified with Lake George and Long Island Sound scenery), were active from the end of the eighteenth until well beyond the middle of the nineteenth century. Later "nature" painters did not confine themselves to the Hudson River valley. Albert Bierstadt (1830-1902) devoted himself to correct and not unimpressive paintings of the magnificent scenery of the Rocky Mountains: *Sierra Nevada* (Corcoran Gallery, Washington), and *The Valley of the Yosemite* (Lenox Collection, New York) are his most famous pictures. Besides, he contributed two large canvases to the pictorial story of his native land: *The Discovery of the Hudson River*, and *The Settlement of California* (Capitol, Washington). Thomas Moran (b. 1837), was also a Rocky Mountain painter, who treated the same scenery his teacher Bierstadt had recorded with more insight in such great canvases as *The Grand Canyon of the Yellowstone* and *Chasm of the Colorado River* (Capitol, Washington). Frederick Edwin Church (1826-1900), Cole's pupil, was a brilliant and "plausible"—which means that his pictures convinced you of their truth—painter of grandiose natural scenes. His vogue passed as newer men came to the fore, but he had great nobility in handling light and color in rainbow, mist, ice-berg and sunset effects. His trips to South America called forth his *Andes of Ecuador, Heart of the Andes* (1859) *Cotopaxi* (1862) and *Morning in the Tropics* (1877), and his *Great Fall at Niagara,* painted in 1857 (Corcoran Gallery, Washington) makes us understand why his paintings were so much admired in their day, and brought extravagant prices from American and European collectors. Church was probably the most famous member of the "Hudson River School".

JOHN LA FARGE AND THE FRENCH INFLUENCE IN THE UNITED STATES

John La Farge (1835-1910), of French parentage, studied drawing with his grandfather, the miniature painter Victor Binsse de St. Victor and is notable for spreading the French naturalist influence of Rousseau, Corot and Millet in the United States as for his own artistic achievement. Though he painted landscapes, still-life scenes and figures (the best-known *The Golden Christ and Nicodemus* and *The Golden Age)* he is most famous as a decorative painter, and for his wonderful control of color and light in mural paintings (*The Ascension,* Church of the Ascension, and paintings in St. Bartholomew's Church, New York), his stained glass windows *(Battle Window,* Memorial Hall, Harvard, and those in many New York and other churches), his panels in the Congressional Library, and elsewhere. In stained glass work he was the first to employ the so-called "opalescent"—translucent fusible glass—instead of "pot-metal glass"—glass colored through while being fused. This was a distinctly "American" invention, and is known as "American glass". He also introduced the custom of painting only hands and faces of figures in stained glass. As a writer and artist the French ideals he advocated were carried on by others in other fields of endeavor. As a decorative artist (though one with an English training), Edwin A. Abbey might also be mentioned with La Farge. Beginning as an illustrator ("Harper's Magazine" published many of his drawings), he turned to mural paintings, and has told the story of *The Holy Grail* in beautiful color and drawing on the walls of the Boston Public Library. In the decorative and mural field might also be mentioned: E. H. Blashfield, Ed. Simmons, H. S. Mowbray, R. Reid, G. W. Maynard, Van Ingen, Miss Violet Oakley and others.

GEORGE INNES

George Innes (1825-1894) born in Newburg, N. Y., largely self-taught, though he made two visits to Paris, is one of the greatest of American landscape painters. He had a distinctly original and distinctly American mind in art, and most of his landscapes represented New York, New Jersey and New England scenes. His *Gray Lowering Day* and his *Niagara,* his beautiful *Delaware Water Gap* are among his finest paintings, and show the French influence. Many of his pictures are in American Museums. William Morris Hunt (1824-1879), who studied first in German Düsseldorf and later came under Millet's influence, and Thomas K. Hicks (1823-1890), as well as, later, Kenyon Cox, the Weirs, Will H. Low, Abbot H. Thayer and others, especially the great American painter John S. Sargent represent the influence of a Paris training.

JOHN SINGER SARGENT

John Singer Sargent (b. 1856) won European fame—he studied with the French portraitist Carolus-Duran in Paris—with his *Portrait of a Young Lady* which the novelist Henry James praised, even before he became known in America. In Europe, as well as in the United States, his sitters included all of the leading men and women in social, literary, artistic and political life. He has not painted the *souls,* the characters of his sitters, so much as wonderfully clever, daring, brilliant conceptions of their *outward* individuality. Two of his best portraits are the *Henry Marquand* (Metropolitan Museum, New York), and *La Carmencita* (Luxembourg), while among his other easel pictures (his fine paintings of scenes in Venice, the Orient and Brittany are less known) is the Spanish *El Jaleo* (Boston Art Museum). As a decorative painter he is represented in the Boston Public Library by the brilliant mural *Pageant of Religion.* Portrait and *genre* painting have also been cultivated by Abbot H. Thayer: *Young Women* (Met. Museum of Art, New York), John W. Alexander, *Study in Black and Green* (Met. Museum of Art, New York), Cecilia Beaux, I. R. Wiles, A. Franzen, Lydia F. Emmet, W. Lockwood, T. Eakins, E. Tarbel, G. de Brush Forest, Robert Henri, Louise Cox, W. Glackens, and numerous others.

THE GERMAN INFLUENCE IN AMERICA

Some exceedingly brilliant American artists have reflected the art training received in the great German art centres of Düsseldorf and Munich.

Alexander H. Wyant (1836-1892) studied with Hans Gude, a distinguished Düsseldorf artist, in Carlsruhe. Wyant, who early lost his health as a consequence of hardship and exposure while on a Government expedition in the West, developed into a landscape artist of rare and poetic talent. Most of his pictures, done in the high altitudes of the Adirondack or the Catskill Mountains, have increased greatly in value since his death, and high prices are now paid for them.

William Merrit Chase (b. 1849) an Indianan, and a pupil of Wagner and Piloty in Munich, painted with distinction in oils, water-color and pastel, and also etched. He is best known as a portrait painter of rare merit, among his sitters being the painters *Whistler* and *Duvenek, Peter Cooper* and *General Webb*. One of his best-known oil paintings is *Ready for the Ride* (Union League Club, New York).

Frank Duvenek (b. 1848) a Cincinnatian, and a pupil of Diez of the Royal Munich Academy, on his return from Europe in the seventies overturned the traditions of the Hudson River School, and transmitted the theories he had learned at the great German art centre to numerous American pupils. He is best known as a figure and landscape painter. Frederick Poeter Vinton, Joseph R. De Camp, John W. Alexander, and others represent the influence of Munich in particular in American art.

THREE UNIQUE AMERICAN ARTISTS

WINSLOW HOMER

Among all American artists perhaps *the most truly American in every way* is the unique marine painter Winslow Homer, born in Boston (1836-1910). He may be called our greatest *ocean* painter. He began as a soldier boy, fighting in Civil War days in the Army of the Potomac, and first established his fame by the stirring, spirited drawings published in "Harper's Magazine" as he sent them from the front. His paintings *Home, Sweet Home* and *Prisoners from the Front* (exhibited in New York in 1865, in Paris 1867), were reminiscences of his war experiences, just as *The Country Schoolroom, Eating Watermelon, The Cotton Pickers, Visit from Old Missus, Sunday Morning*, are fresh, original echoes—for he was a realist and largely self-taught—of his sojourn below the Mason and Dixon line. But greater than all his pictures of boys in blue, New England children and Negroes in the land of Dixie, are his wonderful seascapes of stormy Atlantic billows and the life of the Gloucester fishermen. Many of his pictures were painted along the Maine Coast. *Lost on the Grand Banks, The Life, Eight Bells,* and *Under-*

tow are among the best known, and especial favorites are the splendid, impressive *Northeaster,* with its tremendous heave and movement of crashing waves, and his *The Gulf Stream,* with its rich tropic color, and the figure of the shipwrecked sailor on a raft, both in the Metropolitan Museum of Art, New York. No American artist has painted the many moods of the sea* and the life of the plain folk who dwell on its shores and "go down to the sea in ships", to earn their hard daily bread, with more truth and less sham and convention than Winslow Homer.

JAMES ABBOT MCNEILL WHISTLER

A greater artist in his own impressionistic, highly specialized way than Homer, James Abbot McNeill Whistler (1834-1903), was born in Lowell, Mass., but artistically is more "a man without a country", and reflects in an individual way both French and Japanese influences. Whistler's etchings—he did nearly 300 beautiful copperplates—come first in his art production. But he also painted exquisitely in oils, in water color and in pastel, and lithographed direct on the stone (some 150 lithographs); while as a "decorative" artist the famous *Peacock Room* in the home of Mr. Frederick H. Leland (whom he later quarreled with and painted as the devil, with hoofs and horns) was his greatest achievement.

The Whistler Etchings. Waspish, arrogant, sharp-tongued, Whistler made enemies his life-long and his "The Gentle Art of Making Enemies" (1890) is a clever book, which insists that critics and the public know nothing at all about art. His etchings are mainly notable for their command of the "living line". Among the "French Set", etchings like the *Mustard-Seller;* among the "Thames Set", *London Bridge,* and the old Chelsea riverfront—*The Adam and Eve;* and among the "Venice Set" practically any of the plates which show the drowsy beauty of Venetian waterways, may be mentioned.

Whistler's Oil Paintings. Whistler's oils reflect his theory that first of all, art is an "impression" of charm, not an incident of record. Some wonderful portraits, *Pablo Sarasate,* the great Spanish violinist, *The Little Rose of Lyme Regis,* a girlish figure with a sweet echo of *Mona Lisa's* subtle smile, *Connie Gilchrist, Rose Carder, Portrait of the Painter's Mother* (Luxembourg), *Carlysle* (Glasgow), two Japanese-influenced "white" pictures: *Princess of Porcelain-Land,* and *The Little White Girl* (a study of white on white), *Blue Wave* and *Nocturne, Valpariso Harbor,* and also the "impressionistic"

---

*Other American marine painters include: Henry B. Snell, Charles H. Woodbury, Frederick Waugh, Paul Daugherty, C. H. Fromuth, C. W. Hawthorne (fishermen) and H. Reuterdahl (battle-ship paintings and Navy scenes).

Nocturnes (called *Notes, Arrangements, Symphonies, Harmonies*) each in a different color, especially the *Nocturne in Blue and Silver* (National Gallery) are famous. The Venetian watercolors and the pastels of his middle period are less important than these oils. As an etcher Whistler ranks with Rembrandt, Van Dyck and Claude. As a painter, though Ruskin called one of his Nocturnes "a pot of paint flung in the face of the public", and Whistler recovered only a farthing when he sued him for damages, he is the master of a rare and delicate art. The "salt of sex", as a critic has said, is missing in his work, and though sane, his figures are delicate and vapory. Whistler was an American only technically, and lived his life in Paris and London.

ELIHU VEDDER AND ARTHUR B. DAVIES

Elihu Vedder (b. 1836, in New York City), is one of the most imaginative artists the United States has produced. He first attracted attention in 1884 with a fine series of *Illustrations* to Omar Khayyam's "Rubaiyat". Later he painted *Art in the City of Rome* (Walker Art Gallery, Bowdoin College, Maine), and in the Congressional Library, Washington, five lunettes, symbolizing *Good Government,* as well as a great mosaic *Minerva.* One of his most gripping and imaginative pictures is *The Lair of the Sea-Serpent* (Boston Museum of Fine Arts); and *Young Marsyas, Cumaean Sybil* and *Nausicaa* (J. Pierpont Morgan Coll.), and the vivid *Genii and Fisherman* (Martin Brumner Coll., Boston) must also be mentioned.

Arthur B. Davies, like Vedder, is another great imaginative artist. Like Böcklin he introduces in his landscapes (many are Californian) smiling or sinister, the fabulous beasts and creatures of fancy. The *Sea Wind and Sea,* his *Dream* (Met. Museum, New York) a lovely long-limbed nude figure walking as though in a dream through a romantic landscape, *Maya, The Mirror of Illusions,* where ten nude virgins in a rocky landscape gaze longingly into the water-mirror of Maya, the Mother of Illusions, are among his most striking paintings.

SOME MODERN REPRESENTATIVES IN SPECIAL FIELDS OF PAINTING

Howard Pyle (b. 1853) has devoted himself especially to America in the Colonial period, and as a "decorative" painter is represented by *The Battle of Nashville* (Capitol, St. Paul, Minn.), and *The Landing of Cartaret* (Essex County Court House, Newark, N. J.). E. Irving Couse, Charles Y. Turner, Ralph A. Blakelock (*Indian Fishermen, Ta-wo-ko-kak or Circle Dance,* aside from landscapes) and George De Forest Brush (b. 1855), a Tennesseean (*Aztec King, Moose Hunt, Mourning Her Brave*) devoted themselves to American

THE ROMANCE OF PAINTING

Indian scenes, as have Walter Ufer (*Going East*) and others. The late Frederick Remington and Gilbert Gaul have illustrated the Cowboy and soldier life of the Western plains. George Bellowes is noted for his vivid treatment of groups in action—boxers in the ring and other subjects, with "strong" light effects.

Distinguished names in landscape include the late John W. Thwachtman, Gari Melchers, C. Y. Turner, F. B. Williams, F. W. Benson, Mrs. Johansen, Louis Loeb (deceased) and such "open-air" impressionists as Childe Hassam (*Flag Day, Fifth Avenue, New York, 1918*, a brilliant patriotic picture), and Alexander Harrison: *Arcadia* and that lovely, living water-picture, *The Wave* (Penn. Academy), William M. Chase, Horatio Walker and others too numerous to mention.

Mary Cassatt is known as a painter of "mother" pictures, while Frank D. Millet (deceased) cultivated the "humorous" type. American street and country life have been pictured by Glacken, Sloan, Lucks (*East Houston Street, New York*) and Jerome Myers, and by the deceased artists Eastman Johnson, C. F. Ulrich, E. M. Ward and J. G. Brown.

The nude has been cultivated by men like Fitz, Eaton and Shirlaw (deceased) Simmons, Kenyon Cox, Joseph de Camp, Lillian Genth, Herter, Friescke. H. B. Fuller, R. Reid, R. V. V. Sewell.

Other "specialists" have been: H. O. Tanner (the Biblical subject), F. L. Mora (Spanish and society life), Hugo Ballin (mythology), A. H. Thayer (symbolic figures), T. W. Deming (feminine motives) and E. Tarbell (interiors).

CONCLUSION

Practically every important American city now has its art gallery and American painting, for all that American painting has been influenced by the newer European developments, especially French, is original in subject and motive and can find enough in its own national life and surroundings to inspire its landscape and *genre* paintings, its figure and historical works, and out of his own consciousness the American artist has shown that he can create with a fertility of imagination and fantasy equal to that shown in any other land. Modern art reflects, plus the factor called *individuality*—which is the something original, "out of himself" every real artist puts into his work—all the "trends", "movements", "theories" and "school" ideas the reader has met in this work. The greatest thing for the average, every-day art-lover to remember—for his attitude toward Art should be the same as toward Religion—is to be *tolerant*. Do not condemn an "impressionistic" picture or a "cubist" aggregation of blocks seemingly devoid of sense because you do not get them "off-hand". Others may and do. *Beauty,* in Art, as in Religion and Life, means different things to different people. And anything that has an honest and legitimate claim to the admiration of some other human being (whether or not we ourselves can grasp it) is entitled to respect. For the art-lover, *toleration for the idea of beauty,* no matter how presented, if only it be *sincere,* should be the law.

THE ROMANCE OF MUSIC

HOW MUSIC CAME INTO THE WORLD

(Introduction)

Music came into this world in *sections*. Architecture and Painting are arts of matter, they are *material* arts, because you can *handle* and *see* them. But Music is *immaterial*, because you cannot *touch* it with your hand, you cannot *see* it with your eye. You can only *hear* it.

The *foundation-stone* is the background of all architecture, the *canvas* is the backbone (speaking in the sense of *matter*) of all painting. Music has a "backbone", too—called *Rhythm*. And Music's backbone *rhythm*, might almost be said to have been born *before* music herself. In fact, as already mentioned, Music came into the world in *sections*. This is the way of it:

Out in the forest wilderness, even before the day of the Neanderthal Man perhaps, a hairy, apish creature struck his shaggy breast in joy or rage—struck it "without thinking", and heard a deep, hollow boom. He found the *first rhythm*, the first "regular beat" that gives the "swing" to music. He found music's "backbone", the thing that gives tone a regular *rise* and *fall*, an "accent". Without rhythm Music is as formless as a jelly-fish, it is just "tone". But tone *with* rhythm has a backbone, as flexible and "springy" as a piece of whalebone.

And so the man-ape who found rhythm returned to it and developed it in moments of excitement. He had quicker "beats" when he was angry, slower ones when he was glad. With the regular *cheststrokes*, came a kind of regular *chest-notes*, (notes produced "from the outside") booming notes. And out of this beating of his savage, hairy breast, this regular "beat" of booming sound, that "dared" anyone to fight him, or which roused him to a higher pitch of courage, was the first step toward *all national, patriotic, war and battle music*. It was the very beginning of *all* the music that sets men's pulses beating higher with the *military* spirit.

The next step was the discovery that a hollow tree-trunk, if beaten with a club, gave a fine "boom", and this was the first *drum*. After a while he took his hollow trunk, covered it with a tight-drawn skin at each end, and he had his rhythm and "boom" where he wanted it. He did not need to beat his breast any longer, for the drum is the soul of rhythm. So rhythm is the "measure and beat" which runs through all music like the pulse of life. It is the "flexible backbone" which binds all tone together with a regular swing.

Rhythm came before there was any such thing as a "spoken word". But the Neanderthal Man was developing his "language" of grunts and growls, of strange odd sounds. And when anything excited him he burst out into all sorts of cries and howls of a stronger, shriller kind than he used as a rule. All this "tone" that came from his throat was a sort of thing without beginning or end. He might begin a sort of howl down low in his voice and carry it up high before he stopped. It came out the way toothpaste runs out of a tube, in a long *ribbon of tone-stuff*. But once he had a "backbone" in the way of rhythm for his "tone-stuff", he began to stop *here* and *there* and *the other place,* using the "swing" of his "beat". The first thing you know he had *two* or *three* or maybe *four* real, round "separate tones" cut out from his long "tone-ribbon". His ear learned to know these tones. He "slid up" or "slid down" to them. The primitive men of savage tribes do so to-day. Have you ever heard a "slide trombone" slide? Well, that's the way these first music-makers got to the *hard and fast* notes they had "cut out" from their "ribbon stuff".

And as he kept on learning *talk words,* he began to keep his *song-notes* that he had cut out of his "song-stuff" ribbon, which were a finer and higher "language" to use in talking to his gods. And that was *the beginning of songs and singing*. And the hard and fast notes of this language were its *scale*. There is nothing mysterious about a "scale". The scale of any people is simply the *distinct tones,* going *up* or *down,* that have been "picked out" of that people's "tone-ribbon". Many cave-men of to-day have only a scale of *three* tones or notes. The Chinese have a scale of *five* tones. We use one of *seven* tones.

When rhythm reached the "drum" stage, other things came along to help make it strong: *hand-clapping, stamping of feet, clicking of sticks against each other*. Whenever there is "swing" enough you feel you want to dance. Every one does. When a military band comes down the street playing a rousing good march, we can't help "beating time". When a good orchestra is "jazzing along" in first-rate style, our feet begin to tingle.

Early man always was ready to try something new. He gave right in when the rhythm swept him off his feet and *danced*. And he sang (or yelped) while he danced, while rhythm set up a kind of electric current that tied *singing and dancing* together, and made

THE ROMANCE OF MUSIC

them one and the same thing. And man did not object to using his "god-talk" language of song in dancing, for in the beginning *all* his dances were *religious ones,* danced for the gods: mating dances, harvest dances, hunting dances, war-dances.

But his "singing", his "god-talk" language, he used apart from the dance, too. He began to make *magic* with it. Certain "combinations" of notes ought to be able *to charm the gods,* and get them to do what he wanted.

So the first songs man sung were *religious songs,* they were "magic incantations". They came before love-songs, war-songs, or any other kind of songs in importance. And this was pretty much the way singing and music developed all over the earth. From the *earliest ages* there has been *music of some kind* all over the earth from the Equator to the Poles!

And now for the last section of music to be born. Little by little, man found out that just as he had gotten the rhythm-boom out of a hollow tree trunk, *other kinds of music were hidden in other "things".* And once he had found this out, we began to have *instrumental music,* and to *combine* it with vocal music and rhythm. Some Neolithic Man, the brother or cousin, perhaps, of one of the early "cave-painters", had a "musical gift". He found that he could draw a note out of the *reeds* which grew by the river-bank. And he cut at his reed and "blew" it until he had a "scale", *a tune* of sweet wind notes that he could bring out of the reed whenever he wanted. Soon other fellows were cutting reeds, and the little tunes they drew out of these pipes and flutes, when they played them of an evening, sitting in front of the wretched hut or gloomy cave in which they lived, gave them *the happiness that only beauty can give,* gave them the joy that *Art*—which is a kind of making magic, too, in a way—only can grant. In time *flutes* and *pipes* were made of clay, of wood and, later, of metal. Even *human bones* were used and—such is man!— we can imagine no music sounded *sweeter* in a player's ear than the tones he drew from *the flute made from the leg-bone of some hated foe* he had killed in battle! For the satisfaction of *revenge* gave each note an added sweetness and charm. Did not some of the savage barbarian kings of the early Middle Ages swear their wine *only tasted good* to them when they drank it out of the silver-mounted skull of some bitter enemy? After the *wind* instrument had been found, some keen ear heard the note of music in the *bow-string* as it twanged when the arrow sped and—that was the start of every kind of *string* instrument. To this day the negroes of Angola (Portuguese West Africa) say in their language that they *"are playing the bow"* when they make music. The *more* string instruments and the *fewer* "drum" (*percussive*) instruments a nation uses, the more advanced it is in civilization.

CHAPTER I

MUSIC IN ANCIENT EGYPT

ACCORDING to the ancient Egyptians, the world itself was born *out of music*. Thoth, chief of the eight gods of Hermopolis (he had "created" himself) was supposed to have invented all the arts and sciences. One day he gave a *"great cry"*, a *musical* cry. It was in the voice of *just intonation* (which means *the right pitch*), not too high and not too low, and lo, and behold, *out of space popped up the four gods who made the world!* Without the music of god Thoth's voice the ancient Egyptians would have had *no world to live in*. So they thought, at any rate.

Egyptian religious music was all *"magic music"*. Sounding solemnly in the shadow of mighty temples, *tone turned into a kind of looking-glass,* a mirror that reflected all sorts of events happening on earth and in the world to come. And in the strange legends of the Egyptian gods, music plays an important part. Osiris, lord of the "Blue River, gentle king of the Egyptian underworld" has his gold and crimson *benno* bird, a heron with a glorious voice. The *benno* bird was the symbol of the resurrection (as the lily is with us), and was supposed every thousand years, to *burn to death* in his nest, only to rise, singing, from his own ashes, in Heliopolis, the city of the goddess Isis. Isis herself invented a musical instrument, the *sistrum*.

From 3,000 B.C. on there was music in the land of Egypt. And in what is known as the "New Empire" period,* the Golden Age of ancient Egypt, especially, there was music everywhere. There was music in the *"beer-houses"* standing in dark alleys in Thebes or Memphis and in the *temples* of the great gods. There was music with the *funeral processions* moving along to the king's pyramid, or some humbler tomb in the "city of the dead", and in the handsome gardens or *"parlors"* where the young Egyptian girls of "high society" entertained the young officers of the armies of Rameses II and the other conquerer pharoahs, back on a furlough from Syria.

The priests of the Egyptian crocodile, hippopotamus, bull-monkey-bird-dog-and-cat gods and goddesses all used *magic charm music* in their temples to make the people bestow gifts and offerings. All

* 1500 to 1200 B.C.

singers who "bleat" their trills should know that the *goat* was the animal shape of the bad god Set or Typhoon, whose music was the *music of evil passions* and brutal and depraved instincts. And we may be sure that there was a good deal of "goat-music" in the gay processions of which Herodotus tells us, when the people paraded through the streets, singing to the sound of pipes, carrying obscene emblems.

There even is a *musical pyramid*. It was the tomb of King Ounas, and the Egyptian "picture-writing" on the wall has (among others) a *musical incantation* to protect King Ounas against snake-bite. The syllables given are *meant to be sung,* and it is thought possible that the songs *old as the hills,* on a few notes, which the Egyptian snake-charmers sing to-day, date from that ancient "magic song". The great temples had their own "music schools", where priest-musicians were trained to sing the sacred "formulas" or magic prayer and incantation, and to play the big *twenty-three string temple harps*. They had large temple "orchestras" of harpists, lutenists and lyre players, with leaders or "conductors". On solemn festival days, no doubt, people who thought more of *"music"* than the *"service"* went to some special temple because "the music was *so good* there", just as they do to-day! The Egyptian temple music, the solemn chants of the choirs of priests and the orchestras which accompanied or answered the voices, lingered on as Egypt decayed, until there was but little of it left in the Roman days. *When the religion which had inspired it died away, its music lost the power to move souls!* The whole temple "organization went to pot", and the few priests who were left in temples, getting more and more "out of repair", lived only on "tips". The wealthy Roman "tourists" who went to "see the sights" in Egypt because it was the thing to do, "tipped" the priests who led out Apis, the holy bull to be stared at in ruined Memphis, or coaxed the big crocodile-"gods", with their crystal ear-rings, out of the temple lake at Elephantine. Where great choruses had intoned the hymns to the sun-god, Ammon-Ra, a few half-hearted voices feebly joined in some ancient temple chant. It was a sorry ending.

War-music is like religious music. It does not live any longer than the victories of the race that makes it. The *sistrum* (Isis's invention) was a bar of metal shaped like any horseshoe, with a handle. When "well shaken", the little metal "janglers" fastened to it sounded out with a very "peppy" rhythm. It was first used for the sacred *temple dances,* but there was so much "get up and go" about its rhythm that the Pharaohs drafted it into the army. Military music was not at its best in Egypt before the "New Empire". When war broke out, the "embattled farmers" were conscripted into the ranks, and there was but little in the way of "military bands". But the "New Empire" was an age of "regulars", who drilled on the parade-grounds of their barracks to *regular military music*. In "parades" through the streets of Memphis or Thebes, the bands marched at the head of the regiments, and the naked little street Arabs turned somersaults and handsprings in front of them in the dust thousands of years ago. "Boys will be boys" in any age. Some of the "bandsmen" had *castanets*. For *army* use, instead of being made of wood or ivory, which gave too "soft" a sound, they were made of iron and copper, and had a really stirring ring. The gilded bronze war-trumpets gave out a shrill, piercing note and, together with the battle-cry "Ammon! Ammon! Ammon!" and the crash of sistrum and beat of drum and rattle of bronze war-chariots, helped make the *music of Egyptian victory*. But Egyptian battle-music "faded out" when the Persians conquered the Egyptians, and they gradually lost their "national consciousness", which no military music can bring back, once it is gone.

Private music "in the home"? Among the "upper crust" in the Nile valley music was fashionable. The great court ladies, the leaders of "society", seeing that it was "good form", often enrolled themselves as *khanrits,* volunteer tympanists, in the temple orchestras. (The girl tympanum players of the streets, though, were "no better than they should be", and had a bad name). And when the *Asiatic flute* and the guitar were introduced from Syria with the "New Empire", ladies "took up" the new instruments with enthusiasm, as though they were *ukeleles.* Authorities say that Egyptian music got too sentimental and rather "naughty". But an age of foreign war usually makes for an overplus of sentiment where the "home fires are burning". When man must "work" on the battle-field, lovely woman likes to shed tears of melody in the home. When the men of the nation, just as in the days of the First French Empire or during our own Civil War, spent most of their time in the army, the *sentimental Egyptian girls* played the *sentimental harp* just like the Parisiennes did so many centuries later, or as in American homes, in the North and in the South, women remembered *the absent in song.* Music made the hard task of anxious waiting a little lighter while sons, lovers and brothers with the armies of Amenhopis or Rameses carried the Egyptian standards as far as the Euphrates, and their drums and sistrums dared the Assyrian war-pipes.

The Egyptians were not, as so many think, a stern, solemn race, spending most of their time in the temples. They were a happy, merry, light-hearted and music-loving folk. In fact, they were much like anyone else. They liked their "light beers and light wines" and, *as a race, often drank too much.* In their "beer-houses", they sang drinking songs, just as "Sweet Adeline", in days gone by, often rose above the "steins on the table" in our land. And the *word-echoes* of some Egyptian *love-songs,* though their *music* is gone, have come down through the ages, to show us that a heart beat tenderly under the coarse linen robe of the Egyptian "man in the street", and that he sang out of the fulness of that heart.

And, strange to say, out of all the music which rose and died centuries ago on the still air of the Nile valley, temple chants, love and drinking songs, battle hymns and others, there is a reason to think that *the melody of just one song* still sounds along the Nile banks, as it did 5000 years ago. It is a song of the *chadouf,* the bucket in which the *fellahin,* the farmer who still looks just as his Bronze Age ancestors did, raises the water from the Nile to water his field.

"A song on three notes, which must date from the ancient Pharaohs, is still sung in our own day on the banks of the Nile, from the Delta to Nubia. Half-naked men, with bodies of bronze, beginning their endless task, start it at beginning of day and keep on singing until the evening hour of rest. Surviving all the historic glories of the Nile empire, it shows how *a phrase of music can embalm in tone* a tradition that lasts!"

CHAPTER II

THE LAMENTS OF CHALDEA, THE WAR-PIPES OF ASSYRIA, AND THE MUSIC OF ANCIENT PERSIA

WE do not get much in the way of real "music" before there are cities. When cities and temples rise, then music develops, as in Egypt and in Chaldea. The music of the Sumerians, the oldest Chaldeans, a yellow race which drifted down from the Siberian mountain range to the valley of the Euphrates, was sad and doleful. This was the fault of their religion, for it was a religion of gloom. The Sumerians' sacred tree of Life had "roots of crystal." Unfortunately, these roots went to the centre of the earth, "the dark forest man's heart never has penetrated." And that's where the devils lived, thousands of them, who were the curse of this yellow race's world. For they walked about the earth, and had to be guarded against all the time. So most of the Chaldean temple songs were "magic incantation" songs, to keep these devil-spirits from doing harm. They paid all the more attention to their temple music because they believed with the Egyptians that *every note uttered by the human voice had a special power*. Some tones irritated the gods, others they liked, and with the right "combinations", the singers and players could almost *force* the gods to do their will. The Chaldeans coupled each of the *seven notes* of the musical scale with one of the *seven planets* they worshipped, and their idea of life seems to have been: "Cheer up, the worst is yet to come!" They had big, complicated choral services and "groups" of choral psalms and prayers, and half their temple songs were hymns of *lamentation*. It is not surprising that the *Sumerian* spearmen could not "buck up" against the *Semite* tribes that overran their country, with such a half-hearted religion and such sad music. *After the two races had mingled* when the Semites had gotten the better of them, the empire of Babylon formed, and music brightened up a bit. But *magic song* was still the leading "musical attraction", though not so sad in the *ziggurats,* the temples of Babylon, the "Paris of the ancient East". Yet this temple music of the Babylonians—they had *popular songs* which for vulgarity and frankness of text exceeded anything we know in our own "more refined" day!—could not hold out against the shrill war-pipes of the *Assyrians,* when they came down the Tigris river into

THE WAR-PIPES OF ASSYRIA

the lower valley, and founded one of the greatest military powers of the ancient world.

The Egyptians were a more "civilized" race than the Assyrians, for they had more "string" instruments. The Assyrians ran to "drum" music.* Why? Because, in dead earnest: "it was their nature to". Nine, the Chaldean goddess of music, smiled sadly down on the hymns of lamentation her people sang. But Ishtar, the Assyrian goddess of music, was a goddess of war as well. In Nineveh she was worshipped in the "churches" as a goddess of music and love; but in the city of Arbela, they put flowers on her altar as the giver of victory". War was the one big trade and profession in Assyria.

The Assyrians "went to war" as we "go to work" or "go to business". They were one hundred per cent efficient, for a long time in their business of life, and even arranged their "heaven" on war lines. All the Assyrian gods practically, were gods of war, and the king of Assyria was a "war-lord". And they used music as we did "tanks" or poison gas: to frighten, stun and put the enemy to rout. The Assyrian footmen "struck" the foe to the sound of drum, cymbal and shrill double-flutes. The fierce Assyrian cavalry (the more civilized Egyptians poked fun at their neglect of the bath and their dirty sheepskins) made a music of their own when they charged. A number of small iron bells (like our sleighbells) hung from the harness of their horses and the enemy could *hear* as well as feel an Assyrian cavalry charge. The high, shrill double-flutes were "military fifes". From 1100 B. C. until Assyria was conquered by the Persians, Asia danced to the tune of the Assyrian war-pipes *and paid the piper,* while blood flowed wherever they sounded. Babylonians, Syrians, Phoenicians, Jews, Egyptians and the Greeks of Asia Minor "handed over" their gods and treasures when the war-pipes played. Gold, silver, horses, cattle, lapis-lazuli, guns, spices, war-chariots and slaves—all the loot of the world, poured into Nineveh, the "big town", when the Assyrian boys "came marching home".

No doubt the "regimental bands" were made up of Assyrians. But when it came to other kinds of music, *temple-music* and *social music,* they had no trouble in finding players and singers. In the great war raids whole populations were put to the sword—*but musicians were spared.* These captured singers and players, when the kings "took

* When you hear someone use the word "percussive" or "percussion instruments" when speaking of the orchestra, it means instruments of the "drum kind", where sound is produced by a blow, a "percussion". Our piano, though it has "strings" is a "percussive instrument" and so are all the "traps" in an orchestra.

a day off" from war and went lion-hunting or feasted in their big boastful palaces, supplied the "band". They made the music while the king and his great lords and captains sat over their wine and the virgins of Babylon or Nineveh danced unclothed before a thousand eyes to the sound of harps and Asiatic flutes. In Chaldea *temple music* was more important than the festival music. But in Assyria the great palaces, the homes of *profane music*, were almost more important than the temples, just as they were bigger as buildings. The kings of Assyria, that high-priest of war, ruled all the other priests on his land and the most important music was the *mass of the battle-field* and the *Te Deum of the palace*.

The Assyrians like the Egyptians, the Babylonians and every other race with a "city life", had their street songs and popular songs, but they have not come down to us. And in the end the savage shrilling of the Assyrian war-pipes, preaching the gospel of "Kill! kill!" died out for want of *lung-power*. One of the reasons Assyria fell was that the *native-born soldiers* were gradually disposed in great garrisons over all the immense empire, and the birth-rate went down. An army of Persians and Babylonians took Nineveh in the year 600 B.C., but Nineveh did not fall to the sound of war-pipes calling from the walls in a last heroic stand. It fell to the psalms and *songs of despair* of the Assyrian women—it was their turn to sing penetential psalms now! Babylon was taken by the Persians sixty odd years later. The Bible implies that the king and his lords were surprised by the Persian soldiers while "half-seas over", singing some sort of "Stein Song". But Nabonidus, the last king of Babylon, was an elderly antiquarian, a lover of fine art "museum pieces", who preferred water to wine. And his son, Belshazzar, was a keen-witted fighting man, the last one in the world to be caught by the enemy singing over his cups.

To the blood-thirsty Assyrians, strange to say, we owe the idea of what is now the most generally popular musical instrument of western civilization—the piano. For they seem to have produced the *dulcimer*. It was a shallow box over which strings, struck by little hammers, were stretched—the *"germ idea"* of the *piano Paderewski plays*.

THE MUSIC OF THE ANCIENT PERSIANS

The ancient Persians made more history than music. Outside of battle-music and the sacred songs of the priests, the Magians or Magi, we do not know of much. But to this day high and low "masses" celebrated at the festivals of the Parsees of Bombay keep alive the memory of ancient Persian temple-chants, and they still observe the festival of the last Sassanian king of Iran, Yzdegerd III, with music and ceremonies. Though we have little information about Persian music, their sacred books say that song is a mighty means of waking up the fighting spirit. So, instead of Assyrian war-pipes and Egyptian drums and sistrums, we have the Magian priests going in advance of Persian armies singing of the national heroes to sound of flute and cymbal, to "wake up" the soldiers of the Great King to the right fighting pitch. Xenephon in his political romance, the "Cyropaedia", a fanciful version of the life of Cyrus, who was the first great Persian king and conquerer of Media, the golden Lydia of Croesus, the Greek cities of Asia Minor, Assyria and Babylon, confirms this. And in the old Greek book is another musical remark, that is still true to-day: that "in music it is a new melody, flower-like freshness, that wins popularity".

Yet after the conquests of Cambyses and Darius I had made the Persian a world-empire of the "pep" of the Magian battle-hymns must have been lost. Assyrian and Egyptian armies were mostly "sons of the soil" and not "hired soldiers". But the vast armies with which the Persian kings, from Xerxes to the last Darius, went to war took in all the peoples of the Asian earth. What influence could a hymn from the *Zend-Avesta* exert on the skeptical soul of a Greek? He did not *believe* in what was sung. The names of Persian lords and captains "sound like the chime of gong and cymbal", as one writer has said, and the Magian hymns may have been fine. But what cared the "Libyans clad in leather garments, having javelins hardened by fire", who marched in Xerxes' army, as Herodotus tells us? The gods of the Persians were not *their* gods. The Persian "over-rule" held together the many countries like a golden girdle. But the *one-people spirit* which united the Chaldeans in their gloom and thrilled in the Assyrian war-pipes was not there.

At the courts of the Great King and his lords, however, music was appreciated as one of the pleasures of life, and a means of display. Nararos, a Persian satrap (governor) of Babylon, kept an orchestra of *150 women musicians* to "make music at his meals"; and when Alexander defeated Darius III at Arbela, hundreds of singing girls and musicians of the Great King's harem were captured by his calvarymen in Damascus. But from Darius I to Alexander the Great, Persia struggled with Greece and in all that time she found *no musical weapon* to oppose the Greek war-hymn.

CHAPTER III

MUSIC IN INDIA, THE MONGOL LANDS AND WESTERN ASIA

(India)

In the case of the ancient Hindus climate seems to have had an effect on their music, mind and morals. The torrid sun, and atmosphere which "takes it out of you", a lush riot of wildest vegetation incubated and hatched out the "over-ripe", fantastic and riotous Hundu music and religion.

Drums beat, conch-shells blared and flutes shrilled in Hindu temples in a more riotous, excited way, probably than in Egypt or Chaldea. And music played a big part in the Hindu "heaven".* There Satasvati was the goddess of music, and the inventor of the favorite Hindu Lyre, the *vina*. There is plenty of music, in Indra's paradise. The *handharbas*, seven heavenly maidens, rule the "harmonies" of the seven planets. And the *ragas* and *raginis*, sons and daughters of the lesser gods, rule the musical scales, *the natural expressions of the passions*. The expression of the passions, *the senses*, is the main thing in Hindu music and religion.

In this Hindu mythology, music is put to the *lowest* uses. The Hindu believes that if you "mortify" your flesh, if you undergo all sorts of tortures and "endurance tests", spending your life in *one position*, going almost *without food*, and other nonsense of the kind, you "win merit", and gain power over other human beings and *over the gods themselves*. Owing to this "kink" in the Hindu mind, there are "holy men", fakirs and hermits, who are tormenting themselves all over India to-day, thinking that self-denial carried to excess will "get them somewhere", in heaven if not on earth. Indra, up in his paradise, used to get worried when some of these old saints (?) and hermits, by ill-treating their bodies, got more and more *powerful*. If they got too powerful, some fine day one of them might fly up to heaven and "turn him out". And so—a fine thing for a god to do!—he would send his *apsaras*, the "singing" (?) of his paradise down to earth to tempt and lead astray saintly old hermits trying

---

* No Hindu music has made the god Indra's paradise so "real" to us as the beautiful ballet music of the French composer *Massenet*, in his opera, "The King of Lahore", where he has used Hindu tunes *in our way*.

THE ROMANCE OF MUSIC

to "make good" in their strange way! The music of their divine voices was not only inducement the *apsaras* held out to the hermits to "fall". But it did much to "charm" and help their senses get the better of them. So they would give in to the *apsaras'* "wicked will", and lose all the power years and years of self-torture had given them.

Krishna, the young cowherd god, is one of the most musical of Hindu gods. But a god like Krishna whose chief idea was having a good time with the wives of his *mortal* cowherd companions, does not make music noble! His creed says: *man's love for god is best shown by free indulgence in the natural appetites*. His priests claim that 16,000 *gopis,* lovely maidens of Indra's heaven, each invented a new scale, hoping her own particular "tune" would win her Krishna's favor.

There is Vishnu, who tries to *"humanize* divine worship by bringing it into accord with the experience of human love". There is Siva, another "sense" god, and Kali, the goddess of death. Her image is a naked black woman with a necklace of skulls, and she has abominable secret rites. The worship of these and a hundred other animal, bird and reptile gods is the dark background to the nobler dreams of the Brahmins. Music, in the worship of such gods, led to "sacred orgies" and bloody self-mutilation.

The *Science* of music among the Hindus is fantastic detail and "hair-splitting", with the same wild extravagance their Architecture shows. The Hindus have about *1,000* theoretical "scales" and use all of *twenty.* Where we are satisfied to divide the "steps" or "tones" of our scale into *seven* whole and half tones, they use *twenty-two* "quarter-steps" or tones. The Hindus have nearly as many different kinds of musical instruments, as they have "theoretical scales", drum, wind and string. And, with the race feeling for minute *detail,* certain *forms* of certain instruments can only be used by certain *"classes".* One *kind* of *vina* is used by priests, another *kind* by travelling beggars, a third *kind* by dancing-girls. If a dancing girl were to use a priestly *vina,* who knows what might happen—probably the heavens would fall!

Hindu music seems *least* important in the Hindu temples. The priests of the strange Brahmin gods use it *mainly* in connection with *temple dances.* But the Buddhists' faith makes *no singing and no dancing* a rule of its church. For this reason music is more of a *profane* art, a *popular* art in India, because religiously it "plays second fiddle" to the *dance.* But all over India *popular song* has flourished through the ages (though, owing to the difference in scale, tone, *way* of singing, and a hundred other things we would never recognize a Hindu "popular" song if we heard it). Every one sings, the workman at his work, the elephant-driver, the street "peddler", the man in the field, and the woman in the home. And side by side with the *old songs* from the Sanskrit, are the modern "ballads" born out of the *life of to-day*. The music of Egypt, of Assyria, of Persia, is all *"dead"* music. It does not "connect up" with our modern life. But the music of India does.

Our great composers have used real Hindu tunes (handling them according to our own rules for the science of music) in pieces for *orchestra,* in *operas* and other works. The best-known *Hindu tune used in this way* is the famous *"Song of India"*. A Russian composer, Rimsky-Korsakof, wrote it in one of his operas. It became very popular in Europe and the United States. Fritz Kreisler arranged it for the violin; the greatest singers made *records* of it. And this Hindu tune is the *mother* of a whole tribe of American popular songs, born by changing it here and there a bit, while keeping the tune idea. "Dardanella" is one of other little daughters of Rimsky-Korsakof's "Song of India".

MUSIC IN THE LAND OF THE YELLOW MEN

(China)

The early Chinese did not think of Music as something which expressed the *emotions* of his heart, something working from "inside out". From earliest times music to them was something which worked from "outside in". Its business was to "make people better and happier". Chinese literature tells us strange things of the power of music in the old days. A hymn was composed by the Emperor Shun (2255 B.C.), the *Ta Shao*. When Confucius heard it (500 B.C.) it made such an impression, that to use his own words he "did not know the taste of meat" for three months, it made him a vegetarian! And so powerful for *evil* were the "naughty" songs composed by a Chinese twelfth century minister of state, that they brought about the downfall of the emperor he served. Some of these old Chinese tunes ("magic incantations" like those of Egyptian and Chaldean priests) brought the sacred Phoenix bird down from the skies, set hundreds of storks dancing in the air, called up devils of darkness and storm and carried off the roofs of palaces!

In literature the Chinese everywhere dwell on the *beauty* of music but they also had very practical ideas about it. They considered Music a *useful* art quite as much as an art of *beauty*.

Tso Chun, Confucius's pupil, wants music to have a good *moral* effect. He says "the superior man will not listen to lascivious or seductive airs" (what would he say to the tunes of the Jazz Age?), and that a good man "plays his lute in order to *regulate his conduct* and *not* delight his heart". But through all the ages of Chinese history men made merry with music over their *wine*—the greatest Chinese poets and musicians of the past were as a rule the greatest *topers* and drunkards of China—and many a lute was played without any thought but that of sense of pure enjoyment, for player and listeners.

The Chinese scale is one of *five* tones, and Chinese song has a good strong rhythm "backbone" to hold it together. The tie between the "spoken word" and the "sung word" still exists in the Chinese language. It is a language of *single syllables,* and the *same syllable* has a *different meaning* according to *which* of the *five tones* is put into it when it is pronounced. That is one reason we call spoken Chinese "sing-song" talk, and when a Chinaman gets very poetic or dignified, his *"word"* sounds almost turn into actual *"music"* sounds, and he begins to *"chant"* what he is *saying*.

According to the Chinese, Nature provided *eight* materials to produce musical sounds—*hide* (skin), *stone, metal, clay, wood, bamboo, silk* and *gourd* or *calabash*. So their many musical instruments are made of these things. *Hide* (drums and tambourines), *stone* (jade-stones or agates, hung and struck with mallets), *metal* (gongs and cymbals), *wood* (clappers and castanets) give them *drum* instruments. *Metal* (trumpets) *clay* (ocarina whistles), *bamboo* and *gourd* (flutes) give them wind instruments. *Wood* ("sound-boxes" of string instruments) *silk* (strings), supply zithers, "moon-guitars", fiddles and viols of all kinds, their *string* instruments. Any of us who have been to a Chinese theatre or have heard native Chinese music played find it horrible. This is because we do not understand its *"rules"*, its science, and our ears are not *trained* to take in its *beauties. If you are a Chinaman, the beauties are there to be enjoyed.*

The *practical* importance of music in ancient China was shown by its use in the state and in war. It was no disgrace for a Chinese emperor to be a *good musician,* for the Chinese proverb says: "He who understands music well reigns well." The first *bells* cast in China, by Ling Lun, were not meant to ring wedding chimes. They were for *practical* use—to drive dragons away. And all "serious" music was provided with a set of scientific "laws" and "rules" almost as complicated as that of the Hindus. In the Chinese manual of arms the constant *changes of detail* in drum-beat and trumpet-call which regulated every movement of the troops, was put down at page-length. And in one of the great works of old Chinese literature, the *Tso Chaun,* a soldier tells a friend that he will listen only to the drum that signals the *advance,* and never to the gong that sounds the *retreat.*

MUSIC IN OTHER LANDS OF THE FAR EAST

In Japan, Music, like Architecture, originally came from China. But the Japanese have developed some musical "kinks" of their own. Like Chinese music the music of Japan—the people are passionately fond of music—to us is as *strange and distant as their soul*. The cricket's song—"sonorous, never stopping, gently wearisome, like the falling of a crystal cascade"—is *Nature's* song in Japan; the *human voice* in Japan as in China leans to shrill, mournful melody *harsh* to our ears. Japanese instruments more or less duplicate those of China, and the best known are the *koto*, a big zither with 6 to 16 strings, and the *samisen,* a three-stringed lute.

In the Indo-Chinese countries, music has been influenced by both China and India. In Burma, Cambodia, and Siam the natives have always leaned to the Hindu scales; in Japan, Java and Korea, the Chinese scale of five tones is used.

WHERE OUR MUSIC TOUCHES THE MUSIC OF THE
YELLOW EAST

In Art, as in life to-day, the artist—the man who "makes beauty", either in Architecture, Sculpture, Painting, Music, Opera, the Dance, —always is looking for new "material" and new "color", to use in his work. The architect may find a "suggestion" for a fine American country house in a Hindu temple porch.

The sculptor finds "hints" in some of the strange statuary found in Negro Africa. The opera composer—if the story of his opera happens in China, or in American Indian days, hunts up *"real tunes"* of the time and country, to make his work more "true to life." The great dancers study the carved and painted figures of Egyptian and Indian obelisks and temple walls to find the "simon-pure" gestures and "attitudes" the dancers used in those days to "introduce them" in their own dance-dramas.

That is why Chinese music, like Hindu music, is "live" for us. All we get in the way of "suggestion", from the art of races, tribes and peoples *foreign* to us, and *to our art,* is called "exotic color", or "local color" (both phrases are worth knowing for artistic people use them a great deal). Original "local color" changes, of course, when we are "putting it in" or "laying it on" in *our* art. But it has the value of "contrast", very valuable in all art.

Among operas Saint-Saëns's *Princess Jaune* (The Yellow Princess), Puccini's "Madame Butterfly" and Mascagni's "Iris", Stravinsky's "Nightingale", represent Javanese, Japanese and Chinese "exotic color". Besides many single songs with a "Chinese" flavor, there are big works for full orchestra, like the American composer Edgar Stillman Kelley's beautiful *Alladin Suite;* the Frenchman Bourgault-

Ducoudray's *Rhapsodie Cambogdienne,* and many "popular" marches, intermezzos, etc. in which just enough Chinese "local color" a suggestion of the five-tone scale, a "twinkle" and a few "rhythm-combinations"—are put in to let "Chinese" go into the title of the piece. In all these ways, in high art and low art, *Chinese music* and the *spirit of Chinese music* comes into touch with *our own music and our life.*

MUSIC OF WESTERN ASIA

(Phoenician and Hebrew Music)

The music of the Phoenicians (though the French composer Reyer wrote a grand opera called *Salammbo,* that deals with ancient Carthage, a Phoenician colony, and tried to get "local color" in to it); the Syrians, and old Asia Minor peoples in general has "echoed out" *on the dead air of the past.* We know these peoples used the instruments of Egypt and Assyria, and "magic song" hymns and chants in their temples and in their *social life.* The part *music* played in their lives seems mainly to have been an *ignoble* one. It was a mere just something to help along the gay round of revels with women and wine, and old Greek philosophers pointed out the luxurious peoples of Syria, Phoenicia and Asia Minor generally, as terrible examples for Greek youth.

Thanks to the Old Testament, we know more about the Jewish music in the old days than any other. The Jews were borrowers and imitators when it came to art. They borrowed their music and their musical instruments from nations with whom they were "in touch". Of course, *sacred music* was most important in their lives, and they often "sized it up" in a very *practical* way, like the Chinese. They did more than use it in the temple to "make a joyful noise unto the Lord". For instance, Samuel "organized" regular "bands" of prophets, and trained them to sing (1,000 B. C.) to make the priesthood's power more secure by "rousing ecstasy in the hearts of the listeners".

The greatest opera work with a Jewish "exotic" cast is Saint-Saëns's famous *Samson and Delilah.* A modern Jewish composer, Ernest Bloch living in the United States, has written some big Jewish "poems" for full orchestra: *Schelomo, Hebrew Rhapsody* and *"Orientale".*

CHAPTER IV

MUSIC IN ANCIENT GREEK LEGEND AND LIFE

Music was well represented in Olympus, the "heaven" of the ancient Greek gods. Father Zeus (Jove), was more interested in fair women, and Dionysus (Bacchus) in wine. But Phoebus Apollo was a musician from head to foot; Terpsichore was the goddess of melody and the choral dance; Pan, the shepherd god, looked after music among the Grecian sheep—and goat-herders, and the shepherd flute or "Pan-pipes" he invented were played by his pupil, the god Mercury. And there was Harmonia,* Venus' daughter, still remembered by singing societies all over the country when they are looking for a good name. There was plenty of music in the heaven of Mount Olympus, and in due course of time it came to earth.

Pandora was the Greek Eve, the first woman, and like her Hebrew sister got her husband into trouble. Hephaestus (Vulcan), made her out of earth, and gave her a human voice, and all the other gods and goddesses put together and "fitted her out" with a handsome chest (or jar) of wedding presents, known as "Pandora's Box". But while some gods put in things like Beauty, and *Cunning* and *Cleverness* and *Charm* and *Music,* Zeus very unkindly slipped in all the miseries and evils we have. Her husband, Epimetheus, when Pandora and her chest of wedding gifts reached him, made her open it. Of course all the evil things in it at once flew out (if you are unmusical you will consider Music one of them), together with the good. The only thing that was left in the bottom of the chest was Hope.

Music, being among the gifts which had escaped from the chest, quickly spread over all Greece. There are hundreds of charming Greek stories about the power and lure of music. One, however, is more beautiful than all the rest, and shall serve as an example. It is the tale of *Orpheus and Eurydice*.

Orpheus was a half-human, half-god child of Apollo, (for the Greek gods were always ready to marry on earth as well as in their heaven), and when his fingers swept the strings of his *lyre* (an early form of harp), lions and tigers crept to lick his feet, great trees bowed down their heads to him and the very rocks were so "moved"

---

* The name, meaning "agreement", is the day we use to express "the science and art of music" to this day.

that they melted. It is not strange that Orpheus easily played and sang his way into the nymph Eurydice's heart. She died. Orpheus who loved her more than life itself, frantic with grief, made up his mind to snatch her back from *Hades,* the Greek underworld. Taking his lyre, he went down into the bowels of the earth. There he pleaded so touchingly with his music for Eurydice to be returned to him that dark Pluto, king of the underworld, Proserpine his wife, and all the ghosts shed tears. And she was given back to Orpheus *on condition that he did not look back,* once they had started, till they reached the upper earth. Musicians are a forgetful race, and Orpheus was no exception. He looked back—and poor Eurydice slipped back into Hades, and this time she stayed there! Orpheus did not live long to regret his mistake. Wandering through the Thracian countryside, he met up with some Bacchantes, immoral women of the out-of-doors, inflamed with wine and religion. In their frenzied state Orpheus' music fell on deaf ears. They drowned it with their screams, and tore him limb from limb in their excitement. As happens to most people after they are dead, Orpheus' merits were at once recognized. The Muses turned his lyre into a star, and the legend goes that over the grave where the tattered shreds of his body were buried, the nightingales sang more sweetly than anywhere else in Greece.

The tale of Orpheus shows the love and respect the Greeks had for music, and music, for a fact, played a large part in Greek life. Just as in the United States to-day, the Greek "kiddies" started with music in the public schools, and *Aristophanes,* the play-writer, tells us that every school-boy of Athens had to learn to sing the two leading patriotic songs, "Invincible Pallas" and "A Resounding Cry", in his class-room. It may seem strange to us, when we think of all that "goes along" with "jazz" music nowadays; but in ancient Greece *"young boys were taught good manners by the use of music."* Aristophanes said that "unmusical monsters" were not supposed to "break into" the better circles of society. The great Greek philosophers, *Plato* and *Aristotle,* even held it was the duty of the State "to regulate the use of music in the interests of *national morals*". But the Greek politicians were no better morally than our own. They had their own Tea-Pot Domes under different names, and music does not seem to have made them forget their own selfish interests while pretending to serve those of the State. And we know that Damon, Pericles' music-teacher, so tired out the Athenians with his constant warnings that Athens was going to the dogs because musicians were tampering with the laws of Music, that he was sent out of the country to get rid of him.

The Greeks had a scale of *seven* notes, but *no* harmony. They sang their notes, one after another, in *unison,* and there was solo singing and chorus singing. Instrumental music was represented by *lyre* or cithara players, *aulos* or flute-players, and players on the *syrinx* or shepherd's pipe. But if they had no harmony they had plenty of rhythm "patterns", and in the popular festivals they combined music with the dance and pantomime in a big way. They had *art-music* and *folk-music,* just as we have, but nothing has come down to us out of all the music they had but a few odds and ends of melody and a little string of 30 notes, set to a few lines of the Greek dramatist Euripides—nothing else. Each of the seven Greek *modes* or *scales* was supposed to have a *character* of its own. The *Dorian* Greek mode was stern and severe, excited men to fight and wrought them up to battle, murder and sudden death. If they ever whipped a Greek boy to music, this is the mode they would have used. The *Hypodorian* was proud and glad; the *Ionian* was the "love-mode"; and the *Phrygian* was used in the songs which rose when the drinking-cup, the ancient Greeks used for a stein, was on the table.

Every one seems to have sung or made music in some way in ancient Greece. The thrifty Boetians put the shepherd's pipe to *practical* use on the big stud farms where they raised horses, having noticed that it stimulated breeding. At the big festivals, the Olympian and other "games", there were all sorts of *contests* among the great *singers, harpists* and *flutists* of the day, with splendid prizes offered. The soldiers went into battle singing *patriotic songs,* and there were "Embarkment" songs sung to drown the sobs and cries of loved ones' farewells when they took ship for the wars. The actual words of one of these songs, "The Song of Hybrias the Cretan", by *Athaneus,* have been set by a modern composer as a baritone or bass song, which is popular with all bass singers of our day. The shepherd piped to his flock, the mother sang and crooned to her babe, and the farm-hand sang in the fields in ancient Greece. The children sang in school, the chorus sang in the big dramas, the great artists played in the contests: there was music everywhere.

The Spartans, the greatest "fighting" people of Greece, used music—the *battle song* and the shrill, high *piccolo flute*—as a military weapon. The Spartan soul, like the Spartan money, was iron, and the *Dorian* mode—wild, savage, exciting, as "red" in sound as blood or flame, swayed that iron soul. Every Spartan mother "raised her boy to be a soldier". Spartan boys, from seven to twenty, were brought up in "gangs", but gangs ruled by iron discipline. Their education was a *hardening* process from beginning to end. They slept on beds of course river rushes, with a little, *just a little* thistledown added in winter for warmth. And the battle-songs the Spartan boy learned did for him what a red rag does for a bull when they went into the fight. The *Ephors* (the council of old men which ruled Sparta), took good care that no "soft" music should spoil their boys. Timotheus of Miletus came to Sparta with a twelve-string lyre, and was told that unless he cut *five strings off* at once he had better go away again! The war flute was both the Spartans' fife and drum. Tyrtaeus, a lame poet and musician (650 B.C.), wrote their famous marching songs, which praised bravery and cursed cowardice. When the soldiers sang these popular songs around their camp-fires at night, the captain rewarded the best singer with an extra piece of meat.

Music, too, was used to punish *bachelors* in Sparta. For the State considered that it was every man's duty to help in the good work of raising soldiers. Once a year, in the winter, Spartan bachelors were "rounded up", and made to march naked around the market-place, singing the song of their shame. The *same* bachelors seldom marched *two* years in succession. But all the war-music and battle songs of Greece did not enable her to stand up against the Macedonians, whose word, after Alexander's time, was law in Greece, more or less, till the Romans came.

Alexander the Great (336-323 B.C.), loved both music and wine. When a youth he gave prizes to pipers and harpers, and took so much interest in the art that his father, Philip, once asked him whether "he was not ashamed to know so much about it?" But—the drinking-songs roared at his big drinking-parties, and the camp-songs in which his soldiers "knocked" unpopular commanders have not come down to us. We *do* know that when his heart's friend Hephaestion died, he said: "Let it be dark and silent in Asia!" And not a voice was raised in song, or a flute, harp or pipe sounded for forty days. But his return from his Indian expedition with his army was one great drunken procession.

In the Greek kingdoms Alexander's generals founded in Asia, in Egypt, Syria, and other lands, *a love of music* seemed to go with *weakness of character* on the part of the kings. The Egyptian Ptolemies who best tooted the flute and the Syrian Seleucidi kings who hiccoughed the glad chorus of the cups with the greatest vigor, were the *worst* of their families. And while they enjoyed music and turned it into a royal political vice, with its companions (wine and women) the stern, unmusical Romans were busy conquering the world.

Greek music suggested the modes or scales on which all the music of the Roman Catholic Church is founded. And Greek mythology and legend has inspired many wonderful modern musical works. The story of *Orpheus,* for instance, inspired the composer Gluck to write a wonderful opera by that title and if you ever have heard a record by some great singer of the world-known air *Che faro senza Euridice* (what will I do without Eurydice) you will know how a heart's sorrow can be divinely expressed in tone.

CHAPTER V

MUSIC IN REPUBLICAN AND IMPERIAL ROME

ONE of the first Roman kings, Numa Pompilius, is said to have been a good flutist, but the earlier Romans, like the Spartans, preferred music with their *fights,* rather than with their *meals.* The warlike *tubas,* "straight trumpets", of the legions sounding the attack, were the official music of the Republic. In the Punic Wars (the wars between Rome and Carthage) Hannibal's great war-elephants were maddened for battle by bucketsful of a mixture of pure wine, pepper and incense, and they and his men were "cheered on" by the din of brass cymbals and flutes made of asses' bones. But the songs of the legions drowned out this battle-music, and that of every other nation which opposed them. But in the case of great individual Romans, music-loving Anthony went to destruction to the sound of "flutes and fifes and harps", while unmusical Augustus founded the Roman empire.

With the empire the Romans began to take a greater interest in music, generally. They borrowed much from the Greeks, but as Rome became a world-centre, the music of every race could be heard in its streets. Egyptian priests beat the *sistrum* (the Romans called it the "Isis-clapper"), in Salvation Army style, and drew coins and converts to their shrines. Chaldean star-gazers "advertised" themselves with mystic chants. Asiatic flute-players, who had a very bad reputation, were to be found everywhere. Syrian girls, priestesses of Astarte, the Syrian nature-goddess, combined the profession of timbrel-playing with that of "religious prostitution", an idea particularly horrible to us. The Roman of the wealthy and aristocratic classes "took" music as part of his "classical course", but he no more thought of *making music himself* than the average society man at Palm Beach or Bar Harbor. He had his slaves and wage slaves to make music for him. Martial tells us, however, that it was considered "good form" for a young Roman of the higher classes to be able to hum one of the popular Egyptian melodies about town.

Some of the worst Roman emperors sang—Commodus, Caracalla, Elagabalus. The damnable secrets of the gloomy Emperor Tiberius' palace on the island of Capri are whispered at by Roman historians.

But one of this monster's favorite pastimes was to study up all he could find about the *Song of the Sirens,* the wonderful melody of the Greek mermaids which would have drawn Ulysses overboard to his death, had he not been tied to the mast of the ship when he passed their rocks.

A musical criticism cost the Emperor Caius Caesar his life. Cassius Chaera was a Preatorian captain. Every evening, in the palace, when Caius—the first Roman emperor to sing and dance in public— gave Chaera the password for the night, he would add a few vile insinuations about Chaera's high, woman's voice. The captain, in time, became sick of the insults, drew his dagger one day, and stabbed the emperor to death.

Nero above all others is the Roman "musical" emperor. He made a *vice* of music. In general music, aside from the funeral flutings when the dead were carried to their graves, the solemn song of the temples, the chorus and other singing on the stage, and the "folk-songs", the songs the people sang at work or at play, served only two purposes in Roman life! It was *battle* music or *orgy* music, and as the empire declined there was less of the former and more of the latter. Let us return to Nero the musician.

He was "not a vicious boy", says one historian. But if not, he got over it, and as he grew up could not keep his hands from picking and stealing toward the strings of the lyre, for as the same historian says: "He was clever with his fingers". Nero had a thin, coarse "parlor voice", and took good care of it.* But you know how we all feel about our *own* voice, if we happen to be singers. Nero felt the same way. But he had no reason to feel so! When he was twenty-two his singing drove the birds out of the mulberry trees of the imperial gardens across the Tiber. When (A.D. 64) he sang in the theatre in Naples, Nature destroyed the building with an earthquake and he got out just in time! But Nero's *position* was such that he always had an *enthusiastic* audience. When he appeared in public as a singer or harp-player no one was *allowed to leave the theatre,* and it is claimed that listeners sometimes actually *did* die from boredom and fatigue! Some bright Greeks used to arrange to be carried out by friends as *corpses.* Once Vespasian (who later became emperor) *fell asleep* at one of Nero's concerts; the emperor noticed it, and the poor soldier's life was saved only with difficulty.

Nero made a concert tour of the Greek cities in 25 A.D. Singing, harping, reciting, he naturally took *first prize everywhere,* and came back to Rome with 1808 crowns of honor and parsley wreaths of

* Suetonius tells us that ". . . to preserve his voice he never spoke to his soldiers except by messengers, and would do nothing unless he had his *Phonascus* (Voice Moderator) standing by, to remind him to 'spare his pipes' or put his handkerchief to his mouth."

victory. Of course, Nero is said to have "fiddled while Rome burned", but there were no fiddles in his day. Yet history tends to prove, however, that he did play his lyre and sing a song "improvised" on the spur of the moment, as he watched the city burn. The popular song of the worst kind was a favorite in Rome in Nero's day, for all the naughty songs and eccentric dances of other lands found their way there. We know of *one popular song* that made a great "hit".

It was sung in a play by Attalus, running at the Campus Martius Theatre. When the moment arrived, Datus, a "comic opera" tenor of the day, would make his bow and render the people's favorite. It was called "Good-by Father, Good-by Mother!" and was a "take-off" on Nero, who was supposed to have poisoned his father and drowned his mother.

And yet the good folks of Rome thought the world and all of their professional musicians. History has preserved the story of the first Roman "musicians' strike". In the year 309 B.C. the *Tibicines*, the jolly Etruscan professional temple musicians, got into an argument with the priests of the Temple of Jupiter. For more than a hundred years they had enjoyed their three-day yearly "celebration", at which the wine flowed freely in that temple and all of a sudden the priests (probably there was a question of a wage-increase somewhere in the wood-pile) told them to "hire a hall"! So the flute-players put their flutes in their cases and "went out". They did more than just go on strike, too; they left Rome, and made a nearby town their headquarters. There was not a musician to be had in Rome for love or money. And—there had to be music for weddings, funerals and temple services. It was not long before the priests had to give in. They sent a delegation to the flute-players' retreat, with a lot of carts. The strikers' demands were all agreed to, and when the musicians had all been treated with wine until they could not keep their feet, they were loaded into the carts and brought back home. And all Rome heaved a sigh of relief when the carts full of musicians passed through the city gates.

The great Roman emperors, Vespasian, Titus, Trajan, Marcus Aurelius, Diocletian, Severus, seem to have been unmusical. Elegabalus, a degenerate Syrian, of whom even the hardened old historians of his day write with a blush, "played the flute, blew the trumpet, plucked the lyre and played the organ", as well as sang vile phallic hymns in the Roman temples. But while the orgies of the empire were celebrated to the accompaniment of every kind of voluptuous sound, a newer and *purer* kind of music was coming into human life, the music of *Christianity*. The main thing the Romans did for music was to spread Greek ideas of *tuning*, of *notation*, of "writing down notes", of modes and styles all over the world, because of the immense crowds of musicians who were drawn to the big city.

CHAPTER VI

FROM THE CATACOMBS TO CHARLEMAGNE

(Early Music of Christianity)

IN the very beginning, when the early Christians were scurrying about in Roman catacombs "underneath the ground", they probably did not raise their voices so that they could be heard. There is a time to sing and a time to keep silence! Early Christians, all in all, were probably no fonder of being turned into human torches, or cast to the Coliseum lions, or shortened by a head, than members of any other faith, in spite of all the martyrs whose blood was the seed of the church. So we take it that *"humming"* was as far as they went in early catacomb days.

We do know that Clement of Alexandria (d. 220 A.D.) wrote *the first Christian hymn* we know of, and we know what the musical hymn "material" was that the early Christian brethren used. It consisted of the old Jewish synagogue tunes, often very "taking", for Arius (A.D. 325), a kind of heretic Billy Sunday, made hundreds of converts by means of his "catchy" hymns. These tunes were "made over" according to the Greek and Roman ideas, and in the year 400 B.C., in Rome and in the West, generally, they were *grave* and *serious*. In the East, however, the new *psalms,* written in imitation of those in the Bible, were more apt to be *passionate* and full of *emotion.* In the fourth century we find that Christian hymns were sung in Asia Minor in good, ringing Methodist style, with clapping of the hands and stamping when the singers' hearts overflowed with holy emotions.

It was in the days of the Emperor Septimus Severus that *the patron saint of Christian music* makes her appearance. *Cecilia* was a noble Roman lady, and a Christian. Her story is told in the "Golden Legend". We learn that her husband Valerian (as has been the case with other church singers since) was not Cecelia's *first* interest. She was wrapped up in her *church work* and in good deeds, and when she was "taken up" by the Roman authorities together with Valerian, and they were offered the choice of sacrificing to Jupiter or martyrdom, they chose to die rather than renounce their faith. One line in the "Golden Legend" made St. Cecilia's musical reputation: "And, hearing the organs make melody, *she sang in her heart, only to God."* On the strength of this one line she has become Christianity's patron saint of music,* and there probably is a ladies' choral society in your own town named after her.

With every country, as Christianity spread, "working out" its "service" and "hymn" music in a different way—in Spain, Italy, Greece, Egypt, Syria, etc.—the musical part of the church "service", the *mass* and *"ritual"*, was getting very much mixed up, and this led Pope Gregory the Great (d. 605) once and for all to settle what should be used in the church music. Bishop Ambrose of Milan (d. 397) had already arranged church music in *his* way (it is called the *Ambrosian Chant* to this day) and to this day is used in Milan, by "special permission". In the same way, some Spanish churches have kept their own style of singing certain parts of the Roman Catholic mass, the Mozarabic Ritual. But otherwise, the Gregorian Chant has ruled the music of the Roman Church ever since. The Byzantine Church (the church of Constantinople and the Christian East) when Constantinople fell, already had passed on many of *its* musical ideas to the Greek Catholic Church, in which they have been handed down in Russia, Greece, Armenia and Syria.

At first the Christians fought very shy of *instrumental music.* Flutes and pipes and harps and other instruments were all suspicious, because they went with "orgies", and pagan feasts and wickedness in general. But in their singing in public and singing in private, Christians after a time (about 300 A.D.) began to use the *organ* cautiously: it supported the Gregorian chant, *one note at a time,* and soon the organ was taken in as a regular piece of "church furniture".

Its music was one of the greatest means the Church had of spreading ideas and ideals of Christianity among the heathen. But though the progress of Christianity was steady, it was slow.

Sacred love always has been accompanied by *profane* love in life and in history. *Sacred* song has always sounded side by side with *worldly song,* the popular song. And, strange as it may seem, history records that the Early Christians, fond as they were of their hymns, would not give up their "popular songs". The bishops of the church, from the earliest times to the tenth century, fought the good fight without getting very far ahead. Satan had no trouble in finding popular songs for idle mouths to sing. The Fathers of the Church complained that song was misused in the *agapé,* the "love-supper"

---

* The great painters throughout the ages have been St. Cecilia's press-agents. Carlo Dolci, Raphael and Paul Delaroche have painted her *singing* and *playing the organ.* Dominique (Louvre), shows her *handling the bass viol;* Pierre Mignard paints her *singing* and *playing the harp,* with oboe, clarinet, bass viol and tambourine waiting their turn. Van Eyck has pictured her at the *organ directing* the singing of a chorus of virgins.

of the early days of the Faith. The *idea of the agapé was a beautiful* and *reverent* one: the meeting of the brethren and sisters at a feast where a little simple meal, with devout singing and other exercises, encouraged *spiritual* affection and the brotherly love all should feel for one another. (The *agapé* survives in a way in our "church suppers", Sunday-school straw-berry festivals, etc.) But the hymn which "each was invited to sing" gave way to more profane songs after the meeting. Such noble and pious men as Clement of Alexandria objected to the "little suppers", and Tertullian complains that "the young men misbehaved with the sisters after the *agapé*". It was the same *funeral* services. Once the dead had been put away, the catacombs echoed with the unblushing "hit" of some Roman Irvingus Berlinus, sung by the late mourners. At last the holy fathers of the Church had to *forbid the holding of the agapé,* and in fact, (Council of Vannes) "profane assemblies where love-songs were sung". It is hard to believe that *women* were the chief offenders when it came to the unseemly use of profane popular songs, but the Council of Chalons (650 A.D.) declared that if they did not improve in this respect, they would be *whipped* or *excommunicated*.

The rulers of the barbarian kingdoms which rose on the ruins of the Roman empire took over the *music* of Christianity with Christianity *itself*. Clovis, the murderous king of the Franks, sang. He sang off key, but still he sang—pious hymns! King Dagobert played the organ and sang, and was so fond of music that when he heard the nun Clothilde's beautiful voice behind a barred cloister gate, he fell head over heels in love with her, took her out of the convent by *force*, divorced his queen and married her instead. Clothilde may be said to have been the first of many singers who married well because of their *voices!* Charlemagne did much to encourage sacred music in his vast empire. We are told that "Charlemagne and Saint Louis, King of France, passed entire days singing or listening to those sweet Christian songs of peace and hope which Gregory had introduced." Amid war, murder, pillage and ruin, kings and peoples turned to these lovely melodies for consolation. King Charles the Bald even kept up a big correspondence about music with his musical friends, and composed hymns together with the monks of St. Gall.

THE MUSIC OF THE PEOPLE

But popular song* and popular music, the "music of the people" keeps on going, in spite of all the church can do. In general musical instruments (except the organ) were associated with profane song.

---

*"Popular music", in all ages, in ancient Babylon or Rome, in the Middle Ages or to-day, flourishes beside the *loftier, purer music of the church and of art.*

All the peoples among whom Christianity was gradually introduced had their *bards* or *minstrels*—the Franks, Gauls, Teutons and Scandinavians, Britons and Russians. They kept alive the old *hero songs* of the people, and handed on "folk-songs" from generation to generation. And they kept on doing so even after they had been *baptized*, in spite of the fact that the Church looked on no music except sacred music with approval. So we have all sorts of primitive harps and hurdy-gurdy horns and bagpipes, used only with the people's songs, and the people's dances.

The period we are considering was the golden age of the Irish, Welsh, British and Nordic bards. They did not always put music to good uses for Plutarch tells us that the British Druids drowned the cries and shrieks of human victims they sacrificed on their altars with the sound of songs and musical instruments. But Irish and Welsh bards, like the Norse *skalds,* swept the harp-strings to make the wine taste the sweeter at the drinking-bout, to make the hero fight the harder in battle, or to speed his soul the quicker when he was dying. And they could *set an example* as well as sing it. Ragnar Lodbrag, the Dane, bard as well as king (ninth century), was captured by the Saxon king Ella. He was flung into a dungeon full of vipers, which began to eat him alive. But Ragnar had set his heart on composing a war-song in 29 verses. Before he finished the snakes had devoured his liver—but Ragnar kept right on. It is a story one must take with a grain of salt.

That a knowledge of the harp might be useful in the *military intelligence* service was proved by King Alfred the Great of England, who sneaked into his Danish enemy's camp disguised as a harper, learned all that he needed to know and won a battle the next day as a result. The songs of bards sometimes *even led saints astray,* for St. Dunstan, in his earlier days, was called up before his abbot or "studying the vain songs of his Pagan ancestors!"

CHAPTER VII

MUSIC AND MOHAMMED

THE good Christian bishop Isidore of Seville was sitting quietly in his palace study. He was writing a learned book on Christian hymns. Yet little he thought, as his pen travelled over the page that *while it did so,* a young camel-driver in the Arabian desert (630 A.D.) had "started something" which was to come near to doing away with Christian hymns altogther.

Mohammed had a practical mind where music was concerned. He wanted his followers to devote their attention to their *battle-cry,* the muezzin's *chant,* calling them to *prayer* from the minaret, and the few songs used in the mosque. Tradition says that Mohammed *stopped his ears* whenever he heard a flute! But in his paradise his followers could go as far as they liked; musically, as well as otherwise. The beautiful Mohammedan female angels, the *houris,* sat on verandahs "a hundred years long", before groves of trees loaded with flutes. A breeze from beneath Allah's throne drew enchanting sounds from the branches and the *houris'* voices were sweeter than any known on earth. But, according to Mohammed, it is only those who have *fled* music on *earth* who are received with *music* in heaven!

Politically speaking, Mohammed's idea of music seems to have been *sound.* It is the peculiar chant of the muezzin, the same succession of *tones,* for generations and generations, sung five times a day from the minarets, which holds Islam together with a rosary of sacred notes. But even Mohammed could not hold down the Arabs musically once their civilization had developed. Great, luxurious courts without music seem to have been out of the question in the old days. In spite of the way the Prophet felt about the art of tone, the Mohammedan princes and rulers in all the Eastern lands and in Moorish Spain, kept court musicians, and spent gold lavishly on their music. One Caliph, Yezid, (A.D. 682), passed his days in his palace "drinking wine and minding nothing but his *tabors* (small drums), singing wenches and his dogs". Later caliphs gave every vice a musical accompaniment. But Haroun al Raschid, the caliph of the "Arabian Nights", managed to combine greatness and a love for music. It was nothing to him that the pious priest Xafey had said: "The Prophet Mohammed would have chosen another time for his blessed birth had they played the *taf-taf* and the *dulcimer* (a zither with strings struck with mallets) in his day!" Haroun had his own "Fritz Kreisler", a musician named Isaac ben Mosuli, whose sweet melodies on the Arab *rebab*, an early form of violin, drew tears of emotion from the caliph's eyes. Wherever Isaac went his fame was sure to go, and the kings and sultans of the East weighed his songs with gold.

A pretty tale has come down to us about his marvelous playing. Ismail, Vizier of the Sultan Fekreddouli of Egypt, was a music-lover, and kept an orchestra of professional players for his own entertainment. One day, when he had settled down to enjoy a selection, in came a repulsive looking beggar, all rags and dirt. The vizier's Nubian bouncers rushed forward, ready to do their part but, no sooner had the beggar's hands touched the strings of his *rebab*, than they fell back, and with Ismail and the musicians, listened with thirsty ears to his music. Soon the beggar wove a glad note of devil-may-care joy into his tune and, in a few minutes, the vizier and all his musicians were dancing and jumping, laughing foolishly, and playing catch-as-catch-can with their instruments. Suddenly the beggar changed his tune and now the tears trickled down their cheeks, while some tore their hair and garments with grief, and others wailed and gnashed their teeth in despair. Then, as though to let his audience recover, Isaac ben Mosuli—for it was he in disguise!— played a slumber song so tender that it would have lulled asleep the giant bird, the Roc, in its nest above Sinbad's valley of diamonds. And, while Ismail, his slaves and his musicians all lay fast asleep, as though they had been drinking *hasheesh*, "the herb of joy", Isaac, like the Arab he was, "silently stole away".

Everywhere, in the courts of the Mohammedan kings, music was held in great esteem and cultivated. And—in Mohammed's own Arabian desert, to this day, the camel-drivers sing their songs. The "occupational song", the song sung at work, in fact, is sung all over the East. The "art music" of Mohammedan, of Saracen or Arab civilization, has disappeared with that civilization itself. From the music played in the Mohammedan East to-day, however, we know what it must have been like. Mohammedan music, like ancient Greek music, knows only *melody*. It has no *harmony*. It is interesting to see the *different way* in which the East has developed the *material* of music. Where our music has developed *harmony*, the combining of melodies, the Eastern races have developed music's "backbone", rhythm, the combination of "tunes" and "beats". In Algeria, Tunis, Northern Africa, and other Mohammedan lands, the native orchestras, made up of string, wind and drum instruments all may be playing in a *different rhythm*, in a different time, and with different accents. And, because for hundreds of years the Arab Mohammedan has learned to *hear music* from the *angle of rhythm*, he "gets" what these orchestras are playing, the meaning of their music, and *we do not*. To him it is beautiful, while to us it is only noise and discord. In their singing the Orientals of the Mohammedan East carry out in tone, and in all sorts of elaborate "patterns" of rhythm and notes, the "arabesque" (ornamentation) idea they use in architecture. They will sing one note, and then surround it with a whole group of little "grace"-notes, little ornamental notes, just as a square or circle in their wall decorations will be surrounded and overgrown with all sorts of extra scrolls and graceful lines. These *two* ideas are the main ones in all Mohammedan music: in fact they apply to nearly all Eastern music.

Western composers have drawn on this Mohammedan "eastern color", and created beautiful "Western" music. Two examples are: the lovely little "Anitra's Dance", an *Arabian* dance, in the Norwegian composer Grieg's "Peer Gynt" suite for grand orchestra; you probably have a record of it. And a modern French opera (never heard here, but highly thought of in Paris), the composer Dupont's "Antar", deals with a story of the old desert days, "When Knighthood Was in Flower" so to say, among the proud chiefs of the Arabian desert, before Mohammed's time. Dupont's music is full of this rich "oriental" coloring of sound. It is only another proof of Art's wonderful power to create *new beauty* out of material which, *as it stands*, is *not* beautiful to us. And it shows that Art is the greatest thing in the world for helping one group of races understand something of the spirit and soul of other groups of races.

In a political way it is very interesting to notice that instead of the *national unity* we get from our *patriotic* songs, the Mohammedans get a feeling of *religious unity* (in spite of sects in Islam), much greater than ourselves (Christianity has no religious unity). And in Mohammedan music the *one little tune* the muezzins chant binds together millions and millions of souls with a single melody. Pierre Loti, that great French writer who, though not a musician, has given us a deeper insight into the music of the East than anyone else, declares: "It flings the Mussulman's prayer to the four corners of the skies!" And what he says, speaking of the Turkish mosques of Constantinople in particular, applies to the whole Mohammedan East: "This immortal song, five times a day, planes above the Turkish land and its cities. It expresses in melody a whole religion! . . . So long as this prayer continues to make heads bow about the mosques, Turkey (and every other Mohammedan land) will continue to possess the same superb soldiers, indifferent to death."

CHAPTER VIII

CLOISTER AND HEARTH IN MUSIC

(During the Gothic Ages)

THERE are three kinds of music going along, each "going its own gait", so to speak, during the Gothic Age: the music of the *People;* the music of the *Church;* and the music of Knighthood.

Each of these three kinds of music has its own character, and each borrows and comes in touch with the other and borrows from it, and yet each is different and independent.

THE MUSIC OF THE PEOPLE

A *duet,* two voices singing different notes together, was unknown before the year 1,000 A.D. But what Egyptian Pharaohs and Assyrian kings, Alexander the Great and Nero had never known and enjoyed—the sound of voices singing in *harmony,* in *two—three—* and *four-parts,* was a pleasure the humblest in the land enjoyed during the dark Gothic Ages.

With the attention the Church paid *musical theories* and church *singing,* we would naturally suppose that the first male quartet started in the cloister singing school. Not a bit of it! Profane music, the songs that sprang up naturally among the *toilers,* the workingmen, the farmers, sailors, artisans, the ordinary, everyday "people" of the world, were the first to get away from the *unison* idea, that of every voice and instrument pounding away at *the same note at the same time,* and to develop *harmony.* The invention of part-music is the greatest thing in music the Gothic Age produced. Musically speaking, it was *the* invention of the age, and all future progress in music is based on it, and is an extension of it.

Music was a much bigger and more important thing in the lives of the everyday person in the Middle Ages than it is now. To most of us music is an *incidental.* We like to hear music in church because of reverence, habit, association, and the feeling of the sublime it gives the service. We like our daughter to be able to play or sing as well as the next girl. But unless we are especially "musical", we do not attach very much *importance* to music. Besides, we have the phonograph and the radio. The very air carries the best music by the greatest artists, to us.

In a way we *gain*. For it makes life richer in enjoyment, without our having to lift a finger to work, making music ourselves. In a way we *lose*. What we lose is the pleasure—and it was almost every one's pleasure in the Middle Ages—of making music ourselves. Take a look at the ordinary man's world in Gothic times and you will see why it meant more to him than it does to us. Royalty and nobility were well off, more or less. When there was fighting to be done, they had a Class A equipment, and they had plenty of leisure time. The clergy was well off: they belonged to the greatest institution of the day, could only be tried for offenses against others by themselves, in their own courts, and lived on the fat of the land, whenever there was any fat to be had! But—life in general in these Dark Ages was what Sherman once said war is. In the seventh century Mohammed had stirred up the desert sands. Clouds of wild, fanatic horsemen swooped down on the Christian East—Egypt, Palestine, Syria, Northern Africa, Sicily and Spain only asking to kill or be killed in his name. In the Greek empire, whose capital was Constantinople, ambitious men who wanted to be crowned in St. Sophia's played "tag" with one another. The man who was "tagged", really was "it", for he was stabbed or blinded at once, and then the game went on.

Among the kingdoms which had arisen on the ruins of the Roman empire, the chiefs or tribes, now "kings", and their "nobles", quarreled and fought, murdered and destroyed each other in the same merry way. All over the world the one idea was: if you see what you want, take it. That what you wanted usually belonged *to some one else* made no difference. You simply up with an axe and brained him. Then his relatives got after you, and thus things and people kept moving.

There were millions of quiet people* who only wanted to earn an honest living as best they could. But where they were not plundered bare, they were taxed to death. They toiled, served, sweated, starved and suffered and still—they *sang*! For music was one of the few things their worldly and churchly masters could not take from them. Their world was a world of blood-shed and strife, or terrible calamities, of constant fighting, robbery and ruination. They had no "movies", no theatres, no phonographs, no radio to "take them out of themselves". *Music* was all of this to them and more.

The Church in the Middle Ages was the one great *democratic institution* in the world. In theory at least, master and man, lord and

---

* Besides "professional soldiers" who counted more on "loot" than they did on "wages".

slave were equal in the sight of God. But the very nature of church music held it down to certain things: the church-bells rang for the *solemn* moments of the Christians life: baptism, wedding, death. But life in the Middle Ages was only *too full* of "solemn moments". It was their own "popular music", their folk-music, that the people *enjoyed*.

What was this "popular music" like? There is no doubt that the singing done "in the home", around the hearth, even during the Gothic Age, a coarse and material one, was *clean and decent,* for there *woman* ruled. But outside the house! . . . We have examples of clean, happy choruses of those early times, but there were many as bad as any "popular song" of imperial Rome. Charlemagne had been obliged to pass laws forbidding the singing of indecent songs near churches and in the street. These songs, in what was called the "vulgar" language of the land (to show that they were not sung in *Latin,* the language of the *Church*) were vulgar indeed. Vile were the drinking songs roared in the village tavern, and as for the "love-songs"—Heaven save the mark!—they were indescribable. The trouble with the age was that, except among the knightly class, which developed the ideals of *pure, noble exalted womanhood* in its songs, "love" in our sense of the word, simply did not exist. Everything was placed on a low and brutish physical plane, and this was reflected in the popular song. The Church tried to discourage "genuine" popular songs, whether drinking, love, occupational or any other. But the charcoal burner in the woods, the sailor in the port towns, the village serf, the thousand and one among the toiling masses on which the whole splendid superstructure of medieval life was built up, to cheer their hours of labor or their hours "off", wanted more than pious hymns and canticles.

Otfried, a monk of Weissenburg (843 A.D.) translated verses of the Gospels into the "vulgar" tongue, so that the sailor "home from the seas", might sing them in place of his wild drinking-rounds. Theobaldus of Rouen, another cleric, in the year 1200 A.D. set the lives of the saints to "catchy" popular tunes, in the hope that dissolute and drunken men-at-arms would prefer them to the ribald glees they picked up, but in vain.

Through all the ages profane music, the music of the *world,* has held its own. It does not seem possible musically, for the soul always to walk the high levels. Whatever their moral associations might be, the main thing about this "popular music" or "folk music" was that, aside from part-singing, it kept up the singing of solo melodies to the accompaniment of some instrument, it kept alive the individual race soul in peoples: the Church knows no difference in races. It allowed music to develop in *different* directions: the Church knows but one direction, the heavenward one.

The wandering jongleur or minstrel, an early "professional musician, with a *viéle,* an early ancestor of the violin, across his back, was the "carrier" of popular music, gossip, new ideas and new tales from land to land. He was welcome in the huts of the village and in the castles of the knights. Everywhere in France, Germany, Spain, England, the "wandering folk" as they were called kept the soul of music alive in the people. With zither and harp, viéle (fiddle) and bagpipes, they brought the good, (or bad) new songs into the country hamlets, small towns or cities. They followed the armies of kings and princes, and appeared at the camps to hearten the soldiers with music and song. When the soldiers camped they put up their huts of boughs apart, and played and fiddled, juggled and danced to amuse the soldiers and win a share of their booty. They were "human newspapers". For the minstrels knew the latest political, military and fashionable news long before any one "higher up". These professional minstrels were a race apart, however. They paid no taxes, they owed no duty to king or lord. They were "free as the birds". "Ask the clouds and the winds where they are bound, but not one of the wandering folk", was one of their sayings. But —they were as helpless as the birds, too. On the other hand, they were *outside the law.*

Our "professional" musicians to-day are treated like anyone else. But in the Middle Ages the Church denied them *Christian burial!* Since they were "outside the law", anyone who had a mind to, could kill them. And if anyone else wounded a strolling musician, the latter could only strike back—at the other man's *shadow!* They were children of pleasure and brought pleasure wherever they came, but the Church said: "Player and singer folk are not like other people. They have only a *seeming* of humanity, and might almost be compared to the *dead."* But the strolling musicians and their like had their revenge in their songs. They made cruel fun of the vices of their times, the cruelty of kings and nobles and the abuses and corruption of the Church. In their day, they were what we would now call the "liberal" element in human life.

What music have we to-day out of the music of the Gothic Age that has a live interest for us?

The Church took the idea of *harmony,* of two voices singing different notes together and developed it into *polyphony,* many voices singing different notes together. Notes were written as large "points" in those days, and the art of putting down different "points" or notes to run "counter" to each other was called "counterpoint". Gregorian masses and other church music was written in this elaborate, many-voiced style and then the scientific "music-lovers" took it up and wrote counterpoint to profane words: they turned it into art-music.

But the music of this age *lives* only in the Gregorian hymn and chant of the Roman Church and in certain motets, madrigals, etc., for many voices sung by large choral societies. They are for us only musical Chinese puzzle-patterns, examples in musical mathematics, dry, dull and dead.

The original germs of tunes that sprang up among the people, that were sung and carried by nameless minstrels, exist to-day, changed and hidden in some of the very songs we hear or sing. But they too have passed, and the few that have come down to us have mainly a "historical" interest, which, generally speaking, means that the people are not interested in them at all.

THE TROUBADOURS

The real romance of music in the Gothic Age lies with the troubadours (*trouveries*). For they—kings, great nobles and knights —wrote poetry, composed songs to it and sang their songs to win the love of fair ladies.

With their "accompanists"—the minstrels or *jongleurs,* who played the *vièle* (early fiddle) while their masters sang, these blue-blooded musicians, in intervals of fighting, put over in melody the ideal on which the way we look at women (or should look at them) is based. It is the idea and the ideal that woman is a finer, nobler, better creature than man, and should be treated accordingly. It took music to establish this idea, which the *troubadours* preached in song in France and Norman England, the *trobadores* in Spain, the *Minnesinger* ("love-singers") in Germany; they borrowed many of their tunes from "popular song". The real troubadours were the "amateurs", the *non-professional* musicians of the time, they sang for, as well as of, love. With the coming of the Renaissance, the bloom was rubbed from the cheek of knighthood. Kings and nobles, in most cases had their music "made" for them, but the musical "publicity work" the troubadours had done for lovely women has endured through the ages. If the reader is a woman, she owes these royal and knightly singers a debt of gratitude. Men are more apt to look at what the troubadours did for women in the light of their own experience.

THE MASTERSINGERS

Toward the end of the Gothic Age, the professional musician moves up to a higher level. The wandering minstrels were, to be frank, nothing more or less than musical *tramps* in most cases. In the twelfth century musicians begin to get together in "guilds" or "unions", and we have "Piper Kings" and "Minstrel Kings" and "Kings of the Fiddlers", who try to get a monopoly for their "unions" where the playing of certain instruments is concerned.

THE ROMANCE OF MUSIC

Then, while the Church and the "scientific" musicians went on making Church music and art-music more complicated, and the Troubadours turned the tunes of popular song into glorification of woman, a new idea came up in some of the big German cities. The *tradesmen*, butchers and bakers, cobblers and candlestick-makers, did not see why *knights* should be the only non-professional musicians. So clubs of *Meistersingers* ("master singers") were formed, with secret initiations and secret ceremonies. But—what the "Mastersingers" (with a few exceptions) lacked was the true musical spirit. Their musical contests often degenerated into mere trials of skill. The troubadours sang from the *heart*, the Meistersingers from their *throats*. A real musical genius among them was Hans Sachs (d. 1576), the songful shoemaker of Nuremburg. One of Wagner's greatest operas, "The Meistersingers of Nuremburg" (See "The Romance of Opera") deals with Hans Sachs.

The majority of musical names during the Gothic Ages do not stand for *romance*: they represent *scientific* or *technical* skill and *theoretical* advance. Among the troubadours, King Richard Coeur de Lion of England, Bertrand de Born, the Count de Coucy and the Count of Champagne, are but a few important names among many.

CHAPTER IX

THE RENAISSANCE AND THE BAROQUE AGE IN MUSIC

During the Renaissance, Opera comes into the world (its story is told in a separate volume) developed out of the Miracle and Mystery plays, the "sacred dramas", of the Middle Ages. The Renaissance has its musical kings and queens: Mary Queen of Scots played the virginal, the keyboard forerunner of the piano, better than Queen Elizabeth and this was one of the things Elizabeth never forgave. But there were no troubadours. Henry VIII, whose merry "Hunting Chorus" is still sung, and who played various instruments, had a way with an axe where women were concerned of which no troubadour would have been guilty. King Charles IX of France did not let violin-playing interfere with massacre. But there was much music, instrumental and vocal, at the courts of the pope, the Italian princes, in France, Germany, Spain and elsewhere. The *court conductor* and choirmaster had become an established institution. Leaving aside the musical names which, romantically, and even humanly speaking, mean but little to us, *the great dramatic thing in music* during the Renaissance is the split in the Church, and its effect on the life of the times. Looking at it in a broad way, two great men stand out, musically: *Palestrina*, the glory of Roman Catholic church music and (somewhat later) *Bach*, who built his palace of tone on the foundation of Protestant church music which Martin Luther laid. With the split in the Church came renewed popular interest in its music. Why? Because music, like everything else, was turned into a weapon. It carried the two fighting doctrines along on tone. Each kind of music, Catholic and Protestant, spoke in its own way for the ideas of its own church.

Palestrina wrote masses so beautiful—the "Mass of Pope Marcellus" to this day is said to express all the mystic, heavenly striving and aspiration of the Church—that they never have been excelled. His beautiful "Pope Marcellus" mass was the salvation of the Church's music in his time, so the story runs. Besides the plain Gregorian chant, counterpoint had developed a much richer and more beautiful music for the Church, but Pope Pius IV (1563) made up his mind to act as a new musical broom, and sweep it all out, keeping only the Gregorian chant itself. Then, so legend tells us, and when we hear Palestrina's beautiful music we can believe it, angels came down to the composer's study as he sat mourning in the twilight,* and sang him the divine music his melodies are built upon. And in every Catholic land the composers rallied around the ideal of Palestrina's music, and wrote masses, which, like it, lent the eloquence and beauty of tone to the beautiful mystic and impersonal doctrines of the old Church, which made the human individual, his feelings and ideas, very secondary in importance, and turned altogether to the divine.

But—Protestantism developed another ideal. The tendency of the Protestant Church, in music as in life, was *away from tradition*. It encouraged every man to express *himself,* his feelings, his doubts and hopes. Catholicism in music was the doctrine of the impersonal, the acceptance of reverenced traditions, the beauties of a mystic outlook in life. Protestantism meant the personal examination of questions of faith, a more human and independent manner of thought and expression. Each "system", each type of mind, inclines to one or the other way of looking at things. Each has its advantages (as already has been explained in "The Romance of Evolution, Chapter 25), Martin Luther himself, the founder of Protestantism, was a music-lover of a hearty sort. His famous saying: "Who does not love wine, women and song, remains a fool his whole life long", has been much misinterpreted. Luther was sober and moderate as regards wine, which everyone drank in his day. As to women, he was an irreproachable husband: his marriage to the woman he loved was his heart's protest against what seemed to him the unnatural celibacy the Catholic clergy were supposed to observe. And in music he favored glad secular song as well as sacred. (A little Christmas hymn he composed, printed in octavo form, may still be bought for five cents in any music store). But Luther was no Palestrina. The Palestrina of Protestantism was the great German composer, Johann Sebastian Bach, who, though he was born in the century following the Renaissance (1685), wrote the great *Protestant musical work* in his "Mass in B Minor ", just as Palestrina wrote the great *Catholic* work in his "Mass of Pope Marcellus".

Between the divine creations of master musicians lies the whole terrible period of the religious wars. We cannot, in our day, imagine men killing, burning and bespoiling their fellow-men because of a difference of religious opinion. The last World War has shown, more clearly than anything else, that while the ideal of *nationality* still has power to make peoples commit wholesale murder in defense of

* The German composer Pfitzner has written a famous opera, *"Palestrina"*, dealing with the legend. In it the great church Council of Trent, has been set to music—the first time *a parliament of any kind has been sung in tone.*

what they think *right*, the ideal of *religion* has not. And, perhaps, the thing on which we can pride ourselves most in the Constitution of the United States, is its guarantee of *absolute freedom of religious opinion* to every American. Yet, with the first wars regarding differences of belief which began even before Luther had established Protestantism as a faith and only ended with the expulsion of the Huguenots from France by Louis XIV, music was one of the weapons used on both sides to help fight their battles. The *Veni Creators* of the Paris priests cheered on the St. Bartholomew murderers, just as the *psalms* of Clement Marot (the first Calvinist psalm-writer, d. 1455) encouraged the Huguenots to kill and torture just as their enemies did. Through the *Latin chants* of the Spanish priests who swarmed on the big hulks of King Philip's "Armada", there sounded the refrain of "Kill, kill!" just as "Burn, burn!" echoed in the *Protestant hymns* the people sang when Catholic martyrs were devoured by the flames in the days of Henry VIII and Elizabeth, at Smithfield. The horrible cruelties practiced by both parties during the Thirty Years' War (1618-1648), were committed to the tune of Luther's *Protestant hymn,* "A Mighty Fortress is Our God" on the one side, and the Latin church hymn *Dies Irae* ("Day of Wrath") on the other. This, in the music of the Renaissance and the Age of the Religious Wars, is the great, outstanding dramatic fact—the romantic one: that *music, whose mission in human life is divine,* should have been prostituted to provide a *war-weapon for murderous passions,* that it should have been used as a kind of tonal "poison gas" to destroy the souls of men!

In a short study of the "Romance of Music", a great outstanding fact of this kind grips the imagination. It seems far more important than long lists of names of men whose accomplishments are no longer directly in touch with our own life! So we will remark merely that during the Renaissance and the Baroque Age which succeeded it, music became more and more a factor in human life in every class. Kings, princes, and great nobles encouraged it, and kept large court orchestras. Musicians grew in public esteem. And—folk-song, the song of the people, flourished as never before. In Shakespeare's day, to give an idea of how generally popular music was, a zither or virginals lay around in every barber shop in London, for the customer waiting his turn, to take up and play, just as in our barber-shop today, we have copies of the magazines to elevate our thoughts while waiting for a shave. And, while the organ developed into a finer and nobler instrument in the churches, the earlier string instruments reached the end of their long evolution in the perfected violin and 'cello.

With the Age of the Baroque we find that all music has settled down to definite *forms*. Great "styles", as in architecture, are established: there are the Roman and Protestant temple styles, including the music of their services written and sung according to set rules. And we have *oratorios,* really a kind of "sacred opera", in which the tales from the Bible or the Lives of the Saints" are told in dramatic music; and *cantatas,* which handle secular as well as sacred subjects. We have the "symphonic" style—great works for a combination of *instruments,* some that tell a story, and are known as "program music", because they have a story "program"; others which are *just music,* and are called "absolute music", because they simply express beautiful musical thought *without* any *set* program. We have both for solo instruments (violin, 'cello, piano, etc.), and for groups of instruments forms made up of regular sections (like "chapters", in a book), with a quick or gay "first chapter", a slow, sad or gentle "second chapter", and a third rapid, climax "third chapter". These forms are called "Sonatas". The architectural styles of music become fixed and the succeeding centuries develop, extend and modify them as great creative musicians succeed each other.

CHAPTER X

THE ROMANCE OF SONG

And now, the better to give the true spirit and feeling of Music's romance, we will present from the romantic angle some of the things in music which are most interesting to us all. We will begin with the Romance of Song.

The song, whether long or short, is the smallest and most complete "form" in music. It is the most direct, it is the one we all grasp and understand best, and it is the most *romantic*. For two pages of a song can tell a heart's sorrow or a heart's joy, they can picture every shade of love, the emotion that rules men's lives, they can sing his dreams, his hopes, his despairs! The great songs of the world are the tone-jewels of human feeling. They are the diamonds, sapphires, pearls and rubies of our hope, joy, love and passion in tone. To tell the romance of all songs would call for a book of thousands of pages. We will give an idea of a few.

The songs that all the world has sung and loved, and still loves and sings are of two kinds: folk-songs—songs that spring up like wild-flowers among the people, and *"art-songs"*, songs born of the inspiration of a single mind. There are wonderful songs of either sort, and—when an art song is well enough liked—the people at large take it up and make it their own. Handel's celebrated *Largo* is a song of this kind. The old opera "Xerxes" in which it once occupied a page, has long been forgotten; but the *Largo* still lives as one of the sweetest and purest of sacred melodies. Haydn's Austrian patriotic hymn, "God Save Francis the Emperor", has survived the empire it sings, and its tune—with other words—has served many other nations as a patriotic song and hymn.

The romance of the great songs often is a triple one. Their melody is tied up with the romance of the lives of great composers, of great singers and of great historical times. Sometimes a nation's soul trembles in the notes of a single song. The Swiss "paid soldiers", from the Renaissance, to the eighteenth century, when they heard the famous *Ranz des Vaches,* the "Cow-call Song" of the Alps, would throw down their arms and desert, so great was their homesickness. In the eighteenth century the tune had to be forbidden in the Swiss regiments of the French army. We can buy to-day a copy of

Anne Boleyn's favorite melody, (she was a fine singer, and often sang it in husband Henry's ear) "O deathe, rock me to sleepe!" The words have a kind of ghastly appropriateness. The gouty husband whom she betrayed with the handsome young Mark Smeaton, and who loved to hear her sing the song, was the one who handed Death the axe with which to "rocke" Anne to sleep forever. And we have the sharpest contrasts between the personality or character of some of the greatest song-writers, and the beauty of their songs. Schubert (1797-1828), one of nineteen brothers and sisters, was a poetic, unkempt, disorderly beer-swilling sort of a man, who lived largely from hand to mouth. Yet the greatest of his 634 *lieder* (songs), songs like "Death and the Maiden", and the "Serenade", move the heart to exquisite tears of tenderness. Schumann (1810-1856) became insane and died in a madhouse, but his set of wonderful songs called "Woman's Love and Life", have all the deep truth and *sanity* of purest affection. Schubert's "Erl-King" thrills with the drama only unclouded genius can create. Beethoven suffered from a hereditary blood disease which made him deaf, but his great song "Adelaide", is one of the purest and noblest of love songs, one of those songs that sang itself out of the composer's soul and was caught up by his *inner* ear!

There are songs which have made history. Four songs—Handel's *Largo* may have been one of them—kept the government of Spain running smoothly for nearly a quarter of a century. Every evening, for twenty-two years, Farinelli (his real name was Carlo Broschi), an artificial "male" soprano, tall and thin who looked like a "human spider", sang *the same four songs* for King Philip of Spain (at a salary of $15,000 per year and "extras"). For the king had a streak of melancholy madness, and Farinelli's songs kept him going. The *Marseillaise* and the French Revolution by which it was inspired, cannot be separated. Our own patriotic songs tell the heart story of our War of Independence, our Civil War, the Spanish American conflict and the World War. All the emotional feeling of the South thrills in the strains of "Dixie", as the Northern spirit rings in the "Battle-Hymn of the Republic."

There are great songs we associate with great singers. In England Mme. Catalini, during Napoleon's time, so greatly did her voice stir British patriotism, got $10,000 at a festival to sing "God Save the King!" Jenny Lind and Patti made such songs as "Home, Sweet Home", and "The Last Rose of Summer" take a personal meaning, breathe a personal message to every one who heard them. And today, as in the eighteenth and nineteenth centuries, great singers—a Geraldine Farrar, a Maria Jehitza or a Frieda Hempel, a Caruso or a McCormack—still "make" songs. Some are made, seemingly, for all time, some are made only for the moment—for no matter *how great the singer,* his *voice* can only keep a song popular for a time. It is *song itself* which must have a musical soul, if it is to endure through the ages.

In the romance of song perhaps the most striking thing is the way in which the great general public, the people who listen to songs, whether in concert-halls, at the phonograph or at the radio, play the part of Fate *in deciding* which songs shall live and which shall die. And so we have the strange contradiction that you and I and everyone who buys and listens to and, for the moment, perhaps, *enjoys* the manufactured "popular song" of the day, flings it aside without pity when its season is past. Much has been written and said about the "harmful" influence of popular song; its low musical and text quality; and the damage it does. But the great majority of people who make the commercial success of the popular song possible, are the very ones who "kill the things they love." For nothing, at bottom, is more *sane* and *just* in its estimate of *real worth in music* than *the great general public.* The manufactured products of "Tin-pan Alley" serve to while away an idle hour. Man cannot, either in music, art or religion always tread the clouds. He has to tread the *sidewalk* as well, at times, and step on the accelerator of lighter emotion if only for the sake of contrast. The true, beautiful *American folk-songs* of *Stephen Foster* endure through the centuries: "Swanee River", "Nellie Grey", "Old Folks at Home", "Old Black Joe"; but "Bananas" and "Corner" and "Back Porch" and other maudlin sentimental or passingly humorous songs of a season find their way to music's great garbage-pile of things cast away. And this stern final judgment on the part of the world's great audience of music-lovers when it comes to the very things which are dinned and advertised into momentary popularity is one of the clearest signs of a constant upward trend in good musical taste.

One of the main things that lends romantic quality to the music of songs is *poetry*—the poet's "winged words" to which they are set. Out of the inspiration of the poet's fancy is born the inspiration of the composer's fancy. And, above all the *external romance*—the romance of personality, of singers' lives, of tragic or sentimental circumstances surrounding individual songs—is the romance of the words and music of a song itself! *Association* may set the heartstrings quivering when we hear "Annie Laurie" or "Killarney"; *patriotism* may stir the pulse when we stand or pull off our hats as "The Star-Spangled Banner" rings out. *Tears* may come into our eyes at the singing of "Lead, Kindly Light", but—even without association these songs would be beautiful, tender, stirring, soulful music.

And another noticeable feature in beauty of song is that its beauty has flowed freely through the centuries. It is a spring that

THE ROMANCE OF MUSIC

does not run dry. The unknown composers of folk-song, and the great masters of inspired song-writing alike have given us a deathless treasure. The cheap popular songs the people of Jerusalem sang making fun of their last, weak king (appropriately named *Guy* of Lusignan), as he rode through the streets, have passed like the cheap popular song of our day, once it has jazz-buzzed or sobbed itself out on our ear. But the *great songs* endure through the ages, and new and beautiful songs are added to the treasure already existing with every year. The "high-brow" art-lover need not worry. *Public opinion* is a fair guide to what is good in music. And the fact a man may, for the moment, enjoy an "Arrah, g'wan" song of some kind, by no means proves that he cannot appreciate Gounod's "Ave Maria".

The romance of songs is unending: there are the divine melodies that came to the dying Mozart as he wrote his *Stabat Mater*—songs of a distant land his foot was about to tread. There was the song of Greek Amphion that caused the stones to shape themselves into the walls of Thebes. There were the burning songs of Sappho, the Greek poetess, which singed the lips that sang them. There are the songs of David which calmed the madness of Saul. There are the songs which have gained battles, and which have cost the lives of lovers, songs in which nations have been reborn and to which royal families died out. But Anne Boleyn's "O Deathe, Rocke Me to Sleepe" is, perhaps, one of the most romantic of all. Sung to the gross and repulsive king, no doubt, with her handsome young lover in mind, the beautiful girlish queen could shut her eyes and put her whole soul into the melody with never a thought for the words. And then—retribution! Death "rocked" but once: one blow of the axe and the head that had been Henry's delight fell into the sawdust beneath the scaffold. One wonders whether Anne's pale lips were murmuring the fateful words when it fell, whether the ghost of its tune died in her white throat as the axe-blade struck!

CHAPTER XI

THE ROMANCE OF THE VIOLIN

As the Middle Ages went by the *vièle,* the rude first-draft fiddle of the minstrels, and other early string intruments began to shape up in different ways, as *viols, lutes* and *guitars.* In the lute instruments which were in their glory in the Renaissance and early Baroque Ages, the strings were twanged with the finger-tips but the violin instruments were played "with a bow". The Arab fiddle, the *rebab,* had some effect on the development of our violin. The knights who went crusading in the Holy Land (like the A. E. F. in France), brought home all sorts of things: wives, new ideas regarding manners, morals and dress, and new musical intruments. And between the 16th and the 18th centuries the great violin-makers managed to turn the *viol family into violins.* Out of a great flock of small viols and big viols, the *violin,* the *viola* (a trifle larger), the *'cello* and the *counterbass* have survived the struggle of the fittest. The lute is represented to-day by such instruments as the mandolin, guitar, banjo and ukelele.

The great "families" of violin-makers—Stradivarius, Guarnerius, Amati are chief among them—practiced their trade like the priests of some holy craft. They had their "secrets", of varnish, of wood, of line and curve. The great violinists, however, were the romantic figures in string music. The violin could express every passion in music, like the human voice, and the famous fiddlers soon learned the trick of turning a prince's tears into drops of gold. Among crowned heads themselves, the Austrian imperial house took first rank as musicians. For several centuries nearly every Austrian emperor played either violin or 'cello. The Stuarts—though poor King Charles I scratched a bit on the 'cello—were not very musical. Nor were the French kings: Henry IV may have been able to sing and is supposed to have composed a love-song. He was a great ladies' man; and love-songs were part of his equipment for winning hearts. But Louis XVI had a better ear as a locksmith than as a music-lover. The nobility in every land, and the people as well appreciated the great masters of the strings. They and the kings made it worth while to be a concert violinist.

We can mention only a few among many names of violinists who once moved hearts in the seventeenth and eighteenth centuries. The *sonatas, concertos* (larger and more elaborate sonatas) and *suites* (succession of dance numbers) first played by the violinists, were succeeded by all sorts of single numbers and brilliant arabesque "Variations" on well known tunes, and the violin was *the* instrument of the late seventeenth and early eighteenth centuries, just as the piano was that of the later eighteenth century and the nineteenth.

The Italian Corelli (d. 1713) was the friend of Roman cardinals and honored by the dreadful ex-Queen Christina of Sweden. Vivaldi wrote a concerto whose four parts each described one of the seasons in music: "Spring" was all bird-song, murmuring brooks, thunder and lightning. It showed the slumbering goat-herd with his faithful dog, and a bag-pipe dance between nymphs and shepherds—all on the four strings of his violin. Tartini fell in love with one of his violin pupils and married her in secret. Forced to flee Padua, he went into a monastery, came out again, and was allowed to rejoin his wife. He made such a name for himself that the Emperor Charles VI felt he could not have the Bohemian crown put on his head (1732) in Prague, unless Tartini was there to play at the ceremony. The most romantic episode in Tartini's life he himself has described: "One night I dreamt I had sold my soul to the devil. I handed him my violin to see whether he could play, and he played so beauitful and wonderful a sonata that I was charmed and enraptured. My breath failed me and I woke and seized the instrument to recall some of the wonderful music I had heard. And what I recalled I called my 'Devil Sonata'". Tartini's *Trille du Diable* ("Devils Trill Sonata"), is played by every great violinist to the present day.

In the eighteenth century nearly every court, small or large, had its "court violinist". Spohr, one of the greatest of eighteenth and early nineteenth century violinists, did not have an especially romantic life. He put his romance into compositions, and a big method for the instrument. But in France, where the kings had their own "Band of the Kings' Violins", the titled mulatto fiddler, the Chevalier de Saint-George, son of a French tax inspector and some dark beauty of Guadeloupe, became a court favorite, played for Marie Antoinette, and after raising and commanding a corps of sharpshooters for the French Republican army, died hungry and friendless. Alexander Boucher (more than Baillot, Kreutzer, to whom Beethoven dedicated the "Kreutzer Sonata", Rode, who wrote the famous "Studies", and Gavinies) was a romantic figure among French violinists of the virtuoso age. Most of these violinists, who travelled all over Europe, from Madrid to Petrograd, giving concerts at court and in the large cities, were great self-advertisers. Boucher made the most of a resemblance to Napoleon Bonaparte. He walked, took snuff, blew his nose, put on his hat just as Napoleon did, and

Napoleon—who was the last man in the world to approve of any one who built up a reputation for anything at *his* expense—turned his back on him when he appeared at his court in Paris. This modest fiddler called himself "The Alexander of the Violin" in his "ads", and speeches. His really great gifts as an artist always had to play second fiddle to his love for impressing people with stunts. His wife, who appeared with him in public, was trained to play a "duet" for harp and piano, the harp with one hand, and the piano with the other. But the sort of acrobatic tricks which the real artist of to-day leaves to the "vaudeville" player were the regular thing in the golden days of "virtuosity". And its music was planned first and foremost for showing how brilliantly an artist could play "difficult" things, or how slushily sentimental he could be, instead of trying to move the heart to noble emotions. The poet Heine, who lived in Paris as a music-critic in the early nineteenth century, hits off some of these great virtuosos in an amusing way, while praising others:

"Only Ernst, the poetic Bohemian, can lure such melting, *bleedingly* tender tones from the violin... Batta cried on the 'cello like a child, and pleased the ladies in particular. But he cannot give up his habit of whimpering... Owing to his childish wailing on the 'cello it is said he played himself into a real children's disease, the measles... I once met a ragged old man, the father of a celebrated virtuoso, who begged my paper to publish a notice concerning some noble traits in his boy's life. Among other things he told how his son had played a concert in Southern France, devoting the proceeds to restoring an ancient Gothic cathedral which threatened to tumble down... But he admitted when questioned that his fine son did not do much for him, and even let him starve a bit. I wanted to advise the celebrity to give a concert some day for his poor father's old tumble-down trousers as well as a Gothic cathedral!"

PAGANINI

Paganini is the one great *romantic* hero of the romance of the string instruments. He was the greatest of virtuosos, a real artist, and great both as a trick player and a player musically inspired. And his life of triumph is surrounded by a web of the wildest and most fantastic legends, whose circulation Paganini encouraged during his lifetime because it was "good advertising".

Genoa, where Paganini was born as a ship-chandler's son (1782), was a bad, bad town in his day. A sea-port town to begin with, it was morally one of the most vicious and depraved places in the world, with every form of vice flaunting itself in its sun-baked streets. It did not seem strange, the people whispered, that the devil watched over the boy's birth and joyfully cried: "Ah, my snarer of souls!" when he was born. One person even dreamt that she "saw the devil playing a violin till surrounded by a halo of hellish flame, and then hand the burning instrument to the child!" In 1800 Paganini began the great tours which gave him world fame, after years of hard work. But while he played in the Italian cities so that hard-faced men shed tears they never had expected to weep, and women swooned with emotion his own pleasures were of a baser kind. He hung over the gaming-tables which at that time ran everywhere as a matter of course, panting with excitement; and he began to undermine his health by seeking the society of women of ill repute. In 1805 he stopped at Lucca for a time as court violinist to Prince Bacchiochi and his wife, a sister of Napoleon. Here, in the church, his playing at an evening service one night excited such wild admiration that the priests had to rush into the chancel to restore order. In the palace, on the other hand, his passionate love melodies, so he himself tells us, sometimes caused the Princess Elise to *faint* with pleasure while listening to him. He wandered about Italy from 1808 to 1813, and as he wandered the legends about him grew. Heine sums them up: ". . . he was conductor in Lucca, fell in love with some princess of the theatre, became jealous. . . stabbed the faithless woman in good Italian style, was sent to the galleys in Genoa. . . and finally sold himself to the devil to get away!" And that Paganini knew the advertising value of these gruesome yarns is clear. He was to play in Trieste. The day before, at a dinner party, he jumped up from his chair: "Save me, save me from his ghost!" he cried. "See him, he is shaking the same blood-stained dagger at me with which I stabbed him! . . . She loved me. . . and she was innocent! . . . Alas, two years of prison are not enough! My blood must pay, to the last drop!" The others calmed the seemingly excited man, and he took up his dinner where he had left it with a good appetite. The next day *even the standing room* in the theatre where he was playing his concert had been sold out!

But the scent of the sulphur clung to him. In Vienna, when he played the Rode Concerto they said that he singed the old-fashioned passages of ornamental notes with the flames of hell. In Prague they said he was the Golem, the wandering Jew! In Paris it was claimed that he took part in devil-incantations, and heard *black masses* in order to raise a rich treasure of golden bars and figures, chests of ducats, and caskets of gems in the ruined house where an eighteenth-century magician, the Count of Saint-Germain, had lived. Yet—the same pope who made the great Genoese fiddler a "Knight of the Golden Spur" said, "Paganini plays Gothic cathedrals on his violin, his trills are clouds of incense!" Paganini looked like a starved ghost, thin, bony, his jaw deformed owing to a fracture which had made him have out all his teeth. He had long, skeleton fingers, and a diabolic gleam in his deep-sunken eyes. But when he died—though the "hell-fire" reputation he had was good advertising for earthly concerts, it did not help him gain admission to the heavenly choir after death—the Church of which he died a member finally allowed him to be buried in consecrated ground, which shows that it did not look on him as one of the devil's own.

In 1828 Paganini took the "Witches' Dance"—which he played on one string, cutting off three others with a pair of scissors in sight of the audience—and other numbers, and started to tour Europe. In Vienna the imperial family attended his concert, and everything in Vienna was *a la Paganini* ("in the Paganini style"); dishes on resturant bills of fare, hats, scarves and ribbons for women's wear, pipes, cigars, and snuff-boxes. Even billards were played *a la Paganini.* Concerts in the cities of Austria, Germany and Poland brought him to Paris, and finally to London. There King George IV, a saving monarch, wanted to pay him only *half* his fee of 100 pounds for a private concert in the palace. But the artist said: "Your Majesty can hear me at a much cheaper rate if you care to go to one of the public concerts I am giving!" In 1834 the Genoese master of the strings had reached the height of his glory. The French composer Berloiz dedicated a great symphony to him: *Harold en Italie;* the ex-empress of France, Marie-Louise, gave him a diamond ring; the Marquis de Negro unveiled a marble bust of him in Genoa. But he had invested his money in a big Paris gambling house, and the losses he suffered when the government refused to grant it a license aggravated the lung trouble he had. He died in Nice (1840), leaving his son an estate of $500,000. After death his corpse continued to wander, was shifted no less than seven times, and now rests in the cemetery of Parma. As an artist Paganini was a violinistic comet, but he would have blazed longer in the skies of art if his dissolute habits had not shortened his life. His love for his son Achillion is the great redeeming trait in a character that was a queer mixture of avarice and generosity, lewd living and sublime playing, savagery and nobility. As one writer has said: "Paganini gave the violin the divinest breath of the human voice". Paganini's "Caprices" remain one of the great works of violin literature, and great artists still play his Concertos, and his Variations on the "Carnival of Venice" and other airs.

For long years after Paganini's death great virtuoso violinists rose in the skies of art—Vieuxtemps, Wieniawski, Ernst, and many others —and swept through the countries on wings of brilliant musical display, blazing out in spectacular glory, or paling and dimming into obscurity. But, gradually, *ideals* of violin-playing changed. Technical skill, "showing off one's ability", came to mean *less* than playing with *emotion* and *feeling,* with *soul.* Joachim, in Germany, is a name which stands out in this connection; so does that of Leopold Auer, the teacher of our great violinists of to-day, whose playing we know from *actual hearing* or the disk. So does that of Pablo Casals, who is not alone, probably, the greatest of modern " 'cellists", but also has been called the greatest of *string* masters.

These men and the artists whom they have trained take *technical mastery* of the instrument as a matter of course, technical skill for granted. But they have shown us that the ability to play on the human heart-strings, to raise the enjoyment of the listener to a higher level than the pleasure he feels in watching a clever acrobat, is more important than anything else. And that is why we need not regret even Paganini. For we have the golden glory of Kriesler's tone, the human passion of an Elman, the grace and feeling of a Thibaud, a Heifetz (and, to mention a few Americans) a MacMillen, a Spalding, a White, to give us even more than Paganini, and the great virtuosos of the past gave us.

In chamber-music—the playing of string instruments together in the String Quartet (with first violin, second violin, viola and 'cello acting as the four human voices do in a vocal quartet)—the aim always had been *away from virtuosity,* and in this country, at any rate the Flonzaley Quartet probably stands for its most wonderful exponent.

CHAPTER XII

THE ROMANCE OF THE WIND INSTRUMENTS

THE wind instruments as "concert" instruments, have fallen from their high estate. With the exception of the flute and the cornet, we hardly ever hear them in recital or concert as "solo instruments". Their romance lies mainly in the past, when they were the soul of all battle music, and their romance climaxed in the death-song the great hero Roland blew on his horn,* heard miles away by the Emperor Charlemagne, who rode back only to find him lying dead amid hundreds of Moors he had slain. The flute among all wind instruments is the most romantic one. Some of the worst of men have been the best flute players. It is better, perhaps, that we cannot hear the echo of the depraved Roman Emperor Heliogabalus' flute float down the corridors of the past. The tale of degenerate purple pleasures its tone might tell could only wake horror and repulsion in us. And the flute of Henry VIII should have been made of the blood-red jade the Chinese used for the purpose. Charles IX of France was reproached for playing the violin, an instrument then held fit only for servants, instead of the aristocratic flute, but in general, so far as royalty is concerned, the flute is associated with the most objectionable characters. There is one shining exception in the case of Frederick the Great of Prussia. He could play Bach's Sonatas on his beloved instrument, defeat all the rest of Europe in a war lasting seven years, and when he died leave a well-organized country and a well-filled treasury. But—there is Alphonse VI of Portugal. A mad-man with a strong leaning toward homicide, he was passionately fond of playing the flageolet. Once, when he appeared on his palace balcony to acknowledge the applause of the crowd, he took his flageolet, played a tune on it, and then handed it to a highly respected nobleman and insisted that he play it as well. And history tells us that "the people were so disgusted that they almost laid hands on the royal flageolet player, and dethroned him then and there."

In the eighteenth and early nineteenth centuries the virtuoso flute-player was still in his glory. But the days have long since passed when a wind instrument player like Lebrun (d. 1746), could give a

---

* The story has been told in a beautiful bass song, "The Horn", by the composer Flegier.

concert in Berlin and have it said of him: "Lebrun, the Prince of Oboe, gave a concert which brought him no less than 1200 dollars and besides the King presented him with a hundred gold pieces, and a gold snuff-box." Now the flute-player less often appears as a solo player. Together with the oboist, the horn-player, the clarinetist and the trombonist, he forms the backbone of the orchestra wind group, or joins in the music of the military band. Among the few chances he has of shining in a solo way are those in the opera orchestra, in some famous air like the "Mad Song" from "Lucia", or the "Charming Bird" from the "Pearl of Brazil", where the flute plays a brilliant duet with the human coloratura voice. A new and fine artistic development in wind music, which should do much to make wind virtuosos happy, is the formation of an artistic "wind ensemble" like that of M. Barrère, in which a small orchestra made up entirely of players of wind instruments perform music specially arranged for the combination.

CHAPTER XIII

THE ROMANCE OF THE PIANO

BACH, who did for music what Luther did for the Bible, made it speak a language that would touch the people's hearts, is still regarded as the greatest creator of organ music (aside from his great "Passions" and his "B Minor Mass") in history. But he is not a "romantic" figure. He was a devout, simple man (in spite of his title of Court Composer to the King of Poland and Elector of Saxony), and raised an enormous family of children, and his life was a hard round of duty, church, family and composition. Yet in the great counterpoint form of the *fugue* his "Well-Tempered Clavichord", a collection of Preludes and Fugues for the forerunner of the piano, is still the foundation of all piano playing in the polyphonic style. Real pianos appeared between 1780 and 1790, and most of the famous earlier pianists travelled about like violin virtuosos, and displayed their virtuosity on the ivory keys instead of the strings. The composers Clementi, Dussek, Hummel and Mozart—though we know the last-named best through his great operas—were accomplished pianists and virutosos. Mozart's appearance as a boy (his later life was sad in many respects) may have been among his happiest remembrances. In Cornhill Inn, London, he and his sister Nancy gave concerts on the harpsichord (though his music is mainly written for the piano), and the audiences which crowded to hear them never failed to improve the chance to give the children a tune of some sort to extemporize upon.

Perhaps the most romantic incident of Mozart's life in connection with the piano occurred after a dinner-party at a princely house in Prague. His great opera "Don Giovanni" was to be given the next day, and the sinister ghost-music for the entrance of the "Stone Statue" (the statue of an outraged father whom the libertine has sarcastically invited "to dinner") was still unwritten. Mozart, leaving the table where the champagne bubbled in crystal glasses in the candle-light, stole into a dark and quiet room adjoining, where the piano stood. And there the ghostly terror of the music he drew out of his own soul in a flash of inspiration, made his fellow guests set down the untasted glasses as they listened, so powerful and sinister was its supernatural menace.

But while in Mozart's piano Sonatas, and in those of Beethoven the greatest works of their kind were being produced; while Carl von Weber's "Invitation to the Waltz" expressed the whole poetry of the dance and John Fields, a pathetic Irish pianist, living in Petrograd, wrought his wonderful "Nocturnes" amid the mist of drunkenness, and later, Chopin wrote the masterpieces which never have been equalled, the virtuoso tide ran strongly in the direction of "show pieces". Kalkbrenner, Pixis, Thalberg, Lysberg, Henri Hess, Leopold de Meyer, even Louis Gottschalk, our own Creole pianist who has written such charmingly poetic fancies ("The Last Hope", "Le Bananier"), were pianists of the virtuoso type. Sentimentality and showy brilliance were their strong points. In the early nineteenth century, the great player cherished the tradition that he was somehow different from the rank and file of people. Only too often outrageous manners, the most dissolute mode of life, and stage appearances in a state of intoxication were taken as proof that the artist really was an artist. In this respect the twentieth century insists (except, perhaps, in opera), that the great artist conform to the code of morals which governs life in general. Perhaps that is one reason that there is not so much "romance" in the lives of the great virtuosos of the present day, and more in their music. The romance of piano virtuosity—in its highest and noblest sense—centers around one great figure, that of Franz Liszt. Liszt is to the piano, in a way, what Paganini is to the violin.

FRANZ LISZT

Napoleon I was in the height of his glory when Liszt was born (1811), at Raiding in Hungary. He studied with Karl Czerny, the man who wrote the famous piano studies in "Velocity" and "Agility" which many of those who read these lines will recall with a feeling of hatred. When he appeared as a boy prodigy in Paris, in 1825, he was the pet of the lovely women of the French aristocratic *salons,* and was called "the ninth wonder of the world". And when he heard Paganini in Paris in 1831, he determined to do for the piano and its music what Paganini had done for the violin. This he accomplished with his brilliant "transcriptions" (rewriting a piece for the piano from an orchestral score, or from a song or violin copy) of great opera airs, songs, violin and organ numbers.

Paganini's love affairs were the kind which are passed over without mention but, "the king of pianists", as he was called, was a Louis XIV of music. He loved and was loved by various fair and frail women, intoxicated by the magic of his magnetic personality and his music. It is only fair to Liszt to remark that he did not have to do much "seeking"; all his life long women sought him out. For five years, from 1835-1840, he may have been said to have lived only for the Countess d'Agoult. She was an aristocratic blue-stocking whose pen-name was Daniel Stern. The even tenor of their life was interrupted only by the birth of the three children she gave him, and his occasional concerts in Geneva (they lived in Switzerland), Florence, Milan, Rome and Paris. In 1837 the Emperor of Austria made Liszt a noble, and the noblemen of Hungary presented him with a sword of honor. In 1848 he settled in Weimar, where the Princess of Sayn-Wittgenstein kept house for him informally, and except for concert tours which took in the European capitals, there he remained until 1861, when he retired to Rome for a time, and was made an *abbé*, after he had joined the Franciscan Order. It is generally understood that though the Princess of Sayn-Wittgenstein wished to marry her king of the keyboard, neither her family nor the pianist himself favored the plan, and so Cardinal Hohenlohe quietly had him ordained a priest, thus making marriage an impossibility for him.

Heine, as in Paganini's case, has given us some of the finest glimpses of Liszt's romantic personality. "He is a man whose character is eccentric yet noble, unselfish and without deceit", says the poet. At a concert in Paris ". . . it was a most uplifting sight to see him letting bunches of flowers rain down on him with entire self-possession, and finally, with a gracious smile, thrusting a red camelia into his buttonhole . . . in the presence of some young soldiers who had just come from Africa, where they had seen, not flowers, but bullets rain, and whose breasts were decorated with the red camelias of their own heroic blood." Or again, "A physician I asked to explain the magic Liszt exerts on his public smiled in the strangest manner and said all sorts of things about magnetism, galvanism, electricity, the contagion of a close hall filled with countless wax lights and perfumed and perspiring human beings, of musical cantherides and other things . . ." Het Heine himself cannot have believed this unromantic theory, for elsewhere he says: " . . . his playing at times seems to me *the melodic agony of the world of visions!*"

Liszt cast a glamor of his own romantic personality over the piano and piano music. Before him, to a large extent, it was a "trick instrument" in the hands of the sensational performer. He was the revolutionist in fingering, in ideas, in execution, who made it the most popular individual instrument in the world, and laid the foundation on which *all modern piano-playing* is built. Liszt himself said: "My piano is to me what his ship is to the seaman, what his horse is to the Arab . . . it is my eyes, my speech, my life!"

From Liszt's time on the greatest pianists (many of them his pupils) Rubinstein, Carreño, Von Bülow, Joseffy, d'Albert, Leschetizky, Paderewski, Rosenthal, Hofmann, Bauer, Grainger, Rachmaninoff and countless others, have developed and built out and on the art foundation he laid. He summed up the new art *ideal* which was to take the place of the *virtuoso fallacy* in the pianist's art, and his work in this respect is probably more important than his fine original compositions, his great concert pieces and transcriptions, his great studies, and his "Hungarian Rhapsodies", even his great symphonic poems for orchestra.

Only one other pianist, perhaps, should be mentioned *with* Liszt: Chopin, the "Raphael of the piano". Yet all that Liszt did was strong and sane, its keynote was poetic ardor or virile strength. Chopin, "scented with the praises of good society", was not strong physically. Even when he left Poland, then crushed beneath the Russian yoke, taking with him a bit of his beloved native soil in a silver goblet friends had given him, and went to Paris he was delicate. He never was a great concert pianist because his fragile frame lacked the strength needed for public playing. Perhaps an unfortunate early marriage with a woman named Marie Wodzinska had its share in lending his beautiful compositions—he wrote *only* for the piano—that vein of tender melancholy which is their chief charm. A Beau Brummel, who haunted the *salons* of the highest circles of Parisian society, always wore white kid gloves and a stickpin which matched his tie and shirt, the elegance and distinction of Chopin's music was equalled by that of his personality. The French woman writer, Georges Sand (Mme. Dudevent)—some one said of her that she "collected" lovers as a naturalist does butterflies, and stuck them up and labelled them as "models" for the characters in her novels—fastened on the unfortune Pole, though they had little in common. Chopin's consumption made rapid progress after they had pooled their lives, so to speak. A trip to the island of Majorca in 1839 did not help the composer. A rare letter of Georges Sand gives a glimpse of their life there: Georges Sand tells of many vexations, how they were put out of one house when the nature of Chopin's trouble became known, and how they rented an old convent—Valdemosa:

". . . The sea borders the horizon, formidable heights surround us, eagles pursue their prey even into the orange groves of our garden. Nothing could be more magnificent but . . . wherever nature is gorgeous and beautiful, men are wicked and sordid! . . . Nobody cared to wait upon a consumptive person. Chopin at last obtained his piano, and the walls of the convent cells were enlivened by its melody. Chopin composed some of his masterpieces . . . but we were living amid the clouds . . . the climate became unbearable. Chopin grew worse daily." From Palma to Barcelona, when they left "we travelled in company on the boat with a hundred pigs . . . Chopin arrived at Barcelona spitting blood by basinful, and crawling along like a spectre . . ." After their return to France, Georges Sand, who was tired of him whom she had first called "her dear sick man", broke with him, and Chopin's last year (1847), was one long agony. When he was buried in the Père-Lachaise Cemetery, Paris, a little of the earth he had brought with him from his beloved Poland twenty years before was dropped on his coffin.

But his many pupils were kind. A Miss Stirling sent him 20,000 francs from Edinburgh when she heard he was in want. The Countess Delphine Potocka rushed from the gaming-tables at Nice to brighten his death-bed hours with her singing. He died in the arms of Adolph Gutmann—the pupil to whom he dedicated his C sharp minor Scherzo. Liszt, his friend, has described his last moments: "The final agony began . . . a cold sweat ran from his brow; after a short drowsiness he asked in a voice hardly audible: 'Who is near me?' When told he bent his head to kiss Gutmann's hand, which still supported it—and while giving this last tender proof of love and gratitude, the artist's soul left its fragile clay. He died as he had lived—loving!"

Chopin created the piano "style", as Liszt did the piano technique. Bach, Haydn and Mozart wrote for the clavecin, Beethoven and Liszt made their piano music *orchestral* in effect, and so did the great composer Schumann, at times; but Chopin's passionate romantic *dances* (he wrote no sonatas in the classic form) his *waltzes, mazurkas, polonaises* and his "pure fancy" forms, *preludes, impromptus, ballads, nocturnes, études,* express every human feeling: sorrow, suffering and resignation, joy, love, anger, pride and heroic patriotism. In *emotion* he is the most intense of all composers.

Grieg, in his lovely piano pieces first showed that *nationality* could be expressed in music. He expressed Norway, as our MacDowell and others have expressed the American *Indian,* and John Powell the American *Negro*. Claude Debussy carried on the ideal of Chopin with *color* instead of pure melody of tone as his first thought. The "race spirit" and romance of individual nations have all been expressed by their great composers, since Grieg began to write. But this feeling, too, harks back to Chopin and Liszt. But the "romance" of the piano must now be sought in its music. The artist of an older day took for granted that his life "belonged to the public". The artist of to-day makes a distinction between his "public" and his "private" life. The latter, with whatever "romance" it may have, he regards as his personal, private business. Who shall say he is wrong? And if he seeks "romance" in the great piano music of to-day, and seeks it in the right way, we shall not be disappointed.

CHAPTER XIV

THE ROMANCE OF THE ORCHESTRA

THE most romantic thing about the orchestra is that, just as the Mohammedan mosque is built up on *one spot*—the wall-hollow that turns toward Mecca, so the orchestra is built up on *one idea*—the *balance* of different kinds of tone. In religion, in art, in life, new ideas, new principles are constantly taking the place of old ones. But in the highest and noblest architectural form of music, the combination of all instruments in a whole, in the orchestra, the *romance of the tradition of balance* links the New York, the Chicago and the Boston Symphony orchestras with the old temple orchestras of Chaldea and Egypt. The orchestra, too, stands for the idea of *democracy* in the highest achievement of musical beauty. The great solo singer, the great solo violinist, the great solo musician of any kind is an aristocrat. He stands proudly above the crowd as a member of the nobility of genius. But the orchestra represents *the more democratic, collective effort* of a *number* of artists, each of whom, whether he be a string player, a wind player, a brass player or a "percussion" player puts his own personal ability *second,* and the effect of the orchestra as a *whole first*.

There is romance, too, in the story of the orchestra's development. It is, in music, a clear process of Evolution. First, in old Chaldea, Babylon, Egypt, in Greece and Rome, there was the *backbone of rhythm,* as a foundation—for the orchestra is a building, a great temple or palace—of quivering tone whose outline, whose form, is shaped by the instruments of which it is built. Rhythm is its foundation, and the rhythm foundation of the orchestra building is the great group of the so-called "battery", "percussive" or "struck" instruments, kettle-drums, tympani and other drums, triangles and bells. On the strong rhythm-foundation of these instruments the three other "stories" of the great palace of tone are built up. There is the brass-wind (horns, trumpets, trombones and tuba), the wood-wind (flutes, oboes, clarinets, bassoons, piccolos, and horns of various kinds.) And, at the top, reaching out into the *highest ranges of tone,* are the strings, beginning with the double-basses, and moving up through 'cellos and violas, to the violins. The harp and many other instruments for special effects stand by themselves like rich turret or tower ornaments added to the walls or superstructure of the building.

The conductor is the guiding spirit who out of himself directs and expresses the *collective democratic energy* of this body of artists, each of whom is a *pillar* supporting the orchestral *palace hall*. When he steps on the concert platform the building is *dead*. It is empty, cold, lightless, soundless, a shell. When he takes up his bâton, in one dramatic moment we turn from death to life! When a symphony orchestra begins to play we think of one of the great ice palaces the Russian empresses, Catherine II and Elizabeth, used to put up. They stood towering in the silent and soulless grandeur of huge ice blocks, ghastly crystal monuments with a thousand darkened rooms, lying dull and deathlike beneath the dim rays of the moon. Suddenly, at a signal, they would flame and blaze with thousands of torches and lamps, and the dead, empty building would spring into the pulsing, glowing life of every jewelled color of the rainbow, dazzling, flashing, sparkling, in crimsons, sapphires, emeralds and gold, in a glory of beautiful hues.

The conductor's bâton is raised, and at once the orchestra, the *symphonic building,* springs into glowing, pulsing life. The difference is that its life is the life of *living tone,* its color is the *shifting color of living music.* If you ask for romance, there is nothing more romantic than this miracle, renewed whenever a great symphonic orchestra or an opera orchestra begins to play, and the huge dead, tonal ice-palace of individual instruments flashes out into a life that calls to *our life,* that draws us into it, that makes us share the joy or sorrow, the melancholy or happiness, the glory or the despair its music sings!

The orchestra came into existence with the opera in the early eighteenth century, but the most *ideal* orchestral palace-building is that of the *symphony orchestra.* As its name implies, it is complete in itself, like its music. The opera orchestra is a part of another art palace, one of the trinity of *vocal music, instrumental music* and *dramatic action*s which constitutes *opera.* The "military band", as the name it keeps shows, was once only a war-weapon, a kind of musical "armored tank" of sound, which in the shape of kettle-drummers, trumpeters and cymbalists drove down on the enemy, and rolled him over with its terrific din. Now it has "split off" from itself, like the soft cell-forms of early life and has a twin. The twin is the *band of wind instruments* which plays the same finer kinds of music the symphony orchestra does, arranging its "kinds" of tone within itself, like the orchestra, and using some of its brasses for strings and wood-wind instruments. But what are called *chamber ensembles,* groups of five, six, seven, eight or more instruments, with or without piano, strings, wood-wind and brass, grow out of another germ.

They are extensions of the instrumental four-part group, the *String Quartet.*

If we know how a thing is "made", how it came to be what it is, if we understand how it "shaped up", we can enjoy whatever it has to offer by way of beauty or interest a thousand times better. If we go to a symphony concert or hear an orchestral record, we are too apt simply to take it all for granted. When a record is giving you the Prelude to the "Meistersinger", or the "William Tell" Overture, we should see one of the most romantic pictures music has to offer. Under every South Sea atoll-island, with blue waves curling on silver sands, and green palms nodding over the transparent waters of its inner basin, lies the patient, century-long effort of millions of coral insects, building, building, till the beautiful island rose from the sea. Beneath the wealth of melody and color of sound in every great musical number an orchestra plays, lies the effort, the inspiration of thousands of men dead and gone, each of whom did his part in making the orchestra of to-day what it is. Stamitz, (1750), first shaped the orchestra as a *unified whole,* with the string quartet as its *central point,* and made the violin instead of the wood-wind tone the *lead* tone; Haydn and Mozart in their symphonies, first scored (wrote music) for the instruments in "groups"; Beethoven, in his greater symphonies, first wrote *solo passages* for the individual instruments, bringing out the individuality of each; Weber made the clarinet and horn prominent; Schubert created the lovely "duet" between woodwind instruments; Meyerbeer brought back the *viola d'amore,* the "love-viol", into the orchestra for special effects; all these and hundreds of others, led up to Wagner, Debussy, Strauss and Stravinsky, who have added new beauties in the way of handling tone, and new instruments, and made the modern orchestra what it is.

The music of the orchestra? The music of the orchestra is bound up with a great miracle. It falls, like all music, into two great classes. There is absolute music, music that has no "program", that tells no definite "story", music that is just music, beauty of idea and expression in tone, just as the beauty of a Greek temple lies in its perfection of form.

As in the Arabian Nights the magician with a wave of his wand called up a palace, so the conductor calls up palaces with a wave of his bâton. But—the conductor is the great magician of the two, for he can call up palaces of every period and every kind. Say it is a Haydn or Mozart Symphony: the flexible orchestral building changes shape according to its music. We have Greek temples, white marble pillars gleam beneath blue sunny skies, simple Doric or rich Corinthian. A Beethoven symphony towers with the massive grandeur of the Roman Colisseum. We can see golden Byzantine cupolas in the symphonies of modern Russian composers, Tschaikovsky, Borodine, Rachmaninoff; Gothic cathedral spires in those of Brahms; Chinese pagodas in works like Edgar Stillman Kelley's "Aladdin Suite". All this music without a fixed programme is "absolute" music. It is the music which calls on *us ourselves* to supply the *romantic story*, to dream a day-dream of ideal beauty. It offers us this beauty, and we can interpret it according to our heart's desire. *Absolute music* is the soul of emotion, of every sort of feeling, human and divine, and we can read its meanings according to the book of our own heart.

The other kind of tone palace which the conductor's bâton calls into existence is the tone palace of the *programme piece*, the great *symphonic poem*. Here we have a definite story, a great romance of the past or present, the human passions and emotions connected with human individuals. The programme poem, the great symphonic poem for orchestra, is in music what the great historical novel, the great historical drama, is in literature. Liszt, though there were symphonic poems before him, may be said to have founded the style. Think of it: the whole story of the world's history, the great romances, tragedies and passions, the whole story of mankind, could be told in the splendid programme tone-paintings great masters have created. Beginning with Stravinsky's the "Rites of Spring" (*Le Sacre du Printemps*), will call up early man in primitive Russia, and his bloody rites of sacrifice, the great moments, human and national, of the passing centuries have been caught and fixed by genius in works that move the heart in a thousand and one different ways. And—all this romance, all this beauty is within the grasp of practically every one to-day! Only—if you want to get from it all there is in it, listen to the great music of the orchestra as you would read the pages of a great book. Give it *all* your attention, and you will be rewarded. If you shut your eyes and turn all ear to hear a symphonic poem like Tchaikovsky's "Francesca", the tale of Italy's most tragic lovers will stir your heart. You may not be an "educated" musician. You do not need to be if you know the story, the music itself will make it clear to you. All the romance in the world lies "shut up" in the ice-palace of the silent orchestra, only waiting for the magic wave of the conductor's bâton to set it aglow with a thousand rainbow lights of tone, a thousand colors of harmony, a thousand singing jewels of melody, a thousand changing "shapes" and "forms"!

CHAPTER XV

THE ROMANCE OF MUSIC IN AMERICA

THE old alchemists and astrologers who dabbled in the "black arts" of magic during the Middle Ages claimed that somewhere in space was a spot to which they gave the Latin name of *stagnum oblivionis,* "the pool of forgetfulness", where the years of the past floated about like the clouds in the skies, and could be recalled if one knew the magic spell. There, floating on the sound-waves of those vanished years, echoes all the rich, barbaric, *romantic* music of the America of the early days. What would we hear could we "listen in" on those air-currents of forgotten sound?

We would catch, perhaps, the clarion call of the *first Spanish trumpets,* the first *white man's* note, to sound in a world of *red men.* And we would hear the rich, strange melodies of the Aztecs. Out of the great Sargasso Sea of tone that has passed, would come the threatening dull beat of the great war-drum on the terraces of the war-god's temple in Mexico City, the drum-beat that filled the hearts of the Spanish soldiers with terror. Their string instruments were few in number, but the Aztecs had almost taught their drums to sing! And the sound of sea-shell horns, of flutes of bone and terra-cotta, the rhythm of stone-filled gourds, would mingle with the echo of silver bells. Did not an old writer say: "They are a folk of dancers, priests and children, who would rather hold silver bells in their hands than swords!" When Montezuma went to Cortez' camp did not his minstrels march before him, flinging up into the air and catching again in copper basins their sounding silver balls? Each ball sounded a different note. One sang tenor and another bass, and with them the juggler-musicians played a melody. And the Spaniards laughed, for the tune was just like one that the farmers back in old Castile sang when they spread the manure over the fields! But the echo of silver bells and of conch-shells, of drums and temple choruses fades, and we hear a flute, a single flute that sings a love-song as sweet as any our fancy had imagined.

We are in Peru, on an Andean hillside, with the giant condor floating above us—but Peru in our own day. There the Quichoa shepherd, the descendant of the Incas, still breathes his heart's longing for some village maid into the *huayre-puhura,* the flute of his ancestors, while his shaggy llamas browse about him. But other melodies of romance come sounding up from the "pool of forgetfulness". In the taverns of port towns of the Spanish Main drunken Buccaneer choruses, racy with the vileness of pirate lusts, mingle with the Latin chant of Indian converts in the California missions. The secret Voodoo songs of maddened blacks in Domingan and Haitian jungles cross the love-ditties of old Spain, sung to the guitar under casement windows in Saint Augustine. And, as we move north, everywhere there sounds the chant of the Red Man—the great religious dance choruses, love-songs, war-songs, planting-songs, and the *war-whoop,* the song that compresses laughter, triumph, and the glory of the taken scalp into one shrill note. There are folk-songs from the countryside of Old France in New France; they float down the Mississippi to New Orleans from Quebec. Dutch burghers in New Amsterdam sing "Wilhelmus of Nassau", and the New England Puritans drawl psalms through their noses in Salem and Boston. And while the trappers and woodsmen chorus their rude ballads, the songs like "Sally in Our Alley" that have come from London with the spinets and harpsichords that white fingers play, are raised by fresh girlish voices in the homes of the Colonial gentry.

With the War of Independence our land is filled with the tattoo of the snare-drum and the shrill voice of the fife. When Lord Percy's British soldiers marched to Lexington they played the British regimental band tune to which they had made up words to jeer the patriots and their cause. But when Lord Cornwallis surrendered at Yorktown, and the British bands played "The World Turned Upside Down", our bands retorted with "Yankee Doodle", which we had made our own. With the playing of that national air we pass from the *stagnum oblivionis,* "the pool of forgetfulness", of the romantic music of the past. For the birth of American Independence marks the beginning of an American music that lives to the present day.

From the time of Francis Hopkinson (1737-1784), the *first American composer,* who wrote "My days have been so wondrous free", and James Lyon (1735-1794), the father of the American hymn-writing, to the Civil War, music spreads out in the United States in a hundred different ways. We develop a "folk-song" of our own. You can make up a program to-day, if you wish, that takes in all the romantic songs which one of America's *most romantic historical periods* has produced. The negro slaves brought from Africa turned their old tribal tunes into "plantation spirituals" in the cotton and rice fields of the South; and so fine are they, musically, that they are everywhere sung in concert to-day. Many a gem of folk-song was born of the hard toil and wild carousings of the Mississippi boatmen and French *voyageurs.* In the Appalachians the mountaineers preserved, while changing, the old English ballads that had come over with their forefathers, and these, too, we sing to-day. The Creole songs of New Orleans, with their mixture of French melody and negro rhythm, the old Spanish love romances of *hacienda* days in California, even the ballads of the "Gold Rush" of 1849, have come down to us.

New Orleans had opera as early as 1791, and "The Beggar's Opera" was given in New York in 1750. And music took on a fresh impetus when many German musicians, driven out of their country by the German Revolution of 1848, came to the United States. And then comes another colorful period in our musical history. The "big towns", New York, Boston, Philadelphia, New Orleans, were alive with music during the golden *ante-bellum* (before the war) days. In the North, Barnum, the first great American "advertiser", coined gold with Jenny Lind as well as with Jumbo. There were local choral societies and visiting ones; light-opera and "serious" opera companies came from abroad, and gave "seasons" of opera. In New Orleans the wealthy Southern planters flocked to the city with wives and daughters during the winter opera season. Three times a week, after the French or Italian *prima donna* had taken her last curtain-call and, her arms filled with flowers, had bowed with bobbing crinoline, the great swinging dance-floor was let down over the opera-house parquet, and the ball began—after all gentlemen taking part had been carefully "searched" and any pistols concealed about their persons had been removed! And, both in the North and in the South, the *negro minstrels* were in their glory. Tyrolean "yodlers", Swiss bell-ringers, German dance orchestras could not compete with the genuine American minstrels, whose sentimental and humorous ballads, written by white composers, moved the American heart to tears and laughter.

Stephen Collins Foster (1826-1864), who in the loveliest melodies of this kind created purely American folk-songs, put into them all the sadness, tenderness, and longing of an unhappy and wretched life, its latter years clouded with alcoholic dissipation in a cheap lodging-house, and ending in the free ward of a hospital. We now have other American folk-songs. David W. Guion gives us "Turkey in the Straw", "Sheep and Goat", piano; we have cowboy songs and songs of the Western Indians, idealized, as in Charles Wakefield Cadman's "The Land of the Sky-Blue Waters" and other melodies of the kind, or ruggedly presented, as in Arthur Farwell's piano pieces, "American Indian Melodies", "Pawnee Horses", etc. Masters of orchestral writing have given us the glow and swing of the negro dances of old New Orleans: Henry Gilbert ("American Dances", "Negro Rhapsody", "The Dance in Place Congo"); Dvorak ("New World Symphony") and the soul of the Red Man like Edward MacDowell ("Indian Suite"). The Puritan spirit of old New England is voiced in Edgar Stillman Kelly's "New England Symphony", and for violin and piano we have works like John Powell's "Sonata Virginiaesque" and his piano suite "In the South", which calls up in tone the romance of the South before the Civil War. Coleridge-Taylor and Frederick Burton wrote noble "Hiawatha" cantatas, giving a musical soul to Longfellow's poem. Nor has the "life-rhythm" of the day been forgotten in art-music. John Alden Carpenter of Chicago, has lifted "jazz rhythms" and harmonies to the art plane of his "Krazy-Kat" pantomime music.

As regards "jazz" in art music, there is a kind of "double standard" of taste. If you do *not* care for "jazz", and disapprove of it, you can say that it is a "move back to the jungle", musically speaking, and that we are "dropping to the level of the savage". If it gives you a pleasant tingle, you can always advance the argument that it is "a legitimate expression of the American musical 'soul'", and that it is "interesting" because it stands for the shaping up and expression in music of the *hurry* and *restlessness* and *"surface emotion"* of American city life. You can also add that prominent composers, Debussy, Stravinsky and Milhaud, have written pieces in the "jazz" style.

Since the Civil War the course of American music has been one of steady, consistent development in every field of the art. A steady consistent development and advance, however, is not romantic—except with regard to its *fruits*. And it is in the beautiful tonal fruit of individual American musical inspiration, that we must look for the romance the dingy bark of the tree of knowledge does not suggest. If we do so we will be rewarded. Our garden of music is rich in rare flowers of beautiful melody, flowers as fresh and fragrant as any grown in the hot-houses of French, German or Italian art. All we need do to enjoy the romance of American music in the truest and deepest sense of the word, is to explore our own national garden of music and melody. For it, as well as for the Yellowstone National Park the motto "See America First!" holds good. We will find no music (quite aside from "absolute" music) more romantic than that which the glowing fancy of American composers has called back in new handlings of beauty, in folk-song themes, from the *stagnum oblivionis,* "the pool of forgetfulness", of our historic past.

In the echoes of Zuni cliff-dweller airs, Creole folk-tune from Louisiana, Negro spirituals whose melodies may have served as hymns for some crawling serpent-god of African jungles before plantation slaves "converted" them to the worship of the Most High and a hundred and one others dwell all the romance the heart could wish.

THE ROMANCE OF OPERA

AN OUTLINE OF OPERA

(Introduction)

WHAT IS OPERA?

An opera is a musical drama. It is a dramatic work in one or more acts, in which *music* plays the chief part. It is a drama set to music in such a way that its music and drama might be compared to Siamese twins, so closely are they linked and so dependent is one on the other. In the Middle Ages we have forms of near-opera. First there are the *Mystery Plays* or *Mysteries* given in the fields or town market-places. The Mysteries were stories from the Bible—the Creation, the Flood, the Last Judgment, the life of Christ from the Birth to the Resurrection—acted and accompanied by music. In the thirteenth century came the *Miracle Plays,* dramas of the lives of the saints, but often introducing romantic, heroic and magic incidents anything but religious, and turning to Greek mythology instead of the saints' lives for subjects. The *Mysteries* and *Miracles* at last grew decidedly "profane", and the Church began to disapprove of the wandering "companies", whose stages—they were divided often into three "sections", showing heaven, earth and hell—were dragged from place to place on wheels. With the Reformation the *Moralities* or *Morality Plays* came in ("Everyman" is one which has been successfully revived in our day), and the Mystery and Miracle Plays disappeared. The *Morality* turned vices and virtues into persons (actors) and showed their struggles together on the stage. Plays disappeared. One of the most famous examples of the Morality *Idea,* though it is not a Morality Play, is John Bunyan's "Pilgrim's Progress". In the sixteenth century people began to realize—though the "street plays" were popular—that a drama, instead of being part music, could be musical *throughout,* and this discovery led to the development of the *ballet* on one hand, and of *opera* on the other.

EARLY OPERA

The Renaissance brought the first operas, "dramas for music" as they were called. The first opera, *Dafne* (1549), by Peri, was followed by others, among them Monteverdi's *Orfeo* (1607), and in 1637 *the first opera house* was opened in *Venice*. Opera at once spread from Italy to France and Germany. In France *Lully* and *Rameau* (1683-1764), in Germany *Schutz* and *Keiser* (1674-1739) are the great names; while in Italy itself *Alessandro Scarlatti* (1659-1725), and the German *Handel* (who wrote in the Italian style, and most of whose operas were produced in England) stand out. But none of these earlier operas are operas as we understand the word. They stand in somewhat the same relation to modern operas that the model for the first steam engine does to a modern railroad Mogul, the most complete and developed type of railroad engine. Mostly they were cut and dried "pattern" successions of solo songs, duets, trios and choruses, only meant to show off the vocal brilliancy of the individual singers, and with hardly any dramatic action to give them interest.

THE MODERN OPERA

The first "modern" operas—that is operas in which *dramatic action* and *poetry* have their rightful part in the musical whole, are those composed by *Gluck* (1714-1787). He turned the *undramatic* Italian "serious opera" (*opera seria*) into a real "dramatic opera"; while *Mozart* (1756-1791), turned the lighter form of the Italian opera, the *opera buffa,* "comic opera", into what Rossini called "joyous drama", instead of the inferior Italian type. Later *Rossini* (1792-1868), developed a newer and finer type of Italian *opera buffa,* while *Bellini* and *Donizetti* wrote in the *sentimental* opera style Rossini also cultivated. In France the *opera buffa* shaped up as the *opera comique* ("comic opera" in a special French form of comic opera), with *Boieldieu* (1775-1834) and *Auber* (1782-1871) as its most important composers. Meanwhile *Carl Maria von Weber* (1786-1826) and others developed a German opera kind, the "German romantic opera"; *Meyerbeer* (1791-1864) with *Spontini, Rossini, Halévy* and others created the French "grand historical opera"; and finally *Wagner* (1813-1883), created an *absolutely new operatic form,* which has been used by composers of all nations since his time, the "music drama", in which the orchestra is the main explainer of the musical action, and the individual characters are "identified" and associated with certain melodies (leading themes). The great Italian *Verdi* passed from the style of Rossini to one that approaches the Wagner music drama in his last works.

MODERN OPERA SINCE WAGNER

Modern Opera *since* Wagner reflects any number of different individual ideas and ideas of "schools" or groups of composers who follow certain fixed ideals. The leading *trends*—that is "directions"—followed in modern opera since Wagner are:

Eclecticism. In opera this means that the composer, to express his own original thoughts borrows *ways* and *means* of expression, rhythms, tone-combinations, etc., already existing to use in his own work. There have been great "eclectic" composers: Tchaikovsky, Goldmark, and others who have produced works finely original, using *already established* modes of expression.

Verism. ("Actuality"). The "veristic" opera is always very "theatrical". The dramatic action in it takes first place. Usually it deals with the most terrible passions, brutal loves, murders and crimes among criminals or the scum of humanity. It aims to show life in the raw and usually succeeds. *Verdi* was the first great *verist*. Among many who have followed in his footsteps and made the verist opera the tingling, exciting thing it is in music and action, *Mascagni, Leoncavallo* and *Puccini* stand out among the Italians; *d'Albert* among the Germans, and *Bruneau* among the French.

Nationalism. "National" operas, generally speaking, are those in which the composer has built up his music on the "folk-tune" *themes,* or written in the folk-tune style of some particular country or people. There are many beautiful operas of this kind, written by composers of every land.

Romantic Naturalism. In opera this is an attempt to give "real life" characters and stories a romantic, sentimental treatment, instead of a *brutal natural* one like the verists. *Charpentier's* "Louise" is an opera of this kind.

Impressionism. The "impressionistic" opera is the type of opera created by *Claude Debussy,* a great French composer. They are not brutal. They reproduce "impressions" in music. They have no big sentimental themes, no clear outlines in their music. Vague "color", beautiful *tone,* handled in a delicate and over-refined way is their main feature. The subjects of the "impressionistic" operas are usually "ideal", unreal and symbolic, they do not show life as it is but carry us in music and story to blue lands of dreamy revery.

Symphonic Opera. *Richard Strauss* is the chief composer of this kind of modern opera. He goes further than Wagner in making the orchestra important and turns an opera into a "symphonic poem" with vocal accompaniment. Among his operas are some of the most *effective* ones known.

Expressionism. The "expressionist" opera is chiefly represented by the German composer *Franz Schreker* and his followers. It is a "symbolic" form of opera—that is, *other meanings* underlie the stage action—and rich in color, and "sense-music", it combines the strongest kind of sex-interest (often morbid and unhealthy) with the most fantastic fairytale imaginings in story and music: the modern and the ancient.

Internationalism. Uses a new "world language" in opera, of short, abrupt motives, complex rhythms and endless repetition and is represented by men like *Stravinsky* (Russ.), *Béla Bartok* (Hung.) and modern Italian, German and French composers.

Besides these main *trends* are others which have not as yet become firmly established but which show that composers are always groping for *new ways* and *means* of expressing their thoughts and emotions. As regards *modern opera* in general, since Wagner it might be said, however, that modern opera is more a creation of the *intellect,* while older opera is more a creation of the *heart.*

I

THE TALES OF THE GREAT ITALIAN OPERAS

AÏDA

It. grand romantic opera, 4 acts, by Giuseppe Verdi. Text by Ghislanzoni. Written and performed for the opening of the Suez Canal (Nov. 1869), it is rich in sensuous melodies, in which real Egyptian tunes have been introduced, and its most celebrated air is the love-song *Celeste Aïda* ("Divine Aida").

Aïda, Pharaoh's slave, though an enemy king's daughter, returns the love of Radames, an Egyptian general. But—Pharaoh's daughter Amneris (Act II) has designs on Radames' heart. When he returns from a campaign with Aïda's father Amonasro, the Ethiop king, among his prisoners, Amneris, a rapid worker, has already arranged to marry him. Radames, preferring exile to Amneris' love, is about to flee with Aïda and her father (Act III) when he is caught. Tried for treason he is condemned to death. Led to a living tomb below the temple by the priests, who lay the stone in place, he finds Aïda there. She has come to die with him, and their death song mingles with the sobs of the repentant Amneris, who mourns above the victims wedded to death below.

AMORE DEI TRE RE

(The Love of Three Kings)

It. tragic opera, 3 acts, by Italo Montemezzi. Text by Sem Benelli. Milan, 1913. Very beautiful modern music illustrates a tragic romance of Medieval Italy.

Blind old King Archibaldo, walking his castle battlements, hears Fiora, his son Manfredos' compelled bride, talking to some one. Manfredo, eager to clasp Fiora to his heart returns to the castle, but

THE ROMANCE OF OPERA

the old father's suspicions that Fiora has a lover, weigh his soul. Fiora waves her scarf in farewell (Act II) as Manfredo again leaves. Again the blind king surprises her. Avito, an old lover, is kissing the hem of her robe. He escapes and Fiora refuses to give his name. Then Archibaldo, to avenge his son's honor, strangles her. Manfredo returning is broken-hearted and shrinks from his father's remorse. In the castle chapel (Act III) Fiori lies on her bier while candles burn. Avito comes in and covers her dead lips with burning kisses—only to fall dying: the old king had set a trap and smeared them with poison! Then—when Manfredo enters, and dying Avito forbids him to touch Fiora's lips, he draws death from them in turn. The old king coming in learns with Manfredo's dying breath, that he has slain his innocent son as well as guilty Avito.

BALLO IN MASCHERA
(The Masked Ball)

It. lyric drama, 3 acts, by Giuseppi Verdi. Text by Piave, Rome, 1859. Scribe wrote the original story, to which the French composer Auber set his *Le Bal Masque*. A historical opera, it showed a Swedish king murdered on the stage. In Naples, the government thought it dangerous to see a king so treated, and Verdi's opera was forbidden. In order to get it performed he changed his king to a Governor of Boston, and met no further objection.

In a seventeenth century Boston that never was, Count Richard, the governor loves (not wisely, but too well) his friend Rene's wife. A negro witch, Ulrica, bids Amelia (the wife) pluck a posy from a gallow's-bird's grave at midnight. It will cure her of her budding love for Richard. Richard (Act II) meeting her in the graveyard is attacked by conspirators. But Rene turns up and Richard begs the husband to see his own veiled companion home. The veil is torn off by the conspirators and (Act III) Rene sharpens the dagger of vengeance for his former friend. At the Governor's ball in the Mansion House, Rene runs Richard through with his dagger. But Richard —he already had conquered his ignoble passion—tells him his wife is innocent and dies with a blessing for Massachusetts and his murderer on his lips.

IL BARBIERE DI SIVIGLIO
(The Barber of Seville)

It. comic opera, 2 acts, by Giacomo Rossini. Rome, 1816. Written in two weeks, after a French comedy by Beaumarchais, full of merry melodies and brilliant *coloratura* (passage-work, high note and trill) songs, this opera is still a universal favorite.

Old Doctor Bartolo wants to marry his pretty ward, Rosina. But Count Almaviva already has won her heart as untitled Lindoro. With the help of the cunning barber Figaro he enters the Doctor's house disguised as a soldier, and begins to make love, only to be put out when the old man returns. Again, getting in as a music-teacher (Act II) with the barber's aid, he turns the music lesson into a love-lesson. This time he succeeds in arranging an elopement. But when Bartolo stops it, the lover bribes the notary and signs the wedding contract as the bridegroom, while Bartolo's name appears only as a witness. Weary of trying to stop the course of true love from running smooth, the old Doctor contents himself with Rosina's dowry, and dismisses the lovers with his blessing.

Another famous comic opera by Rossini is *L'Italiana in Algeri* ("The Italian Girl in Algiers") which turns on the amusing adventures of an Italian maid in the Bey of Algiers' harem.

LA BOHÈME

It. tragic opera, 4 acts, by Giacomo Puccini. Text by Giacosa and Illica. Turin, 1896. To sweet and tuneful music the story of Murger's novel of Bohemian life in Paris (the Latin Quarter, 1830), has made this one of Puccini's most popular scores.

Into the bare attic studio which Marcel (artist), Rudolph (poet), Colline (philosopher), and Schaunard (musician) share, the last-named comes with money, real money! It means warmth, food, wine to the starved Bohemians. All save Rudolph hurry off to buy. Enter Mimi, the pretty, consumptive flower-girl who rooms below. Rudolph gives her the candle she came to borrow, but as they stand on the landing before her door both the candles go out . . . they find they love each other, and soon hurry to the Momus Café. It is the first step in one of those idyllic unlegalized unions of carefree Parisian student life. On (Act II) a café scene, follows a meeting (Act III) between Mimi and Rudolph in which they "make up" after a quarrel. In Act IV, as poor students have no money, Mimi and Musetta have wandered off to wealthier admirers. Unable to work because of their memories of their loves, the two lonely Bohemians are talking over old times when in rushes Musetta. Mimi, starving and dying of consumption is below. Flying down the stairs, Rudolph tenderly carries her up and lays her on his bed. They never shall part again he tells her, better to live on stale bread and herring together, than to be parted and suffer. Soothed, Mimi falls asleep, but when Rudolph returns to her side with medicine—she had died!

With a cry of agony he falls across her lifeless body. Their pitiful romance is over!

Leoncavallo's less popular *La Bohème* (Milan, 1897) begins (Act I) with a gay scene in the Café Momus, and shows Musetta being dispossessed and her furniture seized (Act II) when her lover Marcel has left her, while she joyously entertains Bohemian friends in the courtyard. In Act III Marcel and Rudolph turn Musetta and Mimi out of their garret, though Mimi has left rich Count Paul to return to her starving lover. In the last act, Mimi returns to die, and while Musetta runs out and pawns her jewels to buy fuel, poor Mimi expires in Rudolph's arms as the Christmas bells chime.

CAVALLERIA RUSTICANA

(Rustic Chivalry)

It. ("Veristic") opera, 1 act, by Pietro Mascagni. Text after a Verga story, by Targioni-Tozzetti and Menasci. Rome, 1890. The best-known of "veristic" operas, which tell in text and tone, brutal or bloody stories of wild passions, usually among the lowest classes of humanity.

Lola was willing to let Turiddu, a peasant lad, love her. But when he left to serve his time in the army, she married the rich carter Alfio. Turiddu, coming back, tries to console himself with Santuzza, a nice girl who truly loves him, and whom he promises to marry. But Lola is a flirt, and a successful one. Turiddu promises to come to her house, and when poor, jealous Santuzza begs him before the church door not to forsake and dishonor her, he brutally flings her aside. Santuzza tells Alfio that his wife is meet Turiddu. In the village tavern after mass, Alfio bites Turiddu's ear—the Sicilian challenge to mortal combat! Turiddu (sorry, too late, that he took up again with Lola) bids his mother farewell, asks her to look after Santuzza, and goes to his death. When the peasants swarm back to break the news, the curtain falls on Santuzza's swoon.

Mascagni's less important operas include: *L'Amico Fritz*, a tale of Alsatian village loves with a happy ending; *Iris*, a Japanese tragedy in which a poor young girl, betrayed into a house of ill-fame meets a cruel death by dropping into a sewer; *Isabeau*, a fantastic version of the story of Lady Godiva riding unclothed through the town of Coventry; *Lodoletta*, in which a Parisian painter wins a village girl's heart to cast it aside, but repents, his lips pressed to the little red shoe she has worn out wandering to

Don Carlos

It. Tragic opera, 4 acts, by Giuseppe Verdi. Text by Mery and Camilla du Locle. Paris 1867. Historic truth, as in most operas, has not been strictly observed in this work, but the great Russian basso, Chaliapine, has made the tragic rôle of gloomy King Philip II of Spain famous in its American revivals, and it contains much fine music.

Don Carlos, heir to the Spanish throne, loves his step-mother Elizabeth with a sinful passion. While he goes to Flanders, his suspicious father, King Philip instructs Posa to watch his wife. Back in Madrid (Act II) Carlos at the fête in the palace gardens mistakes the Princess of Eboli for his step-mother. Through her the prince's guilty secret is disclosed. Carlos, he had defended heretics at an *auto-da-fe*, or burning, is turned over to the Grand Inquisitor; but Elizabeth (Act III), accused of infidelity, is cleared by the penitent Princess of Eboli. In prison Posa, visiting Carlos, is shot by one of the royal guard, while Carlos turns from his father, who then comes to see him, with loathing. Elizabeth (Act IV) had promised Posa to watch over Carlos. But when they met in St. Just Convent, King Philip, who surprises them, feels sure they have met for no good purpose. So Carlos is sent to his death.

DON GIOVANNI

It. Opera in 2 acts, by Wolfgang Amadeus Mozart. Text by da Pontel (Prague, 1787). This work, as well as *Le Nozze di Figaro*, though by a German composer, was written in Italian, the language preferred by the Viennese Court. No other operatic handling of the subject has ever achieved the popularity of Mozart's score. *Don Giovanni* is one of the most famous operas of all times, climaxing in an unscrupulous libertine's being dragged down to hell by demons. It is rich in beautiful solos, duets and trios, among which the duet "Your Hand in Mine, My Dearest", Don Giovanni's famous serenade, "Appear Love, at Thy Window", and the aria, "Fly Then, My Love" might be mentioned, as also the instrumental "Minuet".

After 2,065 love affairs, Don Juan (Don Giovanni), a Spanish nobleman, tries to seduce Anna, daughter of the commandant of Seville. Her cries bring her father to the scene, but Don Juan kills him with his rapier, and escapes. At an inn on the outskirts of Seville, he meets a former sweetheart, Elvira. She scolds him for his desertion, but Don Juan, leaves his lackey, Leporello, to tell her the story of his master's many loves, and Elvira, broken-hearted, plans revenge. She meets him at a peasant wedding, where Don Juan tries to add Zerlina, the bride, to his string of conquests. Anna and her sweetheart Octavio, masked, and also bent on revenge, are at the wedding. The cries of outraged Zerlina make them rush to kill the libertine, but using his sword, he again makes good his escape. Hearing that Elvira has retained Zerlina as her maid, her former lover serenades his one-time sweetheart, and when she appears, he has his lackey muffle and take her away, while he sings to Zerlina. When set upon by Masetto, the bridegroom, he passes himself off as Leporello. Then he helps them to capture his lackey in the belief that the latter is Don Juan. With his usual good fortune, Don Juan finds himself free again. But now he sees the statue of Anna's father, which speaks to him. Undismayed, Don Juan defiantly invites the statue to a banquet—and the marble statue of the man he has wronged appears and strikes terror to the hearts of the guests. Don Juan, gripped by hands of marble in the dimly lit hall, meets the reward of a misspent life at last, and is dragged by demons to the infernal regions in a burst of flames.

The Stone Guest (1872) by the Russian composer Dargomjsky, in which a sinister progression announces the statue's entrance, is undramatic, though musically fine, and has never been very popular in Russia itself. Nor has the modern German composer Paul Graner's *Don Juans Letztes Abendteuer* "Don Juan's Last Adventure" (1914), been able to compete with Mozart's in popular favor.

DON PASQUALE

It. Comic opera, 3 acts, by Gaetano Donizetti. Text by Gammerano. One of the best of Italian comic operas, with many charming airs to recommend it.

A rich old bachelor, Don Pasquale, cannot make his nephew Ernesto marry as he wants. Huffed, he decides to punish him by marrying himself. Norina, a pretty widow is induced by Malatesta (Pasquale's doctor), to pass herself off as an innocent girl, to captivate and marry the old man. After a mock marriage lets her lay hands on his money her extravagance (according to the plot laid between the doctor and herself) drives poor Pasquale mad. A series of amusing incidents finally leads to the discovery that Norina and Sophronia (the girl Ernesto loves) are one and the same, and the mock marriage confessed to, Don Pasquale gives the reunited lovers his blessing.

L'ELISIR D'AMORE

(The Elixir of Love)

It. comic opera, 2 acts, by Gaetano Donizetti. Text by Romani. Milan, 1832. The graceful romance in Act II, *Una Furtiva lagrima* ("A furtive tear") is one of the most popular songs in all opera.

Nemorino, a poor farmer boy, loves Adina, a rich farmer's daughter, and she smiles on him until—Belcore, a dashing sergeant, courts her. Poor Nemorino now buys an "Elixir of Love" from a quack. But the supposed love potion is Bordeaux wine. It goes to the poor boy's head, Adina sees him intoxicated, and is so shocked that she promises to marry Belcore the next day. Nemorino buys more wine, grows more intoxicated, and enlists under Belcore in despair. But at the wedding feast Adina has a change of heart (Act II), and balks at signing the marriage contract. Meanwhile the rumor spreads that Nemorino's wealthy uncle has died leaving him his heir. At once all the village girls make up to him. And now Adina knows she cannot bear to give him up. The kindly quack explains that Nemorino was not to blame for his fall from grace. She forgives him, and they are about to be married, when Belcore insists that Nemorino must march with the soldiers. But Adina buys his release, and the former lovers are wedded amid the rejoicing of all.

FALSTAFF

It. lyric comedy, 3 acts, by Guiseppe Verdi. Text by Arrigo Boito. Milan, 1893. Falstaff's air, "When I Was a Page", and the "Fairy Music" in the last act are among the best numbers of this fine score, whose story is that of Shakespeare's "Merry Wives of Windsor".

The fat knight Falstaff (Act I) sends his servant to Mrs. Alica Ford and Mrs. Meg Page with love-letters. Insulted (Act II), they plan revenge. Falstaff is lured to the Ford house and there, when Ford's arrival (he is in the plot) is announced, forced to hide under the dirty linen in the big wash-basket. Basket, wash and Falstaff finally are pushed out of the window into the muddy canal below. Falstaff, uncured of flirting, keeps a midnight appointment in Windsor Forest (Act III) but is unmercifully beaten up there by his tormentors, disguised as fairies, imps, flies, wasps and mosquitos. At the end he is let off, promising betterment, and Ford's daughter, who has managed to pair off with her true love in the confusion, instead of the old man of her father's choice, compels a reluctant paternal blessing.

LA FAVORITA

(The King's Favorite)

It. tragic opera, 4 acts, by Gaetano Donizetti. Text by Royer and Waetz. Paris, 1804. The favorite song in this opera, which has some wonderfully touching melodies, is "spirto gentie" (gentle spirit") for tenor.

Fernando, a novice in St. James' Monastery (Castile) cannot fix his mind on his religious duties, for a vision of a beautiful girl disturbs his prayers. So his prior, to whom he confesses, releases him from his vows. Accident leads him (blindfold) to the Island of St. Leon. Here in an entrancing villa lives Leonora, the king's "favorite". A pure love develops between Fernando and Leonora, who hides her shame from him. At last she sends him off with an army commission to win glory, and he plans to claim her hand on his return. In the palace gardens (Act II) the king receives Fernando, who has won the war against the Moors almost singlehanded, while the king has lost his mistress, for a message from the pope declares he must give up Leonora. Unsuspecting Fernando, asked to name his reward, (Act III) begs for Leonora's hand in marriage, and the courtiers snigger as they wed. When his late prior, horrified, explains what Leonora was to the monarch, Fernando curses the king, and leaving Leonora in a swoon, rushes back to the cloister. There, as he is musing on his dead love, Leonora enters in a monk's cowl. When she tells him she had disclosed her shame in a message he never got, he forgives her. But as he plans to fly with her, and babbles gaily of long years of happiness, Leonora dies in his arms with a prayer of thanksgiving on her lips!

LA FIGLIA DEL REGGIMENTO

(The Daughter of the Regiment)

It. comic opera, 2 acts, by Gaetano Donizetti. Text by St. Georges and Bayard, Paris, 1840. Graceful airs and attractive military music mark this score.

The Marchioness Maggiorivoglio and her majordomo have dropped by mistake into a skirmish in the hills. Up come the grenadiers, and Marie, "The Daughter of the Regiment", a pretty sutler girl, waif of the battlefield, where old Sergeant Sulpice found her eighteen years before. Tonio, dragged up as a spy, turns out to have saved Marie's life, and enlists as a soldier for love of her. But—a scrap of paper proves that Marie is the marchioness' child and with a tearful farewell, she leaves the regiment for her new-found mother.

A year later, however, (Act II), the dear old regiment—Tonio is an officer now, of course—returns in the nick of time to Maggiorivoglio Castle to prevent Marie's making an unloved marriage. The aristocrats gathered to celebrate her wedding with a duchess's son scornfully depart, and blue-blooded girl and red-blooded soldier are happily united amid the cheers of the brave grenadiers.

FRANCESCA DA RIMINI

It. tragic opera, 4 acts, by Riccardo Zandonai. Text after D' Ammorzio's drama. Turin 1914. One of numerous operatic settings of a famous love tragedy originally told by Dante. It contains some effective musical scenes and numbers.

Lovely Francesca's brothers, in their castle of Ravenna, plan to marry her to Gianciotto Malatesta of Rimini, an evil cripple, whose handsome brother Paolo is sent to Ravenna as *Gianciotto*, to wed her in his name. Francesca loves Paolo at first sight and gives him a rose. Hating him when she finds herself married to his evil brother (Act II) when after she first comes to her husband's castle of Rimini, she ends by loving him again. Paolo, too, has felt the passion-flame, and (Act III) returns from Florence (whither he had gone) to read the story of the loves of Queen Guinevere and Lancelot with his brother's wife and—to kiss her as they kissed! But a third brother, one-eyed Malatestino, also yearns to possess Francesca and (Act IV), offers to poison her husband to win her favor. When she declines, his vengeful hints rouse Gianciotto's jealousy: the cripple plans to surprise the guilty pair. Finding them together in Francesca's room, the injured husband first mortally wounds Francesca—who flings herself upon his sword as he attacks Paolo—and then stabs his brother. He then breaks his sword—perhaps he thinks of three lives shattered—and envies the dead!

Zandonai's *Conchita* (Milan, 1911) is a violent "veristic" opera. In a Seville cigar-factory, Conchita invites Mateo, a wealthy stranger home, (he had rescued her from a policeman) but sends him off when she finds him giving her Mother money. But Mateo begs her (Act II) to give up earning a living dancing vulgar dances and come and live in a little house of his. At midnight, instead of letting him in, as agreed, she bars him out. When she seeks him out in his own home he beats her brutally. Then Conchita knows she loves him, though she first tries to stab him, and lets him take her in his arms.

LA FANCIULLA DEL OUEST

(The Girl of the Golden West)

It. romantic opera, 3 acts, by Giacomo Puccini. Text after David Belasco's play, founded on Bret Harte's story. New York, 1910.

In the bar-room of the Polka Saloon, in Cloudy Mountain mining camp, California, 1849, the sheriff, Rance, brags that Minnie, "the girl", an orphan who serves at the bar, will marry him on his say-so. Minnie disproves his words with a revolver. when Dick Johnson, of Sacramento (he really is Ramirez, a Mexican bandit, come to rob the saloon) enters, Minnie's heart goes out to him. He, too, loves her at sight, gives up his plan of robbery, and while the men of the camp are off hunting him as Ramirez, accepts the girl's invitation to visit her in her shack. There Minnie dresses prettily for her visitor (Act II) and when a sudden snowstorm blows up, says he may stay in her cabin. A shot rings out in the darkness. Nick, the bartender, Rance, Ashby, and other miners enter, but she has hidden Dick (whom they now know is Ramirez). The men gone, he confesses how he drifted naturally into his criminal life, but Minnie, unable to forgive his deceit, sends him off. Again shots are heard and when Minnie opens the door, Dick falls in, wounded. Hiding him in the loft the girl has almost now convinced Rance he is not in her cabin, when his blood dropping from the rafters on the floor, betrays him. Rance is a passionate gambler: Minnie offers to play him a game of draw-poker—if he wins, he gets both Dick and herself, if he loses she and Dick are free. Minnie cheats and wins, and Rance keeps his word and leaves. On the rim of the forest (Act IV) Dick, caught as he was escaping from the cabin, is about to be lynched when Minnie rushes up. When she pleads eloquently with the "boys", and begs them to spare him because she loves him, they are moved to pity. So they cut him lose, and he and the Girl of the Golden West start eastward together to begin life anew.

I GIOJELLI DELLA MADONNA

(The Jewels of the Madonna)

It. tragic "veristic" opera, 3 acts, by Ermanmo Wolf-Ferrari. Book by Zangarini and Golisciani. Berlin, 1911. A terrible tragedy which expresses the passions of the dregs of present-day Neapolitan popular life in highly dramatic music.

Gaily the people celebrate the Madonna's festival in Naples. Maliella, a "child of sin", reared by Carmela as a daughter to keep a vow, runs out into the street. She is sick of being pent up, she longs for life, gaiety and love, and follows the crowd. Meanwhile Gennaro, her foster-brother, an honest blacksmith, confesses to his mother that he loves her. But when he goes into the street he finds Maliella with Rafaele, the vile leader of the lowest criminals of the town, the Camorrists. Rafaele makes passionate love to Maliella while the Madonna's holy image sways past them and—Maliella, though Gennaro tells her what he is—likes it. She puts the flower Rafaele flings her between her lips. In the garden of her home Maliella, about to run away (Act II) tells superstitious Gennaro that she will stay and love him on one condition—he must rob the Madonna at the altar of her holy jewels and give them to her. He shudders but—Rafaele's serenade rings through the garden. Taking up his tools he goes, and returns with the jewels of the Mother of God! In a burst of physical and religious passion Maliella hangs the sacred necklace around her throat and yields herself to Gennaro. . . In the Camorrist's den (Act III) the scum of the city, male and female, make merry. A low orgy in which the depraved "Apache Dance" is danced climaxes when Maliella, rushing in, shows the stolen jewels of the Madonna. The criminals turn from her with superstitious horror, though Rafaele tries to murder Gennaro, who now comes in, but is prevented. One by one the Camorrists slink out, shuddering. And while Maliella flings herself into the sea, Gennaro, hanging the jewels about the Madonna's image on the wall, stabs himself just as the mob rushes in with pitchforks and clubs to slay him.

Wolf-Ferrari's other operas include: *Le Donne Curiose* ("The Inquisitive Woman") and *L'Amore Medico* (The Lover as Physician), jolly eighteenth century scores and "Susannah's Secret", a one-act opera, in which a husband whose wife is a secret cigarette-smoker, thinks she has a lover when he smells cigarette smoke in her boudoir, but finally discovers the truth.

LA GIOCONDA

It. tragic opera, 4 acts, by Amilcare Ponchielli. Text after Victor Hugo's tragedy "Angelo", by Gorrio. Milan, 1876. The aria "Cielo e mar" (Sky and sea) from this opera, was one of Caruso's most moving "hits".

Sailors, monks and masqueraders praise the Venetian government, in song, while Barnaba, a government spy, talks of folk who dance on their graves. He loves Gioconda, a blind singing girl, and when she repulses him, plans revenge. Gioconda loves Enzo, a Genoese nobleman, but heart-broken, discovers that her lover betrays her with Laura, wife of Alvise, a leader of the Inquisition. Just as Enzo and Laura are about to sail off at dawn in his ship (Act II) Gioconda climbs aboard. Only her feeling and recognizing the rosary Laura wears (the blind girl's mother gave it to her), prevents her from stabbing Alvise's wife. Instead she helps Laura escape before her husband comes, while Enzo sets fire to his ship to prevent its falling into Barnaba's hands. But Alvise learns the truth. He leaves his palace (Act III) after presenting faithless Laura with a cup of poison. When he returns he gives a grand ball (in which is danced the famous ballet called "The Dance of the Hours", where the bright hours of the day are slain in pantomime by the dark hours of the night, to beautiful music). When Enzo denounces him, he draws aside the curtain and shows him dead Laura. But Laura is not dead, only sleeping, for the noble blind girl has changed the poison cup for a sleeping potion. Still loving Enzo, Gioconda promises Barnaba to be his if he will set Enzo free. In a ruined palace by the sea (Act IV) Enzo embraces Laura, while Gioconda is about to commit suicide singing the great *Suicidio* Aria) when—Barnaba arrives. As he grasps her, and the poison falls to the ground, she stabs herself with her dagger, and thus escapes him. Barnaba's revenge is to shout into her dying ear that he has murdered her mother!

LUCIA DI LAMMERMOOR

It. tragic opera, 3 acts, by Gaetano Donizetti. Text after Scott's novel by Cammerano. Naples, 1835. Generally regarded as Donizetti's masterpiece, this opera contains the famous "Mad Scene" with flute obbligato, often sung in concert by coloratura sopranos, and one of the most brilliant songs of its kind.

In the park of Lammermoor Castle (1700 A.D.), Lord Henry Ashton, coaxing his sister Lucia to marry wealthy Lord Arthur Bucklaw, flies into a rage when he finds she loves his mortal enemy, Edgar of Ravenwood. Lucia, later meeting Edgar in the park, parts from him (he is off to France), both swearing to be true to each other. But her brother by means of a forged letter (Act II) makes her believe Edgar is untrue, and she promises to wed Lord Arthur. Just as she has signed the marriage contract in the castle hall, however, Edgar rushes in, and finding the contract signed, thinks Lucia false, and curses her. In the castle (Act III) all are merry, but shortly after bride and groom have retired, comes word that Lucia has killed her husband. Lucia, raving mad, now appears among the guests, and sings her famous "Mad Scene", falling back dying with the last note. When Edgar hears the castle bell toll the death chime, and learns it rings for Lucia, he kills himself in the churchyard, forgetting he is to fight a duel with his dead love's brother.

LUCREZIA BORGIA

It. tragic opera, 3 acts, by Gaetano Donizetti. Text by Romani, after Victor Hugo's drama. "Lucrezia Borgia" is *the poison* opera of the operatic repertory, and Lucrezia appears alternately as the piteous mother wearing her heart on her sleeve, and the pitiless murderess bearing the poison-cup in her hand. Her mother songs are very touching and fine.

Lucrezia leaves her husband's palace—he is Alfonzo, Duke of Ferrara—for Venice. There Gennaro, son of an early marriage, has been raised as a fisher boy, and her mother's heart longs for him. But when the other fisher lads whisper her name (the name is enough) and insult her, he shrinks from the beautiful stranger lady with loathing. Now Gennaro comes to Ferrara, and tears his unknown mother's coat-of-arms from the palace gates. When Lucrezia complains to the Duke he is sentenced to die. The mother, recognizing her son, pleads for him, but the Duke suspecting a love affair, himself puts Gennaro's poison-cup in her hand. Yet as mother and son walk to the door Lucrezia slips him an antidote and begs him to fly. But no—Gennaro must stay! He does not tell his mother it is to go to a great supper party at Prince Negroni's. At the party the revengeful woman has assembled all the fisher lads who had insulted her before her son in Venice, Lucrezia has prepared their wine for them in *her* style! But when she arrives to gloat over her victims, there sits Gennaro. He too, has drunk of the flowing bowl; he too is poisoned! In vain she offers an antidote. There is not enough for all, so the noble boy prefers to die with his friends. In vain she tells him she is his mother, he turns from her in horror and expires. The Duke, arriving, finds all in their last agonies, Lucrezia herself, poisoned by remorse, dying with the rest.

MADAME BUTTERFLY

It. musical tragedy, 3 acts, by Giacomo Puccini. Text after Long's novel and Belasco's play. Milan, 1904. A touching musical tale based on a strange Japanese custom, beautifully melodious and very popular, laid in the present day, with an American hero and a Japanese heroine.

Lieutenant Pinkerton, U.S.N., has taken a villa and wife in Nagasaki, Japan, the latter "Japanese fashion", that is, for the length of his stay in port, as the quaint Japanese custom is. Butterfly, however, his girl wife, takes her marriage seriously, renounces her gods for his God, and the curtain falls as he tenderly consoles her after he has driven off the cursing native priest. Three years later (Act II) in the same villa, Butterfly plays with her fair-haired baby son (he takes after his father). She awaits Pinkerton's return: he said he would come back when he left, and when the cannon sounds from the Navy ship in the harbor she waits for him through the night, though her maid and baby have fallen asleep. Still watching at dawn (Act III) Pinkerton arrived with—an American wife! Pinkerton would like to have his son and poor Butterfly, her heart broken, promises the boy in half an hour. Blindfolding her babe, she gives him an American flag to wave, then stabs herself with her father's sword, the words on whose blade bid its owner die with honor rather than live without. Dragging herself to her baby's side, she breathes her last sigh as Pinkerton returns.

MADAME SANS-GÊNE

(Madame Free-and-Easy)

It. opera in 4 acts, by Umberto Giordano. Text by Simoni, after Sardou's play. New York, 1915. Interesting because it probably is the only opera which presents Napoleon Bonaparte, *who could not sing*, on the opera stage, as a baritone. Stage action and music are dramatic and the "Marseillaise" is introduced in Act I.

Three historical figures, Fouché, Lefèbvre, and the poverty-stricken Napoleon Bonaparte, discuss the progress of the French Revolution in the cellar of the laundry of Catherine Huebscher (Madame Sans-Gêne). After they leave she hides a royalist there, despite the fact that Lefèbre returns to search for him. With Napoleon Emperor, Lefèbvre Duke of Dantzig and a general, and Fouché, head of the Imperial police, Catherine appears as the wife of the general, continually being rebuked at the instance of the Emperor for her lack of etiquette, and her outspoken tongue. Having seriously offended the Emperor's sisters she is summoned before Napoleon. But he, knowing her of old, appreciates her presentation of a still unpaid laundry bill to him, and readily pardons her behavior. He suspects the Austrian Count Niepperg of attempting a clandestine meeting with Marie Louise, the Empress, and orders him executed; but the intervention of Madame Sans-Gêne, who proves his wife's innocence, causes him to praise her for averting a tragedy.

MANON LESCAUT

It. tragic opera, 4 acts, by Giacomo Puccini. Text after Abbé

Prévost's famous novel, "Manon Lescaut". Turin, 1893. The whole opera, which has many a lovely page, is one long, sorrowful duet between the pathetic lovers.

We are in the easy-going eighteenth century. Lescaut—just arrived at the Amiens' Inn—is taking sister Manon to a convent, but is not disturbed when wealthy Geronte, a financier, plots to abduct her. But a younger admirer, Des Grieux, falls in love with her at sight, and before Geronte can prevent they are off together, Paris bound, in the financier's carriage. Alas, we soon find Manon (Act II) in *Geronte's* luxurious Paris mansion! Des Grieux was poor, and Manon liked pretty clothes. But brother Lescaut, when he finds Des Grieux has made money gambling, tells him where Manon flitted when she left his bare little love-nest. Des Grieux appears, she agrees (in a love-duet) to go back to him. But Geronte sends for the police and has her arrested for stealing—she had stopped to gather up the jewels he had given her! Manon in jail in the port of Havre as an "incorrigible" (Act III) is waiting to be shipped to Louisiana. Des Grieux (in vain he had tried to rescue her) grieves so as she is driven aboard that the captain lets him go along. Alas, in the New World, on a bare Louisiana plain, (Act IV), the lovely, wretched girl, worn by weary wandering, dies of exhaustion in her lover's arms as night falls, and Des Grieux faints with grief over her dead body.

The French composer Massenet's *Manon,* 5 acts, (Paris, 1884), is less popular than Puccini's. The lovers elope (Act I) as in the Italian version. But Des Grieux's father (Act II) while Manon arranges to flit to a wealthier love, has his boy seized, and (Act III) there is a fine Seminary Scene where Manon appears to beg him not to become a monk and he offers to marry her, is coaxed back to Paris. There Des Grieux and Manon are arrested (Act IV) in a Paris gambling house for cheating at cards, and on the road near Havre, (Act V) where Des Grieux appears to rescue her, she begs him to forgive her faithlessness and dies in his arms.

MEFISTOFILE

(Mephistopheles)

It. grand tragic opera, in a Prologue, 4 acts and Epilogue, by Arrigo Boito. Text by the composer after Goethe's "Faust", Milan, 1868. The opera "Mefistofile" is the Italian "Faust", telling the story in powerful, original music, and from a different angle than Gounod does.

In the Prologue the Devil makes a wager with God that he will cause Faust to commit all manner of sins and lose his soul. Faust, weary of knowledge, sits reading the Bible in his laboratory in Frankfort. Mephistopheles (the Devil) enters disguised as a friar, and seeing the holy book shrieks with horror. Faust strikes a bargain at his soul's expense, and both disappear in the air on the demon's cloak. At a witches' festival on the Brocken Mountain (Act II) Mephistopheles shows Faust a vision of lovely Marguerite in chains, for Faust's loves with the hapless girl have had terrible consequences. To Marguerite (Act III) in her prison, where she has been sent for the poisoning of her mother and murdering her nameless babe, appears Faust. He urges her to fly with him, but she shrinks from him and dies. Angel voices (off-stage) tell that heaven has received her soul. Faust, now taken to classic Greece by Mephistopheles, forgets his victim in making ardent love to fair Helen of Troy, "the world's desire", amid nature's charms. But in the Epilogue pleasure has turned stale: Faust mourns his past misdeeds. In vain Mephistopheles calls up voluptuous sirens; Faust turns to his Bible. And, as he prays for heavenly aid, angel voices tell him his soul is saved and Mephistopheles foiled!

Boito's *only* other opera, *Nerone* ("Nero") was given in Milan, in May, 1924, with 700 musicians and singers. Toscanini conducting, a performance for which the world of Art had been waiting for 50 years. Nero (Act I) buries the mother he has murdered at night to the sound of Christian voices singing their prayers. Simon Magus, a Christian wonder-worker, (Act II) tries to hold back Nero from his murderous designs on the Christians, who (Act III) are shown in a glorification of the Christain virtues, peace, love and sacrifice. In the last act the vestal virgin Eubria is slain, together with Simon Magus, for protecting the Christians; and the latter set fire to Rome as a grand climax. Seven thousand people camped all night before La Scala Opera House in order to see the first performance and the last top-tier box brought $1,250.

NORMA

It. tragic opera, 2 acts, by Vincenzo Bellini. Text by Romani. Milan, 1831. Every great dramatic soprano has sung the noble air Casta Diva ("Chaste goddess"), one of many fine melodies it contains.

In the Druid's grove Norma refuses to cut the mistletoe and declare war against Rome. Why? She has broken the virgin's vow of the Druid priestesses and secretly married Pollio, a Roman general.

Alas, in spite of two lovely children she has given him, the soldier's fickle heart has turned to another! Adalgisa, also a Druid priestess, is ready to abandon home and altar and fly with him to Rome. But —she first confesses to Norma, and the latter reviles her faithless husband, who comes in at this inopportune moment. Now abandoned Norma (Act II) is in despair. First she decides to slay her sleeping children. Then she decides to yield Pollio to Adalgisa, and burn to death on the funeral pyre. Adalgisa, touched, begs Pollio to return to Norma, but he refuses. Instead he tries to carry Adalgisa off, and Norma strikes the battle-shield, declaring war on Rome. Pollio is seized by Gaulish warriors. Now Norma (alone with Pollio) promises to save him if he will return to his family. But Pollio would rather die. Then Norma calls in priests and people, tells them a priestess has been false to her vows and denounces—herself! Now Pollio finds he loves Norma after all, enough to step on the funeral pyre with her. There both die happy in the flames, commending the children to their grandfather, Crovist.

Bellini's *I Puritani* (Paris, 1835) contains charming melodies, but the libretto is poor. A number of improbable incidents ends in the hero's winning the girl who lost her reason when she thought her lover had eloped with another, and regained it when she found he still loved her.

LE NOZZE DE FIGARO

It. *opera buffa,* comic opera, in 4 acts, by Wolfgang Amadeus Mozart. Text by da Ponte. Vienna, 1786. A charming Rococo comedy set to immortal music, but not the revolutionary comedy of the Frenchman Beaumarchais, on which it is founded, which was a cutting satire on the French nobility. Among a wealth of lovely melodies the great E flat "Figaro" aria, "Ah, open your eyes", might be mentioned.

Figaro the barber loves Susanna, who is maid to the Countess Rosina. Count Almaviva, though he thinks his wife charming, is at heart a gallant, and often flirts with Susanna. He also unjustly suspects his wife of favoring her page Cherubino, for the latter really is passionately in love with his mistress. Several times the Count almost finds them in a compromising situation, only to have it reflect on his own jealousy and, finally, Rosina and Susanna plan to outwit him, and expose his own easy gallantry. Exchanging costumes, they meet Figaro and the Count in the garden, where Almaviva waxes enthusiastic over his wife in the guise of her maid, and the real Susanna, being recognized by her lover, Figaro, is ardently wooed. At the Count's approach Susanna tricks him into thinking she is his

THE ROMANCE OF OPERA 403

wife, and then makes ardent love to Figaro. Almaviva suffers all the tortures of jealousy, until his wife exposes the deception. Then he turns penitent, is forgiven by his Countess and hastens to unite the lovers, Susanna and Figaro.

L'ORACOLO

(The Oracle)

It. tragic opera, 1 act, by Franco Leoni. Text by Zanoni, after Fernald's American drama "The Cat and the Cherub". London, 1905. An effective modern Italian score, its scene of action the Chinatown of San Francisco before the Great Fire, 1906. There is some attractive Chinese "temple-bell" music in the score.

Chim Fen, the Hatchet Row opium dealer, is refused the hand of Ah Yoe, Hoo Tsin, the wealthy merchant's daughter. But young San Luy wins Ah Yoe's smile when he serenades her from the street. On New Year's day the oracle threatens danger to Hoo Tsin's boy heir. Sure enough, vengeful Chim Fen kidnaps Hoo Tsin's little son, hides him in his cellar, and then visiting the unhappy father, promises to find the child if—he gets Ah Yoe's hand. San Luy makes the same offer, and traces the child to the opium dealer's cellar. There Chim Fen kills him in a struggle. While poor Ah Yoe mourns her dead lover, his father avenges his son by killing Chim Fen, while rescuing the baby. Then, when an American policeman comes along, to avoid discovery—though from a Chinese standpoint he had only done justice!—he props up the corpse on the sidewalk. Since the two Mongols seem to be having a pleasant chat, the bluecoat is deceived and passes on.

OTHELLO

It. tragic opera, 4 acts, by Giuseppe Verdi. Text by Boito. Milan, 1887. Written in Verdi's 73d year, after Shakespeare's original, it is one of the finest dramatic scores ever produced, and Iago's "Credo" is one of its most dramatic numbers.

Othello lands after victories over the Turks in Famagosta, Cyprus' capital cheered by the people. Soon Iago, his lieutentant jealous of his comrade Cassio, makes him drunk and Othello, finding Cassio drawing a sword on a brother officer, reduces him to the ranks. After a love scene with Desdemona they enter the castle. Here Iago (Act II), gets innocent Desdemona to plead Cassino's cause, first having told Othello that Cassio has a love-token, a handkerchief Desdemona gave him. Jealous Othello swears to be avenged. After Desdemona's plea in the castle hall has confirmed his suspicions (Act III), Iago tells his chief he has heard Cassio murmur her name in his dreams.

Other devilish tricks of Iago's end in Othello's flinging Desdemona to the ground, whence she is carried fainting to her bed room. There (Act IV), Desdemona sings her beautiful "Willow Song", and her "Ave Maria", and falls asleep. Othello wakes her with a kiss, but when she protests her innocence and love for him, he brutally smothers her with her pillow. Emilio, Iago's husband, now reveals how the innocent lady has been wronged, and Iago slays her; while Othello, in his remorse and grief for the loss of her whom he loved so deeply, stabs himself and dies.

I PAGLIACCI

(The Clowns)

It. tragic, "veristic" opera, 2 acts, by Ruggiero Leoncavallo. Milan, 1892. This horrible, touching companion score to Mascagni's ("Cavalleria") is usually given with it. In a Prologue song, *Ridi, Pagliacci* ("Laugh Clown"), a famous Caruso number, Tonio prepares the audience for the sad fate of two wretched lovers.

A troupe of wandering play-actors enters a Calabrian village. Canio, chief actor and manager, leaves Nedda, his wife, to take a drink in the village inn with Beppo, one of his company. When Nedda cruelly flaunts the love of hunchbacked Tonio, and he hears her promise to run away with Silvio, a rich farmer's handsome boy, the hunchback brings back her husband. But Beppo wrests his dagger from him while Silvio escapes. The play that evening (Act II) reproduces the actual situation between Nedda and her husband. Rage, love and jealousy carry the Clown away. He pleads, begs, stammers, but Nedda will not tell her lover's name and, suddenly, he stabs her. Dying, Silvio, in the audience, leaps forward and catches her in his arms. Canio has his answer: he plunges his dagger into Silvio's breast. As the villagers seize him he seems to wake from a dream and cries: "The farce is over!"

None of Leoncavallo's other scores (except *Zaza*) have held their own. His Renaissance "trilogy" *Crespuculum*, a group of 3 operas, his *Chatterton*, were unsuccessful. His *Bohème* (1897) was cast in the shade by Puccini's; his *Roland von Berlin*, a Hohenzollern "glorification" (1904), is written for the ex-emperor William II of Germany fell flat; and his *Zingari*, a Gipsy opera, and *Reginetta delle Rose*, a fantastic imaginary Balkan kingdom score are forgotten.

RIGOLETTO

It. tragic opera, 3 acts, by Giuseppe Verdi. Text by Piave, after Victor Hugo's drama, "Le roi s'amuse" ("The King

Amuses Himself"). Venice, 1851. Exquisite melodies embellish a tale which has *one* noble character, the lovely and innocent Gilda, amid a crowd of base repulsive figures.

The Duke of Mantua, where women are concerned, knows no law but his own wicked will. Fathers, brothers and husbands curse his name. His vileness is abetted by the hunchbacked court jester Rigoletto. Count Monterone, whom Rigoletto mocks, father of a girl betrayed, cursed him at court. And Rigoletto—who keeps an innocent daughter of his own, Gilda, hidden away from his master—slinks to his hidden home abashed. When her father leaves her, the Duke, disguised as a student, makes love to Gilda. When *he* has left her—alas, not as she was!—Rigoletto returning, finds the courtiers about to kidnap a lady the Duke fancies. Blindfolded, Rigoletto joins them, is led to his *own* house—and *holds the ladder* while his child is abducted for the assassin of her honor! In the Duke's palace, while courtiers mock, father and child embrace, and having heard poor Gilda's confession Rigoletto plans revenge. In Sparafucile, the hired bravo's house, Gilda is surprised to see the Duke (who wishes to add Maddalena, the bravo's sister, to his list of conquests), enter. He sings his famous song *La donna e mobile* ("Woman is fickle"). Rigoletto now comes, arranged the details of the Duke's murder and sends Gilda home. But she returns to hear Maddalena beg her brother to spare the Duke. The bravo says a substitute will answer. So Gilda, to save her seducer, lets Sparafucile, who thinks she is the Duke, stab her in the dark. Rigoletto, returning, and gleefully swinging the sack containing the Duke's body over his shoulder, suddenly hears his vile master's voice singing *La donne e mobile*. Madly he claws open the sack! In it innocent Gilda is breathing her last. She dies in his arms. Monterone's curse is accomplished!

SIBERIA

It. tragic "veristic" opera, 3 acts, by Umberto Giordano. Text by Civinini. Milan, 1903. A gloomy tale of crime and punishment in Czarist Russia.

Stephana, a courtesan, prefers the young sergeant Vassili to her countless other lovers. Vassili, who has loved her thinking her pure and innocent, when he discovers the truth, rushes in at a ball she is giving, and kills his lieutenant, one of the "others." He is condemned to Siberia. At the convict-station on the Siberian border (Act II), Stephana appears and there is a tender meeting. She has obtained leave to share Vassili's fate. In the mines (Act III) Stephana finds Globy, the man who made her what she was. She exposes his infamy to the convicts assembled. In revenge he betrays the convicts' plot to escape to the authorities. At the moment of flight Stephana is shot, and dies in poor Vassili's arms just as liberty and happiness seemed within their grasp.

Siberia is Giordano's best and most artistic work. Three other operas however stand out: There is *Mala Vita* (1892) a scandalous "veristic" score, which is a coarse imitation of *Cavalleria*. *Andrea Chenier* (1896), tells a tale of self-sacrifice in stirring music. Chenier, a poet, and Gerard, a French revolutionary leader, both love Madeleine. When Gerard cancels the order sending Chenier to the guillotine, moved by Madeleine's pleas, the reprieve comes too late. The two lovers die on the scaffold, rejoicing to think that death will unite them forever. *Feodora* (1898), is a breathless drama of Russian horrors under the Czarist government. Count Vladimir, the police spy, has been murdered. Feodora, his fiancée, swears revenge. But (Act II), finding Loris, Vladimir's murderer, shot him for seducing his wife, she falls in love with him. In Act III they are as happy as children in their love, in a villa in the mountains, but—the fact that she has caused the deaths of Loris' mother and brother (before she met him) weighs on Feodora's mind. So, after confession, she takes poison and dies in Loris' forgiving arms.

LA SONNAMBULA

It. sentimental opera, 2 acts, by Vincenzo Bellini. Text by Romani. Milan, 1831. A simple, happy tale, the singing of whose beautiful air *Ah, non giunge,* one of the show pieces (soprano) of Italian opera, is associated with such famous names as Etelka Gerster, Adelina Patti, Jenny Lind, Tetrazinni and Marcella Sembrich. It is no work for a heavy-weight *primadonna*. There always is danger that she will break the plank bridge she has to cross in the last act.

Amina, a Swiss village girl walks in her sleep, as village girls sometimes do, but the rest of the villagers (who do not know it), think a ghost walks. Not even her lover, young Elvino, knows her weakness. One night her sonnambulism (Act II) brings about a compromising situation. She enters the room in the village inn where Count Rudolph is staying. Landlady Lisa, who loves Elvino, at once spreads the scandalous news, and Elvino, shocked, turns from his sweetheart to woo her. Amina's despair makes her sleep-walk more than ever, and this (Act III) proves to her salvation. For the next night, walking out of the mill window (she lives in the old mill), she is seen crossing the mill-pond on a frail plank which bends beneath her steps. Providence watches over the poor village girl, however, and on the hither band, Elvino—convinced of her innocence by the evidence of his own eyes—receives her in his arms!

LA TOSCA

It. tragic "veristic" opera, 3 acts, by Giacomo Puccini. Text by Illica and Giocosa, after Sardou. Rome, 1900. An exciting musical melodrama, with fine lyric passages, which is a universal favorite. The leading rôle of Tosca, the heroine, which is associated in the minds of thousands with the American "singing actress" Geraldine Farrar and the Austrian prima donna Maria Jeritza, is one which calls for acrobatic as well as vocal skill.

While Mario Cavaradossi is busy painting a Madonna in the likeness of his mistress Tosca, in a church (Rome, 1800), the latter comes in and displays profane jealousy amid sacred surroundings. Meanwhile Scarpia, chief of the papal police, has decided to use Tosca's jealousy to get Angelotti (Cavaradossi's friend, whom he has helped escape from the Castle of Sant' Angelo), into his clutches. To the music of a *Te Deum* he shows Tosca a woman's fan, and hints that Mario loves another. When he has captured Mario, Scarpia sends for Tosca. She hears her lover groan. He is being tortured in the next room, and she reveals Angelotti's hiding-place to save him. Now the villainous Chief of Police offers to release Mario if she will be his. Tosca buys her lover's safety: Mario is to be shot with blank cartridges! After Scarpia has written a passport which will pass the lovers out of Rome, she stabs him with a carving-knife as he takes her in his arms, and leaves him with a candle at his head and a cross on his breast. At dawn on the battlements of Sant' Angelo, Mario, is led out to die. But Tosca tells him of the blank cartridges and the passport. Freedom and love will soon be theirs. Alas, the treacherous Scarpia has played her false! The volley rings out, Tosca rushes to Mario after the squad has left, and—finds him dead! Now Scarpia's men, their chief's murder discovered, come running to seize Tosca. But she foils them. With a leap from the dizzy castle terrace into the Tiber below she escapes her earthly judges!

LA TRAVIATA

(Violetta)

It. tragic opera, 3 acts, by Giuseppe Verdi. Text after Dumas' play "The Lady with the Camelias." It is a very sentimental tale of passion presented in a refined "drawing-room" atmosphere, which invests an "unfortunate" woman with sentiments more pathetic than probable.

Violetta, a professional beauty, is loved by Alfredo Germont. He establishes her in a villa near Paris (Act II) and the frivolous girl is surprised to find that for the first time in her life she loves deeply and sincerely. With his charming, consumptive sweetheart, Alfred spends rapturous hours until—his father, visiting Violetta, explains that she is ruining his son's life. The noble girl leaves him and Alfredo, meeting her at a ball in Paris (Act III), insults her publicly because he thinks her untrue. Then, too late, learning (Act IV) of Violetta's sacrifice, he hastens to her side, but the poor Magdalen is dying. She has sung her *Addio del passato* ("Farewell to bright visions") the swan song of her frail, now purified soul. But when Alfredo clasps her in his arms, hope revives. *Parigi, o cara, lasceremo* ("We shall flee from Paris, beloved") they sing, in a dream of the future. But joy kills her. Her racking cough stilled forever, she dies, Alfredo's arms vainly striving to hold her back.

IL TROVATORE

It. tragic opera, 4 acts, by Giuseppe Verdi. Text by Commanaro. Rome, 1853. Perhaps Verdi's best-known and best-liked opera, its lovely airs hackneyed by the playing of organ-grinders the world over, the "Trovatore" melodies, *Stride la vampa* ("Upward the flames roll"), the "Anvil Chorus", the famous *Miserere,* and the "Ah, I have sighed to rest me," might be mentioned.

The Count di Luna, a fifteenth century Spanish noble, burned to death the Gipsy Azucena's mother. Gipsies are revengeful. Azucena stole the Count's baby son and brought him up as her own under the name of Manrico. Manrico is a troubadour. The lady whom he serenades is Leonora. After the serenade, he fights a duel with his brother, the young Count di Luna, another admirer of Leonora. Azucena (Act II) now tells Manrico who he really is. By mistake she had cast her *own* boy into the flames which burned her mother. Then she robbed the Count of his son to make good her loss. After various incidents Manrico appears just in time to rescue Leonora, whom the Count his brother, has abducted. Now the Count captures Azucena (Act II), and when Manrico hears she is to be burned, he hastens to the rescue. Alas, he is defeated, and (Act IV) cast into prison! There, with Azucena (Leonora who has arrived joins her voice to theirs) he sings the famous *Miserere.* Leonora promises herself to the Count, if Manrico go safe, but Manrico reviles her, thinking her untrue. Yet when she dies of the poison she has taken, he recalls his cruel words, and begs her forgiveness. The Count, enraged to think his bride preferred death to himself, has Manrico's head struck off with the axe.

And then Azucena blasts him with remorse and horror by telling him that he has murdered his own brother.

ZAZA

It. lyric comedy, 4 acts, by Ruggieri Leoncavallo. Text after a French play by Berton and Simon. Milan, 1900. A rather vulgar tale of Parisian concert-hall life which, however, has much life and passion, and owes its American popularity mainly to Geraldine Farrar's spirited and dramatic interpretation of the rôle of the heroine.

Zaza is a music-hall dancer. She wagers that she can add Milio Dufresne, indifferent to her charms, to her many admirers, and wins her wager. In winning it, however, she has fallen in love with Dufresne. They live together (Act II) in a charming villa outside Paris, but her love affair interferes with business, so Cascart, her manager, tells her that Dufresne spends his time away from her in Paris, with another woman. The butler lets Zaza into Dufresne's Paris home (Act III), while his unconscious wife has accompanied him to the station to take the train. When Zaza meets Dufresne's little girl she nobly retires without making a scene, though she did not know Dufresne was married. Broken-hearted, the concert-hall artist now returns home. When Dufresne (Act IV) tries to caress her she says: "I have seen Toto!" Furious at his fury, she first declares she has told his wife everything. Then— finding that his love for his wife is real, while she is only a passing fancy to him—she tells him the truth. With one of those noble gestures of sacrifice more frequent in opera than in real life, she sends him back to his family.

II

TALES OF THE GREAT FRENCH OPERAS

L'AFRICAINE

Fr. tragic grand opera, 5 acts, by Giacomo Meyerbeer. Text by Scribe. Paris, 1865. A brown Madagascan queen, unable to win the heart of a sailor lover, generously thrusts him into the arms of the girl he does love, and dies under a poison-tree. One of its most famous arias is: "Oh, paradise of the wave!"

Vasco da Gama, the Portuguese ocean navigator, returns from a hazardous trip to claim the hand of his betrothed, the beautiful Inez, and secure aid for further discoveries. With him are Nelusko, a Madagascan native, and Selika, the latter's sovereign, both captives. The Inquisition, denouncing Vasco for insisting on the existence of lands not mentioned in the Holy Scriptures, condemns him to die. He is released, however, at the plea of the faithful Inez, who pays the unhappy price of marriage to Vasco's rival, Don Pedro, for his release. The latter, in possession of Vasco's plans and slaves, sets sail with his wife, followed by da Gama, and they meet in the Indian Ocean during a terrific tempest. Piloted by Nelusko, they are shipwrecked on the Madagascan coast, where the natives decide to kill all the Christians. But Selika has fallen desperately in love with Vasco da Gama. She saves the sailor by proclaiming him her husband, despite the jealous hate of Nelusko. Da Gama, however, still loves Inez, and betraying his passion on hearing her voice when she is led out to die, Selika, in a wave of generous emotion, permits the lovers to escape on a passing Portuguese ship. Then the Madagascan queen, after watching the sails of the vessels fade on the horizon, inhales the blossoms of the deadly manzanillo tree, rather than live without the love of her choice.

APHRODITE

Fr. tragic grand opera, in 5 acts, by Camille Erlanger. Text by de Gramont, after Pierre Louys' novel of the same name. Paris, 1906. The opera shows in thrilling scenes what love led to in artistic and less polite circles of the Egyptian city of Alexandria, in the year 50 B.C. The music is effective in a spectacular and "accompanimental" way.

In ancient Alexandria, Demetrius, a famous sculptor, has presented his greatest piece of work, the statue of Aphrodite, goddess of love, to the temple. While at the height of his glory he arrogantly scoffs at the prediction of the sorceress Chimairis that he is doomed to commit two murders and come to his own death. But the sorceress knew what she was talking about. Demetrius, in love with a girl of light life, Chrysis, swears to accomplish any demand she may make in order to possess her. And Chrysis promptly asks him to secure for her the famous mirror of rich Bacchus, the ivory comb worn by the wife of the High Priest, and lastly, the holy and matchless necklace of pearls adorning the statue of his own Aphrodite. At a feast in Bacchus' home, Corinne, a slave girl whom Bacchus was about to free, is accused of stealing the mirror Demetrius has stolen, and is immediately crucified. Later on, while the crowds rage at the brutal murder of the High Priest's wife, whom the infatuated artist has killed for her comb, they hear of the sacriligeous theft of the famous necklace of Aphrodite. Demetrius, meanwhile, has presented all three to Chrysis, and has claimed her promise. The mob later sees Chrysis, nude save for the pearls, comb, and mirror, impersonating the goddess Aphrodite on the top of Alexandria's light-house tower. Scandalized at her effrontery, the authorities throw her in jail, and force her to drink poison. As she dies, with slowly benumbed senses, she sees a vision of her lover, Demetrius, as he is quite properly slain by outraged Love.

ARIANE ET BARBE-BLEUE

Fr. "allegorical" grand opera, in 3 acts, by Paul Dukas. Text by Maurice Maeterlinck. Paris, 1907. In this score an ultra-modern French composer has taken the tale of Bluebeard, as told by a Belgian "symbolic" writer, and used it as a text on which to deliver an argument in favor of women's rights in tone. Though the period of the opera is Medieval France, Ariane, its heroine, is practically a modern suffragette.

Bluebeard, of legendary fame, having jailed five former wives in his dungeons, marries Ariane, and entrusts her with seven keys, six of silver, and one, the seventh of gold. The last she is not to use but despite the warnings of her nurse, she decides to open the forbidden door. The nurse, attempting to overcome her desires to use the key, opens six doors with the silver keys, and from each comes a shower of brilliant and costly gems, amethysts, sapphires, pearls, emeralds, rubies and diamonds. Still curious, however, Ariane uses the fateful seventh key and finds a great black chasm, from which come the wailing voices of her five predecessors in Bluebeard's affections. Bluebeard appears and warns her not to lose his love by investigating their fate. He grasps her arm to enforce his arguments, but her cry brings a threatening mob into the castle. Ariane assures them that her husband did no harm and dismisses them. Then, descending the stairs, she comforts the five unhappy wives, and leads them to freedom, bedecking them in the jewels found above. The populace, irritated at Bluebeard's cruelty, now waylay him, and he is brought in bound to Ariane, who bandages his wounds. Then, despite his pleas, she leaves him with his five previous wives. For they, eternally feminine, refuse to avail themselves of the freedom they have just won. Their medieval souls prefer masculine bondage to modern woman's heritage of liberty.

CARMEN

Fr. tragic grand opera, in 4 acts, by Georges Bizet. Text by Mielhac and Halevy, after Prosper Merimée's novel. Paris, 1875. The most famous "Gipsy" opera ever written "Carmen," with its piquant, passionate melodies in the Spanish Gipsy style ("On the Ramparts of Seville," etc.), the exquisite Micaela's "Flower-Song", and its stirring baritone number, the "Toreador's Song," holds its own as one of the finest operas of human passion. Its scene is Seville, Spain, about 1820.

Carmen, a beautiful but morally not scrupulous gipsy cigarette girl, is arrested for pulling the hair of another girl in the factory where she works. Don José, her soldier guard, at once falls a victim to her fascination, and forgets all about his fair-haired sweetheart Micaela, a "good" village girl. He unties Carmen's hands, after making an appointment to meet her at an inn, and she escapes through the crowd. That night Carmen, dancing to the rattle of castanets, tries to make José forget his duty when the bugles of his regiment sound to call him to barracks. He seriously wounds his lieutenant Zungia, who also has an eye on Carmen, and so is forced to flee with her to the camp of a smuggling band in the mountains. After several months of life together Carmen tires of him and prefers the bull-fighter, Escamillo, while José leaves her to go back with Micaela to the bedside of his dying mother. Some time later, outside the bullring in Seville, where Carmen is waiting for Escamillo, whom she has now accepted as her lover, José confronts her. Her taunts rouse him to a fury of despair. He stabs her, maddened because she has betrayed him, just as the bull-fighter Escamillo comes out, victorious, acclaimed by the crowd.

There are many other Gipsy operas. Most of them have been dropped from the active repertoire, but live in their songs and beautiful instrumental numbers, often heard in concert. In the Irish composer Michael Balfe's *Bohemian Girl* (1843), Thaddeus, a noble Pole, after many impossible adventures, gains the heart and hand of Arline, a "mock" gipsy, a child of noble blood, stolen and brought up in a gipsy camp. Ambroise Thomas' *Mignon,* (Paris, 1866) is another aristocratic gipsy, stolen from her father's castle in childhood to find love's long and crooked lane of unkind accident comes to a happy end in a lover's arms. "I Would I Dwelt in Marble Halls" from the first and "Dost Thou Know the Land," from the second opera are melodies which do not die. Wallace's *Maritana* is a tale of Spanish gipsy street singer. A plot to give her a noble name and court position, so that the Spanish king may carry out his villainous designs on her is foiled. She is to marry Don César de Bazan. He is to gain the privilege of being shot instead of hung for leaving his widow. A trick procures his shooting with blank cartridges, the royal villain is foiled, and all ends happily.

Lesser gipsies are: Paderewski's *Manru* (New York, 1901). A gipsy lad, he marries a farmer girl, and deserts her for a gipsy princess only to be poisoned by a rival. The farmer girl drowns herself in a convenient lake. Rachmaninoff (*Aleko*),

Leoncavallo (*Gli Zingari*), F. Schmidt (*Notre-Dame*) are other composers who have added to the store of Romany operas.

LE CHEMINEAU

(The Wayfarer)

Fr. lyric opera, 4 acts, by Xavier Leroux. Text by Jean Richepin. Paris, 1911. The sentimental idealization of a French tramp in effective theatrical music, stressing the idea that "the call of the road" sounds above all others in the heart of the wayfarer.

Le Chemineau, at heart a rover, leaves the farm-girl Toinette, whom he has loved for a harvest-hand's hour, to follow the lure of the open road. So she marries François, a good, honest toiler. Her son Toinet hopes to marry Pierre's daughter Aline, but Pierre, knowing the facts, proclaims him the illegitimate son of Le Chemineau, the roving tramp now gone for over twenty years, and forbids the marriage. François, sickly for years, is surprised when his wife, having gone to meet Toinet, returns with Le Chemineau. He fears he may lose Toinette's love. On Christmas Eve, Aline and Toinet are about to be married, when Pierre, calling on Le Chemineau, promises to make him comfortable for the rest of his life, if he will marry Toinette upon the death of François, who is rapidly failing. But Le Chemineau declines, and François, happy in this knowledge, though he has commended his wife to her former lover, dies thanking him. For Le Chemineau would rather wander the highways than sit at a snug fireside indoors. Force of habit is stronger than sentimental memories. He takes his old cap and leaves his love of golden summer days for the frosts and rains of the out-of-doors.

Leroux's *Vénus et Adonis* (Nunes, 1905), *Théodora* (Monte Carlo, 1905), *William Ratcliffe* (Nice, 1905), *Carilloneur* (Paris, 1912), *Fille de Figaro* (Paris, 1914), *Cadeaux de Noël* (Paris, 1916), and "1914" (Monte Carlo, 1918), a tragic "Great War" opera have none of them been as successful as *Le Chemineau*.

CONTES D'HOFFMANN

(Tales of Hoffmann)

Fr. fantastic opera 3 acts, with a Prologue and Postlude, by Jacques Offenbach. Text by Barbier after the German E. T. A. Hoffmann's novelette. Vienna, 1881. The farce—and comic opera—composer Offenbach's one famous *grand* opera. Though a terrible tragedy, in which many lives were lost, the burning of the Vienna *Ring Theater,* on the day of its first performance for years kept it off the boards—it was considered a "bad luck" work—it is now one of the most popular scores of the operatic repertory. Its music is delightfully melodious and taking, and the famous "Barcarole" duet has gained world-wide popularity.

One night in a wine-cellar the poet Hoffmann is teased by his friends to disclose his love affairs. So Hoffmann tells how he first fell in love with Spalanzani's life-sized doll, who was introduced to him as his daughter, Oympia. She is beautiful, and mechanically perfect, but cold to his advances. Hoffmann views her through the magic glass of Coppelius, a magician, and his mad infatuation continues until, in a furious dance, Olympia breaks to pieces in his arms. His next love develops in a gondola on the waterways of Venice. Its heroine is Giulietta, and in attempting to gain the key to her chamber, he is duped into killing her real lover's rival, and sees the latter, Dapertutto, sailing away with faithless Giulietta on the canal. His third romance is his love for delicate Antonia. She, possessing a glorious voice, is forbidden to sing lest it overtax her. But Dr. Miracle, a wizard, tempts her to sing, and she dies from the strain in Hoffmann's arms. Having thrice loved—for beauty, out of pure passion, and with a high and sacred devotion—Hoffmann now resigns himself to confining his love to the ever faithful Muse.

FAUST

Fr. lyric opera, in 5 acts, by Charles Gounod. Text after Goethe, by Barbier and Carré. (Paris, 1859). Rich in lovely melodies, Gounod's "Faust" is one of the enduring favorites of the opera repertory. The names of Christine Nillson, Adeline Patti, Melba, Calvé and Eames are associated with the singing of the rôle of "Marguerite" in the United States, and those of Campanini, Jean de Reske and Caruso with that of "Faust". Marguerite's "Jewel Song", a brilliant coloratura waltz, and Faust's romance "Hail to Thee Dwelling Pure and Chaste", are probably the favorite vocal numbers.

Faust has grown old in scholarly research. The echoes of joyous youth and love rising to his study from the street fill him with despair. He curses life. Then the devil, in the person of Mephisto, appears and offers him a new life of youth, pleasure and love in return for his soul. Faust accepts his offer and meets and falls in love with an innocent girl, Marguerite, although ordered away by her brother Valentin. With Mephisto's aid Faust, during her brother's absence at war, wins and betrays her trusting heart. On her brother Valentin's return, Faust is forced to fight a duel with him, and kills him unintentionally, through Mephisto's magic. Marguerite, shrinking from her brother's murderer, seeks solace in church. But her conscience so troubles her that she loses her reason and drowns her new-born child! For this she is condemned to die. Faust, now repentant, visits her in her cell accompanied by his satanic adviser. But Marguerite refuses to fly with him, calls on God to forgive her, and expires as the bells toll for her execution. While her soul is carried to heaven by angels, and Faust sinks to his knees in prayer, Mephisto, foiled, is turned away by an archangel's sword. In a gorgeous ballet (Act V) sometimes given, Faust meets all the famous courtesans of olden times.

Hector Berlioz's *La Damnation de Faust* (Paris, 1846) is the second of the important "Faust" operas: Boito's *Mefistofile* is the third. Berlioz's score has more of the true spirit of the Middle Ages than Gounod's, and differences in telling the tale are responsible for three fine numbers: a version of the Hungarian "Rakoczy March", the beautiful and airy "Dance of the Sylphs", and the famous ballad song by Marguerite, "The King of Thule".

GRISÉLIDIS

Fr. lyric opera, 3 acts, by Jules Massenet. Text by Silvestre and Morand. Paris, 1891. Mary Garden created the title-rôle in the United States (New York, 1910). An opera in which a real "personal" Devil, with horns and tail, vainly tries to lead a virtuous wife into temptation, but is foiled. It is not a story of to-day but is supposed to happen in the Middle Ages. Beautiful "Devil Music", where the Evil One summons the imps of hell in a forest, a noble tenor aria, *Ouvrez-vous sur mon front*, and a splendid musical climax (Miracle Scene) stand out.

The powerful Marquis de Saluce falls deeply in love with a simple shepherdess named Grisélidis. He wins her for his wife, despite the fact that she is much in love with a shepherd named Alain, and trusts her implicitly. When a son is born to them, he leaves her to fight the infidel in the Holy Land, despite the warnings of a priest. The Devil wagers with the Marquis before he goes, however, that he can make his wife become untrue. The Marquis, like a true gentleman, puts his faith in her honor. During the Marquis' absence, the Fiend brings her old lover Alain to tempt her, but her baby boy keeps her from yielding. The Devil now spirits the son away, continuing his unsuccessful attempts to cause mischief. And when the Marquis returns he spirits away his weapons. At last the nobleman and his wife, devoutly praying for the restoration of their son, see the triptych over the altar in the chapel open, and there is their child miraculously given back to their arms, smiling in a halo of golden light!

The heroines of Massenet's operas are by no means all of them faithful wives. In *Sapho* (Paris, 1892), we have an artist's model with a past. She wrecks the life of a poor country boy while trying to rise a bit higher in the social scale. In *Hérodiade* (Brussels, 1881), an unhappy mother, jealous of Salome (her daughter, though she doesn't know it) drives the unfortunate girl to kill herself. It contains the famous air: *Il est doux, il est bon* ("He is good, he is kind"). In *Le Cid* (1885) two ladies love Spain's national hero, Rodrigo de Bivar, the "Cid," or "Chief" of Spanish legend. He is driven to kill the father of the one whom he loves and destroy his life's happiness. In *La Navarraise* (1894) a black-eyed Spanish village beauty murders an enemy general to get the money which will make her lover's father consent to their marriage, but the lover dies cursing the bloody wages of her sin. *Don César de Bazan* (1872) tells the same story as Wallace's *Maritana*. *Esclarmonde* (1889) is a Greek enchantress of medieval Constantinople, who wins the love of a Christian knight. It is known as Massenet's most "Wagnerian" score. In *Le Mage,* "The Magian," two girls, one better the other worse, try to win the heart of the Persian prophet Zoroaster. One succeeds, the other dies with a cry of rage. *Cendrillon,* "Cinderella", (1899), is one of the Massenet's few innocent heroines, though in *Cherubin* (1905), a Spanish dancer is abandoned by a young rake who salves the broken heart of another innocent heroine by marrying her as she is about to enter a convent. In *Thérèse* (1907), however, the French Revolution produces a virtuous wife, who goes to the guillotine with her husband rather than survive him. *Ariane* (1906), *Bacchus* (1907), *Don Quichotte* (1910) and other scores are less important.

LA HABANERA

Fr. lyric drama, 3 acts, by Raoul Laparra. Paris, 1908. A modern veristic score in which retribution overtakes a Cain who murders his brother for a dancer's sake.

Pedro and Ramon, brothers, are both in love with Pilar, who is a dancer. Following a drinking bout at the tavern, Ramon provokes a violent quarrel with his brother over his infatuation for Pilar, and stabs him to death. Matters so arrange themselves that the murder remains a mystery, Ramon hiding his guilt by violently declaring the foul murder should be avenged. While dancing the Habanera in his beloved's house, Pedro's ghost appears, visible only to Ramon, and whispers that if the truth is not told by the following day, Pilar, madly beloved by him, will die. Ramon, torn by conflicting emotions, meets Pilar at the cemetery, and proclaims his devotion to the girl who appears to be wavering in her mind. Alarmed, Ramon then confesses his misdeed, and Pilar, unable to bear her misfortune, sinks dead on her lover's grave. Ramon rushes from the spot in a fit of madness.

LES HUGUENOTS

Fr. grand historical opera, 5 acts, by Giacomo Meyerbeer. Text by Scribe and Deschaps. Paris, 1836. The Massacre of St. Bartholomew set to music. It contains many suave and elegant melodies ("Whiter Than Whitest Ermine", tenor; "A Wise and Noble Lady", mezzo; and the duet beginning "Danger Presses", between Raoul and Valentine which is interrupted by the sinister tolling of the bell that signals the massacre to begin).

Raoul de Nangis, a young Huguenot, entertained, during a lull in the strife between his own and the opposing party in a Catholic mansion, offers a toast to an unknown lady whom he has recently rescued from insult. Later, meeting Queen Margarita of Valois, he agrees to obey her wish to help bring about a peaceful ending of hostilities by accepting the hand of the daughter of the Count of St. Bris, a staunch Catholic. Having reason to think that his unknown lady, whom he loves, has been intimate with another, he retracts his engagement when he discovers that she is none other than the girl selected for his marriage. The old Count, her father, swears vengeance. Valentine, his daughter, though greatly offended, when she learns that Raoul's life is endangered, warns him through his servant, Marcel. At the duelling ground Raoul finds out that Valentine is innocent, and the appearance of the Queen restores peace between the combatants. The old Count of St. Bris, however, has promised his daughter to a friend, the Count of Nevers. Before the massacre of St. Bartholomew, Raoul learns of the plot and warns the Queen. Valentine, true to her love, pleads with Raoul to turn to Rome, but his old servant bids him be steadfast in the Protestant faith, and the two unfortunate lovers meet death side by side at the hands of the massacring mob!

JONGLEUR DE NOTRE DAME

Fr. lyric opera, 3 acts, by Jules Massenet. Text by Maurice Lena, after an old French legend. Monte-Carlo, 1902. Another opera whose title-rôle was created in the United States by Mary Garden. Its moral is a musically very lovely admonition that no matter how humble one's little gift or accomplishment may be one should use it for the greater glory of God. The "Juggler", a part originally written for a man was changed to a woman's part and has become a woman's rôle.

Jean, a humble juggler, whilst performing for the crowds on a market-day, arouses the wrath of the monastery Prior by singing parodies on holy songs. Begging forgiveness, he is urged to join the monks, but is unmoved until he sees the rich foods delivered to the monastery kitchen. In a monk's garb he endeavors to do penance for his former mode of life, but is discouraged because he cannot pray to the Virgin in Latin. Boniface, the kindly cook, assures him that prayers, even in French, will be understood. So Jean, one day, divests himself of his robe and goes through his juggling performances, and dances in a respectful attempt to show his reverence, before the Virgin's image. Unknown to him, the Prior, monks and Boniface watch him in amazement and anger. Finally they burst in on him, reproaching him with sacrilege. But Boniface, seeing the Virgin's image come to life, stops them. For the Virgin, moved by the simple montebank's sincere worship, smiles on him with the celestial smile earth does not know. A golden halo trembles about her head, and she leans forward and blesses Jean, whose soul is caught up and translated to a better world as he dies in ecstasy at her feet. The monks, humbled and impressed by the miracle, chant the Beatitude, "Blessed are the meek," as his spirit takes flight.

LA JOTA

Fr. tragic opera, in 2 acts, by Raoul Laparra. Text by the composer. Paris, 1911. A veristic story with a repulsive crucifixion of a priest whose human impulses are stronger than his churchly vows. The *jota,* the national Spanish waltz of Aragon, plays an important part in its music.

In the Spanish Pyrenees, during the year 1835, the Carlist war separates two young and ardent lovers—the Basque, Juan Zumarragua and Soledad, a Spanish girl. Although on different sides of the conflict, they pledge their faith, and are happy until they have to part, dancing their last *jota* together. Juan, a soldier, must join the Carlists, but he leaves his Soledad unwillingly. She, it seems, has unintentionally bewitched the curate Mosen Jago with her beauty and charm. He struggles in vain to save himself from his own sinful desires. When the Carlists descend upon the town, Soledad, and all the inhabitants seek refuge in the Church. There they are overpowered by the enemy, but Soledad is caught up in the arms of her Juan, while the raging curate is nailed to the cross by the amiable Carlists, as though in punishment for the sin he came near committing.

Spanish subjects are favorites in French opera. Ravel's *L'Heure Espagnole,* "The Spanish Hour" (Paris, 1911), is a droll little score in which a Spanish beauty rejects two admirers to favor a third. In Jean Nouguès' *Chiquito* (1909) a young Basque lover escapes assassination only to see his sweetheart die in a hospital.

JOSEPH IN EGYPT

Fr. lyric opera, 3 acts, by Etienne Nicholas Mehul. Text after the Bible. (Paris, 1807). A graceful, old-fashioned French score, written to prove that a Biblical subject could be treated in opera.

Joseph, favorite son of Jacob, is sold by his evil brothers to the Egyptians and, having saved Egypt from famine by his wisdom, rises to the position of Governor in Memphis under the name of Cleophas. But Joseph still retains his affection for his old father. His father, now grown blind, sends his sons into Egypt for food when the tribe is suffering from the famine, and they are received by their brother, who recognizes them at once. Meeting his youngest brother Benjamin and learning that his father still mourns him as lost, he induces them to join him in the honors bestowed upon him by the Egyptians. His brother, Simeon, consumed by grief and conscience-stricken, confesses that he sold Joseph, and the old patriarch curses and disowns his ten sons. But now Joseph makes himself known, and intervening, obtains full pardon for his brothers, who join with him in praising God for His mercies.

Belonging to the same period of earlier French *opéra comique* which produced *Joseph,* are other scores never heard in this country though sometimes given abroad. *La Dame Blanche,* "The White Lady", by François-Adrien Boildieu (Paris, 1825), tells in attractive music a pretty love story drawn from Sir Walter Scott's "Guy Mannering" and "The Monastery". *Zampa* by Herold (Paris, 1831), a gloomy old legend of a statue bride who punishes a wicked pirate, has an attractive overture, still heard in many a "movie" house. Meyerbeer's *Dinorah* or "The Pardon of Ploermel", is a confused tale of the loves of a gold-hunting Breton and an insane girl who wanders through the woods with a pet goat. The libretto is incredibly silly, but there is much charming music in the score, and the instrumental number, "Dinorah's Shadow Dance," is still a favorite.

LA JUIVE

(The Jewess)

Fr. grand tragic opera, 5 acts, by Jacques Halévy. Text by Scribe (Paris, 1835). The pathetic and tragic scenes are the ones which give this score its real dramatic and musical value. The rôle of *Eleazar,* especially, when sung as Caruso sang it, was so human and moving that it has been responsible for frequent revivals of the work.

Eleazar, a rich Jewish goldsmith, is the only one of his faith to do business freely in the town of Constance (1414). This is due to the friendship of Cardinal Brogni. All other Jews in Constance are oppressed. Yet Eleazar nurses a secret hatred against the Cardinal. Prince Leopold, the Imperial Commander-in-Chief, takes the name of "Samuel" to gain the affections of Recha, Eleazar's daughter, and she invites him to her house. The Emperor's niece, the Princess Eudora, purchases a gift from the Jew, to be given to her bridegroom, Prince Leopold. The Prince (Samuel), confesses to Recha that he is a Christian, but—in spite of her father's protests—the girl puts love before duty and returns Samuel's love. Later, accompanying Eudora to the palace to present her gift, Recha recognizes Samuel as Leopold, and denounces him as having lived in unlawful wedlock with a Jewess, herself, a capital offense. Recha, her father, and Leopold are thrown into prison. But poor, loving Recha relents, and her lover is set free on her testimony. The Cardinal entreats Eleazar to help him discover the whereabouts of his long-lost daughter, offering freedom as a reward. Eleazar admits he knows the man who kidnapped her, but will say no more. Recha, refusing to embrace the Christian faith, is led to her death—she is to be cast into a caldron of boiling water. Then Eleazar, with fiendish glee, tells the Cardinal that she is *his* daughter. Happy to think he has made a Christian suffer, Eleazar follows Recha into the boiling water, while Cardinal Brogni falls back senseless.

Jews do not play a leading part in operas as frequently as members of other races, yet Halévy's score is not the only one with a Jewish hero or heroine. Halévy himself did another distinctly Jewish opera, *Le Juif errant,* "The Wandering Jew" (Paris, 1852) but it has not survived. *L'Ebreo,* "The Hebrew" is a "rough and ready" melodrama by Appoloni (1822-1889) once very popular. A modern, instead of a medieval Jewish tale is Erckmann-Chatrian, the French novelist's romance, *Le Juif Polonais,* "The Polish Jew". It is a very dramatic and blood-curdling story and has been set as *Le Juif Polonais* by Camille Erlanger (Paris, 1900) and by the German composer

Karl Weiss (1901), as *Der Polnische Jude*. The Russian pianist-composer Rubinstein's attempts to write "Jewish National Operas"—*Moses* (1894), *The Tower of Babel* (1870), *Sulamith* (1883), *The Maccabees* (1875), etc., have been forgotten. These "sacred operas" were quite undramatic and have vanished from the stage.

LAKMÉ

Fr. lyric tragedy, 3 acts, by Leo Delibes. Text by Gille and Gondinet. (Paris, 1883.) A slight but graceful score which survives in a famous soprano aria, Lakmé's "Bell Song".

Gerald, an English officer on duty in India, meets Lakmé in the forbidden grounds of an Indian temple. The beautiful native loves him at first sight, and warns him of the danger he incurs by trespassing on the holy grounds. He manages to hide while Lakmé's father Nilakantha enters, and overhears the priest denounce the intruding visitor, whose footprints have been discovered. Later, Nilakantha brings his daughter to a street festival, where disguised, he makes her sing, hoping her lover will betray his presence. Gerald, unwisely grasping her in his arms, is stabbed by the girl's priestly parent. But Lakmé tenderly nurses him back to health in a forest hut. He now swears undying devotion, and begs her to give him a drink of the potion which will make his earthly love eternal. As she departs, his friend Frederick appears, and urges him to return to his fiancée and his army duties, a campaign being then in progress. Gerald on the principle of "Out of sight, out of mind"—for Lakmé is not about at the moment—is won over to the side of duty. He refuses to drink the potion when Lakmé returns. In despair she poisons herself, and as her father kneels by her side, implores him to pardon Gerald. The young officer is permitted to go unharmed, and joins the British forces, whose martial music sounds in the distance, off-stage.

The color and picturesqueness of the Hindoo subject has attracted many composers. Massenet's *Le Roi de Lahore*, "The King of Lahore" (Paris, 1877), contains some charming native Hindoo tunes, and is famous for a gorgeous ballet showing the paradise of the god Indra. A young temple priestess, persecuted by a wicked uncle who insists on forcing her inclinations, loses a royal lover by the uncle's treachery. The dead king, allowed to revisit earth by the god Indra, since disappointed love makes him wretched in paradise, dies with the object of his adoration, and is happy. The Czech composer Joseph Mraczek's *Ikdar*—a modern score with a "symbolic" story, might also be mentioned here.

LOUISE

Fr. romantic opera in 4 acts, by Gustave Charpentier. Text by the Composer. (Paris, 1900.) A realistic drama of modern Paris tenement life, in which a young dressmaker is torn between her desire for a life of freedom with her lover, and the "slow" existence of her poor parents. The music successfully pictures the sounds of a great city. The best known air is *Depuis le Jour* ("Since the Day"), sung by Louise to tell her happiness in her love.

Louise, a young girl who lives with her parents on the top floor of a Paris tenement, falls in love with Julien, a young artist who lives across the alley. Her Mother catches them in conversation, and when Louise's Father comes home (he is a laborer), he tries to reason with the girl, telling her that Julien is not a dependable fellow. Mother and daughter quarrel, the first slaps the other's cheek, but Louise promises to try to forget him. In Act II Julien waits near the shop for her (it is early morning and many odd figures shuffle by), to try to persuade her to elope. She refuses, but later, inside the shop, she is sickened by the girls' teasing, and when she hears her lover's voice outside runs to join her life with his. Act III shows the two in a little cottage on the hill of Montmartre (an artists' quarter), where the gay Bohemians come in the dusk to crown Louise "Queen" of their revels. Her Mother appears and, saying that the Father is ill, persuades the girl to come back home. But in the last act Louise again longs for freedom and Paris, and after an argument, her Father orders her out of the house. As she goes, he breaks down and curses the wicked city!

A sequel to this work by the same composer, called *Julien*, was a comparative failure when produced in the New York Metropolitan Opera House. It is a long and rather tiresome story which tells of the later life of Julien after the death of Louise, when he believes he sees her again in four different women, going down the scale to a drab of the streets. He dies in misery in the end. This opera is remarkable for its *fourfold woman's part*. Charpentier has idealized the "freedom" of artistic life. Alfred Brunneau is a modern French realist who preaches socialistic doctrines in some of his operas. *Messidor* (Paris, 1897) expresses a Zola libretto in which socialism and symbolism are paired. Two tales are interwoven. One is a legend of the Christ Child who sits in an underground cathedral beneath the Ariège River. There, as he plays with its sands, they run from his fingers in grains of gold. The other tale is one of a struggle between poor villagers and a greedy capitalist who has ruined them with labor-saving machinery. In *L'Enfant Roi*, "The Child King", the same composer deals with lower middle-class life in Paris in the style of *Louise*. It is a naturalistic tale of a mother of the working class asked to sacrifice for her husband's sake a child which is not his. Fortunately he accepts the child, and forgives the mistake to which it owes its existence.

MAROUF

(The Cobbler of Cairo)

Fr. lyric comedy, 5 acts, by Henri Rabaud. Text by Nepoty, after an "Arabian Nights" tale. (Paris, 1914). An effective modern score which retells a delightful Oriental fairytale in brilliant and colorful music.

Marouf, a Cobbler of Cairo, hounded by a shrewish wife, runs away to sea in despair, and is shipwrecked near Khaitan, somewhere " 'twixt China and Morocco". There he boasts of the riches of his wonderful caravan, "on its way" to him, until the greedy Sultan married him to his daughter. When he admits he is a fraud to the Princess, who loves him, she flees to the desert with him. There he is lucky enough to stumble by chance on a treasure-cavern filled with jewels and a magic ring which forces an obedient spirit to do his will. Marouf now is in a position to produce the imaginary caravan and does so just as the sultan turns up with the vizier who has cast doubts on his veracity. While the Sultan apologizes for his suspicions, the lovers set out to the palace to the tune of the vizier's cries—for he is getting a hundred stripes on the soles of his feet!

MONNA VANNA

Fr. tragic opera, 4 acts, by Henri Fevrier. Text after Maeterlinck's play. (Paris, 1909). To save a starving Italian Renaissance city a young girl goes to the enemy commander's tent dressed only in her long hair and a cloak. He delivers a poetic lecture on love, but does not otherwise take advantage of her unprotected condition. The music is rather commonplace.

During the siege of Pisa, Guido, torn between maintaining the defense of his city, and protecting the populace from the vengeance of the enemy, prepares to meet the popular demand to surrender. An envoy brings a most unusual message. The enemy general will spare the townspeople only on condition that Guido's wife, Monna Vanna, will be sent to him—wrapped only in a cloak! Monna Vanna persuades Guido to accept, although he cannot maintain faith in the fidelity of his wife. She meets the opposing general, Prinzi-

the ideal accomplishment of the impressionist composer. Like "Tristan and Isolde," it is a drama of fatality in love.

Golaud, a mighty hunter, son of King Akel of Allemonde, discovers Melisande grieving at a fountain in the woods, and brings her home to become his bride. But Pélleas, the passionate young brother of Golaud, falls impetuously in love with Melisande. She, awed by the gloominess of the castle, often meets Pélleas at a fountain in the castle park, and finds herself being won by the wild young lover. In one of these meetings she loses her wedding-ring, and Golaud, suffering from a fall from his horse, requests Pélleas to accompany her in search of it. The adventures that befall them create an even greater desire for Melisande in the heart of Pélleas. At last Golaud finds Pélleas in the act of passionately kissing his wife's hair as it hangs from her head in the tower window. Later, Melisande, about to become a mother, rouses such jealousy in Golaud, that he even holds up a little child to spy at her bed-room window. And then, one day, Golaud surprises them together and kills Pélleas with his sword. Melisande, desperately ill at the birth of her son, is approached by the remorseful Golaud, who realizes that she is innocent. She forgives him listlessly, and passes away while the old King cradles the new-born grandchild.

LE PROPHÈTE

Fr. grand opera, 5 acts, by Giacomo Meyerbeer. Text by Scribe. (Paris, 1849.) The tragic tale of a medieval religious fanatic who (1509-1536) introduced communism and polygamy in his New Sion, the city of Munster. There are some fine melodies, and a brilliant ballet. The tenor rôle of the hero, Jean of Leyden, is one associated in this country with Caruso's name. A great aria by *Fides* is still used as an alto "test" aria for alto aspirants who wish to get on the *Opéra* stage in Paris.

In medieval Holland, Count Oberthal, shortly after quelling a revolt of the Anabaptists, is approached by Bertha and John of Leyden for his consent to their marriage. Struck by the girl's beauty, the Count refuses, looking forward to enjoying it himself. He keeps Bertha and John's mother Fides captives in his palace. The Anabaptists see in John a striking resemblance to King David of Holy Writ, and urge him to become their leader and prophet. He refuses until he is forced to release his sweetheart in order to save his mother's life. The Anabaptists then besiege and take the city of Munster which John rules as its King. But his mother believes him dead, and Bertha has sworn vengeance against the Anabaptists who, she thinks, have killed him. Fearing an untimely end, John

Robert must prove himself before he can read the will. But Bertram, inducing him to gamble, wins everything he has, including his horse and armor. Princess Isabella of Sicily loves Robert. She provides him with a horse and arms; but Bertram, planning to win Robert's soul, sends him to secure the magic branch from a ruined abbey. Here, where the spirit of dissolute nuns dance in unholy revelry at midnight (Ballet), he plucks the cypress branch of power. Returning, he enters Isabella's palace and, himself invisible, uses the magic branch to put the assembly to sleep. He means to carry off Isabella, but dropping the branch, the charm is broken. He now is attacked by the guards, but Bertram saves him, and then tries to win his soul in the very vestibule of the Cathedral. But, prompted by Alice, Robert learns that Bertram is his father—the Devil—and turns a deaf ear to his pleas. As the clock strikes twelve, his infernal parent vanishes, and the cathedral door opens, showing Isabella waiting in her bridal robes.

LE ROI D'YS

(The King of Ys)

Fr. tragic grand opera, 3 acts, by Edouard Lalo. (Paris, 1888). It is the composer's one important opera—he also wrote a graceful Oriental ballet, *Namouna*—and is a gloomy story founded on a legend of ancient Brittany. Its music recalls that of Gounod and Wagner.

Ys is a royal city on the Breton Sea. Its king's daughters, Margared and Rozenn, both love Mylio—but Mylio loves only one of the girls, Rozenn. The gift of her heart flouted, Margared in revenge gives Karnac, enemy of her father and his people, the keys to the sluice-gates that hold back the ocean waves from covering the town. Karnac unlocks the gates: the tide rushes in. But just as the city and people are about to be overwhelmed by the waters, Margared's guilty conscience urges her to fling herself into the raging flood to atone for the wrong she has done. St. Corentin, patron saint of Ys, accepts her sacrifice, the waves retire and all are saved. The best scene in the score is that of Rozenn's wedding.

ROMEO AND JULIETTE

Fr. tragic opera, 4 acts, by Charles Gounod. Text by Barbier and Carré. (Paris, 1867.) Aside from "Faust" this is the only other Gounod opera that has survived in the modern repertory. It tells Shakespeare's tragedy of the Veronese lovers in tender and appealing music, and climaxes in their tragic death.

Despite a feud between the Montagus and Capulets, Juliette, a Capulet girl, meets Romeo, a Montagu youth, who attends a ball in disguise. Their love is mutual, swift and complete. Romeo, knowing the difficulties to be overcome, meets his love at Friar Laurent's, who furthers their plans hoping to effect a reconciliation between the warring families. But Tybalt, a Capulet, kills Romeo's friend Mercutio, and is himself killed in a duel with Romeo, who now has to go into banishment. Juliette's father, anxious to have his daughter keep her pledge to marry Tybalt, insists on the union taking place. But good Friar Laurent gives her a sleeping potion, and she is laid on the family tomb. There it is planned to have Romeo rejoin her, and they will escape. Romeo, however, hearing of her supposed death, and not aware that it is a stratagem, takes poison and staggers to her tomb to bid her farewell. At that moment Juliette awakes. Despairing, she sees her lover die in her arms, and, unable to bear her grief, thrusts his dagger into her own breast.

Another famous Shakespearian tragedy set by a French opera composer is *Hamlet* (Paris, 1868) by Ambroise Thomas. It has a famous scene, Ophelia's "Mad Scene," in its last act, very brilliant musically, and often sung in concert. The "Ghost Scene," earlier in the work, is one of its best dramatic moments, and some old Danish tunes are used in the score with great effect.

SAMSON ET DELILA

Fr. tragic opera, 3 acts, by Camille Saint-Saëns. (Weimar, 1877.) Saint-Saëns' one *great* opera, and one of the most popular scores ever composed. In beautiful and passionate music it tells one of the most dramatic stories the Old Testament contains. Its best known air is probably the voluptuous "My Heart at Thy Sweet Voice." A very effective ballet, the "Bacchanale," is included in the score.

The Hebrews, in their revolt against the Philistines, take comfort in the mighty Samson, who cheers them in battle and slays the great Abimelech. But when the Philistines are scattered and the curses of their High Priest have been silenced, Delilah appears on the steps of Dagon's Temple, and in turn overcomes the mighty Samson. He tries to resist her charms, but accepts her invitation to visit her in her home in the valley of Sorek. There, encouraged by the High Priest to deliver the hope of Israel to the Philistines, Delilah greets him warmly. Artfully learning the source of his marvelous strength, she clips his locks while he sleeps. When he wakes he is easily overpowered. The Philistines now blind him and condemn him to work in the mills. Later, he is led to Dagon's Temple during a great feast. But while Delilah and the Philistines taunt him, and the Hebrews reproach him for his weakness, he prays for a return of his former strength. Heaven grants his prayer, and Samson seizes the main pillars of the temple and brings the entire building down upon the heads of his enemies.

THAÏS

Fr. lyric opera, 3 acts, by Jules Massenet. Text by Gallet after a novel by Anatole France. (Paris, 1894.) The title-rôle of Thaïs, originally written for Sybil Sanderson, is associated in the United States with the names of Mary Garden, Geraldine Farrar and Maria Jeritza. Its story may be summed up in a sentence by Henry T. Fincy as the tale of "A courtesan who turned from the god of love to the love of God." The best known number of the passionate and melodious score is not a vocal, but an instrumental one, the famous "Meditation."

Athanael, a desert monk, is shocked by tales of the lives led by the idle rich in Alexandria during early Christian days. The beautiful courtesan Thaïs is the queen of its hey-dey of sin and debauchery. Athanael sees a vision of her, scantily clad, and acclaimed by the multitude as the Goddess of Love, and hastens to the great city to convert her. Nicias, Thaïs' lover of the moment, is giving a great party at his palace, and Athanael visits him. The loose-living millionaire, an old acquaintance, fits out the monk with fine clothes so that Thaïs will receive him. When they meet she tries to tempt the solemn stranger by throwing off her robes. He swoons in horror and rushes off, only to return to her house and be taunted in her luxurious boudoir. But his earnest pleas wake her conscience, and when he leaves he cries out in agony. Her soul has been reborn, and she agrees to go to the convent in the desert after giving away all her ill-gained possessions. In the midst of the desert, Athanael leaves her with some nuns. But in the process of weaning her from earthly to heavenly love, he himself has turned from love sacred to love profane. A vision shows her to him, dying, and he rushes to her side, filled with an uncontrollable earthly passion. While she dies as a saint in his arms, he sinks beside her, wild with despair, crying out to her to live!

WERTHER

Fr. lyric opera, 4 acts, by Jules Massenet. Text by Blau, Milliet and Hartmann. (Vienna, 1892.) A sentimental tale of tragic love based on a Goethe novel. A virtuous German village wife repulses a romantic lover who commits suicide in despair.

It is an opera of refined and delicate workmanship, its choicest musical page the climaxing duet between Werther and his love Charlotte, "Ah, If Only I Can See Your Eyes. . . ." Geraldine Farrar has sung the rôle of Charlotte in New York.

In the town of Wetzler, in the early eighteenth century, Werther meets Charlotte and each loves the other. But Charlotte tells him she is pledged to marry Albert. And Albert, returning from a journey, holds her to her promise. Werther, unable to overcome his passion for Albert's wife, spends his time writing despairing letters to her, and finally visits her in her home. He finds her weeping over one of his letters. Once more they fervently declare their love for each other and embrace. But virtuous Charlotte manages to tear herself from his arms. They must not yield to the yearning of their hearts! Werther leaves her to borrow a pistol from her husband on a flimsy pretext. Albert, the husband, is glad to loan it to him, and has Charlotte deliver it to Werther's messenger. She, surmising the use he will make of it, however, rushes to his home. It is too late. Werther, who has shot himself, dies in Charlotte's arms to the sound of Christmas bells, happy that she carries only his image in her heart.

WILLIAM TELL

Fr. grand romantic opera, 3 acts, by Gioacchino Rossini. Text by Jouy and Bis. (Paris, 1829.) Rarely heard, this French historical opera by an Italian composer on a Swiss legend may be called the only opera by an *Italian* composer whose *Overture* has achieved a world-wide reputation.

In thirteenth century Switzerland, the Austrian tyrant Gessler is defied by the patriot William Tell who aids his fleeing countrymen to escape Gessler's guards. Planning Gessler's overthrow Tell seeks Arnold's help. Arnold is torn between love of Gessler's beautiful daughter Matilda and loyalty to the cause. Finally, however, when his own father is killed by the tyrant's order, he joins Tell. The latter seen during a festival in the courtyard of Gessler's castle, is ordered to shoot an apple from his young son Jemmy's head. He does so and coolly informs Gessler that the second arrow found on his person was meant for his heart had he killed his own son. Gessler now has Tell thrown into prison. But the tyrant's daughter, Matilda, saves young Jemmy, while Arnold delivers the imprisoned hero with a band of patriots. In the fight which ends in the Austrians' defeat, Gessler falls to Tell's arrow and Matilda falls into Arnold's arms, at last united to her lover.

III

TALES OF THE GREAT GERMAN OPERAS

ALESSANDRO STRADELLA

G. romantic opera, 3 acts, by F. von Flotow. Text by Friedrich (Hamburg, 1844.) The Neapolitan musician who is the hero of this opera really existed. He was assassinated in 1682 by a Roman whose sweetheart he had abducted. Its music is graceful and melodious and the "Hymn to the Virgin" (Act III) is still sung.

The Venetian, Bassi, is the guardian of his niece Leonore, whom he wishes to marry. But she, in love with Stradella, elopes with him. They are to be married in a distant Roman village. Two bandits, engaged by Bassi to kill Stradella are won from their purpose by their victim's musical talent. They come upon Stradella as he is singing a hymn to the Virgin supplicating mercy for sinners. The wonderful sweetness of his voice outweighs the lure of Bassi's gold. They cannot draw their daggers, and when he hears Stradella sing, Bassi himself pardons his niece and her lover.

Other scores by "romantic" German composers are numerous. In Konradin Kreutzer's *Das Nachtlager in Granada,* "The Night Encampment in Granada" (Vienna, 1834) a Spanish shepherd's child saves a princely guest who spends the night in a Moorish ruin from being murdered by two herdsmen, and he rewards her by winning her father's consent to her marriage to her lover. Albert Lortzing's *Czaar und Zimmermann,* "Czar and Carpenter" (Leipsic, 1837) shows a flute-playing Peter the Great in a Haarlem (Holland) shipyard. Various adventures lead to the union of another Russian, who has been impersonating Peter, to his sweetheart. *Der Waldschütz,* "The Poacher" (1842), *Undine* (1848), a legendary tale, and *Der Waffenschmied,* "The Armorer" (Vienna, 1846), a medieval story of love currents crossed which flow together in a happy ending are also by Lortzing. In Heinrich Marschner's *Hans Heiling* (1833) an earthly maiden disdains the love of the king of the gnomes, but he foregoes his revenge to return to his subterranean halls. Ludwig Spohr's *Jessonda:* A young Hindoo girl, Jessonda, meets and loves a Portuguese captain. Forced to marry a rajah, she is about to be burned with his body when—she is saved. Later "romantic" operas are Victor Nessler's *Trompeter von Sakkingen* (1884), highly sentimental medieval love story with one favorite air, "It Was Not Thus to Be," often heard as a cornet solo; and Ignatz Brull's (an Austrian) *Das Goldene Kreutz,*

"The Golden Cross" (1875), in its time a world success. A golden cross given a soldier as a marriage token turns up in the hands of the wrong man. The girl is about to enter a convent, when the rightful owner, not slain, as he was thought to be, turns up and the two lovers are happily wed.

ARIADNE AUF NAXOS

(Ariadne at Naxos)

Gr. burlesque opera in one act and a Prologue, by Richard Strauss. Text by Hugo von Hoffmannsthal, after Molière's play "Le Bourgeois gentilhomme." (Stuttgart, 1912.) Contains graceful and some inspired music, including some of the most difficult airs for coloratura soprano *ever written*. Popular in Germany and Austria.

A great lord is planning to give a party (in the original version the "new rich" Jourdain is about to entertain an admired marquise during his wife's absence). His major-domo orders an entertainment for the evening and an opera, "Ariadne," by a young composer, is to be presented. As a climax there is to be a lively sketch by the dancer Zerbinetta, a notorious flirt, and four male actors. Through the caprice of Zerbinetta, however, the five intrude on the serious opera, and a laughable mixture of the sublime and the ridiculous results. The scene shows a desert island where Ariadne, abandoned by her lover, Theseus, is mourning, watched over by dryads. Zerbinetta and Harlequin look out from the wings and tease her, and after some delightful humor, Ariadne, is consoled for Theseus' loss by the arrival of the god Bacchus, and they pledge their love in a final duet.

Richards Strauss' *Guntram* (Weimar, 1894) is a Wagnerian "salvation through sacrifice" drama, which musically out-Wagners Wagner; and his *Teuersnot* (1901) uses a Middle Age scenic setting to present his own satires on the Munich artists opposed to his aims. His *Ariadne* might be called an attempt to revive the old Italian *opera buffa*.

DER BARBIER VON BAGDAD

(The Barber of Bagdad)

Gr. comic opera in 2 acts, by Peter Cornelius. Text by the Composer, after an "Arabian Night's" tale. (Weimar, 1858.) Considered one of the finest musical scores in the Wagnerian humorous (Meistersinger) style. Abdul's love song, "Let Me, at Your Feet" (Act I) and a very effective male chorus, "Salumaliekum", often sung by choral societies, are among its best known numbers.

A young Bagdadee, Nurredin, loves a cruel girl. Sunk in despair, he does not even shave until he hears that his Margiana will see him. As he hurries off, he is stopped by a talkative barber, Abdul Hassan Ali-Eben Bekar, who claims he can foretell the future. He delays the frantic lover until he has to call his servants to his aid, before he can rush off to the rendezvous. While making eloquent love to Margiana, accompanied by the persistent serenade of Abdul, the Cadi, Margiana's father, returns and Nureddin is hidden in a trunk. The Cadi, who wants to marry Margiana to an old friend, and hunting for a thieving servant, accuses Abdul and Nurredin's servants of a plot to steal, when they try to remove the trunk in which their master is hidden. The hubbub arouses the neighborhood, and the Caliph passing by, orders the lid opened, and advises the Cadi to permit the young lovers to marry.

Another fine comedy in this style is Hermann Goetz's *Der Wiederspenstigen Zähmung*, "The Taming of the Shrew," (1784), after Shakespeare's play. Hugo Wolff's *Der Correqidor* (1896) after Alarcon's "The Three-Cornered Hat" (which the Spanish composer de Falla has set it as a ballet), has been called a "Meistersinger translated into Spanish," because of its elaborate polyphonic style. But it is undramatic and seldom heard. E. N. von Reznicek's merry *Donna Diana* (1894) has a very taking overture. Eugen d'Albert's *Die Abreise*, "The Departure" (1898) and his *Flauto Solo*, based on an amusing incident of the youth of Frederick the Great, as well as Leo Blech's *Das War Ich*, "That Was I," (1902), and his *Versiegelt*, "Sealed Up," (1908)—in which the daughter of a magistrate, "sealed up" by his clerk in a closet to be seized for taxes (he had hidden there when visiting the fair widow who owned it) is released by his daughter only after he promises to consent to her marrying her lover—are also among the better-known German humorous operas.

ELECTRA

Gr. "symphonic" opera in 1 act, by Richard Strauss. Text by Hugo von Hoffmannsthal. A sensational and sanguinary tragedy of ancient Greece. The main musical effect of the work lies in the orchestral score.

Queen Klytemnestra and her lover Aegisthus have murdered the King, and exiled the youthful heir to the throne, her son Orestes.

Electra's daughter is a sort of woman Hamlet, and prays for vengeance. Her gentle sister Chrysothemis, however, advises making the best of things. Electra, defiant, hides her feelings from her mother, who complains of fearful dreams at night. Electra then tells her hated mother that the spilling of a woman's blood will cure her and that the rite should be performed by a stranger, "yet, of their house." Consumed with bitterness, she turns on the Queen, and predicts her murder. Chrysothemis now announces the arrival of an old man and a youth bearing tidings of the death of Orestes. Electra refuses to believe this, and despite her sister's plea, plans the murder of her mother. Passionately revengeful, she creeps around the wall of the palace to fulfill her designs, when her exiled brother, Orestes, returns. Accepting the task she has imposed upon herself, she slays his mother, and in the turmoil that ensues, also kills Aegisthus, whom Electra has enticed to his doom. Amongst the faithful servants Electra celebrates Orestes' just vengeance, horrible though it is, and dances a mad dance until she falls senseless.

EURYANTHE

Gr. romantic opera, 3 acts, by Carl Maria von Weber. Text by Helmine von Chezy. (Vienna, 1823.) One of those knightly legends of the Middle Ages which have so great an attraction for the German composer, and famous for a very beautiful Overture, "Euryanthe" contains numerous fine melodies.

Lysiart, Count of Forest, who knows no scruples, provokes Adolar, Count of Nevers so greatly by his assertion that all women are accessible to seduction, that he wagers his entire fortune and estates on the fidelity of his bride-to-be, the beautiful Euryanthe of Savoy. Lysiart agrees to bring back a token of Euryanthe's favor to prove he has won the wager. The girl spends much time in prayer at the grave of Emma, Adolar's sister, who had poisoned herself after her lover's death in battle. The redemption of Emma's soul rests upon bathing a ring belonging to the dead girl with the tears of a virtuous woman shed in extreme need. This, the reason for Euryanthe's faithful visits to the grave, is discovered by Eglantine, who, loving Adolar, conceals her jealousy and wreaks vengeance upon Euryanthe by stealing the ring and giving it to Lysiart. He, in turn, presents it to Count Adolar as the token of his bride's faithlessness. Adolar, in despair, attempts the death of Euryanthe, but the intervention of the King, and the confessions of Eglantine restore his faith in Euryanthe. She forgives him and they are happily united. But Lysiart, who has murdered Eglantine in a frenzy of rage, forfeits not only all he won to Adolar, but pays with his life for his homicide.

Tales of medieval chivalry always have attracted the Teuton composer. Schumann's *Genoveva* (1850) lives on the stage only in Germany. Golo loves the wife of Siegfried, a count who sallies out to fight the Saracens under Carl Martel. He tries to seduce her, but is foiled by his constancy to her husband. Schubert's romantic operas *Fierrabras* and *Alfonso and Estrella* contain charming pages, but their foolish librettos and lack of action prevent their performance. Moderns like H. Pfitzner in *Die Rose vom Liebesgarten* (1901), in *Der Arme Heinrich* (1895) a beautiful romance of a pure maid's sacrifice for a knight she loves; and Siegfried Wagner, in a long series of scores, among which *An Allem Ist Hütchen Schuld*, "It's all the Fault of the Little Cap", (1917), go back to medieval German legend for subjects.

DER FLIEGENDE HOLLANDER

(The Flying Dutchman)

Gr. romantic opera, 3 acts, by Richard Wagner. Text by the composer. (Dresden, 1843). A Dutch captain, during a severe storm off the Cape of Good Hope, swears a sacrilegious oath that he will get around the Cape if it takes him all eternity. So through centuries, his phantom ship, manned by demons and ghosts, sails the seven seas to the terror of all mariners. Only a woman's self-sacrificing love (he is allowed to land once every seven years to seek it) can raise the curse. The most famous musical number is "Senta's Ballad", a spinning song.

The ship of the accursed "Flying Dutchman", with blood-red sails and black masts, slips into a quiet harbor one day and casts anchor. The Phantom Captain is given one opportunity in seven years for his freedom, if he can find a girl who will give up everything for him. Upon landing, the Dutchman seeks shelter with Daland, a sea captain, and meeting his daughter, falls in love with her, and proposes marriage. Daland, bribed by the Dutchman's gold agrees. The girl, musing over the familiar legend of the Flying Dutchman, longs to meet him so that she may, through her fidelity, raise his curse. Eric, her young admirer, tells her of a dream, in which she is carried away by the Dutchman, much to her delight. Meeting him, Senta, Daland's daughter pledges her love, and everything is prepared for the wedding. While the Norwegian ship is alive with light and gayety, there is an ominous silence on the Flying Dutchman's ship, until suddenly lights glow on it, and the waters begin to heave. Now Eric accompanies Senta to the shore, begging her not to go. The Dutch Captain coming upon them, believes she has betrayed him and all is lost. He regains his ship, the bloody sails swell, and the Phantom Ship puts out to sea. Then Senta, in her anguish, flings herself from the rocks into the ocean. The Flying Dutchman's ship sinks as Senta and the Captain, glorying in the lifting of the curse, appear in a vision.

Wagner's "Flying Dutchman" is probably the greatest of all "sea operas", but composers of many nations have written scores in which the ocean plays a part. *Strandrecht* (Leipsic, 1906), or "The Wreckers", by the English woman composer Ethyl Smyth, is a fine, romantic work. A preacher's wife, Thurza, persuades her young lover (it is on the Cornish coast), to light a beacon so that the "wreckers" who include her husband and the rest of the village will be deprived of their hideous profits on the ships wrecked for want of warning. When this is discovered, Thurza and her lover are left bound in a cavern to be drowned by the tide.

The Frenchman Bruneau in *L'Ouragan*, "The Hurricane", (Paris, 1897), develops in "naturalistic" music a gloomy tale of jealousy, love and revenge among the Breton fisherfolk of a wild coast. The Russian Rimsky-Korsakof, in *Sadko* (Moskow, 1897) tells the legend of how Sadko, the minstrel of Novgorod, won the love of the sea-king's daughter beneath the waves. His music sets the sea-king and all his court dancing so madly that tremendous tempests rage along the shores dashing all ships to pieces. Then Sadko escapes with his love to the surface, after the sea-folk have danced themselves dead.

In Schillings' *Moloch* (1907) we have a sea voyage from fallen Carthage to the dim Scandinavian land of Thule, where a Carthaginian takes his fearsome god in an effort to win recruits for his shrine. The ozone of the Adriatic clings to such lighter comic operas as Sir Authur Sullivan's *The Pirates of Penzance*, and *The Gondoliers*, and the Russian César Cui has paid a tribute to the Spanish Main in his buccaneer opera, *Le Flibustier*.

FIDELIO

Gr. opera, 2 acts, by Ludwig von Beethoven. Text by Sonnleithner and Treitschke. (Vienna, 1814). The great Beethoven's one and *only opera*. It was inspired by his indignation at the thought that Mozart had chozen so vile a libertine as Don Juan as the hero of his opera. "I will write an opera whose heroine is a virtuous wife", he thought and did so in "Fidelio". The most famous number in the work is the great area, *Abscheulicher, wo eilst du him?* ("Abominable One, Whither Away"), sung by Fidelio.

Don Pizarro, governor of a Spanish prison, has Don Florestan, a personal enemy, thrown into a dungeon, and plans to let him die of starvation. He circulates the story that Don Florestan has died. Don Florestan's faithful wife Leonore, not believing this, disguises herself as the boy Fidelio, and enters the service of Rocco, the jailer. Marzelline, the jailer's daughter, falls in love with the handsome "youth", and Fidelio, in order to continue her masquerade, agrees to marry her. Suddenly word is received that Don Fernando, Minister of State, is due to inspect the prison, and Don Pizarro, fearful that the Minister will learn that he has used his office and prison to further a personal hatred, decides to have Don Florestan murdered and buried at once. Rocco declines to murder, but consents to dig the grave, and Fidelio, hoping to get some news to her husband, assists in the digging. As the pair enter the dungeon to prepare the grave, Don Florestan sinks exhausted, but is partly revived by the bread which his wife gives him. Pizarro enters, prepared to commit the murder himself. But now Fidelio thrusts herself between them and announces her identity, holding the cowardly Pizarro off with a pistol. Trumpets announce the arrival of Don Fernando. The latter praises the faithfulness of Fidelio, and condemns the murderous governor of the prison, Don Pizarro, to wear the chains taken from his victim. Marzelline, the jailer's daughter, finds comfort in the love of a real boy—Jacquinto, the gate-keeper.

DER FREISCHÜTZ

Gr. romantic opera, 3 acts, by Carl Maria von Weber. Text by F. Kind. (Berlin, 1821). One of the truest "folk operas" ever written, and a score which probably is the composer's best. There are many fine airs and in the orchestra horns are used for nature description, and piccolo flutes for the satanic laughter of hell in the "Wolf's Gorge", with wonderful effect. One of the most famous melodies is "The Bridal Wreath" chorus.

During a sharp-shooting contest to decide who shall succeed Kuno, the head ranger of the Duke of Bohemia, Max loses to Kilian, the peasant. Caspar, Max's brother ranger, knowing that Max loves Agnes, Kuno's daughter, and cannot hope to win her unless he becomes head-ranger, consoles him. Caspar has sold his soul to the Evil One, and wants to win it back again by bringing him another victim. He induces Max to seek help from the Evil One, and although warned by the spirit of his mother, Max appears and consults Zamiel (the Devil). The latter assures him that Agnes would drown herself if he failed at the final shooting-match. So amid lightnings and thunder in the Wolf's Gorge the evil Zamiel moulds seven magic bullets, to be used in the contest. Six are to be shot at whatever tar-

the young farmers are greatly dejected. Some time later the heartbroken Lionel and Plunkett, stopping at a tavern, see the ladies of their heart among a courtly hunting party. But when Lionel throws himself at Martha's feet, she scorns him and says he must be insane. Plunket tries to console him, but in vain. The Queen, seeing a ring Lionel wears, discovers he is of noble birth, and the rightful Earl of Derby. Repentant Martha (Lady Harriet) who now knows she loves Lionel, and Julia again go to Richmond Fair. There all misunderstandings are cleared up and betrothals follow between Lionel and Lady Harriet, Plunkett and Julia.

DIE MEISTERSINGER VON NÜRNBERG
(The Mastersingers of Nuremburg)

Gr. opera, 3 acts, by Richard Wagner. Text by the composer. (Munich, 1868). The story's underlying moral is that individual genius will shake off the fetters of routine and tradition and rise above them. Hans Sachs, as Wagner says, is " the representative of the artistic and creative spirit of the people". A glorious "Overture", a favorite symphony concert number, and the famous "Walther's Prize Song" are the two best-known musical numbers.

The winner of the Nürnberg burghers' "Mastersingers" song-contest is to secure as prize the hand of the lovely Eva, daughter of Pogner the Goldsmith, and pedantic Beckmesser, suitor for her hand, is "marker" in the contest when Walther, a young poet and noble, who loves Eva, sings his offering. Hans Sachs, a philosophical cobbler, ponders over the innumerable bad marks given Walther despite a marvelously sweet voice. When Beckmesser serenades Eva with the song he is to sing the next day, Sachs interrupts him with a jolly catch. He succeeds in confusing Beckmesser to such an extent that the neighbors are aroused, and set upon him with clubs. After the near-riot, Walther, with whom Eva has promised to elope no matter who wins the contest, is dragged into Sachs' shop. Sachs encourages him. Walther spends the night there, and in the morning puts to words and music an idyllic melody he heard the night before in a dream. Beckmesser gets possession of the music, and when the contest begins, mixes it up with his own melody, and makes a fiasco of his attempt. Walther, called upon to sing, gives a wonderful rendition of the song, and wins the Mastersingers' prize as well as lovely Eva's hand.

MONA LISA

Gr. tragic opera, 2 acts, by Max Schillings. Text by Beatrice

Dovsky. (Stuttgart, 1915), A Renaissance tragedy of gripping dramatic power which scored only a qualified success when heard at the Metropolitan Opera House in New York, probably owing to the dissonant modern character of its music. Its heroine is Mona Lisa, whose mysterious smile Leonardo da Vinci has immortalized in his famous painting.

In a house in Florence, once the home of Francesco del Gioconda, Mona Lisa's husband, now a monastic establishment, a lay brother is leading two tourists, an elderly husband and a young bride, through its rooms. He tells the tale of the olden tragedy.

Mona Lisa is treasured by the rich merchant Francesco del Gioconda even above his marvelous collection of pearls. But—he cannot seem to find the key to his obedient wife's heart and love. In a papal messenger sent to purchase a fine pearl the young wife recognizes her former lover, Giovanni. He returns after the other guests have left the house, and they plan to flee, when jealous Francesco returns. Mona Lisa hides Giovanni in the treasure cabinet. But Francesco knows he is there. After cruelly playing with Mona Lisa's anguish he flings the key (he has locked the cabinet as he thinks) into the Arno river, so that his wife's lover shall suffocate. By chance it falls in a boat, and Mona Lisa's step-daughter hands it to her in the morning. Her lover is dead by now. Insane with despair and revenge Mona Lisa innocently pretends she wants a pearl necklace. When Francesco opens the cabinet-safe she pushes him in, locks the door and lets him smother to death as her lover did.

As the monk concludes his story, and the young bride drops a flower at his feet when she leaves with her husband, he stretches out his arm after her departing form and cries: "Mona Lisa, Mona Lisa!"

OBERON

Gr. romantic opera, 3 acts, by Carl Maria von Weber. Text by Theodor Hell. (London, 1826). Webber's last work, completed a month before he died is really a "fairytale opera", which mingles Oriental color and charm with the romance of chivalry. The great vocal number is Rezia's "Ocean Aria", and a genuine Arabian tune has been used for the chorus of Harem Guards. A fine "Overture", and many charming songs, dances and march numbers are features of the score.

Oberon, king of the elves, and his wife Titania cannot be reconciled to each other unless they witness the fidelity of a pair of lovers under the most trying circumstances. Puck, Oberon's servant, selects Huon, a Burgundian knight, for the test. Houn, having slain the son of Charlemagne in a duel, in atonement must visit Bagdad, slay the

The "expressionistic" and "symbolic" operas of the German ultra-modern composer Franz Schreker, are *mystic*, like *Parsifal*. They all develop the motive of *sacrifice* and *renunciation*. But, paired with this is a morbid and fantastic *sex-interest*. In *Der Schatzgräber*, "The Treasure Hunter" (1920), a knight and a woman waver between noble impulse and animal sensuousness in a sequence of fantastic events. In *Die Gezeichneten*, "Branded", (1918), a girl repulses the nobler love of a repulsive hunchback, to yield to the embrace of a libertine on a pleasure island in the gulf of Genoa, though she has heart-disease and knows that the moment she yields to love, she dies. *Das Speilwerk und die Prinzessin*, "The Bell-Chime and the Princess" (1920) is another romance of the struggle between love and lust in the human breast, and *Der Ferne Klang*, "The Distant Tone" (1912) is the tale of Grete, a drunkard's daughter whom her parent tries to sell to a libertine. She escapes, but her longing for her true lover Fritz, who has left her to try and write an opera, is not strong enough to prevent her from gratifying inherited instincts in a life of prostitution. In Venice, Fritz, (a composer seeking an elusive opera theme, "the distant tone") meets Grete, and repulses her with contempt. In the climax, realizing that his hunt for ideal melody has ruined his and Grete's life, he dies in her arms. Death realizes his dream. Schreker's repulsive stories are told in modernist music of great orchestral power and rich effect.

RIENZI

(The Last of the Tribunes)

Gr. tragic opera, 5 acts, by Richard Wagner. Text by the composer. (Dresden, 1842). Rienzi is a people's hero who rescues his people from an aristocratic tyranny only—as is so often the case—to be betrayed in a cowardly way by those whom he sought to free. It was influenced by the French "historical operas" such as Meyerbeer's, Auber's *Muette* and Rossini's *Tell*. While not one of Wagner's greatest scores it has a fine Overture and many melody pages.

Rienzi, leader of the Roman people, is ambitious. He has a plan to restore to the republic the power that once was hers. He takes the part of the oppressed people in their struggles against the nobles. When about to take vengeance on Adriano, a noble, he learns that the latter is the lover of his own sister, Irene, and so spares him. Ruling Rome with an iron hand, he narrowly escapes assassination in a plot. He condemns all those mixed up in it to death, but Adriano, whose father is involved, pleads so warmly in behalf of the condemned that Rienzi relents. Yet the nobles now turn against him, and the people also revolt, shocked by his bloody deeds. Adriano begs Irene to flee when the rebellion against Rienzi begins but, loyal to her brother, she refuses. Both, in the uprising of the people, are stoned to death, Adriano joining them to die by his sweetheart's side.

DER RING DES NIBELUNGEN

(The Nibelungen Ring)

The "Nibelungen Ring" is a vast trilogy of three operas, preceded by a Prologue Opera. Humanity freed and the old Teuton gods perishing is the double theme, with the figure of Fate, which rules both gods and men, ever in the background. They are the operas of "leading motives" and "guiding themes". In the "Rhinegold", the golden treasure of the Rhine-Maidens, which is to curse men and gods, is stolen by Alberich, the evil dwarf. In "The Valkyrie"—the most popular of the four operas—the tragic loves of brother and sister produce the hero of the succeeding score, "Siegfried". He wins his bride and seals the doom of the Teuton gods, realized in "The Dusk of the Gods", in which their heaven, Valhalla, falls, sapped by the lust for power and gold, and a new world of freedom, founded on self-sacrifices rises in its place. In "Rhinegold" the glorious music of the opening scene where the Rhine-Maidens sing beneath the green waves and the "March to Valhalla" stand out. In "The Valkyrie" the "Spring Song, "Siegmund's Love Song" and the "Fire Magic"; in "Siegfried", the famous *Waldweben,* the "Woodland Weaving" music that expresses the myriad voices of forests, and the Love Duets in the final scene stand out. In "The Dusk of the Gods", Siegfried's "Funeral March" is one of the best-known themes.

I

RHEINGOLD

Alberich, dwarf prince of the Nibelungs, by stealth succeeds in snatching from the guardianship of the Rhine-Maidens a portion of the Rheingold, a treasure which they keep watch over under the river. He who fashions from this metal a ring can rule the world. Meanwhile, Wotan and Fricka, in the heaven of the gods, mourn the capture of the daughter Freia by the giants Fasolt and Fafner. Believing that possession of the ring would enable them to win her back again, they visit Alberich, and cajole him into assuming various shapes. When he changes himself into a toad, they overpower him, and he is forced to order the Nibelungs to deliver the ring. However, he curses it and its possessors. Wotan and Fricka use it to buy back lovely Freia, goddess of youth and beauty. But the evil effect of Alberich's curse is at once evident, for the giants Fafner and Fasolt struggle for the Ring, and the titanic combat is ended only with the death of Fasolt. So, with happiness restored to them, Wotan leads his gods and goddesses back to Valhalla over a rainbow bridge; but in the distance is heard the mournful wails of the Rhine-Maidens over the loss of their treasured Rheingold!

II

DIE WAIKÜRE

(The Valkyrie)

The god Wotan and Alberich, the dwarf prince, are both striving to gain the magic Nibelung Ring, now in the hands of the Giant Fafner. Knowing that to succeed in his mission, a hero must be born to carry it out, Wotan contracts many marriages in the hope of begetting a son. Siegmund, by drawing Wotan's sword from a great oak, appears to be the chosen hero, so Wotan tells Brunnhilde, his favorite daughter, and a Valkyrie to protect him. But Fricka, the wife of Wotan, a scold, insists that Wotan punish Siegmund for stealing Sieglinde, whom he loves, from her husband Hunding. In the ensuing pursuit, the young hero is killed, and Brunnhilde carries off Sieglinde on her winged steed to a forest shelter. She predicts that Sieglinde will bear a son who will be the hero Siegfried. Wotan, furious with Brunnhilde for trying to save Siegmund and Sieglinde, condemns her to a magic sleep, surrounded by a hedge fire and to fall to the first man who wakens her. Then, his pity getting the upper hand, he softens his sentence by saying that she shall be won only by a hero who can penetrate the flame hedge which surrounds her. He leaves Brunnhilde as the circle of fire breaks around the summit of the rocks upon which she slumbers.

III

SIEGFRIED

Siegfried, born to perform deeds of strength, lives with an ugly dwarf in the forest. His mother, Sieglinde, who died when giving him birth, left him a broken sword which, when rewelded will permit its maker to slay the dragon Fafner, and regain the Nibelung Ring. Mime the dwarf, is unable to weld the pieces of the sword, as this task is only possible to one who knows no fear. But Siegfried undertakes it successfully, and sallies forth at the god Wotan's suggestion, to dispatch the dragon. Mime, in his own defense, plans to murder the youthful Siegfried, if he kills the dragon and returns the Ring.

Wotan, meanwhile, announces the approach of Siegfried to Alberich, who also plans to kill the slayer of Fafner, and thus gain possession of the Ring. As Wotan blows his horn, the Dragon emerges from his cave and is easily slain by the young hero. With the Dragon's blood spilled on his lips, Siegfried understands the warbling of the forest birds who tell him where to find the Ring, and also warn him of impending danger at the hands of Alberich. Securing the Ring, the victorious youth meets the dwarf Alberich at the mouth of the cave, and puts an end to him. He then learns that the goddess Brunnhilde lies asleep in a magic circle of fire high up among the rocks, and his courage having been tested by the god Wotan, he plunges through the flames and awakens the sleeping Brunnhilde with an ardent kiss. She joyously recognizes in him the hero who will save the world and, goddess though she be, she falls in love with him. This makes her lose her divinity, but glad to be only a woman if she may love him, she sinks happily into his arms.

IV

GÖTTERDÄMMERUNG

(The Dusk of the Gods)

Brunnhilde's magic sleep ends with the coming of Siegfried. They are wed, and live together in a cave until he is restless for further adventure. Leaving the Ring of the Nibelungs, obtained by slaying Fafner, the Dragon, as a pledge, he departs on Brunnhilde's steed, Grane. He visits King Gunther, who lives with his sister Gutrune, and their half-brother Hagen. The latter, son of Alberich the dwarf, plans to restore the Ring to his father, and invites Siegfried to drink a potion which causes him to forget Brunnhilde and fall in love with Gutrune. Siegfried, with no memory of the past, and happy with Gutrune, gives magic aid to King Gunther, and succeeds in bringing Brunnhilde to his castle, taking the Ring from her. She arrives grief-stricken at seeing Siegfried Gutrune's lover; but Siegfried, not remembering her at all, is unable to explain. When Brunnhilde denounces him, Hagen, still intent upon securing the Ring, urges her to take revenge. Siegfried's back having been turned to an enemy, is vulnerable, and while out hunting, the Rhine-Maidens try to persuade him to give up the Ring. He refuses, and they predict his death. Hagen, while the hunting party is in the forest, gives Siegfried a magic drink which restores his memory. He tells of his marriage to Brunnhilde—to Gunther's horror—and Hagen thrusts his spear into his back, killing him. Hagen then kills Gunther in a battle for the Ring, but finds he is unable to take it from Siegfried's finger. Brunnhilde now summons two ravens and sends them to destroy the power of the gods by burning Valhalla. Setting a funeral pyre at Siegfried's bier, she mounts her steed, and rides into the flames, while the Rhine rises and quenches the fire. Rhine-Maidens, riding on the flood, snatch the Ring from the embers, and Hagen, rushing in to seize it is drawn down into the whirlpool. In the distance the gods await their doom in burning Vahalla.

DER ROSENKAVALIER

(The Rose Cavalier)

Gr. "comedy for music", 3 acts, by Richard Strauss. Text by Hugo von Hoffmannthal. (Dresden, 1911). A love-comedy of Vienna in the Baroque days of the Empress Maria-Theresa. Its piquant situations and colorful stage action have made it a favorite, though the popular waltz melody which appears in the score again and again has been called "coffee-house music of the finest workmanship". It is filled with the spirit of Vienna dance tune.

Octavian, lover of the Princess von Werdensberg, and at that moment in her boudoir, dons the garb of a maid when he thinks the Prince has unexpectedly returned from hunting in Silesia. While thus disguised, he attracts the amorous attentions of the uncouth Baron Ochs. Later he is selected to convey the Silver Rose, the customary gift of betrothal, from the Baron to the beautiful Sophia, whom the Baron is to wed. As soon as they meet Octavian and Sophia fall in love with each other. But the girl's father insists on her wedding the Baron, whom Octavian wounds after he has disgusted Sophia by his impudence and loose manners. Using his wits, Octavian now succeeds in implicating the Baron in a succession of amusing though disgraceful scrapes. Then, having proved Ochs' unworthiness, Octavian wins Sophia, his "friend" the Princess relinquishing her young gallant with a sigh.

SALOME

Gr. dramatic opera in 1 act, by Richard Strauss. Text after Oscar Wilde's play by the same name. (Dresden, 1905). Strauss' most *notorious* opera, founded on the play by Wilde, which makes Salome so realistically depraved a character, it was a world sensation when it appeared. Musically it is a brilliant, glowingly colorful and fascinating score, and its famous "Dance of Seven Veils" literally set thousands of veils fluttering in "Salome" dances everywhere among "interpretative dancers" in its hey-day.

While Herod and Herodias are feasting, Narraboth, and his soldiers guard the cistern outside the palace walls, where Jokanaan, the Prophet, (John the Baptist) is imprisoned. Herod fears to kill his prisoner for fear of the Jews' vengeance. But Herodias' beautiful daughter Salome, who spurns the love of Naraboth, and loathes the amorous advances of her mother's husband, leaves the banquet hall for the cool terrace. There she hears the wonderful voice of the Prophet, denouncing sinful Herod and Herodias. She orders Narraboth to bring his prisoner before her. Narraboth obeys her request, then kills himself in a fit of mad jealousy, when Salome makes passionate love to the holy man. Jokanaan now returns to his cistern, and when Herod and Herodias come upon the terrace with their entire court, Salome, whom the Prophet has repulsed, obeys Herod's demand and dances for him on condition that he grant any request she may make. She throws off her seven veils as she dances, until she is nude. (It was this feature of the opera which gave offense at the New York Metropolitan and led to the work's being withdrawn). Then Salome, at her mother's instigation, asks nothing less than the head of Jokanaan. Herod, much disturbed, grants her wish, and when in her depraved lust Salome enters with the head of the holy man on a platter, and presses her living lips to its dead ones, the king, sickened by the sight of her degenerate love, orders his legionaries to smother her with their shields.

TANNHÄUSER

(The Song Contest in the Wartburg)

Gr. romantic opera, 3 acts, by Richard Wagner. Text by the composer. Tannhäuser is an opera whose subject is the redemption of a human soul by love, pure love. Venus represents merely sensuous passion, but her love does not bring true happiness. The love that is capable of self-sacrifice, like that of Elizabeth, who gives up Tannhäuser to save him, is the higher and nobler one that earns salvation. Of all the fine musical numbers in the score, the "Prelude", the "Pilgrims Chorus" the "Entrance March of the Guests", the "Bacchanale" (Ballet) and others, the famous romance "The Evening Star" is probably the best known.

At the annual tournament of minstrels, Tannhäuser excels all others, and as a prize, wins the hand of the adorable Elizabeth, niece of the Landgrave of Thuringia. But he returns to the enchanted grotto of Venus, in a magic hillside, and sinks into her soft white arms instead of claiming his bride. Venus surrounds him with luxury, beauty, and the wiles of her abandoned love, and he gladly stays with her a whole year. Then, tiring of sensual love, he returns to the Wartburg, repentant. Wolfram, his closest friend, reminds him of his Elizabeth, and he essays once more to win her hand

tender passion from the most delicate hints of growing affection to the climax of love's madness and longing are voiced in its music. The one great outstanding number of the score is the immortal *Isolde's Liebstod* ("Isolda's Love-Death").

The ship of Tristan, one of King Mark of Cornwall's knights, brings Isolde to Cornwall to become the bride of his sovereign. But Isolde's lover Morold, had been killed in battle by a Cornish knight. She keeps the splinter of steel from his wound, and finds one day it fits a nick in the sword of Tristan. Ordering her maid, Brangaene, to prepare a poison, she decides to avenge Morold by making Tristan share this drink with her, since she prefers death to marrying old King Mark. Brangaene, however, loving Isolde too much to cause her death, mixes a love potion. Tristan and Isolde drink and love takes possession of their hearts. Tristan, after Isolde's marriage to the King improves Mark's absences to see his sweetheart, until they are surprised by the sudden appearance of the King and jealous Melot, who has betrayed them. Melot mortally wounds Tristan in a fight that follows. While Tristan dies in delirium later on, in his castle in Brittany, Isolde arrives as he is dying, and soon after the King comes to forgive his actions. Kurwenal, Tristan's servant, thinking he wants to kill Tristan, attacks and slays Melot, but falls a victim to the King's soldiers. Poor King Mark finds Isolde at Tristan's death-bed, and offers a prayer for the hapless lovers as she dies of broken heart.

DIE ZAUBERFLÖTE

(The Magic Flute)

Gr. opera in 2 acts, by Wolfgang Amadeus Mozart. Text by Schikaneder. (Vienna, 1791). Musically Mozart's most "folk-wise" score, one overflowing with the loveliest melodies, the opera's fantastic libretto seems devoid of sense unless we remember that it is "symbolic", and that its jumbled story really implies that the young liberal Austrian Emperor Joseph II, a favorer of Free-Masonry, will save Austria from the tyranny of his mother, the Empress Maria Theresia and restored to the Austrian people their heritage of human love and laughter.

Prince Tamino, pursued by a huge serpent, owes his life to the intercession of three attendants of the Queen of the Night. Papageno, his own attendant, appears dressed as a bird, and boasts that it was he who slew the snake. In punishment, his lips are locked. Then the Queen of Night urges the two to free her lovely daughter from the influence of Sarastro, Priest of Isis, and to this end presents them with a magic flute and a chime of bells. In Sarastro's palace they frighten away a Moor who is dragging off Pamina, a beautiful girl. When the Moor returns to attack them, Sarastro appears, punishes the Moor, and decrees that Tamino and his attendant show their worth by undergoing various temple ordeals of silence. Both our adventurers are tempted to break their silence, and eventually Papageno succumbs, but the Prince perseveres though Pamina tempts him. Papageno, who has fallen in love with Papagena, finally uses his magic chimes, and his charming love appears before him. The Prince, with the aid of the Magic Flute, manages to pass through fire and water with Pamina, whose lost confidence in him is restored, and both are united in wedlock by Sarastro, amid general happiness, while the wicked Queen of Night and Amonastro the Moor, are banished.

In an ultra-modern score by Richard Strauss, *Die Frau ohne Schatten,* "The Woman Without a Shadow" (Vienna, 1919), we have an attempt at a "sequel" to Mozart's *Magic Flute.* In a gorgeous Oriental setting, rich in magnificent stage pictures and the glitter of golden and multicolored costumes, the composer presents two couples. One is an emperor and his empress, the other a weaver and his wife. The empress, to save her husband from a magic curse, which will turn him to stone, must have a child. She is a spirit being, can cast no shadow, and cannot bear him an heir. But if she can *buy* some human woman's shadow she will be able to raise the curse. In the end she renounces happiness for her husband and herself rather than purchase it at another's expense—and finds that she has broken the magic spell by her sacrifice.

IV

TALES OF THE GREAT OPERAS OF OTHER LANDS

I

America

Cleopatra's Night

Am. tragic opera, 2 acts, by Henry Hadley. Text by Alice Leale Pollock, after Gauthier's story. (New York, 1920). The romantic episode of the Egyptian commoner who dared to love a queen, and paid for his brief hours of bliss with his life, has been set to colorful music.

Cleopatra's golden bath awaits the queen, while her slave Mardion tells of her love for Meiámoun, a hunter. While Cleopatra's slaves begin to disrobe her for the bath, she laments the loneliness of queens. Immediately an arrow falls at her feet, attached to it a note saying: "I love you!" Cleopatra smiles and sets her foot in the water—then screams, for a man's head appears in her bath! He is her anonymous adorer and the guards are about to kill him, when Cleopatra orders him spared. Mardion recognizes him as Meiàmoun. But the hunter has forgotten his old love, and kneels before the queen, repeating "I love you!" A smile crosses her face. She will grant him "one of Cleopatra's nights"—but he must die at dawn. Mardion hands him a dagger and begs him to commit suicide. When he refuses, she does so instead, and Cleopatra orders her body thrown to the crocodiles, while she leaves for the palace with Meiàmoun. An orgy on the palace terrace, where dancing-girls perform the passion-dances of the East, leaves Meriàmoun depressed. Dawn is near. He draws the curtains, and wishes his night might last forever. Cleopatra starts when the guard enters with the poison-cup. She, too, has a moment's compunction, but—trumpets announce the arrival of Marc Antony—and Meiàmoun drains the fatal cup! Then Cleopatra, while slaves cover the quiet form, goes to meet the Roman to raise to his living lips her own which have just culled the Egyptian's dying kiss.

Henry Hadley's other operas include a short Renaissance score *Bianca* (1918) and *Azora, the Daughter of Montezuma* (Chicago, 1917). The latter is a colorful tale of the Spanish conquest of Mexico. It is a story of Aztec passion, with a climax in which a high-priest's sacrificial knife falls clattering from his hand as he is about to slay two faithful lovers when Cortez bursts into the temple. There are many melodious pages and some charming ballet numbers.

CYRANO DE BERGERAC

Am. dramatic opera, 4 acts, by Walter Damrosch. Text by W. J. Henderson, after Rostand's drama. (New York, 1913).

Roxane, Cyrano de Bergerac's lovely cousin, for whom he nourishes a mad secret affection, shows that she loves Christian. Her cousin Cyrano is afraid to advance his own suit because of his huge and unromantic nose! He fears ridicule, yet men rarely dare it, because of his mastery of the rapier. Writing a love letter to Roxane, he encounters Christian. The latter, despairing of success with Roxane, recklessly subjects Cyrano to public ridicule. Roxane, however, had exacted from him a promise to protect young Christian, so he controls himself. Eventually he tells Christian that Roxane cares for him, and offers him the use of the letter which he himself had written, when Christian complains that he can't write a love letter. Then he loyally aids Christian in his proposal, witnesses his marriage to Roxane, and accompanies him to the battlefield, continuing to write

Christian's ardent love letters for him. Roxane, moved by the heat of these missives, joins them in the field, and just as she discovers that her love has really been won by the letters of Cyrano, both her husband and the faithful Cyrano are fatally wounded in an assault.

She nurses Cyrano at a nearby convent, where he dies, "without a stain upon his snow-white plume", a soldier and a gentleman.

The Scarlet Letter (Boston, 1896), by the same composer, is an operatic setting of Hawthorne's immortal story of Puritan New England by the same name.

MONA

Am. dramatic opera, 3 acts, by Horatio Parker. Text by Brian Hooker. (New York, 1912). A $10,000 prize opera whose rather undramatic character is balanced by many fine pages of high musical quality.

During Roman days in Britain, Mona, last descendant of Boadicea, and Princess of Britain, is chosen to lead her tribe in a desperate revolt against the invaders. Gwynn (his father is the Roman Governor, his mother a British captive), strives for peace and wins Mona's love. Meeting her in a Druid temple, he confesses that he is half a Roman and Mona, though still loving him, has him taken captive, though she does not divulge his secret. In a battle that follows the Romans break the Britons, while Gwynn, escaping, meets Mona and again pleads for peace. He assures her that his position as the Governor's son will bring this about. But Mona, infuriated, thinks him a traitor. After a passionate denunciation she slays him. The Roman Governor, coming on the scene, recognizes in Gwynn his dead son Quintus. Mona, learning that her fury had led her to destroy not only her people's hope for peace, but the only man she loves, is led off a captive.

Horatio Parker's *Fairyland* (Los Angeles, 1915), is an "allegorical" opera. Its story, by Brian Hooker, is staged in an imaginary land of Medieval times, during the 13th century. After many misadventures, (three acts of them), two lovers are about to be cruelly burned on a funeral pyre when, as Rosamund touches Auburn with a magic rose, the powers of the world retreat before them, their chains drop off, the flames of the stake go out and they find themselves the rulers of Fairyland, eternally happy, where wickedness, greed and intolerance of the world cannot reach them.

Frank Patterson's *The Echo* (New York, 1922), one act, is another "allegorical" opera. Its scene is a cave near the seashore. Acantha, sleeping there, is awakened by Theudas' cries, flings him a rope and drags him from the water. The two find they love each other, but Theudas soon forgets Acantha in his eagerness to make the spirits of the cave bring him riches. They bring him gold and gems and put a crown on his head. About to drain the cup that will make him the slave of Cunnan, the spirit queen, Acantha dashes it to the ground. A Bacchanale follows in which Cunnan again woos him, but finally Theudas flings down the cup, and wanders off with Acantha, to know a nobler and purer love.

Here, too, might be mentioned Authur Nevin's *A Daughter of the Forest* (1918). A Father has brought up his Daughter in the forest to be a child of Nature. But—he has neglected to explain that it is well not to be too natural. When, yielding herself to a Lover's arms, she later asks her Father whether Motherhood is a disgrace, he tells her it is when "unblessed by Church". She drowns herself. When her lover returns, repentant, to make her an honest woman, the Father hurries him off again to the battlefield, "where his duty lies", blaming himself for not going more into detail when educating his child along Nature lines. *Poia* (Berlin, 1910) is an opera by the same composer on an American Indian subject which has not been very successful.

NATOMAH

Am. opera, 3 acts, by Victor Herbert. Text by Joseph D. Redding. To a story staged in old California of the Missions and the Royal Grants (1820), the composer has written a colorful and effective musical score, one of whose best numbers is a spirited "Dagger Dance".

Don Francisco, surrounded by servants, friends, and young Alvarado, awaits the coming of his daughter Barbara from her convent school. Natomah, the Indian girl, the last of her race, meanwhile has been telling Paul Merrill, a young American naval lieutenant, the story of her life. But he at once falls in love with Barbara, enthusiastically received by all. Barbara's cousin, Alvarado, and Merrill make ardent advances for the hand of the beautiful girl, but it is plain that she favors the American. This rouses the Spaniard's wrath. He plans to kidnap his cousin. Natomah overhears this, and during the next day's festivities watches while Barbara rejects her Spanish lover. In a thrilling Dagger Dance, Natomah now stabs Alvarado just as he is about to carry out his designs. Then, realizing the hopelessness of her love for Merrill and truly penitent for the murder she committed, she enters a nunnery. Her necklace-charm she gives to Barbara to make her even more lovely on the day she marries the Navy lieutenant.

Victor Herbert's only other essay in grand opera is a graceful one-act score, *Madeleine* (New York, 1913), in which an 18th century Parisian *prima-donno,* after vain attempts to find some one whom she truly loves to dine with her on New Year's eve, at last props up her mother's picture in the vacant chair and falls to, sure at last that true affection bears her company.

ROBIN HOOD

Am. comic opera, 3 acts, by Reginald de Koven. Text by Harry B. Smith. (Chicago, 1890) is not a "grand opera", but remains the composer's outstanding work. It is rich in facile and tuneful melodies, among which the famous romance "O Promise Me", is the favorite.

Robin Hood, leader of the outlaw rangers of Sherwood forest (he is really Robert, Earl of Huntingdon) appears at Nottingham, where he falls in love with Lady Marian (disguised as a page). Incidentally, she hears the sheriff of the town tell Sir Guy, whom he has just put forward as the claimant to Robert's earldom, that he can send the rangers to the gallows. At the archery match Robert, refused his rights by the Sheriff, determines to become an outlaw in earnest instead of in jest, as he had been. He tells Marian he will return to her when King Richard comes back from the Crusades and he can make head against his foes. After a series of adventures, humorous and romantic (Act II), the Sheriff of Nottingham's soldiers (after their leader has set in the stocks as Robin's captive) surprise Robin Hood and his men, and Robin is carried off after giving Marian, who had hunted him in the woods, a farewell embrace. In Act III Sir Guy is to marry Maid Marian. But at the critical moment Robin Hood (who has escaped his bonds) appears, followed by his archers. Yet while—Marian in his arms—his followers urge retreat to the forest, up comes the royal herald with a full pardon for Robin Hood and his men. The return of his estates to the lawful Earl of Huntingdon is foreshadowed in the scene of love triumphant.

The Canterbury Pilgrims, an American "folk" opera, in 4 acts, by Reginald De Koven, (New York, 1917) introduces characters from Chaucer's famous Canterbury tales in a book by Percy Mackaye. On the road to Bath, the "Wife of Bath" plans to win the poet Chaucer for a sixth husband. She wagers him— he is to marry her if she wins—that she can get a brooch from the "Prioress", whom Chaucer really loves. She does and the poet is saved from a loveless union only by King Richard II's

(Chicago, 1924). One of the American operas of high musical and literary quality. The composer's gift of thematic invention is shown in noble and humanly moving melody while his orchestra is handled with masterly skill.

Reginald Warren, misshapen, but a great landowner (1804-5) is deer-hunting on his vast estates in New York. His wife Elinor cherished a hidden passion for her husband's chief forester, Basil. But it remains concealed in her breast, for she is proud and honorable. Basil, too, who owes all to Warren, cannot betray his own love for her. Yet Warren, knowing this, takes pleasure in taunting his wife. Wardwell, a Puritan steward, presuming to warn Elinor against Basil, she summons the latter who drives the Puritan away to carry his tale to Warren, while the honorable lovers agree to part, now that they have admitted their mutual passion. But Warren, believing Wardwell, manages to have Basil shoot and kill Elinor in the morning mist. He knows it is his wife, but tells his forester (who sees Elinor's white scarf) that it is "the white bird", the gull which has been flying about the camp. Basil, when he finds out what Warren has done, kills him with his hands.

II

ENGLISH

English opera, as a whole, does not compare in importance with the three great schools—Italian, French and German. Aside from *The Beggar's Opera* (London, 1728),* immensely popular in its day because in a melodious stringing together of taking English and Scotch ballad tunes by Dr. Pepusch, it made fun of existing social and political conditions, only one other operatic English score has won wide favor. This is a comic and not a grand opera, Sir Arthur Sullivan's, *The Mikado*.

THE MIKADO

Eng. comic opera, 2 acts, by Arthur S. Sullivan. Text by William S. Gilbert. So far as the English speaking peoples are concerned "The Mikado" is probably the most popular comic opera ever written. Its many charming melodies including the well-known "The Flowers that Bloom in the Spring", have made it a perennial favorite.

In the long past yesterdays of Japan, Pooh-bah held the very desirable office of depositant of all state secrets, and also every office in the realm, save only that of Lord High Executioner, the sole paid

* With appropriate changes of text to suit the times it has been successfully revived in recent years.

office, held by his friend Ko-ko. Ko-ko, however, had the delightful monopoly of guardianship over all State wards, and hoped to marry one of them, sweet Yum-yum. She fancies, a younger man, Nanki-poo, seemingly a strolling minstrel, but actually the Mikado's son. He is fleeing from a paternal edict bidding him wed Katisha, an elderly maiden whose charms failed to impress him. Ko-ko becomes delinquent in the matter of executions, and Pooh-bah tells him the Mikado will remove him from office if he does not behead someone within the month. Nanki-poo hearing this, offers himself as a victim, if permitted to marry Yum-yum, and to enjoy a month of happiness with her. Ko-ko consents, but later unearths a forgotten law, calling for the live burial of the wife of any man executed. Ko-ko then describes the execution to the Mikado, who is delighted—until he learns that the victim is his own son. He then decrees that Ko-ko be done to death in boiling oil. But Nanki-poo and Yum-yum showing up very much alive at this juncture, the Mikado remits all penalties, save one—Ko-ko must marry the elderly Katisha!

Sullivan's other comic operas in many cases have almost rivalled The *Mikado's* popularity. *H. M. S. Pinafore* (1878) with its humor, and spirited sea-tunes; *Patience* (1881) which killed the mid-Victorian "aesthetic" craze of which Oscar Wilde was a leader, with tuneful satire; *Princess Ida* (1884) which contains beautiful love songs; *The Yoeman of the Guard* (1888) a "romantic" rather than a "comic" opera, stand out among others. Two grand operas by the same composer, *Ivanhoe* (1891) and *The Rose of Persia* (1900) have not been so successful.

V

RUSSIA

Boris Godounov

Russ. musical folk-drama, in a Prologue and 4 acts, by Modeste Moussorgsky. Text by the composer, after Pushkin and Karamsin. (Petrograd, 1874). One of the most remarkable works in opera literature, and the most characteristically Russian in spirit. It is distinctly a national score and Russian folk-airs have been freely introduced in it. In it the soul of the Russian people is expressed in characters and music, and it is a "naturalistic" opera of the most pronounced kind. Boris' great dramatic Aria (Act II) in which he expresses his remorse, is one of the great single numbers. The great Russian bass Chaliapin has given the rôle of "Boris" its finest interpretation in the United States and elsewhere.

Having foully murdered Dmitri, son of Ivan the Terrible, Boris

Godounov becomes the Tzar of Russia himself. But there is continual unrest among his people and the Poles threaten. They find in a youth named Gregory a resemblance to Dmitri, the assassinated Prince, and support his pretensions. Prince Shouisky tells Boris he has seen the corpse of the real Dmitri, but the people suffering from hunger and pestilence rise, aided by the Poles. Gregory as Dmitri, spurred on by his love for Marina, daughter of a Polish magnate, who is ready to love a Tzar, but not a landless dreamer, defeats the Tzar's forces and proclaims himself Tzar, and when Shouisky brings this dire news to Boris, he falls a victim to his own guilty conscience and goes mad. Just before he dies he recovers his senses long enough to advise his son and heir against his treacherous nobles or *bojars*. Then, haunted by the ghost of the murdered child, he staggers up the steps of his throne and gasps "I am still the Tzar!" as church bells toll and the priests chant his death song, only to fall in a heap and expire, while the nobles of his court watch in fear.

COQ D'OR

Russ. fairy ballet-opera, 3 acts, by Nicholas Rimsky-Korsakof. Text by Bielsky after Pushkine. (Moscow, 1910). An effective and colorful score (the "Cradle Song" is one of the most popular numbers) which is presented by a *double* cast, singers who sit and sing, and dancers who carry out the stage action in pantomime. Looked upon as a satire on the Tzarist government, and on the late Nicholas II, its performance in Russia was for a long time prohibited by the censor. It contains some of the composer's most effective eastern and barbaric music.

The Golden Cock presented to fat-witted King Dodon by his Astrologer, is placed on a village spire, and warns of impending danger. Dodon leads his warriors against the foe. But after coming on his sons' dead bodies on a moon-lit battle-field—they have been slain with the advance guard—he is surprised to see a beautiful woman emerge from a tent. She sings a hymn to the sun. Then she says she is the Queen of Themaka and announces her intention of conquering Dodon's forces. Dodon, captivated by her charms, willingly submits to her designs, beheads his advisor, Polkan, and strives only to amuse her. Upon their return to Dodon's kingdom the Astrologer demands the Queen in return for having given the King the Golden Cock. Dodon, refusing, strikes down the Astrologer with his sceptre, whereupon the Golden Cock descends from his perch and pecks Dodon on the head, killing him. This death revives the Astrologer, and he informs the audience that only he and the Queen are human, the other characters all being creatures of fairyland.

This is Rimsky-Korsakof's only "satiric" opera. The Russian composer Serge Prokofieff, in his *The Loves of Three Oranges* (Chicago, 1921), however, has utilized an old Russian fairytale for his "music of irony".

EUGENE ONEGEN

Russ. opera, "lyric scenes", in 3 acts, by Peter Tschaikovsky. Text by the Composer, after Pushkine. (Petrograd, 1881). A Byronic score with beautiful melodies which gives a true picture of early 19th century Russian life. Pushkine, the author of the tale, himself was killed in a duel. *Eugene Onegin* is the most popular opera the composer wrote. Lenski's air "Ah, I Love Her", stands out.

Eugene Onegin is introduced by his friend Lenski to Olga and Tatiana, daughters of Mme. Larina. He feels an immediate preference for Tatiana, while Lenski is already smitten with the charms of Olga. Tatiana, falling in love with ardent but loose-lived Eugene, tells her passionate emotions to him in a long letter immediately after he departs. He promptly answers her letter in person, saying he is greatly drawn to her, but does not want to marry. Tatiana, at a dance, is made the subject of gossip because of her preference for a man of loose morality. In revenge Eugene makes love to Olga, drawing on his head the wrath of Lenski. Explanations are of no avail. A duel is arranged and Lenski is killed by Eugene. The latter, bitterly regretting the death of his friend, wanders for years before he again meets Tatiana who has married. She loves him as of old, but though he pleads more ardently than before, she remains true to her husband, and Eugene is sent away for ever.

Tschaikovsky's *Pique Dame,* "The Queen of Spades", (Petrograd, 1890) is another picture of Petrograd high society life at the beginning of the 19th century. An officer, a desperate gambler, kills a card-playing old Countess by the shock he gives her when entering her room at midnight to discover the secret of a "lucky card" that makes her win. The old woman's ghost, however, tells him the secret and says it will cause his death. Brooding and distraught he spurns his faithful sweetheart, Lisa, and she drowns herself in the Neva. Then putting his "lucky card", the Queen of Spades, to the test at a gambling session he loses all and seeing the grinning spectre of the dead Countess behind him, kills himself. *Iolanthe* (1892) by the same composer contains some fine musical pages. It is the tale of a blind daughter of King René. Living in a palace in a hidden valley she recovers her sight by a miracle of love when a young adorer finds his way there. Tschaikovsky's *Maid of Orleans* (1881) lives only in one beautiful soprano aria, "Farewell, Forests", often sung in concert.

A LIFE FOR THE TZAR

Rus. tragic opera, 5 acts, by Michail Glinka. Text by Baron von Rosen. (Petrograd, 1836). This work was the first big success of the composer who founded the Russian "nationalist" school of music, which uses folk tunes as the basis of its works. The opera is still a favorite in Russia.

Antonida, daughter of the Russian peasant Ivan Susannin, is wooed by Sobinjin, but will not marry him until a Tzar is elected. The Poles have been defeated in battle, but they rally and march to take the monastery where Romano, now chosen Tzar, is staying. They try to force Susannin to lead them to the Tzar, and they think they have succeeded in bribing his foster-son, Wauja, to betray the whereabouts of the ruler. But Wauja has ridden away to announce the coming of the Poles, and the Tzar escapes. In the last act the ruler enters Moscow and the Kremlin palace, but Susannin, when the Poles find he has led them astray, is killed by them. He gives his "life for the Tzar", and the people mourn the hero, while Antonida and Sobinjin are happily united.

PRINCE IGOR

Rus. heroic opera, 4 acts, by Alexander Borodine. Text after a Russian epic poem by the composer. (Kiev, 1891; New York, 1915). A fine score whose chief beauty is in its beautiful choruses, based on Russian and Tartar folk-song themes. Vladimir's "Serenade", a tender and ardent melody sung before his Tartar love's tent is, perhaps, the most popular single song in the score. The beautiful, part choral, "Tartar Ballet" has been taken over into the repertory of the "Russian Ballet", as a separate work, and has justly become one of its best-liked numbers.

The Russian Prince Igor, with his son Vladimir, leave Kiev to battle against the Tartars, while Galitsky, Igor's brother-in-law, by intriguing and buying public favor manages to mount the vacant throne. But his close friends do much to antagonize the people, and Igor's wife denounces him. She believes that Igor has been killed. He, however, is merely a captive in the Tartar Khan Kontchank's camp, where his son Vladimir has won the heart of the Khan's beautiful daughter, Kontchakovna. In escaping, Igor is forced to leave his son with his Mongol love. He returns to his native city amid the plaudits of the multitude, who have tired of Galitsky's rule. And Vladimir, so attractive is his slit-eyed charmer, would rather lose his freedom than his lovely Tartar mate, whose hand the old Khan bestows on him.

SNIEGUROTCHKA

(The Snowmaiden)

Russ. legendary opera, 3 acts, by Nicholas Rimsky-Korsakof. Text after an old Slavic legend by the composer. (Petrograd, 1882). An opera many of whose charming melodies, notably the "Song of the Shepherd Lehl", are widely known. It is one of the most "racy", most genuinely "native" of Russian operas in its music. The title-rôle was created in the United States by Mlle. Lucretia Bori.

Sniegurotchka, daughter of King Winter and the Fairy Spring, is not content and begs her mother to be allowed to live a mortal life. The Shepherd Lehl is unmoved by her love, and she cannot respond to the ardent wooing of Mizguir, the Tartar merchant, who has jilted Koupava for the Snowmaiden. Mizguir, haled before the Berendei Tzar for his faithlessness, makes Sniegurotchka's loveliness his excuse. The Tzar, when he sees her, promises to give her hand to the man who has won her by sunrise the next day. Meanwhile Sniegurotchka appeals to her mother, who grants her the power of loving like a mortal, although a penalty is attached to the gift. Now Sniegurotchka jubilantly responds to Mizguir's protestations of affection. But when the hot rays of the morning sun fall on her, she melts away in an exaltation of love and longing, while Mizguir in despair casts himself from a mountain peak into a lake.

Russian legends have inspired some of Rimsky-Korsakof's finest scores. *A Night in May* (1880) is a fantastic tale of village life in Little Russia, in which village drunkards, *roussalki* and witches are involved in adventures which end in the happy union of two lovers. *Mlada,* a ballet-opera (1892) deals with a legend of the Baltic Slavs. It is best known by a single melody: "The Song of India", the mother (by different composer fathers) of many "popular" song-children, degenerate offsprings of the lovely original air.

Chistmas Eve Revels—(1895). Vakoula, a Russian village blacksmith loves Oxana, who says she will marry him if he brings her a pair of the empress' shoes. The good-natured ruler gives them to him and he marries his rustic charmer. The plots of the devil and a rival suitor against Vakoula supply much incident. Tschaikovsky has told the same story in an opera called *Roxana's Caprice. The Legend of Tzar Saltan* (1900) is a Russian variation of the story of Cinderella and, contains beautiful folk-melodies. *Kastchei the Immortal* (1902) tells in opera the story Stravinsky has told in his ballet *The Fire-Bird;* and *The Tale of the Invisible City of Kitezh* (1907) is the story of a city made invisible to save it from the Tartars, when beautiful Feoronia after many misadventures becomes the bride of a princely lover.

IV

POLAND, HUNGARY AND BOHEMIA

Stranslav Moninsko's *Halka* (Warsaw, 1847) is the first real Polish "national" opera. Its Overture is still occasionally played. Among more modern Polish opera composers Ludomir Rozycki stands out. He has written in "impressionistic" musical style a legendary music-drama, *Boleslav the Bold* (1909) and a "group" opera, *Eros and Psyche* (Warsaw, 1915) which presents the human meanings of the old tale from Greek mythology in six different historic ages of mankind. The Hungarian "national" opera is Franz Erkel's *Hunyady Lazlo* (1844). The most important recent Hungarian composer is Bela Bartok, who has used folk-melodies in an ultra-modern musical way in his *Bluebeard* opera, *Die Burg des Herzogs Blaubart,* "Duke Bluebeard's Castle" (1911). In Bohemia, though Dvorak in his *King and Charcoal-Burner* (1874), Fibich in his *Hedy* (1896), an opera based on Byron's poem "Haidee", his masterpiece. *The Fall of Ancona* (1900) and Janushek and others have written fine scores, only one Bohemian opera has won world-wide fame.

THE BARTERED BRIDE

Boh. comic opera, 3 acts, by Friederich Smetana. Text by Sabina. (Prague, 1866). The glowing colorful folk character of its racy Bohemian folk-tunes has made the score a general favorite. There are beautiful solo melodies and wild, captivating dances in it. None of the composer's others scores, the historical and legendary *Libussa* (1871), *The Two Widows* (1874) in Auber's style; *The Kiss* (1876), a village comedy; *The Secret* (1878) musically very fine and the impracticable *The Devil's Wall* (1882) have attained the popularity of *The Bartered Bride*.

Though Maria loves Hans, her father has decided to have her marry Wenzel, the stuttering son of a rich farmer, and on the day selected for the betrothal, while her father and the marriage broker are arranging the terms of the wedding, Maria meets Wenzel at an inn. There Maria does her best to induce Wenzel to refuse to marry her. He finally promises, but meanwhile the marriage broker has coaxed Hans into signing an agreement to sell his claim on Maria for a large sum, and consent to Maria's marriage to "Micha's son". Micha, Wenzel's father, and all save Maria are happy. By chance, Wenzel falls in love with a dancer in a travelling show, and refuses to marry Maria, though she (having heard of Hans' treachery) is now willing to wed him. But Micha recognizes in Hans his son by a former marriage. That was why Hans had signed the broker's document. And Hans, in the end not only wins his bride Maria, but also the handsome dowry promised by the short-sighted marriage broker.

V

SPAIN

GOYESCAS

(The Rival Lovers)

Span. romantic opera, in 3 tableaux, by Enrique Granados. Text by Periquet. (New York, 1916). There are musically more important Spanish operas than "Goyescas" ("Scenes in Goya's Style") but it remains the Spanish opera best known in the United States. The Spanish composer Granados built up the score out of his colorful piano pieces. It presents picturesque scenes—suggested by the pictures of the great Spanish painter Goya—of late 18th century Spanish life in Madrid. A beautiful "Fandango" is one of the finest musical numbers.

Majos and *majas,* men and girls of the streets are amusing themselves in Old Madrid. The men play at *pelele,* tossing a figure stuffed with straw on a blanket and the popular *toreador* Paquiro greets his temporary sweetheart Pepa, who drives up in her dog-cart. Just then, Rosario, a blue-blooded Spanish lady, arrives in her sedan chair. She is on her way to keep a rendezvous with her lover Fernando, a captain in the Royal Guard. Pasquiro reminds Rosario of a candlelight ball where he first met her and invites her to attend another with him. Jealous Fernando, overhearing, tells the *toreador* Rosario will go—but only in his company! Meanwhile Pepa, jealous of the bull-fighter plans revenge. At the ball the two men quarrel and a duel is arranged, to take place in Rosario's garden. There Fernando, tearing himself from his lady's arms, goes to meet his foe. A moment later a cry rings out and Rosario rushes into the darkness to reappear supporting Fernando, who totters to a stone bench only to die in her arms.

VI

SCANDINAVIA AND BELGIUM

Among *Danish* operas, Hakon Boerresen's *Eskimo* opera *Kaddera* (Copenhagen, 1921) has probably attracted the most attention. It presents a tale of the primitive love of blubber-eating Greenland Eskimo savages, with a skillful use of their folk-tunes, and relies on the Aurora Borealis to throw the light of romance over a scene where it does not exist. August Enna, (*The Witch, The Little Matchgirl, Cleopatra,* etc.) should also be mentioned.

Among Swedish operas Andreas Hallen's *Herald the Viking* (Leipsic, 1881) and among Norwegian Christian Sinding's *The Holy Mount* (Dessau, 1914), an unconvincing tale of the love affairs of a young monk of a Mount Athos monastery, might be instanced.

Among *Belgian* composers Jan Blocks' *Herbergprinces,* "The Tavern Princess", (Antwerp, 1909) is probably the outstanding opera.

Merlyn, a musician, though betrothed to Reinilde, gets into bad company among tavern friends, and lets himself be won over by the bold and abandoned daughter of the innkeeper, Rita. Home-loving Reinilde turns away other suitors, believing she will succeed in winning Merlyn away from those who are his downfall. After many threats, Rabo, a lout who desires Rita for himself, stirs up a hornet's nest of trouble, and when he finally arouses Merlyn, they fight. Merlyn is beaten and fatally wounded. Just as he dies, news comes that he has won the great national music contest, and he dies in his mother's arms as Reinilde curses Rita as the cause of his death.

THE ROMANCE OF THE DANCE

HOW DANCING CAME TO BE

(Introduction)

The parents of all artistic dancing seem to have been Religion, and Man's Natural Need for Expressing Emotion in Movement. For the cave-man who drew the outline of a mammoth on the wall, the dance was *another way* of expressing *what* and *how* he felt. When he grabbed the tousle-haired cave woman she shared his lair of dried leaves by the hand, and jumped and capered around in his joy at killing some eatable beast, he was laying the foundation of the "social dance". He was expressing pleasure, and taking pleasure in expressing pleasure as he expressed it. Our modern "social" dancing for the pleasure of rhythmic motion in close touch and strict time with some beautiful partner, in a way gives us the same kind of pleasure the cave-man enjoyed. But in this study we have to do, not with "social dancing", but with dancing as an *Art*.

In dancing as an Art, carefully trained "professional" artists use graceful or passionate movement to express the passions of people, the soul of music, stories gay or tragic. The individual "art dancer" is like a *solo* singer or violinist, playing a piece. A *corps de ballet* (a "body of dancers"), is a group which unites to tell a tale of some kind by means of the dance: the *Ballet* is the *Opera* of dancing. In the *Drama*, dancing disappears in natural bodily movement and gesture, with speech as the most important thing in expressing the idea. In *Pantomime,* dancing shades off into a kind of acting drama in which all that is spoken in drama is said in gesture. But in *dancing* proper dance-movement is used to tell a story, with music Rhythm as the backbone of its movement, and *Music* a necessary "helping-along" art to turn rhythm into tone, into sound.

Dancing in this sense, in the case of early man, probably was *religious*—people danced to honor their gods—and the dances of primitive tribes to-day show that dancing in early days was more or less an *act of worship* carried out by moving in rhythm to music's time.

I

In early human life the great tribal dances all turned on the important things *in* life: hunting and harvest, courtship, marriage, and death. They were "pantomime" dances: the dancers "told a story" in dance and gesture. It seems strange to think that early harvest, courtship and marriage dances, "dance prayers" for fertility, human and vegetable, performed by nude savages with the most emotional intensity and (for them) *true religious feeling,* were dances from which we would now turn in horror! For in all these *religious* dances of early man the idea of sexual passion is strongly emphasized. To him this did not appear irreverent. The frank, unmistakeable movements and gestures which he used as an expression of *pious devotion,* were sacred to him in the same way that our movements in church, kneeling, bowing the head, folding the hands in prayer, are to-day. In many cases the sex nature-dance ended in a wild orgy, in scenes of the most gross license. The primitive peoples of earth to-day, if we study the writings of *missionaries* and *travellers,* still carry out these dances which express the intimate relations of the sexes, like those of the *Yabassi* and *Bakeiri* (Kamerun), in this public manner. Some lift the veil which should hang before the door of the nuptial-chamber in dances of the most cynical obscenity. The stomach-muscle dances among the African *Suaheli* and *Ngomas* are accompanied by choruses singing obscene texts. The wild obscenity of the Australian *corroboree* is notorious, and the South Sea islanders, in the *hula-hula, upa-upa* and dances of a similar nature also express "religious" ideas in movements which to us are anything but "religious".

The terribly *enduring effect* of early ideas of unconcealed nature-worship along sex lines, in spite of the bringing of *Christian ideals* of purity and decency to savages so sadly in need of them, is shown by a traveller's account of scenes which vividly contrast Christian and *primitive savage ideals*: It is in the South Sea island of Tahiti where, "After the missionary church of Afareahitu, a beautiful little white coral temple, had been solemnly dedicated with Christian hymns and religious exercises . . . when night fell the Tahitian girls (the very ones no doubt who had been singing 'Lead Me, Gentle Savior!') adorned themselves with brilliant flowers. The sudden pulsing of the drum called them to the *upa-upa,* to which all came running, their hair flying, their bodies hardly covered with muslin tunics—and the dances, mad and lascivious, went on until morning! The Tahitians clapped their hands, and accompanied the tam-tam with a quick, frenzied choral song. Each girl in turn did a step; the music, slow at first, soon grew delirious, and when the exhausted dancer suddenly stopped at a tremendous drum-beat, another rushed forward in her place, surpassing her in shamelessness and frenzy!"

Tahaitian and Hawaiian dances of this kind, in a more subdued form, have been taken over into the art-dancing of our own time. The original negro nature-dances with sex motives, however, have not passed into the modern *art-dance.* Working their way up

the little slipper she has dropped! Clutching it, he sinks unconscious to the ground. In the second act, while red torches flare, and pirates hurry back and forth, loaded with booty, Bryaxis, the pirate chief, has Chloe dance. She dances so prettily that he is about to give rein to his wild passions, and already has seized her when—fauns and satyrs sent by Pan, the shepherd god, invade the stage. The terrified pirates flee, leaving Chloe behind. In the third scene we are back in the green meadows. Daphnis finds his Chloe again and they embrace. Then they pantomime the love-making of Pan and the nymph Syrinx with so much spirit that they pass from tender jest to ardent earnest. They fall into each other's arms as their companions flock up, and they are wedded before the altar of the nymphs, while the ballet ends in a general dance of rejoicing.

L'Apres-midi d'un Faune ("A Faun's Afternoon"). This Dance-Picture by Nijinsky, music by Claude Debussy, made its hero a Greek faun, a mythological half-god, half-man, with a goat's feet, horns and moral character so "natural", that it even shocked Paris audiences (1912), and was censored by the New York police when given in New York (1915). The Faun, first day-dreams harmlessly, but when bathing nymphs appear he chases them about the stage quite too faunishly, and only a pause of astonishment, which lets the nymph he has seized escape, seems to prevent a shocking climax.

DANCING IN ANCIENT ROME

Dancing in imperial Rome was as popular as in modern New York or London. Scipio Aemelianus tells of a dancing school where 500 boys and girls of all classes of society were taught dancing. Professional dancers and pantomime artists received tremendous salaries. Roscius, a male dancer of Cicero's day, made $45,000 a year, a dance-girl named Dionysia $15,000. Rome in the imperial days was an art-centre, though a moral cess-pool. The Romans were not given to dancing in private, but hosts of loose-lived dancing women of all nations added zest to imperial and other banquets with their lascivious dances. In certain big spectacular operas (Jean Nougues' "Quo Vadis", Deodatt de Severac's "Heliogabalus" and De Lara's "Messaline"), we find "Roman ballets". These dances, however, were not really Roman, for the Romans borrowed the dance as they did their other arts, from the nations they conquered. Even in the Roman ballet "Eunice" founded on "Quo Vadis" (Petrograd, 1907), the dances were Greek and Oriental.

IV

DANCERS AND DANCING IN THE MIDDLE AGES

There are two kinds of dancers, and two kinds of dancing in the Middle Ages, sacred and profane. In the Early Church special arrangements were made for dancing in the *choir,* and the first bishops were called *Praesules,* "leaders", because they led the dance on church festival days. Some of the Fathers of the Church claim that the angels *always are dancing,* and that the glorious company of the apostles is really a corps of dancers. But, like the popular song, dancing got a bad name in the *agapé,* the spiritual zeal of the young devotees little by little changing its nature, and the Church stopped all "sacred" dancing. But traces of the early religious dance still linger in Spain, where boys (*the seises*) dance around the altar of the Seville Cathedral on Easter.

When it came to the profane dance, every land had its "city" and its "country" dances. The *Brandon* was danced in France, by young gallants with flaring torches, under their sweethearts' windows at night. In Scotland and Spain there were military "sword dances", in England they danced around the Maypole, in Germany the emperors themselves would tread a measure with the burgomaster's daughter in the Town Hall when they were the guests of some big city. In every land the "wandering folk" of the King's Highway, fiddlers, jugglers, tumblers, gypsies, riff-raff of all sorts, carried with them the women dancers who danced the lewd dances of Cadiz or of the Orient, to please the coarse tastes of the times.

The *Danse Macabre* was the *protest of the weak* in the Gothic Age *against the strong.* It was a taunt the spirit of democracy flung at emperors, kings and nobles whose lives were all splendor, pomp and wealth, ease, comfort and soft living, lordship and command. For —Death makes all men, in imperial purple or in rags, equals! The people of the Middle Ages were down-trodden and oppressed. When the peasants found life unbearable in France, Germany or England, they rose in revolt, committed horrible cruelties, and were slaughtered by thousands by the better-armed and better equipped knights and nobles. They had no newspapers, they had no representation, they dared not speak—but they could *dance* their defiance of tyranny, and did.

The *Danse Macabre,* the "Dance of Death", was sculptured, painted and carved on the walls of churches and cathedrals everywhere during the Middle Ages. It appears a favorite subject for painter and engraver, and among pictured "Death Dances", the grisly series of wood-cuts by Hans Holbein is best known. Death, usually a dancing skeleton with a fiddle, white graveclothes fluttering around his bony limbs, leads a ghastly procession of dancing couples in which pope and peasant, emperor and serf, noble and slave are linked in a horrid semblance of merriment.

MACCABER'S CHURCHYARD ROUND

It seems that in the year 1424, when the English, under the Duke of Bedford held Paris, a strange adventurer named Maccaber suddenly appeared in the city. He took up his lodging in a ruinous old Roman tower adjoining a churchyard. A living skeleton in appearance, he claimed supernatural powers, and inspired terror in the people by his professed knowledge of the black arts. And one fine day the rumor spread through Paris: "They are dancing the Death Dance in the old tower burial ground!" There, at the entrance of the grass-grown church-yard stood Maccaber, a grin on his skeleton face, garbed in a fluttering white robe, and beckoning in the passers-by with his bony fingers. And they came by the hundreds, pouring into the church-yard to dance the ghastly processional dance he led. Round and round the church-yard, while the chill of a fantastic terror ran down their spines, men, women and children trod the grisly measure. And the popularity of the hideous amusement grew and spread. More and more people, day by day, joined the death dancers in a panting, perspiring, mystically and emotionally intoxicated crowd. The churches of Paris stood empty, the courts of justice were deserted, and even the French and English nobles, the Duke of Bedford and the ladies of his court were drawn into the shuddery whirl of that morbid dance. And then—suddenly as he had come, Maccaber disappeared from Paris, in 1425. Had Death himself come for the man, who had turned Death's terrors into a grisly jest? That is something history does not tell us. But his dance remained, and turned up again and again from time to time in popular life. In music the "Dance of Death" has suggested a wonderful work for orchestra, the *Dance Macabre,* by the French composer Saint-Saens, which begins with Death tuning his fiddle, and in which the xylophone makes us hear the rattle of the bones of the dead as they dance until cock-crow stops their unholy waltz.

Kissing was a feature of many of the seventeenth century dances, and added not a little to their popularity with the dancers. The old Spanish *Zarabanda* was so wild and licentious that it rivalled in favor with the equally passionate *Fandango* (both dances derived from old Moorish originals). The Fandango, in fact, was considered so depraved that it was "brought into court" by the Spanish clergy and formally tried.

TILL EULENSPIEGEL

"Till Eulenspiegel", a satiric dramatic ballet in one act, by Waslav Nijinsky, adapted to the symphonic poem of the same name by

Richard Strauss, was given for the first time at the New York Manhattan Opera House, in October, 1916.

Till Eulenspiegel is the model of the fourteenth century peasant, a plain farmer, smarter than the city folk who laugh at him, and not afraid of making nobles and princes look foolish. In the picturesque, market-place of a town in the Middle Ages, with a magnificent Gothic cathedral front at the rear of the stage, Till Eulenspiegel, "the evil conscience of his time", disguised as a clown, then as a knight and then as a learned man, pokes fun at all three in turn. With the "bad boys" of the town to "egg" him on, he first plays all sorts of practical jokes on baker, applewoman, confectioner and merchant. Dressed as a proud knight, he then pretends to be smitten with the haughty dames of lordly castles. They cross the stage in the tremendous tower head-dresses of the day, scorning the town itself, and scorning Till's attentions, much to his secret amusement. As a man of science he leads a group of learned doctors around the stage in a foolish game of "follow my leader" and, as he manages to upset all existing order, and has no respect for any one or anything, he is arrested as a public nuisance.

In court he so outrages the judges that he is condemned to the gallows. The hangman comes, and he swings in the red torch light, while the crowd mills at the foot of the gallows in the darkness. (In the music the flutes play a kind of breathless, fluttery trill, to show that he is suffocating). Suddenly his soul flashes forth among the huddled crowd! Then they regret him. For they feel that he stood for the revolt of the oppressed against the abuses of the nobility, and the pride of the men of learning. And they know he will live forever in their hearts. For his soul is the spirit of humor—the sound, sane, irreverent humor of the people! It makes superstition and tyranny ridiculous and, beyond any hangman's power to destroy, it lives on to the present day.

V

COURT DANCES OF THE RENAISSANCE AND BAROQUE

During the fifteenth and sixteenth centuries, the splendid court dance and ballet was a feature of princely life in all countries. Even the Church celebrated important events by "sacred ballet spectacles", in which marches and all sorts of dances were executed in the public squares. The canonization of Cardinal Charles Borremeo was thus celebrated in Lisbon in 1610, and that of St. Ignatius Loyola in 1622.

The courts of the Italian princes of the Renaissance were dancing courts, and all sorts of dance performances, in which scenes from Greek mythology were presented, were favorites. Lucrezia Borgia was an accomplished dancer, who charmed her venerable father, Pope

THE ROMANCE OF THE DANCE

Alexander VI, with the grace she showed in the dance. And when the Great Council of Trent ended after sitting for many years with a sigh of relief on the part of every one concerned, its conclusion was celebrated with a magnificent ball given by the princes of the Church, at which not only the great lords, but the bishops and cardinals themselves danced with the noblest and most blue-blooded ladies of the age. Catherine de Medicis brought the Italian love for the dance and the ballet to France with her, and the great ballets given by her degenerate son, King Henry III, which were half ballets and half operas, are often regarded as the commencement of opera in France.

THE BALLET DE LA REINE
(The Queen's Ballet)

This was probably the most famous of all the great ballets the Renaissance produced. It was arranged and organized by an Italian named Baltherini, and given in the Paris Louvre, and we read that in one of its entries the effeminate King Henry III danced disguised as a woman. It must have been a ballet in which extreme evening dress was in order, for the chronicles say ". . . . the loveliest ladies of the court were there with their breasts unveiled and hair in disorder."

Seventeen tremendous feasts, and festivals preceded the performance of the "Queen Ballet" at the Louvre, all of them to celebrate the marriage of Henry's favorite, the Duke of Joyeuse. The entire expense of the festivities came to 1,200,000 *écus* (gold pieces) and "The Queen's Ballet" ruined the finances of France, for the sum was beyond all the times could afford. The Ballet itself was a fantastic version of the story of the nymph Circe, in a number of separate parts or entries, full of complimentary allusions to King Henry (Heavens knows he did not deserve them!), and when the many successions of dances were over—which took five and a half hours—and the distribution of gifts to all the great personages of his court had taken place—they had all figured among the actors in the ballet—the royal treasury was as bare as Mother Hubbard's cupboard. The rich costumes of every color, of gold and silver lace and brocade, the luxury of feathers and jewels displayed is marvelled at by the writers of the time. But when in January 1592, the Swiss ambassadors turned up to ask for the payment of the 800,000 *livres* Henry had long owed them for the services of the Swiss mercenary soldiers, he had nothing with which to pay them. Yet it was a "debt of honor", seeing that the Swiss had refused three times the amount to fight for the King of Spain against France.

Philip II of Spain, the Duke of Savoy, the Austrian emperors, all the princes of the age indulged themselves in these magnificent music and dance spectacles and—as a rule the people paid for the piping. In the modern art ballet, the most gorgeous and splendid revival of the Renaissance spirit in the ballet has been in the famous "Legende of Joseph", whose music was written by Richard Strauss, to the text of an aristocratic German religious mystic, Count Kessler, Austrian poet, working together with Hugo von Hoffmansthal. It was given for the first time in Paris, in 1914.

THE LEGEND OF JOSEPH

The story is the story of Joseph, the Joseph of the Bible, but the prophet who wrote it would never recognize it. Put briefly, the dance action of the ballet tells the following tale: Mrs. Potiphar represents the craving for the joys of this world. Joseph stands for innocence, and the pure and simple life. Mrs. Potiphar wearies of the world, and thinks that if she only can win the Hebrew shepherd boy's love she can enter into *his* world of innocence and light. When she sees that her hopes are vain nothing remains for her but to die.

The ballet is staged in Renaissance Italy, instead of ancient Egypt, in costume and scenery. They are those of the Renaissance painter Paul Veronese's great picture "The Marriage at Cana", which shows a splendid court banquet of the painter's day. The Egyptians wear Venetian Renaissance clothes, and the merchants, who sell Joseph to the Potiphars, wear the Oriental garb of the sixteenth century Barbary States.

In a pillared Renaissance hall in Palladia's style, with a marble pavement, Captain Potiphar, like some rich Italian prince watches a blonde slave pour gold-dust—Joseph's purchase price—into the balance of a scale held by the slave-dealer while other slaves bring his lady wife gifts from him: a bowl of uncut gems, a rug, and a brace of Macedonian greyhounds. When she looks bored, Potiphar beckons. Dancers dance a rather frank dance describing the unveiling of bride and bridegroom on their wedding-night, and ten Turkish boxers fight till they have to be whipped apart by Potiphar's armored guards. But when Mrs. Potiphar still remains bored, the leader of the merchants beckons and Joseph (the dancer Massine) is carried in on a litter. He steps forth in a kirtle of white kid-skin, emblem of innocence, and dances a dance supposed to express his search for the Divine. Potiphar's wife is delighted. She hangs a necklace of jewels about his neck and as the servants (the Potiphars having left the hall), clear away the table, dusk deepens, and a footman, torch in hand, leads Joseph away to his little room. There he kneels and prays before retiring. But—his rest is disturbed by the entrance of Mrs. Potiphar. Joseph looks at her with innocent eyes: she strokes his curls, and he, thinking she caresses him as a mother would, lets her do so. But when her lips touch his own, he knows that all is not as it should be. Wrapping his mantle around him, he speeds from his cell. The villainous woman still pursues him, catches him, and raising him from the ground, presses him to her. But tearing himself from her embrace, though he loses his mantle, Joseph defies her charms. Enraged, she tries to strangle him when he repulses her. Then, slaves coming in, she hands him over to them, and faints. Potiphar now enters. In dumb show she accuses Joseph of her own crime, and the torturers enter with their instruments. But now a golden Archangel appears. He touches Joseph's shoulder, and his chains fall from him. While Potiphar's wife stands petrified with shame, the angel visitor leads Joseph away. With a gesture of despair the unfortunate lady then strangles herself with her pearl necklace, and falls back dead in her women's arms. Potiphar shrinks away in horror, and the Archangel and Joseph depart with an air of satisfaction. Such is the Renaissance ballet version of the Biblical story for which Richard Strauss has written music which has very beautiful moments.

VI

THE DANCES OF THE MOHAMMEDAN EAST

The dances of the Mohammedan Orient are practically all "sense" dances. They emphasize the graceful display of bodily beauty in the manner most calculated to inflame the passions, and to excite desire. And so we have the lascivious dances of the *Ouled-Nail*, the girls of that strange Berber tribe which sends its young womanhood out to dance their passion-dances in the *cafés* and *cabarets* of Tunisia, Alexandria and Cairo. There by the practice of prostitution, they scrape together the dowries necessary to establish them as the respected wives of men in their distant village home. Nothing that we can imagine is stranger and more weirdly repulsive than this custom of using the lure of the sense-dance to turn into the gold of a *wedding-dower* the passions the dance has inflamed. And strangest of all is the thought that the woman who has established her family life on such an ignoble foundation is regarded as an exemplary member of society. The better filled her wedding chest, the prouder husband and children are of her.

With the exception of a few religious dances, like those of the "Whirling Dervishes", where religious fanaticism goes mad in motion to the accompaniment of blood-letting with knives, the Mohammedan dances are of the slow sensuous kind, in which the muscles of the stomach and back play a prominent part, and from which their name of *danses du ventre* ("stomach danses") is derived. Sometimes they tell a story, like the "Dance of the Bee", of the Egyptian *almées,* dancers. But this story is a mere pretext for a refined kind of lasciviousness. Its whole point consists in a fancied hunt on the part of the dancer for a bee concealed somewhere inside her garments. As the dance progresses, her search becomes more frantic, one garment after another is torn from her body and flung away until at length the dancer stands revealed in a state of nudity. In such an objectionable dance the bee, of course, is a mere excuse to awaken an interest which can only be condemned.

The Mohammedan Orient type of dance is not one with which our life has many contacts. At the most, dances of this kind, *danses du ventre* may be seen at the lowest kind of "smoker", where coarseness is at a premium, and where the performance would be stopped were the police informed of it. Now and again the report of some especially objectionable dancing of the kind appears in the newspapers, but always with comment which shows that it must be condemned without qualification. In the dance drama, the art ballet, the most famous work illustrating the Oriental dance is the famous ballet "Schéhérazade".

SCHÉHÉRAZADE

"Schéhérazade" is the Introduction story, the Prologue, of "The Arabian Nights" told in dance action (Choreographic Drama), to the music of the great Russian composer Rimsky-Korsakof. It has been seen and heard in New York and other American cities, and was first performed in Paris, in 1910.

In his gorgeous harem the Sultan Shariar praises the faithfulness of his Sultana Zobeide, to his brother. But his brother is a doubting Thomas. Though three *odalisques* (harem dancing girls), dance a body-dance seated on the floor, he is gloomy. "Let us set off on a supposed hunting party and return unexpectedly—then you will see that you are mistaken," he tells the Sultan. No sooner have they gone than a crowd of the Sultan's faithful wives makes the old chief eunuch open three doors: one bronze, one silver, one gold. They lead to the quarters of the stalwart negro slaves. In rush the secret lovers of the harem women, blacks in bronze and silver brocades, while Zobeide's paramour, a giant negro (Nijinsky) stalks through the golden door. In a wild dance of passion the slaves make free with their mistresses in mimicry and gesture which needs no comment to explain itself, until—

Shariar's silent figure shows in the doorway. While his guards cut down the guilty wives and their lovers as they flee about the chamber, faithless Zobeide, clutching her knees, begs for mercy. But the Sultan's brother gently touches the body of her black lover with his foot. The Sultan Shariat's brow darkens, but as he grasps his scimitar, Zobeide plunges his dagger into her breast. The brother who refused to put his faith in woman (at any rate in a harem woman) had proved his case!

VII

AZTEC AND INCA DANCES

No book of the "Romance of the Dance" should omit an account of the dances of the Aztecs of Mexico and the Incas of Peru.

Dancing was an amusement dear to the Aztec heart. The people danced on all occasions, in costumes of skins and feathers, to represent birds and animals. The nobles, who learned the art from childhood, put on their most colorful feather-dresses, of crimson, blue, green and yellow, and hung themselves with their costliest jewels for the dance. This was especially the case in the great ceremonial ballets and festal dances in the market-places of the great cities, in which hundreds of dancers took part. It seems strange to think so, but in that tropical land of barbaric gems and gold, of blood sacrifice and flower-smotherings, of reptile-gods and insect-eaters, we find a breath of the English and American Colonial countryside. In Yucatan, the dancers, in one of their dances, circled around a great pole, fifteen or twenty feet high, from whose top various colored cords ran out, one of which each dancer took in his hand. The people whose priests tore the living heart from the human victim's breast to hold it up in sacrifice to the sun had—*a Maypole dance!*

On the night of the great feast of Huitzilipochtli, the war-god, the most famous of religious ballets took place, when the young men and young women of the nobility danced together, a great dance which was a more refined and artistic form of a "nature" and "fertility" dance of still more savage ancestors. History has prevailed the tale of the last of these great sacred ballets danced in the courtyard of Huitzilipochtli's temple, on the eve of the downfall of the Aztec empire.

THE LAST "INCENSING OF HUITZILIPOCHTLI"

It was on a fair May morning. Six hundred youths, the bravest and noblest in all Mexico, with as many lovely girls of their own class, the boys all in warrior dress, their hair braided in locks, and hung with golden bells, in kirtles and mantles of feather-work, crimson, green, wine-color, blue and gold, flashing with jewels, golden collars on their legs, arms and necks, had carried a kneaded maize-dough image of Huitzilipochtli from a small temple called "The Temple of Thorns" to the courtyard of the Great Temple. In brilliant procession they had passed through the streets of Mexico. They had placed the god's image in a corner of the temple court. Then the priests had tied the dancers lightly together by the hands, so that they stood embracing one another, their arms thrown over each other's necks. For "The Incensing of Huitzilpochtli" as the dance was called, symbolized the relations between the sexes. And unarmed, holding in their hands only greater-roses and golden rattles, they began their sacred dance to the sound of the music of the *huehuetl* trumpets, flutes and conches, and the *teponastlas,* "the singing drums". They were a glorious sight in the rhythmic swirl of their movements, with the sun sending rainbow sparks flashing from gleaming feathers, gold and gems. Suddenly—a musketshot rings out! The Spaniards, who have been watching the dance going on below from a higher terrace of the pyramid-temple, begin the massacre. Swords and battle-axes rage among the unarmed crowd of young men and maidens. Those who try to make the gateways are spiked on the lances of the halbardiers. Not an Aztec boy can scale the courtyard wall of polished stone, and the temple dance-court turns into a crimson lake! An hour—and not one of the happy boys and girls who had begun their dance so light-heartedly, is left alive. The flower of the Aztec nobility died that day, and long after the Conquest the sad ballads of the slaughter were sung in the villages of the Atzec Indians. Nor were the base murderers content with slaughter. When all their victims had been killed, they flung themselves like vultures on the dead bodies to plunder them of their golden bracelets and jewels. It was the last time that "The Incensing of Huitzilipochtli" was danced, for before the year had gone round, the Atzec empire was a thing of the past!

Like the Aztecs, the Peruvians had many dances social, sacred and theatrical. Dancing and drinking, as in Mexico, were the great pleasures of the people. And the great dance known as "The Golden Huasca" takes us back to a land of romance from which the romance has fled.

THE GOLDEN HUASCA

The Great Inca, Hunyac Capac, sits on his throne in the market-place of Cuzco, his capital. From his many-colored royal turban rise the two glowing feathers of the *coraquenque* bird. There are only two *coraquenque* birds in existence. They live in a desert land on the empire's western rim, and provide the ruby plumes for the emperor's headdress. Death is the portion of any Peruvian who captures and slays them. Among the nobles that surround Hunyac Capac the intoxicating crimson drink *sora,* distilled from maize-stalks, is passed in golden cups. And now, in garments of many colors, yellow, blue, crimson, scarlet and black, with brilliant feather headdresses, hung with gold, emeralds, sapphires and turquoises, come the dancers, three hundred in all, from out the Inca's palace. "Huasca" in the Quichua tongue means "a chain", and it is the "chain-dance" they begin. While musicians march ahead, playing bag-pipes and drums, blowing trumpets and *quenas* (double-flutes) each dancer, as he enters the square, catches hold of the hand of the man before him. And then the living chain begins to wind in coiling mazes around the Inca's throne. Like a great serpent it winds, while the crowd sings a chant that keeps time to the music of the dance. But it is not the stately dance itself which makes it the "golden" Huasca. It is the fact that its shifting coils of yellow, black and crimson garments, its blue, green and vermilion featherwork, its rainbow sparkle of precious stones, are all linked by one *central thread of gold*. For the soul of "The Golden Huasca" is its golden heart—the chain of massive golden links, seven hundred feet long, each link as thick around as a big-boned farmer's wrist, that the dancers carry as they dance. It moves with them, it sways to the music and the rhythm, it holds together the many colors of their moving web with a thread of dazzling light, as the sun sparkles on its polished surface. "The Golden Huasca" is another of those ballets the world will never see again! Members of the last Inca household sank "The Golden Huasca" in a lake to hide it from the gold-thirsty Spaniards. It is said that the secret of its hiding places has been handed down in certain families of Peruvian Indians for generations. But there are many lakes in Peru: Colta, San Pablo, Yarhuacocha, Buza, Quillucisa, and hundreds of others. Who would not like to know in which lake, on some rocky ledge, lies the seven-hundred-foot chain of solid gold, pure gold without alloy, pale gold from Peruvian rivers, and red quartz gold from Peruvian mines—each of its links as thick around as a big-boned farmer's wrist?

VIII

ROCOCO DANCES AND BALLETS

Louis XIV, the great king of the Baroque, was the first to make the *Minuet* the leading court dance, and introduce it in his ballets. Lully may be said to have written the first minuet which had any musical value, in 1653, where it was danced for the first time at Versailles by Louis XIV "and one of his mistresses". And it held its own during the Rococo Age. The *Gavotte* and the *Courante,* both danced with powdered hair and court sword at side, as well as the *Branle,* also were carried over from the court of the fourteenth to that of the fifteenth Louis. In fact, the Minuet may be said to have been *the* court dance of the times of Louis XV, and a favorite at the other European courts. It is hard to imagine eighteenth century French court ladies being "prudish", but in the Gavotte, often danced as a sort of second section of the Minuet, the practice of partners kissing at certain points in the dance was dropped in the Rococo Age, and instead of a kiss, they exchanged bouquets.

Though the tastes of Louis XV inclined more to pleasures which could be practiced only in private, there were magnificent fêtes, with dancing and ballets given on occasion. These in honor of Marie-Antoinette's marriage to his grandson Louis (1770) were among the most magnificent, and their splendor and luxury insulted the general wretchedness and poverty of the country. It was in connection with these festivals that the base and cynical Terray, Louis's minister of finance, said a witty thing. The king had asked him how he had "enjoyed the festivities"? "They were magnificent, Your Majesty! *Past all paying for!*" But great court ballets in which the king himself danced as in the day of Louis XIV are infrequent. Louis XV enjoyed visiting the famous "Balls of the Town Hall" in Paris, *incognito* (in disguise). He preferred their unrestrained license and tumult to dancing grave minuets amid an admiring court like his grandfather, the "Sun King". In the art field one of many charming Rococo ballets—though *Mozart's* music to one called "Les-Petits Riens" ("The Little Nothings") is celebrated—will be presented as showing the *spirit* of the age.

LA PAVILLON D'ARMIDE

(Armida's Pavillion)

"Armida's Pavillion" is the Rococo ballet of the Russian Ballet's repertory. Given for the first time in Paris, in 1909, its story is founded on a pretty tale by the French romantic poet and author Théophile Gautier, whose "One of Cleopatra's Nights" has supplied another ballet scenario. The music of "Le Pavillon d'Armide" is by the Russian composer Tcherepnine.

The Vicomte de Beaugency is an eighteenth century French noble. His postchaise breaks down while he is on his way to visit his *fiancée,* and a Marquis who owns a near-by chateau, puts him up for the night in a half-ruined pavillion, hung with tapestry from which the lovely pagan enchantress Armida* smiles down. The Marquis (he dabbles in the black arts), warns de Beaugency that Armida still has powers to charm. But the young nobleman only laughs. Has he not a *fiancée* who is the mistress of his heart? Yet when the great clock in de Beaugency's bed-room strikes twelve, the figure of Love appears. He drives the bronze *Saturn* (Father Time) from the clock—and time stands still! Then the twelve hours of the night, boys in cloth of silver and gold, flock out of the

---

*Armida is heroine of Medieval legend and of the Italian poet Torquato Tasso's great poem "Jerusalem Delivered". A naughty Moslem temptress, her beauty kept the Christian knight Rinaldo from joining the Crusading army, and he had hard work escaping her tender arms. The great painters Van Dyke, Femers and Boucher have painted "Armida".

clock, and when their graceful dance is done Armida, living, glowing, radiant in beauty, steps out from the tapestry as de Beaugency opens his eyes. The background of the tapestry turns into the gardens of Versailles and when the lovely enchantress mourns her Rinaldo's absence to the sound of the harps attendants play, de Beaugency rushes forward, and offers to take his place (alas, what has become of his love for his fiancée?) Armida smiles and leads to a seat, and then the revels begin—one beautiful dance after another until, at last, de Beaugency wins Armida's promise to be his, receives her father, King Hydrao's blessing (he has the face of the magician Marquis!) and as she ties her golden scarf on his throat in a true lover's knot, he swoons with delight. But—suddenly Saturn returns. Time no longer stands still. The figures vanish into tapestry and de Beaugency wakes from his swoon of delight to see the dawn streaming in through the window. His sinister host, the Marquis, now enters and asks how he passed the night. And de Beaugency, thinking he has dreamed a dream is about to reply when —he sees Armida's golden scarf hanging across the face of the clock! He realizes that he has been the sport of evil magic and wizardry, and overcome with horror and repulsion, his heart gives way! He falls lifeless to the ground at his host's feet.

A ballet known, respectively, as *La Camargo, Ruses d'Amour* and *La Fête Galante* is also a favorite Rococo number. It tells in dance a pretty story of which the great *danseuse* Marie Anne de Cupis de Camargo, who enchanted the court and people of France during the reign of Louis XV, is the heroine. Another great dancer, well known in the United States, Mlle. Adeline Genée, has danced it, and its costumes usually are copied from such Rococo painters as Watteau and Fragonard.

IX

SOME GREAT DANCERS OF THE EIGHTEENTH AND NINETEENTH CENTURIES

Beginning with the eighteenth century, we have dancers whose art makes them so famous that their names cannot well be passed over in silence.

There is Marie Sallé, (b. 1707), equally popular in Paris and in London. She wrote two ballets in which she appeared herself. "Pygmalion" (1734) and "Bacchus and Ariadne" (1734), and caused many duels. For enthusiastic young men of fashion crowded in such numbers to her performances that many toes were trodden upon—and the treading resented. Perhaps the most romantic thing about Mlle. Sallé is that in an age in which hardly one dancer was decent—she was a virtuous woman, of irreproachable character!

"La Belle Camargo" ("The Beautiful Carmago"), claimed descent from a Roman noble family on her father's side, and on her mother's from an ancient line of Spanish grandees. As soon as she began to dance in Paris (1726), she became the fashion. Coiffures, hats, shoes, fans—all were *à la Camargo*. She was ravishing in figure as well as graceful on her feet. Voltaire complimented her. Vanloo, Lancret and Pater, great artists all, painted her. And the many titled lovers whom she ruined by her extravagance, including a prince of the blood, Louis de Bourbon, Count de Clermont, never had the heart to reproach her. She appeared—always to everyone's delight—in seventy-eight favorite ballets in her time, and was the first ballet-dancer to shorten her skirt to what is now the regulation length.

Gaetan-Appolino-Balthazer Vestris (b. 1729) a pupil of Beauchamps, the ballet-master of Louis XIV, and the great ballet-master Jean-Georges Noverre created the "academic ballet" of the eighteenth century. Vestris had a good opinion of himself. When a heavy old lady stepped on his toe and apologized, he said: "Hurt me? Why, madam, you have put all Paris in mourning for two weeks!" He often declared his age had produced but three great men: himself, Voltaire and Frederick the Great, and called himself "The God of the Dance". He loved only dancers: his wife Mme. Vestris, and his affinity, Mlle. Alard. The latter, born of poor but dishonest parents (1742), was popular, but had to retire in 1781 because she grew too fat to dance. Their son Auguste became the rage in Paris as his father had been, but neither he nor his father were as important to the ballet and art dance as Noverre, who wrote, directed and produced his ballets in all the royal opera-houses of Europe, and established the ballet as an institution.

La Grande Guimard ("Guimard the Great"). This lady was one of the best and worst of the famous eighteenth century danseuses. But though her life was lived along the easy-going, immoral lines of her profession in those days, *La Guimard* had a kind heart, and was one of the most charitable creatures in the world. Mlle. Guimard was thin. But though the comic actress Sophie Arnould, when she saw her dancing with two male dancers, Vestris and Dauberval, was reminded of "two dogs fighting for a bone", *La Guimard* was the idol of Paris. When she broke her arm in a ballet called "The Fêtes of Hymen and of Love", a mass was said at Nôtre-Dame for her recovery.

Her great successes were won in ballets by Gardel: "Ninette at Court" (1778) "Mizra" (1779), "The Rose-Tree" (1784), "The First Navigator" (1785) and her noble and voluptuous dancing thrilled not alone Paris but London, where the Duchess of Devonshire was her friend. In 1789 she retired from the stage, married a poet.

THE ROMANCE OF THE DANCE

Despreaux, was ruined by the Revolution, and ignored by the Empire. She died in 1816, in fairly comfortable circumstances, though she had been an extravagant creature all her life long. For a time De Jarente, Bishop of Orleans, was her especial friend. He had a list, a "leaf", *feuille* as the French say, of "good livings" good clerical appointments: abbeys, chapels, churches, priories, etc. *La Guimard* used her influence to see that her friends drew prizes. And Sophie Arnould said: "That little silk-worm (Guimard) should be real fat. She was such a good leaf *(felille)* on which to feed!" Yet in the winter of 1768, when the poor were dying of cold and starvation in Paris streets, she took the jewelry the Prince de Soubise sent her, turned it into money, and spent it and more, to relieve suffering.

Among many others these names stand forth in the eighteenth century, and during the Empire that of Mlle. Bigottini, whose dancing is said "to have made the most hardened weep", and with whom the great Napoleon flirted, might also be mentioned.

Salvatore Vigano (b. Naples, 1769) was the greatest ballet-master and designer of the Age of Napoleon, though his name often is overlooked in histories of the dance. He was a genius in planning and carrying out magnificent spectacular ballets with huge numbers of dancers on the stage. In Spain, where toward the end of the eighteenth century he helped stage the magnificent festivals for the coronation of King Charles IV, he married a beautiful Spanish dancer, Maria Medina, and when he had her dance in Vienna, with hardly anything on, in dances taken from Greek bas-reliefs, the Austrian emperor was so smitten that the empress refused to attend her performances. In the great ballet *Richard Coeur de Lion,* which he gave in Vienna, there was a great procession of horsemen in which the horses were so splendidly trained that the *iron horseshoes struck the stage in exact time to the music!* Applauded in all the great cities of Europe, he produced among other ballets the great *I Strelitz** in Venice (1809), a great dramatic work. His *Othello* told Shakespeare's drama in wonderful pantomimes and dances. His *Vestale* was a picture of old Rome ending with the burial alive of Vestal Virgin guilty of a lover. *Psammi* (Egyptian), *La Spada di Kenneth* ("Kenneth's Sword"), *I Titani* ("The Titans") given in Milan (1819) were among Vigano's other famous ballets. He died in 1821, of pneumonia.

A new group of great dancers is associated with the early nineteenth century. Lise Noblet created the great dancing rôle of the "Dumb Girl" in Auber's opera "The Dumb Girl of Portici", Paris (1828), and Mlle. Brocard was so much admired by the late Queen

---

* The Strelitz were the fierce and rebellious guards of the Muscovite tzars before Peter the Great. When they revolted against him he put down their rebellion and "broke" the corps.

Victoria when a little girl that the royal child dressed her dolls in imitation of her. Marie Taglioni (1804-1884), trained by a pitiless father, began her successful career in 1822. She danced not only in the great independent ballets of the day, but in the opera ballets as well. Her dancing of the *Tyrolienne* in Rossini's "William Tell", and the Abbess in the "Ballet of the Nuns", in Meyerbeer's "Robert the Devil", were especially famous. Balzac mentions Taglioni in his novels, and Thackeray in "The Newcomes", says "the young men of his day will never see anything so graceful as Taglioni in *La Sylphide.*"

There were also the two Ellsler sisters, born in Vienna, 1808 and 1810 respectively. Therese, the oldest sister, danced her way into the heart of Prince Adalbert of Prussia. He married her morganatically*—and she retired to family life and a title. Fanny, however, was not far behind her sister. She began her career with the reputation of having been the love of the unfortunate young Duke of Reichstadt, the great Napoleon's son (who lived in Vienna), though it is claimed this rumor was spread by her "press man" and manager to get her talked about. In Vienna, Paris, and London both sisters celebrated triumphs. When they toured America in 1841, the cities in which they danced put up triumphal arches to them, and it is claimed the Mayor of Philadelphia was the first in the traces when their horses were unharnessed after the performance, and they were dragged in triumph to their hotel.

Carlo Blasis (b. 1803) was an Italian Noverre, dancer and balletmaster, and the ballets he made out of certain famous operas, Spontini's "Cortez" and "The Vestal", were famous in their day. He established the ballet reputation of the Milan Opera House, and wrote numerous books on the dance.

Charlotta Grisi (b. 1821), graduated from the Milan Scala Theatre and after winning laurels in Naples, Vienna and London, scored a great success in Paris. Her most famous ballets were "Giselle" and "La Péri", great favorites in their day, the first of which has been revived by the Russian Ballet dancers.

Fanny Cerito, Lucille Grahn, Caroline Rosati, Rosita Mauri and the famous Pepita, the quartet of dancers, Bonfanti, Betty Rigil, Rita Sangalli and Morlacchi, who appeared more than forty years ago in one of the greatest specular ballets this country has ever seen, "The Black Crook", are all names associated with this period, and

* The "morganatic marriage" is an institution which allows a king or prince to have a "heart" as well as a "state" wife. Since these royal unfortunates for "reasons of state" often must marry women whom they do not love, the morganatic or "left hand" marriage has been devised. Morganatic wives are looked upon as real wives in law, and their children legitimate, but they have no claim to royal rights or privileges of any kind.

the "academic" ballet, as is that of the great dancer Adeline Genée.

The greatest dancer of the older tradition in the world today, perhaps is Mme. Anna Pavlova, who travels with her own company, and whose "solo" dances, such as "The Dying Swan", to Saint-Saën's wonderful music, would be hard to surpass. In America, generally speaking, the "solo" dance which follows the art development started by Isadora Duncan, and seeks to picture in dance movement and pantomine the *soul* of certain musical compositions, or calls up the spirit and "feeling" of a certain age, has been very successful. A number of dancers of various nationalities, American English, French, and German have "specialized" in certain dance types and "atmospheres": Miss Ruth St. Denis seems to prefer the "hieratic", the "religious ritual" dance of India and Indo-China; the Armenian danseuse Ohanian has illustrated the Persian dance, and other dances of the Mohammedan East. Again, we have dancers who confine themselves to the national dances of their own land, the famous Carmencita, Spanish; La Argentina, and others, who have appeared in this country. There are special developments too numerous to mention.

Maud Allan, "The Vision of Salome", might be mentioned. The American danseuse Loie Fuller carried the novelty of dances, whose charm lay in the play of colored lights and fluttering draperies, to Paris, and she has remained there ever since. There are some notable "death dances", aside from Mme. Pavlova's "Swan". Isadora Duncan's repertory includes one to Schubert's song "Death and the Maiden"; the American danseuse Lada has illustrated the Sibeeius "Valse Triste" in the same manner (it has been arranged with dramatic words, as a song and a chorus for female voices); and when D'Annunzio's tragic drama "La Pisanella" ("The Pisan Girl") was given in Paris (1913), the famous French dancer Ida Rubinstein danced the part of this unfortunate person, who is punished for loving a young king by being smothered to death with roses.

In the Russian ballet the great names are: ballet-masters; Fokine, Wasla Nijinsky and Adolf Bolm; Karsavina, Trouhanova, Fokina. Topokova, Flodorovana, Kovalevska are famous Russian ballerinas (dancers) and Miassine may be added to the male list.

X

SOME GREAT BALLETS OF OLDER DAYS

Many ballets warmed the hearts and set the blood a-tingle of generations now dead and gone in the sentimental days of the earlier nineteenth cenutry. Once in a great while one or the other is revived, but—they do not mean to us what they meant to those who saw them in their glory, with dancers like Fanny Ellsler, Taglioni and Carlotta Grisi to move them to tears or to passion. Among those which we know now by name only is Leo Delibes' ballet *Sylvia, or the Nymph of Diana* (Paris, 1876), *La Péri*, (Paris, 1843) Théophile Gautier's ballet for which Burgmüller wrote the music, and many another. Taglioni's famous *La Sylphide** (Paris, 1832) is another graceful drama of the older type which has passed into the "lake of forgetfulness". It was the tale of a sylph who falls in love with a young Scotch Highlander, and haunts his dreams until his brain gives way, his fiancée's heart is broken, and "La Sylphide", his unsubstantial love herself, ends unhappily by means of a spell woven around her at a witches' sabbath. A tragic tale. *Les Bayadères, La Gitana, La Fille du Danube* ("The Daughter of the Danube") a Carlotta Grisi ballet, *La Fille de Marbe* ("The Marble Maiden") a Cerito ballet, like hundreds of others seem to have vanished forever. The ballet *Giselle, ou les Willis,* however, has been immortalized by the writings of two great authors, Heinrich Heine, the German poet and Théophile Gautier, the French poet, and revived by the Russian ballet, which gives it a claim to our consideration.

GISELLE

(The Willis)

In our humdrum century a bride is just a bride, nothing more. In fact, we often wonder whether she is lucky in being one! But in the fifteenth century the bride who was torn from the arms of her husband-to-be on the wedding eve by death was considered so unfortunate that a beautiful little legend was woven around her. People thought she became a "Willi", a ghost dancer, who haunted the king's highway and danced to death the unfortunate wanderer she met at night. For, torn from life's joys when most alive, the unfortunate "Willi" could not resign herself to the quiet and silence of the grave.

Giselle is a Courland village maid, the lovely bone of contention between Hilarion, a gamekeeper, and Loys, a young noble living in her hamlet in disguise. The arrival of the Prince of Courland with a gay hunting party brings the rivalry of blue-blooded and the baseborn lover to a head, but—poor Giselle, who had just been preparing to marry young Loys, is a tender and sensitive young creature. For when the Prince recognizes in Loys none other than his old friend

---

* The Russian ballet production *Les Sylphida* ("The Sylphs") tells no story. It is a vague, lovely picture of a group of sylphs who express all the poetry of motion to waltzes, preludes and mazurkas by the most poetic of musicians, Chopin.

THE ROMANCE OF THE DANCE

Duke Albert of Silesia, the shock drives poor Giselle insane! With a despairing glance at her lover she dies.

It is night. The disappointed gamekeeper Hilarion's tears fall on the white cross above Giselle's grave near the forest. He weeps too long. On the stroke of twelve the graves open, and the Willis appear. While Hilarion flees only to be danced to death, off stage, broken-hearted Albert draws near. But Giselle, (she has not joined the rest of her companions) loves him too greatly to dance *him* to death. Instead, she bids him cling to the cross, and when the other ghost dancers return he escapes Hilarion's fate. With the first rosy ray of dawn the spectres vanish. Albert, clutching despairingly at his beloved ghost, sinks unconscious to the ground. There he is found by the Lady Bathilde, his "other" girl, and awakes with good resolves to lead a better and nobler life.

COPPELIA

(The Girl with the Enamel Eyes)

Leo Delibes' beautiful ballet music has made this ballet famous, just as it has his oriental ballet "Naila". It is based on one of Hoffmann's "Strange Tales", as Offenbach's grand opera also is and was first given in Paris in 1876.

Simple Franz, a Hungarian village lad, has lost his heart to a beautiful *automaton,* a mechanical doll that stands in old Dr. Coppelius' show-window, and has forgotten his flesh-and-blood sweetheart, pretty Swanilda. In Coppelius' absence frolicking students break into the shop, where Swanilda has gone to destroy her wooden rival. Coppelius, returning, detains Franz, who has come to make love to the doll while the students flee. Swanilda meanwhile has pushed aside the doll from her pedestal and takes her place, while Coppelius plies Franz with wine. He hopes to get the village boy drunk and then make his life-spark, his strength and vigor, pass into the wooden doll. But when Swanilda comes to life and dances for him, thinking his doll has found a soul, the old magician is delighted. But Franz, sobering up, now is ready to run off with his true love. The artistic Russian Ballet version (instead of making Coppelius a comic figure who sends off the lovers with a blessing) has him die of a broken heart when Swanilda reveals herself as human, for his fondest illusions are destroyed!

Adolph Adam's ballet "The Nuremburg Doll" (Paris, 1852) is another variation of the same story.

Raymonda

A romantic, spectacular ballet by the great ballet-master Pepita

(Petrograd, 1898), "Raymonda" is included in Mme. Pavlova's repertory. It is a slight tale. In a Gothic castle hall, while preparations are going on for Raymonda's wedding to Jean de Brienne, the crusader, a Saracen knight, Abdurrachman arrives. He is charmed by her beauty, and plans to make her his own. But he does not betray his design and all retire. At night, in the green castle gardens, Raymonda (who has strayed out into the moonlight) is suddenly clasped in a rude embrace. It is the Moslem knight. When she swoons, however, he disappears. But when she wakes the poor girl is held prisoner in a fairy ring of elves, and not until dawn is she able to leave the garden. The whole story merely provides chances for elaborate solo and *corps du ballet* dances. The music, by Alexandre Glazounow, is far superior to it.

THE LAKE OF THE SWANS

(Le Lac des Cygnes)

A pantomime ballet for which the great Russian composer Tchaikovsky wrote charming music, "The Lake of the Swans" (Moscow, 1877), has been given both by the classic ballet companies and the Russian ballet.

The story is a tragic tale of the Middle Ages. Prince Siegfried is celebrating his last night as a bachelor. After gay dances a midnight hunting party is proposed. In the forest, Siegfried, separated from his comrades comes across the Lake of the Swans, a jewelled stretch of water where Odette, a princess, and her attendants are held enchanted by the sorcerer Rothbart. For an hour at night they take their true shape. Siegfried and Odette fall in love with each other at once. If he will promise to marry her, she says though she appears before him in his castle as a swan, her true shape will be restored and the magic spell broken. The next day splendid dance performances in the castle, Spanish, Polish, Hungarian, while away the time while Siegfried waits for his Swan princess to appear. But instead comes the magician's daughter Odillia, with Odette's face and shape which she has stolen. As poor deceived Siegfried proclaims the witch his bride, a white swan circles around the castle, with plaintive cries. Then Siegfried knows he has unknowingly betrayed his Odette! He rushes from the castle to the enchanted lake—too late! As he comes to it the white swans headed by Odette their leader, disappear over the surface like vanishing clouds of hope.

THE SLEEPING BEAUTY

(La Belle au Bois Dormant)

The "Sleeping Beauty", the old fairytale we all know, was presented as a ballet with Tchaikovsky's music (Petrograd, 1890), and was first given in the United States by Mme. Pavlova.

Its earlier tableaux, with many charming dance numbers, lead up to the great climaxing scene in which Prince Charming finds his way into the slumbering palace, and wakes the Sleeping Beauty with his kiss, after which she rises and dances a courtly gavotte with him amid general rejoicing. In an older French *Belle au Bois Dormant,* with music by Herold (Paris, 1829), Mlle. Taglioni led the "Dance of the Nymphs".

Among older spectacular ballets there might still be mentioned: such "action ballets" as *The Black Crook,* and its successor *The White Fawn, La Source* (Paris, 1867), in which the most delightful scene was one showing "a silvery glade in the lone forest on whose surface the spirits of springtime appeared to dance." There was the Italian Marenco's glittering *Excelsior,* (Milan, 1890), an "allegorical" spectacle, which showed the struggle between the powers of light and darkness: and the big Italian spectacle ballets *Messaline* and *Sieba* (Sheba). Many ballets still holding a place in the modern repertory are of an older vintage, like the Rococo *La Fille Mal gardé* ("The Girl Poorly Looked After"), and the ballets from many operas—like the *Walpurgis Night* ("Faust"), the wonderful Hindoo Ballet ("King of Lahore"), and the *Spanish ballet* ("Carmen") to mention but a few—are given independently as dance entertainments.

XI

GREAT DANCE-DRAMAS OF THE RUSSIAN BALLET REPERTORY

The important dance-dramas of the modern Russian Ballet may be said to represent the highest point reached by collective dancing as a dramatic art. Many already have been considered under various heads in this volume. The outstanding works of this beautiful repertory which remain follow:

Thamar

Thamar (Paris, 1912), a dance-drama of amorous seduction and tragic murder, after a poem by the Russian poet Lermontoff, to the music of a symphonic poem by Balakireff, is one of the most striking of the Russian ballets.

In her splendid tower chamber, Thamar, the vampire Georgian queen, broods motionless on her couch. Around her in silence are grouped guards and women attendants. Suddenly a girl looks through the great casement window that gives on the winding mountain road and the rushing river Terek below. She whispers to a second, and the second to a third, who in turn whispers to the queen. With a bound Thamar is at the window, waving her long blue scarf to the handsome stranger coming down the mountain road.

The trap is set. Black-robed guards hasten to blindfold the willing victim and lead him to the lovely spider's lair. When Thamar tears the kerchief from his eyes he looks with delight at the beautiful queen and her women. And when Thamar and her graceful dancing girls dance for him he is infatuated. A vague instinct holds him back for a moment, but he drains the wine-cup Thamar offers and follows her to her couch. Yet there she evades his loving arms, and at a sign slaves appear to clothe him in princly robes for further revels. The moment he is gone, the queen's wild guardsmen break into a savage, exultant dance of blood-lust, driving their daggers quivering into the floor. But as the strange youth enters all relapses into repose. While the dancing-girls circle around him in maddening circles, Thamar lures him to one of the walls of the chamber. The dancing-girls suddenly stand motionless, and follow him with their eyes. But the boy does not notice Thamar groping for her dagger while her other hand tenderly clasps his own. He does not see the black mantled guards close around him, nor the panel in the wall move soundlessly in its well-oiled grooves. As the abyss opens before his unseeing eyes, he leans toward the smiling queen, drunk with desire and she thrusts her dagger into his heart with a sudden bound! He reels for a moment on the edge of nothingness then—a push from a guard—and he goes headlong down into the roaring flood of the Terek, hundreds of feet below.

The deadly panel slides back without a sound. Thamar once more broods motionless on her couch. Her guards, dancing-girls and attendants relapse into silence. Suddenly a girl looks through the great casement window, whispers to a second, and the second to a third, who in turn whispers to the queen. With a bound Thamar again is at the window, her long blue scarf waving its welcome to the next victim of her murder-lust!

THE FIRE-BIRD

(L'Oiseau de Feu)

This Russian fairytale ballet (Paris, 1910), scenario by Fokine, music by Stravinsky, is one of the most colorful numbers of the modern repertory.

The moonlight falls on a stunted tree bearing golden apples, standing in a silent forest glade. In the background a wall and barred gates show dimly against the woodland green. Suddenly, across the glade sweeps the Fire-Bird, a glorious dancing figure of flame and gold, after her Ivan Tzarevitch, the Tzar's son, in hot pursuit of the vision of loveliness. He hides. The Fire-Bird, returning,

THE ROMANCE OF THE DANCE 505

is seized and held by him. When her struggles prove vain, she plucks one of her golden feathers, and tells the prince that it will bring her to his aid should he need her. As he takes it she darts from his arms. He raises his bow, but has not the heart to shoot her. Meanwhile dawn has come. The barred castle gates of the evil magician Kostchei the Deathless open. White-robed maidens, the magician's captives, appear. They dance around the tree and play with the golden apples they shake from its boughs. Of course Ivan falls in love with the beautiful Princess, who is one of the captives, and when the signal calls the maidens back to their prison, Ivan shakes the iron gates of the castle with rage, and forces them open. A fantastic mob of figures at once rushes from the magician's stronghold, to a tremendous clangor of sound. There are ghosts, dwarfs, wizards, horrible in shape and glittering with armor and weapons. Last comes Kostchei himself, with his hunchbacked jesters. In vain the captive maidens plead. He begins the magic incantations which will make Ivan his slave when—the prince remembers the Fire-Bird's feather! He holds it out before him, and Kostchei shrinks back. The Fire-Bird appears, and her pure and golden magic drives the demon mob into a wild dance. At its end they drop in a sleep of exhaustion. While Kostchei and its sorcerers sleep, the Fire-Bird leads Ivan to a hollow tree-trunk. Taking out a steel casket, he draws from it the mystic egg containing Kostchei's soul. The magician wakes, and dashes forward, but Ivan, raising the egg flings it crashing to the ground, and kills the "Deathless" sorcerer! As he does so, darkness falls amid the crash of thunder. When the shadows clear Ivan and his love are clinging to each other in rapture amid the magician's rescued captives, while he and his horrid crew have vanished.

THE DANCES FROM "PRINCE IGOR"

The "Prince Igor Dances" of the Russian ballet are the "Tatar Ballet" of the Russian composer Borodine's fine opera "Prince Igor". It is a dance-scene of primitive Mongol tribal life during the twelfth century, and has no "story", properly speaking. The dances of the women and maidens of the Tartar hordes has the *appeal to the senses* which is the essence of the Eastern dance. The dances of the men and boys breathe savage vigor and energy and warlike energy.

Spirals of smoke rise from the low red huts of the wandering tribemen of the steppe. The men of the Tatar horde advance, striking the earth with the ends of their bows, mimicking the shooting of invisible arrows into the skies, surging, crossing and leaping in a wild savage dance. Into their dances the women weave all the indolent seduction of the East, that speaks to the senses rather than to the soul. And the Tartar boys, in their gambols, foreshadow the

506   THE ROMANCE OF THE ARTS

realities of their savage life to come. The ballet is especially fine when given with the original chorus accompaniment, when the "dancers use the musical themes as though they were golden springboards."

Similar in style were the "Scythian Dances" of Isadora Duncan and her pupils (Paris, 1909), from Gluck's opera "Iphigenia in Tauris".

SADKO

Perhaps the finest "Legendary" dance-drama in the Russian repertory is "Sadko". Adolf Bolm,* one of the greatest of modern Russian ballet-masters and dancers, created the New York version (1916), basing his story on an old Russian legend, and his music on a symphonic poem by Rimsky-Korsakof. It is a "sub-marine" ballet, and takes place at the bottom of the sea.

Sadko, the poor wandering *gusly*-player (the gusly was a primitive Russian minstrel harp) of Novgorod, had a stroke of good luck. He played himself into the good graces of Volkova, the Sea-King's daughter, and she gave him power to draw from the sea fishes with fins of pure gold. So he grew rich, built him a white stone palace, and then went to sea with a great ship in order to become even richer. But, coming back from foreign lands with "buckets of red gold, pure silver and fair round pearls", the ship suddenly stopped. Tzar Morskoi, the Sea-king, held it fast and demanded that the minstrel visit him beneath the waves. So Sadko leaped overboard and was drawn down beneath the waters.

In a great hall with walls of purple seaweed, filled with emerald-green light, Sadko swept the strings of his maple-wood harp, and played so bewitchingly that the mermaids and sea-monsters, of the Sea-king's court, and even the Sea-King himself, could not resist his tingling music. Carried away by its rhythms, they *had* to dance, and not until her father sinks dead of exhaustion can Volkova snatch the harp from the minstrel's hands and stop the mad round. As she does so and the strings snap, the troubled waters grow calm, but while the dance was going on the upper waves had risen mountain-high, dashing ships to destruction and tearing down houses along the shore.

But Volkova does not take her father's death to heart. While the sea creatures mourn their dead king, she rises on Sadko's arm from the watery deeps. In the white stone palace in Novgorod she will live happily ever after with her musician lover, for he can give her the human love the cold sea bottoms do not know.

* Adolf Bolm, in order to make his undersea folk dance in the most natural and convincing way, spent hours studying the movements of the fish in the great Oceanographic Museum at Monaco.

PETROUSCHKA

The great burlesque-tragic number of the Russian Ballet repertory is "Petrouschka", scenario by Fokine and music by Stravinsky. It tells the tragedy of a marionette, a mechanical doll which develops a soul.

A winter sun gleams over Admiralty Square in Petrograd (1830), and on an old magician-showman's puppet-booth, for a fair is going on. Suddenly, while the crowd—nurse-maids, coachmen, police agents, Cossacks, grooms, soldiers and a couple of organ-grinders turning the crank—is moving about, the curtain of the booth rises. In separate compartments stand a *Ballerina* (Dancer), a Moor, and Petrouschka, a pierrot. Suddenly all three move woodenly out of their boxes, and to the surprise of the crowd dance in front of the stage till the curtain falls. Their master, the magician-showman, has breathed a kind of life into them!

Then we see Petrouschka's black cell. There the unhappy Pierrot (for he has more of a soul than his companions) curses his master's cruelty and his fate. The Dancer enters, but frightened by his wild cries, leaves again. Now we see the Moor's cell. The Moor is just brute beast. First he plays like an idiot with a cocoanut, then slashes at it with his sabre, and finally worships it. When the Dancer enters his cell she feels more at home. She, like her dusky lover (for after her charming entrance waltz she sits on his knee and their lips cling together) is a creature of sense, not soul. When Petrouschka, who loves the Dancer, enters, his furious rival throws him out of the room. As the Dancer once more seeks the Moor's knee, darkness falls.

The third tableau shows a glowing, colorful succession of beautiful Russian folk-dances: a dance of *droshky* (sleigh) drivers, of nurse-maids, of Russian gypsies, of wild masqueraders. But behind the curtains of the puppet booth grim tragedy is in the making. Suddenly the curtains part: out fly Petrouschka, the Moor and the Dancer. In a whirl of driving snowflakes, while the crowd gapes, the Moor chases poor Petrouschka to the front of the stage, kills him with a slashing blow of his sabre, and disappears with the girl. A police agent now drags up the magician-showman, while the crowd gloats over poor Petrouschka's dying agonies. But when the old magician picks up the supposed dead man—he turns to a sawdust-filled doll in his hands! With a sneering laugh the old sorcerer drags his puppet toward the marionette theatre, but as he nears his booth—the blue, livid ghost of murdered Petrouschka suddenly appears on its top, threatening its master. And the guilty magician's high black hat falls from his head in terror. Unable to face the ghost of the thing he has slain, he flees panic-stricken from the stage.

In its music, its color, its genuine tragic "thrill", the ballet "Petrouschka" is one of the most gripping of all the Russian dance-dramas.

Ballets which are not "marionette" or "puppet" ballets but present pretty scenes of amiable love-making in dance movement without much "story" interest, are: "Papillons" ("Butterflies"), and "Carnaval", whose main attraction is the music by the great composer Schumann which rhythms their dances.

THE SPECTRE OF THE ROSE

The most poetic number, of the Russian repertory is this *pas à deux* (dance scene for two dancers), a "movement version" of a charming poem by Théophile Gautier. It was first danced (Paris, 1911) by Karsavina and Nijinsky, and its music is Weber's "Invitation to the Dance".

A young girl, in a simple white frock, stands in her virginal bedroom (the bed half-disclosed in a corner recess) lost in a happy revery. She is passing in review her hours at the ball from which she has just returned.

Then, through the open French windows of the room, with a graceful bound, leaps the Spectre of the Rose. A light and rhythmic figure, to which cling the crimson and purple petals of all the roses that ever bloomed, he glides to the sleeping girl, and as he calls up the tender, glowing memories of the hours just gone, she rises and with eyes closed, and smiling happily, drifts with her phantom partner through the mazes of the waltz. When she once more wearies and sinks into her chair, the Phantom of the Rose falls adoringly at her feet. He touched her white brow in a kiss of farewell, and with the dying strains of the music leaps through the window and is gone!